CYCLING ITALY

Ethan Gelber
Gregor Clark
Quentin Frayne
Will Marinell

LONELY PLANET PUBLICATIONS
Melbourne • Oakland • London • Paris

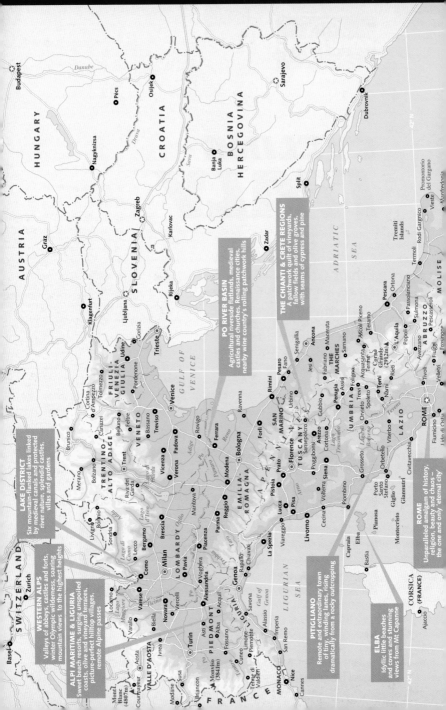

PO RIVER BASIN
Agricultural diversity: wetlands, medieval castles and churches, Renaissance cities, nearby wine country's rolling patchwork hills

THE CHIANTI & CRETE REGIONS
A patchwork quilt of vineyards, fallow fields and olive groves, with seams of cypress and pine

LAKE DISTRICT
Six mountain-flanked lakes linked by medieval canals and protected river nature, splendid castles, villas and gardens

WESTERN ALPS
Valleys of abbeys, castles and forts, winter Olympic wilderness, soaring mountain views to the highest heights

ALPI MARITTIME & LIGURIA
Sweet beach resorts, surging unspoiled coasts, olive and vineyard terraces, picture-perfect hilltop villages, remote Alpine passes

PITIGLIANO
Remote and extraordinary town of tiny, winding lanes, rising dramatically from a rocky outcropping

ROME
Unparalleled amalgam of history, religion, beauty and chaos – the one and only 'eternal city'

ELBA
Idyllic little beaches and coves and stunning views from Mt Capanne

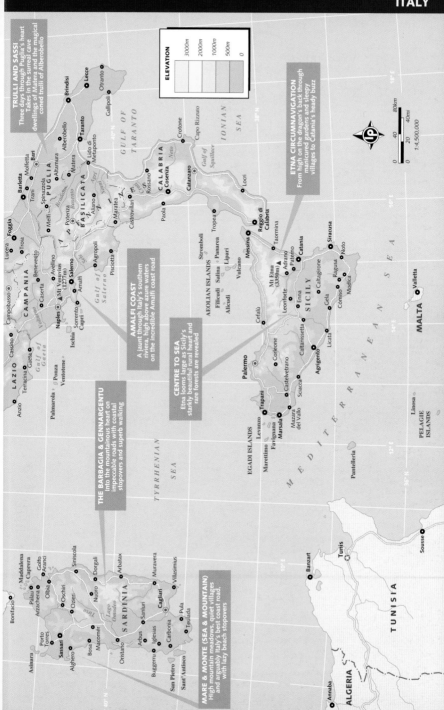

ELEVATION

3000m
2000m
1000m
500m
0

TRULLI AND SASSI
Three days through Puglia's heart. Takes in the surreal cave dwellings of Matera and the magical coned trulli of Alberobello

ETNA CIRCUMNAVIGATION
From high on the dragon's back through manicured gardens and sleepy villages to Catania's heady buzz

AMALFI COAST
A jaunt through Italy's southern riviera, high above azure waters on the incredible Amalfi coast road

CENTRE TO SEA
Etna looms large as Sicily's starkly beautiful rural heart and rare forests are revealed

THE BARBAGIA & GENNARGENTU
Into the mountainous heart on impeccable roads with coastal stopovers and superb walking

MARE & MONTE (SEA & MOUNTAIN)
High mountain meadows, quiet villages and arguably Italy's best coast road, with lazy beach stopovers

1:4,500,000

0   40   80km
0   20   40mi

SEAS & GULFS
TYRRHENIAN SEA
IONIAN SEA
GULF OF TARANTO
Gulf of Squillace
Gulf of Salerno
Gulf of Gaeta
MEDITERRANEAN SEA

PUGLIA
Brindisi
Lecce
Otranto
Gallipoli
Taranto
Alberobello
Bari
Barletta
Molfetta
Trani
Spinazzola
Altamura
Matera
Foggia
Lucera
Troia

CAMPANIA / LAZIO
Campobasso
Benevento
Avellino
Caserta
Naples
Salerno
Amalfi
Sorrento
Capri
Ischia
Mt Vesuvius (1277m)
Cassino
Gaeta
Terracina
Anzio
Ponza
Ventotene
Palmarola

BASILICATA / CALABRIA
Potenza
Melfi
Maratea
Castrovillari
Cosenza
Catanzaro
Crotone
Capo Rizzuto
Rossano
Paola
Locri
Reggio di Calabria
Tropea
Agropoli
Piscotta
Ludo di Metaponto

SICILY
Messina
Taormina
Catania
Siracusa
Noto
Ragusa
Modica
Comiso
Gela
Caltagirone
Enna
Leonforte
Adrano
Paternò
Mt Etna (3350m)
Cefalù
Palermo
Corleone
Castelvetrano
Sciacca
Agrigento
Licata
Caltanissetta
Trapani
Marsala
Mazara del Vallo
Levanzo
Favignana
Marettimo

AEOLIAN ISLANDS
Stromboli
Salina
Panarea
Filicudi
Lipari
Alicudi
Vulcano

EGADI ISLANDS

SARDINIA
Maddalena
Caprera
Palau
Arzachena
Golfo Aranci
Olbia
Siniscola
Dorgali
Arbatax
Muravera
Villasimius
Cagliari
Pula
Teulada
Carbonia
Iglesias
Buggerru
Arbus
Oristano
Santu Lussurgiu
Nuoro
Ozieri
Ottana
Macomer
Bosa
Alghero
Sassari
Porto Torres
Asinara
Bonifacio
San Pietro
Sant'Antioco
Lago Omodeo
Tirso

MALTA
Valletta

TUNISIA
Tunis
Banzart
Sousse

ALGERIA
Annaba

PELAGIE ISLANDS
Linosa
Pantelleria

Cycling Italy
1st edition – July 2003

Published by
Lonely Planet Publications Pty Ltd ABN. 36 005 607 983
90 Maribyrnong St, Footscray, Victoria 3011, Australia

Lonely Planet Offices
Australia Locked Bag 1, Footscray, Victoria 3011
USA 150 Linden St, Oakland, CA 94607
UK 72-82 Rosebery Ave, London EC1R 4RW
France 1 rue du Dahomey, 75011 Paris

Photographs
Many of the images in this guide are available for licensing from
Lonely Planet Images.
w www.lonelyplanetimages.com

Main front cover photograph
The road to Tocco da Casuaria, Abruzzo (John Hay)

Small front cover photograph
Old bikes (Chris Mellor)

ISBN 1 74059 315 4

Contents – Text

LIGURIA, MARITIME ALPS & PO RIVER BASIN 135

ITALIAN ALPS & LAKE DISTRICT 174

DOLOMITES 224

ADRIATIC COAST 252

THE SOUTH & SICILY 290

SARDINIA 325

TRAVEL FACTS 352

The Rides	Duration	Distance	Difficulty
Rome			
The City Centre	3–4 hours	21.5km	easy–moderate
Appia Antica	3–5 hours	52.3km	moderate
Villas, Gardens & Suburbia	3½–6 hours	59.6km	easy–moderate
The Mysterious Etruscans	2 days	109.5km	easy–moderate
Tuscany			
Chianti Region	2 days	101.7km	moderate
Sienese Day Trip	4–7 hours	71.7km	moderate
Hill Town Trek	3 days	150.8km	moderate
Arc to the Sea	3 days	202.4km	moderate
Circling Elba	5–9 hours	92km	moderate–hard
Alpi Apuane	3 days	155.8km	moderate–hard
Southern Odyssey	3 days	172.1km	moderate
Liguria, Maritime Alps & Po River Basin			
Riviera di Ponente	2 days	164.1km	moderate–hard
Cinque Terre & Gulf of Genoa	2 days	130.7km	moderate–hard
Alps to Alpine Sea	3 days	272.1km	hard
Langhe & Roero	3 days	205.8km	moderate
Basso Pinerolese & Saluzzese	5½–10 hours	101.6km	easy–moderate
Lungo Po Argine	3 days	210.2km	easy
Italian Alps & Lake District			
Valle d'Aosta	2 days	125.1km	moderate
Montagne Doc	3 days	244.6km	moderate–hard
Alta Rezia Valleys & Passes	4 days	276.1km	hard
Navigli Milanesi	3 days	245.2km	easy
Central Lakes	5 days	329.2km	easy–hard
Eastern Lakes	3 days	209.3	moderate
Dolomites			
Dolomiti di Brenta	3 days	173.6km	moderate–hard
Adige Valley Bikepath	3–6 hours	66.5km	easy
Heart of the Dolomites	6 days	317.9km	hard–very hard
Alta Pusteria Bikepath	2½–4 hours	40km	easy–moderate
Adriatic Coast			
Triestine Triangle	3 days	212.7km	easy–moderate
Colli Euganei	5–7 hours	77.6km	moderate–hard
Ravenna to Venice	4 days	245.3km	easy
Conero Riviera	3–5 hours	54.9km	moderate
Mystic Mountains, Sacred Hills	6 days	428.3km	moderate–hard
The South & Sicily			
Amalfi Coast	2 days	77.5km	easy–moderate
Trulli & Sassi	3 days	233.5km	easy–moderate
The Gargano	2 days	169.5km	moderate–hard
La Sila	2 days	118.6km	moderate–hard
Lava Magic	2 days	120.8km	moderate
Centre to Sea	2 days	137.1km	hard
Sardinia			
Mare e Monte/Surf & Turf	2 days	108.6km	moderate
Costa Verde & Oristano	3 days	147.4km	moderate
Barbagia & Gennargentu	4 days	293.2km	hard

The Maps

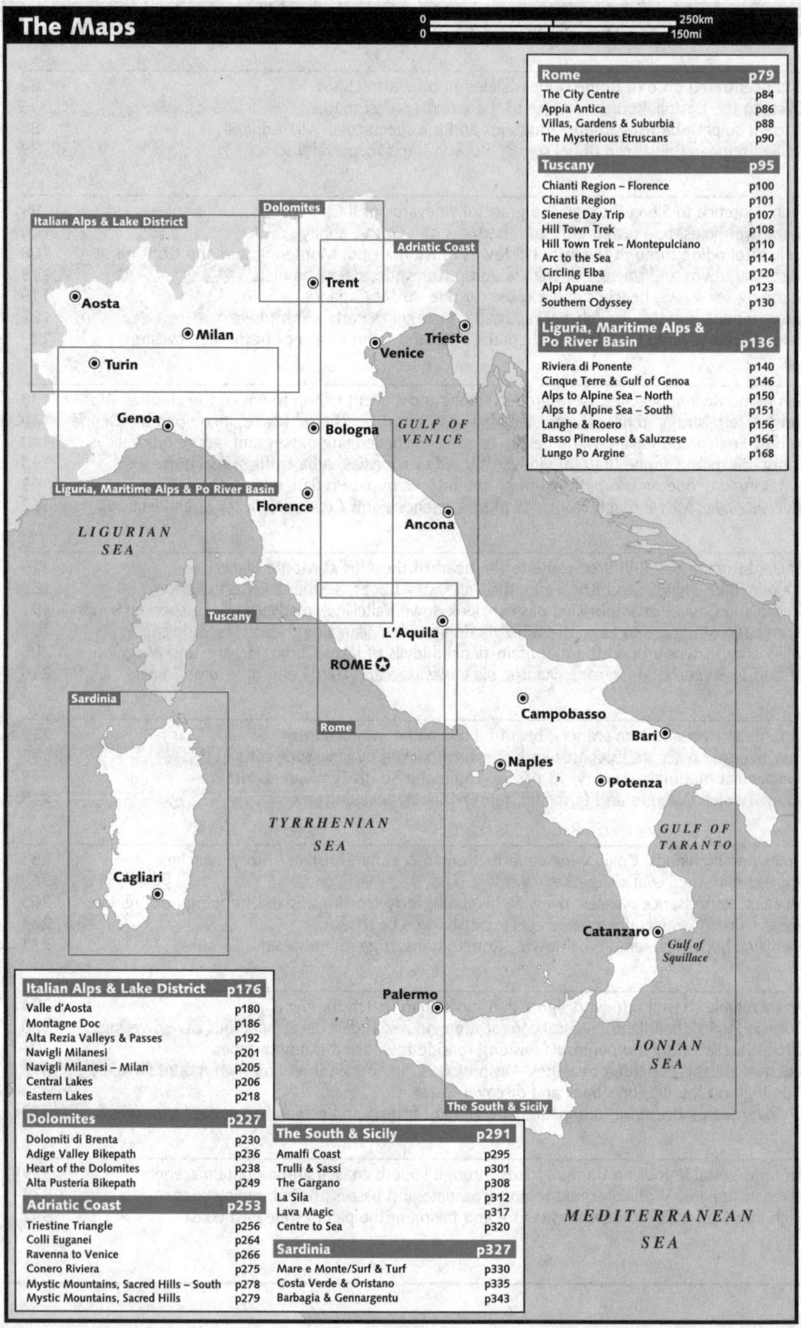
0
250km
0
150mi
Dolomites
Italian Alps & Lake District
Adriatic Coast
Trent
Aosta
Milan
Trieste
Venice
Turin
Genoa
Bologna
GULF OF VENICE
Liguria, Maritime Alps & Po River Basin
Florence
Ancona
LIGURIAN SEA
Tuscany
L'Aquila
ROME
Sardinia
Campobasso
Rome
Bari
Naples
Potenza
TYRRHENIAN SEA
GULF OF TARANTO
Cagliari
Catanzaro
Gulf of Squillace
Palermo
IONIAN SEA
The South & Sicily
MEDITERRANEAN SEA

The Authors

Ethan Gelber

Ethan Gelber is a native New Yorker whose appetite for travel has kept him away from home for nine of the last 15 years. A six-year stint in Europe during which he helped breath life into Blue Marble Travel, a bicycle tourism company, confirmed a passion for pedalling in foreign lands that has not waned. With graduate training in education and international relations, he went on to found BikeAbout, a nonprofit organisation promoting peace and cooperative understanding through cycling and the improved use of technology in learning. To date, he has racked up more bicycling than motorised miles on the roads of 40 countries in five continents. Ethan has written extensively about cycling and travel, primarily through his experience with Blue Marble and BikeAbout, but also as the cycling editor and 'Expert Cyclist' for GORP's (Great Outdoor Recreation Pages) website. Ethan wrote the Facts about Italy, Facts for the Cyclist, Liguria, Maritime Alps & Po River Basin and Alps & Lake District chapters as well as having a hand in the Travel Facts and Health & Safety chapters. This is his first title for Lonely Planet.

Gregor Clark

Gregor Clark started his cycling career with a bang, when at age six he hurtled down a steep New York City street on training wheels and collided with a trash can just short of Broadway. The experience made a lasting impression, and he has been fond of life on two wheels ever since.

Gregor first fell in love with Italy while living in Florence as a teenager. Nowadays splitting his time between Europe, Vermont and the San Francisco Bay area, he is proficient in Portuguese, French, Spanish and German in addition to Italian and has visited more than 50 countries, working as a teacher, European bike-tour leader, and translation rights manager for a publishing company. Since 9 September 1999 he has enjoyed sharing his lifelong passion for languages, travel and the natural world with his mischievous daughter, Maggie.

Gregor wrote the Central and Southern California sections of LP's *Cycling USA: West Coast.* For this book he wrote the Dolomites and Adriatic Coast chapters as well as the Getting There & Away and Getting Around sections in Travel Facts.

Quentin Frayne

With a passion for cycling dating back to early childhood in Melbourne, Quentin now combines road racing, touring and commuting with life as a parent, sharing cycling adventures with his partner Emily and newly arrived daughter Portia.

His 47 years have seen him move from a successful career as hippie vagabond to motorcycle mechanic and racer in the 1970s, to musician, working as a drummer in Perth and Melbourne. A short course in Italian in Siena, Italy, finally led him to university and his current occupation as Language Coordinator in Lonely Planet's Melbourne office.

7

It was ultimately through fast motorcycles and languages that his true love of cycling was born. One too many speeding tickets and a licence suspension meant the bicycle became the easiest way to commute to university, where he was studying for an honours degree in French and Italian. Since then the Laverda hardly gets a look in, and his cycling has taken him to numerous touring destinations in Australia and Italy, and many victories as a veteran road racer. Quentin wrote The South & Sicily, Sardinia and Language chapters. This is his first title for Lonely Planet.

Will Marinell

A teacher, writer and traveller by profession, and an artist and musician by hobby, Will grew up cycling around the Philadelphia area. His love of bicycle touring came years later when, as a junior in college, he lugged his bike to Dublin, where he'd planned to study for the year. It wasn't long before the fern-lined pathways and warm pubs of Eire lured Will away from the library. He spent the better part of that year meandering as far as bike, legs and wallet would carry him. Will is back at the books pursuing a Masters in Education, though he's uncertain whether the scholar or wanderer will win in the end. His wanderlust has led him all around the USA, as well as to Russia, Georgia, eastern Canada, Mexico, most of Western Europe, East Africa and the Asian subcontinent. This is his first title for Lonely Planet. Will wrote the Rome and Tuscany chapters for this book.

FROM THE AUTHORS
Ethan Gelber

To Darren Elder, Sally Dillon, Andrew Bain, Lindsay Brown, Justin Flynn and Glenn van der Knijff, who supported me through this first Lonely Planet experience, many thanks. Bewildering world tragedy made researching and writing this book a challenge that their drive and professionalism overcame. They were not alone in urging purposefulness. Jane Higgins, Padraic Kennedy, Anthony Ziehmke, Greg Green, my family (Sam, Blanche, Linus, Hilary and Bruce, Noah, and even wee Eli) and sundry friends provided crucial buoying spirit and buttressing knowledge, as did Nicolas Clifford, Laura Malone, Tim Suba, Delphine Lyon and Jimi Thomson from Blue Marble Travel.

In Italy, nothing could have been accomplished without a nod from Carl, Emma and (as-yet-unborn) Finn Lyttle. Their hospitality and the warmth of Douglas and Margaret Havers, Valerio Diotto, Giovanna Sassi, Klaus Famira and friends in Apricale and Ventimiglia made Italy feel like home.

A special *grazie* to the informative and forthcoming cyclists and FIAB volunteers I met/communicated with: Marco Danzi, Luigi Riccardi, Gianni Catania, Andrea Marchesini, Enrico Caracciolo, Loris Tissino, Lello Sforza, Michele Mutterle and Marco Centin. Their input was instrumental and enthusiasm great. I hope this guide contributes to furthering the cause of cycling in Italy.

Quentin, Gregor and Will, it has been an awesome collaboration!

Gregor Clark

Warm and heartfelt thanks to Sandro Montanari, Paula Metallo, the Kopsicks, Mia Chambers, Max, Fiorenza, Kristin, Scott, Nate, Erica, Lili, Mimmo, Gianni and Pia, Enzo and his family, and all the others at Coldigioco who made our summer stay in Italy so joyful.

Big thanks also to my co-authors and editors, especially Ethan Gelber for his generous help in locating Italian cycling resources.

Among the countless people who supported me in my research, special mention goes to Cristina Doni, Loredana Miclet, Silvano Vasselai, Gina Aducci and Alisa Hixson. I gratefully tip my helmet to hundreds of other unknown Italians whose native warmth, love of life and desire to help made every kilometre a joy, especially the guys who gave me those extra pushes on the climbs to Passo Pordoi and Tre Cime.

Thanks to Ted and Emma for unfailingly generous hospitality, and to April, Jim, Gabe, Wes, my parents, Janida, Margo, Neil, Orlando, Carl, Iranshid, Jennifer, Paula, and Helen for helping Maggie grow up strong and happy, even when I was off climbing mountain passes.

Finally, loving thanks to my wife Gaen Murphree and daughter Meigan Quetzal Clark, constant supporters and travelling companions, for making me smile and helping me live my dreams.

Quentin Frayne

I've been very fortunate while researching this book to meet some truly wonderful people whose warmth and generosity of spirit kept me sane during many long, hot days in the saddle. In Sardinia, Piero Pintus, Lucio Cadeddu, Paolo Ortu, Gianni, Leonardo and all the folk from Calarinas in Villanova Monteleone. In Puglia, the gang from Bari's Ruotalibera, *il cacciatore* Pasquale in Peschici. Special thanks to Mauro, Giuseppina and Renzo, Sandra and Michele at Tandem, Prati.

A pannier-load of *grazie* to FIAB's vice-president and good friend, Lello Sforza, for support above and beyond the call, and a frigate-load of thanks to the book's ex-captain, Darren Elder. For their friendship and help, special thanks to Maoro, Maria and Bianca, Ethan Gelber, Nicola Wells and Sally D. My chapters I dedicate with *amore, baci ed abbracci forti* to Em, soulmate and supporter *straordinaria*, and to our crazy little bear and *figlia stupenda*, Portia – may she grow to ride fast and far.

Will Marinell

Special thanks, first and foremost, to the Cinelli family for introducing me to the splendours of Italy. Without their generosity, hospitality and advice, my travels would not have been remotely as rewarding (nor as comfortable!). Equal thanks go to Randy Peffer for jumpstarting my writing career. 'Cheers' to Darren Elder for his wisdom and support throughout the preparation and research stages of the guide, as well as to Sally Dillon who seamlessly took over his responsibilities. A warm thanks to my cousin, Chris Spaeth, for outfitting me with his old racing gear. I was definitely the most stylish tourist cycling through rural Italy – no small feat in the fashion capital of the world! In Italy, special thanks go to Marika and Adrea of Florence by Bike for their guidance and their enthusiasm for *Cycling Italia*. Thanks to the countless forgotten rail conductors who helped hoist my unwieldy rig into the bicycle coach. To Nick Butler for embracing both the celebration and pain en route, and to the Higher Power that kept Nick's bike together and got him safely back to Florence. Finally, thanks to my dad and to my family. Chrone's Disease made travelling an arduous and risky affair for my dad. In the summer of 2001, while in the throes of illness, he requested that I leave his side to cycle through Italy. Upon my return, shortly after hearing of my adventures, he passed away. I dedicate my work and research on this book to my dad – a gentle soul, a poet and a loving father.

Maps & Profiles

Most rides in this book have an accompanying map outlining the route and the services provided in towns en route (along with side trips, depending on the map scale). For greater detail, we also recommend the best commercial map available. The Border to Border feature ride is mapped for on-the-road use. You'll find a detailed map for every day of riding, showing the route, towns, services, attractions (look for the star symbol) and side trips. These maps are oriented left to right in the direction of travel; a north point is located in the top right corner of each map. The maps are intended to stand alone but could also be used with a commercial map.

We provide an elevation profile when there is a significant level of climbing and/or descending on a day's ride. These are found at the back of the book with the cue sheets, except for the Border to Border ride, where the profile and cues are placed on the map for that day.

Map Legend

Note: not all symbols displayed below appear in this book

CUE SHEET SYMBOLS

†	Continue Straight	↰	Left Turn	✳	Point of Interest	⚑	Traffic Lights
↱	Right Turn	↖	Veer Left	▲	Mountain, Hill	◆	Roundabout/Traffic Circle
↗	Veer Right	↩	Return Trip	⚠	Caution or Hazard	●●■■	Side Trip/Alternative Route

MAP SYMBOLS

🚲	Bike Shop	🛏	Places to Stay	✳ •	Point of Interest
⛺ •	Camping	ℹ	Information	✕	Restaurant, Café
				🏪	Store, Supermarket
✈	Airport	🏛	Embassy	✉	Post Office
🏰	Castle	🏛	Gallery, Museum	⚑	Ruins
✝	Church	✚	Hospital	■	Tomb

POPULATION

✪ CAPITAL	National Capital	⬤ LARGE Medium	City	Town	Day Start/End town on ride
◉ CAPITAL	State Capital	● Town Village	Town		Urban Area

ROUTES & TRANSPORT

═A1═➤═⪦	Freeway, Tunnel	──●──Ⓜ	Train Line, Station, Metro
═S57═	Primary Road	────□	Tramway, Bus Terminal
═SP76═	Main Road	──────	Bikepath, Track
──────	Secondary Road	├─┼─┼─┤	Cable Car, Chairlift
── ── ──	Unsealed Road	──────	Ferry
←	Lane (one way)		

CYCLING ROUTES

▬▬▬	Main Route
■ ■ ■	Alternative Route
•••••••	Side Trip
▬▬▬	Other Routes
←	Route Direction

HYDROGRAPHIC FEATURES

	Coastline, River, Creek	⊙ ➤	Spring, Rapids
	Canal		Swamp
	Lake	◐	Waterfalls

TOPOGRAPHIC FEATURES

⌂	Cave
	Cliff
▲	Mountain
)(	Pass, Saddle

AREA FEATURES

	Beach		Building
	Mall, Market	❀	Park, Garden

BOUNDARIES

▬ ▪ ▬ ▪	International
── ── ──	Region

Cue Sheets

Route directions are given in a series of brief 'cues', which tell you at what mileage point to change direction and point out features en route. The cues are in a section at the back of the book, with the elevation profiles. These pages could be photocopied or cut out for on-the-road reference and used with a recommended map. (On the Border to Border ride, the cues and profiles are on the corresponding map.) The only other thing you need is a cycle computer.

To make the cue sheets as brief and simple to understand as possible, we've developed a series of symbols (see the Map Legend on p12) and the following rule:

Once your route is following a particular road, continue on that road until the cue sheet tells you otherwise.

Follow the road first mentioned in the cues even though it may cross a highway, shrink to a lane, change name (we generally only include the first name, and sometimes the last), wind, duck and climb its way across the country. Rely on us to tell you when to turn off it.

Because the cue sheets rely on an accurate odometer reading we suggest you disconnect your cycle computer (pop it out of the housing or turn the magnet away from the fork-mounted sensor) whenever you deviate from the main route.

Cue Sheet Example

Cue	
start	Menaggia tourist office
0km	go E on Via Como
0.2 ⬏	Via Lago
▲	4.3km dirt road
13.1 ⬏	SS340
● ●↰	Tremezzo 3.6km ↺
22.7 ▲	800m steep climb
26.4 ■ ■ ↰	alt route: Croce 25km
39.6 ↘ ↰	'to Como'/A2 (dogleg)
40.6 ✳	Como
45.4 ⬏	'to Chiasso'
46.4 ● ●↰	Lago di Oggiono 10km ↺
51.9 ⬈	Via San Primo, Moltrasio
52.1	alt route rejoins (turn left)
76.8 ↘ ✛	(1st exit) Via Garda
76.8 ● 🚦	(20m) Via Corennio Plinio
79.7 ⬈	Via Parco
80.2	Lecco tourist office

the colour band indicates a town

first cue is given as a compass direction: E (east), W (west), NW (northwest) etc ....

potential hazards are detailed

read: *at* 13.1km turn right *for* the side trip *to* Tremezzo indicated distances are for a return trip and are not included in the day's total

climbs are graded as gradual, moderate, hard or steep

read: *at* 26.4 turn left, *for the* alternative route 'to Croce'

read: *at* 39.6km veer left, *following* 'to Como' *road sign,* then right onto the A2 – dogleg (two turns close together)

the town of Como has a point of interest (mentioned in the text)

read: *at* 51.9km veer right *on* Via San Primo, *in the town of* Moltrasio

the alternative route turns left to rejoin the main route

where roundabouts have more/less than four exits the correct exit is also given; not all roundabout and traffic lights are included on the cue sheets, just those where a change of direction is needed

read: 20m *after last turn* turn right *at the* traffic lights *into* Via Corennio Plinio

where possible rides start and/or finish at a tourist information centre

Foreword

HOW TO USE A LONELY PLANET CYCLING GUIDE

The best way to use this Cycling Guide is any way you choose. Some people might link a few days of one ride with a few days of another; others might feel most comfortable following the cue sheets to the letter for an entire tour; or you might use the guide simply to gather ideas on the areas you'd like to explore by bike. Keep in mind that the most memorable travel experiences are often those that are unexpected, and the finest discoveries are those you make yourself.

Our approach is to detail the 'best' rides in each destination, not all possible rides, so if you intend touring for several months you should consider also packing our *Italy* guidebook.

What's Inside Cycling Guides follow roughly the same format as regular Lonely Planet guidebooks. The Facts about the Destination chapters give background information ranging from the history of cycle touring to weather. Facts for the Cyclist deals with the cycle-touring practicalities – it answers planning questions and suggests itineraries. Health & Safety covers medical advice and road rules, while basic maintenance is addressed in Your Bicycle. The Travel Facts chapter will help you make your travel plans and also give handy hints on packing your bicycle. In Italy, where English is not the main language, we include a cyclist-specific Language chapter.

What's left are the rides chapters, broken into geographical regions. Depending on the destination these chapters might cover individual states, countries or traditional provinces.

Ride Descriptions We always start each ride with background information and getting to/from the ride details. Each day's ride is summarized, and the highlights en route are noted in the cues and detailed in the text. At the end of each day our authors recommend the best places to stay and eat, and detail things to see and do out of the saddle. Where possible, each day of a ride starts and ends at a visitor center or somewhere you can get a town map.

Navigating a Cycling Guide The traditional 'signposts' for Lonely Planet guidebooks are the contents (pp1–3) and index (pp379–83). In addition, Cycling Guides offer a comprehensive Table of Rides (pp4–5), providing a quick sketch about every ride featured, as well as an index of maps (p6) showing the regional chapter break-up.

A colour map at the front shows highlights; these are dealt with in greater detail in the Facts for the Cyclist chapter (p30). Each rides chapter also begins with a map showing all the rides for that region.

Lonely Planet's cycling guides are written for cyclists, by cyclists. So, if you know a quieter road than the one we've recommended or want to tell us about your favorite ride, drop us a line. Likewise, if you find a cyclist-friendly cafe or place to stay, or a great bike shop, we'd love to hear about it.

We plan to produce a heap more cycling guides, but if we don't have one to the country you want to cycle in, please let us know and we'll put it on our list.

This Book

This 1st edition of *Cycling Italy* was coordinated in Lonely Planet's Melbourne office by Justin Flynn with help from Jennifer Garrett, Nicola Wells, Craig MacKenzie, Jocelyn Harewood and Melanie Dankel. Anthony Phelan directed the mapping side of things and was superbly assisted by Karen Fry, Helen Rowley, Chris Thomas, Natasha Velleley, Andrew Smith, Jody Whiteoak, Tony Fankhauser, Barbara Benson, Amanda Sierp, Adrian Persoglia and Jacqueline Nguyen. John Shippick steered the book through layout and Vicki Beale took care of the colour wraps. Huw Fowles managed the project from the start until Glenn van der Knijff took control after returning from an overseas jaunt of his own. Cyclist extraordinaire Quentin Frayne expertly wrote the Language chapter and a big *grazie* to Helen Rowley for the climate charts and Wendy Wright for the cover.

UPDATES & READER FEEDBACK

Things change – prices go up, schedules change, good places go bad and bad places go bankrupt. Nothing stays the same. So, if you find things better or worse, recently opened or long-since closed, please tell us and help make the next edition even more accurate and useful.

Lonely Planet thoroughly updates each guidebook as often as possible – usually every two years, although for some destinations the gap can be longer. Between editions, up-to-date information is available in our free, monthly email bulletin *Comet* (w www.lonelyplanet.com/newsletters). You can also check out the *Thorn Tree* bulletin board and *Postcards* section of our website, which carry unverified, but fascinating, reports from travellers.

Tell us about it! We genuinely value your feedback. A well-travelled team at Lonely Planet reads and acknowledges every email and letter we receive and ensures that every morsel of information finds its way to the relevant authors, editors and cartographers.

Everyone who writes to us will find their name listed in the next edition of the appropriate guidebook. The very best contributions will be rewarded with a free guidebook.

We may edit, reproduce and incorporate your comments in Lonely Planet products such as guidebooks, websites and digital products, so let us know if you don't want your comments reproduced or your name acknowledged.

How to contact Lonely Planet:
Online: e talk2us@lonelyplanet.com.au, w www.lonelyplanet.com
Australia: Locked Bag 1, Footscray, Victoria 3011
UK: 72 – 82 Rosebery Ave, London EC1R 4RW
USA: 150 Linden St, Oakland, CA 94607

Introduction

As you turn a corner and lean into a sudden incline, you pass three elderly gentlemen seated in a row on a stone, wall-hung bench. This bend in the road – their bend – hasn't changed a pebble since those black-and-white photo days they lived in full colour, days when they pranced up hills on much heavier, clunkier bicycles. You can see it in the shrewd blue of their heavy-lidded eyes. *'Salve!'* ('Hello!') you say as they lift their gazes in unison. *'Dai, ragazzo!'* ('Give it your all, kid!') says the first. *'Forza!'* ('Be strong!') agrees the second. The third harrumphs encouragingly.

The road is covered with graffiti, like 'Piratatatatatata' to egg on Marco Pantani, *il pirata* (the pirate), when he sweeps through. You are climbing a hill ridden by the world's best cyclists during the Giro d'Italia. Suddenly a multicoloured squadron of day riders clatters by. Each one salutes you in turn, several raising sweaty fists in pedal solidarity. You aren't moving as fast as they are, but you're not meant to. You want to take in the majesty of the morning mountains and breathe the aroma of fresh salami and cheese wrapped in a thick local loaf while seated on a sunny piazza. You want to know that your legs powered you between this tunnel of beech trees and the day-end hotel nestled into an ancient crook of a Renaissance village.

This is why you came to Italy. For the roadside inn, the tinkle of cutlery raking in the fragrant pumpkin pulp folded into pasta shells and the glint of sun through a glass of Chianti. You earn these rewards for the hills you climb. You earn the vistas through luxuriant valleys, dips in the waters of hidden azure Mediterranean coves.

A child races beside you. *'Dove vai?'* ('Where're you going?') he asks. *'Su!'* ('Up!') you reply. *'Perchè?'* ('Why?') he queries. You ask yourself, why are you lugging your life in panniers though this foreign land? *'Perchè sono in Italia!'* ('Why I'm in Italy!) you rejoice. Yes, you are in Italy. And there really is no better way to live Italy than from the saddle of *la bici* (the bike).

Facts about Italy

HISTORY

Italy's history is a patchwork of powerful empires and domination by foreign muscle. From the fall of the Roman Empire in AD 476 until the foundation of the Kingdom of Italy in 1861, the country was never a unified entity. Since then Italy has developed into one of Western Europe's leading powers. The following timeline pinpoints some landmark events in Italian history.

c. 70,000 BC – Paleolithic Neanderthals inhabit the Italian peninsula

c. 1800 BC – start of Bronze Age; peninsula is home to several Italic tribes, including the Ligurians, the Veneti, the Apulians, the Siculi and the Sardi

1300 BC – Etruscans migrate to the peninsula

753 BC – traditional date for foundation of Rome by Romulus (on 21 April)

800–700 BC – peak of Etruscan civilisation, based on the large city-states of the Etruscan League

509 BC – foundation of the Roman Republic

312 BC – construction of the Via Appia (Appian Way) begins

264–241 BC – first Punic War fought between Rome and Carthage over control of Sicily; Rome is victorious

241–218 BC – Rome expels Gauls from the northern peninsula and consolidates what are now the frontiers of Italy

218–202 BC – second Punic War sparked by Hannibal's famous offensive using elephants to cross the Alps, Rome wins again but only after considerable losses

149–146 BC – third and final Punic War deals the final blow to Carthage

91 BC – after Social War, Rome grants citizenship to Etruscan and Italic peoples

73–71 BC – second Social War led by Spartacus ends in disaster for the insurgents

60 BC – first Triumvirate of Pompey, Crassus and Julius Caesar

48 BC – Julius Caesar becomes consul and dictator after Pompey's murder

44 BC – Julius Caesar murdered (15 March)

27 BC – Caius Octavian becomes Augustus Caesar, Rome's first emperor, and rules for 40 years

AD 54–68 – obviously deranged Nero rules the empire

AD 72 – Emperor Vespasian starts the Colosseum

AD 98–117 – the Roman Empire reaches its zenith under Emperor Trajan

313 – Emperor Constantine converts to Christianity and in his Edict of Milan officially recognises it as a religion

364 – Empire split into eastern and western halves

452 – Attila the Hun invades Italy

488–526 – relative peace under Ostrogothic Emperor Theodoric, ruling from Ravenna

527–565 – eastern Roman Emperor Justinian (ruling from Constantinople) reconquers Italy; Byzantine era begins

754 – Franks invade Italy, led by King Pepin, and establish the Papal States

800 – Pepin's son Charlemagne is crowned emperor in St Peter's Basilica in Rome

831 – Muslim Arabs settle in Sicily

962 – Saxon King Otto I is crowned in Roma and founds Holy Roman Empire

1091 – Normans conquer Sicily

1095 – first Crusade is launched

12th century – Frederick I (known as Barbarossa) is Holy Roman Emperor

1220 – Norman rule gives way to Germanic influence when Frederick II (known later as Stupor Mundi, Wonder of the World) crowned Holy Roman Emperor

1232 – beginning of the Inquisition

1268 – control of Sicily passes to France

12th–14th centuries – northern city-states evolve and regional divisions begin to take shape

1282 – Spanish take over Sicily, dividing the south between Spain and France

13th–14th centuries – Dante Alighieri confirms poetic force of Italian vernacular through his *Divina Commedia*; painter Giotti's revolutionary style foreshadows Renaissance

1305–77 – Babylonian Captivity sees Pope move to Avignon, France

1347–48 – the Black Death kills more than one-third of Italy's population

1388–1417 – the Great Schism of two rival Popes, one in Rome, the other in Avignon

1451 – Christopher Columbus born in Genoa

15th century – dawn of the Renaissance

1506 – Pope Julius II employs Bramante to design the new St Peter's Basilica

1508 – Michelangelo is commissioned to paint the ceiling of the Sistine Chapel

1527 – the Sack of Rome by Charles V

16th century – the Counter-Reformation, the Church's response to the Reformation that led to the rise of Protestantism

1582 – Gregorian calendar introduced, fixing 1 January as first day of the year

1651 – Bernini completes *Fontana dei Fiumi*, Baroque masterpiece in Rome's Piazza Navona

1714 – War of Spanish Succession results in control of Italy being passed from Spain to Austria

18th century – the Enlightenment sweeps away the barbarism of the Counter Reformation; the

Grand Tour, undertaken by privileged and adventurous European travellers, familiarises many with Italy's culture and geography

1796 – Napoleon invades Italy

1804 – Napoleon establishes Kingdom of Italy with himself on the throne

1815 – Congress of Vienna reinstates Italy's monarchs and restores its boundaries after Napoleon's defeat (at Waterloo)

1830 – Mazzini founds a nationalist movement, Young Italy, and leads several abortive uprisings

1848 – Italian unification movement gains momentum when Garibaldi returns to Italy from South America

1860 – Garibaldi and his Expedition of One Thousand take Naples and Sicily

1861 – Kingdom of Italy declared and Vittorio Emanuele II proclaimed king; Italy's first parliament convened with Cavour as prime minister

1866 – Venice, wrested from Austria, joins Kingdom of Italy

1870 – Rome reclaimed from Napoleon III and declared capital of Italy; Pope, refusing to acknowledge Kingdom, is later stripped of remaining secular powers

1889 – Italian racer Tomaselli wins Grand Prix de la Ville on a Bianchi bicycle

1894 – Catholics given right to vote; backlash against socialism; male suffrage completed but women denied the vote

1909 – first running of the Giro d'Italia

1914 – WWI breaks out in Europe

1915 – Italy enters the war as an ally of France, Britain and Russia

1919 – Treaty of Versailles restores Trentino to Italy, and hands over Trieste and South Tirol (now Alto Adige) as well; Mussolini founds the Fascist Party

1921 – Fascist Party wins 35 of the 135 parliamentary seats

1924 – Fascist Party wins elections with 64% of the vote; world's first Fascist regime

1925 – opposition parties expelled from parliament; two-thirds of electorate disenfranchised

1929 – Lateran Pact declares Catholicism the sole religion of Italy; Vatican becomes independent state

1940 – Italy enters WWII as an ally of Germany

1943 – Mussolini arrested; king and parliament take control and sign armistice with Allies and declare war on Germany; Mussolini rescued; northern puppet Republic of Salò declared

1944–45 – with Allies moving from the south, Italian Resistance fights German troops in the north

1945 – Mussolini and his mistress captured and shot by partisans; Italy is liberated

1946 – referendum abolishes monarchy; republic is established; newly formed Democrazia Cristiana (Christian Democrats) wins elections

1949 – Fausto Coppi wins both Tour de France and Giro d'Italia

1957 – European Economic Community founded with Italy as a member; beginning of the Economic Miracle (significant industrial expansion and drop in unemployment to mid-1960s)

1968 – student uprisings and the formation of revolutionary groups

1970 – regional governments established; divorce legalised

1980 – right-wing extremists held responsible for explosion in Bologna killing 84 people

1992 – Tangentopoli (a massive corruption scandal) breaks, eventually implicating prominent politicians and businesspeople

1993 – Sicilian godfather, Salvatore Riina arrested after 24 years on the run; Mafia bombs in Milan, Florence and Rome kill several people and damage historic monuments

1994 – right-wing coalition government voted in; media magnate Silvio Berlusconi appointed prime minister

1995 – Berlusconi government collapses

1996 – centre-left coalition government elected; Romano Prodi becomes prime minister

1997 – disastrous earthquake in Assisi damages priceless artistic works and religious buildings; Salvatore Riina sentenced to life in prison

1998 – Italy joins European monetary union

2000 – major nationwide celebrations for Jubilee Year (Holy Year), with vast sums spent to restore many monuments; disastrous floods in the north cause deaths and damage

2001 – Berlusconi elected again and forms Italy's 59th government since 1946; violence at Genoa during World Trade Organisation meeting

2002 – euro replaces lire as Italy's currency

History of Cycling in Italy

Not a da Vinci Italians celebrated the late 1960s discovery of a distinctly bike-like sketch connected to Leonardo da Vinci's *Codex Atlanticus*. It was hailed as proof that an Italian was the first to conceive of the bicycle. Unfortunately, later studies and analyses of the *Codex* image concluded rather convincingly that the rough rendering was a forgery and so Italy withdrew from the Franco–Germanic–Scottish debate about who really invented the bicycle. What *is* clear is that although the first great creative strides were made elsewhere, Italian genius was fundamental to the steady development of *la bicicletta* (the bicycle).

Anche Io (Me Too) The first Italian bicycle manufacturer, Raimondo Vellani of Modena, sent his models to market in

Mazzini

Revolutionary Giuseppe Mazzini (1805–72) was the champion of the Risorgimento (Italian unification movement). Yet, as a result of his fight for Italian unification, he was exiled from his homeland for much of his life.

Son of a Genoese doctor, Mazzini studied at Genoa university until 1827 when he joined southern Italy's secret republican Carbonari movement. Three years later, his political activities forced him to relocate to Marseille (in neighbouring France). Far from giving up the fight, the Genoese rebel founded Giovane Italia (Young Italy), a society of young men seeking the liberation of Italy from foreign and domestic tyranny and its unification under a republican government. Significantly, however, this was to be achieved through education and, where necessary, revolt by guerrilla bands. Secret branches of Giovane Italia were set up in Genoa and other cities – all masterminded remotely by Mazzini.

During the 1830s and 1840s, the exiled freedom-lover organised several abortive uprisings. By 1834 he'd gained an ardent follower in the shape of Giuseppe Garibaldi (1807–1882) who, like Mazzini, was tried in absentia and sentenced to death following an unsuccessful uprising in 1834 in his native Piedmont.

From 1837, Mazzini lived in England, writing articles and soliciting support in a consciousness-raising effort about the Italian question directed at all Europeans.

1867–68; the first Michaux-style *vélocipèdes* (known as a boneshaker because of the rough ride on cobbled streets) came from Carlo Michel of Alessandria at about the same time. In the 10 years that followed, more than 20 workshops set wheels in motion in Milan, Monza, Padua, Novara, Bologna, Turin and Verona.

It wasn't until 1885 that the world got its first glimpse of the Italian genius for bicycle innovation. Following on an 1884 idea, Milan-based Eduardo Bianchi built a bicycle with two equal-sized, tension-spoked wheels (to avoid the perils of the ever larger front wheel of the brakeless 'two-wheel' or bicycle machine) and began a long career as Italy's – and eventually Europe's – foremost bicycle trendsetter and manufacturer. Shortly after, he used iron instead of hard wood for the frame and fork and, by 1888, had substituted pneumatic tyres for the solid rubber predecessors. The resulting 'pneumatic-tyred safety bike', manufactured throughout the north of the country with heroic brand names like Olympia, Frera, Lygie, Taurus, Legnano, Atala, Ganna and Gloria, spread like wildfire. Bianchi's notoriety and place in manufacturing were further assured when, in 1889, Italian cyclist Tomaselli raced a Bianchi to victory in the Grand Prix de la Ville (in Paris), the most important race of the times.

In 1895, the first international Bicycle Exposition was held in Milan and the vastly expanded state of the market, including Italy's newfound manufacturing stature on equal footing with others, was established.

In the history of cycling invention, three more great Italian accomplishments deserve mention, although they came decades later. In 1915, Bianchi committed his company to building bicycles for the WWI *bersaglieri*, a special Italian bicycle army corps. Today Bianchi boasts that the sturdy model produced was the first mountain bike, complete with dual suspension and large pneumatic tyres. In 1927, another Italian great, Tullio Campagnolo, made his mark by inventing the quick-release for bicycle wheels and, in 1930, the *cambio a bacchetta* (rod gear), which inspired the modern front and rear derailleur. These patents were the start of the serious technical advancement in the sport and the dominance of Campagnolo components. Finally, Francesco Moser, the brilliant Italian champion, designed the first disc wheels, with which in 1984 he broke Eddy Merckx's 12-year-old one-hour world record and the 50km/h mark. Today's Italian bicycle manufacturers have continued the legacy, and are now considered to be some of the best and most innovative companies in the world.

Not Exactly a Love Affair Unlike in other European countries where cycling flourished from its earliest days, the history of cycling in Italy was decidedly turbulent. In fact, *il ciclismo* (the cycle) has faced so much of an uphill battle that some historians can't speak of Italian cycling without mentioning *duelli* (duels); cyclists were always up against something.

The first challenge came from the Italian people themselves. Except during the cycling glory years of the fascist 1930s and after WWII in the 1940s to 1950s, cyclists faced rampant *ciclofobia*, a widespread fear of and hostility towards bicycles, and all of the ideas they espoused: modernisation, emancipation, liberalisation etc. City folk considered the bicycle dangerous, a nuisance and meddlesome, and rural dwellers feared the invasion it made possible from the city. One famous writer-reporter named Lombroso even wrote a defamatory treatise supporting a popular theory linking the bicycle with delinquency (since the bicycle could be used to flee the scene of a crime). Even legislators erected obstacles: highly restrictive laws (the earliest from 1818)

governed the handling of a bicycle, imposed taxes on its use and required its registration with authorities (and even licence plates).

Despite this, two-wheel *appassionati* (an Italian term for people who have a real passion for something) gave in to their zeal, and two organisations formed at the end of the 19th century. Although fundamental to the advancement of cycling, they also fed directly into the duel paradigm since few good words passed between them. In 1884, hardened speedsters and racers – those practicing *ciclismo agonistico* (agonistical or athletic cycling) – rallied around the Unione Velocipedistica Italiana (Italian Velocipedallers Union, UVI). Around 10 years later, frustrated, leisure-minded enthusiasts

Giro d'Italia

The Giro d'Italia is Italy's answer to the Tour de France. First run in 1909 (four years after the Tour got its start), the Giro, sometimes called the 'Feast of May', is cycling's second-greatest multistage race and Italy's biggest annual sporting event, attracting hundreds of thousands of spectators to the roadside and watched on television by more than 100 million people worldwide.

The newspaper *Gazzetta dello Sport*, formed in 1896 by the merger of *Il Ciclista* and *La Tripletta*, announced in 1908 that it would sponsor the yearly event. The attempt to increase its readership paid off, as it jumped from two to three issues a week for the first Giro and then became a daily for the Giro of 1913. The *Gazzetta's* distinct pink colour became a part of the race when, starting in 1931, a special *maglia rosa* (pink jersey) was awarded to the overall leader at the end of each stage, to be worn the following day. Other jerseys are donned by other leaders: the best hill climber wears green; the rider with the most consistent (by rank, not time) daily finishes gets the cyclamen jersey; and a sky-blue bib is presented to the rider with the most 'intergiro' points won at predetermined intermediate positions along the rides (and usually requiring excellent sprinting abilities).

The first Giro ran for 2448km in eight stages, starting and finishing in Milan. The winner, Luigi Ganna, took the top purse of 5325 lire, four times the race director's yearly salary. By contrast, the 2002 edition (run per tradition from mid-May into early June) covered 3334km in 20 day-stages (plus two rest days) and a short prologue. It began in the Netherlands (only the seventh time it has started outside of Italy), and went through Belgium, Luxembourg and France in celebration of the introduction of the euro, the EU's single currency. The total prize money was €1.03 million.

Some of the Giro d'Italia's most unusual moments include the 1925 start of Alfonsine Strada, the only woman ever to compete with the men – she completed the course but not before the official cut-off time; in 1930, after winning four out of five years (and taking second the fifth year), Alfredo Binda was paid an amount equal to the winning purse *not* to ride – he nevertheless returned to the winner's podium one more time in 1933; 1933 was also the first year the race was timed; in 1954, after riders climbed the Passo del Bernina at a 'tourist's pace', race directors withheld trophies due to 'insufficient *spirito agonistico* (athletic spirit)'; an Italian has won the Giro 58 of its 84 years; the Giro has been cancelled only nine times, 1915–18 for WWI and 1941–45 for WWII.

The Giro today is more than just a race. Before and after the riders come through, a parade of more than 1000 vehicles covers the same distance: a show of sponsors one hour ahead of the racers; television cameras, race monitors, team cars and many other support crew just behind the racers; and a drove of others far behind.

of *ciclismo turistico* (cycling tourism) heeded the call of the Touring Club Ciclistico Italiano (Italian Cycle Touring Club, TCI), whose monthly *Rivista Mensile* carried news and inspiration to stalwart tourers. For years, the rivalry between UVI and TCI set cycling against itself, a battle that subsided only when new and powerful external duelling partners – first soccer and then the automobile – forced the cycling world to form a somewhat united front.

Social Revolution Despite the setbacks, *la bicicletta* is an undeniable part of Italian history. As the first affordable means of individual transport, it revolutionised Italian life. Women, who took to cycling in respectably large numbers, were liberated by it. Workers traditionally confined to local markets could search further afield. The first of the *bersaglieri* units was formed to accelerate the speed of message delivery during army manoeuvres. Even the moneyed gentry, with time on their hands, turned to the opportunities the bicycle opened. The greatest early example of this is the nearly 750km Milan–Rome *gita turistica* (tourist excursion) organised in 1895 by TCI and attended by Queen Margherita herself. She travelled in a private carriage, but was preceded by a parade of 70 elegant, saddle-mounted gentlemen in dress coats and bowler hats. The 1901 TCI tour in Sardinia made an equivalent splash, welcomed in every town by banners, bands and cheering locals throwing flowers.

In 1904, TCI celebrated its 10th anniversary with a Festa turistica della Nazione (National Tourist Feast), a pageant of 10,000 cyclists in Milan followed by a massive banquet for 3400 people. TCI, in addition to demonstrating the harmless and practical value of the bicycle, had been producing the world's first cycle-tourism maps with elevation charts and cue sheets not unlike those in this book. TCI was also the first group to lobby for improved roads, left to deteriorate after the railroad proved effective, and even bike paths.

In 1905, there were 242,000 bicycles (and 5000 motorcycles and 4000 automobiles) on the roads of Italy. By 1913, more than 1.5 million bicycles were in use. For thousands of Italians, owning a bicycle was a quality of life improvement.

Il Ciclismo Agonistico Meanwhile, the UVI laboured in its own camp to promote cycling as a tough athletic undertaking. Taking its inspiration from France and in cooperation with the newspaper *Il Gazzetta dello Sport*, it developed Italy's very own long-distance road race calendar, including rides that are today's classics: the Giro di Lombardia (1905), the Milan–San Remo one-day epic (1907) and Giro d'Italia (1909), Italy's greatest race (see the boxed text, p19).

Of perhaps greater importance than the actual races are the famous Italian personalities and grand cycling champions who dominated the sport. True to the tradition of duelling in *ciclismo*, the masters in the saddle always emerged in pairs and battled heroically for victory in ways that sometimes polarised and always electrified the nation. The duelling cast of characters is a rollcall of legends, starting with Giovanni Gerbi, the *diavolo rosso* (red devil), who triumphed in the first Giro di Lombardia, but whose race-end antics gave the first Milan–San Remo to his French rival, Lucien Petit Breton. This was followed by Girardengo versus Binda, Binda versus Guerra (and Olmo), Bartali versus Coppi (the greatest contest of all, see the boxed text on p21), Bartali versus Magno, Adorno versus Gimondi, Gimondi versus Motta, Moser versus Saronna, and Bugno versus Chiappucci. In one of the latest wheel-to-wheel battles, Marco Pantani, *il pirata* (the pirate), gave the 1999 Giro d'Italia to Ivan Gotti, when, at the end of the penultimate stage, he was removed from the race after testing positive for performance-enhancing drugs.

And Today? The bicycle continues to duel for its survival. Seen as a fascist vehicle in the 1930s, its nonpolitical utilitarian value came to the fore in an economically and materially depressed Italy. Once feared for its symbolic power, the bicycle was later adopted by neo-realist cinematographers and futurist artists to represent hope, renewal, opportunity and advancement. As a curious sign of the times, today the bicycle is sometimes thought of as a steed from which to fight the speed of modernisation.

Still, the bicycle rolls on (there are an estimated 20 million bikes hidden in Italian garages). Mountain bikes hit the hills in the 1990s (see the boxed text 'Mountain Biking', p40-1). Races grow in stature led by the Federazione Ciclistica Italiana (which took over from the UVI). And cycle-tourism lobbies continue to demand quality, protected bikepaths, and recognition from the same stubborn automobile-minded lawmakers, urban planners and fellow citizens who have stumped them since the 1880s (the Federazione Italiana Amici della Bici picked up where TCI left off after the latter dropped the 'Ciclistico' from its name).

GEOGRAPHY

Italy is one of the world's most easily recognised countries. Its high-heeled, knee-length boot shape embraces an area of just over 300,000 sq km and is caressed by four Mediterranean sub-seas: the Adriatic to the east, Ionian in the south, Tyrrhenian between Sardinia and France's Corsica, and Ligurian lapping the northwestern Riviera.

Italy's terrain is 75% mountainous, divided between two major ranges: the Alps and the Apennines. The Alps dominate the north, rising from the Gulf of Genoa on the French–Italian border and arcing east to the Adriatic Sea like a heavy lifted eyebrow. The Alps comprise three groups of peaks: the Maritime and Western Alps between Genoa and Valle d'Aosta; the Central Alps reaching east to Alto Adige; and the Eastern Alps of the Dolomites and Julian and Carnic Alps. The highest all-Italian summit is Gran Paradiso (4061m) in Valle d'Aosta; nearby Mont Blanc (4807m) and Monte Rosa (4634m) straddle Italy's borders with France and Switzerland respectively. Both Sardinia and Sicily also have significant mountain groups, and Sicily hosts Europe's highest active volcano, Mt Etna (3261m).

The 1220km-long Apennines are like a craggy boot-length zipper from Liguria to

Bartali versus Coppi

Italy's grand champions of the pedals accomplished incredible things, repeatedly winning Italy's greatest marathons, but also dominating the sport at an international level. Greatest among the great were two riders who for more than 10 years exhilarated the country with their individual exploits, but also split the nation into two fan camps, roaring for the triumph of personal favourites in the cycling duel of the century.

Florentine Gino Bartali (1914–2000) was the first to hit the scene. Considered 'the pious' one, he rode 175 victories in 25 years (including the Tour de France in 1938 and 1948, the Giro d'Italia in 1936, 1940, 1947 and 1950, the Milan–San Remo four times, the Giro di Lombardia three times, and was four times Italian national champion, but never world champ). He raced his last of eight Tours de France when he was 39 and placed 11th. But his domination of the late 1930s came to an abrupt end when, in 1940, his Legnano team hired the man he would have to do battle with: Il Campionissimo (the champion of champions), the most beloved of all racers, Fausto Coppi (1919–60).

Coppi was born in Novi Ligure to a poor farmer and at the age of 14 became a delicatessen bicycle delivery boy tackling the hills in his area with aplomb. He won his first race at 19, went semi-professional at 20 and was victorious in his first Giro d'Italia when he was 21, the youngest winner ever. From 1940 to 1959 (except 1943 and 1944 when he was a prisoner of war), he won 151 races, including the Tour de France two times (1949, 1952), the Giro d'Italia five times (1940, 1947, 1949, 1952 and 1953), the Milan–San Remo three times, the Giro di Lombardia five times, Paris–Roubaix once, and was world campion in 1953. He was the first rider ever to win the Tour and Giro in the same year (1949), when he also won the Milan-San Remo and Giro di Lombardia. Known as the *airone* (heron) due to his grace in the saddle but unease out of it, Coppi, who died young (age 40) of untreated malaria, was the soul of cycling.

Both men hit the scene while cycling was in favour, both men carried it to the heights over which they rode, both men's careers were interrupted by WWII, and yet both men had the strength and character to lift their war-shattered lives, careers and, with them the nation, back to soaring heights. Together and separate, united but divided, they were in many ways the spirit of the nation. For more about this incredible time, read Bartali's memoires, *Tutto sbagliato tutto da rifare* (All Wrong, All to Be Redone).

Calabria and even into Sicily. Corno Grande (2914m) in Abruzzo's Gran Sasso d'Italia group is its zenith. Smaller Apennine spur ranges include the marble Apuan Alps in northwest Tuscany, the volcanoes in the south and the limestone uplands on the Amalfi Coast–Sorrento Peninsula.

The densely settled, industrial Po plain (Pianura Padana) is Italy's vast and peerless lowland. Water from scores of rivers and some of Italy's 1500 lakes drains into the meandering Po River, Italy's longest, which in turn empties into the Adriatic through a broad delta south of Venice. The largest inland bodies of water are the northern glacier-carved lakes of Garda, Maggiore and Como.

The coastline is varied, though notably short on sandy beaches. This is similar to Italy's Tyrrhenian Sea islands: Sicily and, off its north coast, the scattered Aeolian Islands; a group near Naples, including Capri; Sardinia; and the handful between Corsica and the coast, notably Elba.

CLIMATE

Italy has six main climatic regions, mainly determined by mountain influence.

Adriatic Region The climate has a continental character because the shallow Adriatic Sea's waters can't trap the summer heat and therefore has little influence. Winters are characterised by cold northeast winds.

Alpine Region The climate is strongly influenced by altitude, with long, cold winters and short, cool summers. Rainfall is greater in summer, especially in the pre-Alpine areas, although thunderstorms are frequent from May to October. It can snow at any time of year, although mostly from December to March. It is, in general, warmer and drier at the western end due to the snow line's higher elevation.

Apennine Region Continental tendencies prevail here too. Winters are cold and snowy. Rain is abundant from autumn to spring, and always heavier on the Tyrrhenian slopes. Summers tend to be hot and dry.

Ligurian–Tyrrhenian Region A maritime climate prevails, ruled by frequent, heavy rain (much less in summer). Winters are cool but milder than in the surrounding hills. Summers can be hot and humid, although there is usually a narrow annual temperature range.

Mediterranean Region Summers are hot and dry. Rainfall is heavy, especially in winter, which is relatively mild. The annual temperature range is limited.

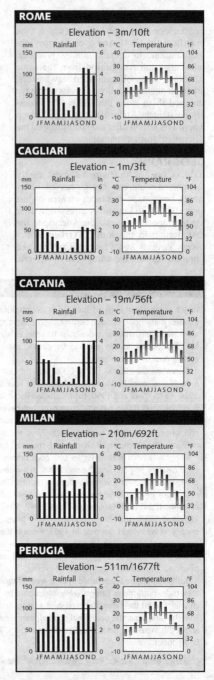

Windy Italy

Of the confusing tangle of gusts and zephyrs, four prevailing winds in Italy have actually been given names, a hint that they are more than just gentle breezes.

The **föhn** is a widespread mountain phenomenon. Moist air rises across windward slopes, condenses as rain or snow and shrouds ridges in cloud. The air then surges down the leeward slope, becoming increasingly warm and dry. Lake district windsurfers love it, but depending on the lay of the land, it can be a curse to cyclists. A bewildering cousin of this wind blows *up* most mountain valleys starting early in the afternoon and hindering otherwise happy-go-lucky descents.

The **mistral** is confined to the northwest and Sardinia; it's a cold, dry northwesterly which rushes down between the Pyrenees (on the Franco–Spanish border) and the Alps.

In contrast, the southerly and southeasterly **sirocco** is usually hot and humid and makes life uncomfortable in the south during spring and autumn. It develops as a dry wind over the Atlas Mountains in North Africa. By the time it reaches Italy, it's laden with sand and Mediterranean moisture.

The **bora** roars across the Adriatic coast from the Albanian mountains as a cold dry easterly wind, gusting to 100km/h, usually during winter.

Elsewhere, winds are hard to fix with regional prevailing tendencies. Examining which way roadside trees are leaning is a good way of determining how local conditions blow.

Po Region Winters are cold and snowy, and summers warm and sultry. Rainfall is highest in spring and autumn. The climate is milder in the pre-Alpine and lake areas.

ECOLOGY & ENVIRONMENT

Since prehistoric times, humans have left evidence of time spent in Italy. Forests have been felled, marshes drained, hills terraced and clearings levelled to make way for industry, housing, pastures, orchards and crops. In fact, truly wild country is rare these days, accounting for less than 20% of the territory (as determined by the Word Wide Fund for Nature), and mainly confined to the remote reaches of Sardinia and the highest mountains. Pollution problems caused by industrial and urban waste are far too common, fouling air, water and land. Rampant rubbish is a particularly trenchant example of this.

Conservation

The Italian government's record on environmental issues is poor. Although Il Ministero dell'Ambiente (Ministry for the Environment) was established in 1986, environmental laws are not adequately enforced. For example, environmental groups claim that one of the reasons for the devastating impact of flooding in northern Italy is that riverbank deforestation and building controls have been far too slack. (Find out more about government's activities, in Italian, at **w** www.minambiente.it.)

Environmental organisations have had some success in arousing awareness about a wide range of issues, though their membership remains small. Recycling practices are being taken more and more seriously, partly due to lobbying and campaigns led by associations like Lega per l'Ambiente (Environmental League). Car-free days in city centres have gained widespread support. Hunting curbs and quotas are being instituted. And the year 2002 was declared International Year of Mountains by the UN, giving environmental lobby groups a case for launching awareness-raising campaigns.

Some active environmental organisations include:

Club Alpino Italiano (☎ 02 205 72 31,
  w www.cai.it) Via Petrella 19, 20124 Milano
Lega Italiana Protezione Uccelli (LIPU, Italian
  League for Bird Protection; ☎ 06 397 30 903,
  w www.lipu.it) Via Monte Grappa 18, 20124
  Milano
Lega per l'Ambiente (Environmental League;
  ☎ 06 86 26 81) Via Salaria 403, 00199 Roma
World Wildlife Fund (WWF; ☎ 06 84 49 71,
  w www.wwf.it) Via Po 25/c, 00198 Roma

National Parks & Reserves

Italy has slowly developed an extensive system of protected areas since the first national park was set aside in 1922. A concerted drive to expand the number of parks and bring protected areas from today's 6% of the country up to 10% has been moderately successful. The three principal categories of protected areas are *parchi nazionali* (national parks), *parchi naturali regionali e interregionali* (regional and interregional natural parks), and *riserve naturale statale e regionale* (state and regional natural reserves). At the time of writing, there were 20 national parks (with four more on the way), 130 regional parks, 150 state reserves and 270 regional reserves, as well as a variety of 230 wetlands, special protection zones and special conservation areas, plus 33 Unesco-designated World Heritage sites. Many of the rides in this book pass through or near some of these natural oases. Find out more about Italy's protected areas through the website of the Federazione Italiana Parchi e Riserve Naturali (Italian Federation of Parks and Reserves; w www.parks.it).

FLORA & FAUNA
Flora
Italy's two most distinctive floral zones are alpine and Mediterranean.

Alpine flora has been affected most by Ice Ages, so today's alpine flora actually consists of relatively recent arrivals. In the mountains the growing season (essentially the snow-free period) becomes shorter with increasing altitude, and therefore Alpine plants take longer to recover from any setback in their growth cycle. Mountain bikers and hiking cyclists should keep this in mind, and take particular care to avoid damaging the fragile flora of the Alps.

In the Mediterranean region, the long presence of humans on the Italian peninsula has resulted in widespread destruction of original forests and vegetation, and their replacement with crops, orchards, flower farms and *macchia*, a scrub that blankets the once-forested foothills in the south. There are, however, still isolated and protected pockets of naturally occurring early vegetation.

Fauna
As with the flora, many animals that now inhabit the Alpine region migrated there after the Ice Ages. Some came from Arctic regions, while others were originally inhabitants of central Asia. Italy is home to remarkably little dangerous fauna. It has only two poisonous snakes, the adder and the viper.

Many animals found in the Alps are also common in the Mediterranean zone. In reality, not that many wild animals remain in Italy's most populous areas – most have been hunted relentlessly – but you might spot a deer, a wild boar, a fox or other smaller mammals from the road in remote areas.

GOVERNMENT & POLITICS
Italy is a parliamentary republic, headed by a president who appoints the prime minister. The parliament consists of two houses – a 315-seat senate and a 630-strong chamber of deputies – both with equal legislative power. Neither house has formal precedence over the other. The seat of government is in Rome. The president, who serves a seven-year term, was last elected in 1999 and resides in the Palazzo del Quirinale. The Chamber of Deputies sits in the Palazzo Montecitorio and the Senate in the Palazza Madama, near Piazza Navona.

Italian politics are still reeling from a decade of scandals that seriously polarised the political party spectrum. Tagentopoli (literally 'kickback cities') broke in early 1992 when a political functionary was arrested on charges of accepting bribes in exchange for public works contracts. Since then, extensive investigations known as Mani Pulite (Clean Hands) have implicated thousands of top politicians, officials and businessmen. At the same time, organised crime continues to haunt everyone.

ECONOMY
Italy's economy lay in ruins at the close of WWII, but the country wasted little time in setting about repairing the damage. By the early 1960s, a boom known as the Economic Miracle catapulted Italy back into the markets. Today, services and public administration account for nearly two-thirds of GDP, industry one-third, and shrinking agriculture the few remaining percentiles. Tourism is a particularly important source of income.

Italy currently holds a spot in the top 10 of largest economies in the world. This is true despite massive public debt, widespread political corruption, an arcane legal and tax system, and a fabled Italian penchant for friendly (ie, grey market) transactions. For these reasons, many foreign firms have avoided investment in Italy.

Against many expectations, Italy succeeded in qualifying for inclusion in the European common market's single currency (the euro) that became legal tender (replacing the lira) on 1 January 2002. A lot remains to be seen about how the new market will evolve, especially given the worldwide economic slump of 2001–02. The signs are really quite mixed. Encouragingly, Italy's economy is improving again despite being hampered by decreasing industrial growth, shrinking agricultural vitality, relatively high taxes and unemployment, persistent prosperity gaps between the north and south, and a political system eternally mired in wrangling.

POPULATION & PEOPLE

Italy's population stood at an estimated 57,716,000 in 2002. The growth rate (0.05%) is one of the lowest in Europe – surprising given the Italians' traditional orientation towards children and the family.

The most densely populated urban areas are around Rome, Milan and Naples, and the most populous regions are Piedmont, parts of Lombardy, Liguria, Veneto and Friuli–Venezia Giulia, where industry is concentrated and earning potential is high.

Italy has traditionally been a country of emigrants, with nationals travelling to many parts of the world, mainly the USA, Australia and Canada, in search of work. In recent years, however, the tide has turned.

Large numbers of immigrants have arrived from Africa and Eastern Europe.

ARTS
Music

The Italians have played a pivotal role in classical music history. They invented the system of musical notation used today, the piano and even the violin.

Impressive is the list of great Italian *musiciste* (musicians) from St Ambrose, the 4th-century bishop of Milan, to today's tenor celebrity Pavarotti. In the 16th century, Cremona's Monteverdi was the earliest successful composer in an operatic musical revolution. He was inspired, among other things, by the first modern violin, built in 1566 by Amati (1511–77), also from Cremona. Other famous Cremonese violinmakers include Rugeri (1620–95), Guarneri (1626–98) and Stradivari (1644–1737).

In the 17th and 18th centuries, instrumental music really found its voice. Corelli (1653–1713), Vivaldi (1675–1741) and Sammartini (1700–75) experimented with form, paving the way for 19th-century superstars like Paganini (1782–1840), Verdi (1813–1901), Puccini (1858–1924), Bellini (1801–35), Donizetti (1797–1848) and Rossini (1792–1868). Verdi's *Aïda*, *La Traviata*, *Oberto* and *Otello*, Bellini's

---

Fashion & Design

Milan's meteoric rise to European fashion capital began in the 1960s. By 1971, Italy's largest fashion show had also made the leggy leap to the north. Milan's most notable fashion houses are Giorgio Armani – which set up shop in 1975 and revolutionised the industry with *prêt à porter* (ready to wear) collections – Gucci, Prada, Laura Bijoti and Krizia, Valentino, Versace and Moschino.

The Camera Nazionale della Moda Italiana (CNMI) oversees Italian fashion. Milan's annual 10- to 12-day fashion bonanzas are seasonal, the most prestigious being the February/March and September/October Milano Collezioni Donna, where the world's top designers unveil their women's collections. The men's fashion show – Milano Collezioni Uomo – occurs in January and June/July. In early 2000 the Milano Freestyle debuted, a show devoted to designer sportswear.

Too often unnoticed as a form of expression, consumer design also has its place as an Italian art. The first Internazionale d'Arte Decorativa Moderna was held in 1902 in Turin, after which the centre shifted to Milan. Some Italian greats of decorative art include: Gio Ponti (1891–1979), the architect of Italian design; Piaggio, producer of the famous Vespa scooter; and Milan furniture producer, Zanotta, creator of the beanbag chair. Early 1960s pop art was strong in Italy, as was the subsequent Radical avant-garde movement that erased all traces of rationalism and helped Italian design make its mark internationally.

The 1980s brought the consolidation of Milanese design houses such as Alchimia, Memphis, Design Group Italia and Zanotta. More than 1000 pieces are on display in Kartell's recently opened Milan museum.

Norma and Puccini's *Madame Butterfly* all premiered at La Scala, Milan's world-famous opera house.

Contemporary Italian music is definitely not the world's best, much of it reminiscent of the 1960's least-endearing ballads. Its roots in *canzone Napoletana* (Neapolitan songs) gave Italian 19th-century popular music a distinct and appealing flair, which has been lost by modernday genres.

Literature

Italy's literary tradition is as rich as its thickest sauces. The classical Latin period began in the 1st century BC, with standout writers like Cicero (106–43 BC) and romantic poet Catullus (c. 84–54 BC). During the reign of Augustus (27 BC–AD 14), the period's most famous luminaries emerged: Virgil quilled *The Aeneid*, Ovid completed *Metamorphoses* and Horace chronicled the emergence of the new empire.

Although the dark times of the early Middle Ages were not as productive, the 14th century brought hope. When San Tomasso d'Aquino (Saint Thomas Aquinas, 1224–74) was penning his learned theses, Latin had ceased to be a living language and Dante (1265–1321), perhaps the greatest figure in Italian literature known best for his *Divina Commedia*, confirmed the Florentine form of Italian vernacular as a serious poetic medium. Two other wordsmiths of the time were Petrarca (Petrarch, 1304–74), whose lyric *Il Canzoniere* permanently influenced Italian poetry, and Boccaccio (1313–75), author of *Il Decamerone* and the first Italian novelist.

Amid the Renaissance frenzy of nonliterary treatises, *Il Principe* (The Prince), the political treatise of Machiavelli (1469–1527), and scientific theories of Leonardo da Vinci (1452–1519) have proved the most enduring.

Tragedy dramatised 18th-century literature, which resulted in Alfieri (1749–1803) creating a new genre – tragic poetry. Poetry remained the main avenue of literary expression until Alessandro Manzoni (1785–1873) released his *I Promessi Sposi* (The Betrothed), an epic historical novel with a barely disguised, strong nationalist flavour that rallied the nation. In theatre, Goldoni (1707–93) tried to reinvigorate stages through a combination of realism, literary discipline and the *commedia del-l'arte* (art of comedy) tradition of improvisation based on a core set of characters.

Italy's richest contribution to modern literature has been through the novel and short story. Turin especially has produced a wealth of authors, like Walt Whitman-influenced Pavese (1908–50), anti-Fascist Carlo Levi (1902–75) and Auschwitz survivor Primo Levi (1919–87). Palermo-born Ginzburg (1916–91) spent most of her life in Turin.

Other well-known writers are Turin's fantastical Cuban-born Calvino (1923–85), Rome's Moravia (1907–90) and Morante (1912–85), Sicilian Sciascia (1921–89), Milan-based intellectual Eco, Pisa's Tabucchi and Milanese opera-buff Capriolo.

Turin's Baricco is one of Italy's boldest contemporary writers, as is 1998 Strega-prize winner (for his *Microcosmi*) Magris. Other names to watch are Loy and Del Giudice.

In other genres, poetry's ardent nationalist Gabriele d'Annunzio (1863–1938) is in a class all his own, while three more mainstream noteworthy poets are Ungaretti (1888–1970) and Nobel laureates Montale (1896–1981) and Quasimodo (1901–68). A contemporary of d'Annunzio, the theatre's Sicilian Nobel-prize winning Pirandello (1867–1936) threw into question every theatrical preconception. The controversial work of modern theatre's Dario Fo (also a Nobel prize laureate) is laced with political and social critique.

Architecture

Italy has scores of architectural masterpieces preserved from every historical period. The earliest good specimens – usually stone temples – date from the 1st century BC and use construction techniques later perfected by the imperial Romans. The earliest significant Christian remains are from the 4th century, when emperor Constantine built churches using Roman models. Rome's 4th- and 5th-century San Giovanni in Laterano became the model for baptistries around the world, and stark 5th-century Basilica di Santa Sabina is one of the best preserved period churches. The basilicas in Ravenna and Venice are more Byzantine in style.

The Romanesque period (c. 1050–1200) was a revival of Roman influence (size and design). Pisa's marble cathedral, baptistry and (leaning) bell tower are Italy's most stunning examples.

Gothic architecture's pointed arches and vaults didn't make as great a mark, although Siena's *duomo* (cathedral) is arguably the most sumptuous Gothic cathedral ever built and Milan's *duomo* is nothing short of truly spectacular.

Renaissance times (c. 1400–1600) brought a love of domes, vaults and arches. Florence's *duomo* was the first major architectural achievement of the period, followed by hundreds of villas and palaces, especially in Rome. The construction of St Peter's Basilica in Rome occupied most of the notable architects of the High Renaissance (Raphael, Peruzzi and the da Sangallos) and coincided with the Counter-Reformation, during which both art and architecture were at the service of the Church.

The two great architects of the Baroque years were Gian 'Lorenzo Bernini (1598–1680) and his rival Francesco Borromini (1599–1667). Rome was their private battleground. Bernini, patronised by Pope Urban VIII, transformed the city most, his churches, palaces, piazzas and fountains are landmarks to this day. Elsewhere, Guarini (1624–83) was turning Turin into the Baroque capital it still claims to be.

A flurry of creative architecture marked the early 18th century, finding neoclassical expression in Rome's Scalinata di Spagna (Spanish Steps) and Fontana di Trevi (Trevi Fountain), and Milan's Piermarini-designed Teatro alla Scala (La Scala).

The beginning of modern architecture in Italy was epitomised by the late-19th-century shopping galleries, the most sumptuous and distinctive being Milan's iron-and-glass roofed Galleria Vittorio Emanuele II. The 20th-century Art Nouveau movement (called Lo Stilo Liberty) had scarcely begun before Mussolini and the Fascist era inaugurated grandiose building projects like Milan's Stazione Centrale.

Italy's two leading contemporary architects are Renzo Poano and Paolo Portoghesi.

Painting & Sculpture

Italy's first known paintings and sculptures – Etruscan wall images and carved stone sarcophagi, Greek tomb decorations and etched ceramic motifs and figurines, extensive Roman-era works, and 5th- and 6th-century religious mosaics – have been preserved in museums and *in situ* (in excavations and churches) throughout the entire country.

The tradition of decorating churches continued into the Middle Ages, first with mosaics and then, in the 10th and 11th centuries, also with frescoes and sculptures. From the 12th century on, panel painting and relief carvings became increasingly important, especially in Tuscany.

The Renaissance was an impossibly rich time for painting and sculpture. From the 13th century when Cimabue (c. 1240–1302) blurred the distinction between Gothic and Renaissance styles in his frescoes in Assisi's Basilica di San Francesco to Caravaggio's move toward a new 16th-century Baroque naturalism, hundreds of experimental masterly artworks were produced all over the country by Giotto (1266–1337), Donatello (1386–1466), Ghiberti (1398–1455), Mosaccio (1401–28), Fra Angelico (c. 1400–55), Botticelli (1445–1510), della Francesca (c. 1410–92), Signorelli (c. 1441–1523), Mantegna (c. 1431–1506), da Vinci (1452–1519), Ghirlandaio (1449–94), Rosselli (1439–1507), Raffaello (Raphael, 1483–1520), Michelangelo (1475–1564), Tiziano (Titian, 1493–1576), Tintoretto (1518–94), Veronese (c. 1528–88) and many, many more.

When Baroque realism supplanted previous leanings, canvases by Reni (1575–1642) and Domenichino (1581–1641) came to the fore. Da Cortona (1596–1669) was also in demand for his frescoes, as were the trompe l'oeil perspectives of dal Pozzo (1642–1709). As well as being a brilliant architect, the greatest sculptor of the times was undoubtedly Bernini.

The innovations in painting since Italian unification follow the European trend away from realism. The years from 1855 to 1865 were the heyday of Macchiaioli (Italian pointillism), which foresaw the rise of Italian symbolism. After that, futurism, inspired by urbanism and industrialisation, had much in common with cubism and influenced De Chirico (1888–1978).

Cinema

The Italian film industry was born in Turin in 1904. Screenings of silent black and white pictures had already taken place as early as 1896, but it was years before Italy's answer to Hollywood, Cinecittà, really took off. Unfortunately, by 1930, the industry was virtually bankrupt so Mussolini nationalised it. After WWII, filmmakers used Cinecittà's huge lots, but by the early 1960s, location shooting had taken precedence.

Italy's greatest gift to cinema is neorealism, characterised by a simplicity and sincerity peculiar to Italian cinema. Director Roberto Rossellini (1906–77) gave it life in 1945 with the first of a trio of postwar films. Vittorio de Sica (1901–94) later produced, among others, *Ladri di Biciclette* (Bicycle Thieves, 1948), about a man's battle to keep his family afloat.

Other great directors include: Visconti (1906–76), the 'aristocrat' of Italian cinema whose work steered in neo-realism; Zeffirelli (born 1923); Fellini (1920–94); and Sergio Leone (1929–89). Modernday masters are the indomitable Bertolucci, Tornatore, Moretti and now Roberto Benigni, the Tuscan comedic actor turned director whose *La Vita è Bella* (Life is Beautiful, 1998) won three Oscars.

The silver screen's Italian greats count Rudolph Valentino, Marcello Mastroianni, Vittorio Glassman, Anna Magnani, Massimo Troisi, Gina Lollobrigida, Sophia Loren, and now Benigni and Isabella Rossellini.

SOCIETY & CONDUCT

Traditional/historical differences sometimes run deep in Italy, a country that has been united for less than 150 years after centuries of rotating foreign domination. In fact, many local dialects and cultures have survived despite everything, including today's centralised government, population drift to the cities and impact of tourism. It is, therefore, fairly pointless to talk about Italian society as one unified entity. Most Italians have a strong sense of *campanilissimo* (loosely translated as an attachment to one's belltower) – identification with their region or town – than with their nation, except perhaps at international sporting events. An Italian is always first and foremost a Sicilian or Milanese before pronouncing him/herself an Italian. However, when meeting foreigners, Italians reveal a national pride not obvious in their relationships with each other.

Traditional Culture

Genuine instances of traditional cultural practices are largely confined to remote Alpine valleys and uplands, as with the Walser people in the western Alps. In most cases, the base culture is not stereotypically Italian.

The caricature Italian (seen by an outsider) is passionate, animated and prone to wild gesticulation, manic driving and a love of food. Italian journalist Luigi Barzini defined his compatriots as a hard-working, resilient and resourceful people, who are optimistic and have a good sense of humour. If there is a 'national' stereotype, this is probably closer to the truth. Italians are passionately loyal to their friends and families, and have a strong distrust of authority. Still, traditions are being eroded by modern attitudes. One in three

The Mafia

In Italy, the term 'mafia' can be used to describe five distinct organised crime groups: the original Sicilian Mafia, also known as the Cosa Nostra; the savage Calabrian 'ndrangheta; the Camorra of Naples; and two relatively new organisations, the Sacra Corona Unita (United Holy Crown) and La Rosa (the Rose), in Apulia. These groups operate both separately and together.

The Sicilian Mafia has its roots in the oppression of the Sicilian people and can claim a history extending back to the 13th century. Its complex system of justice is based on the code of silence known as *omertà*. Mussolini managed to virtually wipe out the Sicilian Mafia, but from the devastation of WWII grew the modern version known as Cosa Nostra, which has spread its tentacles worldwide and is far more ruthless and powerful than its predecessor. It is involved in drug-trafficking and arms deals, as well as finance, construction and tourist development, not to forget public-sector projects and Italian politics.

In the early 1990s, two anti-Mafia judges, Falcone and Borsellino, were assassinated in Palermo in separate bomb blasts. One early result of the feverish anti-Mafia activity that followed was the arrest of Salvatore 'Toto' Riina, the Sicilian godfather. In 1997, Riina was sentenced to life imprisonment in 1997 for his role in the deaths of the judges. The man believed to have taken over after Riina's arrest and also implicated in the judges' deaths, Giovanni ('The Pig') Brusca, was arrested in May 1996 (and imprisoned for 30 years in 1999).

married couples has no children and one in nine children is born out of wedlock.

Social Graces

Italians tend to be very tolerant but, despite an apparent obsession with (mostly female) nakedness, especially in advertising, they're not exactly free and easy. In some parts of Italy, particularly in the south, women will be harassed if they wear skimpy or form-fitting clothing. Read more about this under Women Cyclists (p37).

Dress modestly in churches – no shorts, short skirts or bare shoulders. At major religious attractions, like St Peter's in Rome, dress codes are strictly enforced.

Topless sunbathing, while not uncommon, is not always acceptable. Also, walking the streets near beaches in a bikini or skimpy bottom, bare-chested or bare-footed is sometimes frowned upon. Take your cues from others.

RELIGION

Under the terms of the 1929 Latern Pact between Mussolini and the Catholic Church, in return for Papal recognition of the Italian state, Rome and an independent Vatican were declared the centre of the Catholic world and Catholicism the Italian state religion. However, in 1985, the treaty was renegotiated and references to Catholicism as state religion were removed.

This was seen as law and politics catching up with reality. Although today around 85% of Italians profess to be Catholic and the fabric of Italian life is profoundly influenced by the Catholic Church, surprisingly few Italian Catholics practise their religion. Church attendance has dropped from 70% after WWII to 25%. That said, the very full calendar of religious festivals remains popular and travelling with the intention of catching a few is wise.

Of the remaining 15% of the population, Muslims, evangelical Protestants, Jehovah's Witnesses and other small groups, including a Jewish community in Rome and Waldenses (Valdesi; Swiss-Protestant Baptists) in Piedmont, live freely under a constitution guaranteeing equal freedom before the law to people of all religious faiths.

Facts for the Cyclist

SUGGESTED ITINERARIES
One Week
With so little time, it is best to concentrate on one area. From Milan, head for any of the Heart of the Dolomites, Alta Rezia, Central Lakes and Eastern Lakes plus Dolomiti di Brenta rides. From Rome, attach the one-day City Centre pedal to the Mystic Mountains or Sardinian Barbagia & Gennargentu rides, or combine the Chianti Region, Sienese Day Trip and Hill Town Trek for an all-Tuscany tour. If you're headed south after you've been to Rome, check out the Amalfi Coast and Trulli & Sassi Tour.

Two Weeks
Now we're talking! In the north, strong thighs looking for mountain highs scoot from Heart of the Dolomites and Dolomiti di Brenta through Alta Rezia to the Central Lakes. There's a bit of everything if you traipse from the Valle d'Aosta south through Montagne Doc and the Alps to Alpine Sea to Liguria di Ponente and Langhe & Roero. Novices can go from Milan to Venice in the Po basin of the Navigli Milanesi, Lungo Po Argine and Ravenna to Venice rides. Add the one-day Euganeian Hills for good measure. North of Rome, make a mid-boot traverse by adding the Mystic Mountains and Conero Riviera rides to the one-week all-Tuscany tour. Alternatively, run the hills of the Riviera from Circling Elba through Southern Odyssey, Arc to the Sea and the Apuan Alps, finishing in Cinque Terre & the Gulf of Genoa. In the south, after time in and around Rome, do the four southern mainland rides, or combine Sicily and Sardinia for the best of the islands.

One Month
This is enough time for a southern sweep including Rome and *everything* in Sardinia, Sicily and the south. In the other direction, after Rome, combine the two-week Riviera run with either of the two-week mountain sweeps. In the centre, turn the mid-boot traverse into an Adriatic jaunt by adding to the former the Ravenna to Venice, Euganeian Hills and Triestine Triangle rides.

Two Months
In 60 days, you can see a little of all of Italy. After a selective southern sweep, make the mid-boot traverse and Adriatic jaunt as far as Venice. Cut north through the Dolomites/Alps on the mountain high through the Central Lakes. From Turin, trip into the Western Alps and then to the Riviera for a slide down its coast back into Tuscany.

WHEN TO RIDE
Italy, although thrust deep into the tempering Mediterranean arena, has many climate zones. For the most part, the best biking times throughout the country are spring (April to early July) and autumn (September to October), when a fair and stable barometer is most likely and days can last until 9pm.

In northern mountain zones, the ideal pedalling window is slightly shorter (beginning in mid- to late May and ending in early to mid-October) to allow for the melting of late-spring high-pass snows and avoid the sharpened winter bite of late autumn's teeth. (Note that light, lingering snow can fall over the highest ground at any time of year.) Balmy autumn afternoons, when crop bounty is most plentiful, bring a fascinating assortment of local religious and harvest *fiere* (festivals).

In the south – a land of mild winters, early spring high temperatures and long balmy autumns – winter trips are not impossible,

Why don't you just change down?

Highlights

Picking the best of anything in Italy is perilous. Legendary regional rivalries make singling out one province's qualities like giving it an unofficial leg up in an unremitting king-of-the-hill quarrel. But, of 7600km of coast, only a few can top the list, and every hectare of 301,302 sq km can't be equally mind-boggling. Here then are the highlights of a country where every pedal turn is more than likely to please.

Best Coastal Scenery
The 50km Amalfi Coast (p294) thoroughfare – a narrow road engineered along soaring limestone sea bluffs and elegant isolated resort towns – gets congested in peak season, but is nothing short of sensational. An equally eminent shorefront motorway clings for 77km to the vineyard-covered slopes of rugged Ligurian Parco Nazionale delle Cinque Terre (p144). Island addicts will agree that the 92km Circling Elba (p119) is spectacular.

Best Mountain Scenery
Every day in the Heart of the Dolomites (p238) outdoes itself – gorges, glaciers, rocky spires, tarns and top-of-the-world panoramas – culminating in Day 5's breathtaking Sella Ronda circuit. The same can be said about the remote Barbagia & Gennargentu (p342), 'real' Sardinia's central-east high region. Montagne Doc (p185) country, the Calabrian La Sila Mountains (p312) and junior Alps – Maritime (p149), Ligurian (p138) and Apuan (p122) – are less relentlessly tremendous, but keep riders rapt for days.

Best Ascent
Isn't the best ascent a descent? Not to hill lovers in the central northern border massifs. The six-day Heart of the Dolomites (p238) endeavour crosses 13 of the area's most famous passes, and the four-day Alta Rezia (p191) vaults five *passi alpini* (alpine passes), including Italy's supreme 48-switchbacked saddle on the 'highest road in Europe': the 1826m and 25km climb to Passo dello Stelvio.

Best Descent
Some come short and steep, others go on forever. Day 2 of the Alta Rezia (p191) romp loses 1922m in 37.7km from the Passo di Gavia. Day 3 in the Alps to Alpine Sea (p149) drops 1871m in 54.8km from the Colle di Tenda to the sea. The Stelvio (p193) descent is a steep 1554m in 22.2km. Leaving Sardinia's Gennargentu (p342) plain or Sicily's Centre to Sea (p320) is like riding the face of a 1000m wave!

Flattest Ride
Italy's most substantial (and historic) lowland is the pancake-flat Po plain (Pianura Padana) around the Po River. The three-day Lungo Po Argine (p167) riverside ride, pedalled in conjunction with the four-day float from Ravenna to Venice (p265), makes for 455km of level land broken only by autostrada overpasses and short ramps to the tops of dikes.

Most Remote
Tourist hordes often overrun Tuscany, but the three-day Southern Odyssey (p129) has blissfully few cars. The Mystic Mountains (p277) ride's most tranquil segment is in the Sibillini Mountains, particularly the bit through the ridge-ringed bowl of Piano Grande. High in the Maritime Alps, the mountain traverse of the Alps to Alpine Sea (p149) ride receives more bovines than bipeds.

Best Historical Tour
Everything is part of ancient history in Rome, where the City Centre (p82) orientation spans hundreds of years in just 21km. Two day trips out of Rome hit a wider circle of monuments, as does the six-day Mystic Mountains (p277) walled-city march through time.

especially in Sicily and Sardinia. Inland especially, unexpected frosts, heavy rains and even snow may still occur. Also be prepared to adjust to short hours of daylight – the sun sets as early as 5pm.

The hottest months, July and August, are best left to the throngs of car-bound tourists and vacationers. Not only is it sweltering everywhere (particularly on the islands, throughout the south, and all coastal and lowland areas), competition for accommodation is fierce, even quiet roads are busy and service-industry patience is at a low ebb.

WHAT TO BRING

The well-paved *vie* (roads) of Italy are perfectly suited to road bikes or stocky touring/hybrid frames with slick tyres. (If you put slicks on your wheels, you may also wish to bring foldable knobbies for the eventual off-road ride.) After that, as a general rule, keep gear to a minimum. If you can't decide if you need it, don't bring it. Every gram is noticeable on hills, and if you do end up needing something, you can certainly buy it in Italy. It is, however, important to carry adequate protection from the elements. If you're camping or hostelling, you will, of course, need more equipment than if you stay in hotels. See the Your Bicycle chapter (p47) for handy tips about how to prepare your bike and pack your panniers. The Health & Safety chapter includes a First-Aid Kit checklist (p45).

Clothing

Ideally, pack clothes that are light and dry quickly. Clothes that you can wear on or off the bike, such as a plain black thermal top, help keep your load to a minimum.

Go with the padded bike shorts (knicks) designed to be worn without underwear to prevent chafing. If you don't like Lycra, get some 'shy shorts' – ordinary shorts with padded, lightweight knicks inside. In colder weather, wear Lycra tights over your knicks or padded thermal 'longs'. Another option is a pair of Lycra, individual leg warmers, easily removed when the temperature rises.

The Mediterranean sun can be brutal; don't underestimate the seriousness of sunburn and long sleeves as the best protection. Strong sunblock lotion is indispensable.

Cycling clothing should be light and breathable. Some tops made of synthetic fabrics, like Coolmax and Intercool, are designed to keep cyclists from overheating. Silk is another alternative. Cotton is cool, but dries slowly, making it useless in the cold and wet. Choose bright or light-coloured clothing, which is cooler and maximises visibility.

Sunglasses are essential, not only to minimise exposure to UV radiation, but also to shield your eyes from dust and insects. A helmet with a visor also affords some protection, as does a bandana to soak up sweat.

Be aware of the danger of exposure, especially during cooler months and at higher elevations where weather conditions can change rapidly. Layering (wearing several thin layers of clothing) is the most practical way to dress. Start with a lightweight cycling or polypropylene top, followed by a warmer insulating layer, such as a thin fleece vest (light and quick drying) and then a rainproof, windproof jacket. Fine-wool thermal underwear is an excellent alternative to synthetic fibres.

Some excellent waterproof, yet 'breathable' cycling jackets are available. Gore-Tex is probably the best-known fabric in use, although others, such as Activent, are excellent for light rain (but not a steady downpour).

Fingerless cycling gloves reduce the impact of jarring that can cause nerve damage. They also protect against sunburn and grazes in the event of a fall.

In cold weather you may want full-finger gloves (either thin polypropylene gloves worn over bike gloves, or more wind- and rain-resistant ones). You can also buy thermal socks and neoprene booties to go over your shoes, and help keep blood in your toes on frigid mornings. A close-fitting beanie (winter hat) worn under your helmet will help keep you warm.

Helmets are not compulsory by law, but you shouldn't ride without one. Your helmet should sit so that only 3cm to 4cm of forehead is exposed, and should be fastened firmly but not tight. If it has been in a crash, replace it.

Cycling shoes are ideal footwear (or, next best, stiff-soled ordinary shoes) because they transfer the power from your pedal stroke directly to the pedal. Spongy-soled running shoes are inefficient and may leave your feet sore. More and more people swear by cycling sandals – stiff-soled sandals with room for a pedal cleat. They're nice and cool in summer and they dry quickly in the rain; just make sure you apply sunscreen to exposed skin.

Buying & Hiring Locally Almost all of the thousands of bike shops are small independent businesses focusing on a single market. In fact, many bike stores are so specialised they sell only certain brands based on retail arrangements with one or more of Italy's famous bicycle manufacturers or distributors. Any shop will carry the components or accessories you need, but not necessary the specific brand you desire. Even the gear will probably be branded to match the retailer(s) featured by the store. Some of the larger boutiques do, however, have eclectic collections worth checking.

Prices vary to wild extremes – shoddy stopgap materials are very cheap, but the top-end models of high-profile brands can be extraordinarily expensive. Very general price ranges are:

bike shorts/knicks *(pantaloni corti)* €25–50
helmet *(casco)* €20–100
mountian bikes €400–2500
panniers *(borse viaggio)* €75–250
road/racing bike *(bici corsa)* budget €770–1100, mid-range €1200–1800, topend €1800–6500
summer jersey *(maglia estiva)* €30–50
touring bike *(bici turistica)* **& city bike** €250–1500
winter jersey *(maglia inverno)* €60–100

If you are planning on buying a bicycle in Italy, it is absolutely essential that you research the brands, models, frame types and materials, components and prices before you leave home. You can make purchases directly from the manufacturers through their attached outlets, most of which have excellent multilingual websites. The best place to start your research is the Ancma – Associazione Nazionale Ciclo Motociclo Accessori (w www.ancma.it) – with links to all major companies. If you would rather have a jinxed part fixed than have to replace it, count on routine repairs (tune-ups, truing) costing approximately €18 per hour. Upscale city shops and/or very involved mends will run a little higher (up to €3 more per hour), a bit less (minus €3 per hour) in a country shop.

For more general equipment purchases, begin by investigating Italy's major department store chains – Standa, Upim, Oviesse and Rinascente. They carry basic outdoor clothing, but you should consult with tourist offices for the names of stores specialising in gear of this nature.

If you are planning on renting once you arrive in Italy, shop carefully. Bicycle hire is common in areas where cycling is a hot pastime, but quality can sometimes be questionable. Average costs to keep in mind are as follows:

city bike (without gears) €11/18/42 per day/weekend/week
hybrid €20/38/93 per day/weekend/week
mountain bike (full suspension) €21/37/100 per day/weekend/week
mountain bike (without suspension) €16/29/78 per day/weekend/week
racing/road bike €25/48/104 per day/weeend/week

In many cases, a deposit is required, like a credit card slip equal to the cost of the bicycle or an important personal document (passport).

Most places will provide some sort of basic lock, but it is a good idea to bring your own. Bike theft is a problem, especially in cities. Almost no places hire panniers, and many bikes do not have a rear rack. Be prepared: bring a day pack and elastic cords (bungee or occy straps). For longer rides, find a bicycle with racks and bring your own panniers. Helmets for adults and children are rarely available for hire and if they are, they're not very good.

ORGANISED RIDES

Italy is an extremely popular destination for organised cycle tours. Companies throughout the world offer a range of tours of varying duration and difficulty. Most have websites and will send you enticing full-colour brochures. Prices vary from company to company, depending on the standard of accommodations and meals provided. Many companies listed here also have European offices.

The USA & Canada
Andiamo Adventours (☎ 800-549-2363, fax 831-477-2979, w www.andiamoadven tours.com) 930 Corcoron Drive, Santa Cruz, CA 95062.

Equipment Check List

This list is a general guide to the things you might take on a bike tour. Your list will vary depending on the kind of cycling you want to do, whether you're roughing it in a tent or planning on luxury accommodation, and on the time of year. Don't forget to take on board enough water and food to see you safely between towns.

Bike Clothing
- ☐ cycling gloves
- ☐ cycling shoes and socks
- ☐ cycling tights or leg-warmers
- ☐ helmet and visor
- ☐ long-sleeved shirt or cycling jersey
- ☐ padded cycling shorts (knicks)
- ☐ sunglasses
- ☐ thermal undershirt and arm-warmers
- ☐ T-shirt or short sleeved cycling jersey
- ☐ visibility vest
- ☐ waterproof jacket & pants
- ☐ windproof jacket or vest

Off-Bike Clothing
- ☐ change of clothing
- ☐ spare shoes or sandals
- ☐ swimming costume
- ☐ sun hat
- ☐ fleece jacket
- ☐ thermal underwear
- ☐ underwear and spare socks
- ☐ warm hat and gloves

Equipment
- ☐ bike lights (rear and front) with spare batteries (see torch)
- ☐ elastic cord

- ☐ camera and spare film
- ☐ cycle computer
- ☐ daypack
- ☐ medical kit* and toiletries
- ☐ sewing/mending kit (for everything)
- ☐ panniers and waterproof liners
- ☐ pocket knife (with corkscrew)
- ☐ sleeping sheet
- ☐ small handlebar bag and/or map case
- ☐ small towel
- ☐ tool kit, pump and spares**
- ☐ torch (flashlight) with spare batteries and globe – some double as (front) bike lights
- ☐ water containers
- ☐ water purification tablets, iodine or filter

Camping
- ☐ cooking, eating and drinking utensils
- ☐ clothesline
- ☐ dishwashing items
- ☐ portable stove and fuel
- ☐ insulating mat
- ☐ matches or lighter and candle
- ☐ sleeping bag
- ☐ tent
- ☐ toilet paper and toilet trowel

* see the boxed text 'First Aid Kit' (p45)
** see the boxed text 'Spares & Tool Kit' (p67)

Dear Mum, The tour is rather hard and filled with deprivation. Please send more money...

DON HATCHER

Operates week-long cycling and hiking tours, including some family-friendly itineraries.

Backroads (☎ 800-462-2848, 510-527-1555, fax 510-527-1444, W www.backroads.com) 801 Cedar St, Berkeley, CA 94710-1800. Has week-long cycling and walking tours, including trips for families and solo travellers.

Bike Riders Tours (☎ 800-473-7040, 617-723-2354, fax 617-723-2355, W www.bikeriders tours.com) PO Box 130254, Boston, MA 02113. Offers week-long tours, including 'guest chef' and self-guided trips.

Blue Marble Travel (☎ 215-923-3788, fax 923-3766, W www.bluemarble.org) 222A Race St, Philadelphia, PA 19106-1910. Offers one- to five-week tours featuring Italy alone or in combination with other European countries.

Butterfield & Robinson (☎ 800-678-1147, 416-864-1354, fax 416-864-0541, W www.butter field.com) 70 Bond St, Toronto, M5B 1X3, Canada. Features upscale biking and walking tours, including some family trips.

Ciclismo Classico (☎ 800-866-7314, 781-646-3377, fax 781-641-1512, W www.ciclismocla sico.com) 30 Marathon St, Arlington, MA 02474. Operates one- to two-week tours all over Italy.

ExperiencePlus! Specialty Tours (☎ 800-685-4565, 970-484-8489, W www.xplus.com) 415 Mason Ct, Fort Collins, CO 80524. Leads one-to two-week cycling and walking tours, including trips for singles and families.

Italian Cycling Center (☎ 215-232-6772, W www.italiancycling.com) 2117 Green St, Philadelphia PA 19130-3110. Provides moderately priced accommodations at its headquarters in northern Italy, with guided loop rides daily for three different categories of cyclist (touring cyclists, fitness cyclists, and racers). Visitors can stay for as long or short as they wish, and non-cycling companions are also welcome.

La Corsa Tours (☎ 800-522-6772, W www.la corsa.com) 935 Washington St, Suite 101, Hoboken, NJ 07030. Specialises in challenging nine- and 10-day tours for avid cyclists.

Randonnée Tours (☎ 800-465-6488, 204-475-6939, fax 204-474-1888, W www.randonnee tours.com) 100–62 Albert St, Winnipeg, Manitoba R3B 1E9, Canada. Specialises in self-guided cycling and walking tours.

Van Gogh Tours (☎ 800-435-6192, 802-767-3457, fax 240-368-5596, W www.vangogh tours.com) PO Box 221, Rochester, VT 05767. Offers week-long cycling and walking tours.

VBT (☎ 800-245-3868, 802-453-4811, fax 802-453-4806, W www.vbt.com) PO Box 711, Bristol, VT 05443-0711. Leads deluxe week-long tours for cyclists of all levels.

The UK

Cycle Rides (☎ 01225 428452, 0800 389 3384, W www.cycle-rides.co.uk) PO Box 2440, Bath BA1 6XG. Formerly known as Bike Tours, this company operates a couple of tours.

Australia

Alpine Cycle Tours (☎ 02-9403 1651, 0416 219 491, fax 02-9402 0387, W www.alpinecycle tours.com) PO Box 473, Terrey Hills, NSW 2084. Offers some challenging two-week tours in the Alps of northern Italy, Austria and Switzerland.

MAPS

The best map for cycling in Italy is a Touring Club Italiano (TCI, W www.touring club.it) 1:200,000 *grande carta stradale d'Italia*. There are 15 overlapping regional foldouts (€6.20 each) roughly corresponding to Italy's division into 20 major regions. The attention to details like secondary and tertiary lanes, elevation markings, measured distances and arrows showing every hill's direction and severity of incline are invaluable. Parks and scenic roads are also clearly represented. When in Italy, pick up TCI maps in Milan (☎ 02 535 99 71, e in fotouring@touringclub.it) at Corso Italia 10 and in Turin (☎ 011 562 72 07, e ne gozio.torino@touringclub.it) at Piazza Solferino 3b.

If map expenses are too great, every province distributes free road maps through its tourist offices. Scales and quality vary, but for the most part, these maps more than suffice and make those destructive notes, folds, rips and rain drenches less costly.

For the grand, national overview, Michelin's 1:1,000,000 map No 988 covers the whole country. For slightly more detail, two 1:400,000 area maps – Nos 428 and 431 – cover the mainland, while No 432 contains Sicily and No 433 Sardinia (US$8.95 to US$9.95 each). TCI publishes a decent 1:800,000 map covering Italy, Switzerland and Slovenia.

DIGITAL RESOURCES

There's no better place to start your explorations than the Lonely Planet website (W www.lonelyplanet.com). You'll find summaries on Italy, postcards from other travellers and the Thorn Tree bulletin board, where you can ask questions before you go and dispense advice when you get back. You can also find travel news and updates to many of our most popular guidebooks, and the subwwway section links you to the most useful travel resources elsewhere on the web.

'W' in Italian is pronounced 'voo' and English-speakers always smile when being read a web address by an Italian.

Some useful websites with English pages include:

Italian State Tourist Board (W www.italian tourism.com) Regional and city guides, searchable databases, news and lots of links

Windows on Italy (W www.mi.cnr.it/WOI/woi index.html) Has simple, fast-loading indexes with links to contemporary and historical information.

Italians R Us (W www.italiansrus.com) A guide to Italian culture, with proverbs, recipes, photos, articles and plenty of links.

Italian Tourist Web Guide (W www.itwg.com) Current travel and tourism information, including searchable databases of hotels and tour packages, regional/city guides and maps.

Italy Cyber Guide (W www.italycyberguide.com) Pages most useful for many black-and-white maps and short historical biographies.

Centro Turistico Studentesco e Giovanile (W www.cts.it) Links for young people and students researching tourism, the environment and community.

Some cycling websites (most in Italian only) include:

Federazione Italiana Amici della Bici (W www .fiab-onlus.it) The best resource for bicycle tourists, with bike-lobbying news, calendars, affiliate lists, lots of links, some English pages.

Federazione Ciclistica Italiana (W www.federci clismo.it) Reams of official federation news and information (calendars, results, local contacts etc) regarding all areas of nontourist cycling.

Associazione Italiana Città Ciclabili (W www .cittaciclabili.it) Organisation news, affiliate lists and links.

Massimo Peverada Percorsi di MTB (W www .peverada.it/mtb) Vast MTB resource with links to organisations, events and more.

BOOKS
Lonely Planet
The *Italian phrasebook* lists all the words and phrases you're likely to need. Another

essential read is *World Food Italy*, a full-colour book with information on Italian cuisine, as well as the whole range of Italian food and drink. *Walking in Italy* is useful for those wanting to explore Italy's great outdoors on foot. *Italy*, *Rome*, *Florence*, *Venice*, *Tuscany*, *Sicily*, and *Milan, Turin & Genoa* are recommended for those planning further travel in Italy.

Cycling
Ediciclo (W www.ediciclo.it) is one of Italy's niche-leading publishers of cycling maps and guidebooks (only in Italian). Titles fall into four categories: *passi e valle d'Europa* or 'European passes and valleys', *treni e bici* about trips that include the use of 'trains and bikes', *natura e arte* or 'nature and art' (including two excellent books covering the Milan area) and an impressive array of mountain biking guides.

For thorough and thoughtful information about cycle touring, check out Dennis Coello's excellent *Touring on Two Wheels: The Bicycle Traveler's Handbook* or the more recent *Essential Touring Cyclist* by Richard Lovett. Reams of information about cycling in general fill *Sloane's Complete Book of Cycling* by Eugene Sloane. *Bicycling Magazine's 900 All-Time Best Tips* by Ed Pavelka is a remarkable and cheap cycling how-to with hints from the pros. *Bicycling Medicine* by Arnie Baker MD covers nutrition, physiology, injury prevention and treatment. Women in the saddle will appreciate Susan Weaver's *A Woman's Guide to Cycling*.

If bicycle maintenance is not a strong point, try *Anybody's Bike Book* by Tom Cuthberston.

General
For a potted chronicle of the country's past, try *Concise History of Italy* by Vincent Cronin, *History of the Italian People* by Giuliano Procacci or, particularly recommended, *A History of Contemporary Italy: Society and Politics 1943–1988* by Pail Ginsborg.

The Mafia is the subject of a number of titles, including *The Honoured Society* by Norman Lewis, *Excellent Cadavers: The Mafia and the Death of the First Italian Republic* by Alexander Stille and *Midnight in Sicily* by Peter Robb.

NEWSPAPERS & MAGAZINES

If you read Italian, there is a vast library of regularly published bicycling magazines at your disposal. Cycle tourers (and hikers) will have plenty to sink their teeth into with *Itinerari e Luoghi* (🅦 www.itinerarieluoghi .it) and *Cicloturismo*. Racing fans will get their fill with *Bici Sport*, *La Bicicletta* (🅦 www.cycling.it) and *Granfondo* (🅦 www .granfondo.com). Mountain-bike aficionados will not be disappointed with *Tutto Mountain Bike* (🅦 www.gruppobeditore .it/tuttomtb) and *Bici da Montagna* (🅦 www .cycling.it). *Ciclismo* is the best magazine for general cycling.

RADIO & TV

Of the three state-owned radio stations (🅦 www.radio.rai.it), RAI-2 (846 AM or 91.7 FM) broadcasts news in English at three minutes past the hour from 1pm to 5pm.

The state-run television channels are Rai 1, Rai 2 and Rai. The main commercial stations are Canale 5, Italia 1, Rete 4 and Telemontecarlo (TMC), which broadcasts CNN nightly around 3am. BBC World, Sky Channel, CNN and NBC Superchannel are available by satellite.

PHOTOGRAPHY & VIDEO

Film from reputable international manufacturers is available everywhere in shops and at film store outlets. Film processing quality and speed are improving after years of neglect (poor quality and slow results), but it may still be best to carry completed rolls home to a trusted shop.

A *pellicola* (roll) of 24/36 100 ASA print exposures costs around €3.50/4.50 and processing €7/10. Slide film (36 exposures) costs approximately €6, plus €5 to process. Prices are highly competitive, so shop around away from the tourist flocks. Tapes for video cameras can be found at film stores or shops selling camera and video equipment.

Lonely Planet's *Travel Photography: A Guide to Taking Better Pictures* by Richard I'Anson might help in capturing the perfect snapshot.

WOMEN CYCLISTS
Attitudes Towards Women

Italy isn't a especially dangerous country for women, but for women travelling – and certainly cycling – alone will often find themselves plagued by unwanted attention from men. Many Italian men find lone females (especially of the athletic, foreign variety) completely irresistible and cannot understand why an attraction isn't mutual. As a general rule, they seem to believe all women are beautiful objects in desperate need of manly attention, sometimes protectively paternalistic, usually crassly (and comically) smarmy. Basically, most of the attention falls into the nuisance category.

Although women cycling alone are less common than men, they are not unheard of. And, in areas noted for their cycling communities, a refreshing number of women are seen on the road, sometimes solo, but usually in groups of friends out for a ride. These groups, and, in general, all Italian two-wheelers, are supportive and respectful of women cyclists.

Safety Precautions

Use common sense. When faced with a persistent paramour, avoid becoming aggressive. Ignoring all advances, politely explaining you have a *marito* (husband) or *fidanzato* (boyfriend), or walking away can work. If all else fails, approach the nearest member of the police or *carabinieri*.

Steer clear of walking alone in deserted or dark streets, or cycling at night through remote urban areas; look for centrally located hotels. Also, avoid wearing skimpy clothing, although this may be difficult when biking. In the saddle, a form-fitting Lycra uniform will draw attention, some whistles and plenty of passing comments, but rarely anything truly importunate. Once off the bike, pull on a pair of loose shorts and a less-revealing top to blend in with the surroundings. This is especially true further south, where harassment can increase with conservatism.

Try 🅦 www.women.it (in Italian only) when searching for women's organisations and resources in Italy. La Città delle Donne (🅦 www.netescapeinitaly.com/donneiso) is also useful.

CYCLING WITH CHILDREN

Many of the routes described in this book – particularly those rated easy or easy–moderate – are suitable for children. Opt for routes that will suit the child's ability, provide ample distractions along the way and allow for frequent breaks. Keep plenty of snacks and water on hand, especially given the universally followed lunchtime shutdown of all food shops other than restaurants and children's fickle appetites.

It is particularly important to think about roads in Italy. The reputation of Italian drivers is not undeserved and fretting constantly about safety will not be pleasurable for you or the children. Ponder routes that are primarily on bikepaths, riverside *argine* (dikes) or *alzaie* (tow paths) and back roads.

CYCLING ORGANISATIONS

The Federazione Italiana Amici della Bici (Italian Bike-Friends Federation or FIAB; ☎/fax 02 693 11 624, ⓦ www.fiab-onlus.it), c/o Ciclobby in Milan, is a national lobbying organisation promoting the use of bicycles for tourism and to respect the environment. FIAB and its 60 or so volunteer-managed local affiliates are also the number one resource for pedalling tourists. FIAB is part of the European Cyclists' Federation.

The Federazione Ciclistica Italiana (Italian Cycling Federation; ☎ 06 368 57 255)

has a secretariat at Rome's Olympic stadium but real power in its regional offices that govern International Cycling Union events (major road and off-road races), including all the *giri* (lap) and World Cup contests. Participation in FCI activities requires payment of membership dues.

The Scuola Nazionale Maestri di Mountain Bike (National Mountain Bike Masters School, see the boxed text 'Mountain Biking', p40-1) and its directly allied Associazione Mountain Bike in Italia are as close as Italy gets to coordinating organisations for mountain biking. The Scuola's *centri nazionali* (national centres) teach mountain bike skills and promote their use on endless trails and through organised rallies/races.

City cyclists should throw weight behind Associazione Italiana Città Ciclabili (Italian Cyclable Cities Association; ☎ 02 66981 818) an organisation lobbying for cyclists' rights in the urban jungle. For young people, Unione Italiana Sport per Tutti Lega Nazionale Ciclismo (UISP; Italian Sports for All Union National Cycling League; ☎ 051 22 83 90, ⓦ www.uisp.it) plays a role in developing

Touring with Children

Children can travel by bicycle from the time they can support their head and a helmet, at around eight months. There are some small, lightweight, cute helmets around, such as the L'il Bell Shell.

To carry an infant or toddler requires a child seat or trailer. Child seats are more common for everyday riding and are cheaper, easier to move as a unit with the bike and let you touch and talk to your child while moving. Disadvantages, especially over long distances, can include exposure to weather, the tendency of a sleeping child to loll, and losing luggage capacity at the rear. The best makes, such as the Rhode Gear Limo, include extra moulding to protect the child in case of a fall, have footrests and restraints, recline to let the child sleep and fit very securely and conveniently onto a bike rack.

With a capacity of up to 50kg (versus around 18kg for a child seat), trailers can accommodate two bigger children and luggage. They give good, though not always total, protection from sun and rain and let children sleep comfortably. It's also handy to be able to swap the trailer between adults' bikes. However, a trailer will make dodging the region's many potholes ever harder! Look for a trailer that is lightweight, foldable, brightly coloured with a flag, and that tracks and handles well.

Be sure that the bike to which you attach a child seat or trailer is sturdy and low-geared to withstand – and help you withstand – the extra weight and stresses. Seats and trailers are treated as additional luggage items when flying.

recognised alternative races, especially in the off-road disciplines.

CYCLING ROUTES
Route Description

This guide covers some of the best areas for cycle touring in Italy. The rides do not traverse the territory, but offer a selection of distinct routes through Italy's incredibly varied countryside. Rides range from one to six days in length, allowing visitors to choose one or more day trips or short routes (by hiring a bicycle) as part of a noncycling itinerary, select a few routes in a couple of regions, or link several rides together for an extended tour. There are routes suitable for novices and experienced riders.

In most cases, the rides have been designed to make carrying food and camping gear optional. Each ride is broken into a set number of days, with accommodation and food options available at each day's destination.

Ride Difficulty

Each ride is graded in terms of distance, terrain, road surface and navigational ease.

The grade appears in the Table of Rides (p4-5) and at the start of each ride.

Grading is unavoidably subjective, especially in Italy where hills and mountains cover 75% of the country and make *everything* a challenge. The degree of difficulty on any ride may, in addition to the factors already mentioned, be a function of weather, pannier weight, accompanying children, pretrip training and how tired or hungry you are.

Easy These routes involve a handful of riding hours that can be easily broken up to fill out the day. The terrain is *mostly* flat and the roads have good sealed surfaces or short spans of easy gravel. Navigationally straightforward (with signed bikepaths or simple directions), they make for experiences suitable for young children.

Moderate These rides present a moderate challenge to someone of average fitness. They include some hills, days filled with much more time in the saddle than out, and may involve difficult unsealed roads and/or complex navigation.

Touring with Children

From the age of about four, children can move on to a 'trailer-bike' (effectively a child's bike, minus a front wheel, which hitches to an adult's bike) or to a tandem (initially as 'stoker' – the rider at the back – with 'kiddy cranks', or crank extensions) – this lets them help pedal. The tandem can be a long-term solution, keeping you and your child together and letting you compensate if the child tires.

Make sure you are aware and careful of children rushing into touring on a solo bike before they can sustain the effort and concentration required. Once they are ready and keen to ride solo, at about age 10 to 12, they will need a good quality touring bike, properly fitted (A$400, US$250, UK£160 up).

Bike touring with children requires a new attitude as well as new equipment. Be sensitive to their needs – especially when they're too young to communicate them fully. In a seat or trailer, they're not expending energy and need to be dressed accordingly. Keep them dry, at the right temperature and protected from the sun. Keep their energy and interest up. When you stop, a child travelling in a seat or trailer will be ready for action, so always reserve some energy for parenting. This means more stops, including at places for children to play. Older children will have their own interests and should be involved in planning a tour. Before setting off on a major journey, try some day trips to check your set-up and introduce your child to cycling.

Children need to be taken into account in deciding each day's route – traffic and distances need to be moderate and facilities and points of interest adequate. Given the extra weight of children and their daily needs, you may find it easier to opt for day trips from a base. The very fit and adventurous may not need to compromise to ride with children, but those who do will still find it worthwhile.

As with other activities, children bring a new perspective and pleasure to cycle touring. They tend to love it.

Alethea Morison

Mountain Biking

Mountain biking didn't catch on immediately in Italy. In the mid-1980s, bicycle manufacturers did not see just how important the new industry-boosting phenomenon was. As demand increased, Italian strategists made poor decisions, as remarked in 1990 by the *Gazzetta dello Sport*, like importing cheap mountain bike brands, adding Italian components and then placing them in show rooms as Italian models. The legacy of Italian quality was sacrificed to a booming market in second-rate sales and few attempts at innovating. Fortunately, this trend has been reversed and Italian manufacturers are now producing extremely high-performance mountain bike models.

Organisational Force

The primary on-the-ground institutional force promoting proper mountain biking in Italy is the Scuola Nazionale Maestri di Mountain Bike (☎ 02 335 14 342), Fraz. Villair 15, La Salle, Valle d'Aosta. Founded by the Associazione Mountain Bike in Italia (AMI) in 1997, it fulfilled need created by a rise in organised ecological bicycle tourism. Since proper guides were required to accompany off-road ride groups, the insufficient number of people with proper skills had to train others. And so the Scuola was born and continues to thrive, spreading the mountain bike gospel in collaboration with the AMI and through its Centri Nazionali di MTB and Centri Servizi. At the time of writing, there were 211 diplomaed *accompagnatori* (tour guides) and 60 *maestri* (teachers) from 20 certified schools in 17 regions.

Other organisations, like UISP's Lega Nazionale Ciclismo and the Federazione Ciclistica Italiana (ⓦ www.federciclismo.it) have also been successful at responding to piquing mountain bike interest among Italians. However, there are still almost no consistently podium-quality Italian riders on the international mountain biking circuit.

All organisations have been working since the outset with authorities in mountain bike trail areas to try and ensure that the environment and trail etiquette are respected.

Where to Ride

Mountain biking is most popular in the northern Italian regions where the flats meet hills, the hills meet the mountains and the mountains have no equal. However, more and more mountain biking groups and clubs are identifying, registering and mapping trails throughout the country.

Hard These are for fit riders who want a challenge. They involve long daily distances and/or challenging climbs, may negotiate rough and remote roads, and present navigational challenges.

Times & Distances

Each ride is divided into stages intended to be tackled in one day. Because individual riding speed varies, these should be used as a guide only. They only take into account actual riding time – not time at rest stops, taking photographs, eating or visiting attractions – and are generally based on an average riding speed of between 10km/h and 18km/h.

ACCOMMODATION

Italy has lodgings to suit all tastes and budgets. Only a few are mentioned for each of the destination cities described in this book,

but there are usually quite a few more. For expanded lists, always check with tourist offices.

If you know your cycling limits and ability to stick to an itinerary, advance reservations are always smart, particularly during peak seasons (around Easter, Christmas to New Year, and in July and August). Some hotels will require fax confirmation and a small deposit, small price to pay to avoid pulling into a city after a long day in the saddle and spending hours searching for a vacancy. If you have reserved and are running late, always call ahead to confirm that you're on your way and mention you're travelling by bicycle. This is important. After 7pm or 8pm, many hotel proprietors will give away a room if they haven't heard from a client.

Some places have a secure garage for bicycles; others will squeeze them into a wine cellar, leave it in the dining room or even let

Mountain Biking

Two of the sport's more popular multi-part professional race events taking advantage of the profusion and diversity of trails are the AMI Trofeo and the Coppa Italia Mountainbike Maffei. In 2002, the Trofeo covered nearly 240km using routes in Liguria (mountain bike classic Trofeo Laigueglia), lower Piedmont's Po-side Monferrato Bike, upper Piedmont's upper Po Valley Valpolonga and finishing with one of the greatest alpine rides, the Tour dell'Assietta. A relative newcomer to the mountain-biking racing scene, the FCI-registered Coppa Italia Mountainbike Maffei five-part series also stays mostly in northern Italy (Liguria, Lombardy's Valmalenco, the Dolomites), but offers some farther-flung Umbrian and Puglian rides too.

For nonprofessional tourers, one of Italy's most outstanding multiday rides begins at the Colle di Tenda (1871m) on the high-elevation, former border–patrol road through the Maritime Alps and runs east and then south all the way to the coast at Ventimiglia. The two-day 110km Via di Crinale (Crest Road) usually follows a wide, graded route that takes in a string of 19th-century Italian forts/barracks and panoramic views, and dips below 1500m only once in the first 90km. Three segments (like the walk along treacherously narrow *via ferrate* or iron ways cut into a sheer cliff) require great care and some technical riding. This isn't a ride for beginners. There's a convenient midway overnight stop below the trail at Colle Melosa.

Further north, in Valle d'Aosta, Courmayeur is the start of an unrivalled, week-long, three-country circumnavigation of Mont Blanc. Ask for information at the tourist office in Aosta or Courmayeur (☎ 0165 84 20 60) or contact the Scuola di Mountainbike MB Aventure (☎ 0165 86 97 06, W www.mbaventure.it).

West of Turin at the top of the Susa and Chisone Valleys are a number of fantastic knobby-wheel challenges. Ask at information in Bardonecchia about the Percorso 'Simone Perino', and in Sestriere (☎ 0122 75 54 44) about mountain-bike rental for the Via dei Saraceni or the Tour dell'Assietta (W www.tourassietta.it/mappa), the latter one of northern Italy's most infamous competitive off-road rides.

In the eastern Alps, the Alta Rezia zone has scores of kilometres of trails. Ask at tourist offices for the Alta Rezia *Bike/Trekking Guide*. The 27km Val Grosina Orientale, 44km Laghi di Concano and 32km Val Alpisella rides are particularly scenic.

---

you bring it to your room. There are, however, some places that refuse bicycles, so always ask first.

Camping

Most camping facilities in Italy are major complexes with swimming pools, tennis courts, restaurants and supermarkets. They're graded according to a star system and prices can be surprisingly high (some of the highest in Europe), especially during peak season. Count on €6.50 to €10 per person.

Camping grounds are common near water and in the mountains, and are usually a few kilometres outside town. Roadside (free) camping is officially illegal, although out-of-season discreet campers should be OK. For use of private property, always ask owners.

The two best web-based lists of Italian camping grounds are W www.camping.it and Easy Camping (W www.icaro.it).

Rifugi

If you're planning any mountain hiking or biking, get information on local area *rifugi* (mountain hostels). Open only from June/July to September, they cost €11 to €21 per person (B&B). Meals are usually available, but somewhat expensive. Always book ahead.

Hostels

Ostelli per la goiventù (youth hostels) are run by the Associazione Alberghi per la Giuventù (AIG), which is affiliated with Hostelling International (HI). The cost is €10 to €15 per person (breakfast usually included, dinners for €8). An HI card, while not always required, is recommended (see Visas & Documents, p352).

Many hostels are beautifully located (some in castles and villas), have bars, kitchens and even reasonably priced restaurants.

Bicitalia – the National Cycling Network

One of FIAB's most ambitious projects is Bicitalia, the *rete ciclabile nazionale* (national cycling network). Ten different routes have been proposed, covering the length and breadth of the nation for a total of about 12,000km. FIAB's objective is to work with local administrations and bicycle organisations in the selection of appropriate paths and little-trafficked roads, so that cyclists can appreciate the finest of Italy's natural resources without missing any of its primary attractions.

At present, only 500km (from the Brenner pass at the Austrian border to the Cisa pass just north of La Spezia) of the first route – the Ciclopista del Sole (Cycle Route of the Sun) from the Austrian border to Sicily – has been mapped, but none has been signposted. Most of the route is on minor roads. Three of 10 planned 1:100,000 maps (€4.65 each) are available through Ediciclo (see Books, p35).

The nine other proposed rides consist of five *grande vie* (major routes) – Via del Po e delle Langhe, Via Pellegrini, Ciclovie del Triveneto, Via Romea and Via Adriatica – and four *vie dei due mari* (sea-to-sea connecting routes) – Romagna to Versilia, Conero to Argentario, Via Salaria and Via dei Borboni.

For more about Bicitalia, see FIAB's website at **W** www.fiab-onlus.it.

Accommodation is usually in segregated dormitories. Most hostels are closed from 9am to 3.30pm and have 11.30pm/midnight summer curfews.

For information about hostels (and booking), contact the AIG head office (☎ 06 487 11 52, **W** www.hostels-aig.org), Via Cavour 44, Rome.

Agristurismo
This is an increasingly popular holiday on a working farm. The term also refers more to restaurants in restored farm complexes with rooms available for rent. Prices are higher than at hostels but usually (although not always) less than equivalent quality in hotels. Ask at tourist information offices about the nearest *agriturismo* facilities or contact Agriturist (☎ 06 685 23 42, **W** www.agriturist.it) or Terranostra (☎ 06 468 21, **W** www.terranostra.it).

Free Home-Stays
A increasing number of international networks of people willing to provide free hospitality to travellers registered with the network is starting to add a personal dimension to travel not available at hotels. Servas (**W** www.servas.org) is the largest and most established set of contacts, with around 1500 members in Italy alone. Other establishments that cater specifically to cyclists include the Warm Showers Registrar (**W** www.rogergravel.com/wsl/vh_a.html) and of course FIAB's very own Ospitabici (**W** www.fiab-onlus.it/ospitabi.htm).

Hotels, Pensiones & Alberghi
Pensiones and *alberghi* are the same things – hotels. Quality can vary enormously. One-star establishments are very basic and without a private bathroom/shower. Standards at two-star places are often only slightly better, although bathrooms are en suite. Three-star dwellings have reasonable but variable norms, while four- and five-star hotels are usually part of high-quality chains.

A *camera singola* (single room) is uniformly expensive, usually costing from €21, whereas a *camera doppia* (double with two beds) or *camera matrimoniale* (double with a double bed) usually starts around €31.

Other *alloggi* (lodgings), including *locande* (inns), *affittacamere* (rooms for rent) and B&Bs, are mostly but not always cheaper and rarely included on regular hotel lists.

Italy Bike Hotels (☎ 0541 64 04 10, **W** www.italybikehotels.it) is a new hotel consortium formed especially for bicycle tourists. It has a growing list of three- and four-star lodgings. A less-expensive version is reachable at ☎ 02 720 01 180.

FOOD
One of the principal reasons for cycling in Italy is the after-grind ability to eat great quantities of some of the world's most incredible food. Whole lifetimes could be devoted to savouring Italian delectables.

Regional Food
What the world regards as Italian cooking is really a collection of unique regional *cucine*

(cuisines), each with its own style, and vast differences between north and south.

Among the country's best known dishes are lasagne and spaghetti Bolognese, the latter eaten in Italy with tagliatelle and called *al ragù*, both from Emilia-Romagna. In Trentino-Alto Adige the Austrian influence is strong and you'll find *canederli* dumplings made with stale bread, cheese and perhaps liver. Polenta (corn meal) with all kinds of sauces and/or *fontina* cheese is very popular in Valle d'Aosta. Two Ligurian specialties are pesto, a sauce or paste of fresh basic, garlic, oil, pine nuts and sharp cheese, and focaccia, a flat bread. In Tuscany the locals use plenty of olive oil and herbs, and regional dishes are noted for their simplicity, fine flavour and use of fresh produce. One local favourite is *bistecca fiorentina*, a huge T-bone steak 3cm to 4cm thick.

As you go further south, the food becomes spicier, and the cakes and pastries sweeter and richer. A pizza in Naples (where it was created), and local fish around Amalfi and Sorrento shouldn't be missed. In Sicily, try the *pesce spada* (swordfish); eggplant is popular here, in pasta sauces or as *melanzane alla siciliana*, filled with olives, anchovies, capers and tomatoes. Sardinia's treats include *carte musica*, thin crisp bread eaten warm with oil and salt, and *pecorino sardo*, a sharp sheep's cheese sprinkled on pasta.

Where to Eat A *tavola calda* has self-service-style offerings of inexpensive instant meat, pasta and vegetable dishes; there is no extra charge for sitting down. A *rosticceria* usually offers cooked meats and other take-away food. Of course, a pizzeria serves pizza, but usually also has a full menu of pasta, fish and meat dishes; the best pizzas are *al forno* – cooked in a wood-fired oven. An *osteria* is a classic local bistro, usually a bar, offering a simple menu emphasising local food. A trattoria is essentially a more homely, less expensive version of a *ristorante*, which, in turn, has more professional service, and a greater range of dishes, though not necessarily of a higher standard. Don't judge the quality of any eating establishment by how it looks.

Ristorante/trattoria menus are usually posted outside where you can check prices.

There is always a *pane e coperta* cover charge (around €1.50) and, perhaps, a service charge (around 15%).

Vegetarians will have no problems eating in Italy. Specialist vegetarian restaurants are fairly rare, but vegetables, pasta, rice and pulses are staples of the Italian diet. Most eateries have a good selection of *contorni* (vegetables) and *insalate* (salads), as well as meat-free *antipasti* (appetisers), soup, rice and pasta dishes and pizzas.

Smoking is allowed in eating places in Italy; expect other patrons to light up before, during and after a meal.

Eating Habits Italians rarely eat a sit-down *colazione* (breakfast). A swift coffee or cappuccino and a *cornetto* (croissant) or other pastry taken standing in a café is enough.

Pranzo (lunch) is the main meal of the day and pre-empts everything (most shops close for the long lunch-siesta break). Full meals start with *antipasti*. Next come the *primi piatti* (first courses), usually of pasta or risotto, followed by the *secondi piatti* (second courses), usually of meat or fish. Italians will tack on an *insalata* (salad) or *contorni* (vegetable side dishes), and round off the meal with fruit, or occasionally a *dolce* (dessert), and *caffè* on the way back to work.

The *cena* (evening meal) was traditionally a simple affair, but in recent years has grown in importance as lunch becomes more and more work-impeded.

In between meals, snack-happy Italians may indulge in a *panino* or *tremezzino* (little sandwich), slice of pizza or *merenda* (cake or biscuit).

DRINKS
Nonalcoholic Drinks

Drinking coffee is an essential Italian ritual. Ask for a *caffè*, perhaps *decaffeinato*, and you will get the classic small espresso. On a chilly morning try it *corretto* (corrected) with a dash of grappa; in summer, it could be *freddo* in cold milk. Other forms see it *lungo* like the traditionally diluted American coffee, *macchiato* with a dash of milk, and *ristretto* (restricted) to the first few bitter dribbles out of the machine. Don't forget the famous cappuccino and the milkier (but less foamy) *caffè latte*.

By contrast, *tè* (tea) with *limone* (lemon) or with *latte* (milk) is limp and not widely drunk, although it goes well with late afternoon *pasticcini* (small cakes). *Cioccolato caldo* (hot chocolate) is a common winter teaser, but mostly with the young.

Tap water is reliable throughout the country, despite what locals say. Most Italians prefer bottled *acqua minerale* (mineral water) anyway, either *frizzante* or *con gas* (sparkling) or *naturale, senza gas* (still). If you want tap water, quietly insist on *acqua normale* or *acqua del rubinetto*. This will be the case when you want to fill your water bottle at a bar or café as part of your regular attention to hydration.

Supermarket shelves and bar refrigerators are loaded with *succo di frutta* (fruit drink), soft drinks, excellent *tè freddo* (ice tea) and one Italian specialty, *Elisir di Rocchetta*, a thirst-quenching special mineral water that comes in unusual flavours.

On the Ride Water from village fountains and farm trough taps is safe to drink unless an *'acqua non potabile'* sign suggests otherwise. There are also mineral springs all over the place. Water from streams and rivers – even in the mountains – will almost certainly be polluted (see Water, p47).

Alcoholic Drinks

For the great majority of Italians, wine is an integral part of a meal. This is scarcely surprising in a country that produces 20% of the world's wine. What is surprising is how much more there is than the Barolo, Amarone, Lambrusco and Chianti export successes. Consult local tourist offices for abundant information about regional nectars.

Before and after dinner, sample a bitter *aperitivo* or sweet *digestivo*. The most famous are all post-meal quaffs: potent grape-based grappa, almondy *amaretto* and, around Amalfi and in the Lake District, *limoncello* made from fresh lemons, pure alcohol, sugar and water.

Birra (beer) is mostly popular with younger people. The most common Italian brews – Dreher, Moretti and Peroni – are light lagers ideal for quenching a fierce all-day-in-the-saddle thirst.

Health & Safety

Keeping healthy on your travels depends on your predeparture preparations, your daily health care and diet while on the road, and how you handle any medical problem that develops. Few touring cyclists experience anything more than a bit of soreness, fatigue and chafing, although there is potential for more serious problems. The sections that follow aren't intended to alarm, but they are worth a skim before you go.

Before You Go

HEALTH INSURANCE
Make sure that you have adequate health insurance. For details, see Travel Insurance in the Visas & Documents section in Travel Facts chapter.

IMMUNISATIONS
You don't need any vaccinations to visit Italy. However, it's always wise to keep up-to-date with routine vaccinations such as diphtheria, polio and tetanus – boosters are necessary every 10 years and protection is highly recommended.

FIRST AID
It's a good idea at any time to know the appropriate responses in the event of a major accident or illness, and it's especially important if you are intending to ride off-road in a remote area. Consider learning basic first aid through a recognised course before you go, and carrying a first-aid manual and small medical kit.

Although detailed first-aid instruction is outside the scope of this guidebook, some basic points are listed in the section on Traumatic Injuries later in this chapter. Undoubtedly the best advice is to avoid an accident in the first place. The Safety on the Ride section on p57 contains tips for safe on-road and off-road riding, as well as information on how to summon help should a major accident or illness occur.

PHYSICAL FITNESS
Most of the rides in this book are designed for someone with a moderate degree of cycling

---

First-Aid Kit

A possible kit could include:

First-Aid Supplies
- [ ] bandages & safety pins
- [ ] butterfly closure strips
- [ ] elastic support bandage for knees, ankles etc
- [ ] gauze swabs
- [ ] latex gloves
- [ ] nonadhesive dressings
- [ ] scissors (small pair)
- [ ] sterile alcohol wipes
- [ ] sticking plasters (Band Aids)
- [ ] syringes & needles – for removing gravel from road-rash wounds
- [ ] thermometer (note that mercury thermometers are prohibited by airlines)
- [ ] tweezers

Medications
- [ ] antidiarrhoea, antinausea drugs and oral rehydration salts
- [ ] antifungal cream or powder – for fungal skin infections and thrush
- [ ] antihistamines – for allergies, eg, hay fever; to ease the itch from insect bites or stings; and to prevent motion sickness
- [ ] antiseptic powder or solution (such as povidone-iodine) and antiseptic wipes for cuts and grazes
- [ ] calamine lotion, sting relief spray or aloe vera – to ease irritation from sunburn and insect bites or stings
- [ ] cold and flu tablets, throat lozenges and nasal decongestant
- [ ] laxatives
- [ ] nappy rash cream
- [ ] painkillers (eg, aspirin or paracetamol/cetaminophen in the USA) – for pain and fever

Miscellaneous
- [ ] insect repellent, sunscreen, lip balm and eye drops
- [ ] water purification tablets or iodine

Getting Fit for Touring

Ideally, a training programme should be tailored to your objectives, specific needs, fitness level and health. However, if you have no idea how to prepare for your cycling holiday these guidelines will help you get the fitness you need to enjoy it more. Things to think about include:

Foundation You will need general kilometres in your legs before you start to expose them to any intensive cycling. Always start out with easy rides – even a few kilometres to the shops – and give yourself plenty of time to build towards your objective.

Tailoring Once you have the general condition to start preparing for your trip, work out how to tailor your training rides to the type of tour you are planning. Someone preparing for a three-week ride will require a different approach to someone building fitness for a one-day or weekend ride. Some aspects to think about are the ride length (distance and days), terrain, climate and weight to be carried in panniers. If your trip involves carrying 20kg in panniers, incorporate this weight into some training rides, especially some of the longer ones. If you are going to be touring in mountainous areas, choose a hilly training route.

Recovery You usually adapt to a training programme during recovery time, so it's important to do the right things between rides. Recovery can take many forms, but the simple ones are best. These include getting quality sleep, eating an adequate diet to refuel the system, doing recovery rides between hard days (using low gears to avoid pushing yourself), stretching and enjoying a relaxing bath. Other forms include recovery massage, spas and yoga.

If you have no cycling background this programme will help you get fit for your cycling holiday. If you are doing an easy ride (each ride in this book is rated; see Cycling Routes on p39, aim to at least complete Week 4; for moderate rides, complete Week 6; and complete the programme if you are doing a hard ride. Experienced cycle tourists may start at Week 3, while those who regularly ride up to four days a week could start at Week 5.

Don't treat this as a punishing training schedule: try cycling to work or to the shops, join a local touring club or get a group of friends together to turn weekend rides into social events.

	Monday	Tuesday	Wednesday	Thursday	Friday	Saturday	Sunday
Week 1	10km*	–	10km*	–	10km*	–	10km*
Week 2	–	15km*	–	15km*	–	20km*	–
Week 3	20km*	–	20km†	25km*	–	25km*	20km†
Week 4	–	30km*	–	35km*	30km†	30km*	–
Week 5	30km*	–	40km†	–	35km*	–	40km†
Week 6	30km*	–	40km†	–	–	60km*	40km†
Week 7	30km*	–	40km†	–	30km†	70km*	30km*
Week 8	–	60km*	30km†	–	40km†	–	90km*

* steady pace (allows you to carry out a conversation without losing your breath) on flat or undulating terrain
† solid pace (allows you to talk in short sentences only) on undulating roads with some longer hills

This training programme shown is only a guide. Ultimately it is important to listen to your body and slow down if the ride is getting too hard. Take extra recovery days and cut back distances when you feel this way. Don't panic if you don't complete every ride, every week; the most important thing is to ride regularly and gradually increase the length of your rides as you get fitter.

For those with no exercise background, be sure to see your doctor and get a clearance to begin exercising at these rates. This is especially important for those over 35 years of age with no exercise history and those with a cardiac or respiratory condition of any nature.

Kevin Tabotta

fitness. As a general rule, however, the fitter you are, the more you'll enjoy riding. It pays to spend time preparing yourself physically before you set out, rather than let a sore backside and aching muscles draw your attention from some of the world's finest cycle touring countryside.

Depending on your existing level of fitness, you should start training a couple of months before your trip. Try to ride at least three times a week, starting with easy rides (even 5km to work, if you're not already cycling regularly) and gradually building up to longer distances. Once you have a good base of regular riding behind you, include hills in your training (you'll appreciate hill fitness in parts of France) and familiarise yourself with the gearing on your bike. Before you go you should have done at least one 60km to 70km ride with loaded panniers.

As you train, you'll discover how to adjust your bike to increase your comfort – as well as any mechanical problems.

Staying Healthy

The best way to have a lousy holiday (especially if you're relying on self-propulsion) is to become ill. Heed the following simple advice and the only thing you're likely to suffer from is that rewarding tiredness at the end of a full day.

Reduce the chances of contracting an illness by washing your hands frequently, particularly after working on your bike and before handling or eating food.

HYDRATION

You may not notice how much water you're losing as you ride, because it evaporates in the breeze. However, don't underestimate the amount of fluid you need to replace – particularly in warmer weather. The magic figure is supposedly 1L per hour, though many cyclists have trouble consuming this much – remembering to drink enough can be harder than it sounds. Sipping little and often is the key; try to drink a mouthful every 10 minutes or so and don't wait until you get thirsty. Water 'backpacks' can be great for fluid regulation since virtually no physical or mental effort is required to drink. Keep drinking before and after the day's ride to replenish fluid.

Use the colour of your urine as a rough guide to whether you are drinking enough. Small amounts of dark urine suggest you need to increase your fluid intake. Passing reasonable quantities of light yellow urine indicates that you've got the balance about right. Some other obvious signs of dehydration include headache and fatigue. For more information on the effects of dehydration, see Dehydration & Heat Exhaustion on p52.

Water

Tap water is almost always safe to drink in Italy. However, the intestinal parasite *Giardia lamblia* has been found in water from lakes, rivers, streams and drinking fountains. Giardia is not common but, to be certain, water from these sources should be purified before drinking. For more information on giardiasis, see Infectious Diseases on p53.

The simplest way of purifying water is to boil it thoroughly. Vigorous boiling for five minutes should do the job.

Simple filtering will not remove all dangerous organisms, so if you can't boil water treat it chemically. Chlorine tablets will kill many pathogens, but not giardia. Iodine is very effective in purifying water and is available in tablet and liquid form, but follow the directions carefully and remember that too much iodine can be harmful. Flavoured powder will disguise the taste of treated water and is a good thing to carry if you are spending time away from town water supplies.

Sports Drinks

Commercial sports drinks such as Gatorade and PowerAde are an excellent way to satisfy your hydration needs, electrolyte replacement and energy demands in one. On endurance rides especially, it can be difficult to keep eating solid fuels day in, day out, but sports drinks can supplement these energy demands and allow you to vary your solid fuel intake a little for variety. The bonus is that those all-important body salts lost through perspiration get re-stocked. Make sure you drink plenty of water as well; if you have two water bottles on your bike (and you should), it's a good idea to fill one with sports drink and the other with plain water.

If using a powdered sports drink, don't mix it too strong (follow the instructions) because, in addition to being too sweet, too many carbohydrates can actually impair your body's ability to absorb the water and carbohydrates properly.

NUTRITION

One of the great things about bike touring is that it requires lots of energy, which means you can eat more of Italy's fabulous food. Depending on your activity levels, it's not hard to put away huge servings of food and be hungry a few hours after.

Because you're putting such demands on your body, it's important to eat well – not just lots. As usual, you should eat a bal-anced diet from a wide variety of foods. This is easy in Italy, with so much fresh food widely available (see Food Italy on p42).

The main part of your diet should be carbohydrates rather than proteins or fats. While some protein (for tissue maintenance and repair) and fat (for vitamins, long-term energy and warmth) is essential, carbohy-drates provide the most efficient fuel. They are easily digested into simple sugars, which are then used in energy production. Less-refined foods like pasta, rice, bread, fruits and vegetables are all high in carbohydrates.

Eating simple carbohydrates (sugars, such as lollies or sweets) gives you almost immediate energy – great for when you

Avoiding the Bonk

The bonk, in a cycling context, is not a pleasant experience; it's that light-headed, can't-put-power-to-the-pedals weak feeling that engulfs you (usually quite quickly) when your body runs out of fuel.

If you experience it the best move is to stop and refuel immediately. It can be quite ser-ious and risky to your health if it's not addressed as soon as symptoms occur. It won't take long before you are ready to get going again (although most likely at a slower pace), but you'll also be more tired the next day so try to avoid it.

The best way to do this is to maintain your fuel intake while riding. Cycling for hours burns considerable body energy, and replacing it is something that needs to be tailored to each in-dividual's tastes. The touring cyclist needs to target foods that have a high carbohydrate source. Foods that contain some fat are not a problem occasionally, as cycling at low inten-sity (when you're able to ride and talk without losing your breath) will usually trigger the body to draw on fat stores before stored carbohydrates.

Good on-bike cycling foods include:

• bananas (in particular) and other fruits
• bread with jam or honey
• breakfast and muesli bars
• rice-based snacks
• prepackaged high carbohydrate sports bars (eg, PowerBar)
• sports drinks

During lunch stops (or breakfast) you can try such things as spaghetti, cer-eal, creamed rice, pancakes, baked beans, sandwiches and rolls.

It's important not to get uptight about the food you eat. As a rule of thumb, base all your meals around carbohydrates of some sort, but don't be afraid to also indulge in local culinary delights.

DON HATCHER

need a top-up (see the boxed text 'Avoiding the Bonk'); however, because they are quickly metabolised, you may get a sugar 'high' then a 'low'. For cycling it is far better to base your diet around complex carbohydrates, which take longer to process and provide 'slow-release' energy over a longer period. (But don't miss the opportunity to indulge guiltlessly in pastries and that delicious cheese every now and then …)

Cycle Food: A Guide to Satisfying Your Inner Tube, by Lauren Hefferon, is a handy reference for nutrition and health advice with practical recipes.

Day-to-Day Needs

Eat a substantial breakfast – wholegrain cereal or bread is best, if you can find them in France – and fruit or juice for vitamins. You're unlikely to get cooked breakfasts in hotels or hostels, but if you're camping and cooking your own, include carbohydrates (such as porridge, toast or potatoes). Try to avoid foods high in fat (such as croissants), which take longer to digest.

Bread is the easiest food for lunch, topped with ingredients like cheese, peanut butter, salami and fresh salad vegetables. If you're in a town, filled baguettes make for a satisfying meal (fries [chips] – or pizza, with their high fat content, will feel like a lump in your stomach if you continue straight away).

Keep topping up your energy during the ride. See the boxed text 'Avoiding the Bonk' on the previous page.

Try to eat a high carbohydrate meal in the evening. If you're eating out, Italian or Asian restaurants tend to offer more carbohydrate-based meals.

Rice, pasta and potatoes are good staples if you're self-catering. Team them with fresh vegetables and ingredients such as instant soup, canned beans, fish or bacon. Remember that even though you're limited in terms of what you can carry on a bike, it's possible – with some imagination and preparation – to eat delicious as well as nutritious camp meals.

AVOIDING CYCLING AILMENTS
Saddle Sores & Blisters

While you're more likely to get a sore bum if you're out of condition, riding long distances does take its toll on your behind. To minimise the impact, always wear clean, preferably padded bike shorts (also known as 'knicks'). Brief, unfitted shorts can chafe, as can underwear (see Clothing under What to Bring on p32). Shower as soon as you stop and put on clean, preferably nonsynthetic, clothes. Moisturising or emollient creams or baby nappy rash cream also help guard against chafing – apply liberally around the crotch area before riding. For information on correctly adjusting your bike seat, see the Your Bicycle chapter on p47.

If you do suffer from chafing, wash and dry the area and carefully apply a barrier (moisturising) cream.

You probably won't get blisters unless you do a very long ride with no physical preparation. Wearing gloves and correctly fitted shoes will reduce the likelihood of blisters on your hands and feet. If you know you're susceptible to blisters in a particular spot, cover the area with medical adhesive tape before riding.

Knee Pain

Knee pain is common among cyclists who pedal in too high a gear. While it may *seem* faster to turn the pedals slowly in a high gear, it's actually more efficient (and better for your knees) to 'spin' the pedals – that is, use a low enough gear so you can pedal quickly with little resistance. For touring, the ideal cadence (the number of pedal strokes per minute) ranges from 70 to 90. Try to maintain this cadence even when you're climbing.

It's a good idea to stretch before and after riding, and to go easy when you first start each day. This reduces your chances of injury and helps your muscles to work more efficiently.

You can also get sore knees if your saddle is too low, or if your shoe cleats (for use with clipless pedals) are incorrectly positioned. Both are discussed in greater detail in the Your Bicycle chapter.

Numbness & Backache

Pain in the hands, neck and shoulders is a common complaint, particularly on longer riding days. It's generally caused by leaning too much on your hands. Apart from discomfort, you can temporarily damage the nerves and experience numbness or mild

Stretching

Stretching is important when stepping up your exercise levels: it improves muscle flexibility, which allows freer movement in the joints; and prevents the rigidity developing in muscles that occurs through prolonged cycling activity.

Ideally, you should stretch for 10 minutes before and after riding and for longer periods (15 to 30 minutes) every second day. Stretching prepares muscles for the task ahead, and limits the stress on muscles and joints during exercise. It can reduce post-exercise stiffness (decreasing the recovery time between rides) and reduce the chance of injury during cycling.

You should follow a few basic guidelines:

- before stretching, warm up for five to 10 minutes by going for a gentle bike ride, jog or brisk walk
- ensure you follow correct technique for each stretch
- hold a stretch for 15 to 30 seconds
- stretch to the point of discomfort, not pain
- breathe freely (ie, don't hold your breath) and try to relax your body whenever you are stretching
- don't 'bounce' the stretch; gradually ease into a full stretch
- repeat each stretch three times (on both sides, when required)

Do not stretch when you have an injury to a muscle, ligament or tendon (allow it to heal fully), as it can lead to further injury and/or hinder recovery. Warming up the muscles increases blood flow to the area, making it easier to stretch and reducing the likelihood of injury.

The main muscle groups for the cyclist to stretch are: quadriceps, calves, hamstrings, lower back and neck. Use the following stretches as a starting point, adding extra stretches that are already part of your routine or if you feel 'tight' in other areas (eg, add shoulder rolls if your shoulders feel sore after a day's cycling).

Quadriceps

Facing a wall with your feet slightly apart, grip one foot with your hand and pull it towards the buttocks. Ensure the back and hips are square. To get a better stretch, push the hip forward. You should never feel pain at the knee joint. Hold the stretch, before lowering the leg and repeating the stretch with the other leg.

Calf

Stand facing a wall, placing one foot about 30cm in front of the other. Keep the heels flat on the ground and bend the front leg slowly toward the wall – the stretch should be in the upper-calf area of the back leg. Keep the back straight and bend your elbows to allow your body to move forward during the stretch. Hold the stretch; relax and repeat the stretch with the other leg.

Hamstrings

Sit with one leg extended and the other leg bent with the bottom of the foot against the inside of the extended leg. Slide your arms down the extended leg – bending from the waist – until you feel a pull in the hamstring area. Hold it for 15 seconds, before returning to the start position. Keep the toes pointed up; avoid hunching the back.

Lower-Back Roll

Lie on your back (on a towel or sleeping mat) and bring both knees up towards the shoulders until you feel a stretch in the lower back. Hold the stretch for 30 seconds; relax.

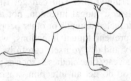

'Cat Stretch' Hunch

Another stretch for the lower back. Move to the ground on all fours (hands shoulder-width apart; legs slightly apart), lift the hips and lower back towards the sky until you feel a stretch. Hold it for 15 seconds; return to start position.

'Cat Stretch' Arch

One more stretch for the lower back. With hands and knees in the same position as for the Cat Stretch above, roll the hips and lower back toward the ground until you feel a stretch. Hold it for 15 seconds; return to start position.

Neck

Gently and smoothly stretch your neck each of the four ways: forward, back and side to side. Do each stretch separately. (Do not rotate the head in a full circle.) For the side stretches, use your hand to pull the head very gently in the direction of the stretch.

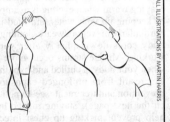

ALL ILLUSTRATIONS BY MARTIN HARRIS

paralysis of the hands. Prevent it by wearing padded gloves, cycling with less weight on your hands and changing your hand position frequently (if you have flat handlebars, fit bar ends to provide more hand positions).

When seated your weight should be fairly evenly distributed through your hands and seat. If you're carrying too much weight on your hands there are two ways of adjusting your bike to rectify this: either by raising the height of your handlebars or, if you are stretched out too much, fitting a smaller stem (talk to your local bike shop). For more guidance on adjusting your bicycle for greater comfort, see the Your Bicycle chapter.

Fungal Infections

Warm, sweaty bodies are ideal environments for fungal growth, and physical activity, combined with inadequate washing of your body and/or clothes, can lead to fungal infections. The most common are athlete's foot (tinea) between the toes or fingers, and infections on the scalp, in the groin or on the body (ringworm). You can get ringworm (which is a fungal infection, not a worm) from infected animals or other people.

To prevent fungal infections, wash frequently and dry yourself carefully. Change out of sweaty bike clothes as soon as possible.

If you do get an infection, wash the infected area at least daily with a disinfectant or medicated soap and water, and rinse and dry well. Apply an antifungal cream or powder like tolnaftate. Expose the infected area to air or sunlight as much as possible, avoid artificial fibres and wash all towels and underwear in hot water, change them often and let them dry in the sun.

Staying Warm

Except on extremely hot days, put on another layer of clothing when you stop cycling – even if it's just for a quick break. Staying warm when cycling is as important as keeping up your water and food intake. Particularly in wet or sweaty clothing, your body cools down quickly after you stop working. Muscle strains occur more easily when your body is chilled and hypothermia can result from prolonged exposure (for prevention and treatment, see Hypothermia on the next page). Staying rugged up will help prevent picking up chest infections, colds and the flu.

It's not advisable to cycle at high altitude during winter; however, you *can* get caught suddenly in bad weather at any time of year, especially in the mountains. No matter when you go, always be prepared with warm clothing and a waterproof layer. Protect yourself from the wind on long downhill stretches – even stuffing a few sheets of newspaper under your shirt cuts the chill considerably.

Medical Problems & Treatment

ENVIRONMENTAL HAZARDS
Sun

You can get sunburnt quite quickly, even on cool or cloudy days, especially during spring and summer and at higher altitudes.

Take sun protection seriously – unless you want to be fried and increase your chances of heatstroke and skin cancer:

- Cover yourself up: wear a long-sleeved top with a collar, and a peaked helmet cover – you may want to go the extra step and add a 'legionnaire's flap' to your helmet to protect the back of your neck and ears. Make sure your shirt is sunproof: very thin or loosely woven fabrics still let sun through. Some fabrics are designed to offer high sun protection.
- Use a high protection sunscreen (30+ or higher). Choose a water-resistant 'sports' sunscreen and reapply every few hours as you sweat it off. Protect your neck, ears, hands, and feet. Zinc cream is good for sensitive noses, lips and ears.
- Wear good sunglasses; they will also protect you from wind, dust and insects and are essential protection against sticks and flying objects if you're mountain biking.
- Sit in the shade during rest breaks.
- Wear a wide-brimmed hat when off the bike.

Mild sunburn can be treated with calamine lotion, aloe vera or sting-relief spray.

Heat

Treat heat with respect. Italy is temperate but can get very hot in the south in summer, so don't set yourself a demanding touring schedule as soon as your arrive; take things lightly until you acclimatise.

Dehydration & Heat Exhaustion Dehydration is a potentially dangerous and easily preventable condition caused by excessive fluid loss. Sweating and inadequate fluid intake are common causes of dehydration in cyclists, but others include diarrhoea, vomiting and high fever – see Diarrhoea at the bottom of this page for details on appropriate treatment in these circumstances.

The first symptoms are weakness, thirst and passing small amounts of very concentrated urine. This may progress to drowsiness, dizziness or fainting when standing up and, finally, coma.

It's easy to forget how much fluid you are losing via perspiration while you are cycling, particularly if a strong breeze is drying your skin quickly. Make sure you drink sufficient liquids (see Hydration p47). You should refrain from drinking too many caffeinated drinks such as coffee, tea and some soft drinks (which act as a diuretic, causing your body to lose water through urination) throughout the day; don't use them as a water replacement.

Dehydration and salt deficiency can cause heat exhaustion. Salt deficiency is characterised by fatigue, lethargy, headaches, giddiness and muscle cramps; salt tablets may help, but adding extra salt to your food is probably sufficient.

If one of your party suffers from heat exhaustion, lie the casualty down in a shady spot and encourage them to drink slowly but frequently. If possible, seek medical advice.

Heatstroke This serious and occasionally fatal condition can occur if the body's heat-regulating mechanism breaks down and the body temperature rises to dangerous levels. Continuous periods of exposure to high temperatures and insufficient fluids can leave you vulnerable to heatstroke.

The symptoms are feeling unwell, not sweating very much (or at all) and a high body temperature (39°C to 41°C or 102°F to 106°F). Where sweating has ceased, the skin becomes flushed and red. Severe, throbbing headaches and lack of coordination will also occur, and the sufferer may be confused or aggressive. Eventually the victim will become delirious or convulse.

Hospitalisation is essential, but in the interim get the casualty out of the sun, remove their clothing, cover them with a wet sheet or towel and then fan continuously. Give them plenty of fluids (cool water), if conscious.

Cold
Hypothermia This is a real danger in Italy's mountains because of the changeable weather.

Hypothermia occurs when the body loses heat faster than it can produce it and the core temperature of the body falls. It is surprisingly easy to progress from very cold to dangerously cold due to a combination of wind, wet clothing, fatigue and hunger, even if the air temperature stays above freezing.

Symptoms of hypothermia are exhaustion, numb skin (particularly toes and fingers), shivering, slurred speech, irrational or violent behaviour, lethargy, stumbling, dizzy spells, muscle cramps and powerful bursts of energy. Irrationality may take the form of sufferers claiming they are warm and trying to take off their clothes.

To prevent hypothermia, dress in layers (see Clothing under What to Bring on p32). A strong, waterproof outer layer is essential. Protect yourself against wind, particularly for long descents. Eat plenty of high-energy food when it's cold; it's important to keep drinking too – even though you may not feel like it.

To treat mild hypothermia, get the person out of the wind and/or rain, remove wet clothing and replace it with dry, warm clothing. Give them hot liquids – not alcohol – and some high-kilojoule, easily digestible food. Do not rub victims: instead, allow them to slowly warm themselves. This should be enough to treat the early stages of hypothermia; however, medical treatment should still be sought, urgently if the hypothermia is severe. Early recognition and treatment of mild hypothermia is the only way to prevent severe hypothermia, a critical condition.

Hay Fever
If you suffer from hay fever, bring your usual treatment, as the pollen count in Italy is very high in May and June.

INFECTIOUS DISEASES
Diarrhoea
Simple things like a change of water, food or climate can cause a mild bout of diarrhoea, but a few rushed toilet trips with no other symptoms are not indicative of a major problem. More serious diarrhoea is

caused by infectious agents transmitted by faecal contamination of food or water, by using contaminated utensils or directly from one person's hand to another. Paying particular attention to personal hygiene, drinking purified water and taking care of what you eat are important measures to take to avoid getting diarrhoea while touring.

Dehydration is the main danger with any diarrhoea, particularly in children or the elderly, as it can occur quickly. Under all circumstances, the most important thing is to replace fluids (at least equal to the volume being lost). Urine is the best guide to this – if you have small amounts of dark-coloured urine, you need to drink more. Weak black tea with a little sugar, soda water, or soft drinks allowed to go flat and diluted 50% with clean water are all good. With severe diarrhoea it's better to use a re-hydrating solution to replace lost minerals and salts. Commercially available oral re-hydration salts should be added to boiled or bottled water. In an emergency, make a solution of six teaspoons of sugar and a half teaspoon of salt in a litre of boiled or bottled water. Keep drinking small amounts often. Stick to a bland diet as you recover.

Gut-paralysing drugs such as diphenoxy-late or loperamide can be used to bring relief from the symptoms, although they do not actually cure the problem. Only use these drugs if you do not have access to toilets, that is, if you *must* travel. These drugs are not recommended for children under 12 years of age, or if you have a high fever or are severely dehydrated.

Seek medical advice if you pass blood or mucus, are feverish or suffer persistent or severe diarrhoea.

Another cause of persistent diarrhoea in travellers is giardiasis.

Giardiasis

This intestinal disorder is contracted by drinking water contaminated with the giardia parasite. The symptoms are stomach cramps, nausea, a bloated stomach, watery and foul-smelling diarrhoea, and frequent gas. Giardiasis can appear several weeks after you have been exposed to the parasite. The symptoms may disappear for a few days and then return; this can go on for several weeks. Seek medical advice if you think you have giardiasis but, where this is not possi-

ble, tinidazole or metronidazole are the recommended drugs. Treatment is a 2g single dose of tinidazole or 250mg of metronidazole three times daily for five to 10 days.

Rabies

Rabies is a fatal viral infection, but is rare in Italy. It is contracted by a bite from an infected animal, which could be a dog, pig, cat, fox or bat: their salvia is infectious. Once symptoms have appeared, death is inevitable, but the onset of symptoms can be prevented by a course of injections with the rabies vaccine, which you will need irrespective of whether or not you have been immunised.

Tetanus

This disease is caused by a germ that lives in soil and in the faeces of horses and other animals. It enters the body via breaks in the skin. The first symptom may be discomfort in swallowing, or stiffening of the jaw and neck; this is followed by painful convulsions of the jaw and whole body. The disease can be fatal. It can be prevented by vaccination.

BITES & STINGS
Dogs & Pigs

You're bound to encounter barking dogs while riding in Italy, and some are likely to be untethered. In some regions you're also likely to come across pigs by the side of the road, emboldened by tourists feeding them. As rabies exists in Italy (see Infectious Diseases), all dogs and pigs should be regarded as dangerous, and preventative action taken to avoid them. Ride through their territory quickly and, for dogs, try shouting at them. A squirt from the water bottle or tap with the bike pump may provide added deterrent if the animal won't take the hint – though use the pump as a last resort, especially if the owner is in sight.

Bees & Wasps

These are usually painful rather than dangerous. However, anyone allergic to these can suffer severe breathing difficulties and will need medical care.

Calamine lotion or a commercial sting relief spray will ease discomfort, and ice packs will reduce the pain and swelling. Antihistamines can also help.

Snakes

A bite by any adder or viper in Italy is unlikely to be fatal. Even so, if bitten, wrap the bitten limb tightly, as you would for a sprained ankle, and immobilise it with a splint. Keep the victim still and seek medical assistance; it will help if you can describe the offending reptile. Torniquets and sucking out the poison are now totally discredited.

WOMEN'S HEALTH

Cycle touring is not hazardous to your health, but women's health issues are relevant wherever you go, and can be a bit more tricky to cope with when you are on the road.

If you experience low energy and/or abdominal or back pain during menstruation, it may be best to undertake less strenuous rides or schedule a rest day or two at this time.

Gynaecological Problems

If you have a vaginal discharge that is not normal for you with or without any other symptoms, you've probably got an infection.

• If you've had thrush (vaginal candidiasis) before and think you have it again, it's worth self-treating for this (see the following section).
• If not, get medical advice, as you will need a laboratory test and an appropriate course of treatment.
• It's best not to self-medicate with antibiotics because there are many causes of vaginal discharge, which can only be differentiated with a laboratory test.

Thrush (Vaginal Candidiasis) Symptoms of this common yeast infection are itching and discomfort in the genital area, often in association with thick white vaginal discharge (said to resemble cottage cheese). Many factors, including diet, pregnancy, medications and hot climatic conditions can trigger this infection.

You can help prevent thrush by wearing cotton underwear off the bike and loose-fitting bicycle shorts; maintaining good personal hygiene is particularly important when wearing cycling knicks. It's a good idea to wash regularly, but don't use soap, which can increase the chance of thrush occurring. Washing gently with a solution of 1tspn salt dissolved in 1L warm water can relieve the itching. If you have thrush a single dose of an antifungal pessary (vaginal tablet), such as 500mg of clotrimazole is an effective treatment. Alternatively, you can use an antifungal cream inserted high in the vagina (on a tampon). A vaginal acidifying gel may help prevent recurrences.

If you're stuck in a remote area without medication, you could use natural yoghurt (applied directly to the vulva or on a tampon and inserted in the vagina) to soothe and help restore the normal balance of organisms in the vagina.

Avoid yeasty products such as bread and beer, and eat yoghurt made with acidophylis culture.

Urinary Tract Infection

Cystitis, or inflammation of the bladder, is a common condition in women. Symptoms include burning when urinating and having to urinate urgently and frequently. Blood can sometimes be passed in urine.

If you think you have cystitis:

• Drink plenty of fluids to help flush the infection out; citrus fruit juice or cranberry juice can help relieve symptoms.
• Take a nonprescription cystitis remedy to help relieve the discomfort. Alternatively, add a teaspoon of bicarbonate of soda to one glass of water when symptoms first appear.
• If there's no improvement after 24 hours despite these measures, seek medical advice because a course of antibiotics may be needed.

TRAUMATIC INJURIES

Although we give guidance on basic first-aid procedures here remember that, unless you're an experienced first aider and confident in what you're doing, it's possible to do more harm than good. Always seek medical help if it is available, but if you are far from any help, follow these guidelines.

Cuts & Other Wounds

Here's what to do if you suffer a fall while riding and end up with road-rash (grazing) and a few minor cuts. If you're riding in a hot, humid climate or intend continuing on your way, there's likely to be a high risk of infection, so the wound needs to be cleaned and dressed. Carry a few antiseptic wipes in your first-aid kit to use as an immediate measure, especially if no clean water is available. Small wounds can be cleaned with an antiseptic wipe (only wipe across the wound once with each). Deep or dirty wounds need to be cleaned thoroughly:

- Clean your hands before you start.
- Wear gloves if you are cleaning somebody else's wound.
- Use bottled or boiled water (allowed to cool) or an antiseptic solution like povi-done-iodine.
- Use plenty of water – pour it on the wound from a container.
- Embedded dirt and other particles can be removed with tweezers or flushed out using a syringe to squirt water (you can get more pressure if you use a needle as well) – this is especially effective for removing gravel.
- Dry wounds heal best, so avoid using antiseptic creams that keep the wound moist; instead apply antiseptic powder or spray.
- Dry the wound with clean gauze before applying a dressing – alternatively, any clean material will do as long as it's not fluffy (avoid cotton wool), because it will stick.

Any break in the skin makes you vulnerable to tetanus infection – if you didn't have a tetanus injection before you left, get one now.

Bleeding Wounds

Most cuts will stop bleeding on their own, but if a blood vessel of any size has been cut it may continue bleeding for some time. Wounds to the head, hands and at joint creases tend to be particularly bloody. To stop bleeding from a wound:

- Wear gloves if you are dealing with a wound on another person.
- Lie the casualty down if possible.
- Raise the injured limb above the level of the casualty's heart.
- Use your fingers or the palm of your hand to apply direct pressure to the wound, preferably over a sterile dressing or clean pad.
- Apply steady pressure for at least five minutes before looking to see if the bleeding has stopped.
- Put a sterile dressing over the original pad (don't move this) and bandage it in place.
- Check the bandage regularly in case bleeding restarts.

Never use a tourniquet to stop bleeding as this may cause gangrene – the only situation in which this may be appropriate is if the limb has been amputated.

A dressing will protect the wound from dirt, dust and flies. Alternatively, if the wound is small and you are confident you can keep it clean, leave it uncovered. Change the dressing regularly (once a day to start with), especially if the wound is oozing, and watch for signs of infection.

If you have any swelling around the wound, raising the affected limb can help the swelling settle and the wound to heal.

It's best to seek medical advice for any wound that fails to heal after a week or so.

Major Accident

Crashing or being hit by an inattentive driver in a motor vehicle is always possible when cycling. When a major accident does occur what you do is determined to some extent by the circumstances you are in and how readily available medical care is. However, remember that emergency services may be different from what you're used to at home. And, as anywhere, if you are outside a major town they may be much slower at responding to a call, so you need to be prepared to do at least an initial assessment and to ensure that the casualty comes to no further harm. First of all, check for danger to yourself. If the casualty is on the road ensure oncoming traffic is stopped or diverted around you. A basic plan of action is:

- Keep calm and think through what you need to do and when.
- Get medical help urgently; send someone to phone ☎ 118.
- Carefully look over the casualty in the position in which you found them (unless this is hazardous for some reason, eg, on a cliff edge).
- Call out to the casualty to see if there is any response.
- Check for pulse (at the wrist or on the side of the neck), breathing and major blood loss.
- If necessary (ie, no breathing or no pulse), and you know how, start resuscitation.
- Check the casualty for injuries, moving them as little as possible; ask them where they have pain if they are conscious.
- Don't move the casualty if a spinal injury is possible.
- Take immediate steps to control any obvious bleeding by applying direct pressure to the wound.
- Make the casualty as comfortable as possible and reassure them.
- Keep the casualty warm by insulating them from cold or wet ground (use whatever you have to hand, such as a sleeping bag).

Safety on the Ride

ROAD RULES

Italian road rules are outlined in the *Codice della Strada* (Road Code), and written essentially for motor vehicles. However, there are a number of points that apply specifically to bicyclists. General rules are:

- Ride on the right side of the road.
- Ride in single file, and always keep to the extreme right, unless you are turning left or passing.
- Obey all traffic lights and road signs, and use hand signals to indicate turns. Avoid sudden movements.
- Never ride the wrong way down a one-way street.
- Always yield to pedestrians.
- Do not ride on footpaths unless there is road construction or cobblestones, in which case you must ride slowly and give priority to pedestrians.
- Keep a suitable distance from parked cars.

For a list of commonly seen road signs, see the Language chapter.

Road Use

Cyclists may use all roads except *autostrade* (autoroutes), *strade statali* (state roads) when posted signs specifically prohibit two-wheel motorless vehicles, and roads parallelled by a compulsory bike path. A round blue sign with a white bicycle symbol indicates a *pista ciclabile* (bicycle path). You are obliged to use it, especially if it is signed with the word *obligatorio* (compulsory). The end of a pista ciclabile is indicated by the same sign, with a red line through it.

Priority to the Right

The most confusing – and dangerous – traffic law in Italy is the notorious 'priority to the right' rule, under which any car entering an intersection (including a T-junction) from a public road on your right has right-of-way no matter how small the road.

There is one notable exception to this rule: Cyclists merging or turning from a bike path onto a road must yield to vehicles. Add to this that, right or wrong, most cars reluctantly give way to cyclists, and this basically means that cyclists should always yield to all vehicles at intersections, even if approaching from the right, and even if traffic on your right has a stop or yield sign and you are on a priority road. Note that a yellow diamond edged with white indicates a priority (usually major) road; adjoining (small) roads are marked with stop and give-way signs.

Rotatorie/Rotonde (Roundabouts)

Roundabouts (traffic circles) are probably the least 'bicycle-friendly' things you'll encounter on Italian roads. Italian road engineers *love* them; they're everywhere.

At most larger roundabouts, *priorità a destra* (priority to the right) has been suspended so that the cars already in the roundabout have right of way. This circumstance is indicated by yield signs displaying a circle made out of three curved arrows.

As a cyclist, use extreme caution. Road decorum calls for you to enter the roundabout and move left to allow enough room for cars to exit (if you are not taking the first exit). However, many Italian cyclists remain in the centre of the outside lane (to discourage drivers' overly aggressive manoeuvring). When you approach your exit, indicate with a right hand turn signal to let cars know you are exiting. Make certain that the driver of the car behind you or to your right has seen you.

MANDATORY BICYCLE EQUIPMENT

Italian law mandates that bicycles must have two functioning brakes, a bell (audible for 30m), a red reflector on the back and yellow ones on the pedals. Starting 30 minutes after sunset and when visibility is poor, cyclists must turn on a white light at the front and a red one at the rear.

Rider Safety

Although helmets are not compulsory in Italy, we strongly recommend you wear one whenever in the saddle. Make sure it fits properly: It should sit squarely on your head with the front low on your brow to protect your forehead. It should be snug, but not tight, once it has been fastened, and there should be no slack in the straps. If it has been in a crash, replace it.

Whether it is day or night, it is always a good idea to wear brightly coloured clothing, and at night garments with reflective strips. Do not hesitate to use your bell or voice to make your presence felt.

TOURING DANGERS & ANNOYANCES
Road Conditions

Some Italian roads look like they haven't been retouched since chariots were in vogue. This is especially true in out-of-way rural reaches, where some of the least-run roads have deteriorated to or been left with gravel surfaces. Keep this in mind when you are planning what thickness tires to use.

Cobblestones are the other major road nuisance. Many steep mountain lanes and most Italian cities include areas paved with rough square stones separated by ruts wide and deep enough to catch, trip and mangle a cyclist's wheels. This is particularly true in Naples. Steer carefully and pedal slowly

Tips for Better Cycling

These tips on riding technique are designed to help you ride more safely, comfortably and efficiently:

- Ride in bike lanes if they exist.
- Ride about 1m from the edge of the kerb or from parked cars; riding too close to the road edge makes you less visible and more vulnerable to rough surfaces or car doors being opened without warning.
- Stay alert: especially on busy, narrow, winding and hilly roads it's essential to constantly scan ahead and anticipate the movements of other vehicles, cyclists, pedestrians or animals. Keep an eye out for potholes and other hazards as well.
- Keep your upper body relaxed, even when you are climbing.
- Ride a straight line and don't weave across the road when you reach for your water bottle or when climbing.
- To negotiate rough surfaces and bumps, take your weight off the saddle and let your legs absorb the shock, with the pedals level (in the three and nine o'clock positions).

At Night
- Only ride at night if your bike is equipped with a front and rear light; consider also using a reflective vest and/or reflective ankle bands.

Braking
- Apply front and rear brakes evenly.
- When your bike is fully loaded you'll find that you can apply the front brake quite hard and the extra weight will prevent you doing an 'endo' (flipping over the handlebars).
- In wet weather gently apply the brakes occasionally to dry the brake pads.

Climbing
- When climbing out of the saddle, keep the bike steady; rock the handlebars from side to side as little as possible.
- Change down to your low gears to keep your legs 'spinning'.

Cornering
- Loaded bikes are prone to sliding on corners; approach corners slowly and don't lean into the corner as hard as you normally would.
- If traffic permits, take a straight path across corners; hit the corner wide, cut across the apex and ride out of it wide – but never cross the dividing line on the road.
- Apply the brakes before the corner, not while cornering (especially if it's wet).

(especially on steep curvy downhills) when you encounter this.

Italian Driving Habits

Italian drivers (and not just the men) are famous for their aggressive behind-the-wheel shenanigans. Their reputation for unrestrained recklessness is not entirely undeserved. However, before levelling the standard accusations at them, it is important to understand a little Italian driving culture.

Why do Italian drivers steer so close? Actually, they don't think they do. They are accustomed to the tight corners of narrow Italian streets and roads. They are not swerving menacingly at you; rather, they are nimbly and ably guiding their vehicles into spaces through which they confidently know they will fit. If you handle your bike with the same self-assurance and dexterity – following your line, making no sudden moves – you will have no trouble. That

---

Tips for Better Cycling

Descending
- Stay relaxed, don't cramp up and let your body go with the bike.
- A loaded bike is more likely to wobble and be harder to control at speed, so take it easy.
- Pump the brakes to shed speed rather than applying constant pressure; this avoids overheating the rims, which can cause your tyre to blow.

Gravel Roads
- Avoid patches of deep gravel (often on the road's edge); if you can't, ride hard, as you do if driving a car through mud.
- Look ahead to plan your course; avoid sudden turning and take it slowly on descents.
- Brake in a straight line using your rear brake and place your weight over the front wheel if you need to use that brake.
- On gravel, loosen your toe-clip straps or clipless pedals so you can put your foot down quickly.

Group Riding
- If you're riding in a group, keep your actions predictable and let others know, with a hand signal or shout, before you brake, turn, dodge potholes etc.
- Ride beside, in front or behind fellow cyclists. Don't overlap wheels; if either of you moves sideways suddenly it's likely both of you will fall.
- Ride in single file on busy, narrow or winding roads.

In Traffic
- Obey the rules of the road, and signal if you are turning.
- Look at the wheels to see if a car at a T-junction or joining the road is actually moving or not.
- Scan for trouble: look inside the back windows of parked cars for movement – that person inside may open the door on you.
- Look drivers in the eye; make sure they've seen you.
- Learn to bunny hop your bike (yes, it can be done with a fully loaded touring bike; just not as well) – it'll save you hitting potholes and other hazards.

In the Wet
- Be aware that you'll take longer to slow down with wet rims; exercise appropriate caution.
- When descending apply the brakes lightly to keep the rims free of grit/water etc and allow for quicker stopping.
- Don't climb out of the saddle (unless you want a change); shift down a gear and climb seated.

On Bikepaths
- Use a bell or call out to warn others of your approach on bikepaths.

said, there is no real excuse for the Italian engine-revving love of overtaking at high-speeds on the blind curves of winding mountain roads.

Why do Italian drivers keep cutting you off? They don't think they are. They see what they consider to be a space between (in front of or alongside) you and a vehicle or turn and so accelerate into it. It doesn't help that Italian law actually permits cars to overtake bicycles near an intersection. However, once again, if you pedal with deliberate and clear motions and look around you at intersections, you should run no risks.

Why do Italian drivers ignore traffic rules? Actually, although the problem used to be rampant, there are fewer and fewer scofflaws today, especially in cities where automotive congestion is a serious problem and traffic laws are more and more strictly enforced.

Vespas & Motorbikes
The one exception to the rules of thumb cited above is the vespa or motorbike driver. Motorbikes are the Italian teenager's transport of choice. And they scoot and zigzag and weave with abandon all over Italy. There is nothing you can do about it except exercise extra caution when you are around them.

RIDING OFF-ROAD
Trail etiquette requires mountain bikes to yield to hikers and equestrians. But it's more important just to use common courtesy while on the trail. Bike paths are often shared with pedestrians; ring your bell or give a holler before passing on the left.

The Off Road Cyclist's Code recommends you minimise impact by carrying out all human-made elements brought into a wilderness area; stay on trails and take care to avoid soil erosion (muddy trails are more vulnerable); never scare animals; control your speed; and wear a helmet at all times.

Although most rides are not too far from civilisation, always remember one of the first rules about offroading: never go alone. It's not uncommon for people to go missing, either through injury or after losing their way. It's best to go in small groups – four is usually considered the minimum. This way, if there's an accident, one person can stay with the casualty and the others can go for help.

Always tell someone where you are going and when you intend to be back – and make sure they know that you're back! Take warm clothing, matches and enough food and water in case of emergency repairs.

Carry a map and take note of the surroundings as you ride. If you get really lost, stay calm and stop. Try to work out where you are or how to retrace your route. If you can't, or it's getting dark, find a nearby open area, put on warm clothes and find or make a shelter. Light a fire and help searchers by making some obvious signs (eg, creating smoke, displaying brightly coloured items or making symbols out of wood or rocks).

EMERGENCY PROCEDURE
The uncertainties associated with emergency rescue in remote wilderness areas should make it clear how important careful planning and safety precautions are, especially if you are travelling in a small group.

If you or one of your group has an accident (even a minor one), or falls ill during your travels, you'll need to decide on the best course of action, which isn't always easy. Obviously, you will need to consider your individual circumstances, including where you are and whether you have some means of direct communication with emergency services, such as a mobile phone (cell phone). Some basic guidelines are:

- Use your first-aid knowledge and experience, as well as the information in this guide if necessary, to make a medical assessment of the situation.
- For groups of several people, the accepted procedure is to leave one person with the casualty, together with as much equipment, food and water as you can sensibly spare, and for the rest of the group to go for help.
- If there are only two of you, the situation is trickier, and you will have to make an individual judgement as to the best course of action.
- If you leave someone, mark their position carefully on the map (take it with you); you should also make sure they can be easily found by marking the position with something conspicuous, such as bright clothing or a large stone cross on the ground. Leave the person with warm clothes, shelter, food, water, matches and a torch (flashlight).
- Try attracting attention by using a whistle or torch, lighting a smoky fire (use damp wood or green leaves) or waving bright clothing; shouting is tiring and not very effective.

YOUR BICYCLE

Fundamental to any cycle tour you plan is the bicycle you choose to ride. In this chapter we look at choosing a bicycle and accessories, setting it up to best accommodate your needs and learning basic maintenance procedures. In short, everything you need to gear up and get going.

CHOOSING & SETTING UP A BICYCLE

The ideal bike for cycle touring is (strangely enough) a touring bike. These bikes look similar to road bikes but generally have relaxed frame geometry for comfort and predictable steering; fittings (eyelets and brazed-on bosses) to mount panniers and mudguards; wider rims and tyres; strong wheels (at least 36 spokes) to carry the extra load; and gearing capable of riding up a wall (triple chainrings and a wide-range freewheel to match). If you want to buy a touring bike, most tend to be custom-built these days, but Cannondale (w www.cannondale.com) and Trek (w www.trekbikes.com) both offer a range of models.

Of course you can tour on any bike you choose, but few will match the advantages of the workhorse touring bike.

Mountain bikes are a slight compromise by comparison, but are very popular for touring. A mountain bike already has the gearing needed for touring and offers a more upright, comfortable position on the bike. And with a change of tyres (to those with semi-slick tread) you'll be able to reduce the rolling resistance and travel at higher speeds with less effort.

Hybrid, or cross, bikes are similar to mountain bikes (and therefore offer similar advantages and disadvantages), although they typically already come equipped with semi-slick tyres.

Racing bikes are less appropriate: their tighter frame geometry is less comfortable on rough roads and long rides. It is also difficult to fit wider tyres, mudguards, racks and panniers to a road bike. Perhaps more significantly, most racing bikes have a distinct lack of low gears.

Tyres Unless you know you'll be on good, sealed roads the whole time, it's probably safest to choose a tyre with some tread. If you have 700c or 27-inch wheels, opt for a tyre that's 28–35mm wide. If touring on a mountain bike, the first thing to do is get rid of the knobby tyres – too much rolling resistance. Instead, fit 1–1½ inch semi-slick tyres or, if riding unpaved roads or off-road occasionally, a combination pattern tyre (slick centre and knobs on the outside).

To protect your tubes, consider buying tyres re-inforced with Kevlar, a tightly woven synthetic fibre very resistant to sharp objects. Although more expensive, Kevlar-belted tyres are worth it.

Pedals Cycling efficiency is vastly improved by using toe clips, and even more so with clipless pedals and cleated shoes. Mountain-bike or touring shoes are best – the cleats are recessed and the soles are flexible enough to comfortably walk in.

Fold & Go Bikes

Another option is a folding bike. Manufacturers include: Brompton (w www.bromptonbike.com), Bike Friday (w www.bikefriday.com), Birdy (w www.birdybike.com), Slingshot (w www.slingshotbikes.com) and Moulton (w www.alex moulton.co.uk). All make high-quality touring bikes that fold up to allow hassle-free train, plane or bus transfers. The Moulton, Birdie, Brompton and Slingshot come with suspension and the Bike Friday's case doubles as a trailer for your luggage when touring.

Touring Bike

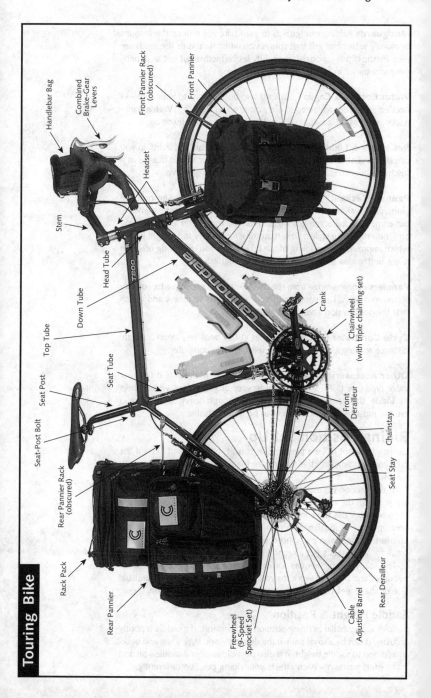

Handlebar Bag

Combined Brake-Gear Levers

Front Pannier Rack (obscured)

Front Pannier

Headset

Stem

Head Tube

Down Tube

Top Tube

Seat Tube

Seat Post

Seat-Post Bolt

Rear Pannier Rack (obscured)

Rack Pack

Rear Pannier

Freewheel (9-Speed Sprocket Set)

Cable Adjusting Barrel

Rear Derailleur

Seat Stay

Chainstay

Front Derailleur

Crank

Chainwheel (with triple chainring set)

Mudguards Adding mudguards to your bike will reduce the amount of muddy water and grit that sprays you when it rains or the roads are wet. Plastic clip-on models are slightly less effective but not as expensive, and they can be less hassle.

Water Bottles & Cages Fit at least two bottle cages to your bike – in isolated areas you may need to carry more water than this. Water 'backpacks', such as a Camelbak, make it easy to keep your fluids up.

Reflectors & Lights If riding at night, add reflectors and lights so you can see, and others can see you. A small headlight can also double as a torch (flashlight). Flashing tail-lights are cheap and effective.

Pannier Racks It's worth buying good pannier racks. The best are aluminium racks made by Blackburn. They're also the most expensive, but come with a lifetime guarantee. Front racks come in low-mounting and mountain bike styles. Low-mounting racks carry the weight lower, which improves the handling of the bike, but if you're touring off-road it is a better idea to carry your gear a bit higher.

Panniers Panniers range from cheap-and-nasty to expensive top-quality waterproof bags. Get panniers that fit securely to your rack and watch that the pockets don't swing into your spokes.

Cycle Computer Directions for rides in this book rely upon accurate distance readings, so you'll need a reliable cycle computer.

Other Accessories A good pump is essential. Make sure it fits your valve type (see p68). Some clip on to your bicycle frame, while others fit 'inside' the frame. Also carry a lock. Although heavy, U- or D-locks are the most secure; cable locks can be more versatile.

Riding Position Set Up

Cycling is meant to be a pleasurable pursuit, but that isn't likely if the bike you're riding isn't the correct size for you and isn't set up for your needs.

In this section we assume your bike shop did a good job of providing you with the correct size bike (if you're borrowing a bike get a bike shop to check it is the correct size for you) and concentrate on setting you up in your ideal position and showing you how to tweak the comfort factor. If you are concerned that your bike frame is too big or small for your needs get a second opinion from another bike shop.

The following techniques for determining correct fit are based on averages and may not work for your body type. If you are an unusual size or shape get your bike shop to create your riding position.

Saddle Height & Position

Saddles are essential to riding position and comfort. If a saddle is poorly adjusted it can be a royal pain in the derriere – and legs, arms and back. In addition to saddle height, it is also possible to alter a saddle's tilt and its fore/aft position – each affects your riding position differently.

ALL ILLUSTRATIONS BY MARTIN HARRIS

Saddle Tilt Saddles are designed to be level to the ground, taking most of the weight off your arms and back. However, since triathletes started dropping the nose of their saddles in the mid-1980s many other cyclists have followed suit without knowing why. For some body types, a slight tilt of the nose might be necessary. Be aware, however, that forward tilt will place extra strain on your arms and back. If it is tilted too far forward, chances are your saddle is too high.

Fore/Aft Position The default setting for fore/aft saddle position will allow you to run a plumb bob from the centre of your forward pedal axle to the protrusion of your knee (that bit of bone just under your knee cap).

Fore/Aft Position: To check it, sit on your bike with the pedals in the three and nine o'clock positions. Check the alignment with a plumb bob (a weight on the end of a piece of string).

Saddle Height The simplest method of roughly determining the correct saddle height is the straight leg method. Sit on your bike wearing your cycling shoes. Line one crank up with the seat-tube and place your heel on the pedal. Adjust the saddle height until your leg is almost straight, but not straining. When you've fixed the height of your saddle pedal the cranks backwards (do it next to a wall so you can balance yourself). If you are rocking from side to side, lower the saddle slightly. Otherwise keep raising the saddle (slightly) until on the verge of rocking.

The most accurate way of determining saddle height is the Hodges Method. Developed by US cycling coach Mark Hodges after studying the position of dozens of racing cyclists, the method is also applicable to touring cyclists.

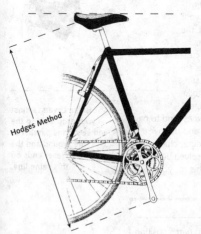

Hodges Method

Standing barefoot with your back against a wall and your feet 15cm apart, get a friend to measure from the greater trochanter (the bump of your hip) to the floor passing over your knee and ankle joints. Measure each leg (in mm) three times and average the figure. Multiply the average figure by 0.96.

Now add the thickness of your shoe sole and your cleats (if they aren't recessed). This total is the distance you need from the centre of your pedal axle to the top of your saddle. It is the optimum position for your body to pedal efficiently and should not be exceeded; however, people with small feet for their size should lower the saddle height slightly. The inverse applies for people with disproportionately large feet.

If you need to raise your saddle significantly do it over a few weeks so your muscles can adapt gradually. (Never raise your saddle above the maximum extension line marked on your seat post.)

Handlebars & Brake Levers

Racing cyclists lower their handlebars to cheat the wind and get a better aerodynamic position. While this might be tempting on windy days it doesn't make for comfortable touring. Ideally, the bars should be no higher than the saddle (even on mountain bikes) and certainly no lower than 75mm below it.

Pedals

For comfort and the best transference of power, the ball of your foot should be aligned over the centre of the pedal axle (see right).

If using clipless pedals consider the amount of lateral movement available. Our feet have a natural angle that they prefer when we walk, run or cycle. If they are unable to achieve this position the knee joint's alignment will be affected and serious injury may result. Most clipless pedal systems now have some rotational freedom (called 'float') built in to allow for this, but it is still important to adjust the cleats to each foot's natural angle.

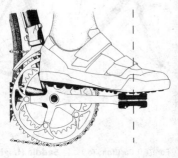

Pedal Alignment: The ball of your foot should be over the centre of the pedal axle for comfort and the best transfer of power.

Comfort Considerations

Now that you have your optimum position on the bike, there are several components that you can adjust to increase the comfort factor.

Handlebars come in a variety of types and sizes. People with small hands may find shallow drop bars more comfortable. Handlebars also come in a variety of widths, so if they're too wide or narrow change them.

With mountain bike handlebars you really only have one hand position, so add a pair of bar-ends. On drop bars the ends should be parallel to the ground. If they're pointed up it probably means you need a longer stem; pointed down probably means you need a shorter stem.

On mountain bikes the **brake levers** should be adjusted to ensure your wrist is straight – it's the position your hand naturally sits in. For drop bars the bottom of the lever should end on the same line as the end section.

Getting the right **saddle** for you is one of the key considerations for enjoyable cycling. Everybody's sit bones are shaped and spaced differently, meaning a saddle that suits your best friend might be agony for you. A good bike shop will allow you to keep changing a new (undamaged) saddle until you get one that's perfect. Women's saddles tend to have a shorter nose and a wider seat, and men's are long and narrow.

If you feel too stretched out or cramped when riding, chances are you need a different length **stem** – the problem isn't solved by moving your saddle forward/aft. Get a bike shop to assess this for you.

Brake Levers: Adjust your drop bars so the end section is parallel to the ground and the brake lever ends on this same line.

🔧 Record Your Position

When you've created your ideal position, mark each part's position (scratch a line with a sharp tool like a scribe or use tape) and record it, so you can recreate it if hiring a bike or when reassembling your bike after travel. The inside back cover of this book has a place to record all this vital data.

MAINTAINING YOUR BICYCLE

If you're new to cycling or haven't previously maintained your bike, this section is for you. It won't teach you how to be a top-notch mechanic, but it will help you maintain your bike in good working order and show you how to fix the most common touring problems.

If you go mountain biking it is crucial you carry spares and a tool kit and know how to maintain your bike, because if anything goes wrong it's likely you'll be miles from anywhere when trouble strikes.

If you want to know more about maintaining your bike there are dozens of books available (*Richard's 21st Century Bicycle Book*, by Richard Ballantine, is a classic; if you want to know absolutely everything get *Barnett's Manual: The Ultimate Technical Bicycle Repair Manual* or *Sutherland's Handbook for Bicycle Mechanics*) or inquire at your bike shop about courses in your area.

Predeparture & Daily Inspections

Before going on tour get your bike serviced by a bike shop or do it your-self. On tour, check over your bike every day or so (see the boxed text 'Pre-Departure & Post-Ride Checks' on p71).

Spares & Tool Kit

Touring cyclists need to be self-sufficient and should carry some spares and, at least, a basic tool kit. How many spares/tools you will need depends on the country you are touring in – in countries where bike shops aren't common and the towns are further spread out you may want to add to the following.

Multi-tools (see right) are very handy and a great way to save space and weight, and there are dozens of different ones on the market. Before you buy a multi-tool though, check each of the tools is usable – a chain breaker, for example, needs to have a good handle for leverage otherwise it is useless.

Adjustable spanners are often handy, but the trade-off is that they can easily burr bolts if not used correctly – be careful when using them.

The bare minimum:
- [ ] pump – ensure it has the correct valve fitting for your tyres
- [ ] water bottles (2)
- [ ] spare tubes (2)
- [ ] tyre levers (2)
- [ ] chain lube and a rag
- [ ] puncture repair kit (check the glue is OK)
- [ ] Allen keys to fit your bike
- [ ] small Phillips screwdriver
- [ ] small flat screwdriver
- [ ] spare brake pads
- [ ] spare screws and bolts (for pannier racks, seat post etc) and chain links (2)

For those who know what they're doing:
- [ ] spoke key
- [ ] spare spokes and nipples (8)
- [ ] tools to remove freewheel
- [ ] chain breaker
- [ ] pliers
- [ ] spare chain links (HyperGlide chain rivet if you have a Shimano chain)
- [ ] spare rear brake and rear gear cables

Always handy to take along:
- [ ] roll of electrical/gaffer tape
- [ ] nylon ties (10) – various lengths/sizes
- [ ] hand cleaner (store it in a film canister)

Fixing a Flat

Flats happen. And if you're a believer in Murphy's Law then the likely scenario is that you'll suffer a flat just as you're rushing to the next town to catch a train or beat the setting sun.

Don't worry – this isn't a big drama. If you're prepared and know what you're doing you can be up and on your way in five minutes flat.

Being prepared means carrying a spare tube, a pump and at least two tyre levers. If you're not carrying a spare tube, of course, you can stop and fix the puncture then and there, but it's unlikely you'll catch that train and you could end up doing all this in the dark. There will be days when you have the time to fix a puncture on the side of the road, but not always. Carry at least two spare tubes.

1 Take the wheel off the bike. Remove the valve cap and unscrew the locknut (hex nut at base; see Valve Types) on Presta valves. Deflate the tyre completely, if it isn't already.

2 Make sure the tyre and tube are loose on the rim – moisture and the pressure of the inflated tube often makes the tyre and tube fuse with the rim.

3 If the tyre is really loose you should be able to remove it with your hands. Otherwise you'll need to lift one side of the tyre over the rim with the tyre levers. Pushing the tyre away from the lever as you insert it should ensure you don't pinch the tube and puncture it again.

4 When you have one side of the tyre off, you'll be able to remove the tube. Before inserting the replacement tube, carefully inspect the tyre (inside and out); you're looking for what caused the puncture. If you find anything embedded in the tyre, remove it. Also check that the rim tape is still in

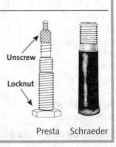

🔧 Valve Types

The two most common valve types are Presta (sometimes called French) and Schraeder (American). To inflate a Presta valve, first unscrew the round nut at the top (and do it up again after you're done); depress it to deflate. To deflate Schraeder valves depress the pin (inside the top). Ensure your pump is set up for the valve type on your bike.

Unscrew

Locknut

Presta   Schraeder

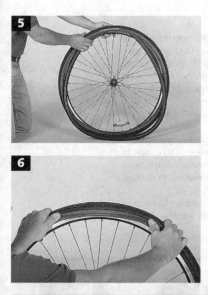

place and no spoke nipples (see p76) protrude through it.

5 Time to put the new tube in. Start by partially pumping up the tube (this helps prevent it twisting or being pinched) and insert the valve in the hole in the rim. Tuck the rest of the tube in under the tyre, making sure you don't twist it. Make sure the valve is straight – most Presta valves come with a locknut to help achieve this.

6 Work the tyre back onto the rim with your fingers. If this isn't possible, and again, according to Murphy's Law, it frequently isn't, you might need to use your tyre levers for the last 20cm to 30cm. If you need to use the levers, make sure you don't pinch the new tube, otherwise it's back to Step 1. All you need to do now is pump up the tyre and put the wheel back on the bike. Don't forget to fix the pucture that night.

Fixing the Puncture

To fix the puncture you'll need a repair kit, which usually comes with glue, patches, sandpaper and, sometimes, chalk. (Always check the glue in your puncture repair kit hasn't dried up before heading off on tour.) The only other thing you'll need is clean hands.

1. The first step is to find the puncture. Inflate the tube and hold it up to your ear. If you can hear the puncture, mark it with the chalk; otherwise immerse it in water and watch for air bubbles. Once you find the puncture, mark it, cover it with your finger and continue looking – just in case there are more.

2. Dry the tube and lightly roughen the area around the hole with the sandpaper. Sand an area larger than the patch.

3. Follow the instructions for the glue you have. Generally you spread an even layer of glue over the area of the tube to be patched and allow it to dry until it is tacky.

4. Patches also come with their own instructions – some will be just a piece of rubber and others will come lined with foil (remove the foil on the underside but don't touch the exposed area). Press the patch firmly onto the area over the hole and hold it for 2–3 minutes. If you want, remove the excess glue from around the patch or dust it with chalk or simply let it dry.

5. Leave the glue to set for 10–20 minutes. Inflate the tube and check the patch has worked.

Chains

Chains are dirty, greasy and all too often the most neglected piece of equipment on a bike. There are about 120 or so links in a chain and each has a simple but precise arrangement of bushes, bearings and plates. Over time all chains stretch, but if dirt gets between the bushes and bearings this 'ageing' will happen prematurely and will likely damage the teeth of your chainrings, sprockets and derailleur guide pulleys.

To prevent this, chains should be cleaned and lubed frequently (see your bike shop for the best products to use).

No matter how well you look after a chain it should be replaced regularly – about every 5000–8000km. Seek the advice of a bike shop to ensure you are buying the correct type for your drivetrain (the moving parts that combine to drive the bicycle: chain, freewheel, derailleurs, chainwheel and bottom bracket).

If you do enough cycling you'll need to replace a chain (or fix a broken chain), so here's how to use that funky-looking tool, the chain breaker.

1 Remove the chain from the chainrings – it'll make the whole process easier. Place the chain in the chain breaker (on the outer slots; it braces the link plates as the rivet is driven out) and line the pin of the chain breaker up with the rivet.

2 Wind the handle until the rivet is clear of the inner link but still held by the outer link plate.

3 Flex the chain to 'break' it. If it won't, you'll need to push the rivet out some more, but not completely – if you push it all the way out, you'll have to remove two links and replace them with two spare links. If you're removing links, you'll need to remove a male and female link (ie, two links).

4 Rejoining the chain is the reverse. If you turn the chain around when putting it on you will still have the rivet facing you. Otherwise it will be facing away from you and you'll need to change to the other side of the bike and work through the spokes.

Join the chain up by hand and place it in the breaker. Now drive the rivet in firmly, making sure it is properly lined up with the hole of the outer link plate. Stop when the rivet is almost in place.

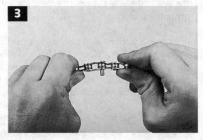

5 Move the chain to the spreaders (inner slots) of the chain breaker. Finish by winding the rivet into position carefully (check that the head of the rivet is raised the same distance above the link plate as the rivets beside it). If you've managed to get it in perfectly and the link isn't 'stiff', well done!

5

Otherwise, move the chain to the spreaders on the chain breaker and gently work the chain laterally until the link is no longer stiff.

If this doesn't work (and with some chain breakers it won't), take the chain out of the tool and place a screwdriver or Allen key between the outer plates of the stiff link and carefully lever the plates both ways. If you're too forceful you'll really break the chain, but if you're subtle it will free the link up and you'll be on your way.

Chain Options

Check your chain; if you have a Shimano HyperGlide chain you'll need a special Hyper-Glide chain rivet to rejoin the chain. This will be supplied with your new chain, but carry a spare.

Another option is to fit a universal link to your chain. This link uses a special clip to join the chain – like the chains of old. You'll still need a chain breaker to fix a broken chain or take out spare links.

Pre-Departure & Post-Ride Checks

Each day before you get on your bike and each evening after you've stopped riding, give your bike a quick once-over. Following these checks will ensure you're properly maintaining your bike and will help identify any problems before they become disasters. Go to the nearest bike shop if you don't know how to fix any problem.

Pre-Departure Check List
- ☐ brakes – are they stopping you? If not, adjust them.
- ☐ chain – if it was squeaking yesterday, it needs lube.
- ☐ panniers – are they all secured and fastened?
- ☐ cycle computer – reset your trip distance at the start.
- ☐ gears – are they changing properly? If not, adjust them.
- ☐ tyres – check your tyre pressure is correct (see the tyre's side wall for the maximum psi); inflate, if necessary.

Post-Ride Check List
- ☐ pannier racks – check all bolts/screws are tightened; do a visual check of each rack (the welds, in particular) looking for small cracks.
- ☐ headset – when stationary, apply the front brake and rock the bike gently; if there is any movement or noise, chances are the headset is loose.
- ☐ wheels – visually check the tyres for sidewall cuts/wear and any embedded objects; check the wheels are still true and no spokes are broken.
- ☐ wrench test – pull on the saddle (if it moves, tighten the seat-post bolt or the seat-clamp bolt, underneath); pull laterally on a crank (if it moves, check the bottom bracket).

Brakes

Adjusting the brakes of your bike is not complicated and even though your bike shop will use several tools to do the job, all you really need is a pair of pliers, a spanner or Allen key, and (sometimes) a friend.

Check three things before you start: the wheels are true (not buckled), the braking surface of the rims is smooth (no dirt, dents or rough patches) and the cables are not frayed.

Begin by checking that the pads strike the rim correctly: flush on the braking surface of the rim (see right and p59) and parallel to the ground.

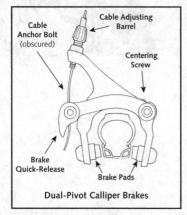

Dual-Pivot Calliper Brakes

Calliper Brakes

It's likely that you'll be able to make any minor adjustments to calliper brakes by winding the cable adjusting barrel out. If it doesn't allow enough movement you'll need to adjust the cable anchor bolt:

1 Undo the cable anchor bolt – not completely, just so the cable is free to move – and turn the cable adjusting barrel all the way in.

2 Get your friend to hold the callipers in the desired position, about 2–3mm away from the rim. Using a pair of pliers, pull the cable through until it is taut.

3 Before you tighten the cable anchor bolt again, check to see if the brake lever is in its normal position (not slack as if somebody was applying it) – sometimes they jam open. Also, ensure the brake quick-release (use it when you're removing your wheel or in an emergency to open the callipers if your wheel is badly buckled) is closed.

4 Tighten the cable anchor bolt again. Make any fine-tuning to the brakes by winding the cable adjusting barrel out.

 Brake Cables

If your brakes are particularly hard to apply, you may need to replace the cables. Moisture can cause the cable and housing (outer casing) to bond or stick. If this happens it's often possible to prolong the life of a cable by removing it from the housing and applying a coating of grease (or chain lube) to it.

If you do need to replace the cable, take your bike to a bike shop and get the staff to fit and/or supply the new cable. Cables come in two sizes – rear (long) and front (short) – various thicknesses and with different types of nipples.

Cantilever Brakes

These days most touring bikes have cantilever rather than calliper brakes. The newest generation of cantilever brakes (V-brakes) are more powerful and better suited to stopping bikes with heavy loads.

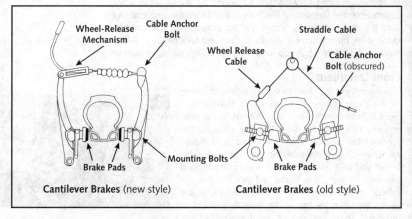

Cantilever Brakes (new style)   **Cantilever Brakes** (old style)

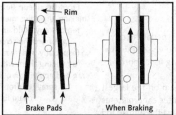

Cantilever Brake Toe-In: This is how the brake pads should strike the rim (from above) with correct toe-in.

On cantilever brakes ensure the leading edge of the brake pad hits the rim first (see left). This is called toe-in; it makes the brakes more efficient and prevents squealing. To adjust the toe-in on cantilever brakes, loosen the brake pad's mounting bolt (using a 10mm spanner and 5mm Allen key). Wiggle the brake pad into position and tighten the bolt again.

If you only need to make a minor adjustment to the distance of the pads from the rim, chances are you will be able to do it by winding the cable adjusting barrel out (located near the brake lever on mountain bikes and hybrids). If this won't do you'll need to adjust the cable anchor bolt:

1 Undo the cable anchor bolt (not completely, just so the cable is free to move) and turn the cable adjusting barrel all the way in. Depending on the style of your brakes, you may need a 10mm spanner (older bikes) or a 5mm Allen key.

2 Hold the cantilevers in the desired position (get assistance from a friend if you need to), positioning the brake pads 2–3mm away from the rim. Using a pair of pliers, pull the cable through until it is taut.

3 Before you tighten the cable anchor bolt again, check to see if the brake lever is in its normal position (not slack as if somebody was applying it) – sometimes they jam open.

4 Tighten the cable anchor bolt again. Make any fine-tuning to the brakes by winding the cable adjusting barrel out.

Gears

If the gears on your bike start playing up – the chain falls off the chain-rings, it shifts slowly or not at all – it's bound to cause frustration and could damage your bike. All it takes to prevent this is a couple of simple adjustments: the first, setting the limits of travel for both derailleurs, will keep the chain on your drivetrain, and the second will ensure smooth, quick shifts from your rear derailleur. Each will take just a couple of minutes and the only tool you need is a small Phillips or flat screwdriver.

Front Derailleur

If you can't get the chain to shift onto one chainring or the chain comes off when you're shifting, you need to make some minor adjustments to the limit screws on the front derailleur. Two screws control the limits of the front derailleur's left and right move-ment, which governs how far the chain can shift. When you shift gears the chain is physically pushed sideways by the plates (outer and inner) of the de-railleur cage. The screws are usually side by side (see photo No 1) on the top of the front derailleur. The left-hand screw (as you sit on the bike) adjusts the inside limit and the one on the right adjusts the outside limit.

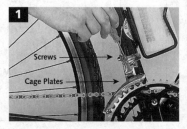

Front Derailleur: Before making any adjustments, remove any build up of grit from the screws (especially underneath) by wiping them with a rag and applying a quick spray (or drop) of chain lube.

After you make each of the following adjustments, pedal the drive-train with your hand and change gears to ensure you've set the limit correctly. If you're satisfied, test it under strain by going for a short ride.

Outer Limits Change the gears to position the chain on the largest chainring and the smallest rear sprocket. Set the outer cage plate as close to the chain as you can without it touching. Adjust the right-hand limit screw to achieve this.

Inner Limits Position the chain on the smallest chainring and the largest rear sprocket. For chainwheels with three chainrings, position the inner cage plate between 1–2mm from the chain. If you have a chainwheel with two chainrings, position the inner cage plate as close to the chain as you can without it touching.

Rear Derailleur

If the limit screws aren't set correctly on the rear derailleur the conse-quences can be dire. If the chain slips off the largest sprocket it can jam between the sprocket and the spokes and could then snap the chain, break or damage spokes or even break the frame.

The limit screws are located at the back of the derailleur (see photo No 2). The top screw (marked 'H' on the derailleur) sets the derailleur's limit of travel on the smallest sprocket's (the highest gear) side of the free-wheel. The bottom screw ('L') adjusts the derailleur's travel towards the largest sprocket (lowest gear).

Outer Limits Position the chain on the smallest sprocket and largest chainring (see photo No 3). The derailleur's top guide pulley (the one

Guide
Pulleys

closest to the sprockets) should be in line with the smallest sprocket; adjust the top screw ('H') to ensure it is.

Inner Limits Position the chain on the largest rear sprocket and the smallest chainring (see photo No 4). This time the guide pulley needs to be lined up with the largest sprocket; do this by adjusting the bottom screw ('L'). Make sure the chain can't move any further towards the wheel than the largest sprocket.

Cable Adjusting Barrel

If your gears are bouncing up and down your freewheel in a constant click and chatter, you need to adjust the tension of the cable to the rear derailleur. This can be achieved in a variety of ways, depending on your gear system.

The main cable adjusting barrel is on your rear derailleur (see photo No 5). Secondary cable adjusting barrels can also be found near the gear levers (newer Shimano combined brake-gear STI levers) or on the downtube of your frame (older Shimano STI levers and Campagnolo Ergopower gear systems) of some bikes. Intended for racing cyclists, they allow for fine tuning of the gears' operation while on the move.

Raise the rear wheel off the ground – have a friend hold it up by the saddle, hang it from a tree or turn the bike upside down – so you can pedal the drivetrain with your hand.

To reset your derailleur, shift gears to position the chain on the second smallest sprocket and middle chainring (see photo No 6). As you turn the crank with your hand, tighten the cable by winding the rear derailleur's cable adjusting barrel anti-clockwise. Just before the chain starts to make a noise as if to shift onto the third sprocket, stop winding.

Now pedal the drivetrain and change the gears up and down the freewheel. If things still aren't right you may find that you need to tweak the cable tension slightly: turn the cable adjusting barrel anti-clockwise if shifts to larger sprockets are slow, and clockwise if shifts to smaller sprockets hesitate.

Replacing a Spoke

Even the best purpose-made touring wheels occasionally break spokes.
When this happens the wheel, which relies on the even pull of each
spoke, is likely to become buckled. When it is not buckled, it is considered true.

If you've forgotten to pack spokes or you grabbed the wrong size,
you can still get yourself out of a pickle if you have a spoke key. Wheels
are very flexible and you can get it roughly true – enough to take you
to the next bike shop – even if two or three spokes are broken.

If you break a spoke on the front wheel it is a relatively simple thing
to replace the spoke and retrue the wheel. The same applies if a broken
spoke is on the nondrive side (opposite side to the rear derailleur) of the
rear wheel. The complication comes when you break a spoke on the drive
side of the rear wheel (the most common case). In order to replace it you
need to remove the freewheel, a relatively simple job in itself but one that
requires a few more tools and the know-how.

If you don't have that know-how fear not, because it is possible to
retrue the wheel without replacing that spoke *and* without damaging
the wheel – see Truing a Wheel (below).

1 Remove the wheel from the bike. It's probably a good idea to
remove the tyre and tube as well (though not essential), just to make
sure the nipple is seated properly in the rim and not likely to cause a
puncture.

2 Remove the broken spoke but leave the nipple in the rim (if it's not
damaged; otherwise replace it). Now you need to thread the new spoke.
Start by threading it through the vacant hole on the hub flange. Next
lace the new spoke through the other spokes. Spokes are offset on the
rim; every second one is on the same side and,
generally, every fourth is laced through the other
spokes the same way.

3 With the spoke key, tighten the nipple until
the spoke is about as taut as the other spokes on
this side of the rim. Spoke nipples have four flat
sides – to adjust them you'll need the correct
size spoke key. Spoke keys come in two types:
those made to fit one spoke gauge or several. If
you have the latter, trial each size on a nipple
until you find the perfect fit.

Truing a Wheel

Truing a wheel is an art form and, like all art forms, it is not something
mastered overnight. If you can, practise with an old wheel before
leaving home. If that's not possible – and you're on the side of the road
as you read this – following these guidelines will get you back in the
saddle until you can get to the next bike shop.

1 Start by turning the bike upside-down, so the wheels can turn
freely. Check the tension of all the spokes on the wheel: do this by

squeezing each pair of spokes on each side. Tighten those spokes that seem loose and loosen those that seem too tight. Note, though, the spokes on the drive side of the rear wheel (on the same side as the freewheel) are deliberately tighter than the non-drive side.

2 Rotate the wheel a couple of times to get an idea of the job at hand. If the wheel won't rotate, let the brakes off (see p72).

3 Using the chalk from your puncture repair kit, mark all the 'bumps'. Keep the chalk in the same position (brace the chalk against the pannier rack or bike's frame) and let the bumps in the wheel 'hit' the chalk.

4 In order to get the bumps out you'll need a constant point of reference – to gauge if the bumps are being removed. Often, if it is not a severe buckle, you can use a brake pad. Position the brake pad about 2–3mm from the rim (on the side with the biggest buckle).

5 With your spoke key, loosen those spokes on the same side as the bump within the longest chalked area, and tighten those on the opposite side of the rim. The spokes at the start and the finish of the chalked area should only be tightened/loosened by a quarter-turn; apply a half-turn to those in between.

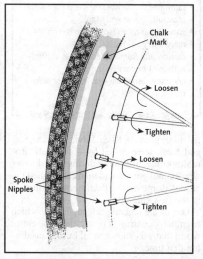

Chalk Mark

Loosen

Tighten

Loosen

Spoke Nipples

Tighten

6 Rotate the wheel again; if you're doing it correctly the buckle should not be as great. Continue this process of tightening and loosening spokes until the bump is as near to gone as you can get it – as the bump is removed turn the nipples less (one-eighth of a turn on the ends and a quarter-turn in between). Experienced exponents can remove buckles entirely, but if you can get it almost out (1mm here or there) you've done well.

7 If the wheel has more than one bump, move onto the second-longest chalk mark next. As each bump is removed you might find it affects the previous bump slightly. In this case, remove the previous chalk mark and repeat Steps 4–6. Continue to do this until all the buckles are removed.

Don't forget to readjust the brakes.

If you've trued the wheel without replacing the broken spokes, have them replaced at the next bike shop.

Rome

'I now realise all the dreams of my youth,' wrote Goethe on his arrival in Rome in the winter of 1786. Perhaps Rome today is more chaotic, but it's certainly no less romantic or fascinating. In this city, a phenomenal concentration of monuments, history and legend coexists with an equally phenomenal concentration of people busily going about everyday life.

Rome is a city of about four million and, as the capital of Italy, it is the centre of national government. Tourists usually stay in the historic centre, avoiding the sprawling suburbs.

While the look of central Rome is defined most obviously by the baroque style of many fountains, churches and palaces, there are also ancient monuments, and beautiful churches and buildings of the medieval, Gothic and Renaissance periods, along with the architectural embellishments of the post-Risorgimento and Fascist eras.

Though not for the faint of heart, cycling in Rome can be a thrilling adventure and a great way to see the sights in a relatively short time. The rides to the outskirts of town lead to unquestionably spectacular attractions. That said, getting to these attractions requires navigating along some heavily trafficked and, at times, unaesthetic routes.

History

In Rome there is evidence of two of the great empires of the Western world: the Roman Empire and the Christian Church. From the Roman Forum and the Colosseum to the Basilica di San Pietro and the Vatican, and in almost every piazza lies history on so many levels that the saying 'Rome, a lifetime is not enough' must certainly be true.

It is generally agreed that Rome had its origins in a group of Etruscan, Latin and Sabine settlements on the Palatino, Esquilino and Quirinale hills. These and surrounding hills constitute the now-famous seven hills of the city. Ancient Romans put the date of their city's foundation as 21 April 753 BC and, indeed, archaeological discoveries have confirmed the existence of a settlement on the Palatino in that period.

However, it is the legend of Romulus and Remus which prevails. According to legend,

In Brief

Highlights
- Discovering Rome's **historic city centre**
- Winding through the wooded hills, lakes and estates of the **Castelli Romani**
- Visiting **Hadrian's Villa** near Tivoli
- Exploring the **Etruscan tombs** of Cerveteri and Tarquinia

Terrain
Hilly, both in the city centre and surrounding countryside. Many city roads are cobbled and slippery.

Special Events
- **Festa de Noantri** street theatre, music and food (last two weeks in July), Trastevere
- **Festa di San Giovanni** dancing and eating (late June)
- **Holy Week** procession through the city (main events on Good Friday and Easter Sunday)
- **Italian Cultural Heritage Week** many museums, monument and galleries in Rome are open for free (usually mid-April)

Cycling Events
- **Giro del Lazio** (September), Lazio region

Food & Drink Specialities
- *saltimbocca alla Romana* (veal fillet with prosciutto, wine and sage)
- *abacchio al forno* (spring lamb with rosemary and garlic)
- *carciofi alla Romana* (artichokes stuffed with mint or parsley and garlic)
- *granita* (crushed ice with lemon or other fruit juices)

the twin sons of Rhea Silvia and the war god Mars were raised by a she-wolf. Romulus killed his brother during a battle over who should govern and then established the city of Rome on the Palatino, with himself as the first king.

Out of the legend grew an empire which eventually controlled pretty much the entire world that was known to all Europeans during that time.

Tourists wandering around the city with their eyes raised to admire its monuments should know that about 4m under their feet exists another city, with traces of other settlements deeper still. The Basilica di San Pietro, for instance, stands on the site of an earlier basilica built by Emperor Constantine in the 4th century over the necropolis where San Pietro was buried. To know this helps in interpreting and understanding this chaotic city.

Natural History

The Comune di Rome covers approximately 150,000 hectares, of which 37% is urban development, 15% is parkland and 48% covers farmland. Rome's most notable geographical features are its seven hills:

the Palatino, Campidoglio, Aventino, Celio, Esquilino, Viminale and Quirinale. Two other hills, the Gianicolo, which rises above Trastevere, and the Pincio, above Piazza del Popolo, were never actually part of the ancient city.

From the Giancolo, it is possible to identify each of Rome's seven primary hills. It is also a good vantage point from which to observe the Tiber (Tevere) winding through town. Its source in the Apennines, the river snakes through Rome before emptying into the sea at Ostia.

Due to the large number of private gardens once owned and maintained by Rome's elite, the city is decorated with exotic fauna, not to mention 1300 native species.

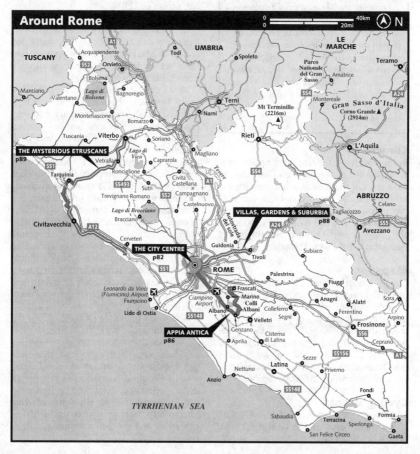

Warning

Cycling in Rome is likely to be a positive and memorable experience – if approached with a thirst for excitement, and a generous dose of cautious wisdom. Enjoy Rome's *When in Rome* says it best: 'Roman drivers are not at all accustomed to seeing bicycles on their streets, so don't assume that they see you or will make room for you. And when you see a green light in front of you, it doesn't necessarily mean that the intersection is clear! Many Roman drivers read a yellow light as speed up instead of slow down.'

Riding in Rome *can* be fun, and if you have a good map and take your time manoeuvring about, the city will quickly seem less overwhelming than it first appears.

That said, you'll enjoy it more if you're well aware of the dangers: heavy traffic and pollution, colossal roundabouts, slick cobbled streets, crowds of pedestrians, high incidents of petty crime and a dearth of racks on which to safely lock bikes. Always, always, always wear a helmet. If leaving your bike to check out a point of interest, lock it up securely and take *everything* with you – computers, lights, tools etc.

Climate

In July and August, Rome's average temperature is in the mid- to high 20°Cs), although the impact of the sirocco, a hot, humid wind from Africa, can produce stiflingly hot weather in August, with temperatures in the high 30°Cs for days on end. Winters are moderate and snow is rare. October, November and December are the wettest months.

Maps

Lonely Planet's *Rome City Map* is waterproof, lightweight and handy. The City Centre ride starting on p82 can be followed almost entirely with this map. The most comprehensive road map of the city is the Michelin (1:10,000) map *Roma*, though it is unwieldy. There is no good map for the rides into the outskirts of the city. The best is Touring Club Italiano's 1:200,000 map *Lazio*.

Cycling Events

For information on International Cycling Union rides, such as the Giro del Lazio, visit **w** www.uci.ch.

Information

The main APT office (☎ 06 48 89 92 53), Via Parigi 5, opens from 8.15am to 7pm Monday to Friday and 8.15am to 1.45pm Saturday. There are also APT branch offices at Rome's central train station, Stazione Termini (☎ 06 487 12 70) and at Fiumicino airport (☎ 06 65 95 44 71).

A good alternative is Enjoy Rome (☎ 06 445 18 43, **w** www.enjoyrome.com), Via Marghera 8a (just northeast of Stazione Termini), a private tourist office brimming with information about the city and its environs. The office opens from 8.30am to 2pm and 3.30pm to 6.30pm Monday to Friday and from 8.30am to 2pm Saturday. It publishes a very useful *When in Rome* city guide and offers a guided three-hour bike tour of the city centre (€21).

Both APT and Enjoy Rome offer free hotel reservation services, as does HR Hotel Reservations (☎ 06 699 10 00), which has booths at Stazione Termini (opposite platform 10) and Fiumicino airport and is open from 7.30am to 9.30pm daily.

Roma c'e is a weekly booklet published every Thursday. *Wanted in Rome* is a fortnightly English-language magazine for foreign residents.

Good bike shops in Rome include Cicli Collalti (☎ 06 68 80 10 84), Via del Pellegrino 80a (closed Monday), a friendly place for quick, competent repairs; Romeo Cycling Shop (☎ 06 482 19 47, **e** info@romeobicycleshop.com) Via Torino 5 (closed Sunday), a modern, well-run store close to Stazione Termini; and Lazzaretti (☎ 06 855 38 28, **e** fratellilazzaretti@libero.it), Via Bergamo 3a. A whopping 83 years in business, the latter bike shop is often too busy building bikes to perform repairs for tourists; however, it has an excellent parts shop and stocks free *Pedala e Cammina nei Parchi* brochures.

Sherwood Iniziative (☎ 06 70 47 64 91, **w** www.biciebike.org), Via la Spezia 79, is an Italian community organisation that schedules organised walks and bike rides (for both mountain and road bikes). Sherwood's *Pedala e Cammina nei Parchi* calendar – which can be picked up for free at the Lazzaretti bike shop or printed from Sherwood's website – lists useful dates, itineraries and contact information (all in Italian).

Things to See & Do

It would simply be absurd to document all of Rome's sights and attractions in a cycling guide designed to be lightweight and portable. Rome quite possibly has a greater number of historic, religious and artistic attractions than any city in the world! The good news is that the city centre covers a relatively small geographic area, so many points of interest can be spotted and visited on the City Centre ride detailed later in this chapter.

Places to Stay

Finding accommodation in Rome can be tiring, especially during the summer tourist season. Many hotels accept bookings in advance, although some demand a deposit for the first night. Prices generally go down if you stay for more than three days.

All of Rome's camping grounds are a fair distance from the city centre. **Seven Hills** (☎ 06 30 31 08 26; Via Cassia 1216; per tent/person €4.60/7.70; open mid-Mar–end Oct) is north along the Tiber. Ride past the Stadio Olimpico to the Piazzale Ponte Milvio to find Via Cassia. **Village Camping Flaminio** (☎ 06 333 26 04; Via Flaminia 821; per tent/person €6.50/7), is closer to the city centre. Tents and bungalows are available for hire.

The Associazione Italiana Alberghi per la Gioventù (Italian Youth Hostels Association; ☎ 06 487 11 52), Via Cavour 44, has information about all youth hostels in Italy and will assist with bookings to stay at universities during summer. You can also join Hostelling International (HI) here. **Ostello Foro Italico** (☎ 06 323 62 67; Viale delle Olimpiadi 61; with/without HI card €13/15.50, including breakfast & shower; closed 9.30am-noon) is a mediocre HI hostel about 7km from Stazione Termini with a bar, restaurant and garden. Meals cost about €8. **Colors** (☎ 06 687 40 30; Via Boezio 31; dorm beds/doubles €15.50/72) near the Vatican is new, with kitchen area, Internet access, laundry service and terrace.

The accommodations listed following are clustered around Stazione Termini – the departure point for rides in this chapter.

For a budget pensioni or hotel, the popular **Fawlty Towers** (☎ 06 445 03 74; Via Magenta 39; dorm beds/singles/doubles €18/44/67) offers hostel-style accommodation. Operated by Enjoy Rome, it has excellent shared facilities and plenty of information. Friendly **Hotel Ascot** (☎ 06 474 16 75; Via Montebello 22; singles/doubles with bathroom €41/57) has quiet, tiny, old-fashioned rooms. Ask for a room on the 2nd floor. Management may allow bikes in rooms.

Hotel d'Este (☎ 06 446 56 07; e d.este@italyhotel.com; Via Carlo Alberto 4b; singles/doubles €134/196) is a stone's throw from Santa Maria Maggiore and is one of the better mid-range hotels in the area, with a pleasant rooftop garden and beautifully furnished rooms.

Places to Eat

Open 24 hours, **Conad** supermarkets are on the lower level of Stazione Termini and at the Tiburtina train station. A large, cheap fruit and vegetable **market** is on the north side of Piazza Vittorio Emanuele. Other **markets** are located at Campo de' Fiori; Piazza Testaccio; and on Via Andrea Doria, north of the Vatican.

Caffè Greco (Via dei Condotti 86) and **Babington's Tea Rooms** (Piazza di Spagna 23) are fashionable (and expensive) places to drink coffee or tea.

La Piazza, a self-service restaurant in the Stazione Termini complex, serves reasonably good food at cheap prices. **Da Gemma alla Lupa** (Via Marghera 39; full meal around €18) is a nice, simple trattoria with budget prices. **Trattoria da Bruno** (Via Varese 29; full meal around €20) has a pleasant atmosphere and excellent home-made gnocchi (€5); great value. **Andrea** (☎ 06 482 18 91; Via Sardegna 24-28; full meal about €52), close to Via Vittorio Veneto, is one of Rome's most popular top restaurants.

Getting There & Away

See Getting There & Away starting on p357 in the Travel Facts chapter for advice about getting to/from Rome.

Air To get to the city from Fiumicino airport take the aeroporto–Stazione Termini direct train (€8.80, 30 minutes, hourly or half-hourly). The train arrives and departs at Stazione Termini. Buy tickets from vending machines at Fiumicino and Stazione Termini, and from the Alitalia office at Stazione Termini. Another train stops at Trastevere, Ostiense and Tiburtina stations (€5.60, 30 to 45 minutes, every 20 minutes).

From Ciampino airport, the blue Cotral bus operates services to the Anagnina Metro station (30 minutes, about every one to 1½ hours), from where trains run to Stazione Termini (combined bus and train ticket is about €2).

Late or very early arrivals have little option other than to bike or take a taxi. Taxis have limited space for bikes, other than minivans, which have just enough room for a bike bag. Try Cooperativa Radio Taxi Romana (☎ 06 35 70) or La Capitale (☎ 06 49 94). Fares are calculated on the basis of time, distance and luggage. Expect to pay around €50 from either airport to the city. If you telephone for a taxi, the meter starts upon receiving your call.

Bicycle If you're eager to hop on the bike, and have enough daylight for potential wrong turns, you can ride to/from either airport (leave about 1½ hours for either ride). From Fiumicino, the least trafficked route is along the SS201 (the ancient Via Portunense), which deposits you near Trastevere. From Ciampino, head northwest on Via Appia Nuova until the first roundabout, then head southwest briefly on Grande Raccordo Anulare before turning right onto Via Appia Antica (see the Appia Antica Ride on p86), which leads to the heart of Rome's city centre. Note, the latter ride should only be attempted with a hearty road bike or a mountain bike.

The City Centre

Duration	1½–2½ hours
Distance	21.5km
Difficulty	easy–moderate
Start/End	Stazione Termini

A great way to get down the lay of the land and see many of Rome's most spectacular sights, this ride is an exciting and hair-raising sampler of one of the planet's most fascinating cities. Within minutes, you'll be smack in the middle of the ancient city centre, marvelling at how old and new worlds collide and intertwine to form the chaotic, charming wonder that is present day Rome. Among zillions of other sights, this route whisks you past the Colosseum, the Roman Forum, the Vatican, the green hills and breathtaking

views of Trastevere, the Pantheon, Piazza Navona and the Trevi Fountain.

PLANNING
When to Ride
Sunday morning, when traffic is lightest, is the best time to tackle Rome's centre. During August, with fewer Romans in town, car traffic is lighter, but the swarms of tourists are thicker.

What to Bring
Avoid cleated shoes not suited to walking as the route involves walking bikes and frequent dismounts. Bring a good bike lock (or two), so you can investigate attractions; avoid carrying anything that can be stolen

THE RIDE
Starting from Stazione Termini's southwest exit, turn right onto Via G Giolitti then left down bustling Via Cavour, heading past **Basilica di Santa Maria Maggiore**, built in the 5th century during the time of Pope Sixtus III. Inside is a series of mosaics from the 5th century. Via Cavour ends at the **Roman Forum**, the ancient Roman commercial, political and religious centre. Though the Forum cannot be explored by bike, much of it can be viewed from outside its walls.

Proceed towards the **Colosseum**, which looms ominously outside the Forum grounds. This massive structure once seated more than 80,000 spectators who came to delight in the bloody gladiator competitions. Pass the **Arch of Constantine**, built in AD 312 to honour Constantine's victory over Maxentius. Join Via di San Gregorio VII, turn right onto Via dei Cerchi, and pass **Circus Maximus**, the 600 BC chariot-racing venue that once drew 200,000 to 300,000 spectators. Today it is a nondescript, dusty jogging track.

Take a minute to explore the 12th-century, seven-storey bell tower of **Chiesa di Santa Maria in Cosmedin** on Piazza Bocca della Verità. Inside, under the portico, is the famous **Bocca della Verità** (Mouth of Truth), a round mask that probably covered an ancient drain. Legend says that if you put your right hand into the mouth while telling a lie, it will snap shut.

Take a first glimpse of the Tiber as you head north past **Teatro di Marcello**, completed in 11 BC. Once the blindingly white **Monumento a Vittorio Emanuele II** comes into view, glance right to the steep staircase (and winding street) to Michelangelo's **Piazza del Campidoglio**. Both the piazza and the monument are worth investigating.

Bend around onto Via dei Fori Imperiali for a quick glance at the ruins of **Foro di Cesari** before taking a hairpin turn back towards **Trajan's Markets** and **Trajan's Vast Forum**. Trajan's Column depicts battle scenes between the Romans and Dacians and is regarded as one of the finest remaining examples of Roman sculpture.

Pass through the Piazza Venezia and head towards **Campo de' Fiori**, an attractive piazza with a flower/vegetable market, and the former site of Inquisition executions. Nearby is the **Palazzo Farnese**, a magnificent Renaissance building that is now the French embassy.

Breeze by a slew of historic places of worship en route to the most significant: **Basilica di San Pietro** in the Vatican. For information on visiting Basilica San Pietro and/or the Vatican, contact the tourist booth (☎ 06 698 844 66) in Piazza San Pietro. While crossing the Tiber to Piazza San Pietro, check out **Castel Sant'Angelo**, which was originally Hadrian's mausoleum, and later a fortress.

Back at the river, proceed south along the western bank towards Trastevere. Consider poking around one of Rome's most colourful neighbourhoods for a lunch spot. **Da Lucia** and **Da Otello in Trastevere** are both excellent. Climb to **Chiesa di San Pietro in Montorio**, built on the spot where St Peter was supposedly crucified upside down. The famous architectural gem, **Tempietto di Bramante**, adjoins the church. Further uphill is **Fontana dell'Aqua Paola**, built by Pope Paul V in 1608 to showcase the workings of a restored aqueduct. **Piazza Garibaldi** (82m) offers one of the best panoramic views of the city and some lovely, shady vegetation.

The next stop, back on the other side of the river, is **Piazza Navona**. Lined with baroque palaces, this beautiful piazza contains three fountains, including Bernini's masterpiece **Fontana dei Quattro Fiumi** (Fountain of the Four Rivers), in the centre, depicting the Nile, Ganges, Danube and the Rio Plata. Facing the piazza is **Chiesa di Sant'Agnese in Agone**, its facade designed by Bernini's bitter rival, Borromini.

Walk your bike through the (officially pedestrian) Piazza Navona and across the street to the **Pantheon**, Rome's best-preserved ancient building. The original temple was built by Marcus Agrippa in 27 BC and dedicated to the planetary gods. The dome is considered the most important achievement of ancient Roman architecture.

Walk to **Colonna Antonina** in **Piazza Colonna**, which was erected after the death of Marcus Aurelius in AD 180 to commemorate his victories over the barbarian tribes of the Danube. Continue walking to the baroque **Trevi Fountain**, designed by Nicola Salvi in 1732 and one of Rome's most famous monuments. The custom is to throw a coin into the fountain (over your shoulder while facing away) to ensure you return to Rome.

Palazzo del Quirinale, on the piazza of the same name, is the official residence of the president, and formerly the summer residence of the popes. Along Via del Quirinale are two excellent examples of baroque architecture: the churches of **Sant'Andrea al Quirinale**, designed by Bernini, and **San Carlo alle Quattro Fontane**, designed by Borromini.

Proceed to the ritzy Via Vittorio Veneto and into the lovely **Villa Borghese** park, a pleasant picnic place (consider walking across the hectic intersection just inside Porta Pinciana). Turn left onto Viale dell'Obelisco, then right onto Viale G D'Annunzio. Wind down to **Piazza del Popolo**, where, three roads converge to form a trident at what was the main entrance to the city from the north. In the piazza's centre is an obelisk brought by Augustus from Heliopolis in ancient Greece, and moved here from the Circus Maximus.

South of the piazza is **Mausoleum of Augustus**, built by the emperor for himself and his family. Further east are the famous **Spanish Steps** – long a gathering place for foreigners.

Pass through **Piazza Barberini**, noting the spectacular **Fontana del Tritone** (Fountain of the Triton) and **Fontana delle Api** (Fountain of the Bees), both by Bernini.

Turning right onto Via Orlando, you'll notice **Fontana della Aqua Felice**, completed in 1586 to mark the terminus of the Aqua Felice aqueduct, and **Chiesa di Santa Maria della Vittoria**, which houses the once controversial sculpture, *The Ecstasy of St Theresa*, by Bernini. Also controversial were Mario Rutelli's scantily clad nymphs in **Fontana delle Naiadi** in **Piazza della Republica**. Shortly past the piazza is Stazione Termini.

ROME

The City Centre

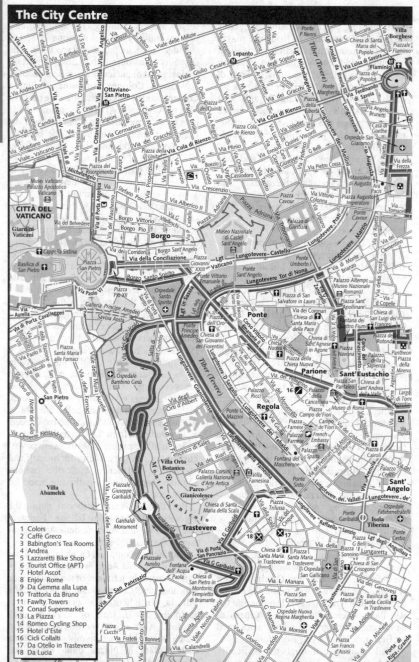

1 Colors
2 Caffè Greco
3 Babington's Tea Rooms
4 Andrea
5 Lazzaretti Bike Shop
6 Tourist Office (APT)
7 Hotel Ascot
8 Enjoy Rome
9 Da Gemma alla Lupa
10 Trattoria da Bruno
11 Fawlty Towers
12 Conad Supermarket
13 La Piazza
14 Romeo Cycling Shop
15 Hotel d'Este
16 Cicli Collalti
17 Da Otello in Trastevere
18 Da Lucia

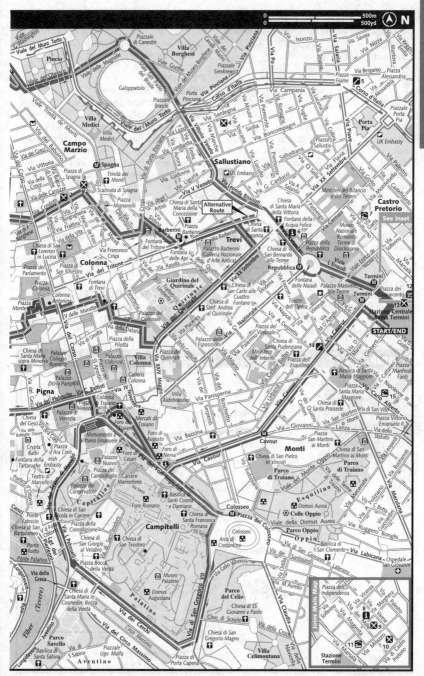

ROME

ROME

Appia Antica

Duration	3–5 hours
Distance	52.3km
Difficulty	moderate
Start	Stazione Termini
End	Frascati

This ride offers an extraordinary blend of history and beauty. Fascinating attractions, such as the extensive catacombs of San Callisto and San Sebastiano contrast with the tree-lined winding roads and posh resort towns of the Castelli Romani.

HISTORY

Known to ancient Romans as the *regina viarum* (queen of roads), Via Appia Antica runs from Porta di San Sebastiano, near the Baths of Caracalla, to Brindisi, on the coast of Puglia. It was started around 312 BC by the censor Appius Claudius Caecus, but did not connect with Brindisi until around 190 BC. The first section of the road, which extended 90km to Terracina, was considered revolutionary in its day because it was almost perfectly straight and cambered for drainage purposes. Sections of the original ancient roadway were excavated in the mid-19th century and remain in place.

PLANNING
When to Ride

Sunday is the best day to cycle this route, as part of the Appia Antica is closed to vehicles. However, some attractions (such as Catacombe di San Sebastiano) are closed on Sunday. The private road to the catacombs opens between 8.30am and noon and 2.30pm and 5pm daily, except Wednesday.

Maps

There are no great maps for this ride. Lonely Planet's *Rome City Map* will get you started along the Appia Antica, and Touring Club Italiano's 1:200,000 map *Lazio* provides just enough detail of the Castelli Romani region to be somewhat helpful.

GETTING TO/FROM THE RIDE

From Frascati, trains run regularly to Rome's Stazione Termini (€1.70, 30 minutes, hourly).

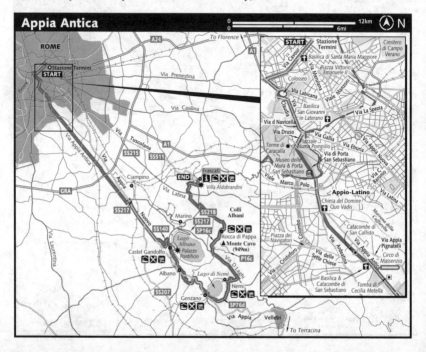

THE RIDE

Enjoy glimpses of Rome's city centre attractions on the way to Via Appia Antica. From Porta San Sebastiano, the route follows the cobbled (but relatively flat) Appia Antica past various points of interest. Spend the afternoon exploring the charming, hilly towns of the Castelli Romani before catching a train back to Rome from Frascati.

If you haven't visited the **Colosseum** or **Baths of Caracalla**, this route swings by both. Ride along Via Appia Antica through **Porta San Sebastiano** (4.3km), the largest and best preserved gateway to the city. At the fork between Appia Antica and Appia Ardeantina, **Chiesa del Domine Quo Vadis?** (5.2km), a church built at the point where St Peter is said to have met Jesus. Proceed straight at the fork onto the scenic, private road that leads to the **Catacombs of San Callisto** (6.2km; ☎ 06 51 30 15 80), the largest and most famous of the catacombs, and the **Basilica and Catacombs of San Sebastiano** (6.8km; ☎ 06 788 70 35). Outgoing car traffic must exit left at 6.9km, as the road becomes one way, but cyclists can proceed carefully, watching for the few oncoming

Warning

Though the sections of Via Appia Antica's original cobble are impressive testaments to the road's durable construction, they make for a somewhat bouncy ride and it's recommended that you have 1) a tough road bike with puncture-resistant tyres, 2) a mountain bike, or 3) spare tubes and a firm grasp of how to change a tyre.

On a completely different note, the ruined tombs and scrubby forests that line the outskirts of the Appia Antica, though relatively innocuous, are the notorious haunts of prostitutes and those seeking their services. Though this ride ends before the road becomes offensively seedy, it's wise to monitor what lies ahead, and to avoid riding in the evening.

cars. Further along are the well-preserved **Circo di Massenzio** (7.2km) and picturesque **Tomb of Cecilia Matella** (7.3km), plus a section of original Appia Antica cobble. After departing the Appia Antica, there's an unavoidable section of highway (Via Appia Nuovo, 16.2km), so stay to the shoulder.

Appia Antica

Cue

start		Stazione Termini		▲		9.2km gradual climb
0km		go NW on Via G Giolitti		22.1	↱ 🚏	SS140, to 'Castel Gandolfo'
0.1	↰	Via Cavour		25.4	✱	Castel Gandolfo
1.5	↰	Via dei Fori Imperiali			↙	unsigned road
1.9	↰	unsigned road (before Colosseum)		27.7	↱	Via G Matteotti 'to Genzano'
2.2	↑	onto Via di San Gregorio VII		31.9		Genzano
2.7	↰	Via Terme d Caracalla		32.9	↘	SP76d 'to Nemi'
3.5	↑	Piaz Pompilio on V Appia Antica		36.7	⚠	30m tunnel
4.3		Porta San Sebastiano		37.9	↰	SS217 'to Roma'
5.2	✱	Chiesa d Domine Quo Vadis?		41.5	↰	'to Rocca di Pappa'
	↑	unsigned road (through gate)		42.7	↰	SP16c 'to Frascati'
6.2	✱	Catacombe di San Callisto		44.1		Rocca di Pappa
6.8	↰	Via Appia Antica		44.4	↑ ✦	SS218 'to Grottaferrata'
	✱	Bas & Cat S Sebastiano		48.9	↙ ✦	(2nd exit) 'to Frascati'
6.9	⚠	oncoming traffic		51.8	✱	Villa Aldobrand.
7.2	✱	Circo d. Mass.		51.9	↑	through Piazzini Marconi
7.2	✱	Tomba d. C. Matella		52.1	↰	Via L Bonaparte
15.9	↰	'to Via Fioranello'		52.3		Frascati train station
16.2	↙ ✦	Via Appia Nuovo				

Elevation

ROME

A pleasant, tree-lined stretch, characteristic of the rest of the afternoon, leads to Castel Gandolfo. Just outside of the town is the dazzling summer residence of the Pope, **Palazzo Pontificio** (25.4km), before continuing through the other quaint towns in the Castelli Romani: Genzano (31.9km); Rocca di Pappa (44.1km); and Frascati (51.8km), which has several interesting **churches** and the magnificent **Villa Aldobrandini**. To explore the villa grounds, get a free permit from the IAT tourist office (☎ 06 942 03 31) at Piazzale Marconi 1. Frascati's cosy train station is just down the hill from the Piazzale Marconi.

Villas, Gardens & Suburbia

Duration	3½–6 hours
Distance	59.6km
Difficulty	easy–moderate
Start/End	Stazione Termini

This ride, for better and worse, reveals more of Rome's splendour and squalor than any day trip out of the city. Why do it? Though there are few traces of the original road, this route follows the ancient pathway of Via Tiburtina to Tivoli, the resort town of wealthy Romans. History buffs will relish the opportunity to retrace the route that Hadrian travelled to reach his magnificent summer compound, Villa Adriana – a must-see sight. This ride also offers the promise of Villa d'Este's fountains and gardens. Unfortunately, the getting there and back is not as scenic, with suburban sprawl lining much of Via Tiburtina (complete with about 100 McDonald's), not to mention a dusty stretch

past marble mines. If you want a *real* slice of Rome, this ride is a fascinating option.

HISTORY

No one is sure exactly how old Via Tiburtina is. It was in use during the time of the Roman republic, though was not completed until the 3rd century AD. The road's start was moved to its present location during the rule of Aurelian – who came to power in AD 270 – in an effort to fortify the city. Once an important thoroughfare that linked wealthy Romans with their summer retreats, the road became overrun by invaders in the Middle Ages, who used Tivoli as a base for attacking Rome. Today the only trace of the ancient road is Mammolo Bridge, the right span of which is original – built by the Byzantine general Narses during the republican era. Unfortunately, most of the original bridge was blown up by the French in 1849, in an attempt to end Garibaldi and Mazzini's republican revolution. The bridge was restored several years later.

Perhaps Via Tiburtina's most famous patron was the Roman Emperor Hadrian (ruled AD 117–138), who most likely commuted between his government seat and his gargantuan country estate in Tivoli along this very road. One of the most extraordinary Roman rulers, Hadrian was a cunning and disciplined military general, a brilliant architect and an eloquent public speaker. Perhaps best known for his extensive travels and his mission to define and fortify the empire's boundaries, Hadrian also remodelled Agrippa's Pantheon in downtown Rome, designed his own holiday villa in Tivoli, oversaw the modernisation of Rome's legal system, and wrote poetry in his spare time. Hadrian ruled at the height

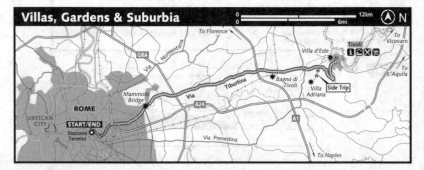

of the empire, when Rome's prosperity and functionality, and the empire's relative peace, had all reached a zenith. After choosing a successor – his adopted son, known today as Antonius Pius – Hadrian passed away in Naples at age 62. Though Hadrian hasn't thrown a bash at his Tivolian estate for more than 2100 years, the chance to tromp around the ruins of his villa compels countless visitors to retrace his steps from Rome to Tivoli along Via Tiburtina.

PLANNING
When to Ride
It is particularly important to avoid summer weekends, as the route becomes clogged with holidaying Romans. (However, the Tivoli Baths open daily and cost €8.30, or €9.30 on Sundays.) Also avoid morning and evening rush, when tons of suburban residents commute on the Via Tiburtina between the city and suburbs.

Plan your ride to include at least two hours to explore Villa Adriana (Hadrian's Villa).

Maps
This route is a straight shot and so a map is not essential. However, the Michelin map *Roma* (1:10,000) follows Via Tiburtina for about 6km from Stazione Termini, and Touring Club Italiano's 1:200,000 map *Lazio* covers the route.

THE RIDE
Departing from the Via Marsala side of Termini, this ride is relatively flat until about 3km from Tivoli, upon which the route winds gradually upwards to the city.

Admire **Mammolo Bridge** (7.2km; see History p88) on the way out of Rome. The ancient sulfur **Tivoli Baths** (21.4km) were

famous among wealthy Romans for their supposed healing powers and were mentioned by Virgil in the *Aeneid*. After a short, but tiring, climb into Tivoli (29.8km), the breathtaking gardens of **Ville d'Este** provide a moment of cool respite. The villa was built in the 16th century for Cardinal Ippolito d'Este on the site of a Franciscan monastery.

Leave plenty of time for a 2.7km side trip to the ruins of the **Villa Adriana** (*admission* €6.2). Constructed AD 118–34, Hadrian's Villa was one of the largest and most sumptuous in the Roman Empire. The model in the visitors centre gives an idea of the extent of the complex. To find the ruins, turn left at a busy intersection (34.4km) just after the descent from Tivoli (the sign is only visible from the other direction). After visiting the Villa, retrace the route back into Rome, with a slight diversion onto Via Cesare de Lollis at 57.6km, which ends at Stazione Termini.

The Mysterious Etruscans

Duration	2 days
Distance	109.5km
Difficulty	easy–moderate
Start	Cerveteri
End	Viterbo

Just a short train ride north of Rome, in the gently rolling farmlands of Lazio, are some of the most fascinating and best-preserved Etruscan sights in the country. Until their nautical trade routes were seized by the Greeks (5th century BC) and their culture absorbed by the more powerful Romans (1st century BC), Etruscans were known as skilled navigators, traders and artists. This route visits the mysterious tombs and ruins of Cerveteri and Tarquinia – two of the main city-states in the Etruscan League (peaked from 7th to 6th century BC) – and Viterbo, Lazio's medieval gem. Both days offer fairly easy riding past 18th- and 19th-century coastal villas, as well as wheat fields and ruined aqueducts.

Villas, Gardens & Suburbia

Cue	start	Stazione Termini
	0km	SE on Via Marsala
	0.7 ⬏	Vialle de Porta Tiburtino
	1.0 ⬑	Via Tiburtina (at P. Tiburtino)
	7.2 ✳	Mammolo Bridge
	21.4 ✳	Bagno di Tivoli
	26.0 ▲	3.7km moderate climb
	⬑	(20m) to 'Villa d'Este'
	29.8 ✳	Tivoli
	retrace outward route	
	34.4● ● ⬑	Villa Adriana at traffic light, 2.7km ↺
	retrace outward route	
	57.6 ↗	Via Cesare de Lollis
	59.6	Stazione Termini

PLANNING
The ride could be extended to include exploration of the three large lakes surrounding Viterbo: Bracciano, di Vico, and Bolsena

ROME

(which offers the most tourist conveniences). Cyclists continuing to Tuscany may consider heading north from Cerveteri to Orbetello to join the Southern Odyssey ride (p129).

When to Ride
Anytime! Unlike many, this ride is suitable even for the summer's peak tourist season. Accommodation is not hard to find and the attractions and roads are less crowded than those on other rides in this chapter.

Maps
Touring Club Italiano's 1:200,000 map *Lazio* covers the ride.

What to Bring
A torch (flashlight) is useful for the eerie Etruscan tombs.

GETTING TO/FROM THE RIDE
Regular services run between Cerveteri/Ladispoli train station (6.5km south of Cerveteri) and Rome's Termini (€3, about 45 minutes, hourly).

Trains from Viterbo's Porta Fiorentina station to Rome are regular, though indirect and oddly timed. The standard service to Rome runs direct to Ostiense, for a connecting train to Termini (€4.10, about 2¼ hours, hourly). Other services involve changing trains (mainly in Orte) to a service for Termini.

THE RIDE
Cerveteri
Ancient Caere was founded by the Etruscans in the 8th century BC and enjoyed a period of great prosperity as a commercial centre from the 7th to the 5th centuries BC. The main attractions are the tombs known as *tumoli*: great mounds of earth with carved stone bases. Treasures taken from the tombs can be seen in the Musei Vaticani, the Museo di Villa Giulia and in Paris, at the Louvre.

Information The Pro Loco tourist office (☎ 06 99 55 19 71), Piazza Risorgimento 19, is open from 10am to 1pm Tuesday to Sunday. It can provide useful and interesting information about the area's history. Rome's proximity to Cerveteri makes the capital city the logical place to stay; the tourist office can provide information about places to stay and eat in Cerveteri.

Things to See & Do The small **Archaeology Museum** (☎ 06 994 13 54; *Piazza S Maria*) houses an interesting display of pottery and sarcophagi.

The main necropolis area, **Banditaccia** (☎ 06 994 00 01), is about 3km west of town. Take a guidebook or brochure from the tourist office since the signs detailing the history of the main tombs are in Italian, and follow the recommended routes to see the best-preserved tombs. One of the more interesting is **Tomba dei Rilievi** from the 4th century BC, decorated with painted reliefs of household items. Others worth seeing are **Tomba dei Capitali** and **Tomba dei Vasi Greci**.

Day 1: Cerveteri to Tarquinia
3½–6½ hours, 64.4km
With a train ride in the morning and an early stop at a point of interest, it may be early afternoon before the cycling really begins. The rest of the day entails sailing along on flat, easy roads past pleasant villages, attractive beaches, and one unfortunate industrial patch.

Don't miss the **Etruscan tombs**, reached on a 3.8km side trip at the beginning of the

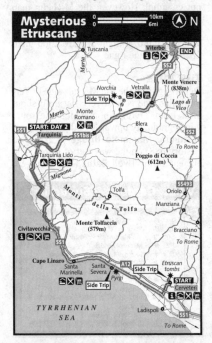

ride. Soon after leaving Cerveteri, the route follows the well-travelled, but not unpleasant, SS1. Take another (1km) side trip at 24.6km to visit the castle of **Santa Severa**, the pretty beach on which it stands, and, next door, the ruins of **Pyrgi** (closed Monday), one of the region's busiest ports during the 6th and 5th centuries BC. The ruins are to the left as you approach the castle; ring the bell at the gate marked 'Pyrgi Antiquarium Pyrginese'.

The ride becomes increasingly scenic as the road hugs the coast and passes through attractive towns such as **Santa Marinella** (31.2km). There's little reason to visit **Civitavecchia** (41.6km), a busy port and industrial centre.

Past Civitavecchia's grimy industrial zone, the route becomes markedly prettier as it winds through the marshy coastal flats towards hilltop **Tarquinia** (64.4km).

Tarquinia

Believed to have been founded in the 12th century BC, and home of the Tarquin kings who ruled Rome before the creation of the republic, Tarquinia was an important economic and political centre of the Etruscan League. The town has a small, medieval centre that with a good Etruscan museum, but the major attractions here are the painted tombs of the burial grounds.

Information The APT office (☎ 0766 85 63 84), Piazza Cavour 1, opens from 9am to 7pm Monday to Saturday, supposedly year round, but don't count on afternoon hours in winter.

Bike repair shop Bettosti Giovanni Battista (☎ 07 66 84 09 38) is at Via Cesare Battisti 3 (closed Sunday).

Things to See & Do The 15th-century Palazzo Vitelleschi houses the **Museo Nazionale Tarquiniese** (☎ 0766 85 60 36; Piazza Cavour) and a significant collection of Etruscan treasures, including frescoes removed from the tombs. If you plan to visit the tombs the next morning, *don't* view the fresco display on the top floor, as it will just take away from the excitement of exploring the actual site.

Wander through town and visit the 13th-century **Chiesa di San Francesco** (Via Porta Tarquinia) and the beautiful Romanesque

Chiesa di Santa Maria di Castello, in the citadel at the northwest edge of town.

Tarquinia's famous **painted tombs** are at the necropolis, which is a suggested early stop on the Day 2 route to Viterbo. Almost 6000 tombs have been excavated, of which 60 are painted, but only a handful are open to the public. DH Lawrence, who studied the tombs before measures were taken to protect them, wrote extensive descriptions of the frescoes he saw, and it is well worth reading his *Etruscan Places* before seeing the tombs. Excavation of the tombs started in the 15th century and continues today.

Places to Stay & Eat The camp site **Tusca Tirrenia** (☎ 0766 86 42 94; Viale delle Neriedi; open May-Oct) is 5km from the medieval town beside the sea at Tarquinia Lido.

Hotel San Marco (☎ 0766 84 22 34; Piazza Cavour 10; singles/doubles €50/65), with spacious comfortable rooms, is the best bet in the medieval section. It has a good **restaurant**. In the newer part of town **Hotel all'Olivo** (☎ 0766 85 73 18; Via Togliatti 15; singles/doubles with breakfast €50/80) also has a fine **restaurant**.

Mysterious Etruscans – Day 1

Cue

start		Ladispoli/Cerveteri stazione
0km	↱	Via Taranto
0.2	↱	unsigned road (stop sign)
1.9	↰	SS1 to 'Cerveteri'
2.7	↱ 🅗	to 'Cerveteri'
5.5	↰	to 'Museo Etrusco'
6.4	↰	unsigned road (after park)
6.5		Cerveteri tourist office
	✳	Archaeology Museum
retrace route from tourist office		
6.5	↱	(40m) at park (downhill)
6.7	↗	to 'Sasso' (at end of park)
6.8	↗	to 'Necropoli Etrusco'
8.3	✳	Etruscan tombs
retrace route to SS1		
13.3	↱	SS1 to 'Santa Marinella'
24.6 ●●		Santa Severa/Pyrgi 1km ↻
31.2		Santa Marinella
41.6		Civitavecchia
42.6	↗	to 'Tarquinia'
43.5	↰	to 'Grosseto' (over bridge)
48.5	↰	to 'Bagni S. Augostino'
51.6	↱	to 'Tarquinia Lido'
57.8	↱	to 'Tarquinia'
63.1	↰	unsigned road (towards town)
63.3	↗	'Tarquinia' sign
64.0	↰	unsigned road (petrol station)
64.0	↱	(30m) just past petrol station
64.1	↰	Viale Luigi Dasti
64.3	↰	Piazza Cavour
64.4		Tarquinia tourist office

Situated at Tarquinia Lido, **Hotel Miramare** (☎ 0766 86 40 20; Viale dei Tirreni 36; singles/doubles €52/65) is a good budget choice.

Of the few places to eat in Tarquinia, **Trattoria Arcadia** (Via Mazzini 6) has good, cheap meals. The free map from the tourist office lists several pizzerie.

Day 2: Tarquinia to Viterbo
2½–4½ hours, 45.1km

The ride begins with a visit to the fascinating Etruscan necropolis before settling into a pleasant and easy ramble over gently rolling farmland to Viterbo – a major attraction in itself.

Perhaps the most famous of all Italian necropolises, the beautifully painted tombs of the **Etruscan burial site** (1.6km; see Things to See & Do, p91) are a must-see. The snack bar in the park is an excellent place to stock up on delicious local panini.

If your appetite for Etruscan history has yet to be satiated, consider a 12km side trip (22.8km) to **Norchia**, another ancient necropolis, perched dramatically on a rocky outcrop. Otherwise, continue to **Vetralla** (31km) a small, attractive medieval town worth a quick poke around.

Allow plenty of time to get lost in Viterbo's tangle of streets, churches, piazzas and fountains.

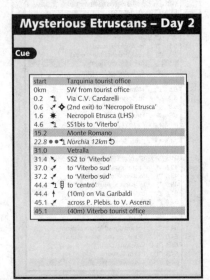

Mysterious Etruscans – Day 2

Cue

start	Tarquinia tourist office
0km	SW from tourist office
0.2	⤴ Via C.V. Cardarelli
0.6	⤴ ◆ (2nd exit) to 'Necropoli Etrusca'
1.6	✳ Necropoli Etrusca (LHS)
4.6	⤴ SS1bis to 'Viterbo'
15.2	Monte Romano
22.8	●●⤴ Norchia 12km ↺
31.0	Vetralla
31.4	↘ SS2 to 'Viterbo'
37.0	⤴ to 'Viterbo sud'
37.2	⤴ to 'Viterbo sud'
44.4	⤴ ⌷ to 'centro'
44.4	↑ (10m) on Via Garibaldi
45.1	⤴ across P. Plebis. to V. Ascenzi
45.1	(40m) Viterbo tourist office

Viterbo

Founded by the Etruscans and eventually taken over by Rome, Viterbo developed into an important medieval centre and in the 13th century became the residence of the popes. Papal elections were once held in the town's Gothic Palazzo Papale.

Although badly damaged by bombing during WWII, Viterbo remains Lazio's best preserved medieval town. Apart from its historical appeal, Viterbo is famous for its therapeutic hot springs.

Information The Porta del Parco tourist office (☎ 0761 32 59 92, e portavt@isa.it), on Via Ascenzi 4, is open daily from 10am to noon and 4.30pm to 6.30pm. It's easier to find, has more convenient hours, and offers more helpful advice than the APT office (☎ 0761 30 47 95) on Piazza San Carluccio. The Porta del Parco office offers a hotel booking service by phone, email and in person. ATMs are sprinkled throughout town; one is on Piazza del Plebiscito.

Things to See & Do Adjoining 15th- and 16th-century palaces enclose **Piazza del Plebiscito**, the most imposing of which is **Palazzo dei Priori**, with an elegant fountain in its courtyard. Many rooms are decorated with frescoes.

The 12th-century **Cattedrale di San Lorenzo** on Piazza San Lorenzo was rebuilt in the 14th century to a Gothic design. Also on the piazza is **Palazzo Papale**, built in the 13th century with the aim of enticing the popes away from Rome.

The Romanesque church on **Piazza Santa Maria Nuova** was restored after bomb damage in WWII. The cloisters are worth a visit. Via San Pellegrino takes you through **Medieval Quarter** into **Piazza San Pellegrino**. The extremely well-preserved buildings on this piazza comprise the finest group of medieval buildings in Italy.

Built in the early 13th century, **Fontana Grande**, Piazza Fontana Grande, is the oldest and largest of Viterbo's Gothic fountains.

Chiesa di San Francesco, a Gothic building, was also restored after WWII. The church contains the tombs of two popes: Clement IV (died 1268) and Adrian V (died 1276).

Museo Civico (☎ 0761 34 82 75) houses the lovely painting Pietà by Sebastiano del

Piombo, along with a Roman sarcophagus which is said to be the tomb of Galiana, a beautiful and virtuous woman who was murdered by a Roman baron after she refused his advances.

The sulphurous Bulicame pool, Viterbo's best known hot spring, was mentioned by Dante in his *Divine Comedy*. Once frequented by the Romans, these public medicinal pools, known today as **Terme dei Papi**, are about 3km from Viterbo on the Strada Bagni. The Porta del Parco tourist office can provide directions to the springs, as well as information about the spa facilities nearby.

Places to Stay & Eat If you aim to spend the night in Viterbo, try the budget **Hotel Roma** (☎ 0761 22 64 74; Via della Cava 26; singles/doubles with bathroom & breakfast €39/57), just off Piazza della Rocca. Slightly more up-scale is **Hotel Tuscia** (☎ 0761 34 44 00; Via Cairoli 41; singles/ doubles with breakfast €52/83).

For a reasonably priced meal seek out **All' Archetto** (Via San Cristoforo; full meal €13), off Via Cavour. **Il Richiastro** (Via della Marrocca 18; soups €4, pasta €5, meat courses €8) serves hearty food based on ancient Roman recipes and has outside tables in summer.

Tuscany

The people of Tuscany (Toscana) can rightly claim to have just about the best of everything – architecture, art, beautiful countryside and some of Italy's finest produce and wines. It was from Tuscany, about 600 years ago, that the effects of the Renaissance began to ripple out across Europe.

The works of Donatello, Michelangelo, Leonardo da Vinci and other 15th- and 16th-century Tuscan masters remain models for artists worldwide. Tuscan architects – notably Brunelleschi, responsible for the magnificent dome of Florence's duomo (cathedral), and Leon Battista Alberti, who designed much of the facade of the Basilica di Santa Maria Novella – have had an enduring influence on the course of architecture.

Most people are attracted to Tuscany by the artistic splendour of Florence (Firenze) and Siena, or to view the Leaning Tower of Pisa, but Tuscany also features some of Italy's most impressive hill towns, including San Gimignano, Volterra, Cortona and Montepulciano.

The Etruscan sites in the south, around Pitigliano, will take you away from the mainstream tourist itinerary. Southern Tuscany also boasts some of Italy's best beaches – near Orbetello and on Isola d'Elba. Those seeking more mountainous terrain will enjoy the Alpi Apuane in the Garfagnana region.

HISTORY

The Etruscans founded Florence in about 200 BC. It later became the Roman Florentia, a strategic garrison built to control the Via Flaminia. The city suffered during the barbarian invasions of the Dark Ages.

The first conflicts between the pro-papal Guelfi (Guelphs) and the pro-imperial Ghibellini (Ghibellines) started in the mid-13th century. The plague of 1348 halved the city's population. In the late 14th century, Florence was ruled by the Guelfi under the Albizzi family. Among the families opposing them were the Medici, whose influence grew as they became the papal bankers.

In the 15th century, Cosimo de' Medici became Florence's ruler. Alberti, Brunelleschi and Donatello flourished under his patronage. Cosimo was followed by his grandson,

In Brief

Highlights
- **Florence** and **Siena**, and the vineyards of the **Chianti** region in between
- The hill towns of **Montalcino**, **Montepulciano**, **Cortona** and **Pitigliano**
- **Elba's** idyllic beaches and panoramic views
- Quaint mountain towns of the **Alpi Apuane**

Terrain
Rolling hills in the Chianti and Crete regions; flatter in the south near Pitigliano and Orbetello and along the coast by Viareggio; steep climbs and descents in the mountainous Alpi Apuane.

Special Events
- **Il Palio** horse race (July and August), Siena
- **Explosion of the Cart** fireworks display (Easter), Florence
- **Feast of St John** festivies for Florence's patron saint (June), Florence

Cycling Events
- **Giro di Toscana** (TBA), Tuscany region
- **Gran Fondo della Versilia** (TBA), Viareggio
- **Gran Fondo del Brunello** mountain-bike race (TBA), Montalcino
- **Sbiciclettata** community event (mid-June), Grosseto

Food & Drink Specialities
- *crostini* (grilled bread covered with chicken-liver pâté)
- *cinghale* (wild boar, often served in pasta dishes or as a sausage)
- *panaforte* (dense dried-fruit-and-nut tart)
- *Chianti Classico* (a blended red-and-white wine

Lorenzo il Magnifico, whose rule (1469–92) ushered in the Italian Renaissance. Lorenzo favoured philosophers, but also sponsored Botticelli, Leonardo and Michelangelo. In 1492, the Medici bank failed and the family was driven out of Florence. Girolamo Savonarola, a Dominican monk, led a puritanical republic until he was fried as a heretic in 1498.

After Florence's defeat by the Spanish in 1512, the Medici returned to the city but were expelled, this time by Emperor Charles V, in 1527. Charles later allowed the Medici to return to Florence, where they ruled for another 200 years.

In 1737, the Grand Duchy of Tuscany passed to the House of Lorraine, which retained control for the most part until it was incorporated into the Kingdom of Italy in 1860.

Florence was badly damaged during WWII by the retreating Germans. Floods ravaged the city in 1966.

NATURAL HISTORY

If you regard Tuscany's coast as the base, the region forms a rough triangle covering 22,992 sq km. Crammed within that triangle are a variety of land forms, from mountains in the north and east to relatively flat plains in the south, from islands off the coast to rolling hills in the interior.

Much of the coast is flat, with the exception of a stretch south of Livorno and the Monte Argentario peninsula. The northern flank of the region is closed off by the Apennines and the Alpi Apuane.

In all, two-thirds of Tuscany is mountainous or hilly. Lower hill ranges rise in the south and are separated by a series of low river valleys, the most important being the Arno. The Arno rises in the Apennines, flows south to Arezzo, and then meanders northwest. Once an important trade artery, traffic on the river today is virtually nonexistent.

TUSCANY

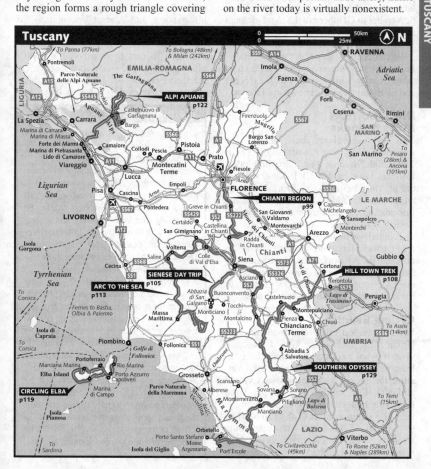

Of the islands scattered off Tuscany's coast, the central and eastern parts of Elba, along with Giannutri and parts of Giglio, are reminders of an Apennine wall that collapsed into the sea millions of years ago. Western Elba and parts of Giglio are the creation of volcanic activity.

CLIMATE

Tuscan summers are hot and oppressive. From late June to September, highs of 35°C are common. The Chianti region is the hottest. Temperatures along the coast are marginally lower. Mountainous areas, such as the Alpi Apuane, are cooler though wetter.

Spring and autumn are the nicest times of year, though rainfall in November can be heavy. Specifically, April to early June and September to October are the most pleasant months. Average daytime highs around 20°C to 25°C are ideal for cycling.

Winter is chilly across the region. Snowfalls and temperatures around zero are possible in inland hilly areas (such as Siena and Cortona). It rarely snows in Florence.

INFORMATION
Maps & Books

The best general reference map of the region is Touring Club Italiano's (TCI) 1:200,000 *Toscana*. For individual rides, Edizioni Multigraphic's 1:100,000 individual province maps, *Carta Stradale Provinciale*, provide additional detail. For more information on Tuscany and Florence, see Lonely Planet's *Florence* and *Tuscany*.

To purchase maps and books in Florence, try Feltrinelli International, Via Cavour 12r, opposite the APT office; and Internazionale Seeber, Via de' Tornabuoni 70r; for maps only, Geographica on Via dei Cimatori 16r (near Palazzo Vecchio) is the best bet.

Cycling Events

For information on International Cycling Union rides, such as the Giro di Toscana, visit w www.uci.ch/english/index.htm. To learn more about the Gran Fondo della Versilia, the race's website (w www.versili abike.it). For information on the Gran Fondo del Brunello and mountain biking in the Val d'Orcia, contact Club Orso on Bike (☎ 347 05 35 63 8, w www.bikemonta lcino.it). The Sbiciclettata is a bike ride/ecological walk/party from Grosseto to Istia d'Ombrone and back. For information, call the event's founder Romolo Domenicioni (☎ 0564 41 38 52).

Information Sources

For itineraries and events in Florence, check out w www.firenze.turismo.toscana .it. For train times and prices, w www.tren italia.it is excellent. Go Tuscany's site, w www.firenze.net/events has tips on places to stay and an events calendar. For useful information about cycling around the city, including the locations of the city's bike lanes and several ride itineraries, check out w www.florencebikepages.com. FIAB is a bicycle advocacy group that coordinates affiliated clubs. Its website (w www.fiab onlus.it) has links to maps, accommodation information, and contact information for local cycling clubs, many of which organise rides on Sunday morning.

Unione Italiana Sport per Tutti's (UISP) office (☎ 055 658 35 01, w www.uisp.it), Via Francesca Bocchi 32, Florence, schedules and coordinates cycling events in Italy.

Warning

Tuscany's popularity as a tourist destination makes for a steady stream of traffic between the major regional attractions, especially from late June to August. Take a glut of foreigners unfamiliar with the roads and mix in hordes of Italians fleeing the cities on vacation, and you have a recipe for traffic-induced disaster. Be particularly alert when entering and leaving Florence and Siena. Though the routes detailed in this chapter avoid the most congested areas, all paths to and from these two cities can become clogged in summer.

Because many of the inner-city roads are closed to automobile traffic, scooters predominate in town centres. Though this arrangement may appear advantageous to cyclists, scooter drivers seem, surprisingly, the most likely to shave cyclists too close for comfort.

Cyclists in Tuscany will enjoy some of the best road surfaces in Italy. That said, most secondary roadways are characterised by hairpin switchbacks and a dearth of safe shoulders on which to ride. Though the most dangerous spots along the routes are highlighted in the cue sheets, cyclists should be conscious of these two conditions at all times.

GATEWAY CITY
Florence

In a valley on the banks of the Arno River and set among low hills covered with olive groves and vineyards, Florence (Firenze) is immediately captivating. Cradle of the Renaissance and home of Machiavelli, Michelangelo and the Medici, the city seems incomparably laden with art, culture and history. The French writer Stendhal was so dazzled by the magnificence of the Basilica di Santa Croce that he was barely able to walk for faintness. He is apparently not the only one to have felt overwhelmed by the beauty of Florence – Florentine doctors supposedly treat a dozen cases of 'Stendhalismo' a year.

Information The main APT office (☎ 055 29 08 32) is just north of the duomo at Via Cavour 1r. The Comune di Firenze (city council) operates a tourist office (☎ 055 21 22 45) on Largo Alinari, just outside the southeastern exit of the train station, Stazione di Santa Maria Novella. The Comune di Firenze has another office (☎ 055 234 04 44) at Borgo Santa Croce 29r. Inside the train station, you can pick up basic information at the Consorzio ITA office (☎ 055 28 28 93). The office's main role is to book hotels.

Two useful websites devoted to the Chianti region are ⓦ www.chianti.it and ⓦ www .chiantinet.it.

Banks and ATMS are scattered everywhere throughout the city centre, including several inside the train station.

The best bike shops in town are Giuseppe Bianchi (☎/fax 055 21 69 91) on Via Nazionale 130r; and the family-run Cicli Conti (☎ 055 57 92 08) in the northeastern part of the city on Via Marconi 120. To rent a road or mountain bike, contact Florence by Bike (☎ 055 48 89 92, ⓦ www.florenceby bike.it), Via San Zanobi 120. It can supply you with panniers and extra gear if necessary.

Things to See & Do Florence's small city centre may be more conducive for self-guided walking, rather than cycling, tours. That said, some pleasant rides can be had along the banks of the Arno and through the city centre. The wealth of sights within the old centre make a short summary of things to see and do near impossible. Here are just a few of the major sights to hit by bike or foot.

Basilica di Santa Maria Novella, just south of the train station, was begun in the late 13th century as the Florentine base for the Dominican order. The church and cloisters house some of the city's best frescoes.

Basilica di San Lorenzo on the Piazza Madonna degli Aldobrandini is considered one of the most harmonious examples of Renaissance architecture.

The **Cappelle Medicee** are entered via Piazza Madonna degli Aldobrandini. **Cappella dei Principi** (Princes' Chapel) was the principal burial place of the Medici rulers.

The **duomo's** pink, white and green marble facade will stop you momentarily in your tracks. This stunning piece of architecture is also famous for Brunelleschi's tiled dome – a dominant feature of Florence's skyline. Although now severely cracked and under restoration, it remains a remarkable achievement of design. When Michelangelo went to work on the Basilica di San Pietro, he reportedly said: 'I go to build a greater dome, but not a fairer one.' The duomo took almost 150 years to complete. The view from the summit over Florence is unparalleled.

On the Piazza di Santa Croce is the **Basilica di Santa Croce**. The piazza was once used for the execution of heretics, but today it is lined with souvenir shops. Along the south wall (to your right as you enter the church) is Michelangelo's tomb.

The area around **Piazza della Signoria** was the hub of the city's political life through the centuries and is now surrounded by some of its most celebrated buildings. Ammannati's huge **Fountain of Neptune** sits beside the Palazzo Vecchio, and flanking the entrance to the palace are copies of Michelangelo's *David* (the original is in the Galleria dell' Accademia) and Donatello's *Marzocco*, the heraldic Florentine lion (the original is in the Museo del Bargello).

Palazzo Vecchio, built between 1298 and 1314, is the traditional seat of Florentine government. Its **Torre d'Arnolfo** is 94m high and is as much a symbol of the city as the duomo.

Uffizi Gallery is in the **Palazzo degli Uffizi**, which originally housed the city's administrators, judiciary and guilds. The Galleria degli Uffizi houses the world's greatest collection of Italian and Florentine art.

Along Via degli Speziali is the **Piazza della Repubblica**. Originally the site of a Roman forum, it is now home to Florence's most fashionable and expensive cafés.

The 14th-century bridge, **Ponte Vecchio**, has been draped in the glittering wares of jewellery merchants since the time Ferdinando I de' Medici ordered them here to replace the town butchers, who jettisoned unwanted leftovers into the river. The views of and from the only bridge to survive Nazi explosives in 1944 are every bit as beguiling as you might expect.

No tour of Florence is complete without a visit to the **Galleria dell'Accademia**. It houses paintings by Florentine artists spanning the 13th to 16th centuries, but its main draw is Michelangelo's *David*, carved from a single block of marble when the artist was aged only 29. Originally in the Piazza della Signoria, the colossal statue now stands in an alcove at the end of the main hall on the ground floor.

The views of the city's skyline from the **Piazzale Michelangelo** and/or the **Forte di Belvedere** are stunning and should not be missed.

Places to Stay Establishments close to the train station are most convenient if you intend to cycle the Chianti Region route. For this reason, the majority of the accommodation is listed in this area. Florence's small geographic size, however, makes it a short trip to the ride's start no matter where you end up. Book ahead in the summer and for the Easter and Christmas–New Year holiday periods.

The Consorzio ITA office in the train station can check the availability of rooms and make bookings. The fee ranges from €2.50 to €8 for one- to five-star places. The APT office has a list of *affittacamere* (private rooms).

Some establishments in Florence have courtyards or garages where bikes can be stashed, but most do not. Be prepared to pay €5 to €8 to store bikes in a car-parking garage. At least there, they will be safe from Florence's talented thieves!

Campeggio Michelangelo (☎ 055 681 19 77; *Viale Michelangelo 80; open Apr-Oct)*, just off Piazzale Michelangelo, south of the Arno, is the closest camp site to the city centre. **Villa Camerata** (☎ 055 61 03 00; *Viale Augusto Righi 2-4)* is next to Ostello Villa Camerata.

The HI **Ostello Villa Camerata** (☎ 055 60 14 51; *Viale Augusto Righi 2-4; B&B €12.50, dinner €7.50; open 7am-9am & 2pm-midnight)* is one of the most beautiful hostels in Europe. It accepts HI members only. About 4.5km from the Stazione di Santa Maria Novella, ride east along the Arno then northeast on Via Campofiore. **Ostello Archi Rossi** (☎ 055 29 08 04; *Via Faenza 94r; large dorm/smaller dorm per person €13.50/21)* is a good option, closer to the train station.

Many of the budget hotels around the train station are well-run, clean and safe, but there are also a fair number of seedy establishments. **Hotel Aldobrandini** (☎ 055 21 18 66; *Piazza Madonna degli Aldobrandini 8; singles/doubles €57/83)* is in a handy location, though bikes must be stored in the Garage Giglio (€5.50 per night) next door. **Pensione Bellavista** (☎ 055 28 45 28; *Largo Alinari 15; doubles €70)* is at the start of Via Nazionale and has small, but knockout, bargain rooms with balconies and a view of the duomo and Palazzo Vecchio. **Albergo Azzi** (☎ 055 21 38 06; *Via Faenza 56; singles/doubles €36/52, doubles with bathroom €73)* is a simple, comfortable place with helpful management.

For mid-range accommodation, **Pensione Accademia** (☎ 055 29 34 51; *Via Faenza 7; singles with shared bathroom €67, doubles with private bathroom €103)* offers pleasant rooms in an 18th-century mansion with stained-glass doors, carved wooden ceilings, breakfast and TV. For a top-end hotel, **Machiavelli Palace** (☎ 055 21 66 22; *Via Nazionale 10; singles/doubles €124/201)* is a 17th-century mansion with beautiful rooms.

Places to Eat Many tourists fall into the trap of eating at the self-service restaurants that line the streets of the main shopping district between the duomo and the Arno. If time permits, be adventurous and seek out the little eating places in the Oltrarno (roughly the downtown area from the duomo to Ponte Vecchio) and near Piazza del Mercato Centrale in the San Lorenzo area, where you'll eat authentic Italian food. Remember to calculate cover (average about €1 to €2 per person) and service charges (15%) when budgeting.

The streets between the duomo and the Arno harbour many **pizzerie** where you can buy takeaway pizza by the slice for around €1 to €2, depending on the weight. Another option for a light lunch is **Antico Noè**, a legendary sandwich bar through the Arco di San Piero, just off Piazza San Pier Maggiore. It is take-away only. Just opposite is **Il Nilo** where you can get felafel or shawarma sandwiches for €2 to €3. **Gilli** (Piazza della Repubblica; coffee at the bar €1, outside table €2.60) is one of the city's finest cafés.

Eating at a good trattoria can be surprisingly economical – a virtue of the competition for customers' attention. For lunch, try **Mario** (Via Rosina 2r; lunch €3-5), a small bar and pasta trattoria near Piazza del Mercato Centrale. For dinner, **Hostaria il Caminetto** (Via dello Studio 34; pasta €5, mains €6.50; closed Wed) has singing waiters and a small, vine-covered terrace. **Trattoria il Contadino** (Via Palazzuolo 55; set menu €8, including wine) is good value for money. **Da il Latini** (Via dei Palchetti 4; pasta €3, mains €7.50) is an attractive trattoria just off Via del Moro. **Sostanza** (Via del Porcellana 25r; mains from €9.50) offers traditional Tuscan cooking and is one of the best spots in town for bistecca alla Fiorentina (a rich, white oxen steak, usually served rare).

Getting There & Away Seeing as it is such a popular tourist attraction, Florence can easily be reached by land or air.

Air Florence is served by two airports. Amerigo Vespucci (☎ 055 306 17 00), a few kilometres northwest of the city centre at Via del Termine 11, caters to domestic and European flights. Galileo Galilei (☎ 055 50 07 07), near Pisa, is one of Italy's main international airports. Several airlines are represented in Florence, including Alitalia (☎ 055 2 78 88), Lungarno Acciaioli 10–12r; TWA (☎ 055 239 68 56), Via dei Vecchietti 4; and British Airways (☎ 147 81 22 66).

Bus Lazzi (☎ 166 84 50 10), Piazza Adua 1, next to the train station, runs services to/from Rome. Lazzi forms part of the Eurolines network of international bus services. You can, for instance, catch a bus to/from Paris, Prague or Barcelona from Florence. A detailed brochure of all Eurolines services is available from the Lazzi ticket office. The SITA bus station (☎ 055 21 47 21), Via Santa Caterina da Siena 15, is just to the west of Piazza della Stazione. There is a direct, rapid service to Siena. Direct buses serve other smaller cities throughout Tuscany.

Train Florence is on the Rome–Milan line, which means that most of the trains for Rome, Bologna and Milan are Intercity or Eurostar Italia, which do not carry bikes. *Diretto* and *regionale* trains, however, both take bicycles and run between Florence and Rome (€14.50, 3¾ hours, every two hours). It is possible to catch a train from the Galileo Galilei airport to Florence (€4.70, 1½ hours, hourly), but not from Amerigo Vespucci.

Chianti Region

Duration	2 days
Distance	101.7km
Difficulty	moderate
Start	Florence
End	Siena

Originating in Florence, this ride is a logical and attractive route on which to begin a tour of Tuscany. Though some of the climbs are tough, the total distance per day makes these rides only moderately challenging. Just a few kilometres from Florence, the excitement and bustle of the city give way to the rolling vineyards and olive groves of the Chianti region, the centre of Tuscany's world-famous wine industry. Stop to sample the local wines en route to Greve in Chianti, and pay a visit to the castle of Montefioralle and the magnificent abbey, Badia di Passignano. Day 2 swings through the lovely hamlets of Radda and Castellina in Chianti before descending into Florence's Gothic rival – and one of Tuscany's most charming cities – Siena.

PLANNING
When to Ride
See the Climate section on p96 for information on the best weather conditions. In addition to climate concerns, consider the tourist season. Florence and Siena are swamped in July and August, making accommodation very difficult to secure. April to early June and September to October are the most pleasant times to cycle.

TUSCANY

Maps

Because the ride crosses two provinces (Florence and Siena), there are not any highly detailed maps of the route. The best map for this ride is Selca's frustratingly hard to find 1:70,000 *Il Chianti*. Ask for it at APT tourist offices or contact the Provincia di Firenze office (☎ 055 27 60 1), Via Cavour 37, in Florence. TCI's *Toscana* (see the Maps & Books section on p96) is adequate.

What to Bring

Don't underestimate the power of the scorching Tuscan sun in July and August. If you're embarking on this ride in summer, bring a healthy supply of sunscreen and several large water bottles.

ACCESS TOWN

See Florence (p97).

THE RIDE
Day 1: Florence to Greve in Chianti

2½–4½ hours, 46.7km
This ride trades the splendour of Florence's Renaissance art, cathedrals and gardens for greener pastures as it crosses the Arno in search of the Chianti region's undulating hills and acclaimed vineyards. There is a short, optional stretch of unpaved road at the end of the ride.

Take a brief detour at the **Porta Romana** (3.8km), an imposing city gate that once marked the outer limits of Florence, down the Via Romana to explore the **Boboli Gardens**.

Chianti Region – Florence

PLACES TO STAY
3 Ostello Archi Rossi & Alberghi Azzi
4 Pensione Bellavista
5 Machiavelli Palace
10 Hotel Aldobrandini
11 Pensione Accademia

PLACES TO EAT
6 Mario
13 Trattoria il Contadino
14 Sostanza
15 Da il Latini
17 Hostaria il Caminetto
18 Gilli
19 Il Nilo
20 Antico Noè

OTHER
1 Florence by Bike
2 Giuseppe Bianchi
7 APT Tourist Office
8 Feltrinelli International Bookshop
9 Basilica di San Lorenzo
12 Basilica di Santa Maria Novella
16 Seeber Internazionale Bookshop
21 Geographica
22 Libreria Succursale TCI
23 Uffizi Gallery
24 Galleria dell'Accademia

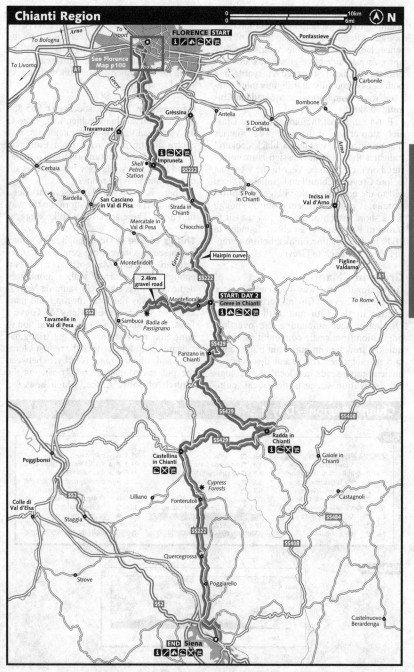

Chianti Region

0 ——— 10km
0 ——— 6mi

N

To Bologna
To Livorno
Arno
To Airport
FLORENCE START
See Florence Map p100
Pontassieve
Carbonile
A1
Greve
Bombone
Grèssina
Antella
S Donato in Collina
Travarnuzze
Shell Petrol Station
Impruneta
SS222
Cerbaia
Pesa
Bardella
San Casciano in Val di Pisa
Strada in Chianti
S Polo in Chianti
Incisa in Val d'Arno
Arno
Mercatale in Val di Pesa
Chiocchio
Montefindolfi
Greve
Hairpin curve
Figline Valdarno
A1
2.4km gravel road
SS222
Montefioralle
START: DAY 2
Greve in Chianti
To Rome
Tavarnelle in Val di Pesa
SS2
Sambuca
Badia de Passignano
SS429
Panzano in Chianti
SS429
SS408
Poggibonsi
SS429
Radda in Chianti
Castellina in Chianti
Gaiole in Chianti
Colle di Val d'Elsa
SS2
Lilliano
Cypress Forests
Fonterutoli
Castagnoli
SS484
Staggia
SS222
SS408
Quercegrossa
Strove
Poggiarello
SS2
Castelnuovo Berardenga
END Siena

Continue by climbing out of the city to the south, enjoying splendid views of Florence's skyline. After about 7km, the bustle of Florence fades as the route winds steadily upwards past airy olive groves towards **Impruneta** (15.5km). Terraced vineyards line both sides of the hilly, and slightly more travelled, route from Impruneta to **Strada in Chianti** (20.8km).

For a sample of the famed Chianti Classico, stop at one of the dozens of wineries that produce the vintage; a black cockerel indicates that Chianti Classico is manufactured on the premises. Veer to the west just before **Greve in Chianti** and grunt up a steep hill to the ancient castle-village of **Montefioralle**. If your equipment is sturdy enough for a short stretch of gravel, pay a visit to **Badia di Passignano**, an abbey founded in 1049 by Benedictine monks, before retracing the route back to Greve.

Greve in Chianti

Approximately halfway between Florence and Siena, Greve in Chianti sprung into existence in the 13th and 14th centuries. Originally accommodating the overflow population from castle communities, Greve quickly grew into an important trade centre and marketplace. The recent discovery of ancient grape seeds in a local archaeological excavation suggests that local, culti-

vated vineyards have been in existence for nearly 23 centuries. Today, Greve serves as the centre for tourist excursions into the Chianti region in search of wine and olive oil. Greve is also popular with trekkers, as there are a number of pleasant mule tracks suited to ambling.

Information The tourist office (☎ 055 854 62 87, e info@chiantiechianti.it), Viale G da Verrazzano 59, is just outside the city centre on the main road from Florence. Staff will book accommodation, recommend local vineyards for wine and olive oil tasting, and provide maps.

There is a Monte dei Paschi di Siena bank and ATM on Viale Vittorio on the way into town. There are no local bike shops.

Things to See & Do Though there's not a lot to see in Greve's old centre, a wander through **Piazza Matteotti** is pleasant enough. Now adorned with a monument dedicated to navigator Giovanni da Verrazzano, this was the local meeting and marketplace for centuries. Many of Greve's finest lunch and dinner spots, in addition to **wine** and **craft shops**, line the triangular 'square'. Stop for a taste of the region's local wine and culinary treats. Nearby, in between the piazzas Matteotti and Trieste, is the **Church of Santa Croce**, which houses a

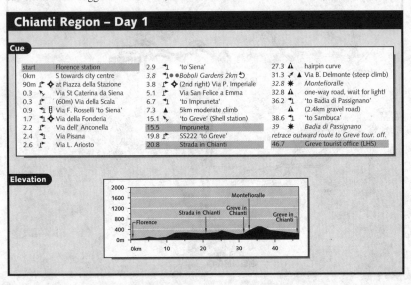

Chianti Region – Day 1

Cue

start	Florence station	2.9	'to Siena'	27.3	▲	hairpin curve	
0km	S towards city centre	3.8	●Boboli Gardens 2km ↻	31.3	↗ ▲	Via B. Delmonte (steep climb)	
90m	at Piazza della Stazione	3.8	✦ (2nd right) Via P. Imperiale	32.8	✱	Montefioralle	
0.3	Via St Caterina da Siena	5.1	Via San Felice a Emma	32.8	▲	one-way road, wait for light!	
0.3	(60m) Via della Scala	6.7	'to Impruneta'	36.2	'to Badia di Passignano'		
0.9	Via F. Rosselli 'to Siena'	7.3	▲	5km moderate climb	▲	(2.4km gravel road)	
1.7	Via della Fonderia	15.1	'to Greve' (Shell station)	38.6	'to Sambuca'		
2.2	Via dell' Anconella	15.5	Impruneta	39	✱	Badia di Passignano	
2.4	Via Pisana	19.8	SS222 'to Greve'	retrace outward route to Greve tour. off.			
2.6	Via L. Ariosto	20.8	Strada in Chianti	46.7	Greve tourist office (LHS)		

Elevation

15th-century triptych by Bicci di Lorenzo. The tourist office can provide details and directions for several walking or mountain-biking treks in the surrounding countryside, including one which links the ancient castles of Uzzano and Montefioralle, considered the oldest settlement in the Chianti hills, with the wooded hilltop San Michele Park via Roman and Etruscan pathways.

Places to Stay & Eat Budget accommodation is not the area's strong point and you'll need to book well ahead, since it is a popular area for tourists year-round. Albergo e Ristorante Giovanni da Verrazzano (☎ 055 85 31 89; Piazza Matteotti 28; singles/doubles €52/67) is worth a look, but Del Chianti (☎ 055 85 37 63; Piazza Matteotti 86; singles/doubles €83/93) is less interesting. The tourist office recommends the working farm, Casa Nova (☎/fax 055 85 34 59; Via di Uzzano 30; doubles with breakfast €70), just outside of Greve. Omero (☎ 055 85 07 16; e luca.casprini@trident.nettuno.it;singles/doubles €42/57) is a cheaper option, though about 7km from Greve in Passo dei Pecorai. There is a restaurant and a well-stocked café attached to the hotel.

Greve's Coop supermarket is located on Viale Vittorio, the main street through town. For lunch or dinner, try the delightful Nerbone di Greve restaurant, Caffé Le Logge, or

Caffé Lepante, all of which are moderately priced and located on Piazza Matteotti.

Day 2: Greve in Chianti to Siena
3–5½ hours, 55km

The familiar themes of vineyards and olive groves continue en route from Greve to Siena. The terrain is similar to the previous day: undulating hills with occasional steep climbs up to the hill towns.

The quiet, virtually traffic-free SS429 offers a stretch of easy riding before climbing up to the charming Radda in Chianti (21.9km). Park your bike at the base of Via Roma, just near the Cose Vecchio restaurant, and take a quick stroll through Radda's quaint main drag. Radda boasts one of the region's best tourist offices (☎ 0577 73 84 94) at Piazza Ferrucci 1. Stop in for information on winery tours and local walks. Radda's speciality meat and cheese shops, near the base of Via Roma, make a nice place to grab a quick bite.

Castellina in Chianti (33.5km) also boasts plenty of medieval charm, fine restaurants and modern conveniences. Hold on for a rip-roaring descent past cypress forests (37km) as you rush towards the distant marble domes and red-brick towers of Siena that lie on the horizon. In Siena (55km), delight in the architectural marvels of the main square, Il Campo, and the ornate Gothic cathedral.

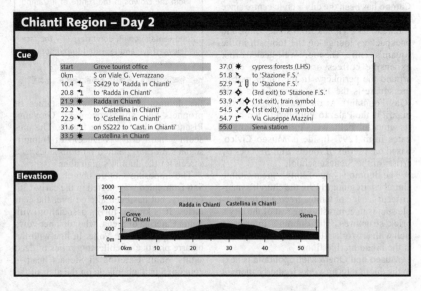

Chianti Region – Day 2

Cue

start	Greve tourist office	37.0 ✳	cypress forests (LHS)
0km	S on Viale G. Verrazzano	51.8 ↘	to 'Stazione F.S.'
10.4 ⌐	SS429 to 'Radda in Chianti'	52.9 ⌐ ⌂	to 'Stazione F.S.'
20.8 ⌐	to 'Radda in Chianti'	53.7 ◆	(3rd exit) to 'Stazione F.S.'
21.9 ✳	Radda in Chianti	53.9 ↗ ◆	(1st exit), train symbol
22.2 ↘	to 'Castellina in Chianti'	54.5 ↗ ◆	(1st exit), train symbol
22.9 ↘	to 'Castellina in Chianti'	54.7 ⌐	Via Giuseppe Mazzini
31.6 ⌐	on SS222 to 'Cast. in Chianti'	55.0	Siena station
33.5 ✳	Castellina in Chianti		

Elevation

Elevation profile (metres): 0m, 400, 800, 1200, 1600, 2000. Labels: Greve in Chianti, Radda in Chianti, Castellina in Chianti, Siena. Horizontal axis (km): 0km, 10, 20, 30, 40, 50.

TUSCANY

Siena

Siena is, without doubt, one of Italy's most enchanting cities. Its medieval centre bristles with Gothic buildings such as the Palazzo Pubblico on Il Campo (Siena's main square) and a wealth of artwork is contained in its numerous churches and small museums. Like Florence, Siena offers an incredible concentration of attractions.

Siena also makes a good base from which to explore central Tuscany, in particular the medieval towns of San Gimignano and Volterra. Note, however, that it can be difficult to find budget accommodation in Siena unless you book ahead. In August and during the city's famous twice-yearly festival, **Il Palio**, it is impossible to find accommodation without a reservation.

Information The APT office (☎ 0577 28 05 51, e aptsiena@siena.toscana.it) is at Piazza del Campo 56. ATMs are scattered throughout Siena, the highest concentration being on Banchi di Sopra. The best bike shop is Rossi Bike (☎ 0577 483 06) Via Camollia 204–206 just near the Porta Camollia. Siena has a local cycling club, Amici della Bicicletta F. Bacconi (☎ 0577 451 59) at Via Campanisi 32 (affiliated with the FIAB) that organises rides to nearby attractions.

Things to See & Do The magnificent **Il Campo** has been the city's civic centre since the mid-14th century. Tourists gather in the square to take a break from sightseeing, and backpackers lounge on the footpath in the square's centre. The more well-heeled drink expensive coffees or beers at the cafés around the periphery. In the upper part of the square is the 15th-century **Fonte Gaia** (Gay Fountain). At the lowest point of the piazza is the **Palazzo Pubblico** (town hall). Its graceful belltower, **Torre del Mangia**, dates from 1297. Inside is **Museo Civico**, based on a series of rooms with frescoes by artists of the Sienese school.

The **duomo** is one of Italy's great Gothic churches. Begun in 1196, the church's magnificent facade of white, green and red marble stands in contrast to the rest of the city's brick structures. The duomo's interior is rich with artworks. Its most precious feature is the inlaid marble floor.

Museo dell'Opera Metropolitana is next to the duomo. Its artworks formerly adorned

Il Palio

This spectacular event, held twice yearly on 2 July and 16 August in honour of the Virgin Mary, dates back to the Middle Ages and features a series of colourful pageants, a wild horse race around Il Campo and much celebrating in the streets.

On a rotating basis, 10 of Siena's 17 *contrade* (town districts) compete for the coveted *palio* (a silk banner). Each of the contrade has its own traditions, symbol and colours. The centuries-old local rivalries make the festival very much an event for the Sienese, though the horse race and pageantry attract larger crowds of both Italians and tourists.

On festival days, Il Campo becomes a racetrack, with a ring of packed dirt around its perimeter serving as the course. Starting at about 5pm, representatives of each contrada parade around the city in historical costume, each bearing their individual banners. For not much more than one exhilarating minute, the 10 horses and their bareback riders tear three times around Il Campo with a speed and violence that makes your hair stand on end. Even if a horse loses its rider, it is still eligible to win and, since many riders fall each year, it is the horses in the end that are the focus of the event. There is only one rule that riders do not interfere with the reins of other horses.

Join the crowds in the centre of Il Campo four hours before the start if you want a place on the barrier of the track. If you can't find a good vantage point, don't despair – the race is televised live and repeated throughout the evening on TV.

the duomo, including the 12 statues of prophets and philosophers by Giovanni Pisano that decorated the facade. The museum's main draw is Duccio di Buoninsegna's *Maestà*, painted on both sides as a screen for the duomo's high altar.

The imposing Gothic church **Chiesa di San Domenico** was started in the early 13th century, but has been altered over the centuries. It is known for its association with Santa Caterina di Siena, who took her vows in its Cappella delle Volte. In line with the bizarre practice of collecting relics of dead saints, Santa Caterina di Siena's head is contained in a tabernacle on the altar of the

Cappella di Santa Caterina. Also in the cappella are frescoes by Sodoma depicting events in the saint's life.

West along Via del Paradiso from Piazza Matteotti is Piazza San Domenico, from where you can see the massive **Fortezza Medicea**, built for Cosimo I de' Medici.

The city hosts **Siena Jazz** (☎ 0577 27 14 01), an international festival each July and August, with concerts at the Fortezza Medici as well as at various sites throughout the city.

Places to Stay For help finding a room, contact the APT or Siena Hotels Promotion (☎ 0577 28 80 84), Piazza San Domenico.

Colleverde (☎ 0577 28 00 44; Strada di Scacciapensieri 47; 1 night adult/child €10.50/ 5.20 plus €13 for a site; open late Mar–early Nov) is a camping ground north of the centre. **Guidoriccio** (☎ 0577 5 22 12; Via Fiorentina 89, Località Stellino; B&B €12, full meal €7.20) is a non-HI youth hostel about 2km northwest of the city centre. Leave the city by Via Vittorio Emanuele II, which is an extension of Via di Camollia.

In town, **Hotel Le Tre Donzelle** (☎ 0577 28 03 58; Via delle Donzelle 5; singles/doubles €24/39, doubles with bathroom €50) has clean, simple rooms and a secure garage for bikes. **Locanda Garibaldi** (☎ 0577 28 42 04; Via Giovanni Dupré 18; singles/doubles €24/44) is just south of Il Campo. **Piccolo Hotel il Palio** (☎ 0577 28 11 31; Piazza del Sale 19; singles/doubles €67.50/83) has bland rooms with bathroom. Bikes aren't allowed inside, but there's an outdoor stand nearby. The three-star **Hotel Minerva** (☎ 0577 28 44 74; Via Giuseppe Garibaldi 72-80; singles/doubles €47/62) is a more upmarket affair, with small, clean rooms with spectacular views. Lock bikes (for free) in the Fiat garage next door.

Places to Eat There are **Crai supermarkets** scattered around the town centre, including one at Via di Città 152–156 and another on Via Cecco Angiolieri. **Nannini** (Banchi di Sopra 22) is one of the city's finest cafés. The cheap self-service **Spizzico-Ciao**, where you can eat well for €10.50 or less, is on Il Campo. **Hostaria il Carroccio** (Via del Casato di Sotto 32; pasta €5.50) is south of Il Campo and serves excellent pasta. **Osteria del Castelvecchio** (Via di Castelvecchio 65) is more expensive but highly regarded by locals. **Al Marsili** (Via del Castoro 3; 1st course €4.50, 2nd course €8) is one of the city's better-known restaurants. **Ristorante da Mugolone** (Via dei Pelligrini 8; 1st course €5.50, 2nd course €8-13) is an excellent restaurant with local specialities. **La Pizzeria di nonno Mede** (Via Camporegio 21; pizza €5.50) has a spectacular view of the duomo and serves the best pizza in town.

Getting There & Away The Tra-in/SITA bus office (☎ 0577 20 42 46) is located underneath the Piazza A. Gramsci on La Lizza. Regular buses leave for Florence (€6.50, 1¼ hours, hourly) and other destinations in the Crete and Chianti regions. Daily SENA buses also connect Siena with Rome (€13.50, three hours, up to seven daily). The Siena APT office and the bus station have timetables.

The frequency of train times and the ease of transporting a bike by train, make this the preferable travel option. Siena's station is just north of the city centre on Piazzale Rosselli. To get to Rome, it is necessary to change in Chiusi (Siena–Chiusi €4.70, 1½ hours, half-hourly; Chiusi–Rome €8, two hours, every other hour). Siena to Florence (€5.10, 1½ hours, hourly) is an easy jump, though some lines change in Empoli, adding another 30 minutes to the journey.

Sienese Day Trip

Duration	4–7 hours
Distance	71.7km
Difficulty	moderate
Start/End	Siena

If you're based in Siena and are lucky enough to have a spare afternoon, consider this delightful, day-long ramble through the Sienese countryside to the ruined abbey of San Galgano. The day's many attractive characteristics include directions that are straightforward and easy to follow; kilometres of cycling through sunflower fields and farmland; the opportunity to dine at some of the area's best restaurants; and an afternoon spent among the tranquil ruins of one of the country's finest and most spectacular Gothic buildings.

TUSCANY

PLANNING
Maps

The free *Siena APT* map handed out at the main APT office in Siena is adequate for this ride, as is Itografia Artistica Cartographica's 1:150,000 *Siena: Carta della Provincia*, which can be purchased at most tourist offices and bookstores.

ACCESS TOWN

See Siena (p104).

Farm with a Mission

The Sienese Day Trip also passes one of Tuscany's most lovely, interesting and ambitious working farms, Tenuta di Spannocchia (☎ 0577 75 21, Ⓦ www.spannocchia.org). Situated on 1200 acres of vineyards, olive groves, fields and forests, Spannocchia is also a wildlife sanctuary, a centre for educational programmes and conservation projects, and an *agriturismo* (tourist accommodation on farms) that offers both daily and long-term accommodation possibilities.

An organic farm for the past 800 years, written records trace Spannocchia's existence to around the mid-13th century. The villa's grand, crenellated tower is believed to date back even further to the 12th century. In addition to acres of farmland and protected forests, the remains of the Santa Lucia monastery and the Romanesque bridge, Ponte Della Pia, can also be found on the estate's grounds.

Spannocchia sponsors various farming, gardening and architectural internships. As well, the estate hosts a number of independent archaeological, art and cooking programmes. Those seriously interested in gathering information about the estate or staying at Spannocchia, should call in advance for rates and information. To stay, you must be a member of the Spannocchia Foundation (€28). The membership, good for one year, helps support the farm and includes a subscription to the organisation's newsletter. Those wishing to explore the grounds or purchase any of the farm's organic products (wine, olive oil, honey etc) may simply drop by. Keep in mind that it's a working business, and there's much to be done.

THE RIDE

Winding in and out of Siena can be a bit tricky, but after crossing the bridge at 4.9km, and merging onto the SS73 immediately afterwards, this ride is a breeze. The first 20km on the way to San Galgano are gently rolling, the last 15km are steeper but manageable.

After only about 10km, the busy medieval streets of Siena give way to seemingly endless stretches of wheat and sunflower fields. Consider a side trip through a sea of yellow flowers to one of the finest local restaurants, **Ampugnano** (13.6km), situated beside the area's tiny airstrip. A bit further along the route is the 13th-century **Ponte della Pia** (20.3km), once an important point on the 'Massetana' road, which linked Siena with Massa Marittima in the Middle Ages. The bridge can be crossed by foot, and adventurers may want to tromp around in search of the nearby ruins of the **Santa Lucia** monastery. Further down the road, the privately owned estate/farm/wildlife sanctuary/*agriturismo*, **Tenuta di Spannocchia** (21.8km) is one of the more fascinating operations in Tuscany.

The ride gets a bit more challenging at this point, with some steep, switchbacked inclines and descents, though it's not long before the turn-off for the **Abbazia San Galgano** appears and the colossal grey walls of the ruined Gothic abbey loom solemnly on the horizon. A former Cistercian abbey, San Galgano's

---

Sienese Day Trip

Cue

start		Siena station
0km		SE towards Siena
0.3	↑ 🚦	Via G. Mazzini
1.0	↑ 🚦	Via G. Garibaldi
1.5	↗	Via di Camollia
1.6	↰	Via dei Gazzini
1.7	↱	Via R. Franci to fortezza
1.8	↗	Via Armando Diaz (past fort)
2.3	↘	to 'tutte le direzione'
2.5	↰	Via C. Battisti ('tutte le direzione')
4.7	↗ ✦	to 'Sovicille'
13.6 ●●		*Ristorante Ampugnano 4km ↻*
20.3	✳	Ponte della Pia bridge (LHS)
	✳	Santa Lucia monastery
21.8 ●●	↰	*Tenuta di Spannocchia 4km ↻*
33.6	↱	to 'Abbazia San Galgano'
35.8	↰	to 'Abbazia San Galgano'
35.8	✳	(50m) Abbazia San Galgano
retrace outbound route to Siena		
71.7		Siena station

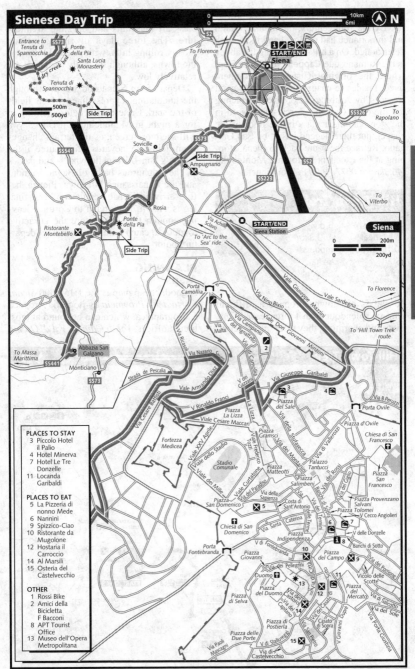

Sienese Day Trip

0 — 10km
0 — 6mi

(↑) N

To Florence

START/END
Siena

To Rapolano

SS326

To Viterbo

SS52

SS223

[Inset: Side Trip detail]

Entrance to Tenuta di Spannocchia
SS73
Ponte della Pia
dry creek bed
Santa Lucia Monastery
Tenuta di Spannocchia
0 — 500m
0 — 500yd
Side Trip

Soville
SS73
Side Trip
Ampugnano

Rosia

Ristorante Montebello

Ponte della Pia
Side Trip

To Massa Marittima
SS441
Abbazia San Galgano
Monticiano
SS73

TUSCANY

[Inset: Siena]

START/END
Siena Station

Via Achille Sclavo
To 'Arc to the Sea' ride

Siena

0 — 200m
0 — 200yd

To Florence

To 'Hill Town Trek' route

Porta Camollia
1

Via Nino Bixio
Viale Giuseppe Mazzini
Viale Sardegna

Via Malta
Via Campansi del Pignattello
Viale Don Giovanni Minzoni

2

Via di Camollia
V de Garzoni
Via Nazario Sauro
Via Ricasoli

Via Giuseppe Garibaldi

3
4
Via B Peruzzi
Porta Ovile

Piazza del Sale
Via della Sapienza

Strada de Pescaia
Vale Armando Diaz

V Rinaldo Franci
Piazza La Lizza
La Lizza
Viale Cesare Maccari

Piazza d'Ovile
Chiesa di San Francesco
Piazza San Francesco

Via Cesare Battisti
Fortezza Medicea

Piazza Gramsci
Viale XXV Aprile
Viale dello Stadio
Viale Curtatone
Viale dei Mille

Piazza Matteotti

Palazzo Tantucci
Piazza Provenzano Salvani
V Cecco Angiolieri

Stadio Comunale

Piazza Salimbeni
Banchi di Sopra
Piazza Tolomei

Piazza San Domenico
X 5

Costa di Sant'Antonio

Piazza Indipendenza
6
7
V delle Donzelle
8

Chiesa di San Domenico

Via Santa Caterina
Via della Sapienza
Via di Città

Piazza Tolomei
Via Banchi di Sotto

Porta Fontebranda

Via di Fontebranda
10
Via del Pellegrini
Piazza del Campo
X 9

Piazza Giovanni

11
13
Duomo
Via di Stalloreggi
Piazza del Duomo
12
14

Piazza del Mercato

Vicolo delle Scotte
Via di Salicotto
Via del Sole

Piazza di Selva

Via del Capitano
Via di Città
Casato di Sopra

Piazza di Postierla

V Giovanni Dupré
Via di Porta Giustizia

Piazza delle Due Porte

15 X

Via Paolo Mascagni
V di Stalloreggi
Via di Castelvecchio
Casato di Sotto

PLACES TO STAY
3 Piccolo Hotel il Palio
4 Hotel Minerva
7 Hotel Le Tre Donzelle
11 Locanda Garibaldi

PLACES TO EAT
5 La Pizzeria di nonno Mede
6 Nannini
9 Spizzico-Ciao
10 Ristorante da Mugolone
12 Hostaria il Carroccio
14 Al Marsili
15 Osteria del Castelvecchio

OTHER
1 Rossi Bike
2 Amici della Bicicletta F Bacconi
8 APT Tourist Office
13 Museo dell'Opera Metropolitana

monks were among Tuscany's most powerful. By the 16th century, the monks' wealth and importance had declined and the church deteriorated. On a hill overlooking the abbey is the Romanesque **Cappella di Monte Siepi** where the original Cistercian settlement lived. Inside the chapel are badly preserved frescoes by Ambrogio Lorenzetti depicting the life of St Galgano. A real-life 'sword in the stone' is under glass in the floor of the chapel, put there, legend has it, by San Galgano. Retrace the route back to Siena, stopping at the excellent **Ristorante Montebello** *(46.3km; ☎ 0577 79 90 86)* for dinner.

Hill Town Trek

Duration	3 days
Distance	150.8km
Difficulty	moderate
Start	Siena
End	Cortona

Tuscany's hill towns promise a different kind of splendour than Florence or Siena. Cosy and charming, they offer quaint seren-

ity and dramatic views rather than world-class art museums and dazzling architecture. The three days of riding include mostly rolling hills, with steep climbs into the towns, although the daily distances are relatively low.

Depart from Siena and wander through the undulating, cypress-lined wheat fields of the stark Crete region before settling in for a night in Montalcino. On Day 2 you will see more green, as the terrain changes from fields to vineyards – the source of the region's famed Brunello wine – and passes by the sulphurous baths of Bagno Vignoni and the Renaissance hill town, Pienza, before arriving in Montepulciano. The final leg is a short, flat stretch to Cortona, leaving enough time to explore the attractive town or to catch a train to your next departure point.

PLANNING
Maps

A good, cheap map is the 1:150,000 *Siena: Carta della Provincia* by Itografia Artistica Cartographica, which can be found at most tourist offices. *Val di Chiana, Val d'Orchia*

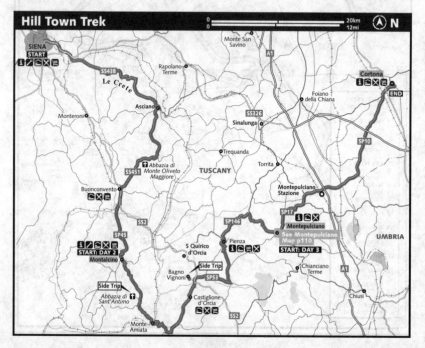

by Edizioni Multigraphic (1:50,000) has mountain-bike trails and can be purchased at bookstores.

ACCESS TOWN
See Siena (p104).

THE RIDE
Day 1: Siena to Montalcino
3½–6 hours, 57.9km

The scenery along this stretch varies from stark and barren to green and fertile, but is dramatic throughout. The ride is hilly, with some particularly tough stretches between Asciano and the Abbazia di Monte Oliveto Maggiore. The final 6km is also steep.

The departure from Siena station is a bit hectic. Proceed straight through five round-abouts, following signs for Arezzo. About 10km from Siena, busy arterial roads give way to the spacious wheat fields and olive groves of **Le Crete**. Peaceful and breathtaking, the landscape in this tiny geographic region radiates violet or golden hues depending on the season. Cypress-lined roads meander to the **Abbazia di Monte Oliveto Maggiore** (35.5km), where things look considerably less parched. The abbazia, a 14th-century monastery, is famous for its **Signorelli and Sodoma frescoes**, the later of which are considered controversial due to their effeminate portrayals of religious

icons. The monastery is open from 9.15am to noon and 3.15pm to 6pm daily.

Enjoy a rip-roaring descent (on excellent pavement) into Buonconvento. A few flat kilometres offer a moment of respite before the challenging, though visually stunning, grunt up to **Montalcino**, one of Tuscany's quaintest hill towns. To find the tourist office, make a sharp left hairpin turn from Piazza del Popolo towards Piazza Garibaldi. The office is on the left.

Montalcino
A pretty town perched high above the Orcia valley, Montalcino is best known for its wine, the Brunello. Produced only in the vineyards surrounding the town, it is said to be one of Italy's best reds.

Information The Pro Loco tourist office (☎ 0577 84 93 31, ⓦ www.digitamiata.com/promontalcino), Via Costa del Municipio 8, is just off Piazza del Popolo, near the towered Palazzo Comunale. The office sells Club Orso on Bike's *Biking in Val d'Orcia*, a mountain-biking guide to the region, for €7.80. There's an ATM in Piazza del Popolo and several others sprinkled throughout town.

LM Bike (☎ 0577 84 82 82), Viale Piero Strozzi 31, operates out of the town's only petrol station (IP). The store has a modest

TUSCANY

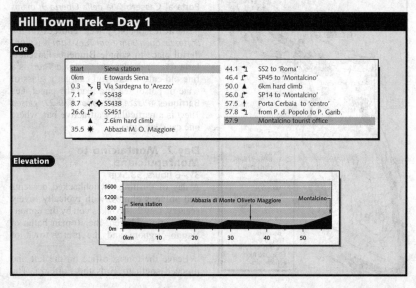

Hill Town Trek – Day 1

Cue

start	Siena station		44.1 ↰	SS2 to 'Roma'
0km	E towards Siena		46.4 ↳	SP45 to 'Montalcino'
0.3 ↘ ⍿	Via Sardegna to 'Arezzo'		50.0 ▲	6km hard climb
7.1 ↗	SS438		56.0 ↳	SP14 to 'Montalcino'
8.7 ↗ ◆	SS438		57.5 ↑	Porta Cerbaia to 'centro'
26.6 ↳	SS451		57.8 ↰	from P. d. Popolo to P. Garib.
▲	2.6km hard climb		57.9	Montalcino tourist office
35.5 ✳	Abbazia M. O. Maggiore			

Elevation

supply of gear and performs minor repairs for €15 to €20 per hour. It also rents mountain bikes (€13 to €15.50 per day).

Things to See & Do Plenty of *enoteche* (wine bars) around town provide you with the chance to taste and buy Brunello, as well as the other main local wine, the Rosso di Montalcino.

The **Fortezza** (Piazzale Fortezza), an impressive 14th-century fortress that was later expanded under the Medici dukes, dominates the town's southern end. You can sample and buy local wines in the *enoteca* inside, from where you can also climb up to the ramparts of the fort.

Museo Civico e Diocesano d'Arte Sacra (☎ 0577 84 60 14; Via Ricasoli), housed in the former convent of the neighbouring **Chiesa di Sant' Agostino**, contains an important collection of religious art from the town and surrounding region. Among the items on show are a triptych by Duccio di Buoninsegna and a *Madonna col Bambino* by Simone Martini.

To visit the local vineyards get a list from the tourist office as many are only open on weekends and some require a booking. The

office can also provide a full list of Brunello producers and information on good years.

Places to Stay The hotel possibilities in Montalcino are limited but adequate, and the surrounding countryside is dotted with *agriturismos*. The tourist office has complete lists.

Il Giardino (☎/fax 0577 84 82 57; Piazza Cavour 4; doubles with bathroom €52) is the best bet, with a small courtyard for bikes. **Albergo Il Giglio** (☎/fax 0577 84 81 67; Via Soccorso Saloni 5; singles/doubles €47/68) has comfortable rooms and is an excellent choice. **Hotel dei Capitani** (☎ 0577 84 72 27; Via Lapini 6; doubles €100) is a little more expensive and also has a little less atmosphere. **Agriturismo Aiole** (☎/fax 0577 88 74 54; Strada Provinciale 22 della Grossola; doubles with breakfast €57) is a pleasant, quiet B&B with a pool located just off the route from Montalcino to Castiglione d'Orcia.

Places to Eat There's a **Coop supermarket** on the corner of Via Sant'Agostino and Viale della Liberta. You'll eat well at **Ristorante Il Giardino** (Piazza Cavour 1; dinner €25; closed Wed), next to the hotel of the same name. **Trattoria Sciame** (Via Ricasoli 9; mains around €7; closed Tues) has straightforward, well-prepared meals. **Osteria Porta al Cassero** (Via della Liberta 9; mains around €5; closed Wed) has home-made pasta at reasonable prices. **Enoteca** (in the Fortezza; open 9am-6pm Tues-Sun) is a wonderful place to sample Brunello. **Fiaschetteria** (Piazza del Popolo 6; closed Thur) is a fine old café where you can get a glass of wine or pot of tea and read the paper. **Les Barriques** (Piazza del Popolo 20-22; closed Tues) is a particularly attractive bar, where one can also dine.

Day 2: Montalcino to Montepulciano

3½–6 hours, 58.5km
A day of thrilling, switchbacked descents and arduous climbs, with typically lovely scenery, Day 2 also takes you by the famous Sant'Antimo church, the Roman baths of Bagno Vignoni and the pretty town of Pienza.

Leave the tourist office on the left and proceed south towards the Fortezza. The

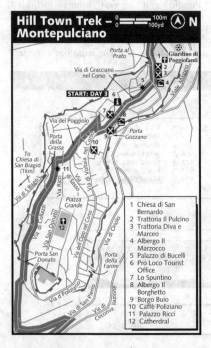

Hill Town Trek –
Montepulciano

0 —— 100m
0 —— 100yd N

1 Chiesa di San Bernardo
2 Trattoria Il Pulcino
3 Trattoria Diva e Marceo
4 Albergo Il Marzocco
5 Palazzo di Bucelli
6 Pro Loco Tourist Office
7 Lo Spuntino
8 Albergo Il Borghetto
9 Borgo Buio
10 Caffè Poliziano
11 Palazzo Ricci
12 Cathedral

hilltop vantage point and pleasant scenery make up for the chunky pavement (caution!) on the descent out of Montalcino. At 9.4km, visit the 12th-century Romanesque **Abbazia di Sant'Antimo**, built on the site of a monastery founded by Charlemagne in AD 781. The climb to Castiglione d'Orcia is hard work, but the view on the descent to **Bagno Vignoni** (29.9km) is generous compensation. Visit the picturesque **hot-spring pool** built by the Medici before pedalling to **Pienza** (43.7km), a superb example of Renaissance architecture and town planning. See the central square, Piazza Pio II, and the cathedral and Palazzo Piccolomini located on it, before grabbing a bite at one of the pizzerie on Piazza Dante Alighieri.

Enjoy a relatively flat, vineyard-lined stretch en route to Montepulciano (58.5km), until the final 500m – a brutally steep final incline. Finding the tourist office in Montepulciano is an ordeal. Be patient and enjoy meandering through this little maze of a town.

Montepulciano

Set atop a narrow ridge of volcanic rock, Montepulciano, like Montalcino, combines Tuscany's superb countryside with some of the region's finest wines. This medieval town is the perfect place to spend a quiet day or two.

Information The Pro Loco tourist office (☎ 0578 75 73 41) is on Via di Gracciano nel Corso, next door to the Chiesa di Sant'Agostino at the lower (northern) end of town. There are a few banks with ATMs scattered about the town, including a Banca Toscano across from the tourist office. There are no bicycle shops in Montepulciano centre.

Things to See & Do Most of the main sights are clustered around Piazza Grande, although the town's streets boast a wealth of palaces and other fine buildings.

At the northernmost end of town, near Porta al Prato, is the 18th-century **Chiesa di San Bernardo**. Nearby is the late-Renaissance **Palazzo Avignonesi** by Giacomo da Vignola. Several other **mansions** line Via di Gracciano nel Corso including the **Palazzo di Bucelli** at No 73. Its facade features Etruscan and Latin inscriptions.

Piazza Michelozzo (in front of the tourist office) is dominated by the Renaissance facade of Michelozzo's **Chiesa di Sant' Agostino**. In front is a medieval tower house, **Torre di Pulcinella**, topped by the town clock and the figure of Pulcinella (Punch of *Punch & Judy* fame), who strikes the hours.

In the Renaissance **Palazzo Ricci** on Via Ricci is one of the town's wine *cantine* (wine cellars), the Cantina Redi.

TUSCANY

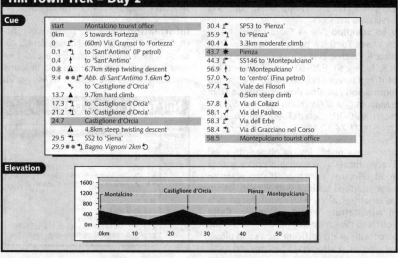

Hill Town Trek – Day 2

Cue

start	Montalcino tourist office		30.4 ↱	SP53 to 'Pienza'
0km	S towards Fortezza		35.9 ↰	to 'Pienza'
0 ↱	(60m) Via Gramsci to 'Fortezza'		40.4 ▲	3.3km moderate climb
0.1 ↰	to 'Sant'Antimo' (IP petrol)		43.7 ✴	Pienza
0.4 ↑	to 'Sant'Antimo'		44.3 ↱	SS146 to 'Montepulciano'
0.8 ▲	6.7km steep twisting descent		56.9 ↑	to 'Montepulciano'
9.4 ●●↱	Abb. di Sant'Antimo 1.6km ⟳		57.0 ↘	to 'centro' (Fina petrol)
↘	to 'Castiglione d'Orcia'		57.4 ↰	Viale dei Filosofi
13.7 ▲	9.7km hard climb		▲	0.5km steep climb
17.3 ↰	to 'Castiglione d'Orcia'		57.8 ↑	Via di Collazzi
21.2 ↰	to 'Castiglione d'Orcia'		58.1 ↙	Via del Paolino
24.7	Castiglione d'Orcia		58.3 ↱	Via dell Erbe
▲	4.8km steep twisting descent		58.4 ↰	Via di Gracciano nel Corso
29.5 ↰	SS2 to 'Siena'		58.5	Montepulciano tourist office
29.9 ●●↰	Bagno Vignoni 2km ⟳			

Elevation

Piazza Grande marks the highest point of the town and features the austere **Palazzo Comunale**, a 13th-century Gothic building. From the top of the 14th-century tower, on a clear day, you can see the Monti Sibillini to the east and Siena to the northwest. To climb the tower you'll need to get permission from the guardian first.

Also on the piazza is the **Palazzo Contucci**, now a wine cellar. The **cathedral**, on the southern side of Piazza Grande, contains a triptych above the altar depicting the Assumption, by Taddeo da Bartolo.

Outside the town wall, about 1km from Porta della Grassa, stands **Chiesa di San Biagio**, a fine Renaissance church built by Antonio da Sangallo il Vecchio and consecrated in 1529 by the Medici pope Clement VII.

Places to Stay Accommodation in Montepulciano is limited, so plan ahead. The tourist office has a list of *affittacamere* (rooms for rent) if the hotels are booked.

Albergo Il Marzocco (☎ 0578 75 72 62; *Piazza Savonarola 18; singles/doubles with bathroom & breakfast €83*) is an excellent, though pricey, accommodation option, with a locked garage for bikes. **Albergo Il Borghetto** (☎ 0578 75 75 35; *Via Borgo Buio 7*) has comparable prices and is also a pleasant place to rest.

Places to Eat There are no major supermarkets in town, so stock up at a small *alimentari* (grocery shop) along the Via Gracciano nel Corso.

Lo Spuntino (*Via di Gracciano nel Corso 25; closed Tues*) has pizza by the slice. **Trattoria Il Pulcino** (*Via di Gracciano nel Corso 108; full meals €20-30; closed Fri*) is a decent restaurant. Popular with locals and tourists and just next door is **Trattoria Diva e Marceo** (*Via di Gracciano nel Corso 92; full meals €20-30; closed Tues*). **Borgo Buio** (☎ 0578 71 74 97; *Via Borgo Buio 10; closed Thur in summer, Sun evening & Mon lunch in winter*) is a rustic, low-lit place with good Tuscan meals at reasonable prices with a good selection of wines. It can organise wine and food tastings with various Italian personalities, along with occasional courses in wine-tasting. For good coffee, **Caffè Poliziano** (*Via di Voltaia nel Corso 27*) is the place with its magnificent views and pleasant interior. It also serves pastries and food.

Day 3: Montepulciano to Cortona
2–3½ hours, 34.4km

Flatter and slightly less dramatic than the previous two days, Day 3 is a significantly shorter and easier ride. After a quick, thrilling descent out of Montepulciano, cruise along at about 300m until the final ascent into Cortona.

On a clear day, Cortona is visible from Montepulciano. To spot your destination, glance off to the northeast as you scream out of Montepulciano towards the plains below. Gentler hills and stretches of newer pavement make this ride a breeze. The landscape is mainly **wheat fields**, **vineyards**, **olive groves** and **sunflowers**. After about 20km, Cortona looms grandly above you on an intimidating ridge. Fortunately, there are several gradual ascents into the centre of town. Though this route follows a slightly longer approach, the grade is manageable, making the climb a pleasure rather than a chore. Take the afternoon to see Cortona at a leisurely pace, or catch a train to your next destination.

Cortona
Set into the side of a hill covered with olive groves, Cortona, which has changed little since the Middle Ages, offers sensational views across the Tuscan and Umbrian countryside. It was a small settlement when the Etruscans moved in during the 8th century BC and it later became a Roman town.

Information The APT tourist office (☎ 0575 63 03 52), Via Nazionale 42, can assist with a hotel list and the useful *Cortona* brochure, a complete guide to tourist essentials. There are several ATMs on Via

Hill Town Trek – Day 3

Cue		
start		Montepulciano tourist office
0km	↑	NE on Via di Grac. nel Corso
0.2	↑	SP17 to 'Perugia/Cortona'
	⚠	4.6km steep descent
5.7	↙	to 'Montepul. S. NE' (at fork)
6.1	↰	to 'Montepulciano Stazione'
9.3	↙	Via Modena/SP10 to 'Cortona'
21.8	↑	to 'Cortona'
28.9	↰	to 'Cortona'
29.2	↱ 🄱	Via L. Signorelli/SP34
33.2	↱	to 'Centro Nazionale'
34.2	↑	Via Nazionale (at Piazza Garibaldi)
34.4		Cortona tourist office (LHS)

Nazionale, including one on Piazza Garibaldi just as you enter the town. There are no bicycle-servicing shops in Cortona.

Things to See & Do Start in Piazza della Repubblica with the crenellated **Palazzo Comunale**. To the north is Piazza Signorelli, named after the artist and dominated by the 13th-century **Palazzo Casali**. Any hint of its medieval grandeur has been obscured by the facade added in the 17th century. Inside is the **Museo dell'Accademia Etrusca** (☎ 0575 63 72 35), which displays Etruscan artefacts discovered near Cortona.

Museo Diocesano (☎ 0575 62 830) is in the former church of Gesù. It contains a fine, if limited, collection of artworks, including a remarkable Roman-era sarcophagus made of Carrara marble, along with a series of paintings by Luca Signorelli.

At the eastern edge of the city centre is the **Chiesa di Santa Margherita**, which features the Gothic tomb of St Margaret. Further up the hill is the 16th-century **Fortezza Medicea**, built for the Medici.

Every year for about a week from late August into the first days of September, Cortona becomes a big Mostra Antiquaria, one of Italy's main antique furniture fairs. Getting a room in Cortona around then is virtually impossible without a reservation.

A few kilometres out of town, back towards the Camucia train station, is the weather-beaten **Chiesa di Santa Maria del Calcinaio**. Note how the main body of the church is free of columns and is basically a two-storey structure topped with tabernacle windows – all unusual elements.

Places to Stay The city has several cheap hotels and a hostel, and finding a room shouldn't be a problem. **Ostello San Marco** (☎/fax 0575 60 13 92; Via Guiseppe Maffei 57; B&B €10.50; open 15 Mar–15 Oct) is an attractive HI hostel east of Piazza Garibaldi. **Albergo Athens** (☎ 0575 63 05 08; Via Sant' Antonio 12; singles/doubles €24/42) is the next cheapest option, with smallish, straightforward rooms. A great, though pricier, bet is **Albergo Italia** (☎ 0575 63 02 54; Via Ghibellina 5; singles/doubles with bathroom, TV, air-con & phone €60/90), an old mansion just off Piazza della Repubblica. There is a locked garage across the street for bikes. **Hotel San Michele** (☎ 0575 60 43 48; Via Guelfa 15; singles/doubles with phone, TV & minibar €83/130) is the luxury option in town.

Places to Eat Piazza della Repubblica hosts a **produce market** each Saturday and several grocery shops dot the area. **Trattoria Dardano** (Via Dardano 24; full meals around €20; closed Wed) serves a delicious ravioli al burro e salvia (butter and sage ravioli). Il **Cacciatore** (Via Roma 11; full meal & wine €28; closed Wed) is one of the city's better restaurants and offers local specialities. **Pane e Vino** (Piazza Signorelli 27; meals €20-25) is a huge and hugely popular dining hall in the heart of Cortona. You may find you have to queue. **Osteria del Teatro** (Via Giuseppe Maffei 5; full meal around €30; closed Wed) is the pick of the crop. Your meal could include ravioli ai fiori di zucca (pumpkin-flower ravioli).

Getting There & Away Because Cortona is on the Rome–Florence train line, it is quite easy to get to/from either location. It's a bit tougher to get back to Siena. Cortona/Camucia is the closest train station to Cortona (about 4km downhill from town, off the road to Montepulciano). Regionali and diretto trains run to Florence (€6, 1¼ hours, hourly) and diretto trains to Rome (€9, 2¼ hours, every two hours). To return to Siena, first take the Florence–Rome train to Chiusi, then change for Siena (€6.50, 2¼ hours, every two hours).

Arc to the Sea

Duration	3 days
Distance	202.4km
Difficulty	moderate
Start	Siena
End	Massa Marittima

Heading northwest out of Siena and arcing towards the sea, this ride visits the tourist destinations of San Gimignano and Volterra before settling in to some less-explored countryside near Massa Marittima. Terrainwise, expect typically rolling hills, with short, steep climbs into the towns. The low daily mileage makes this ride only moderately difficult.

TUSCANY

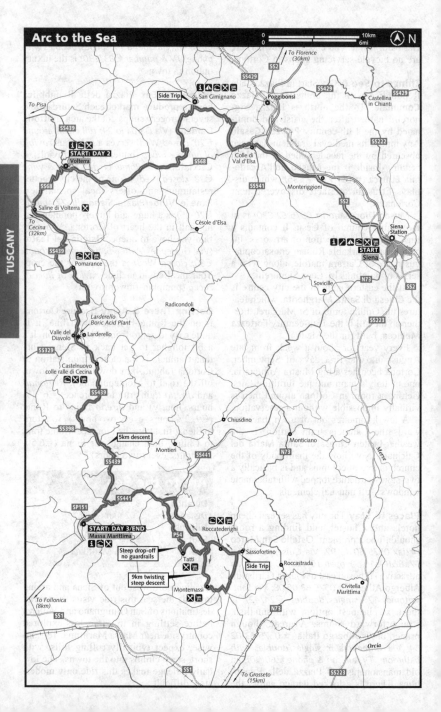

The walled medieval fortress, Monteriggioni, is a short hop from Siena, and the famed towers of San Gimignano a quick trip from there. Day 1 ends in atmospheric Volterra. Day 2 is a pleasant-enough jaunt to the sleepy 8th-century mining town of Massa Marittima. The last day is a loop that explores some of the most picturesque, undiscovered hill towns in Tuscany: Montemassi, Sassofortino and Roccatederighi. Enjoy a day of cycling through sleepy hamlets and along deserted roads. This area is known by Tuscans for its thick forests, hiking trails and wildlife.

Although this route doesn't deposit you right at the edge of the sea, Massa Marittima is situated within easy striking distance of the coast. Follonica, the nearest point on the shore, is a quick downhill spin, and Piombino, where ferries depart for Elba, is an easy (but unattractive) ride. Because the ride to Piombino is unappetisingly industrial, it has not been documented as Day 4 of this route. However, tagging on a trip to Elba is an excellent option. To get to Piombino, simply follow the signs out of Massa Marittima to Follonica, then take the coastal route (not the SS1) northwest all the way to Piombino.

Consider your pre-/post-ride itinerary before embarking on this trip, as it's difficult to get to/from Massa Marittima. This route works well if you're planning a visit to Elba or continuing on to Rome. Getting from Massa Marittima to Florence or Siena is an ordeal.

PLANNING
When to Ride
Visiting San Gimignano in July or August can be a permanently scarring travel experience, as tourist hordes clog the narrow streets, and entrance lines to attractions wind endlessly about. Any other time is preferable.

Maps
The map for the Hill Town Trek can also be used for this ride: 1:150,000 *Siena: Carta della Provincia*. Touring Club Italiano's *La Via Francigena in Provincia di Siena* is also good and is free at the Siena tourist office.

ACCESS TOWN
See Siena (p104).

THE RIDE
Day 1: Siena to Volterra
3½–6½ hours, 65.4km
One of the most popular and interesting routes in Tuscany, Day 1 combines pleasant riding with two exceptional points of interest. The ride is fairly flat to San Gimignano, but gets a bit harder (and prettier) from there. Though the second half of the route is hilly, the undulations don't rise or fall more than about 150m at a time.

From Siena, at 12.3km, is the 13th-century, medieval stronghold of **Monteriggioni**, the walls and towers of which constitute one of the most complete examples of a **fortified bastion** in Tuscany. Slightly off the road, it's easy to bike right past Monteriggioni. Look for it off to the right at 11.6km, then keep your eyes peeled for the turn-off. Continue by ambling along through sunflower fields towards the famed, towered skyline of **San Gimignano**, a side trip not to be missed. To reach San Gimignano, continue straight at the roundabout (35.7km), instead of following the route to the left. Plan on spending several hours in San Gimignano. For a list of attractions, enter the old city at Porta San Giovanni and walk your bike to the Pro Loco tourist office (☎ 0577 94 00 08) on Piazza del Duomo.

Leaving San Gimignano, the route twists and turns through lush olive groves and farmland before reaching the ancient Etruscan

Arc to the Sea – Day 1

Cue		
start		Siena station
0km		W Via Achille Sclavo
1.1	↱ 🚻	SS2 to 'Firenze'
12.3	✳	*Monteriggioni (RHS)*
13.4	↰	to 'Colle Val d' Elsa'
22.6	↱	to 'San Gimignano'
22.8	↱	to 'San Gimignano'
22.9	↰	to 'San Gimignano'
26.1	↱	to 'San Gimignano'
31.8	↰	to 'San Gimignano 5km'
35.7 ●●↑		*San Gimignano 1km* ↺
	↰ ✦	to 'Volterra'
47.8	↱	SS68 to 'Volterra 15km'
64.0	↱	Via Porta a Selci (at obelisk)
64.2	↑	Via Don Minzoni/Via Gramsci
65.2	↰	Via Giacomo Matteotti
65.3	↱	into Piazza dei Priori
65.4		Volterra tourist office

town of **Volterra**, which offers plenty of attractions of its own, and some of Tuscany's best budget accommodation.

Volterra

Straggling high on a rocky plateau, Volterra's medieval ramparts give the windswept town a proud and forbidding air. Originally an Etruscan settlement, Volterra was absorbed into the Roman confederation around 260 BC.

Information The tourist office (☎ 0588 8 61 50), Piazza dei Priori, is in the centre of town. ATMs can be found in the Piazza dei Priori, and along the Via Gramsci as you enter town. There are no bicycle repair shops in Volterra, so have any repairs done before leaving Siena.

Things to See & Do A €6 ticket, valid for a year, covers visits to Museo Etrusco Guarnacci, Pinacoteca Comunale and Museo Diocesano di Arte Sacra. The Roman theatre and Parco Archeologico are free.

Piazza dei Priori is surrounded by austere medieval mansions. The 13th-century **Palazzo dei Priori** is the oldest seat of local government in Tuscany and is believed to have been a model for Florence's Palazzo Vecchio.

The **cathedral**, built in the 12th and 13th centuries, is on Via Turazza. Inside, highlights include a small fresco by Benozzo Gozzoli.

The **Pinacoteca Comunale** (Via dei Sarti 1), in the Palazzo Minucci Solaini, houses a modest collection of local, Sienese and Florentine art.

All of the exhibits in the fascinating **Museo Etrusco Guarnacci** (Via Don Minzoni) were unearthed locally, including a vast collection of some 600 funerary urns.

Further along Via Minzoni is the entrance to the **Fortezza Medicea**, built in the 14th century and altered by Lorenzo the Magnificent, and now used as a prison.

Just west of the fort is the pleasant **Parco Archeologico**, whose archaeological remains have suffered with the passage of time. This is where the heart of the ancient city, the Acropolis, was located. Little has survived, but the park is a good place for a picnic.

Palazzo Viti (Via dei Sarti) affords a glance into the luxury enjoyed by the wealthy business class in Tuscany.

On the city's northern edge is a **Roman theatre**, a well-preserved complex that includes a Roman bath.

The **Balze**, a deep ravine created by erosion, about a 10-minute ride northwest of the city centre, has claimed several churches since the Middle Ages, the buildings having fallen into its deep gullies. A 14th-century monastery is perched close to the precipice and is in danger of toppling into the ravine. To get there, head out of the northwest end of the city along Via San Lino and follow its continuation, Borgo Santo Stefano and then Borgo San Giusto.

Places to Stay In the Monastero di Sant' Andrea, **Casa per Ferie Seminario** (☎ 0588 8 60 28; Viale Vittorio Veneto; doubles with bathroom €33) is one of the best deals in Tuscany. Rooms are large and clean. Book in advance as it's popular with student groups. You can lock your bike in the entrance courtyard. **Ostello della Gioventù** (☎ 0588 8 55 77; Via del Poggetto 3; dorm beds €16), a non-HI hostel near the Museo Etrusco Guarnacci, is also a great deal. **Albergo Etruria** (☎/fax 0588 8 73 77; Via Giacomo Matteotti 32; singles/doubles with bathroom €41/62) is a good bet if you want a more traditional hotel room.

Places to Eat With a great set menu (two-course dinner, side dish and dessert) with a range of pasta and meat choices head to **Da Beppino** (Via delle Prigioni 13; set menu € 13; closed Wed). **L'Incontro** (Via Giacoma Matteotti 18) is a cheerful place for breakfast, a coffee during the day, or a drink or two in the evening. **Pozzo degli Etruschi** (Via delle Prigioni 28-30; pasta €5, meat dishes €10, full dinner with wine €30) is directly across from Da Beppino and has a first-rate *tiramisú* (a famous Tuscan dessert).

Day 2: Volterra to Massa Marittima

4–6½ hours, 66.8km

Though the Day 2 ride is a bit longer kilometre-wise than Day 1, the lack of significant points of interest along the route make it substantially shorter in duration. Like the previous day, the second half of the ride is more scenic. Again, the terrain is rolling, with one steep climb about halfway through the ride (28km). Unlike the vineyard terraced hills in the Chianti region, however, the Maremma's hills are adorned with grand chestnut, beech and evergreen oak forests.

Pass through Saline di Volterra (11km), which takes its name from the nearby salt mines (the source of its wealth in the 19th century), and Pomarance (23.7km), a largely industrial town, before encountering a tough (and surreal) climb past the colossal boric acid plant near Larderello (34.2km). Located in the **Valle del Diavolo** (Valley of the Devil), Larderello's geothermal vents once terrified passing travellers. Today, it is Italy's largest boric acid producer. Though this sight may sound less than appealing, twisting around past the maze of zigzagging steam tunnels is more bizarre and fascinating than offensive, and the view north at the giant condensation towers from **Castelnuovo colle valle di Cecina** (38.7km) is one of the more stunning old-world-meets-new scenes in Tuscany. Stop here for a bite to eat.

From Castelnuovo, the ride is more 'naturally' scenic, with sweeping views of the **forested mountains** to the south and east. The riding is easier, too, with less climbing and little traffic until the final, modest ascent (64.5km) into **Massa Marittima**. To reach the tourist office, proceed across Piazza Garibaldi to the steps; the office is at the bottom of the steps on the right.

Massa Marittima

This is, perhaps, the most interesting town in the Maremma region of Tuscany. Dating back to the 8th century, the walled nucleus of the old town was in place by the 12th century. The medieval town thrived on the local metal mining industry until the plague hit in 1348 and mining ended 50 years later. Only in the 18th century, with the draining of marshes and re-establishment of mining, did Massa Marittima come back to life.

Information Ufficio Turistico (☎ 0566 90 27 56) is just off Piazza Garibaldi on Via Norma Parenti 22. The Banca Toscana at Piazza Garibaldi 17 has an ATM. There are no bike repair shops in the town centre. The nearest place to get repairs done is at Sumin (☎ 0566 91 91 11) at Zona Industriale in Valpiana, 5km away on the road to Follonica.

Things to See & Do The heart of medieval Massa is Piazza Garibaldi, dominated by the imposing bulk of the **cathedral** in Pisan Romanesque style. It is thought Giovanni Pisano designed the church, although much of the work may have been carried out by Sienese workmen. The inside is graced with substantial remnants of frescoes and several paintings, including a *Madonna delle Grazie* by the workshop of Siena's Duccio di Buoninsegna.

TUSCANY

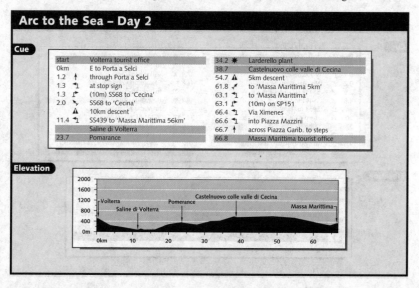

Arc to the Sea – Day 2

Cue

start	Volterra tourist office	34.2 ✳	Larderello plant
0km	E to Porta a Selci	38.7	Castelnuovo colle valle di Cecina
1.2 ↑	through Porta a Selci	54.7 ⚠	5km descent
1.3 ↰	at stop sign	61.8 ↗	to 'Massa Marittima 5km'
1.3 ↱	(10m) SS68 to 'Cecina'	63.1 ↰	to 'Massa Marittima'
2.0 ↘	SS68 to 'Cecina'	63.1 ↱	(10m) on SP151
⚠	10km descent	66.4 ↰	Via Ximenes
11.4 ↰	SS439 to 'Massa Marittima 56km'	66.6 ↰	into Piazza Mazzini
	Saline di Volterra	66.7 ↑	across Piazza Garib. to steps
23.7	Pomarance	66.8	Massa Marittima tourist office

Elevation

Also on the Piazza Garibaldi is the 13th-century **Palazzo del Podesta**, which houses the **Archaeology Museum**, visited above all for Ambrogio Lorenzetti's *Maestà*.

The Città Nuova (New Town) is dominated by the **Torre del Candeliere**, in turn joined to defensive bastions in the wall by the so-called **Arco Senese** (Sienese Arch). You can enter the tower and bestride the arch – the views over the Città Vecchia (Old Town) are best in the early morning.

Places to Stay Overnight options are thin. If you find them all full, the tourist office may be able to help organise something in the surrounding area. **Hotel Il Girifalco** (☎/fax 0566 90 21 77; Via Massetana Nord 25; singles/doubles €37/62) is the best bet. It is about 500m from the town centre, back towards Volterra and has a pool, nice rooms, a good breakfast and a garage for bikes. **Hotel Il Sole** (☎ 0566 90 19 71; Corso della Libertà 43; singles/doubles €46/65) is the best choice in the town centre.

Places to Eat As surprising as the lack of accommodation is the concentration of above-average restaurants. Even the touristy places on Piazza Garibaldi are quite good. **Trattoria Vecchio Borgo** (Via Butigni 12; tris di primi for 2 €20; closed Mon) serves appetising fare. **Ristoro Il Gatto e La Volpe** (Vicolo Ciambellano 12; mains €10-14; closed Mon) offers a divine *filetto tartufato* (fillet steak prepared with truffles) for €13. **Osteria da Tronca** (Vicolo Porte 5; full meals €26-30; closed Wed) is another fine choice. **Le Catene-Vanni** (Piazza Garibaldi 4; pizza & pasta €5) offers a tasty Caprese appetiser and a gorgonzola pizza to die for, not to mention a commanding location in the main piazza.

Getting There & Away To get back to Siena, consider cycling or bussing. Buses are irregular, so check times at the tourist office. The trip usually takes about two hours, and the terminal is on Via Valle Aspra. To get to Florence or Rome, the train is a better option.

The nearest train station is Follonica on the coastal Rome–Turin (Torino) line. Cycling to Follonica is a 20km breeze – it's downhill or flat all the way. *Diretto* trains run to Rome (€11.50, about three hours, every two to four hours). To get to Florence, take the Rome–Turin train north to Pisa, then change for Florence (€9, three hours, every two hours).

Day 3: Massa Marittima Circuit
4–7 hours, 70.4km
Finally a corner of Tuscany that no-one else has found! It's unlikely that you'll encounter any tourists after leaving Massa Marittima, even in summer. Along with the reward of tranquillity, Day 3 offers a challenge as well –

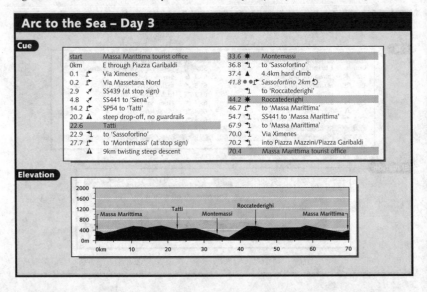

Arc to the Sea – Day 3

Cue

start	Massa Marittima tourist office	33.6 ✳	Montemassi	
0km	E through Piazza Garibaldi	36.8 ↰	to 'Sassofortino'	
0.1 ↱	Via Ximenes	37.4 ▲	4.4km hard climb	
0.2 ↱	Via Massetana Nord	41.8 ●●↱	Sassofortino 2km ↻	
2.9 ↙	SS439 (at stop sign)	↰	to 'Roccatederighi'	
4.8 ↙	SS441 to 'Siena'	44.2 ✳	Roccatederighi	
14.2 ↱	SP54 to 'Tatti'	46.7 ↱	to 'Massa Marittima'	
20.2 ⚠	steep drop-off, no guardrails	54.7 ↰	SS441 to 'Massa Marittima'	
22.6	Tatti	67.9 ↰	to 'Massa Marittima'	
22.9 ↰	to 'Sassofortino'	70.0 ↰	Via Ximenes	
27.7 ↱	to 'Montemassi' (at stop sign)	70.2 ↰	into Piazza Mazzini/Piazza Garibaldi	
⚠	9km twisting steep descent	70.4	Massa Marittima tourist office	

Elevation

this is the longest and toughest day of the ride. Lighten your load as much as possible.

Descend out of Massa Marittima heading northeast before branching off the main roads and winding southeast along quieter trails. Though the paving along this route is generally good, the lack of guard rails is unnerving. Watch out for sections of switchbacked road that have steep drop-offs and no rails (20.2km)! Tatti (22.6km) is a nice town for a quick visit or a cup of coffee, and **Montemassi** (33.6km) is a medieval village composed of the intimidating Montemassi Castle and several pleasant cafés and restaurants. Heading north again, grunt uphill towards Sassofortino and Roccatederighi. Consider a quick side trip to castle-adorned hill town **Sassofortino** before continuing on to **Roccatederighi** (44.2km). One of the most well-preserved medieval villages, Roccatederighi is perched on a rocky outcropping and has views of the valley and towns below. Enjoy a climb through the village to the 10th-century **Chiesa di San Martino Vescovo**.

Meander back towards Massa on a different, but equally appealing, wooded road, before retracing your steps along the main roads back into Massa Marittima.

Montemassi, Sassofortino & Roccatederighi

Known as 'Roccastrada's Villages', these picturesque towns dot the tops of the hills to the west of Roccastrada, the larger primary town in the district. Because Day 3 follows a loop that begins and ends in Massa Marittima, no accommodation information for these villages has been provided. However, if you're interested in spending a night in a medieval hill town, or in trekking along the district's eight trails, visit ⓦ www.comune .roccastrada.gr.it or call the Commune di Roccastrada (☎ 0564 56 11 11).

Circling Elba

Duration	5–9 hours
Distance	92km
Difficulty	moderate–hard
Start/End	Portoferraio

Elba rises out of the Tyrrhenian Sea like the sharpened top of a volcano. Indeed, the central and eastern parts of the island are remnants of an Apennine wall that collapsed into the sea and the western part of the island was created by volcanic activity. For cyclists, the geological origins of the island translate into steep climbs, thrilling descents and stunning sea views. Elba, 28km long and 19km across at its widest, is a cyclist's, trekker's and sunseeker's Mecca. This day-long circuit around the island is a great way to sample its offerings.

Among Elba's attractions, all of which can be visited during this ride, are Portoferraio's walled old town, the stunning views from the top of Monte Capanne, the cosy beaches near Marciana Marina, and the enchanting towns of Marciana and Capoliveri.

HISTORY

Elba has been inhabited since the Iron Age. Ligurian tribespeople were the island's first inhabitants, followed by Etruscans, Greeks from Magna Graecia and Romans, the richer of whom began building holiday villas. Centuries of peace under the Pax Romana were compromised during the barbarian invasions, when Elba and the other Tuscan islands became refuges for those fleeing mainland marauders. By the 11th century, Pisa was in control and built fortresses to help ward off attacks by Muslim raiders operating out of North Africa. In the 16th century, Cosimo I de' Medici founded the port town of Cosmopolis (today Portoferraio). Napoleon was exiled to Elba, arriving in 1814 and staying only a year before attempting another shot at imperial greatness. Iron remained the major industry until WWII when facilities were hit hard by the Allies and never recovered. By the beginning of the 1980s, tourism had arrived to take the place of mining and smelting.

PLANNING
Maps

The handy, pocket-sized *Isola d' Elba* is an excellent 1:35,000 map produced by Vivaldi Editori-Ingenia with cycling and walking routes. The directions which accompany the map, however, are virtually useless. The map can be purchased at almost any bike shop or *tabaccheria* (tobaccanist's shop).

ACCESS TOWN
Portoferraio

Known to the Romans as Fabricia and later Ferraia, this small port was acquired by

TUSCANY

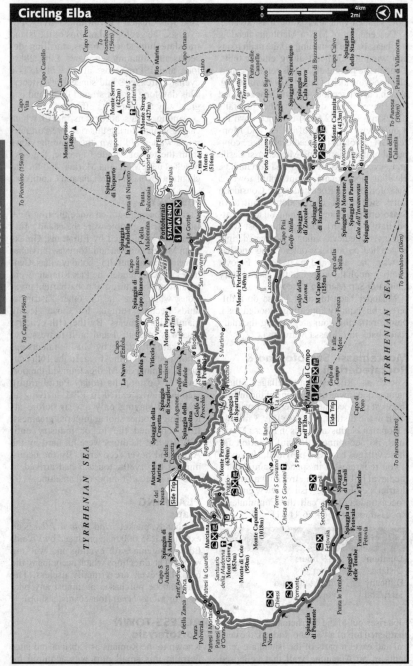

Circling Elba

Cosimo I de' Medici in the mid-16th century. It was from this time that the fortifications, and town that exists today, took shape. The walls link two forts (Stella and Falcone) on high points and a third tower closing the port (Linguella). The new part of Portoferraio encompasses the modern ferry port, but is of little interest.

Information The main APT tourist office (☎ 0565 91 46 71), Calata Italia 26, can assist with accommodation and provides a list of shops that rent and repair bikes. Pick up the free map of Portoferraio as well. The Associazione Albergatori Isola d'Elba (☎ 0565 91 47 54), Calata Italia 20, can help you find a room.

There are banks and ATMs on Calata Italia and Via Giosue Carducci in the new part of town, and in the Piazza Cavour in the old town.

The best bike repair shop in town is Cicli Brandi (☎ 0565 91 41 28) on Via Carducci 33. To rent a mountain bike, try either Cicli Brandi or TWN (☎ 0565 91 46 66), Viale Elba, which has six stores scattered around the island.

Things to See & Do Wander around the **forts** of Falcone. Below the walls of Forte Falcone is a narrow, but fetching, sliver of beach known as **Le Viste**.

In the old town, up on the bastions between the two forts, you'll also encounter **Villa dei Mulini**, one of the residences where Napoleon mooched about. It features a splendid terraced garden and his library. A ticket, which can be bought at the door, costs €5.

The ticket also allows your admission to **Villa Napoleonica di San Martino**, Napoleon's summer residence, set in hills about 5km southwest of the town. The villa houses a modest collection of Napoleonic paraphernalia and also hosts an annual exhibition based on a Napoleonic theme.

The Linguella fortifications, down by the old town's port, house the modest **Museo Civico Archeologico** (☎ 0565 93 73 70), which contains a display of ancient nautical relics.

Places to Stay & Eat The closest camping grounds are about 4km west of Portoferraio, in Acquaviva. **Campeggio La Sorgente** (☎ 0565 91 71 39; per adult/tent €12/10) and

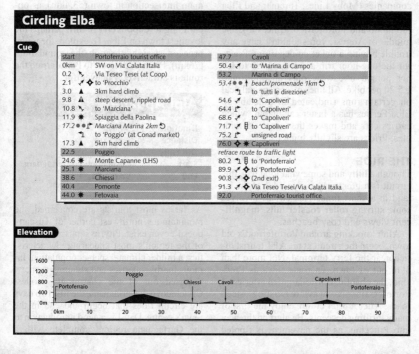

Circling Elba

Cue

start	Portoferraio tourist office		47.7		Cavoli
0km	SW on Via Calata Italia		50.4	↙	to 'Marina di Campo'
0.2	↘	Via Teseo Tesei (at Coop)	53.2		Marina di Campo
2.1	↗ ◆	to 'Procchio'	53.4 ●●↑		*beach/promenade 1km* ↻
3.0	▲	3km hard climb		⤺	to 'tutti le direzione'
9.8	⚠	steep descent, rippled road	54.6	↙	to 'Capoliveri'
10.8	↘	to 'Marciana'	64.4	↳	to 'Capoliveri'
11.9	✳	Spiaggia della Paolina	68.6	↙	to 'Capoliveri'
17.2 ●●↳		Marciana Marina 2km ↻	71.7	⚡	to 'Capoliveri'
	⤺	to 'Poggio' (at Conad market)	75.2	↳	unsigned road
17.3	▲	5km hard climb	76.0	◆ ✳	Capoliveri
22.5		Poggio	*retrace route to traffic light*		
24.6	✳	Monte Capanne (LHS)	80.2	⤺ ↘	to 'Portoferraio'
25.1	✳	Marciana	89.9	↗ ◆	to 'Portoferraio'
38.6		Chiessi	90.8	↙ ◆	(2nd exit)
40.4		Pomonte	91.3	↙ ◆	Via Teseo Tesei/Via Calata Italia
44.0	✳	Fetovaia	92.0		Portoferraio tourist office

Elevation

Acquaviva *(☎ 0565 91 55 92; per adult/tent €12/12)* are easily found. On the southern shore, the Lacona area has many camping options.

Albergo Ape Elbana *(☎ 0565 91 42 45; Salita de' Medici 2; singles/doubles with bathroom & breakfast €52/73)* is in the old town. **Villa Ombrosa** *(☎ 0565 91 43 63; Via De Gasperi 3; singles/doubles with bathroom €86/135)* may insist that you take half-board, which is OK as its restaurant is good.

Ristorante Villa Ombrosa *(Via De Gasperi 3; full meal around €23)* serves good Tuscan dishes. **Trattoria da Zucchetta** *(Piazza della Repubblica 40; full meal around €26; closed Tues)* is a Neapolitan eatery in the old town and has been operating since 1891. **Stella Marina** *(Banchina Alto Fondale; closed Wed)* is on the waterfront towards the ferry terminal. This place isn't cheap, but it serves some good local and Genoese dishes, especially seafood. **Il Baretto** *(Calata Mazzini 21; drinks around €6)* is a nice harbourside bar.

Getting There & Away Unless you're flying directly into Elba, the only way to get there is by ferry from Piombino. Several companies (Moby Lines, Toremar and Elba Ferries) operate ferries and have offices in Piombino and Portoferraio. Unless it is the middle of August, you shouldn't have any trouble buying a ticket on departure. Prices for the one-hour trip are around €6 to €8 per person one way, plus an additional €5.20 per bike. All lines offer a special deal on certain runs (indicated in timetables). Elba Ferries has a faster catamaran, which carries cars and makes the trip in 25 minutes. Prices are slightly higher.

THE RIDE

Though a hilly and somewhat long day, this circuit is a great way to see a lot of the island in a short time. This circuit involves some stirring **roller coaster hills**, **magnificent views** and **cosy beaches**.

After knocking around Portoferraio's old town, begin the circuit at the APT tourist office near the ferry terminal. Not more than 3km out of town, en route towards Procchio, the chaotic, traffic-jammed arteries of Portoferraio give way to twisting, steep roads. After a brief climb, enjoy the first of many thrilling descents. Be alert on the way into Procchio, as the pavement is rippled

and dangerous (9.8km). From Procchio to Marciana Marina, the road hugs the **dramatic cliffs**. Keep an eye out for signs indicating beaches, as some of the prettiest (and smallest) coves lie along this stretch. The **Spiaggia della Paolina** (11.9km) can be visited by locking up your bike and scrambling down the steep steps. You may want to take a quick minute to rest and explore the attractive town of **Marciana Marina** (17.2km) before the relentless climb up to Marciana (25.1km). For a stunning **panoramic view** of the island, stop in the car park on the left about 500m before Marciana (24.6km) for a **cable car ride** to the top of **Monte Capanne** (€11.36 return, about one hour). Alternatively, or additionally, a quick spin (on foot) around picturesque Marciana is rewarding.

From Marciana to Marina di Campo (53.2km), the road offers **spectacular views** of the **Tyrrhenian Sea**. At 44km, **Fetovaia** has a broad, sandy beach, if you're looking to cool off. The **waterfront cafés**, **promenade** and **beach** in **Marina di Campo** are worth a side trip. To do so, leave the route momentarily by proceeding straight at the main intersection in town (53.4km), as opposed to turning left. The route continues by climbing to **Capoliveri** (76km), perhaps the loveliest town on Elba. To explore the town, proceed straight through the roundabout (76km). From Capoliveri to Portoferraio the route is attractive, if uneventful.

Alpi Apuane

Duration	3 days
Distance	155.8km
Difficulty	moderate–hard
Start	Castelnuovo diGarfagnana
End	Viareggio

As far as most tourists are concerned, the mountainous northwest corner of Tuscany doesn't even exist. Pity, as it possesses some of the region's most endearing characteristics: a milder climate, sparser population, famous marble quarries and stunning scenery.

Based out of the charmingly modest Castelnuovo di Garfagnana, the first two days are circuit rides that begin and end in the town's centre. Day 1 is a good introduction to the Garfagnana region, complete with a

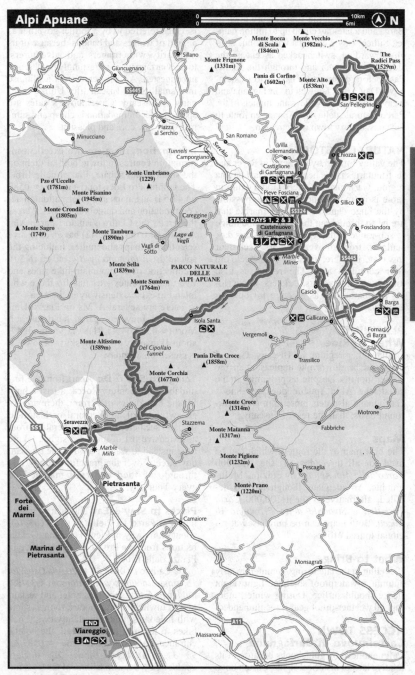

memorable stop in the 10th-century town of Barga and a late-day climb up to hilltop hamlet, Sillico. Day 2 entails a wicked, but visually rewarding, switchbacked ascent up the side of a mountain and through the Radici Pass before plummeting back into Castelnuovo. Day 3 bids farewell to Garfagnana and weaves through the valleys and tunnels of the Parco Naturale delle Alpi Apuane en route to the coastal party town of Viareggio.

NATURAL HISTORY
The valley formed by the Serchio River and its tributaries is the heart of the Garfagnana region. Garfagnana's international claim to fame is its marble industry, made possible by the huge deposits of white marble that are laced throughout the Alpi Apuane range (a sub-range of the Apennines). To this day, sculptors from all over the world seek their raw materials here, just as Michelangelo did four centuries ago. The region is also known among cyclists, trekkers, horse riders and naturalists as a centre for outdoor activity.

PLANNING
When to Ride
Unlike other regions in Tuscany, Garfagnana can be downright unpleasant in the winter months. Despite its proximity to the coast, the Alpi Apuane does get snow. Garfagnana also gets more rain, on a year-round basis, than the rest of Tuscany.

Maps
The best map of the region, which can be used for all three days, is the 1:50,000 *Parco delle Alpi Apuane* by Edizioni Multigraphic. An adequate, though far less detailed, alternative is the 1:100,000 *Carta Turistica e Stradale della Provincia di Lucca*. Both maps can be purchased at regional tourist offices.

What to Bring
If cycling in the late spring, summer or early autumn, a waterproof shell and lightweight fleece should suffice. During winter, more rugged weather-proof gear is recommended.

ACCESS TOWN
Castelnuovo di Garfagnana
Left unnoticed by guidebooks because of its relative lack of historical sights, Castelnuovo

deserves recognition as the charming town it is. Once referred to by a former governor as a 'land of wolves and bandits' because of its popularity with robbers and adventurers, today Garfagnana is refreshingly modest and uncongested. A visit here offers a glimpse into small-town Tuscan life. Unlike other parts of Tuscany, Castelnuovo's cafés are spacious, accommodation is cheap and summer days stay cool and pleasant.

Information There are two excellent information centres in town, both of them on the small, main square, Piazza delle Erbe. The helpful Pro Loco tourist office (☎ 0583 64 43 54) has maps and information on accommodation and outdoor activities. Across the street, the Centro Visitatori Parco Alpi Apuane (☎ 0583 64 42 42) has an extensive selection of maps and guides, including the splendid *Garfagnana by Bicycle* (€16.50), a collection of 22 mountain-bike rides and five touring routes – a must for those who intend to cycle extensively in the area.

There are several ATMs on Piazza Umberto. For bicycle repairs, head to Cicli Mori (☎ 0583 64 45 51), Via Vannugli 47, about 1km away on the outskirts of town. It is closed on Monday.

Things to See & Do Apart from the formidable 14th-century **Rocca**, a castle built for the Este dukes of Ferrara, there are not an awful lot of architectural or historical gems to see here. Enjoy the liberation from an extensive list of must-see sights, taking time instead to wander around the pleasant city streets, over the graceful **bridges**, and through the **food and craft market** held every Thursday.

Places to Stay & Eat The nearest camping is at **Parco La Piella** (☎ 0583 629 16), about 4km away in Pieve Fosciana. Get directions from the Pro Loco tourist office in Piazza delle Erbe.

Da Carlino (☎ 0583 64 42 70; Via Garibaldi 15; singles/doubles with bathroom €31/52; full meals €18) is the best hotel and restaurant in town, boasting modest rooms (some with balconies) and mountain views. Lock bikes to the iron fence beneath the hotel's entrance. **La Vecchia Lanterna** (☎ 0583 63 93 31; Via Nicola Fabrizi 26; singles/doubles €21/31, with bathroom €31/52; full *meals €15-18)* is a less attractive, but adequate, option on the southwest side of town. **La Credenza** *(Via Farini 2; pastas & pizzas €3-5)* is just off Piazza Umberto and has fine, inexpensive fare.

There's a **Conad** supermarket on Via Valmaira near the sports complex, and the **Maria Antonietta Castelli Supermercato** is in town next to La Credenza.

Getting There & Away If coming from Lucca, hopping on a CLAP bus is a viable option (€6, about one hour, every two hours). You'll be charged for two tickets – one for you, one for your bike.

From Florence, catch a train on the Florence–Viareggio line to Lucca (€4.50, 1¼ hours, hourly) then change to the Lucca–Aulla line, on which Castelnuovo is a stop (€3, one hour, hourly). Rome to Castelnuovo is more difficult. First take the Rome–Turin line to Pisa (€15.50, four hours, every two hours), then the Pisa–Lucca line (€2, 30 minutes, hourly), and finally take the Lucca–Aulla line to Castelnuovo.

Bicycle Though the distance is manageable, cycling from Lucca to Castelnuovo is not recommended. The road is narrow and heavily travelled by overloaded, marble-hauling tractor trailers.

THE RIDE
Day 1: Garfagnana Circuit
2½–5 hours, 48km

An excellent introduction to the Garfagnana valley, Day 1 offers a manageable sampler of tough climbs, exciting descents and spectacular views. The ride's relatively short length makes it possible to linger in some of the pleasant towns, such as Barga and Sillico, along the route. The toughest climb comes late in the day, so save enough strength for a difficult switchbacked ascent to Sillico.

With your back to the tourist office, proceed northeast towards the river and main road (SS445). After leaving Castelnuovo, the route climbs steeply, providing picturesque glimpses of the town. After 3.7km, consider a side trip to **Cascio**. An important military fortification in the 17th century, today Cascio is a quaint village town with a nice view. The ascent into **Barga** follows a shady, tree-lined roadway, with its fair share of steep switchbacks. In Barga (14.5km), visit the medieval town centre and pay a visit to the crenellated duomo and its exquisitely carved pulpit. Appreciate the view across the valley of the Parco Naturale delle Alpi Apuane before heading back towards Castelnuovo. Use caution after turning onto the SS445 (20.5km), as there is a small shoulder and the road is heavily travelled by trucks.

TUSCANY

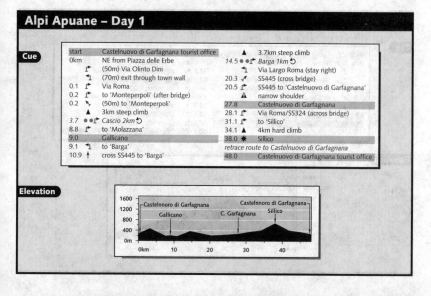

Alpi Apuane – Day 1

Cue

start	Castelnuovo di Garfagnana tourist office	
0km	NE from Piazza delle Erbe	
↱	(50m) Via Olinto Dini	
⬏	(70m) exit through town wall	
0.1	↱ Via Roma	
0.2	↱ to 'Monteperpoli' (after bridge)	
0.2	↘ (50m) to 'Monteperpoli'	
▲	3km steep climb	
3.7	● ●↱ Cascio 2km ↻	
8.8	↱ to 'Molazzana'	
9.0	Gallicano	
9.1	⬏ to 'Barga'	
10.9	↑ cross SS445 to 'Barga'	

▲	3.7km steep climb	
14.5	● ●↱ Barga 1km ↻	
⬏	Via Largo Roma (stay right)	
20.3	✗ SS445 (cross bridge)	
20.5	↱ SS445 to 'Castelnuovo di Garfagnana'	
▲	narrow shoulder	
27.8	Castelnuovo di Garfagnana	
28.1	↱ Via Roma/SS324 (across bridge)	
31.1	↱ to 'Sillico'	
34.1	▲ 4km hard climb	
38.0	✹ Sillico	
retrace route to Castelnuovo di Garfagnana		
48.0	Castelnuovo di Garfagnana tourist office	

Elevation

Pass through Castelnuovo heading towards Pieve Fosciana, before turning onto a quiet back road and climbing up to **Sillico** (38km), a charming, sleepy hamlet perched on the side of a mountain. Lock your bike in the car park and wander through the town's twisting cobbled alleys before sipping a coffee at the café just above the car park. Retrace your steps back to Castelnuovo, taking extra care while navigating the steep descent's hairpin curves.

Day 2: The Radici Pass
3–5 hours, 50.4km

A difficult but rewarding ride, Day 2 reminds cyclists that, though Tuscany's mountains may be puny compared to their mightier relatives in the Dolomites, they're still a branch of the Alps! In 18km this route rises 1300m. It sounds daunting, but don't forget that this is a circuit ride and what goes up must come down; the promise of more than 30km of downhill excitement makes the uphill grind more palatable.

The route proceeds out of the Piazza delle Erbe towards Pieve Fosciana, retracing the last third of the Day 1 route. After about 4km, the tough climbing begins. Settle in for 14km of relentless, switchbacked climbing. **Chiozza** (10.1km) is a good place to catch your breath, enjoy the view and refill water bottles – there's a fountain in the

car park at La Grotta Pizzeria. In summer, **raspberries** line the next segment of road, not to mention meadows of waving grass, wildflowers and patches of woods. After passing a cluster of sturdy, weather-worn homes on the left, the ascent becomes savage – the incline angle exceeding 15%! Alas, **San Pellegrino** (16.8km), known as the 'balcony of Garfagnana' for its dramatic location, provides a much-needed reason to dismount. Visit the **Don Luigi Pellegrini Ethnographic Folk Museum**, an interesting collection of historic folk art and farming equipment housed in a medieval villa. Wander around on foot here and grab a bite to eat. Enjoy beautiful views to the west of the peaks in the Parco Naturale delle Alpi Apuane. Occasionally, the notorious 'sea of fog' blankets the valley below.

After sailing through the **Radici Pass** (19.4km), bomb downhill to **Castiglione di Garfagnana** (43km), where it's worth exploring the medieval city walls, 12th-century fortress, and the 13th-century **Chiesa di San Michele** before returning to Castelnuovo di Garfagnana.

Day 3: Castelnuovo di Garfagnana to Viareggio
3–5½ hours, 57.4km

Day 3 leaves the cosy cafés and alleyways of Castelnuovo behind in search of Viareggio's

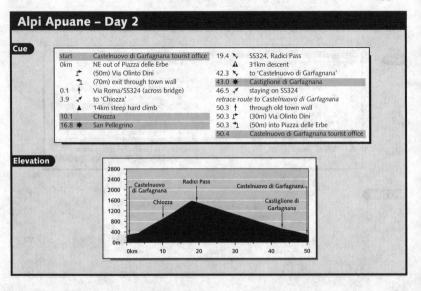

Alpi Apuana – Day 2

Cue

start	Castelnuovo di Garfagnana tourist office		19.4 ↘	SS324, Radici Pass
0km	NE out of Piazza delle Erbe		▲	31km descent
↱	(50m) Via Olinto Dini		42.3 ↘	to 'Castelnuovo di Garfagnana'
↰	(70m) exit through town wall		43.0 ✳	Castiglione di Garfagnana
0.1 ↑	Via Roma/SS324 (across bridge)		46.5 ↗	staying on SS324
3.9 ↗	to 'Chiozza'		*retrace route to Castelnuovo di Garfagnana*	
▲	14km steep hard climb		50.3 ↑	through old town wall
10.1	Chiozza		50.3 ↱	(30m) Via Olinto Dini
16.8 ✳	San Pellegrino		50.3 ↰	(50m) into Piazza delle Erbe
			50.4	Castelnuovo di Garfagnana tourist office

Elevation

fun and sun. Though less than 60km away, Viareggio is Castelnuovo's antithesis, and the culture shock will undoubtedly leave some feeling overwhelmed. The riding is moderately easy, with a steady climb for the first 20km, followed by a long, slow descent to sea level.

Just a few kilometres out of Castelnuovo, watch with fascination (or horror) as bulldozers create mini-avalanches in the **marble mines** (about 2km) on the left. Though the mines are far enough away from the road to feel secure, their presence prompts an important safety precaution: this ride cuts through a steep gorge. Despite the valley walls being secured with mesh retaining wire, large chunks of rock still find their way onto the road. Keep your eyes peeled and wear a helmet!

Meander through the ferny woods of the **Parco Naturale delle Alpi Apuane** to **Isola Santa** (13.1km), a picturesque town on the edge of a man-made lake. **Da Giacco** (☎ 0583 66 70 48) is an excellent restaurant at which to sample local fare, or grab a cup of coffee, hunk of chocolate or a loaf of dark bread. Enter the spooky, 1125m-long **Del Cipollaio tunnel** at 19.1km for an experience more akin to spelunking than cycling. Though the tunnel is lit well enough to cycle without a headlight, turning on a flashing tail light to alert motorists is wise.

Enjoy spectacular views on the descent past **marble-cutting mills** (40km), where huge car-sized hunks of rock are sliced into thin slabs for kitchen counters and bathroom walls. Upon dead-ending into the sea, head towards **Viareggio**, passing the dizzying profusion of bars, beach clubs, discos, and two- to four-star hotels that line the strip.

Viareggio

Italy's second Carnevale capital after Venice, Viareggio is the leading resort town on the northern Tuscan coast. The town's architectural wonders are limited to some pleasing Liberty (Art Nouveau) edifices, mostly on or a block or two back from the palm-lined Passeggiata, the (almost) waterfront boulevard. To some, Viareggio epitomises the ultimate party for which they've been searching. Others find the town a nightmare realised. If beach clubs and block-rockin' beats aren't your bag, proceed directly to the train station and escape to greener pastures. Both Lucca and Pisa are but a hop, skip and jump away.

Information The main APT tourist office (☎ 0584 96 22 33) is at Viale Carducci 10. Staff speak several languages, but they do not make hotel bookings. The office opens from 9am to 1pm and 4pm to 7pm Monday

TUSCANY

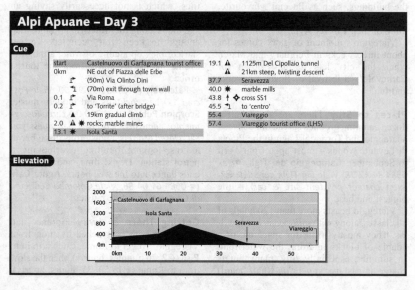

Alpi Apuane – Day 3

Cue

start	Castelnuovo di Garfagnana tourist office		19.1 ▲	1125m Del Cipollaio tunnel
0km	NE out of Piazza delle Erbe		▲	21km steep, twisting descent
↱	(50m) Via Olinto Dini		37.7	Seravezza
↰	(70m) exit through town wall		40.0 ✳	marble mills
0.1 ↱	Via Roma		43.8 ↑ ✧	cross SS1
0.2 ↱	to 'Torrite' (after bridge)		45.5 ↰	to 'centro'
▲	19km gradual climb		55.4	Viareggio
2.0 ▲ ✳	rocks; marble mines		57.4	Viareggio tourist office (LHS)
13.1 ✳	Isola Santa			

Elevation

to Saturday, from Easter to the end of September. For the rest of the year (except the excitable time of Carnevale), it opens only in the morning. In summer, a smaller office also operates at the train station from 9am to 1pm daily.

There are ATMs at both the tourist office and the train station, but no bicycle repair shops in town.

Things to See & Do The city is arranged roughly north to south on a grid pattern. South of the pleasure-boat lined Canale Burlamacca, stretch the enticing woods of the **Pineta di Levante**. Another smaller wood, the **Pineta di Ponente**, occupies a large chunk of the northern end of town. Beyond it, Viareggio blends into the next beach resort of Lido di Camaiore. Apart from strolling along the tracks in the Pineta di Levante, around the Canale Burlamacca and along Via Regina Margherita, there's not much to occupy your time but the beach.

The **beach** will cost you plenty. It has been divided up into *stabilimenti*, individual lots where you can hire change cabins, umbrellas, recliners and the like. You have to avail yourself of at least a recliner (€13 per person).

A good deal of the waterfront was developed in the 1920s and 1930s, and some of the buildings, such as Puccini's favourite, the Gran Caffè Margherita, retain something of their Liberty style.

Viareggio's moment of glory comes for about three weeks in February and March when the city lets its hair down for **Carnevale** – a festival of floats, fireworks and fun.

Places to Stay There are about half a dozen camping grounds spread out between Viareggio and Torre del Lago in the Pineta di Levante woods – most open from April to September. **Campeggio dei Tigli** (*☎/fax 0584 34 12 78; Viale dei Tigli; per adult €7, extra charges per tent site & car*) is the biggest and best.

Viareggio boasts more than 120 hotels of all classes, along with *affittacamere* and villas. They mostly jostle for space on, or a couple of blocks in from, the waterfront. In summer, especially July, many hotels charge at least *mezza pensione* (half-board)

and often *pensione completa* (full board). Two places stand out from the crowd: **Albergo Villa Bruna** (*☎ 0584 310 38; Via Michelangelo Buonarroti 10; rooms/full board €30/50*) is a quiet place with clean rooms and it insists you take full board in July and August. **Hotel Garden** (*☎ 0584 4 40 25; Viale Foscolo 70; singles/doubles with TV, phone & minibar €83/119, full board €103*) is expensive, quality accommodation. Management prefers if you to take full board in summer, but may not insist on it.

Places to Eat If you dodge full board in the hotels, there are plenty of restaurant options around town. The waterfront places tend to be expensive and uninspiring.

Brasserie Stuzzichino (*Viale Foscolo 3; closed Wed*) serves all sorts of snacks, salads and full meals. The speciality of the house is the amazing range of salads. **Sergio** (*Via Zanardelli 151; closed Mon*) is Viareggio's favourite roast chicken joint and also serves other meals plus a decent selection of wines. **Barcobestia** (*☎ 0584 38 44 16; Via Copponi 289; full meals €31; closed Mon*) serves fish specialities. The decor is modern seafarer (with portholes). Be sure to book ahead.

Entertainment Viareggio is one of Tuscany's better places for a night out on the tiles, which is not necessarily saying an awful lot. There is an endless stretch of bars and clubs along the waterfront – more than enough to keep you occupied. To get started, pick up a copy of *Note*, a monthly events listing brochure, from the tourist office.

Patchouly (*☎ 0368 353 99 00; Viale Foscolo 17*) has cocktails and modern music. **Scorpion Pub** (*☎ 0584 310 06; Largo Risorgimento; admission €6 Fri & Sat unless you eat, closed Mon*) is a boisterous disco/bar in a crass-looking building overlooking a petrol station. Drink, dine, and on weekends dance into the wee hours. **Agorà Café** (*☎ 0584 61 04 88; Viale Colombo 666, Lido di Camaiore*) has live music.

Getting There & Away Florence and Rome can both be reached by train from Viareggio. To get to Rome, catch a train to Pisa (€2, 20 minutes, hourly), then the slow train to Rome (€15.50, 3½ hours, hourly).

Fontana dei Quattro Fiumi (Fountain of the Four Rivers), Piazza Navona, Rome

Campo de' Fiori market, Rome

Castel Sant'Angelo, Rome

JON DAVISON

Isola d'Elba, Tuscany

DAMIEN SIMONIS

Abbazia di Sant'Antimo, Montalcino, Tuscany

DIANA MAYFIELD

Il Campo, Siena, Tuscany

JOHN HAY

Vineyards, Chianti region, Tuscany

If Florence is your destination, take the Viareggio–Florence line (€5.50, about two hours, hourly). Another option is to go to Florence via Pisa, which takes about the same amount of time and is comparably priced.

Southern Odyssey

Duration	3 days
Distance	172.1km
Difficulty	moderate
Start	Orbetello
End	Montalcino/Buonconvento

From the natural beauty of Orbetello's shady Feniglia isthmus to Pitigliano's architectural splendour to Montalcino's lofty vineyard views, this three-day route offers more in the way of scenic diversity than, perhaps, any other ride in Tuscany. With its remote, dramatic landscape and historic points of interest, this ride qualifies as a 'southern odyssey' to be sure.

Depart from the sleepy coastal town of Orbetello, heading inland past flat, scrubby fields and farms towards the dramatic, rocky spectacle that is Pitigliano. Day 2 entails a quick morning exploration of Etruscan tombs before venturing off the beaten path, through the hilly stretches west of Monte Amiata (Tuscany's highest peak at 1736m). Day 3 is a shorter, easier route that takes cyclists through the famous hill town of Montalcino, where they can spend the night and link-up with the Hill Town Trek route, or zip into Buonconvento for the next train to Siena.

PLANNING
Maps
Unfortunately, due to its relatively long distance, and the fact that it is not a highly travelled route, there aren't any great maps to consult for this ride. The most helpful is probably Touring Club Italiano's 1:200,000 *Toscana*.

ACCESS TOWN
Orbetello
Once an island, the Monte Argentário promontory came to be linked to the mainland by an accumulation of sand that is now the isthmus of Orbetello. The tiny, oval-shaped town of Orbetello is located in the middle of this narrow strip. Further sandy bulwarks form the Tombolo della Giannella and the Tombolo di Feniglia to the north and south. They enclose a lagoon that is now a protected nature reserve.

Information The Pro Loco tourist office (☎/fax 0564 86 04 47), Piazza della Republica 1, across from the cathedral, provides accommodation and dining information, as well as a free map of the city.

ATMs line the Corso Italia.

Though there are no specific bicycle repair shops in Orbetello, Mandragora Gastone (☎ 0564 86 77 90), Via Vittorio Veneto 2, will perform modest repairs.

Things to See & Do Orbetello's main attraction is its **cathedral**, which has retained its 14th-century Gothic facade despite being remodelled in the Spanish style in the 16th century. Other reminders of the Spanish *presidio* (garrison) that was stationed in the city include the fort and city wall. Parts of the latter belong to the original Etruscan wall.

The best place for observing the birdlife (as many as 140 species have been identified) is out along the **Tombolo della Feniglia**. Though there are narrow beaches on both shores, the beach on the southern, seaward shore – known as the Duna Feniglia – is the more popular.

At night, locals repeatedly cruise the main drag, **Corso Italia**, to stretch their legs and catch up on the gossip.

Time permitting, you may want to explore the hilly Monte Argentário peninsula. **Porto Ércole**, in a picturesque position between two Spanish forts, retains some of its fishing village character. The main tourist office (☎ 0564 81 42 08) is in Porto Santo Stefano at Corso Umberto 55.

Places to Stay & Eat On the southwest fringe of Duna Feniglia beach, **Camping Feniglia** (*☎ 0564 83 10 90; near Porto Ercole; per adult €8, plus tent fees from €5-10 depending on tent size & season*) is the closest and best camping ground. It also rents four- and six-person bungalows by the week.

Piccolo Parigi (*☎ 0564 86 72 33; Corso Italia 169; singles/doubles €31/54, with bathroom €36/62*) is conveniently located, with adequate rooms and a garage across the street for bikes. The pleasant rooftop

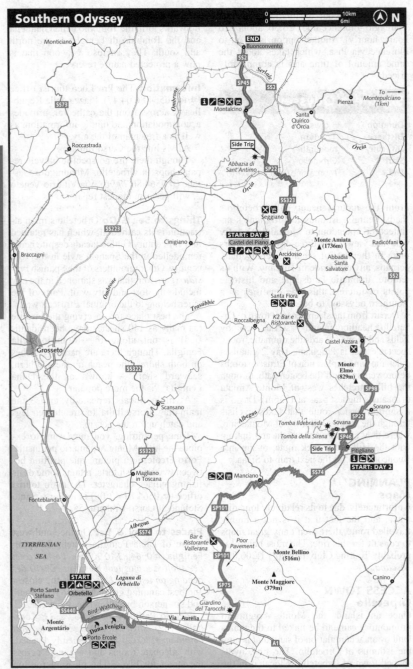

Southern Odyssey

0 — 10km
0 — 6mi

N

Montciano

Roccastrada

SS73

SS223

Braccagni

Grosseto

SS322

Scansano

SS323

Magliano
in Toscana

Fonteblanda

TYRRHENIAN
SEA

Porto Santa
Stéfano

Monte
Argentário

Orbetello

SS440

Laguna di
Orbetello

Bird-Watching

Duna Feniglia

Porto Ércole

END
Buonconvento

SS2

SP45

SS2

Serlate

Ombrone

Montalcino

Santa
Quirico
d'Orcia

Pienza

To
Montepulciano
(1km)

Side Trip

Orcia

SP22

Abbazia di
Sant'Antimo

Orcia

SS323

Seggiano

START: DAY 3
Castel del Piano

Arcidosso

Monte Amiata
▲ (1736m)

Radicófani

Abbadia
Santa
Salvatore

SS52

Cinigiano

Ombrone

Trasúbbie

Santa Fiora

Roccalbegna

K2 Bar e
Ristorante

Castel Azzara

Monte
Elmo
(829m) ▲

SP98

Sorano

SP22

Albegna

Tomba Ildebranda
Tomba della Sirena

Sovana

SP46

Side Trip

Pitigliano
START: DAY 2

Manciano

SS74

Albegna

SS74

SP101

Bar e
Ristorante
Vallerana

Poor
Pavement

SP101

Monte Bellino
(516m)

Monte Maggiore
(379m)

Canino

SP75

Giardino
del Tarocchi

Via Aurélia

A1

START

A1

terrace and café are pluses. **Albergo La Perla** (☎ 0564 86 35 46; Via Volontari del Sangue 10; singles €37, doubles with bathroom €62) has no-frills, cheap, pokey singles; it's just outside the walls of the old town on the road back to the mainland.

Osteria del Lupacante (Corso Italia 103; full meals around €26; closed Tues) offers true Sicilian cooking. The spaghetti *alla messinese* (Messina style) comes with swordfish, tomato, peppers, sunflower seeds and spices. The pasta courses are generous and will satisfy the average appetite. **Il Cavallino Bianco** (Corso Italia 184-190; pizzas around €6) is across from Piccolo Parigi and is an excellent place for pizza and cold beer. **Osteria il Nocchino** (Via dei Mille 64; meals €8-16; closed Wed) is another sound choice, though with about as much seating capacity as a glorified matchbox.

Getting There & Away The Orbetello/Monte Argentario train station is easily reached from Rome on the Rome–Turin *diretto* line (€7, two hours, every two hours). From Florence, the fastest route entails either going to Pisa first, then hopping on the Turin–Rome line, or taking a sluggish *diretto* from Florence to Rome (€14.50, 3¾ hours, every two hours) on the Milan–Rome line, before turning and heading back north to Orbetello via Rome–Turin.

THE RIDE
Day 1: Orbetello to Pitigliano
4½–8 hours, 82.9km

Although Day 1 is long, the first two-thirds of the ride are relatively flat, making for easy pedalling. Rather than distance or elevation, stretches of horribly paved roads can make this leg of the journey tiring. The good thing is that the scenery is spectacular, and the roads are virtually (and refreshingly) traffic-free.

Begin by cruising across the flat isthmus of the **Duna Feniglia** (4.2km) under a serene canopy of pine trees. The best **beaches** are to the right, while **bird-watching** is better to the left. Cyclists with extremely thin tyres take caution, as the trail is dirt and loose gravel, with some sharp pebbles in the mix. After leaving Duna Feniglia, the route skirts the border of the protected coastal flood plain before turning inland towards Pitigliano. If at all possible, visit **Giardino del Tarocchi** (33.2km; ☎ 0564 89 51 22; ⓦ www.nikidesaintphalle .com; admission €10.50, open 14 May–20 Oct), artist Niki de Saint Phalle's psychedelic mosaic wonder. It's open from 2.30pm to 7.30pm daily, making the timing of the visit difficult given the length of the ride.

Grin and bear some sections of chunky pavement (38km to 45km and 49.1km to 52.2km), stop at the excellent **Bar e Ristorante Vallerana** (47.1km) for lunch and enjoy unparalleled views of Pitigliano

TUSCANY

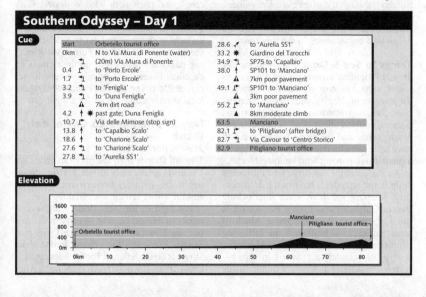

Southern Odyssey – Day 1

Cue

start	Orbetello tourist office		28.6 ↗	to 'Aurelia SS1'
0km	N to Via Mura di Ponente (water)		33.2 ✳	Giardino del Tarocchi
↰	(20m) Via Mura di Ponente		34.9 ↱	SP75 to 'Capalbio'
0.4 ↱	to 'Porto Ercole'		38.0 ↑	SP101 to 'Manciano'
1.7 ↰	to 'Porto Ercole'		⚠	7km poor pavement
3.2 ↰	to 'Feniglia'		49.1 ↱	SP101 to 'Manciano'
3.9 ↰	to 'Duna Feniglia'		⚠	3km poor pavement
⚠	7km dirt road		55.2 ↱	to 'Manciano'
4.2 ↑ ✳	past gate; Duna Feniglia		⚠	8km moderate climb
10.7 ↱	Via delle Mimose (stop sign)		63.5	Manciano
13.8 ↑	to 'Capalbio Scalo'		82.1 ↱	to 'Pitigliano' (after bridge)
18.6 ↑	to 'Charione Scalo'		82.7 ↰	Via Cavour to 'Centro Storico'
27.6 ↰	to 'Charione Scalo'		82.9	Pitigliano tourist office
27.8 ↰	to 'Aurelia SS1'			

Elevation

(81km) on the descent into the surrounding river valley. The climb into the town centre is short but steep. For the tourist office, wind into the old city and proceed down Via Cavour and through Piazza della Republica; it's on the right at the start of Via Roma.

Pitigliano

The visual impact of this town is unforgettable. It seems to grow organically out of a high volcanic rocky outcrop that towers over the outlying valley. The gorges that surround the town on three sides constitute a natural bastion, completed to the east by the fort.

In the 15th century, a Jewish community began to grow here, a tendency that accelerated when Pope Pius IV banned Jews from Rome in 1569. In 1622, the Jews of Pitigliano moved into a tiny ghetto, where they remained until 1772. From then until well into the following century, the local community of 400 flourished, and Pitigliano was dubbed Little Jerusalem. By the time the Fascists introduced their race laws in 1938, most Jews had moved away (only 80 or so were left, precious few of whom survived the war).

Information The tourist information office (☎ 0564 61 44 33) is at Via Roma 6, just off Piazza della Repubblica, and is supposedly open from 10am to noon and 3pm to 5pm Monday to Friday (from 10am to noon on Sunday), though it's often closed in winter.

A Banca di Credito Coopertivo ATM stands next to the tourist office. There are no bicycle repair shops in the tiny town.

Things to See & Do It is a joy to wander around Pitigliano's narrow lanes. Perched as it is on a sharp outcrop surrounded by gorges, the place seems like it could have inspired Escher. Twisting stairways disappear around corners, cobbled alleys bend out of sight beneath arches and the stone houses seem to have been piled up one on top of the other by a giant drunk playing with building blocks.

As you enter the town, the first intriguing sight is the aqueduct, built in the 16th century. Keeping watch over the interlocking Piazza Garibaldi and Piazza Petruccioli is the 13th-century **Palazzo Orsini**. Much of what you see was built over the following centuries. Now seat of the local bishopric, it is a true citadel, a city within a city – fortress, residence and supply dump. Inside

you will find the **Archaeology Museum**, with an instructive display rather than just the usual glass containers full of all sorts of unexplained ancient odds and ends.

If you wander down Via Zuccarelli deep into town, you will see a sign pointing left to the **synagogue**. The structure had largely gone to seed until 1995, when it was restored using old photos. If you want to visit (unless it's open when you walk by), call Dottore Luigi Cerroni (☎ 0347 789 20 33). It is closed on Saturday and Jewish holidays.

The town's cathedral dates back to the Middle Ages, but its facade is baroque and its interior has been modernised. Older is the oddly shaped **Chiesa di Santa Maria**.

Ask at the tourist centre for the free map of the mysterious **Etruscan caves** and roadways. Several are just a short walk from town.

Places to Stay & Eat The only hotel in the town centre is **Albergo Guastini** (☎ 0564 61 60 65; Piazza Petruccioli 4; singles/doubles with bathroom €34/57). Rooms are clean and comfortable, and there's a reasonable restaurant. There's nowhere to store bikes other than locked up outside. **Hotel Valle Orientina** (☎ 0564 61 66 11; Località Valle Orientina; singles/doubles €31/52) has fine rooms; it's 3km outside town on the road to Orvieto.

Osteria Il Tufo Allegro (☎ 0564 61 61 92; Vico della Costituzione 2; just off Via Zuccarelli; full meal with wine & dessert €30; closed Tues) is definitely the place to eat. The gnocchi di zucca al tartufo bianco (pumpkin gnocchi with white truffle) is a delight (although pricey at €18). **Il Forno** (Via Roma), just past the tourist office on the right, is an excellent bakery with breads, sweets, focaccias etc. **Jerry Lee Bar** (Via Roma 28) is where local young people gather for a night out.

Day 2: Pitigliano to Castel del Piano

2½–4½ hours, 46.1km
Though shorter than the previous day, Day 2 is also significantly hillier. Traffic continues to be virtually nonexistent, however, and the views remain breathtaking.

It's hard to hit your stride with several points of interest coming so early in the day, but the **Etruscan tombs** (5.5km) just past Sovana are worth the detour. **Tomba della Sirena** is on the left, and **Tomba Ildebranda** is about 200m down the road on the right. After a quick visit, enjoy an afternoon of alternating climbing and coasting, taking particular note of the views north and east from **Castel Azzara** (14.4km). There are hair-raising descents to prepare for: one comes complete with uneven pavement and hair-pin turns (26km to 30km), the other is less dangerous but worth anticipating (40km to 42.4km).

K2 Bar e Ristorante (25.5km) and the cafés, markets and restaurants in **Santa Fiora** (34.5km) are some of the only places to grab a bite on this remote stretch of road. After the climbing is over (40km), cruise effortlessly into **Castel del Piano** (46.1km).

Castel del Piano

Castel del Piano is a friendly town nestled near the base of Tuscany's highest mountain, the volcanic Monte Amiata (1736m). As such, it serves as a base for Italians (not many tourists make the trek here) who've come to enjoy the area's hiking and mountain-bike trails. It is a quiet, pleasant little town, with a main square, Piazza Garibaldi, and a winding, maze-like old city.

Information The Pro-Loco tourist office (☎ 0564 97 35 34), which claims to be open year-round, is just off Piazza Garibaldi at Via G. Marconi 9.

Several ATMs and banks line the Viale Vittorio Veneto.

Motofficina Giallini Loriano (☎ 0564 95 56 11), Pizza RG Carducci 9, mainly a motorcycle/scooter sales and repair shop, will perform repairs. It carries a modest supply of bike parts. Entry is on Viale Dante Alighieri, next to Punt Sma supermarket.

Things to See & Do Most visitors spend little time in the towns, opting to explore the nearby forests, streams and waterfalls of **Monte Amiata**. In winter, several downhill and cross-country ski trails open on the snowcapped peak. Wildlife lovers hope to spot the mountain's resident foxes and deer.

The most interesting sector of Castel del Piano town is the **Centro Storico** (Old City Centre), which is worth a quick wander. After taking in the dramatic view of nearby hill town **Seggiano** from **Piazza Garibaldi**, walk to the **Piazza Madonna**, taking note of the **Chiesa dell'Opera**, also known as the Church of Proposituria di Saints Nicholas and Lucia, and **Chiesa della Madonna delle Grazia**. The former houses some Nasini family paintings of local importance and a wooden crucifix from the 16th century. Proceed under the **Tower Clock** through the Porto dell'Orologio arch and along the Via Basilica. Pass the sparsely decorated, rural facades of the **Chiesa di Santo Leanardo** and the **Chiesa Piccina** as you amble through the dark, winding old town.

TUSCANY

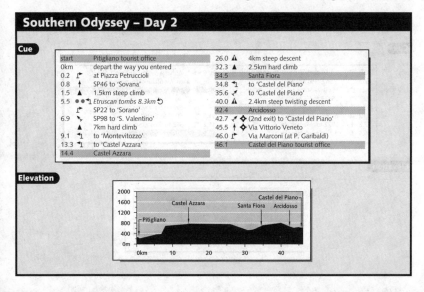

Southern Odyssey – Day 2

Cue

start	Pitigliano tourist office		26.0 ⚠	4km steep descent	
0km	depart the way you entered		32.3 ▲	2.5km hard climb	
0.2 ↱	at Piazza Petruccioli		34.5	Santa Fiora	
0.8 ↑	SP46 to 'Sovana'		34.8 ↰	to 'Castel del Piano'	
1.5 ▲	1.5km steep climb		35.6 ↗	to 'Castel del Piano'	
5.5 ●●↰	Etruscan tombs 8.3km ↺		40.0 ⚠	2.4km steep twisting descent	
↱	SP22 to 'Sorano'		42.4	Arcidosso	
6.9 ↖	SP98 to 'S. Valentino'		42.7 ↗ ◆	(2nd exit) to 'Castel del Piano'	
▲	7km hard climb		45.5 ↑ ◆	Via Vittorio Veneto	
9.1 ↰	to 'Montevitozzo'		46.0 ↱	Via Marconi (at P. Garibaldi)	
13.3 ↰	to 'Castel Azzara'		46.1	Castel del Piano tourist office	
14.4	Castel Azzara				

Elevation

Places to Stay & Eat The nearest camping is at **Camping Amiata** (☎ 0564 95 51 07; Via Roma 15; per person/tent €6/8.50), on your left as you enter town.

Albergo Impero (☎ 0564 95 53 37; Via Roma 7; singles/doubles €26/42, with bathroom €37/55) is the best and most spacious accommodation in town, with a large lawn, decent restaurant and a shed in the back to put the bikes. **Albergo Stella** (☎ 0564 95 53 91; Via Pozzo Stella 24; singles/doubles with bathroom €31/52) is a dingier but adequate alternative. Lock your bike outside or on the porch if the staff let you. **Albergo Da Venerio** (☎/fax 0564 95 52 44; Piazza RG Carducci 18; singles/doubles with bathroom €21/36) is the cheapest decent option in town, located conveniently across from the Coop supermarket.

Ristorante Impero (Via Roma 7; mains €6-9; closed Wed) is a decent, quiet restaurant that caters to an older clientele. **Antico Frantoio** (Corso Nasini 31; pizzas & pastas about €5; closed Tues) is an excellent brick oven pizzeria with a quiet backyard garden. Try the salciccia e cipolla (sausage and onion) pizza. Pasta dishes are less exciting, but decent.

There are two supermarkets in town, the **Punt Sma** (Viale Dante Alighieri 6a) and the **Coop** (Piazza RG Carducci 2a), and a great bakery, **Panificio Amiata** (Via D Santucci 27), on the right towards Montalcino.

Day 3: Castel del Piano to Montalcino/Buonconvento

2½–4½ hours, 43.1km

The easiest day of the journey, Day 3 allows enough time to explore the famed hill town of Montalcino or catch a train to Siena before nightfall. The day contains equal amounts of ascending and descending, the toughest portion of which begins at 16.4km and continues to Montalcino (29.8km). After Montalcino, it's virtually all downhill to Buonconvento.

The 12th-century Romanesque church, **Abbazia di Sant'Antimo** (20.7km), built on the site of a monastery founded by Charlemagne in AD 781, is the first significant point of interest along the way. Definitely pay **Montalcino** (29.8km) a visit. The notorious (and pricey) Brunello wine is produced here. Plan on spending at least one or two hours exploring the town and soaking in the grand views. See the Hill Town Trek section on p108 for more information on Montalcino.

If spending the night in a cosy hill town seems less appealing than seeking out a place with a bit more bustle, scream downhill to Buonconvento. It's easy to catch a train to Siena at the dusty brick train station (with green shutters and a bold 'F.S.' adorning the facade), on the right-hand side (43.1km).

Montalcino

See Montalcino (p109).

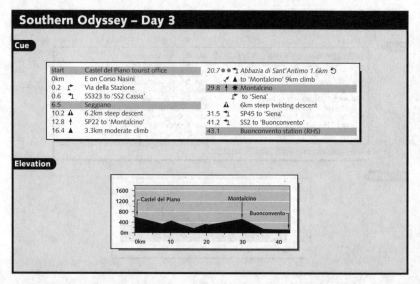

Southern Odyssey – Day 3

Cue

start	Castel del Piano tourist office	20.7 ● ● ⌐	Abbazia di Sant'Antimo 1.6km ↺
0km	E on Corso Nasini	⤴ ▲	to 'Montalcino' 9km climb
0.2 ⌐	Via della Stazione	29.8 † ✳	Montalcino
0.6 ⌐	SS323 to 'SS2 Cassia'	⌐	to 'Siena'
6.5	Seggiano	▲	6km steep twisting descent
10.2 ▲	6.2km steep descent	31.5 ⌐	SP45 to 'Siena'
12.8 †	SP22 to 'Montalcino'	41.2 ⌐	SS2 to 'Buonconvento'
16.4 ▲	3.3km moderate climb	43.1	Buonconvento station (RHS)

Elevation

Liguria, Maritime Alps & Po River Basin

This chapter covers a lot of ground, some of it rolling coastal, some mountainous, and some as flat as a pancake. But that, in many ways, is why Italy is so enticing. Over a 150km span, you can rise from a floodplain's swelter to the nip of an exposed mountain pass, and still finish the day smoothing out any muscular wrinkles in the warm welcome of the Mediterranean's waters.

GATEWAY CITIES
Genoa
Travellers who write off Genoa (Genova) as a dirty port town and bypass it for coastal resorts do the city and themselves a disservice. Once a mighty maritime republic and supposedly the birthplace of Christopher Columbus, Genoa, known as La Superba (literally 'The Proud'), has admittedly lost some of its gloss over the centuries, but none of its fascination. After decades of neglect, the Porto Antico (Old Port) and the entrancing labyrinth of narrow *carrugi* (alleys) at the heart of the once-seedy old city have undergone an extensive and effective makeover.

Information The APT Genoa main office (☎ 010 57 67 91, ⓦ www.apt.genova.it), off central Piazza de Ferrari at Via Roma 11/3, is open daily. There are also offices in the Principe train station (☎ 010 246 26 33) and at the Porto Antico.

Banks are located all over town, with good concentrations around Piazza de Ferrari and in Via Garibaldi.

The Genovese FIAB-affiliated association, Circolo Amici della Bicicletta (☎ 010 362 13 57, ⓦ www.megaone.com/adbgenova) has a full calendar of cycling activities open to all. Also check with Nuovo Centro Sportivo (☎ 010 254 12 43) at Piazza dei Garibaldi 18, which rents bicycles. A very good bicycle shop, Olmo (☎ 010 56 20 25), is in the new part of town at Piazza Rossetti 19r.

Things to See & Do Flanked by the neo-classical facade of the WWII-bombed

Teatro Carlo Felice, the imposing **Borsa** (former stock exchange and now an Art Nouveau haven), **Palazzo dell'Accademia** and **Palazzo Ducale** (seat of the city's rulers from the 13th to 16th centuries and now home to a small jazz museum), renovated Piazza de Ferrari is Genoa's focal point. A stone's throw to the southwest are baroque **Chiesa del Gesù**, which showcases masterpieces by Guido Reni and Peter Paul Rubens, and, further east along Via di Porta Soprana, is **Porta Soprana**, a restored 12th-century gate from the once-unassailable city walls. Back northwest across Piazza Matteotti in Via San Lorenzo is the 12th-century Gothic facade of **Cattedrale di San Lorenzo**. In the cathedral's sacristy is **Museo del Tesoro**, which has the platter upon which Salome is said to have received John the Baptist's head.

Via San Lorenzo, a lovely pedestrian street, cuts through the middle of the old city to the **Porto Antico** and its Piazza delle Feste. Having benefited most from the city's facelift, the port is now Genoa's strongest drawcard with the **Acquario** (supposedly Europe's largest aquarium – 5000 marine animals in 61 tanks); **Il Bigo**, an odd, 200m panoramic lift; **Museo Nazionale dell'Antardide**, a museum devoted to Antarctica; and a **pavilion** about the sea and seafaring.

Parallel to San Lorenzo to the north is **Via Garibaldi**, a must-see street lined with some magnificent, sand-washed palace-museums. Nearby is the inspiring **Palazzo Spinola**, once owned by one of the Republic's most formidable and feared dynasties and now housing Italian and Flemish Renaissance works or art.

Similar surprises await in the area south of Via San Lorenzo, called the **Castello**, as they do in mansion-studded **Via Balbi**, which runs to the main train station. East, in the newer part of town, are large gardens, museums, and portico- and shop-lined **Via XX Settembre**. In the panoramic hills behind the city recline 13km of 17th-century city walls. Take the funicular from Largo della Zecca to **Righi** and follow trails to forts along the ramparts.

Places to Stay The closest camping ground is **Villa Doria** (☎ 010 696 96 00; *Via al Campeggio Villa Doria 15; per person/tent €6/7*), west of town on the road to Pegli. The Hostelling International (HI) **Hostel Genoa** (*☎/fax 010 242 24 57; e hostelge@iol.it; Via Costanzi 120; B&B with card €13; dinner €8*) is to the north, in Righi (follow signs north from Piazza Acquaverde).

One choice budget lodging in the old city is **Hotel Major** (☎ 010 247 41 74; *e hotel major_ge@yahoo.it; Vico Spada 4; singles/doubles €30/40*); cheap and quite friendly. **Hotel Doria** (*☎ 010 247 42 78; Vico dei*

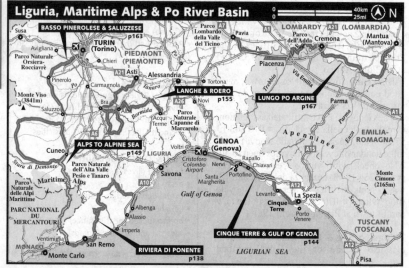

Liguria, Maritime Alps & Po River Basin

0 — 40km
0 — 25mi

N

BASSO PINEROLESE & SALUZZESE p163

LOMBARDY (LOMBARDIA)

Susa
Avigliana
Parco Naturale Orsiera-Rocciavrè
TURIN (Torino)
Chieri
PIEDMONT (PIEMONTE)
Pinerolo
Asti
Alessandria
Tortona
Parco Lombardo della Valle del Ticino
Pavia
Parco dell'Adda
Cremona
Mantua (Mantova)
Piacenza
Po

Monte Viso (3841m)
Saluzzo
Carmagnola
Bra
Alba
Novi
LANGHE & ROERO p155
Via Emilia
Parma
LUNGO PO ARGINE p167

Cuneo
Parco Naturale dell'Alta Valle Pesio e Tanaro
ALPS TO ALPINE SEA p149
LIGURIA
Acqui Terme
Parco Naturale Capanne di Marcarolo
Voltri
GENOA (Genova)
Rapallo
Chiavari
A p e n n i n e s
EMILIA-ROMAGNA
Monte Cimone (2165m)

Parco Naturale delle Alpi Marittime
Maritime Alps
Cristoforo Colombo Airport
Nervi
Savona
Santa Margherita
Portofino
PARC NATIONAL DU MERCANTOUR
Albenga
Alassio
Imperia
Gulf of Genoa
Levanto
Cinque Terre
La Spezia
Porto Venere
TUSCANY (TOSCANA)

MONACO
Ventimiglia
San Remo
Monte Carlo
RIVIERA DI PONENTE p138
CINQUE TERRE & GULF OF GENOA p144
LIGURIAN SEA
Pisa

Garibaldi 3; singles/doubles €16/26) is tucked down a dim alley off Via XXV Aprile. Near the Brignole station, **Albergo Barone** *(☎/fax 010 58 75 78; Via XX Settembre 2/23; singles/doubles €18/23)* is on the 3rd floor of a big-roomed old building.

For a little more money, try **Hotel Cristoforo Colombo** *(☎/fax 010 251 36 43; ⓦ www .hotelcolombo.it; Via Porta Soprana 27; singles/doubles €65/85)*, a charming place in a beautiful part of the old city. One of the grand old establishments of Genovese hospitality is **Hotel Bristol Palace** *(☎ 010 59 25 41; ⓦ www.hotelbristolpalace.com; Via XX Settembre 35; singles/doubles with breakfast €123/142)*.

Places to Eat Self-caterers will have a ball, especially in the old city thick with **trattorias** and **specialty shops**. Try the tastes in and around Via Indoratori. Otherwise, there is a huge **Supermercato Standa** *(Via Antonio Cecchi 83)*, a five-minute walk from Piazza della Vittoria.

For quick, cheap eats in the old city, head to the waterfront around Piazza Caricamento; if you're near Brignole, stick to Via San Vincenzo. More formal, sit-down opportunities also exist. Pizza fans should visit **Taverna da Michele** *(Via della Libertà 41)* for its peaceful and atmospheric terraces. Although kitschy, **Ugo Il Pirata** *(Via Finocchiaro Aprile Camillo 34; closed Mon dinner)* is excellent value with particularly good homemade pastas. For a true *pesto genovese*, in the old town go to **Antica Trattoria Sa Pesta** *(Via del Giustiniani 16; closed Sun & Mon dinner)* or **La Taverna di Colombo** *(Vico della Scienza; closed Mon)*.

Add a few euros to the dinner budget and gastronomic horizons expand. Just off Via Garibaldi, **I Tre Merli** *(☎ 010 247 40 95; Vico della Maddalena 26; dinner €16-26; closed Mon)* is an old stand-by, as is shabby-looking **Ostaja dò Castello** *(☎ 010 246 89 80; Salita Santa Maria di Castello 32; dinner €21-26; closed Tues)*. Near Piazza Dante, one always-packed eating institution is **Trattoria alle Due Torri** *(☎ 010 251 36 37; Salita Prione 53-55; dinner €19-26; closed Sat lunch & Sun)*.

Getting There & Away Cristoforo Colombo international airport is at Sestri Ponente, 6km west of the city. For general flight information call ☎ 010 601 54 10.

The main train station is Piazza Principe at the northwestern edge of the old city, although most trains also pass through the Brignole station on Piazza Verdi east of the old town. Regular services connect with Ventimiglia, Acqui Terme and Asti, Turin, Milan, La Spezia and Rome. Genoa's main long-haul bus station is on Piazza della Vittoria south of the Brignole station.

Expressway A12 runs east from Genoa down the coast to Tuscany. The A7 goes north to Milan and A26 heads directly to the lakes of Lombardy (with a connection to Turin via the A21). Ventimiglia, to the west, is the terminus of A10 along the Ligurian coast.

Genoa's port is an important embarkation point for ferries to Spain, Sicily, Sardinia, Corsica and Elba. During summer, there is also local service to towns east on the Riviera di Levante. Check for times at Cooperativa Battellieri del Porto di Genova (☎ 010 26 57 12).

Cuneo

The largest city in the province of the same name, Cuneo is the self-proclaimed 'green capital' of Piedmont (Piemonte). The compact old town lies in the northern *cuneo* (wedge), perched atop an impressive butte overlooking the Stura di Demonte and Gesso rivers, and the western edge of the Po plain. Cuneo's foundations were laid in the 12th century. Known as the 'city of the seven sieges', Cuneo's history has been replete with conflict from the medieval period to the modern era.

Information The IAT office (☎ 0171 69 32 58, ⓦ www.cuneotourism.com) is at Via Roma 28 in the old town.

Banks line Corso Nizza, the main street south of Piazza Galimberti.

The best bike shop is Ciclo Pepino e Chiapale (☎ 0171 69 09 85), which you will find at Corso Kennedy 13.

Things to See & Do Cuneo's kilometres of arcaded streets – built as protection from winter's bitter cold and freezing rains – and medieval alleys are a stroller's delight. Start at the huge **Piazza Galimberti** and turn into porticoed Via Roma for a trip as far as **Contrada Mondovi** (Mondovi Lane), which best preserves the old city. Left is the 17th-century **duomo** (cathedral), as is, further down Via

Roma, **Palazzo Municipale**. Climb the 13th-century **Torre Civica** for a bird's-eye view of the area. More elegant **palazzi** flank the street, all the way to the tip of the *cuneo*. Off to the west, **Museo Civico**, covering the history of Cuneo and its environs, is located inside the 13th-century **San Francesco cloister**.

Places to Stay & Eat About 1km south of the centre is **Campeggio Bisalta** *(☎ 0171 49 13 34; Fraz. Castagnaretta, Via S. Maurizio 33; tent site for 2 €10.50)*. **Hotel Ligure** *(☎ 0171 68 19 42; Via Savigliano 11; singles/doubles €44/62, dinner from €16)* is a central, well-run and friendly place. **Albergo Cavallo Nero** *(☎ 0171 60 20 17; Piazza Seminario 8; singles/doubles €42/52)* is near the market. For a knockout night of luxury, **Lovera Palace** *(☎ 0171 69 04 20; W www.loverapalace.com; Via Roma 37; singles/doubles €105/141; gourmet dinner €35)* can't be beaten.

Supermarkets are near Piazza Galimberti *(Via Ponza di San Martino)* and an easy walk from the train station *(cnr Corso IV Novembre & Via Felice Cavallotti)*. Of the surprising number of restaurants in Cuneo, on the cheap end, **Ristorante Capri** *(Via Seminario 2; closed Wed)* is cosy. On the main road, try the pasta at **Vecchio Zuavo** *(Via Roma 23; closed Wed)*. **Ristorante Alta Italia** *(Corso IV Novembre 20bis)* is near the train station and serves solid standard fare. Go for the fish dishes at **Pizzeria Tramonti** *(Corso Ferraris 11; closed Wed)*.

Getting There & Away Almost-hourly trains chug south to Ventimiglia (two hours) and north to Turin (1¼ hours). There are also six trains a day (Monday to Friday) north to Saluzzo. Infrequent buses from Cuneo service the Stura valley.

Expressway A6 between Turin and Savona comes closest Cuneo (use the Carru exit).

Liguria

Seaside Liguria is best known for its *riviera*, which simply means 'coast' or 'shore.' However, if properly inflected and crowned with a capital 'R', the words '*the* Riviera' call much more to mind. But don't be misled into thinking that coastal charm makes for perfect, pan-flat pedalling. Rising dramatically to impressive heights a few kilometres inland, the Maritime Alps (Alpi Marittime) – sometimes also called the Ligurian Alps east of Colle di Tenda – and the Apennines (Apennini) give the Riviera its climate and its agricultural richness. It is into these mountains a cyclist must venture for an honest appreciation of Liguria.

HISTORY

Liguria has been blessed and cursed as a transit land caught between Rome and all points north and west. Since prehistory, Ligurians have seen Neanderthals, Cro-Magnon man, the Carthaginians, Romans, Goths, Vandals, Byzantines, Lombards, Franks, Saracens, Germans, French, Spanish and Austrians climb through their mountains and move along their shores. Despite this tumult, Liguria grew into its own. With Genoa in the lead as one of Italy's four great maritime powers, Liguria used the Crusades, the discovery of the New World (Columbus was Ligurian) and the wars of succession to forge an identity. It wasn't until the 19th century when two more locals, Mazzini and Garibaldi, began the Risorgimento, leading to Italy's unification, that Liguria joined the rest of the peninsula.

NATURAL HISTORY

One of Liguria's most enduring qualities is its natural diversity. The 'eternal spring' of the *riviere* and the proximate classic mountain climate have allowed for a marvellous mix of flora. From the profusion of coastal flowers to the higher terraced gardens, and further into the hills where trees proliferate and give way to upper-elevation fields, you can see it all in just a few hours of cycling. The steep-walled valleys and coastal precipices are also perfect for the cultivation of olives, grapes, citrus and a variety of vegetables – foods and their by-products (olive oil, wine, pesto) for which the area is justly famous.

Riviera di Ponente

Duration	2 days
Distance	164.1km
Difficulty	moderate–hard
Start	Ventimiglia
End	Albenga

To the west of Genoa stretches the Riviera di Ponente, the Alp-squished 'coast of the setting sun' that boasts about 3000 botanical species, the papal palms, delicious light wines and arguably the best olive oils in Italy. Here you will find magnificent beach Meccas for sun worshippers; evidence of the Roman 'Salt Roads'; picture-perfect fortified towns; splendid mountain panoramas; and acres of planted, terraced valley slopes.

PLANNING
When to Ride
Spring and autumn are best for biking, with days light and mild enough for outdoor enjoyment, free from summer hordes, and full of festivals. Summer, too, is good, if very hot and crowded.

Maps & Books
The Touring Club Italiano (1:200,000) *Liguria* map (€6.20) is best, although the free Regione Liguria (1:250,000) provincial map available at tourist offices is a good alternative. Ask for other free Regione Liguria maps: two *Itinerari ciclabili dell'entroterra* maps, produced by Claudio Zaccagnino, and *Ligurianatura* (1:250,000), produced by the Parks and Natural Reserves Department.

For local history and culture, the Rivieri dei Fiori APT distributes two free booklets in English, both called *La Terra dei Colori*. Olive fans should get the free *La Strada del Vino e dell'Olio dale Alpi al mare* information packet.

ACCESS TOWN
Ventimiglia
The last Italian city before the French border, Ventimiglia was founded in the 2nd century. It has three distinct parts: the hilltop medieval town, the commercial *centro* (centre) and a new apartment-building spread. People pressing towards more noteworthy beaches and towns usually skip Ventimiglia; for this reason alone, it should be given its due.

Information The IAT office (☎/fax 0184 35 11 83, w www.apt.rivieradeifiori.it) is on the main drag at Via Cavour 61. Most banks are in Via Roma and Corso Repubblica. A good bike shop, Cicli Action, is at Corso Genova 18a, 500m east of the central traffic light.

Things to See & Do Unearthed artefacts are housed in the Forte dell'Annunziata's **Archaeology Museum**. In the narrow streets of the medieval city, admire the 11th- and 12th-

century **Cattedrale dell'Assunta** and its octagonal baptistery, the **Convento delle Canonichesse**, and the first-millennium crypt of the **Chiesa di San Michele**. Also enjoy the majestic **palazzi** on the main Via Garibaldi. Three levels of **fortifications** dating back to the 12th century rise above the town.

Places to Stay & Eat Along the Fiume Roia just north of downtown is **Camping Roma** (☎ 0184 23 90 07; w www.campin groma.it; Via Freccero 121; tent sites per adult €9.50).

Villa Franca (☎ 0184 35 18 71; Corso Repubblica 12; singles/doubles €26/36) is Ventimiglia's best find: simple rooms, straight down from the train station. Nearby, **Hotel XX Settembre** (☎ 0184 35 12 22; Via Roma 16) and **Hotel Calypso** (☎ 0184 35 15 88; w www.calypsohotel.it; Via Matteotti 8) both have singles/doubles from €35/50. **Hotel Al Mare** (☎/fax 0184 23 20 55; Vico Pescatori 7; singles/doubles from €31/42) is five minutes east of the centre.

For self-caterers, a **supermercato** (cnr Via Roma & Via Ruffini), the **central covered market** (Corso Repubblica) and other specialty stores litter the centre. The Friday market extravaganza runs along the Roia. Otherwise, Ventimiglia is awash in passable places to eat. Cheap **sandwich places** line Via Stazione and spill over into Via Hanbury. Choose from seafood menus posted along the seaside Passeggiate Oberdan, Cavallotti and Marconi. Another concentration of **trattorias** includes the western stretch of Via Roma and parallel Via Aprosio.

Getting There & Away Ventimiglia is on the main coastal train line that runs through Genoa (three hours) and Nice (45 minutes), with hourly services to/from both cities. Ventimiglia is also the terminus of a nearly hourly train service from Turin (3½ hours) via Cuneo (1¾ hours).

If driving from Nice (38km) or Genoa (152km), use the Ventimiglia exit from expressway A10. Expressways from the north (Turin – 134km, Milan – 134km) intersect A10 east of Ventimiglia.

Bicycle Ventimiglia is an enjoyable, rolling 41km from Nice along the *basse corniche* (coastal road) via downtown Monte Carlo and Menton.

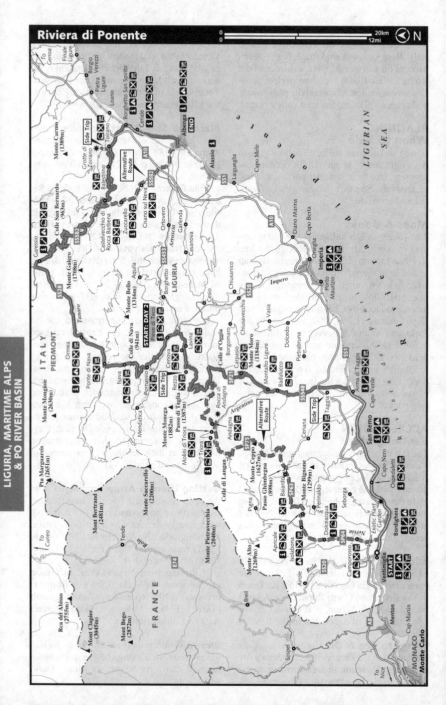

THE RIDE
Day 1: Ventimiglia to Pieve di Teco
4½–8 hours, 76.8km

Today is a back breaker. The ride is long and involves a lot of climbing, especially the alternative route. An early start is advisable. However, the end-of-day reward is a fabulous pitch headlong into the heart of nature-rich alpine Liguria.

Liguria's most famous road, the Via Aurelia, glides along part of one of Italy's most famous stretches of coast, the Riviera dei Fiori. Ventimiglia and beach-abundant, villa-rich **Bordighera** are at the start of a gentle, coastal pedal along a busy road past the **Exotic Plant Garden** to **San Remo** (17km). The latter's medieval centre, art and architecture, villas and gardens, port and century-old casino were instrumental in attracting bygone British holidaymakers and making the Riviera a hot vacation destination. It's still a hectic tourist target.

Now come the hills. From **Arma di Taggia's** beaches, there is a 27.5km crank up to **Colle d'Oggia** (1167m, 52.8km). The gentler inclines of the lower Valle Argentina –

fields of small, black *taggiasca* olives that have lent detour-worthy **Taggia** (28km) and its olive oils such notoriety – give way to steeper, wooded and less forgiving slopes. But the views are tremendous.

Think ahead about lunch: Badalucco (36.5km), Montalto Ligure (41km) and Carpasio (46.5km) are the last chances for prepared food until Rezzo (68.8km).

From the top of Colle d'Oggia, Pieve di Teco is 24km away, all downhill. The quiet low-traffic descent, into the prime **valley** named after the slate-roofed town of **Rezzo**, is through western Liguria's largest forest, an area used for animal grazing since the earliest days of written history.

Alternative Route: Ligurian Hills
5–8 hours 72.8km

For the stout of lung and thigh, this alternative route drives over a dramatic, wooded panoramic road to the 1504m pass near Monte Ceppo and the 1387m Passo di Teglia. In its lower reaches, it's blanketed by a patchwork of mute olive and sun-bright grape greens, and peppered lightly with stone-clad medieval villages. At its heights,

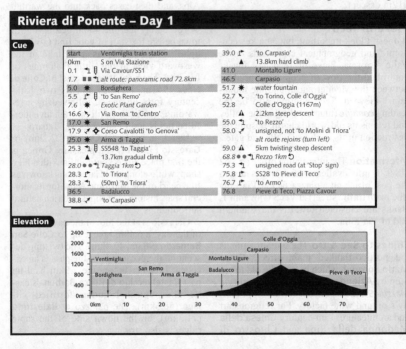

Riviera di Ponente – Day 1

Cue

start	Ventimiglia train station	39.0	↱	'to Carpasio'
0km	S on Via Stazione	▲		13.8km hard climb
0.1	↰ 🅱 Via Cavour/SS1	41.0		Montalto Ligure
1.7	■■↰ alt route: panoramic road 72.8km	46.5		Carpasio
5.0	✳ Bordighera	51.7	✳	water fountain
5.5	↱ 🅱 'to San Remo'	52.7	↘	'to Torino, Colle d'Oggia'
7.6	✳ Exotic Plant Garden	52.8		Colle d'Oggia (1167m)
16.6	↘ Via Roma 'to Centro'	▲		2.2km steep descent
17.0	✳ San Remo	55.0	↰	'to Rezzo'
17.9	↗ ◆ Corso Cavalotti 'to Genova'	58.0	↙	unsigned, not 'to Molini di Triora'
25.0	✳ Arma di Taggia			alt route rejoins (turn left)
25.3	↰ 🅱 SS548 'to Taggia'	59.0	▲	5km twisting steep descent
▲	13.7km gradual climb	68.8	●●↰ Rezzo 1km ↻
28.0	●●↰ Taggia 1km ↻	75.3	↰	unsigned road (at 'Stop' sign)
28.3	↱ 'to Triora'	75.8	↱	SS28 'to Pieve di Teco'
28.3	↰ (50m) 'to Triora'	76.7	↱	'to Armo'
36.5	Badalucco	76.8		Pieve di Teco, Piazza Cavour
38.8	↙ 'to Carpasio'			

Elevation

there is the beauty of remote open-field vistas to the near-distant Maritime Alps. Plan ahead for lunch – there is nothing available for the last 36.5km – and be realistic about time since this is a tough route that will take longer than you may think.

From the eastern edge of Ventimiglia, head north into the Nervia valley, considered the most beautiful in the western Riviera, and home to the medieval, castle-crowned villages of **Dolceacqua** and **Isolabona**. At Isolabona (11.7km from the turn), turn right towards hilltop-village gems **Apricale** (244m, 14.3km) and **Baiardo** (851m, 25.8km). From Baiardo, continue right to Passo Ghimbegna (898m, 27.3km) and then left to **Monte Ceppo** (40.3km). A steep plunge from the panoramic view ends at the main road (1078m, 47.5km) and a right turn to **Molini di Triora** (433m, 59.9km). Lunch here, bracing for the **Passo di Teglia**. Leave plenty of time – two hours or more – for the steep 12km climb of 950m, especially the 7km stretch 'paved' with bone-rattling, loose-rock gravel. The Rezzo valley and a left onto the main route await on the far side, after a 4.5km and 412m descent.

Pieve di Teco

It doesn't look important, but, at a key economic and geographical crossroads in the Valle Arroscia, Pieve di Teco has always controlled the flow of people and produce between the Mediterranean and the mountains. Pieve di Teco continues to be the leading *comune* (municipality) in the valley and retains its old-world charm, despite the destruction of its medieval walls and gates.

Information The information office (☎ 3 62 78/9, e info@vallearroscia.com) is next to the post office on a piazza facing Via Eula (the main traffic street) at Via S Giovanni 1. Banks are clustered towards the southern end of Via Eula.

Things to See & Do The star attraction is the portico-flanked main street, **Corso Mario Ponzoni**, which bisects the old town. Stop by **Azienda L'Angelo dei Sapori** *(Via Mazzini 9)*, the storefront for the Lupi family's oil and wine factory. For religious art and architecture, 15th-century **Chiesa della Madonna della Ripa** and **Chiostro di**

Sant'Agostino preserve some of the city's lost significance, as does the curiously pillarless main **cathedral**.

Places to Stay & Eat At the north end of town is the somewhat dowdy **Albergo Del-l'Angelo** *(☎ 0183 3 62 40; Piazza Carenzi 11; singles/doubles €21/31)*. It has a lunch restaurant only (closed Friday). **Albergo de Filippi** *(☎/fax 0183 36 65 97; Via Eula 35/37; singles/doubles €41/52)* is on the main car thoroughfare and has a welcome bar and restaurant (closed Monday).

Markets and **specialty food shops** are in Corso Ponzoni. On Piazza Cavour, **bars** and a **quick-serve pizza** place have cheap eats for the hasty. Other places for meals are **Il Portico/Trattoria d'Olio** and **Pizzeria 'Da Rita'** *(closed Thur)*, both on Corso Ponzoni, and **Pizzeria dal Maniscalco** *(Via Roberto Manfredi)*.

Day 2: Pieve di Teco to Albenga
5–9 hours, 87.3km

Today's ride is longer but not as hard as yesterday. The route climbs three medium-length passes, all within sight of the towering Alps, and then eases back into the warmth and colour of the seashore.

You barely feel the 400m getting out of town before the start of your first (10.7km) uphill. Pause in **Pornassio** to take in the westward view of the 'little Dolomites of Liguria'. The busy, touristy crest of **Colle di Nava** (941m, 11.1km) and its two 18th-century **forts** lie ahead, followed by a rewarding, gentle downhill through lavender-filled fields and Piedmont's Val Tanaro.

Lunch in medieval **Ormea** (22.2km) or **Garessio** (35.9km) is a pleasure. Ormea is the first place since Ventimiglia with a bike shop, while elongated Garessio is known as 'the pearl of the Maritime Alps' for its mineral spas, historical vestiges and rich natural surroundings.

Garessio is at the foot of the easiest climb of the day, a 6.4km breeze up to **Colle San Bernardo** (963m, 42.4km). The twisting descent on the ocean side of the pass is an excellent breather before the 7.9km haul up past **Castelvecchio di Rocca Barbena's** castle and typical Ligurian fortified village (58.6km). The palazzo at **Balestrino** (71.3km), on the down side of the same ridge, is also striking.

Back in the seaside flats, a small road hugs the coast to Albenga's doorstep. The ancient towers of this monument-rich city appear long before the square near a modern suspension bridge at the heart of town.

As an alternative to the third climb, the road from Colle San Bernardo continues all the way down to the coast at Albenga. On the way, brake for the perfect medieval village of **Zuccarello**, once the most important town in the Neva valley.

Side Trip: Grotte di Toirano
6km return

More than 200 million years ago, underground rivers carved the Varatella system of 70 caverns into an otherworldly tangle of calciferous wonders in the karstic dolomite complex outside the village of Toirano. Who knows what hibernating bears, Paleolithic Neanderthals and their later Cro-Magnon cousins (who left footprints behind!) thought of these formations? There are 1280m of galleries open to the public. It's open from 9am to noon and 2pm to 5pm daily.

To get there, just before the right turn towards Borghetto San Spirito on the out-skirts of Toirano (75.9km), turn left onto Via Carretto, signed for 'Grotte di Toirano'. Turn left again after 30m and then follow signs 3km to the cave entrance.

Albenga

Historically, Albenga is one of the most important cities of coastal Liguria; its physical history – vestiges remain from Roman, Byzantine, medieval, Renaissance and Baroque times – is, in many ways, the story of Liguria. The silting up of the Cento River has today left a fertile cultivated plain and an extensive beach.

Information The IAT office (☎ 0182 55 84 44, **w** www.italianriviera.com) is just off Piazza del Popolo at Viale Martiri della Libertà 1. Many banks are on Piazza del Popolo and adjacent Piazza Petrarca. The best bike shop is Bike Race (☎ 0182 5 07 72) at Via Genova 71.

Things to See & Do Other than indulging in beach fun, stick to the *centro storico* (historic centre). Start at Piazza San Michele, dominated by three 13th-century brick

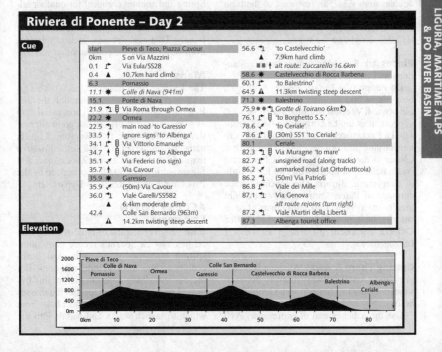

Riviera di Ponente – Day 2

Cue

start	Pieve di Teco, Piazza Cavour	
0km	S on Via Mazzini	
0.1	↰	Via Eula/SS28
0.4	▲	10.7km hard climb
6.3		Pornassio
11.1	✷	Colle di Nava (941m)
15.1		Ponte di Nava
21.9	↰ 🍴	Via Roma through Ormea
22.2	✷	Ormea
22.5	↰	main road 'to Garessio'
33.5	↑	ignore signs 'to Albenga'
34.1	↱ 🍴	Via Vittorio Emanuele
34.7	↑	ignore signs 'to Albenga'
35.1	↙	Via Federici (no sign)
35.7	↑	Via Cavour
35.9		Garessio
35.9	↙	(50m) Via Cavour
36.0	↰	Viale Garelli/SS582
	▲	6.4km moderate climb
42.4		Colle San Bernardo (963m)
	⚠	14.2km twisting steep descent

56.6	↰	'to Castelvecchio'
	▲	7.9km hard climb
	■ ■ ↑	*alt route: Zuccarello 16.6km*
58.6	✷	Castelvecchio di Rocca Barbena
60.1	↱	'to Balestrino'
64.5	⚠	11.3km twisting steep descent
71.3	✷	Balestrino
75.9	● ● ↰	*Grotte di Toirano 6km* ↻
76.1	↱ 🍴	'to Borghetto S.S.'
78.6	↗	'to Ceriale'
78.6	↱ 🍴	(30m) SS1 'to Ceriale'
80.1		Ceriale
82.3	↰ 🍴	Via Muragne 'to mare'
82.7	↱	unsigned road (along tracks)
86.2	↙	unmarked road (at Ortofrutticola)
86.2	↰	(50m) Via Patrioti
86.8	↱	Viale dei Mille
87.1	↰	Via Genova
		alt route rejoins (turn right)
87.2	↰	Viale Martiri della Libertà
87.3		Albenga tourist office

Elevation

towers. They are clustered near the 11th-century Romanesque **Cattedrale di San Michele** and 5th-century Byzantine **baptistry**. Two museums have entrances nearby: the artefact-filled **Civico Museo Ingauno** and **Museo Navale Romano**, devoted principally to items salvaged from a 1st-century Roman ship. Otherwise, walk the streets lined with 16th- and 17th-century **palazzi**, or trot 10 minutes east of Piazza Garibaldi along Viale Pontelungo to the 13th-century **Ponte Lungo**, built to span the former bed of the Cento River. Olive-oil lovers will enjoy the permanent display on olive cultivation at Via Mameli 7.

Places to Stay There are 16 **camping grounds** spread along the seashore. Tent sites for two run from €25 to €45.

Albenga's best bargains are **Hotel Torino** (☎/fax 0182 5 08 44; Viale Italia 25), on the main street to the beaches, and **Hotel Italia** (☎ 0182 5 04 05; Viale Martiri della Liberta 8) opposite the information office. Both have singles/doubles from around €30/45.

For slightly more, try **Hotel Concordia** (☎ 0182 5 02 63; Viale Patrioti 46; singles/doubles from €33/58), just west of the train station. Charming **Hotel Ancora d'Oro** (☎ 0182 5 18 56; Via Sauro 90; singles/doubles €35/55) is right on the water.

Places to Eat Most hotels have restaurants and cafés.

Da Puppo (Via Torlaro 20) has Albenga's best pizzas and *farinata*. Elsewhere in the old town, **Il Vecchio Mulino** (Via Torlaro 13) is good, as is hip **La Linguaccia** (Via Cavour 40). **La Pazzazucca** (Via Torlaro 34) caters to vegetarians and organic food aficionados. Closer to the beach, **Pizzeria Al Cantuccio** (Viale Italia 4) is family-run and has a little of everything. **Birreria alle Macine**, at the entrance of Parco Minisports, serves light meals in a beer hall ambiance. For a splurge, be sure to reserve ahead at **Antica Osteria dei Leoni** (☎ 0182 5 19 37; Via Lengueglia 49).

Getting There & Away Albenga is on the principal coastal railway, midway between Ventimiglia (1½ hours) and Genoa (1½ hours).

Use the Albenga exit of expressway A10 if driving.

Bicycle Ventimiglia is 72km west of Albenga along seaside SS1. Genoa is approximately 90km to the east on the same road.

Cinque Terre & Gulf of Genoa

Duration	2 days
Distance	130.7km
Difficulty	moderate–hard
Start	La Spezia
End	Genoa

East of Genoa unfolds the Riviera di Levante, laced in by the northern Apennines, and harbour to storybook villages along the Paradiso Gulf, Gulf of Tigullio and the World Heritage-listed Cinque Terre. Two days of pedalling up steep, vineyard-covered slopes and down to sultry, soft-sand beaches will only whet your appetite. Oh, and the food! You will never be able to eat enough to satisfy your hunger for variety.

PLANNING
When to Ride
Spring and autumn are ideal for outdoor adventuring; days are still long, the light is bright, and the temperature is no longer beastly. That said, crowds flock to this area even well outside the peak summer months.

Maps
The Touring Club Italiano (1:200,000) *Liguria* map (€6.20) is best, although the free Regione Liguria (1:250,000) provincial map available at tourist offices is a good alternative. Ask for other free Regione Liguria maps: two *Itinerari ciclabili dell'entroterra* maps, produced by Claudio Zaccagnino, and *Ligurianatura* (1:250,000), produced by the Parks and Natural Reserves Department.

ACCESS TOWN
La Spezia
It isn't high on the list of must-see Ligurian centres, but La Spezia's facade is an uninspiring hodgepodge of 19th- and 20th-century architecture and industrial ports. But there is something appealing about this bypassed naval centre, perhaps that the masses have skipped it. It's also a perfect base from which to launch walks and pedals into the magical surrounding countryside.

Information The main APT/IAT (☎ 0187 77 09 00, ⓦ www.aptcinqueterre.sp.it) is near the waterfront at Viale Mazzini 45. For advance information about the Cinque Terre, write to ⓔ parconazionale5terre@libero.it. Banks have branches on Via Chiodo. The city's best bike shop is Bellotto (☎ 0187 2 03 54) at Viale Italia 109, 500m east of the tourist office.

Things to See & Do The compact historical core has the city's principal attractions. Two blocks east of Piazza Cavour, on Via Prione, **Museo Amedeo Lia** houses an extensive private art collection in the former 17th-century Convento dei Paolotti. On the hill above the museum, **Castello San Giorgio** contains the Roman, primitive and prehistoric collections of the Archaeology Museum. At Piazza Chiodo are the **Museo Navale**, one of Italy's most important naval museums, and **Museo d'Arte Contemporanea**. For determined strollers, make a circuit taking in pedestrian Via Prone, Piazza San Agostino, palm-lined Passeggiatta Morin, the botanical **Giardini Pubblici** and arcaded Via Chiodo.

Places to Stay There are no camping grounds at La Spezia; try neighbouring Arcola and Lerici. Also ask IAT offices about *agriturismo* (tourist accommodation on farms) options. One of the nearest hostels is **Ostello Cinque Terre** (☎ 0187 92 02 15; ⓦ www.cinqueterre.net/ostello; Via Riccobaldi 21; dorm beds €20; meals €12) in Manarola.

Albergo Parma (☎ 0187 74 30 10; Via Fiume 143; singles/doubles without bathroom €28/45) is a few steps from the train station. **Albergo Venezia** (☎ 0187 73 34 65; Via Paleocapa 10; basic singles/doubles €26/52) is a nearby three-star hotel. Closer to the centre is adequate but dingy **Albergo Teatro** (☎/fax 0187 73 13 74; Via Carpenino 31; singles/doubles €28/46). **Albergo Il Sole** (☎ 0187 73 51 64; ⓔ albergo.ilsole@libero.it; Via Cavallotti 31; singles/doubles without bathroom €31/39) is around the corner and a step up in quality.

Places to Eat For homemade meal makings, shop at the daily **market** on Piazza Cavour. **Casalini** (Via Prione 91) is one of many excellent bread/pastry stores on Via Prione.

Many **fast-food joints** lurk on Via Fiume, near the train station. In the vicinity of the central hotels, try **Ristorante di Bayon** (Via Cavallotti 23; set menu €14.50). **Trattoria da Luciano** (Via Colombo 27) is cheap and has large servings, including local specialty *mesc-ciua* (soup of chick peas and spelt). **Trattoria Toscana da Dino** (Via da Passano 17) is known for its seafood. **Ristorante All'Incontro** (Via Sapri 10) has affordable, tasty pasta.

Getting There & Away La Spezia is on the coastal Genoa–Rome train line, which is connected to Milan and Turin via Genoa (one to two hours), and to Pisa (one to 1½ hours). The slowest of the frequent services from Genoa makes local stops the length of the Paradiso Gulf, the Gulf of Tigullio and the Cinque Terre. ATC buses cover the short distances to Lerici and Portovenere.

During summer and on most weekends, La Spezia is accessible by ferry from Genoa. Check for times and details in La Spezia at Navigazione Golfo dei Poeti (☎ 0187 73 29 87) and in Genoa at Cooperativa Battellieri del Porto di Genova (☎ 010 26 57 12).

If driving, expressways A12 and A15 intersect just outside of La Spezia. Use the La Spezia exit from A12 (connecting Genoa and Pisa) or the Stagnoni terminus of A15 (from Parma).

Bicycle Pisa is approximately 75km from La Spezia along the busy SS1 or the touristy, seaside SS432. Parma is a more difficult 125km ride on the SS62 over the 1039m Passo della Cisa.

THE RIDE
Day 1: La Spezia to Sestri Levante
4½–8 hours, 77.3km

Today is spent in Parco Nazionale delle Cinque Terre, a protected, spread of precipitously steep terraced vineyards, olive groves, cluster pines and forests of chestnuts. The only road climbs to a perch high above the coast and the five ravine-lining fishing villages of Riomaggiore, Manarola, Corniglia, Vernazza and Monterosso (the *Cinque Terre* or Five Lands) before dropping to lunch and the lapping of waves at Levanto. A swim is *de rigueur* before the

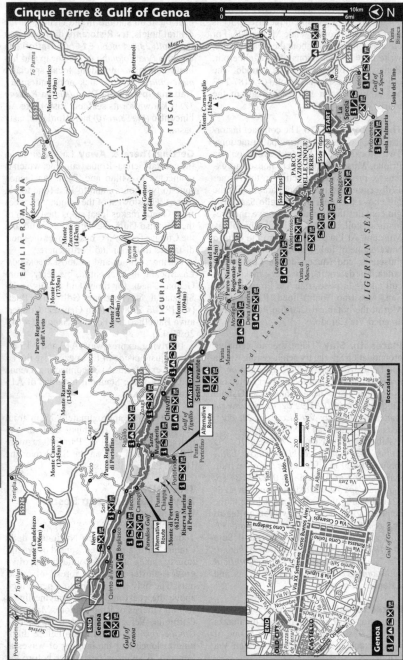

grind up 615m to Passo del Bracco and a screaming plunge back to sea level at Sestri Levante.

From La Spezia, head for the hills. And hills there are: 300m up from the city limits to a lookout over the whole of the **Cinque Terre** and then 25km of (sometimes steeply) 'rolling' terraced terrain through some of Italy's most extraordinary countryside. The turns for the villages fly by. Visit each seaside settlement at your own peril; every metre down is a metre met again coming up.

Take lunch in **Levanto** (41.5km), the only seaside town to which all roads necessarily lead. If there is time after a beach break, check out the medieval **Castello San Giorgio**, **Chiesa della Costa** and **Loggia Medievale**, off Piazza del Popolo in the eastern part of town.

Then it's back to work. A long, stiff climb leads away from the coast to **Passo del Bracco** (615m, 58.5km). The start of the climb is particularly brutal and almost shadeless, but the sweet views and abundant nature are worth it. From the Passo del Bracco almost 20km of windy descent finishes in the heart of civilisation at Sestri Levante.

Sestri Levante

Sestri Levante shares the shores of the Gulf of Tigullio with famous neighbours Chiavari, Rapallo and Portofino. The bay's beauty, climate and bounty have held the attention of the nobility for centuries and today draw more than one million visitors a year. Rich in artistic and religious significance, Sestri Levante's past is particularly well evoked by the yesteryear Genovese gentry's grandiose villas, now also symbolic of the region's present-day splendour.

Information The IAT office (☎ 0185 45 70 11, ⓔ infoapt@apttigullio.liguria.it) and banks are on the central roundabout, Piazza San Antonio. For bike business, go to Bo (☎ 0185 4 47 25) at Via Nazionale 417a.

Things to See & Do As with all of the communities on the Gulf of Tigullio, the sea and coast is the primary distraction. **Beaches**, **boats**, and **scuba** and **bathing establishments** keep people busy all day, every day. For a change of pace, there are excellent one-day **hikes** in Parco Nazionale delle Cinque Terre and on the promontory at Portofino.

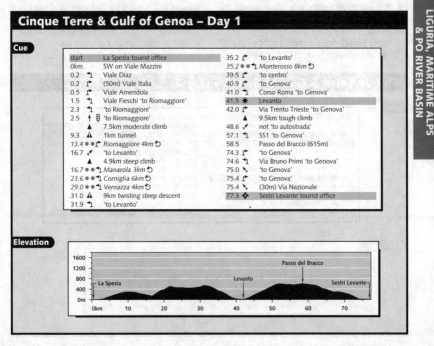

Cinque Terre & Gulf of Genoa – Day 1

Cue

start	La Spezia tourist office	
0km	SW on Viale Mazzini	
0.2	Viale Diaz	
0.2	(50m) Viale Italia	
0.5	Viale Amendola	
1.5	Viale Fieschi 'to Riomaggiore'	
2.3	'to Riomaggiore'	
2.5	'to Riomaggiore'	
▲	7.5km moderate climb	
9.3	1km tunnel	
13.4 ● ●	*Riomaggiore 4km* ↺	
16.7	'to Levanto'	
▲	4.9km steep climb	
16.7 ● ●	*Manarola 3km* ↺	
23.6 ● ●	*Corniglia 6km* ↺	
29.0 ● ●	*Vernazza 4km* ↺	
31.0 ▲	9km twisting steep descent	
31.9	'to Levanto'	
35.2	'to Levanto'	
35.2 ● ●	*Monterosso 8km* ↺	
39.5	'to centro'	
40.9	'to Genova'	
41.0	Corso Roma 'to Genova'	
41.5 ✳	Levanto	
42.0	Via Trento Trieste 'to Genova'	
▲	9.5km tough climb	
48.6	not 'to autostrada'	
57.1	SS1 'to Genova'	
58.5	Passo del Bracco (615m)	
74.3	'to Genova'	
74.6	Via Bruno Primi 'to Genova'	
75.0	'to Genova'	
75.4	'to Genova'	
75.4	(30m) Via Nazionale	
77.3 ◆	Sestri Levante tourist office	

Elevation

Elevation profile (metres): markers at La Spezia (0km), Levanto (~41.5km), Passo del Bracco (~58.5km), Sestri Levante (~77km). Y-axis: 0m, 400, 800, 1200, 1600. X-axis: 0km, 10, 20, 30, 40, 50, 60, 70.

In town, a number of the area's famous villas can be admired. Viale Rimembranza's **Villa Balbi** and the promontory-dominating **Villa Gualino** both double as luxury accommodations. The grounds of Grand Hotel dei Castelli share the tip of the peninsula with **Convento della Santissima Annunziata** and **Palazzo Negrotto Cambiaso**, majestic architectural wonders (now civic buildings) overlooking the lovely beach on the Bay of Silence.

Places to Stay Sestri Levante has more than 30 hotels.

Camping Fondeghino (☎ 0185 40 92 09; Loc. Villa La Rocca 59; tent sites €20) is not the closest camping ground, but in contrast with those nearer, it's clean and peaceful.

Albergo La Neigra (☎ 0185 4 17 56; Viale Roma 49; singles/doubles €27/45) is near the train station and has no private toilets, but a good value restaurant. Jointly run **Albergo Principe** and **Albergo Roma** (☎ 0185 4 10 41; e hotelromaprincipe@libero.it; Viale Mazzini 38 & 42; singles/doubles with bathroom €42/52) are across from the tourist office. In the centre of town, **Villa Jolanda** (☎/fax 0185 4 13 54, w www.villaiolanda.com; Via Pozzetto 15; singles/doubles from €40/60) is right on the peninsula.

Grand Hotel dei Castelli (☎ 0185 48 57 80; w www.rainbownet.it/htl.castelli; Via

Penisola 26; singles/doubles €160/200) is the height of luxury.

Places to Eat A wide variety of food options is clustered on the isthmus on Via Rimembranza and the main alleyway (Via XXV Aprile). **Trattoria Da ü Galetü** (cnr Viale Dante & Viale Rimembranza; set menus €10 & €25) is a step back from the water. Nearby, on Via Rimembranza, **Il Coccodrillo**, **Don Luigi** and **Pizzeria Riri** are popular, the last two especially for pizza. Try the stoccafisso (salted cod in a crispy batter or tasty sauce) and other sea fare at **La Cantina del Polpo** (Piazza Cavour 2) and **Polpo Mario** (Via XXV Aprile). For dessert, slurp a glass of the Cinque Terre's unique dessert wine, Sciacchetrà, or sample gelato at **Baciollo** and **Gelataria 83** on Via XXV Aprile.

Day 2: Sestri Levante to Genoa
3–6 hours, 53.4km

This is a short and relatively easy ride. The route skirts the shore the length of the Gulf of Tigullio, gains some altitude as it summits the ridge behind Monte di Portofino and then drops back to roll along the Paradiso Gulf's edge all the way to downtown Genoa.

Riding on this morning's road has resulted in many cricks in cyclists' necks. It's just too hard not to look at the azure waters

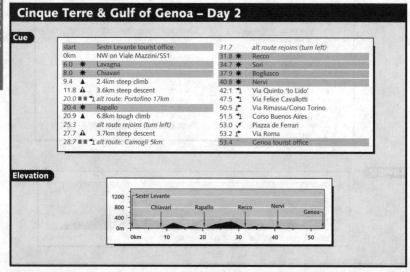

Cinque Terre & Gulf of Genoa – Day 2

Cue

start	Sestri Levante tourist office		
0km	NW on Viale Mazzini/SS1	31.7	alt route rejoins (turn left)
6.0 ✳	Lavagna	31.8 ✳	Recco
8.0 ✳	Chiavari	34.7 ✳	Sori
9.4 ▲	2.4km steep climb	37.9 ✳	Bogliasco
11.8 ⚠	3.6km steep descent	40.8 ✳	Nervi
20.0 ■■↰	alt route: Portofino 17km	42.1 ↰	Via Quinto 'to Lido'
20.4 ✳	Rapallo	47.5 ↰	Via Felice Cavallotti
20.9 ▲	6.8km tough climb	50.5 ↱	Via Rimassa/Corso Torino
25.3	alt route rejoins (turn left)	51.5 ↰	Corso Buenos Aires
27.7 ⚠	3.7km steep descent	53.0 ↗	Piazza de Ferrari
28.7 ■■↰	alt route: Camogli 5km	53.2 ↱	Via Roma
		53.4	Genoa tourist office

Elevation

of the Mediterranean. Fortunately, the Tigullian shore is a perfect place to stop and soak sore muscles into submission. The beaches at **Lavagna** and **Chiavari** (8km) are wide and welcoming.

Rapallo (20.4km), at the far end of the gulf, is a major resort with some fine **Roman ruins**. Most people don't stop here, preferring the quieter, haughty lustre of **Santa Margherita** and **Portofino**, and chance encounters with the rich and famous. Both villages are worth the extra kilometres for the boasting value, hikes on the promontory, and vistas from Portofino's **castle** and **lighthouse**.

Back on the main road, the hill over Portofino's promontory will raise a sweat. On the way back down, detour through **Camogli** (28.7km) for its well-decorated buildings gleaming along the port like a homing beacon for wayward sailors. The town's 12th-century **Castello Dragone** and **Chiesa di Santa Maria Assunta** draw quite a crowd.

The next 10km roll the length of the Paradiso Gulf through beachfront communities of great renown: **Recco**, the 'gastronomic capital of Liguria' boasts Italy's best focaccia; **Sori** has its beaches; **Bogliasco** is celebrated for its mimosas and castello; and **Nervi** is a cultural pole of art museums, and summer ballet and film festivals.

Nervi (40.8km) is at the eastern edge of Genoa, whose central fountain-graced Piazza de Ferrari is only 12.2km away.

Genoa
See Genoa (p135).

Maritime Alps

The Maritime Alps (Alpi Marittime) are a spur of snowcapped giants that reach down from Colle della Maddalena the length of the southern French-Italian border and splash into the Mediterranean Sea, rippling the landscape for hundreds of kilometres. The sierra also sweeps southeast as the Ligurian Alps before giving way to the Ligurian Apennines behind Genoa. Veiled in a quiet and wild obscurity but easily accessible, the Alpi Marittime are rich in culture, lush forests, rugged ridges, and glacial valleys sheltering high meadows.

HISTORY
The valleys on either side of the Maritime Alps have been populated since the Bronze Age, when pastoral peoples (the 'ancient Ligurians', whose rock engravings from about 1800 BC to 1500 BC have been uncovered) first cherished their value. Best known during Roman times for the Sentiero del Sale (Salt Road), a sea-to-scree trade route that passed through the Maritime Alps, the area was also recognised for its Gallic cultural unity, which found full voice in the Middle Ages through a single language – *langue d'Oc* – and a palpable Occitan identity. It wasn't until the 1713 Treaty of Utrecht that the region's lands (then part of the Savoy state) were divided. In recent years, especially since borders have dissolved in the European Union, interest has resurged in long-forgotten, cross-border Occitan culture.

NATURAL HISTORY
Despite the cultural unity in the Maritime Alps, its position at a geographical and geological crossroads is characterised by a large variety of landscapes, plants and animals. In contrast to the solid and squat white-granite massifs in Parco Naturale delle Alpi Marittime to the west, to the east are wind-carved and mottled limestone giants rooted over extensive networks of karstic caves in Parco Naturale dell'Alta Valle Pesio e Tanaro. To the south, the middle slopes rich in a Mediterranean abundance unusual at such elevations (warmed by the tempering effect of the sea) give way (in less than 10km) to sparse, northern Alpine pastures and plants. Even animals rarely seen in lower climes – chamois, ibex, Alpine marmot – are a mere bray away from their woodland neighbours – deer, boar, fox, badger, marten and hare.

Alps to Alpine Sea

Duration	3 days
Distance	272.1km
Difficulty	hard
Start	Cuneo
End	Ventimiglia

Three tough passes in three tough days. This isn't a routine route, but wow is it dazzling. Four valleys – Varaita, Maira, Grana and Stura – radiate westwards from Cuneo and divide the terrain of the first two days. These verdant valleys are only the overture and entr'acte of a rich experience in a high-altitude theatre starring the remote, awesome slopes of Colle di Sampeyre, Colle d'Esischie and Colle Faunaria/dei Morti. As a thigh-busting epilogue, Day 3 is a pedal over Colle di Tenda and down the scenic Roia Valley to the sea.

PLANNING
When to Ride
Relative to the northern Alps, the weather slap in the Maritime Alps is softened by the proximate Mediterranean climate. However, we are still talking about mountains: chilly and rainy springs, brisk autumns, and cold and snowy winters. The best time for two wheeling is from May to October, although even at the height of summer, in the higher elevations, nights (and many days) can be chilly, rainy, foggy and even snowy.

Maps
The Touring Club Italiano (1:200,000) *Liguria* or *Piemonte* maps (€6.20) are best. The free Regione Liguria (1:250,000) and Cuneo (1:200,000) provincial maps available at tourist offices are also good. For the Day 3 of the ride, look for the superb, free *Ligurian Alps – Franco-Italian hiking itineraries* (1:50,000) map by the Provincia di Imperia/Conseil Général des Alpes-Maritimes.

ACCESS TOWN
See Cuneo (p137).

THE RIDE
Day 1: Cuneo to Marmora-Vernetti
5–9 hours, 89.5km
A total of 2198m of climbing on the first day alone dissuades many from thinking about this ride. Don't let it. There *is* a lot of uphill today, but most is packed into a single 1336m plod to Colle di Sampeyre. The first part of the day (preceding the pass) is a mellow 50km stint up the Varaita valley. After the *colle* (the lowest point of a ridge connecting two mountain peaks) there is a 1355m nosedive to the floor of the Maira valley, followed by a salt-in-wound trudge up 354m in 4.7km to the hotel door.

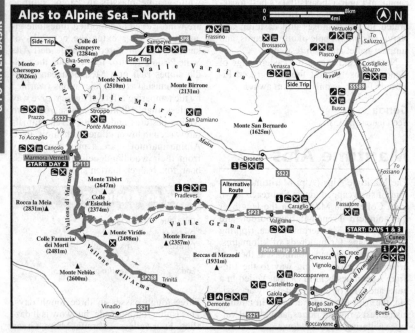

LIGURIA, MARITIME ALPS & PO RIVER BASIN

Alps to Alpine Sea – South

The first 23.8km are no challenge. A straightforward ride on a wooded plain and through small villages leads into the mountains, finding form in the morning haze. Admire the **castles**, baroque **churches** and medieval **towers** at Busca (17.5km) and Costigliole (23.3km).

From Costigliole, the easy alpine-valley atmosphere of Varaita makes the next 27.5km upward roll to Sampeyre seem easy. Take the short, snack detour into the market centre of **Venasca** (31.8km) for its famous bread and salami.

Sampeyre (51.3km) is an ideal place for a rest and lunch before assaulting the pass. Stroll the length of the main street to take in some local attractions: **medieval buildings**, an **ethnological museum** and the **Chiesa dei SS Pietro e Paolo**. Self-caterers and bonk-prone snack fiends should stock up in Sampeyre. Other than a small store in Canosio, there are no good markets until tomorrow afternoon at Demonte.

Now, take a deep breath. There's no way around what lies ahead: 15.9km of killer climb. Unfortunately, the shade doesn't last long, giving way to open alpine meadow and falling-rock scree slopes. Small hillside settlements advertise local produce, but the artisans are often off tending to fields and wandering flocks.

If the barren Colle di Sampeyre (2284m, 67.6km) seems like an anticlimax, remember that there's a downhill! The road wiggles down through panoramic reaches to the tree line at the head of the **Vallone di Elva** (make the detour to Elva Serre for food and fresh water, the first since Sampeyre). Ahead unfurls one of the most magnificent descents in the Alps.

The lush Valle Maira lies at the bottom. Ponte Marmora (84.8km – whose restaurant and fountain are important if those at Elva were bypassed) is just ahead to the right, at the turn uphill for Marmora-Vernetti.

The Vernetti *borgata* (burg) of Marmora and an evening of rest are now just 4.7km away. Appreciating the natural splendour may be tough on this short and sheer final climb, but the **Vallone di Marmora** is simply stunning.

Marmora-Vernetti

Marmora-Vernetti is a remote mountain hamlet overlooking the confluence of two small rivers and their valleys. Facing Marmora, across a deep, open dip and towered over by the Monte Cassorso massif, is the slightly larger village of Canosio. For local information, check the bulletin board outside Pensione Ceaglio.

Things to See & Do People come here for quiet, mountain charm. That's about all there is: pleasant **hikes**, isolated *trune* (stone shelters) and small summer-becalmed winter resorts. Some of Marmora's higher *borgate* do have fine old buildings, particularly the 15th-century **Chiesa di San Sebastiano** on the path leading to Torello. The Canosio *comune* also has some charming old structures and a prominent **parochial church**.

Places to Stay & Eat The only accommodation option in Marmora-Vernetti is **Trattoria/Pensione Ceaglio** (☎ 0171 99 81 17; Frazione Vernetti 5; half-pension €34; dinner €13). Fortunately, the rooms are comfortable, and dinners copious and excellent. There is a small **alimentari** (grocery shop) in Canosio.

Day 2: Marmora-Vernetti to Cuneo
4½–7½ hours, 75.3km

Today is the recompense for yesterday's labour. Just 17.9km away, at the top of the Vallone di Marmora, Colle Faunaria/dei Morti is the green light for 25.1km of tearjerking descent to the Stura valley and then a 32.3km rolling spin back to Cuneo.

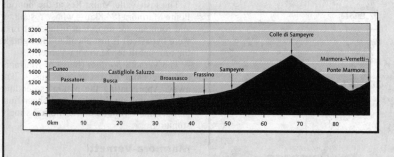

Alps to Alpine Sea – Day 1

Cue

start	Cuneo tourist office	43.5		Frassino
0km	SW on Via Roma	47.1 ▲		4km moderate climb
0.5	Piazza Galimberti	51.3 ●●↱		Sampeyre 0.4km ↻
0.7 ↱ ⏚	Corso Marcello Soleri bikepath	51.4 ↰		'to Colle di Sampeyre'
1.0	(2nd exit) Viadotto Soleri	51.7 ▲		15.9km very hard climb
2.1 ◆	(2nd exit) 'to Caraglio'	67.6		Colle di Sampeyre (2284m)
2.3 ↱ ⏚	Via del Passatore 'to Busca'		▲	16.2km steep descent
7.0	Passatore	71.5 ↱		unsigned, not to Stroppo
15.0 ↱	'to Busca'	75.0 ↱		unsigned, not to Elva
16.9 ◆	(3rd exit) SS589 'to Saluzzo'	75.0 ●●↰		Elva Serre 0.4km ↻
17.5 ✳	Busca	83.8 ↱		SS22 'to Acceglio'
23.3 ✳	Castigliole Saluzzo	84.8		Ponte Marmora
23.8 ↰	'to Piasco'		↰	'to Marmora'
	▲	23.3km gradual climb	88.8 ↑	'to Marmora'
25.8 ◆	(3rd exit) 'to Sampeyre'	89.3 ↱		'to centro'
31.8 ●●↰	Venasca 1km ↻	89.5		Marmora-Vernetti Pensione Ceaglio
34.8	Brossasco			

Elevation

The upslope begun yesterday is continued today: up some extreme inclines through fly-thick, shaded woods to the wide curve at the top of the Vallone di Marmora. On the far side of an intermediate pass – **Colle d'Esischie** (2374m; 16.4km) – there is a choice between a left to the descent via Valle Grana (one of Italy's steepest) or a right to **Colle Faunaria/dei Morti** (2481m, 17.9km), visible 1.4km away up to the right. (The Valle Grana alternative route drops 1535km in 20km to Pradleves and then continues down 250m and 13.2km to Caraglio, before a right on SS22 across the edge of the flatlands to Cuneo.)

From Colle Faunaria/dei Morti, the city of **Demonte** (43.3km), the first urban centre since Sampeyre, is nestled 1701m below at the bottom of the Vallone dell'Arma.

Only interrupt the plummet for a bite at the makeshift food kiosk (26km) or for fresh water from a fountain in the lower valley.

After Demonte, the converted military road on the far side of the valley is a nicer, car-free alternative to the main thoroughfare. Above Gaiola, when this same principal truck route abruptly crosses your country lane, shift back to the north side of the river for a quiet spin through the villages of Castelletto and Roccasparvera. The high plateau on the far side of the river is the mesa the northern tip of which is Cuneo, just 15km away.

Day 3: Cuneo to Ventimiglia
7–11 hours, 107.3km

Today's route is another classic up-and-down toil-and-reward ride. The morning

---

Alps to Alpine Sea – Day 2

Cue

start	Marmora-Vernetti Pensione Ceaglio		45.5 ↰	'to Festiona'
0km	N to main road		47.4 ↖	'to Cuneo'
0.2 ↱	'to Demonte'		48.2 ↑	'to Cuneo'
▲	16.2km tough climb		56.6 ↰	unsigned SS21
1.7 ↑	'to Passo del Faunaria'		58.0 ↱	'to Roccasparvera'
3.3 ↰	with hairpin		61.8 ↰	'to Vignolo'
7.7 ▲	1km very steep climb		65.0 ↰ 日	SS22 'to Cervasca, Caraglia'
16.4	unsigned Colle d'Esischie (2374m)		65.7 ↑	'to Cuneo'
16.5 ↱	'to Valle Stura'		66.6 ↱	'to S. Croce'
▲	1.4km steep climb		70.2 ↱	'to Cuneo'
■ ■ ↰	*alt route: Valle Grana 41.6km*		71.7 ↱	Via Maira bikepath 'to Cuneo'
17.9	Colle Faunaria/dei Morti (2481m)		*71.7*	*alt route rejoins (stay straight)*
▲	25.1km steep descent		72.6 ↘	bikepath ends
26.0 ✳	bar/restaurant		73.2 ↗ ◆	Viadotto Soleri 'to centro'
36.3	Trinita		74.2 ↑ ◆	Corso Marcello Soleri
43.0 ↰	unsigned SS21		74.5 ↰ 日	Piazza Galimberti
43.3	Demonte		74.8 ↱	Via Roma
43.6 ↱	'to Festiona'		75.3	Cuneo tourist office
43.6 ↰	(50m) 'to Festiona'			

Elevation

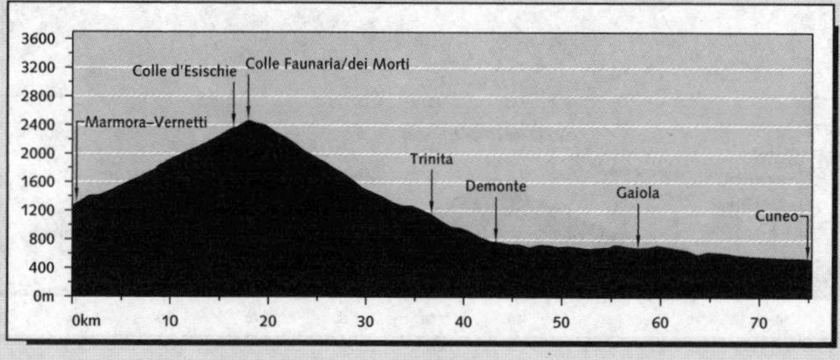

task is a punishing 42.5km slog up 1337m to Colle di Tenda; the afternoon breathtaker is a 64.8km drop the length of the Roia River valley to sea level. A passport may be necessary for the quick dip into France.

From downtown Cuneo, the road leads through commercial sprawl to Borgo San Dalmazzo (7.5km) at the bottom of the Vermenagna valley. Shift gears for a long climb and landscape appreciation. When days grow short, this awesome green spread turns wintry white and attracts hordes of skiers.

At **Limone Piemonte** (27.3km), if the legs won't go where the ego urges, a little train barrels through the mountain you would otherwise go over (erasing 32km, almost 900m of climbing and a difficult 550m descent). The one-stop rail trip (10 trains a day; all take bikes) to Tende in France takes about 20 minutes (€2). It is worth arguing about not having to pay for a bike ticket over such a short distance. Sending your panniers unaccompanied through the mountain by train is, unfortunately, not an option. The station in Limone Piemonte is above town on its northern edge. As you enter town, take the first left towards the *centro*, then turn left again just before the first roundabout. In Tende, after leaving the station, turn left on the main road to rejoin the main route.

True mountain gluttons must be prepared with food, drink and determination. Ahead lies a stout 14.7km hike up 890m, the last 8.2km on 17 windswept switchbacks – very tough. Near the top, the paved road turns gravel over a penultimate ridge and then

Alps to Alpine Sea – Day 3

Cue

start	Cuneo tourist office	▲	7.6km twisting steep descent	
0km	SW on Via Roma/SS20	▲	7.6km loose gravel road	
7.5	Borgo San Dalmazzo	50.1 ↰	rejoin main road (no sign)	
7.9 ↙ ◆	(3rd exit) 'to Limone P.'	▲	7.7km steep descent	
8.5 ↙ ◆	(1st exit) 'to Limone P.'	59.8	Tende	
10.2 ↙ ◆	(2nd exit) 'to Limone P.'	63.6 ● ● ↰	*Fontaines church 14km* ↻	
10.9 ↰	Via T. Aime 'to Robilante'	63.8	St-Dalmas-de-Tende	
▲	16.9km gradual climb	71.8 ↑	Fontan	
11.4	Roccavione	75.0 ■ ■ ↙	*alt route: Gorges de Saorge 0.9km*	
14.6	Robilante	75.9	*alt route rejoins (turn right)*	
16.5 ↙	rejoin main road	80.8	Breil-sur-Roya	
22.0	Vernante	89.6 ✳	Italian border	
27.3	Limone Piemonte	94.2 ↰	'to Airole'	
27.8 ▲	6.5km moderate climb	98.9 ↱	rejoin main road (no sign)	
34.3 ↰	'to Tre Amis, Limone 1400'	99.6	Trucco	
▲	8.2km very hard climb	104.2↰	'to Roverino'	
41.5 ▲	0.4km gravel road	106.8↙ ◆	(4th exit) 'to stazione'	
41.6 ↙	unsigned road	107.3	Ventimiglia tourist office	
42.5	Colle di Tenda (1871m)			

Elevation

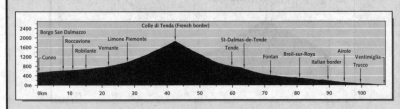

finally to **Colle di Tenda** (1871m, 42.5km) at the unmarked French border. Unfortunately, the downhill is almost as brutal as the climb: 7.6km of loose gravel through tight hairpins – take care!

Pavement reappears (50.1km) at the start of the **Roia valley**. Take in the precipitous valley walls, dramatic gorges and pastel cliffside villages.

The side trip through **la Brigue** (5km return) and up 160m to the ornately frescoed **Notre Dame des Fontaines** (14km return) is worth it only if there's time. But the 900m alternative route through the **Gorges de Saorge** (75km) isn't to be missed. Clamber over the low barrier blocking the road.

Almost 5km after crossing back into Italy (89.6km), the second tunnel is off limits to bikes! The left turn to Airole is an odd wandering road that disappears once (forge through the dirt section) and even passes through a local rubbish dump.

From the intersection back with the main road (98.9km), it's only 8.4km through the flat lower valley to the coast at Ventimiglia.

Ventimiglia

See Ventimiglia (p139).

Wine Country

Look longingly into a bottle of Italy's best northern red wine and the imaginary sight of undulating, vineyard-covered hills and ancient stone villages, the smell of busy agriculture and the feel of feet-squished grapes almost seem real. So how about a trip to and through the real thing? Well, Langhe, Roero and Monferrato *are* the real thing. Barolo, Barbaresco, Moscato, Asti and Dolcetto – the names alone ring like the crystal into which they are decanted. Add the unforgettable cities of Acqui Terme, Alba, Bra and Asti, and there is nowhere better.

HISTORY

Traces of the region's first inhabitants date back to the Neolithic times. The Romans also frequented this fertile area, and plentiful evidence remains of life in the centuries that followed, from ancient hilltop surveillance towers to medieval castles, churches and buildings, baroque and Gothic palaces, and

much more. This is a land that has been fought over, divided between and passed through the hands of the area's wealthiest and most powerful people, as well as the Savoys, Spanish, Austrians, Napoleonic French and Russians, before landing back in Italian territory. Curiously, although wine production dates back to before the Roman arrival, written mention isn't made until the 14th century.

NATURAL HISTORY

The soil of this unique area is the result of millions of years of layered underwater deposits. Alternating drifts of clay and sand settled at the bottom of the Padano Gulf, an arm of the then larger and deeper early Mediterranean Sea. Later, an uplifting of the land thrust this ground above water and bent the hardened strata into today's hills. Wind and water erosion have continued to shape the terrain. Water (rivers), in particular, having coursed eastwardly, gave the hills a characteristic shape: steep but stable, dry and exposed to the southeast versus gently inclined, higher in water content and less stable to the northwest. These contrasting slopes of nutrient-rich soils and differing degrees of exposure to the elements are ideal for the growing of grapes, as well as forests and pastures whose rich earth gives birth to highly prized truffles, hazelnuts, cheese and flowers.

Langhe & Roero

Duration	3 days
Distance	205.9km
Difficulty	moderate
Start	Acqui Terme
End	Asti

The best way to see the astonishing vineyard-covered landscape of Langhe and Roero is from high places. And the only way to get to these high places involves sweat. There is plenty of that on this magnificent three-day trek through the most famous wine towns in the area and the endless fields of grapes that gave them their celebrity.

PLANNING
When to Ride

The full impact of the Po plain weather patterns, especially the hot summers, is felt here. Thus, the best pedalling times are

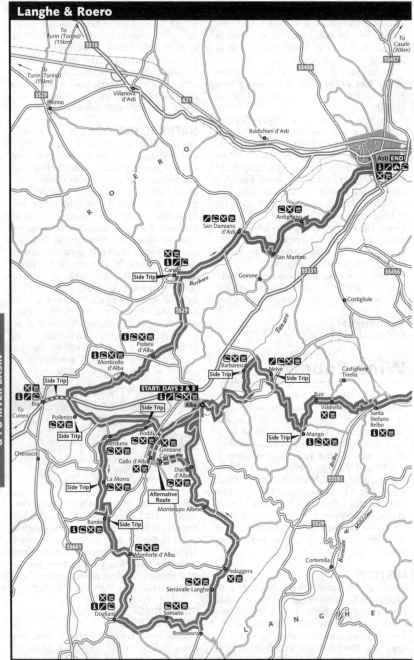

Langhe & Roero

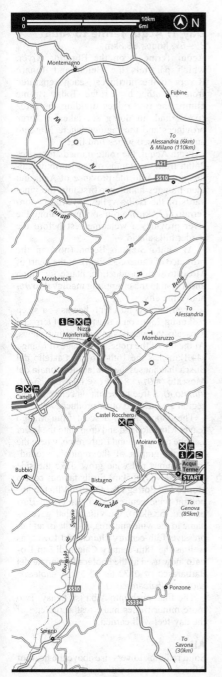

spring and autumn. Keep in mind that during the autumn festival and harvest season, hotels fill quickly, especially in September during Asti's madcap and medieval Palio.

Maps & Books
For overall coverage, Touring Club Italiano's (1:200,000) *Liguria* or *Piemonte* maps (€6.20) are best, although the provincial maps of Asti, Alessandria and Cuneo, available at information offices, are free and fine, especially the *Terre e Vini d'Asti* (1:160,000) map.

Keep an eye out for free brochures and maps, particularly those dealing with wine trails. The inexpensive Associazione Trekking in Langa *Carte dei Sentieri* for Barolo and Barbaresco are particularly good, as is the Cassa di Risparmio-sponsored *Invitation to the Roero* booklet.

ACCESS TOWN
Acqui Terme
This town's strategic position at a sulphurous thermal water source on a trade route (later the Roman Via Emiliana) between the Po plain and the Mediterranean brought it attention long before Romans bathed. Acqui Terme was, however, a famous spa town during Roman times, and eventually controlled by the Monferrato family after the tumultuous medieval period. In 1708, the city went to the House of Savoy and then followed the standard bumpy road to Italian unification. Acqui is deep in Alto Monferrato, the higher elevations of a hilly zone of woods alternating with fields of the Moscato d'Asti white grape.

Information The IAT office (☎ 0144 32 21 42, w www.acquiterme.org) is northwest of the city centre at Via Ferraris 5. There are a few banks nearby, and more in Corsos Vigan and Dante. The Atola bike shop is at Corso Cavour 70, near the information office.

Things to See & Do At the centre of the city, on Piazza Bollente is a **water fountain** from which gushes *la bollente*, naturally heated water (75°C). A short distance towards the south, in streets lined with medieval buildings, a wide ramp leads up to the 11th-century **Duomo di San Guido**, overshadowed by the **Castello dei Paleologi**

with its **Archaeology Museum** and free **bird garden**. Outside of town are the arched remains of a **Roman aqueduct**, and south across the Bormida River is the **Terme di Acqui** spa area, surrounded by the small lake of Antiche Terme and its park. **Spa treatments** are available around Piazza Italia.

Places to Stay & Eat Acqui Terme is awash in affordable accommodation, almost all of it lined up on Viale Einaudi. Its nine one- and two-star hotels all have similar services (including restaurants) and prices: singles/doubles without bathroom for €26/36 and with bathroom €30/44. Two-star **Albergo Svizzera** (☎ 0144 32 29 89; Viale L. Einaudi 25; singles/doubles €21/29) is good value for money. In the centre of town choices are more limited. **Albergo Bue Rossi** (☎ 0144 32 27 29; Corso Cavour 64; singles/doubles without bathroom €18.50/31) is the cheapest and dowdiest. **Albergo San Marco** (☎ 0144 32 24 56; Via Ghione 5; singles/doubles with bathroom €28/44) is more upscale.

Almost all hotels have good attached restaurants. Elsewhere in town, for cheap eats head to the **pizzerie** in Piazza Addolorata and Via Mazzini. Also on Via Mazzini are **Osteria da Bigât** (Via Mazzini 30-32; closed Wed), the town favourite for classic farinata, and **Osteria Ca' del Vein** (Via Mazzini 14; closed Mon), where regional cuisine is the focus.

Getting There & Away The rails through Acqui Terme are infrequently used: the Savona–Alessandria service passes less than 10 times a day in each direction (30 minutes from Alessandria, 1½ hours from Savona) and the Asti–Genoa service about a dozen (one hour from Asti, 1¼ hours from Genoa).

Drivers coming from Turin should use the Asti Est exit of expressway A21. From Genoa, take the A26 Ovada exit. From Milan, A7 to A26/7 goes to the same A26 Ovada exit.

Bicycle Acqui Terme is an easy 35km pedal from Alessandria on the SS30, a hilly 50km from Asti via the SS456, a difficult 60km from Savona on the SS334 and a no-nonsense 25km from Ovada.

THE RIDE
Day 1: Acqui Terme to Alba
3½–6½ hours, 66.8km

Acqui Terme is on the Bormida River, which parallels the Belbo and Tanaro Rivers to the northwest, each separated from the other by a ridge. Today's route climbs the two ridges dividing the three rivers, and, in doing so, takes in three provinces and the regions where Moscato and Barbaresco wines find life.

From Acqui, the route immediately rises 240m from the depths of the Bormida valley, crosses into the province of Asti, and then plunges handlebar-first into the vineyards of the Belbo valley. At Nizza Monferrato (17.5km), a run southwest along the river provides a welcome rest before the harder hills ahead.

At Santo Stefano Belbo (now in the province of Cuneo, 32.2km), at the heart of Moscato wine production, pause for lunch and a visit to the crumbling **medieval tower** above the city.

Then the second climb begins – a steep 5.3km up 258m on a twisty road of terraced Moscato vineyards and outstanding views. At the top of the ridge, the village of Mango (44.1km) has the 16th-century **Castello dei Busca** that houses the **Enoteca Regionale del Moscato** (☎ 0141 8 92 91, e enotecamango@ infinito.it), a free presentation centre for the region's wines and other products.

The 280m, 5.9km descent from Mango leaves Moscato land and drops into the lower Langhe region around Barbaresco, where the Nebbiolo grapes of the region's second-most-famous red wine grow. Take the side trip to Neive (50.5km) for its famous **centro storico** and **Bottega dei Quattro Vini** (an important wine centre). Also don't skip Barbaresco (55.4km), the village that gave its name to the wine and area, and site of an impressive 13th-century **church** and **tower**, as well as the 18th-century **Chiesa di San Donato**, now used as the **Enoteca Regionale del Barbaresco** (☎ 0173 63 52 51, e enoteca@ enotecadelbarbaresco.it).

The final push into Alba isn't easy. Two more minor ridges make rest at the end of the day feel well earned.

Alba

Solid redbrick towers rise above the heart of Alba, a wine town with good evidence of its medieval past. Alba's modern claims to fame, in addition to wine, include its late-autumn white truffle crop and festival, and a *palio* (race) on donkeys. Towards the end of WWII, the town's citizens proclaimed Alba an independent republic for 23 days after partisans liberated it from the Germans.

Information The main IAT (☎ 0173 3 58 33, W www.langheroero.it) is on the northwestern outskirts of the city in Palazzo delle Mostre on Piazza Medford 3. There is another office (☎ 0173 36 25 62, W www.turismodoc.it) in the centre at Via Vittorio Emanuele 19. There is a cluster of banks on Piazza Savona. Cicli Gagliardini (☎/fax 0173 44 07 26), just off Piazza Garibaldi at Via Ospedale 7, is an excellent bike shop. La Bicicletta, Via Vittorio Emanuele 23d, sells bike clothing only.

Things to See & Do The 14th- to 15th-century **Cattedrale di San Lorenzo** dominates central Piazza Risorgimento. Also on the square are the porticoed **Palazzo Comunale** and two of the city's many medieval **towers**.

For traces of Alba's Roman origins, visit the **Museo Federico Eusebio** *(Via Paruzzo 1)*. Otherwise, you can stroll down the commercial *via maestro*, Via Vittorio Emanuele.

Places to Stay & Eat On the northern edge of town, **Leon d'Oro** *(☎ 0173 44 19 01; Piazza Marconi 2; singles/doubles €42/60)* is Alba's only inexpensive accommodation and a good one at that. Otherwise, ask at the tourist information offices about *affitta-camere* (rooms for rent) or try upscale **Hotel Savona** *(☎ 0173 44 04 40; W www.hotel savona.com; Via Roma 1; singles/doubles €60/90)* at the other end of town.

Osteria dei Sognatori *(Via Macrino 8; closed Wed)* has an at-home atmosphere (no written menu) and big servings. On the nearby piazza, **Ristorpizza Lattuga** *(Piazza Pertinace 8; closed Mon)* is inexpensive and open late, but rather sterile. **Pizzeria La Duchessa** *(Via Ospedale 5; closed Wed)* has excellent pizza (starting at €6.20) and basic Italian fare on a broad terrace. **La Torre** *(☎ 0173 44 16 47; Via Cavour 3; closed Mon)* is good for gourmet, wallet-friendly, candlelight terrace meals.

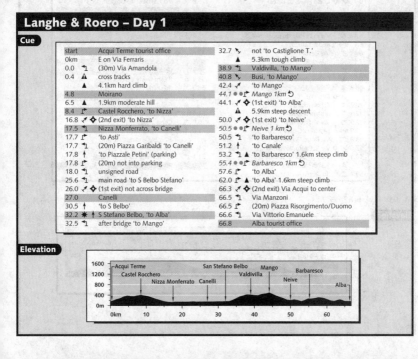

Langhe & Roero – Day 1

Cue

start	Acqui Terme tourist office	32.7 ↘		not 'to Castiglione T.'
0km	E on Via Ferraris	▲		5.3km tough climb
0.0 ↱	(30m) Via Amandola	38.9 ↰		Valdivilla, 'to Mango'
0.4 ⚠	cross tracks	40.8 ↘		Busi, 'to Mango'
▲	4.1km hard climb	42.4 ↙		'to Mango'
4.8	Moirano	44.1 ● ● ↱		Mango 1km ↻
6.5 ▲	1.9km moderate hill	44.1 ↙ ◆		(1st exit) 'to Alba'
8.4 ↱	Castel Rocchero, 'to Nizza'	▲		5.9km steep descent
16.8 ↙ ◆	(2nd exit) 'to Nizza'	50.0 ↙ ◆		(1st exit) 'to Neive'
17.5 ↰	Nizza Monferrato, 'to Canelli'	50.5 ● ● ↱		Neive 1 km ↻
17.7 ↰	'to Asti'	50.5 ↰		'to Barbaresco'
17.7 ↰	(20m) Piazza Garibaldi 'to Canelli'	51.2 ↑		'to Canale'
17.8 ↱	'to Piazzale Petini' (parking)	53.2 ↰ ▲		'to Barbaresco' 1.6km steep climb
17.8 ↱	(20m) not into parking	55.4 ● ● ↱		Barbaresco 1km ↻
18.0 ↰	unsigned road	57.6 ↱		'to Alba'
25.6 ↰	main road 'to S Belbo Stefano'	62.0 ↱ ▲		'to Alba' 1.6km steep climb
26.0 ↙ ◆	(1st exit) not across bridge	66.3 ↙ ◆		(2nd exit) Via Acqui to center
27.0	Canelli	66.5 ↰		Via Manzoni
30.5 ↑	'to S Belbo'	66.5 ↱		(20m) Piazza Risorgimento/Duomo
32.2 ✳ ↑	S Stefano Belbo, 'to Alba'	66.6 ↰		Via Vittorio Emanuele
32.5 ↰	after bridge 'to Mango'	66.8		Alba tourist office

Elevation

Day 2: Alba Circuit
4–7 hours, 71.3km

Today's route sweeps through lower Langhe, three times up (as much as 450m) over hills in the region's *alto* area, and then back down a long sunset-view ridgeline to Alba. Fortunately, panniers can be left at the hotel or carried empty for wine purchases.

From Alba, speed west through an uninspiring strip to where hints of distant hilltop castles are a bright harbinger of brilliant things to come. Detour for a moment through Roddi (6.4km), the first of the 11 Barolo-producing *comuni*, for a peak at its 13th-century **bell tower** and medieval **castle**.

After some brief but steep rollers, the first of the three climbs begins. Only 4.2km long, the ascent of 450m is an early lesson

in humility. Treats along the way include the **Piazza Don Borgna** in Verduno (10.5km) and the in-the-fields feel of the rural road; stop and taste some sour grapes to discover why they are not for eating. The view from **La Morra's** Piazza Castello at the ridge summit is out to a heart-stoppingly beautiful amphitheatre of Langhe hills. Make sure there is film in the camera. La Morra (13.9km) also has an elegant **bell tower**, the **Castello della Volta**, a 17th-century **church**, and a **Cantina Comunale** for the tasting and purchase of local wines.

To the lowlands south of La Morra is Barolo (19.9km), the village that gave its name to the wine now known as 'the king of wines, the wine of kings'. The 10th-century **Castello di Barolo** contains the **Enoteca**

Langhe & Roero – Day 2

Cue

start	Alba tourist office		19.9 ●●↰	*Barolo 1km* ↻	
0km	S on Via Vittorio Emanuele		19.9 ↑	'to Monforte'	
0.2 ↱	Via Roma		▲	5.9km moderate climb	
0.3 ↰	Via Sacco		23.7 ↰	'to Monforte'	
0.4 ↙◆	Via L. Enaudi bridge 'to Barolo'		25.7 ✳	Monforte d'Alba	
0.7 ◆	Corso Piave 'to Barolo'		25.8 ↙	Via Garibaldi 'to Dogliani'	
1.4 ↑	'to Barolo'		32.7 ✳	Dogliani	
4.4 ↱	'to Roddi'		↰	Via Codevilla 'to Bossolasco'	
5.4 ↰	'to Roddi'		33.7 ▲	10km tough climb	
6.1 ↘	Via Prati Riva 'to municipio'		35.2 ↑	'to Bossolasco'	
6.4 ●●↰	*Roddi 1km* ↻		38.7	Somano	
6.4 ↱	Via Cavour		43.6 ↙◆	'to Alba'	
7.1 ↘	downhill		47.6	Serravalle Langhe	
7.3 ↱	Strada Roddi–Verduno 'to Verduno'		50.2	Pedaggera	
9.7 ▲	0.6km steep climb		53.1 ▲	8.6km twisty descent	
10.5 ✳	Verduno		56.9 ↰	'to Diano'	
↙◆	(3rd exit) 'to La Morra'		63.2	Diano d'Alba	
10.7 ▲	3.2km moderate climb		▲	6.8km steep descent	
12.3 ↰	unsigned road		64.0 ■■↰	*alt route: Grinzane Cavour 12km*	
12.9 ↰	Via V. Emanuele 'to La Morra'		70.0 ↰	Corso Langhe	
13.9 ●●↑	*La Morra Centre 0.5km* ↻		71.0 ↑◆	into Piazza Savona	
13.9 ↱	Via Roma 'to Barolo'			*alt route rejoins (turn left)*	
17.0 ↙◆	Via S. Pietro 'to Barolo'		71.1 ↰	Via Alfieri	
18.1 ↰	Via XXV Aprile 'to Barolo'		71.1 ↱	(15m) Via Vittorio Emanuele	
▲	1.3km steep descent		71.3	Alba tourist office	
19.4 ↱	'to Barolo, centro'				

Elevation

Portofino, Liguria

San Remo market, Liguria

Vineyard, La Morra, Piedmont

Levanto, Cinque Terre, Liguria

Como and the Bergamo Alps, Lombardy

Monumento al Ciclista, Como

Alta Rezia high roads

Piazza Chanoux, Aosta, Valle d'Aosta

Regionale del Barolo (☎ 0173 5 62 77) in its cellars and museums on its upper floors.

Hill two is the easiest and drives to the view at Monforte d'Alba (25.7km), a village at the southern edge of the Barolo hills and site of another medieval **castle** and 13th-century **tower**. On the downhill side is a dramatic change in scenery; the former full spread of vineyards is periodically interrupted by trees and pastures fundamental to the production of the region's cheeses and hazelnuts. Dogliani (32.7km), at the bottom of the hill, has a fine medieval centre, complete with a **castle** and **tower**.

The last climb of the day is a toughie: up 420m over 11km. It pushes to the crest of a long ridge. The route stays high for a few kilometres and takes in the full Langhe spread to the west (the same surveyed from the east this morning) before the final 18km, 541m descent back to Alba. An alternate route from Diano d'Alba (63.2km) to the **medieval castle** and **Enoteca Regionale Piemontese di Grinzane Cavour** in Grinzane Cavour drops to the valley floor at Gallo d'Alba, from where Alba is an easy ride.

Day 3: Alba to Asti

3½–6½ hours, 67.8km
Where the wine hills of Langhe cover the southern sweeps of the Tanaro River, Roero rules the north. Not as well known or frequented as Langhe, Roero nevertheless has its attractions. The route today twice climbs 100m, but is essentially a rollicking ride on

back roads through rolling hills of vineyards, forested former estates and fields.

From Alba, take the same Roddi road as yesterday, but skirt the village's heights, choosing instead the direction of Bra on the north side of the Tanaro River. Don't skip the fascinating side trip to **Pollenzo** (13.5km), site of the rich Roman community of Pollentia, which preceded the founding of nearby Bra. Visit the village's **Palazzo Traversa Museum**. The city of Bra, visible at the top of a hill to the west, is the third (after Asti and Alba) of the area's great wine centres. The side trip to Bra's many medieval and Renaissance **churches** and **palaces**, and its **museums** should not be idly dismissed.

Stretching for miles from Bra to the northeast is the **Rocche of Roero**, the rocky outcropping bisecting the region. The route today stays below it (and its most famous vineyards and castle-topped towns), riding the more gentle rollers within turret-viewing distance of Monticello d'Alba's medieval **Castello dei Conti Roero** all the way to Canale (35.1km), main town of Roero's 24 *comuni*. Visit Canale's 14th-century **Castello dei Malabaila**, three 18th-century **churches** and the **Enoteca del Roero** (☎ 017 397 82 28; e *enoteca.roero@areacom.it*).

Although the road east officially leaves the Roero region and dips into the province of Asti and its Monferrato wine estates, the route climbs into hills whose draping vineyards still feed the Roero wine cycle. This is the most picturesque part of the ride.

How to Know a Barolo

Barolo wine is the Langhe region's premium potion. It and others in the area have been awarded one of Italy's precious quality seals: DOC (Denominazione di origine controllata) or DOCG (Denominazione di origine controllata e controllata). A product of the Nebbiolo grape, Barolo's prominence as the 'the king of wines, the wine of kings' began in the early 19th century when the last marquess of Barolo, Giulia Colbert, asked the Count of Cavour to help enhance her cellar. With the aid of a French specialist, they developed a robust, complex, full-flavoured and fragrant red like those in vogue in Bordeaux. A true Barolo is still unlike most of its lighter Italian kin. The most exceptional 20th-century Barolo wine years are 1922, 1931, 1947, 1971, 1982, 1990 and 1997, and the most recent 'grand' years are 1970, 1978, 1985, 1989 and 1996.

Other worthy wines in Langhe include **Barbaresco**, another vigorous red, the poor cousin of which is believed to have been produced during Roman times; **Barbera**, a lately improved red reputed for its complexity; **Dolcetto**, the local, long-standing red table wine; and **Moscato d'Asti**, a sweet white dessert wine whose bubbly spumante is legendary. To learn more about native brews, contact Turismo in Langa (☎ 0173 36 40 30, W www.turismoinlanga.it) or any of the *enoteche* (wine bars) mentioned in the ride descriptions.

The day's final leg is a steep downhill from Antignano (56.4km) back to the banks of the Tanaro River and then a painless spin into downtown Asti.

Asti

Settled long before it was made a Roman colony in 89 BC, Asti has a rocky history. An independent city-state in the 13th and 14th centuries, it was subsequently passed around between Spain, Austria, Napoleon's France and finally the Savoys, prior to Italy's unification.

Information The Asti information office (☎ 0141 53 03 57, **w** www.terredasti.it) is under the southern arches of Piazza Alfieri 34. Banks can also be found on this piazza.

Asti's bike gurus work at Piemontesina (☎ 0141 59 22 92) to the west of Piazza Alfieri at Corso Vittorio Alfieri 361.

Things to See & Do Asti isn't as small as it sometimes feels and is rich in history. The short list of top sites is led by the 14th-century Gothic **cathedral** on Piazza Cattedrale and **Chiesa di San Secondo**, on Piazza San Secondo named after Asti's patron saint. Two elegant medieval buildings, **Palazzo dei Tribunali** (Court House) and **Palazzo del Consiglio di Città** (Council House), make the Piazza Statuto impressive. During the late 13th century, the region became one of Italy's wealthiest, and more than 100 **towers** and **palaces** stand as reminder of this glorious past.

Sidebar: LIGURIA, MARITIME ALPS & PO RIVER BASIN

Langhe & Roero – Day 3

Cue

start	Alba tourist office	
0km	S on Via Vittorio Emanuele	
0.2	Via Roma	
0.3	Via Sacco	
0.4	Via L Enaudi bridge 'to Barolo'	
0.7	Corso Piave 'to Barolo'	
1.4	'to Barolo'	
4.4	'to Roddi'	
5.4	'to Bra'	
6.6	'to Bra'	
11.1	'to Bra'	
13.5	Pollenzo 1km	
15.0	Bra 7.8km	
15.0	cross SS231 'to Monticello'	
15.4	'to Monticello'	
▲	1.9km steep climb	
20.5	'to Monticello B(orgo)'	
20.7	'to Piobesi'	
22.2	(2nd exit) 'to Piobesi'	
24.4	'to Piobesi'	
25.2	'to Piobesi'	
26.1	'to Alba'	
26.3	Piobesi, Piazza S Pietro (no sign)	
26.4	Via S Rocco (around church)	
28.2	SS29 'to Canale'	
30.7	'to Canale'	
33.3	'to Canale'	
35.1	Canale 2km	
35.1	'to S Damiano'	
40.1	'to S Damiano'	
41.1	'to centro'	
42.0	San Damiano d'Asti	
42.1	with traffic	
42.5	'to Govone'	
43.2	'to Govone'	
46.1	'to Govone'	
48.8	'to Govone'	
49.1	'to S Marino'	
49.6	'to S Marino'	
51.6	Via Alfieri 'to Asti'	
51.9	Via Asti 'to Antignano'	
56.4	Antignano	
▲	4.1km steep descent	
65.7	(2nd exit) SS458 'to Torino'	
65.9	'to Acqui T'	
66.3	Corso Venezia	
66.7	Corso Savona 'to centro'	
67.3	Corso Luigi Einaudi	
67.5	'to centro' around Campo del Palio	
67.7	Viale alla Vittoria 'to info'	
67.8	Piazza Vittorio Alfieri	
67.8	(50m) Asti tourist office	

Elevation

On the third Sunday of every September, 21 madcap jockeys spur their horses around Campo del Palio for a wild, medieval race known as the **Palio**. The festival was revived in 1967 and dates back to the 13th century. The Palio comes at the end of a month-long series of **food and wine festivals**.

Places to Stay & Eat Festival time in September makes finding a place to stay difficult. **Campeggio Umberto Cagni** (☎ *0141 27 12 38; Via Valmanera 152; tent sites for 2 €10.50*) is the nearest camp site, off Corso Volta. **Albergo Antico Paradiso** (☎/fax *0141 21 43 85; Corso Torino 329; singles/doubles with bathroom €39/69*) is the cheapest hotel, but a good distance away at the northwestern edge of town. **The Cavour** (☎/fax *0141 53 02 22; Piazza Marconi 18; singles/doubles without bathroom €31/44*) is in town near the train station. Ask at the tourist office for *agriturismo*, *affittacamera* and B&B options.

Asti is a culinary centre of more than 60 restaurants to suit most budgets. Ask for specifics at the tourist information office, or explore the blocks under the arcades around Piazza Alfieri and the streets around Piazzas San Secondo, Statuto and Marconi, as well as the connecting Via Cavour. Many **supermercati** (supermarkets) and **alimentari** are located here too.

Getting There & Away Asti is on the Turin–Alessandria–Genoa line and is served by hourly trains in both directions (55 minutes to Turin, 1¾ hours to Genoa).

Expressway A21 links Asti with Turin (60km) and Alessandria (40km). Cyclists can easily cover the same distances on smaller but busy roads.

Po River Basin

The Po River is Italy's longest at 652km, and the primary artery of the country's most important industrial and agricultural region. The upper and middle reaches of the Po – the area constituting its catchment basin – are strikingly different. Their histories, monuments and environments are, in many ways, only linked by the blue aqueous strip of the great river. The following two rides provide a cyclist with some of the best to be had in both.

HISTORY

The upper and middle reaches of the Po are in the Piedmont and Lombardy regions, adjacent areas with remarkably different histories. On the one hand, in Piedmont, the distinct mountain cultures of the Alps were deeply influenced by the French and Swiss and dominated by the House of Savoy (with its capital in Turin). Milan, on the other hand, has always been the heart of Lombardy since as far back as the time of Romanised Cisalpine Gaul and the Germanic Langobards. While Peidmont enjoyed stability, the Lombards, when under attack by the Franks, formed the Lombard League, which, after its collapse, resulted in centuries of dispute between powerful families and their political and religious allies. Over the last two centuries before Italian unification, Piedmont joined Lombardy while successions of conquering foreign powers passed through. Now, Turin and Milan are Italy's industrial poles.

NATURAL HISTORY

The source of the Po River is in the Piano del Re on the slopes of Monviso, 40km west of Saluzzo. From its high-elevation peat bogs through the steep-cut valley of the pre-Alps, the river emerges onto a vast plain and begins its meandering flow to the Adriatic, collecting the contents of scores of waterways. The whole plain used to be the floor of the Tethys Ocean, the larger precursor to what is now the Mediterranean Sea. Sediment accumulated over millennia and, after the water level dropped, was shaped by glaciers, wind and water. Rice and other grains, sugar beet and fruit are now the most important crops exploiting the nutrient-rich soil. Industry too has benefited from the advantages of the river and its plain.

Basso Pinerolese & Saluzzese

Duration	6–10 hours
Distance	101.6km
Difficulty	easy
Start	Turin
End	Saluzzo

The lower reaches of the upper Po River are an in-between zone: neither rocky and raging with ripping currents, nor silted,

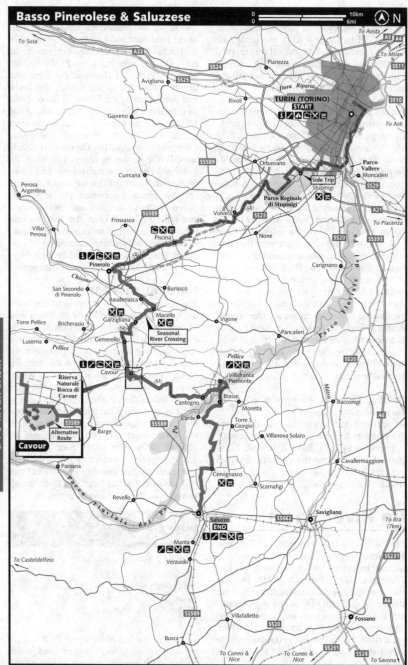

serpentine and somnolent. So it is with the region's history: not too turbulent, not too tame. This one-day ride along marked bicycle routes through the *basso* (lower) Pinerolese and Saluzzese flats at the base of the Alps takes in the best of this transitional zone.

PLANNING
When to Ride
The Po plain can get uncomfortably sultry during summer. The best pedalling seasons are spring and autumn.

Maps
For overall coverage, Touring Club Italiano's (1:200,000) *Liguria* or *Piemonte* maps (€6.20) are best. Otherwise, try the free provincial (1:200,000) map of Cuneo available at tourist offices. That said, since most of this route is on bikepaths not always marked on maps, for the Turin to Villafranca leg use the free bike maps available from Provincia di Torino's Servizio Turismo e Sport (☎ 011 861 26 39, w www.provincia.torino.it) at Via Maria Vittoria 12, 10123 Torino. From Villafranca, the free Città di Saluzzo *Percorsi cicloturistici del Saluzzese* brochure/map is indispensable.

ACCESS TOWN
See Turin (p174).

THE RIDE
Today's seemingly complex route is made simple by a profusion of bikepath signs along country lanes. Plus, from start to finish, today's ride is flat. It's an easy day of easier pleasure, even over the frequent but short unpaved bits.

In Turin, go south on the bikepath along the western bank of the Po River. This bikepath can be baffling, but as long as the river is to the left, all is well. When, in Parco Vallere (7.5km), bikepath signs disappear, cross the open field to the park headquarters building at the far corner. Bicycle signs reappear at the bike-friendly pedestrian bridge spanning the highway.

Excellent bike signs along the wandering *ciclopista* Stupinigi–Vallere lead unfailingly to Stupinigi (15.8km). Take time here to explore the sprawling grounds and rococo buildings of the Savoys' **Palazzina di Caccia** and the **Castello di Moncalieri**.

From Stupinigi, follow the signs to Pinerolo on another bikepath: the *ciclostrada* Pinerolo-Stupinigi. This route is even more indirect and sometimes on lovely, unpaved forest lanes. There are a number of turns where signs are either absent or obscured; all of these are addressed in the cue sheet. Copious use of the Provincia di Torino map outlining this ride is advised.

Pinerolo (47.7km), the terminus of the bikepath, is a significant township and perfect lunch spot (see Pinerolo, p190, for more information).

South of Pinerolo unfurls a richly historical spread of small agricultural towns knitted together by yet another web of bikepaths: the *ciclostrade basso pinerolese*. Wind through cornfields, past the 15th-century **castello** in Macello and the **Santuario di Montebruno** in Garzigliana, to Cavour (65.8km). In Cavour, an alternative route includes a return climb (the only one of the day) to the top of **Rocca di Cavour** for an unimpeded 360° view of the surrounding plain. To make the detour, in Cavour (65.6km), follow signs to Rocca di Cavour. After 500m, turn left on the steep Strada Communale della Rocca and strain 1.5km up 140m to the top. Descend on the same road, but turn left at the bottom to continue around the hill, staying left and close to the rock until you rejoin the bikepath to Villafranca (66.8km).

The final leg of the bikepath to Villafranca is only complicated by a few missing signs, explained in the cue sheet.

Villafranca Piemonte (80.4km) is on the west bank of the Po River. Cross here and hug its east bank on a gravel path through the quiet Amici del Po park. You will feel lost, but persevere. At Brasse, pavement and a new set of bikepaths (with a chipmunk logo) begin, with excellent directions to Saluzzo through long stretches of well-tended fields.

Saluzzo
Once a medieval stronghold and regional capital, Saluzzo maintained its independence until the Savoys possessed it through a 1601 treaty with France. Saluzzo nevertheless remained an important agricultural centre and is today a historical gem, having preserved many vestiges of a rich past. One of Saluzzo's better-known sons was General Carlo dalla Chiesa, whose implacable pursuit of the Mafia led to his assassination in 1982.

Information The tourist office (☎ 0175 4 67 10, ⓦ www.terredelmarchesato.it) is on the main street at Via Torino 51a. Many banks can also be found on this busy strip. Associazione ciclistica Ij'Npaotà (Via Deportati Ebrei 5, ⓦ www.ijnpaota.org) is Saluzzo's FIAB affiliate. Visit La Bici (☎ 0175 24 81 60) at Via Savigliano 53/55 to untangle bicycle brambles.

Things to See & Do Cobbled lanes, some (like Salita al Castello) lined with medieval houses, twist up to **La Castiglia**, the sombre castle of the Marchesi, Saluzzo's erstwhile rulers. From the top of the restored 15th-century **Torre Civica** there are commanding views over burnt-red tiled rooftops. Pass the convent of San Giovanni on the square of

the same name to get to **Museo Civico di Casa Cavassa**, a renovated 16th-century noble's residence. Two religious landmarks – the Gothic **cathedral** and **Chiesa di San Giovanni** – are also worth a turn. Nearby in Manta, the frescoes of **Castello dei Marchesi di Saluzzo** will refine an understanding of life in medieval Saluzzo.

Places to Stay & Eat There is no cheap accommodation in Saluzzo. **Albergo Persico** (☎/fax 0175 4 12 13; Vicolo Mercati 10; singles/doubles €39/57) is very comfortable. **Perpoin** (☎ 0175 4 23 82; Via Spielberg 19; singles/doubles €52/77) is nicer still. Both have restaurants.

For the hasty and do-it-yourselfers, try the lower part of town (especially along Via

LIGURIA, MARITIME ALPS & PO RIVER BASIN

Basso Pinerolese & Saluzzese

Cue

start	Turin tourist office		48.6	↱	Via Bignone/Baudenasca (no sign)
0km	SE across Piazza Castello		53.3	↘	Stradale dei Paglieri (no sign)
0.4	↘ 🚲 Via Verdi bikepath		55.4	✱	Macello
1.5	↱ 🚲 Lungo Po Cadorna bikepath		57.1	⚠	seasonal river crossing
3.0	↑ Parco del Valentino bikepath		58.4	✱	Garzigliana
7.5	↰ cross bridge to Parco Vallere		61.1	↱	bikepath 'to Gemerello'
	⚠ 1.9km dirt bikepath		65.6	↖	bikepath 'to Villafranca'
8.0	↗ diagonally cross open field			■ ■ ↱	alt route: Rocca di Cavour 5.1km
9.4	⚠ bikepath bridge over highway		65.8	✱	Cavour
15.8	↱ bikepath 'to Pinerolo'		66.2	↱	bikepath 'to Villafranca'
	⚠ 0.4km gravel bikepath		66.8		alt route rejoins (turn right)
15.8	● ● ↑ Stupinigi 1km ↺		71.9	⚠	1.4km gravel bikepath
16.7	↰ bikepath 'to Pinerolo'		73.5	↘	unsigned bikepath (at house)
17.5	↑ bikepath		77.3	↱	unsigned bikepath (at tree)
	⚠ 5km hard-packed earth		80.4		Villafranca Piemonte
17.8	↑ cross road to rejoin bikepath		80.6	↱ 🚲 Via Mattetti 'to Moretta'
19.0	↱ unsigned bikepath (at 'T')		81.3	↱	1st path after bridge (unsigned)
20.9	↱ unsigned bikepath (before farm)			⚠	2.4km gravel bikepath
25.6	⚠ 2.8km gravel bikepath		83.6	↑	new bikepath signs (chipmunk logo)
28.7	↰ Via Dante (unsigned bikepath)		89.0	↱	'to Cervignasco'
29.4	Volvera		94.7	↱	Cervignasco, bikepath No 1
32.7	⚠ 1.6km gravel bikepath		95.9	↰	unsigned (at three-sided shrine)
38.6	⚠ tracks		100.6	↰ 🚲 SS589 'to Saluzzo'
	↱ immediately after tracks		100.8	◆ (1st exit) Via Torino 'to centro'
47.5	↰ 🚲 Viale C. d'Italia/Corso Bosio		101.3	↰ 🚲 Corso Italia
47.7	✱ Pinerolo		101.6		Saluzzo, Piazza XX Settembre
48.0	↰ 🚲 Via Vigone (cross tracks)				

Elevation

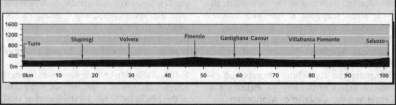

Torino) for **supermarkets** and cheap pizzerie and **birrerie** (pubs). Otherwise, **Taverna San Martino** (*Corso Piemonte 109; closed Tues dinner & Wed*) is the most economical sit-down in town. Up in the old *centro*, pricier **L'Ostu du Baloss** (*Via Gualtieri 38; closed Sun & Mon lunch*) has expensive regional food, while **Osteria dei Mondagli** (*Piazza Mondagli; closed Wed*) has more typical Italian fare.

Getting There & Away Saluzzo is on a small rail spur between Savigliano and Cuneo. There are six trains a day Monday to Saturday to Cuneo (all take bikes) and an hourly weekday service to Savigliano. Both legs have three trains on Sunday. Buses are sometimes substituted and don't guarantee bike transport. There are hourly buses to/from Turin.

Bicycle Savigliano, on the main train line between Cuneo and Turin, is an easy 13km pedal from Saluzzo, and Cuneo is only 32km by the most direct route (SS589).

Lungo Po Argine

Duration	3 days
Distance	210.2km
Difficulty	easy
Start	Pavia
End	Mantua (Mantova)

The Po River took many millennia to shape the wide, fertile plain through which it meanders. Humankind has been swifter in making its mark on the land. Prone to flooding, the Po's path has over the years, been lined by a series of *argine* or dikes, and a considerable riverside lowland zone called a *golena*, both used for water-level control and agricultural purposes. Any bicycle trip *lungo* (along) the Po must take advantage of the tranquil *argine* paths, dense riparian nature and rich accompanying history. This three-day pedal, easily completed in two by the ambitious, is along some of the best of the Po's flow.

PLANNING
When to Ride
The lower elevations in Italy, particularly in the flats of the Po River basin, get uncomfortably muggy during summer, particularly in July and August. The best pedalling seasons are the spring and autumn.

Maps & Books
For overall coverage, the Touring Club Italiano (1:200,000) *Lomabrdia* map (€6.20) is best. The free Regione Lombardia (1:400,000) *Lombardia* map and *Lombardia – Tourist map of rivers* can also be used with the free provincial maps of Pavia, Piacenza, Cremona and Mantua, available at tourist offices.

Regione Lombardia also produces a superb *Cycling along the Po* brochure and map, while the Cremona APT has three thin but thorough cycling guides (in Italian only) for the areas around Cremona, Casalmaggiore and Crema.

ACCESS TOWN
Pavia
Originally Roman Ticinum, Pavia is on the Ticino River just north of its confluence with the Po. Now just a satellite of Milan, Pavia was once its rival as the capital of the Lombard kings until the 11th century. During the Renaissance, however, the city became a pawn of power politics, was occupied by Spain in the 16th century, Austria in the 18th century and finally France from 1796 to 1859. Today it's a thriving industrial, agricultural and educational centre.

Information Pavia's IAT/APT (☎ 0382 2 21 56, ⓦ www.apt.pavia.it) is to the northwest at Via Filzi 2. Banks are on Corso Cavour between the station and Piazza della Vittoria. A good bike shop, AZbici (☎ 0382 46 86 80), is at Viale Monte Grappa 18c on the route leaving town to the east.

Things to See & Do Start with the forbidding **Castello Visconti** (built in 1360) watching over the northern end of the medieval city. Walk south on Corso Strada Nuova past the ancient **university** (Columbus studied here) to the majestic **covered bridge**. Off the corso to the west, stop in at the 14th- to 19th-century **duomo** topped by the third-largest dome in Italy, and to the east, visit **Basilica di San Michele** (circa 1090) where Barbarossa was crowned Holy Roman emperor in 1155. About 10km north of town is the not-to-be-missed **Certosa di**

Pavia, a fabulous 14th- to 15th-century Carthusian monastery (church, cloister and palace) and one of the most notable Italian buildings produced during the Renaissance.

Places to Stay & Eat Just west of town, **Campeggio Ticino** (☎ 0382 52 70 94; Via Mascherpa 10; tent sites for 2 €15) is rather noisy.

Hotel Stazione (☎ 0382 3 54 77; Via Bernardino de Rossi 8; singles/doubles without bathroom €31/42) is spare and rumbled by passing trains. Two-star **Albergo Aurora** (☎ 0382 2 36 64; Viale Vittorio Emanuele II 25; singles/doubles with bathroom €45/70) is right in front of the station.

Pizzeria Capri (☎ 0382 2 00 67; Corso Cavour 20; closed Tues) has simple and affordable pizza and pasta. For hearty local cuisine – like *risotto con le rane* (risotto with small frogs) – explore Via Milazzo in the *basso borgo* on the far side of the covered bridge. **Osteria della Malora** (Via Milazzo 79; dinner €25; closed Mon) is a good terraced example.

Getting There & Away Pavia is on the main, frequently served train line between Milan (30 minutes) and Genoa (1½ hours). It's also linked to Alessandria (1½ hours) and Codogno (one hour) by smaller spurs.

The best choice for drivers is the Pavia extension of expressway A7 (between Milan and Genoa) from the Bereguardo exit. The A21 between Turin and Piacenza passes nearby too (head north from the Casteggio-Casatisma exit).

Bicycle See the Navigli Milanesi ride (p201). Otherwise, Pavia is 35km from Milan on the busy SS35 or SS412.

THE RIDE
Day 1: Pavia to Cremona
5½–10 hours, 99.2km

One important feature of the Po plain is that it's flat, very flat. In fact, the steepest roads on today's ride are mere ramps, linking 'low' roads through extensively cultivated fields to the elevated *argine* paths along which part of the route runs. It's easy touring made marvellous by the natural beauty and serenity of the surroundings.

Head east from Pavia then south across the Po-spanning, century-old, 1km-long

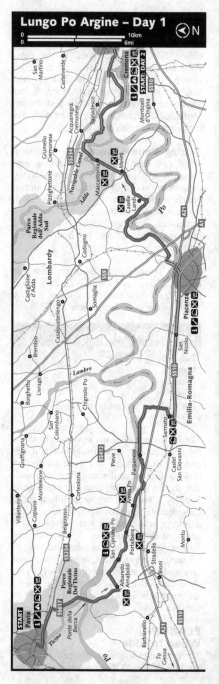

Lungo Po Argine – Day 1

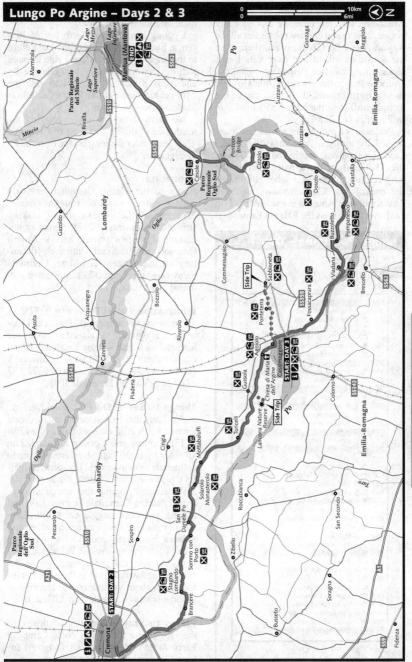

LIGURIA, MARITIME ALPS & PO RIVER BASIN

Ponte della Becca (10.5km). At Albaredo Arnaboldi, turn left onto the first of many *argine*. This raised embankment goes all the way to Arena Po (26.6km) and then, after the road dips inland and over a highway, picks up again after Parpanese (33.8km). Unfortunately, after Sarmato (46.1km) and its vast **fortifications**, there is no choice but to fight traffic on the busy SS10 for 15km to Piacenza (63.2km).

Piacenza is a prosperous town often overlooked by tourists. Its central Piazza dei Cavalli is fabulous, dominated by **Il Gotico**, the 13th-century town hall. Nearby, the 12th-century **duomo** is a sober building at the end of Via XX Settembre, although **Basilica di Sant'Antonio** is even older (11th century). Don't miss the **Palazzo Farnese** on

Piazza Cittadella, home to three museums, including the **Museo Civico**.

Cycling again, head north out of Piacenza, back to the far side of the Po. Return to the *argine* for a meandering ride through rich agricultural country between the Po and Adda Rivers. Make sure to visit the 14th-century fortress-like **Rocca Castello** at Maccastorna (79.3km).

No maps show the *argine* hugging the north side of the Po just west of Cremona. They lead under the long bridge over the Po to Cremona.

Cremona

Home of the violin, Cremona jealously maintains its centuries-old status as premier exponent of the delicate art of making stringed instruments. All of the great violin-making dynasties started here – Amati, Guarneri and Stradivari. Until the 14th century an independent city-state, Cremona today boasts a compact but impressive medieval city centre.

Information The APT office (☎ 0372 2 32 33, [w] www.aptcremona.it), Piazza del Comune 5, is opposite the cathedral. Banks are here and on Corso Vittorio Emanuele II and Corso Palestro, both off Piazza Stradivari. A good bike shop is Bici Gaboardi (☎ 0372 2 37 81), Corso Vittorio Emanuele II 45.

Things to See & Do Piazza del Comune is the heart and tourist nexus of medieval Cremona. It's a 1st-class example of a 12th- to 13th-century urban centre surrounded on all sides by significant structures: the main **cathedral**; its adjoining 111m **Torrazzo** (belfry), touted as Italy's tallest; the **Bertazzola**, a Renaissance loggia; the octagonal **baptistry**; **Palazzo Comunale** or town hall; and a small porticoed **Loggia dei Militi**. Elsewhere throughout the city are **churches** and **palaces** from many eras. Violin-lovers can view a few instruments in Palazzo Comunale, but for real indulgence, go to the **Museo Stradivariano** in Via Palestro. For information about visiting one of the 90-odd violin workshops, check with APT staff.

Places to Stay & Eat Just southwest of the city centre along the Po is **Camping Parco Al Po** (☎ 0372 2 12 68; Lungo Po Europa 12a; tent sites from €13).

Lungo Po Argine – Day 1

Cue

start		Pavia tourist office
0km		E on Viale Matteotti
0.5	↱ 🅗	Corso Strada Nuova
1.1	↰ 🅗	Corso Garibaldi/SS234
6.1	↱	SS617 'to Stradella'
10.5	✳	Ponte della Becca
15.3	↱	argine 'to San Cipriano Po'
20.1		San Cipriano Po
20.4	↰	argine 'to Portalbera'
22.3	↰	'to Portalbera'
24.1		Portalbera
	↑	'to Arena Po'
26.6		Arena Po
	↰	'to Parpanese'
30.1	↰	'to Parpanese'
33.8		Parpanese
	↰	argine 'to Tosca'
46.1	✳	Sarmato
46.1	↰	'to Piacenza'
46.9	↰	SS10 'to Piacenza'
61.7	↑ ❖	(3rd exit) Via G Taverna
62.7	↙ 🅗	Via Garibladi
63.1	↰ 🅗	Largo C Battisti
63.2	✳	Piacenza Piazza Cavalli
	↑	Via Cavour/SS9 'to Milano'
65.4	↱	unsigned road (argina)
69.6	↰	'to Meleti'
75.3		Meleti
	↑	'to Maccastorna'
79.3	✳	Maccastorna
81.3	↱	'to Acquanegra'
82.3	↱	near Canottieri d'Adda
86.2	↰	argine
	⚠	8.6km gravel path
94.8	↱	argine 'to Cremona'
96.8	↰	Via del Porto bikepath
97.3	↙ ❖	(2nd exit) Corso V. Emanuele
98.9	↑	cross Piazza Stradivari
99.2		Cremona tourist office

Albergo Touring (☎ 0372 3 69 76; Via Palestro 3; singles/doubles €21/47) is the cheapest hotel near the centre. **Albergo Giardino di Giada** (☎/fax 0372 43 46 15; Via Brescia 7; singles/doubles with shared bathroom €26/ 31) is near farther-flung Piazza della Libertà and has a good inexpensive Chinese-Italian restaurant. Back in the centre, two three-star hotels are surprisingly reasonable with singles/doubles costing €39/57: **Hotel Astoria** (☎ 0372 46 16 16; Vicolo Bordigallo) in a small lane near Piazza Cavour; and **Albergo Duomo** (☎ 0372 3 52 42; Via Gonfalonieri 13) just off Piazza del Comune.

For an affordable pizza fest, head to **Pizzeria da Tonino** (Via Antico Rodano; pizzas from €5.20; closed Wed), hidden in a side alley off Corso Campi. Both **Marechiaro** (Corso Campi 49; closed Tues) and **La Bersagliera** (Piazza Risorgimento 17; closed Wed) have similarly priced pizza and standard Italian fare. A full meal at **Ristorante Centrale** (Via Petrusio; closed Thur) could include local specialty *bollito* (boiled meats) drenched in *mostarda* (sweet mustardy goo) for €21.

Day 2: Cremona to Casalmaggiore
3–5 hours, 49.1km

Like yesterday, there is little today to challenge the thighs. In fact, the route is even easier since there is no stretch on a main road and the distance is less, leaving time for exploration in Cremona, relaxed riding and the side trip from Casalmaggiore.

From central Cremona, head back to the banks of the Po and turn east into and through the fluvial countryside of Stagno Lombardo. On the water there may be a variety of boats since the navigable Po begins at Cremona. On land many *cascine* (large farms) have settled between colourful fields of crops and wildflowers, *bodri* (ponds) and canals, and protected nature reserves.

Follow cue sheet directions carefully (using a map) between Stagno Lombardo (15.3km) and Mottabaluffi (32.8km), since many of the turns are unsigned. After Mottabaluffi the route is easy, small agricultural towns (many with fine 18th-century villas and churches) are more common and the riverbank nature is more splendid. Of particular note are: **Lancona Nature Reserve** (42.4km), a humid wooded area considered

the most typical of the region, 300m off the main route outside of Gussola; and the baroque **Chiesa Santa Maria dell'Argine** on the right 1km before Casalmaggiore.

The last few kilometres pass quickly once Casalmaggiore's unmistakable skyline comes into view.

Side Trip: Sabbioneta
14km return

Once settled in Casalmaggiore, make the side trip to Sabbioneta, the 16th-century 'little Athens' of the Gonzaga clan. Planned and built on a Roman model, it's an almost perfect, intact Renaissance town.

From Casalmaggiore's Piazza Garibaldi, take Via Cavour to the outskirts. After crossing the main road, turn right on Via Matteotti and follow signs to Sabbioneta.

Casalmaggiore
Once a fully fortified village, Casalmaggiore was founded at a strategically important location on the banks of the Po River and in the midst of some of Italy's most fertile land. As long ago as the 11th century, Casalmaggiore grew in notoriety due to an

Lungo Po Argine – Day 2

Cue

start	Cremona tourist office
0km	W on Via Baldesio/Viale Po
1.9	✔ ✦ (3rd exit) Via del Porto bikepath
2.4	↰ Largo Marinai d'Italia bikepath
3.7	▲ 3.9km gravel towpath
5.5	↑ through gate
7.6	↰ unsigned road (pavement begins)
7.7	↑ 'pista ciclabile per Brancere'
12.4	↰ unsigned road not to Cà Provaglio
12.8	↑ 'to Stagno Lombardo'
14.6	↰ 'to Stagno Lombardo'
15.3	Stagno Lombardo
	↰ 'to La Pioppa'
16.3	↑ not 'to La Pioppa'
19.3	↰ 'to Via Po'
19.5	↰ not 'to Via Po'
20.4	↰ unsigned road (before farmhouse)
21.4	↰ unsigned road (near little canal)
23.1	↰ unsigned road (in centre Sommo)
24.5	↰ not 'to Isola'
24.6	San Daniele Po
	✔ unsigned road
25.3	↰ Via G. Marconi 'to Motta Baluffi'
29.1	↰ Via Argine Cremona 'to Solarolo M'
32.8	Mottabaluffi
37.4	✔ just before Toricelli
42.4	● ● ↕ Lancona Nature Reserve 0.6km ↩
47.8	✳ Chiesa di Maria dell'Argine
48.8	↘ Via Romani
48.9	↖ Via Baldesio
49.1	Casalmaggiore, Piazza Garibaldi
49.1	● ● ↕ Sabbioneta 14km ↩

abundance of local freshwater springs. Today Casalmaggiore is a small *borgo* towered over by its duomo, visible from great distances on the Po plain.

Information The tourist office (☎ 0375 4 00 39) is on the central square at Piazza Garibaldi 6. Banks are nearby on the same square. For bicycle repair, MD Cicli (☎ 0375 20 13 78) is at Via Bixio 69a.

Things to See & Do Life in this small community revolves around Piazzas Garibaldi and Turati. Within easy reach are the imposing 18th-century **Duomo di Santa Stefano** and the majestic neogothic **municipal building**. In the medieval commercial city centre at the **borgo superiore** (at the end of Via Baldesio) are a number of elegant **palazzi** and the unusual **Costume Jewellery Museum**. On the eastern outskirts of town, the 15th-century **Beata Vergine della Fontana** sanctuary is worth the walk.

Places to Stay & Eat The cheapest accommodation, **Albergo La Rotonda** (☎ 0375 4 15 57; Via Volta 8; singles/doubles €26/47) has simple rooms. About 2km to the west in Agoiolo, **Albergo La Favorita** (☎ 0375 4 24 80; Via Provinciale Bassa 40; singles/doubles €19/36.50) has a popular local restaurant (closed Sunday). **City Hotel** (☎ 0375 4 21 18; Via Cavour 54/56;singles/doubles €39/72.50) and its somewhat upscale dining room draw a happy weekend crowd. Two more trendy eating spots are **Pizzeria Vecchia Roma** (Via Bixio 34; closed Wed) and **Ristorante Il Bersagliere** (Via Favagrossa 17; closed Tues), both with affordable pizzas and pastas.

Day 3: Casalmaggiore to Mantua
3½–6 hours, 61.9km
Like the two previous days' routes, this ride is flatter than flat and, for 42.2km, hugs the banks of the Po River, on its *argina maestro*, to its confluence with the Oglio River. From there, Mantua is only 19.7km away.

The first and only trick of the day is getting to the *argine* south of Casalmaggiore. Cycle beyond the train and car bridges over the Po to the unsigned gravel ramp at Canottieri Eridanea. It leads to the top of the dyke.

The subsequent run along Via Argine del Po to Cizzolo is interrupted only by man-

made sites: the stuccoed 17th-century **Santi Rocco e Sebastiano church** in Viadana (11.4km), Italy's melon capital; the 16th-century **porticoed square** in Pomponesco (18.6km); and the 15th-century **parish church** at Dosolo (22.4km). All three villages are good places to lunch.

Past Cizzolo (33.8km), after rejoining car traffic, the route swings through a lovely **poplar grove** and then, at Torre d'Oglio on the mouth of the Oglio River, crosses a curious **pontoon bridge** (42.2km).

From Cesole (44.9km) the road turns inland for a straight shot to Mantua.

Mantua
On the shores of lakes Superiore, Mezzo and Inferiore (a widening of the Mincio

Lungo Po Argine – Day 3

Cue

start		Casalmaggiore, Piazza Garibaldi
0km		W on Via Baldesio
0.2	↱	Via Romani
0.3	↰	Via Italia 'to Lido Po'
1.4	↰	leave river before train bridge
1.5	↱	'to tuttele direzioni'
1.8	↱	unsigned (at Canottieri Eridanea)
1.9	↰	Via Argine Po (no sign)
4.8	⚠	6.6km gravel
11.4	✳	Viadana
	↱	SS358
11.6	↑ 🚲	'to Guastalla'
11.7	↘	'to Mantova'
13.1	↱	Via Villa Scasse 'to Dosolo'
13.5	↗	Via A. Corbari 'to Buzzoletto'
14.4	↰	Via Argine Po
18.6	✳	Pomponesco
22.4	✳	Dosolo
29.7	⚠	3.6km gravel argine
33.4	↰	unsigned road (after gravel ends)
33.8		Cizzolo
34.6	↱	Via C. Poma
36.9	↰	Via Argine Po
38.0	↱	unsigned road
39.3	↱	'to Cesole'
42.2	⚠	Oglio River pontoon bridge
44.6	↱	Via Scuole 'to Mantova'
44.9		Cesole
45.3	↰	'to Mantova'
56.2	↑	'to Mantova'
57.2	↗ ◆	(1st exit) 'to Mantova'
58.2	↗ ◆	Via Chicianuova 'to Mantova'
59.6	↱ 🚲	Via Achille De Giovanni
60.5	↘ 🚲	'to centro'
60.8	↱ 🚲	Corso V. Emanuele
61.5	↑ 🚲	Via Umberto I
61.9		Mantua tourist office

River) is serene and beautiful Mantua (Mantova). Settled by the Etruscans in the 10th century BC, Mantua's greatest years (known as 'La Gloriosa') were under the House of Gonzaga during the Renaissance and ended with the arrival of the Austrians in 1708. Mantua joined the rest of Italy in 1866. The old city is on a small peninsula at the heart of which is a string of five piazzas capped at the northern end by the Palazzo Ducale complex.

Information The APT office (☎ 0376 32 82 53, Ⓦ www.aptmantova.it) is at Piazza Mantegna 6, on the corner touching the market-busy Piazza delle Erbe. A good cluster of banks can be found in Via Umberto I.

Bike repairs (but no parts) can be done at La SEB di Stradiotto Mauro (☎ 0349 403 69 08) at Via Arrivabene 29. Be sure to phone first. Check with the FIAB affiliate, Amici della Bicicletta (☎ 0376 26 31 30, Ⓔ dandy50@libero.it) about local ride groups.

Things to See & Do The centre of the old city is medieval Piazza Sordello, site of the **duomo** and the incomparable **Palazzo Ducale**, also known as the Reggia dei Gonzaga. Behind the palazzo's facade is a city within the city, an extensive complex of open piazzas and structures, including **Castello di San Giorgio**. On the city's other squares are a number of significant monuments: Piazza Mantegna's **Basilica di Sant'Andrea**, Piazza delle Erbe's **Rotonda di San Lorenzo** (and **Palazzo della Ragione**) and Piazza Broletto's **Palazzo Broletto**. Finally, at the southern edge of the city, not to be missed is the architecturally wacky **Palazzo del Te**, a superb example of Renaissance Mannerism.

Places to Stay The HI **Ostello Sparafucile** (☎ 0376 37 24 65; Via Legnaghese, Lunetta di San Giorgio), a modern facility set in one of Mantua's former city gates, is 1km to the east across the bridge by the Palazzo

Ducale. There is also a **camp site** (☎ 0376 37 24 75; tent sites from €4) within the grounds.

Albergo ABC Superior (☎ 0376 32 33 47; Ⓔ hotel.abc@tin.it; Piazza Don Leoni 25; singles/doubles €66/99) is directly across from the train station and the cheapest in-town hotel. In Cittadella, 2km north across the Via Mulini bridge, **Albergo Peter Pan** (☎ 0376 39 26 37; Piazza Giulia 3; singles/ doubles €45/70) is a modern alternative. Back downtown, comfortable **Hotel Due Guerreri** (☎ 0376 32 25 33; Piazza Sordello 52; singles/doubles with bathroom €70/108) has rooms with views over the square.

Places to Eat Opposite the train station, **Pizzeria Europa** (Via Bettinelli; pasta from €4.50; closed Thur) has basic pizzas. **Pizzeria Al Quadrato** (Piazza Virgiliana 49; closed Mon), overlooking the eponymous park, is a very popular and pleasant place. Check out **Antica Osteria Fragoletta** (Piazza Arche 5; meals from €21; closed Mon) just off Lungo Lago dei Gonzaga for large servings. One of the city's better restaurants is **Ristorante Pavesi** (Piazza Erbe 13; menus from €21; closed Thur) in the centre of town. In the same neighbourhood, **La Masseria** (Piazza Broletto 7; closed Mon) and **Leoncino Rosso** (Via Giustiziati 33; closed Sun) are good-quality alternatives.

Getting There & Away Located on a secondary north–south rail line between Verona and Modena and a west–east line that runs through Cremona to/from Padua, Mantua isn't an important rail junction. Trips to every major hub usually require at least one change of train.

Drivers can use two Mantova exits from *autostrada* A22 between Brennero and Modena, which intersects A4 (from Milan to Venice) near Verona.

Bicycle A direct, albeit trafficky, route to Verona is approximately 40km north on SS62. Parma is about 60km to the southwest via SS420.

Italian Alps & Lake District

GATEWAY CITIES

Turin

A gracious city of wide boulevards, elegant arcades and grand public buildings, Turin (Torino), the Savoy capital from 1574 and for a brief period after unification the seat of Italy's parliament, rests in regal calm beside a pretty stretch of the Po River. Touting itself as Europe's capital of baroque, the city definitely has the air of a capital *manqué* rather than some provincial outpost.

Information The main tourist office (☎ 011 53 51 81, ⓦ www.turismotorino.org) at Piazza Castello 161 is open 8.30am to 7.30pm daily, as is a smaller booth (☎ 011 53 13 27) at Stazione Porta Nuova.

Banks are along Via Roma and on Piazza San Carlo.

Turin's cycling sector has been well developed. Write to Provincia di Torino's Servizio Turismo e Sport (☎ 011 861 26 39, ⓦ www.provincia.torino.it), Via Maria Vittoria 12, 10123, for the free bicycling maps.

Bici & Dintorni (☎/fax 011 88 89 81, ⓦ www.biciedintorni.org) is the FIAB affiliate of urban cyclists promoting two-wheeling in Turin. It has a busy calendar of organised activities open to anyone (sometimes for a small fee). For repairs, go to the shops near Piazza della Repubblica. Try Tuttobici (☎ 011 521 32 36) at Via Cottolengo 2; Risico (☎ 011 248 25 19) at Corso Brescia 44; or Qualiotto (☎ 011 521 30 94) at Via Mameli 4. Amante e Casella (☎ 011 54 06 41) is a big store west of the centre at Corso Matteotti 61.

Things to See & Do The nucleus of Turin's historic centre is **Piazza Castello**. Bordered by porticoed promenades, it's dominated by **Palazzo Madama**, a 13th- and 18th-century, part-medieval, part-baroque 'castle' that houses the **Museo Civico d'Arte Antica** (City Museum of Ancient Art). To its northwest, the baroque **Chiesa di San Lorenzo** is more impressive from the inside than outside. Through imposing gates is the austere, but lavish, apricot-coloured, 17th-century **Palazzo Reale** (Royal Palace) and its **Giardino Reale**

In Brief

Highlights
- **Monte Blanc** cable car into the heart of the Alps
- Astounding 10th-century **Sacra di San Michele** abbey
- Lago di Como's **Madonna del Ghisallo** cyclists' shrine
- Lakeside and canal-side **villas** and **botanical gardens**
- **Stelvio Pass** and other Alta Rezia high roads and valleys

Terrain
Forested flats along the Milanese canals; undulating hills and steep-sloped pre-Alps cut by wide rivers and sterling lakes; pitched climbs into valley uplands; snowscaped high passes in Alta Rezia.

Special Events
- **Eurochocolate** five-day cacaomania (January), Turin
- **Battle of the Oranges** (February), Ivrea
- **Navigli Festival** (first fortnight in June), Milan
- **Bataille des Reines** cow wrestling pageant (October), Aosta Valley

Cycling Events
- **Bimbimbici** (early May), national bike day
- **Alta Rezia Bike Rally** (July), Bormio
- Tours of **Lombardy** and **Piedmont** (October)

Food & Drink Specialities
- polenta (corn meal)
- *tortelli di zucca* (pumpkin-filled pasta)
- *pizzoccheri* (buckwheat pasta and vegetables)
- *risotto alla Milanese* (saffron-infused risotto)
- Valtellina cheeses, coffee and chocolate
- *zabaglione* (traditional Italian dessert custard)

(Royal Garden). To the east is the **Armeria Reale** (Savoy Royal Armoury).

North of Palazzo Reale is Turin's **Duomo di San Giovanni**, a cathedral displaying a replica of the holy **Shroud of Turin** (the original is usually kept out of sight in the **Cappella della Santa Sindone**). Further still are the remains of a 1st-century **Roman amphitheatre** and, a few steps beyond, the **Porta Palatina** red-brick Roman-era gate. Across the road at Via XX Settembre is the enormous **Museo d'Antichità** (Antiquities Museum).

The hip, young scene is around Turin's regal squares – particularly café-lined **Piazza San Carlo** and southwest of Piazza della Repubblica, as well as on **Via Po** between Piazza Castello and Piazza Vittorio Veneto. Don't miss the panoramic views from atop the indescribable architectural wonder, and symbol of Turin, called **Mole Antonelliana** (just north of Via Po). South of Piazza Vittorio Veneto, in Parco del Valentino, are the mock French-style 17th-century **Castello del Valentino** and a **medieval castle and village** constructed for the Italian General Exposition of 1884.

Outside of town are the early 18th-century **Basilica di Superga**, built on a hill to the northeast; the **Palazzina di Caccia di Stupinigi**, a vast Savoy hunting lodge to the southwest; and, to the west, the **Castello di Rivoli**, once the Savoy family's preferred residence.

For much more about Turin's attractions, in particular its many **museums** like the **Palazzo Carignano**, seat of Italy's first parliament, and the **Museo Egizio** (perhaps the world's third-best Egyptian museum after those in Cairo and London), see Lonely Planet's *Milan, Turin & Genoa*. Planning on visiting three or more museums within 48 hours? Invest in a Torino Card available at tourist offices for €15 for 48 hours or €17 for 72 hours.

Places to Stay Despite 48 one-star hotels in Turin, finding a room can be surprisingly difficult. This is especially true for people with a bicycle in tow, since many hotels are on the upper floors of apartment buildings with tiny, or no, lifts (elevators).

Campers will find **Villa Rey** (*☎/fax 011 819 01 17; Strada Val San Martino Superiore 27; per site/person €5/6)* in the hills 3km east of town. **Ostello Torino** (*☎ 011 660 29 39; Via Alby 1; B&B per person €12, dinner €8)* is also east of the Po overlooking Parco del Valentino.

Albergo Canelli (*☎ 011 53 71 66; Via San Dalmazzo 7; singles/doubles €24/32)* is ageing, but quiet, central and very cheap. **Albergo Mobledor** (*☎ 011 88 84 45; e mobledor@libero.it; Via Accademia Albertina 1; singles/doubles €31/47)* runs a tight ship just off Via Po. **Albergo San Carlo** (*☎ 011 562 78 46; e albergosancarlo@iol.it; Piazza San Carlo 197; singles/doubles from €55/80)* is top of the budget list with a hard-to-beat location.

An exception to a clot of dreary hotels is **Hotel Bellavista** (*☎ 011 669 81 39; Via Galliari 15; singles/doubles €45/70)*, an airy top-floor establishment near the train station.

Places to Eat For self-caterers, the **Di per Di** supermarket chain has stores all over town. Otherwise, try the large **Metà Metà** *(Via Giovanni Giolitti 16; closed Wed afternoon & Sun)*. **Speciality food shops** are in Via Mercanti and Via Garibaldi.

The Italian version of fast food is **Brek** *(meals €11)*, with outlets in Piazza Carlo Felice 22 and Via Santa Teresa 32b. **Mamma Mia** *(Via Parini 9; closed Sat & Sun lunch)* serves Turin's best and most popular pizzas, for around €5 to €8.

Two mid-range restaurant favourites are in the trendy area northwest of Piazza Castello: **Tre Galline** (*w www.3galline.it; Via Bellezia 3f; closed Sun & Mon lunch)* and **I Tre Galli** (*w www.3galli.com; Via S. Agostino 25b; closed Sun)*. Dedicated vegetarians have **Il Punto Verde** *(Via San Massimo 17)*. Nearby **Caffe Guglielmo Pepe** *(Via della Rocca 19)* is a bastion of Turinese society. Further north, **Porto di Savona** (*w www.portodisavona.com; Piazza Vittorio Veneto 2; closed Mon & Tues lunch)* is an old and trusted standby.

Pepino *(Piazza Carignano 8)* and **Fiorio** *(Via Po 8)* are Turin's oldest and most legendary *gelaterie* (ice cream parlours).

Getting There & Away Turin has a number of options for a quick getaway.

Air Turin is served by Caselle international airport (*☎ 011 567 63 61)*, 16km northwest of the city. Buses and trains also run frequently to Milan's Malpensa airport.

Train & Bus The main train station is the southern Stazione Porta Nuova on Piazza

Carlo Felice. Regular trains connect with Modane, Aosta, Domodossola, Milan, Genoa, and Cuneo and Ventimiglia. Many also stop at Turin's western Stazione Porta Susa, behind which is the main bus station (☎ 011 433 25 25) at Corso Inghilterra 3.

Car Turin is at a major *autostrada* junction. The A4 connects with Milan, the A5 with Aosta, the A6 with Savona and the Ligurian coast and the A21 with Piacenza (and onward to Genoa on the A7).

Milan

Milan (Milano) is synonymous with style. Smart and slick at work or play, the Milanese run their busy metropolis with efficiency and aplomb. It's Italy's economic engine room, the powerhouse of world design and a leading fashion centre. It's also a city for city-lovers, and an efficient orientation centre for anyone recently arriving or soon to depart.

Information The main IAT/APT office (☎ 02 725 24 301, ⓦ www.milanoinfo tourist.com) is open daily next to the cathedral at Via Marconi 1. There is a branch office (☎ 02 725 24 360) at Stazione Centrale. The Comune di Milan also operates a weekday information bureau (☎ 02 869 07 34) in the nearby Galleria Vittorio Emanuele. All sell the visitors guide *Milano – Dove, Come, Quando.*

ATMs dispense cash all over town, particularly on important shopping strips and in heavily touristed areas.

Interested in organised cycling activities? Check with Milan's very active FIAB affiliate, Ciclobby (☎/fax 02 693 11 624, ⓦ www.associazioni.milano.it/ciclobby). Its offices are due north of the Garibaldi train station at Via Borsieri 4e. Otherwise, the Provincia di Milano produces Italian-language cycling brochures. Look for *Percorsi Ciclo Turistici nella Provincia di Milano, Itinerari nel verde (Guida ai Parchi della Provincia di Milano)* and *Le strade azzurre in bicicletta.* Ediciclo's *In bicicletta nei dintorni di Milano,* both the *nord* (north) and *sud* (south) volumes, are also very good.

One of the most central bike shops is Rossignoli (☎ 02 80 49 60) north of Castello Sforzesco on Via Garibaldi 71. Near the central station (and start of Day 2 of the Navigli Milanesi ride) is AWS (☎ 02 670 72 145) at Via Ponte Seveso 33. In the south, near Piazza XXIV Maggio (and the terminus of the other Navigli Milanesi ride days), try I Signori del Ciclismo (☎ 02 894 01 498) at Via Ferrari 2. Check with Ciclobby for others.

Things to See & Do Milan's navel is the Piazza del Duomo, lorded over by the

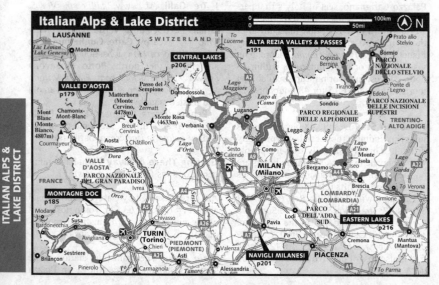

14th- to 15th-century late-Gothic **duomo** (the world's fourth largest) and scrutinised by the **Palazzo Arcivescovile** and **Palazzo Reale**. The northern stairs of the cathedral lead to its roof terrace for the best panorama of the city. Immediately to the north of the duomo is the cruciform, café-lined, steel-and-glass **Galleria Vittorio Emanuele II**. The celebrated 18th-century **Teatro della Scala** is through it to the north.

A short walk west of the duomo is **Pinacoteca Ambrosiana**, Milan's finest art museum and old library. Da Vinci's *The Last Supper* can be seen at the **Cenacolo Vinciano**, the refectory adjoining **Chiesa di Santa Maria delle Grazie**, in Corso Magenta much further west.

Northwest of the duomo is a wide pedestrian promenade called **Piazza Mercanti**, a medieval marketplace flanked by the red-brick, vaulted **Palazzo delle Regione** (1233) and the **Palazzo Affari al Giureconsulti**, Milan's 19th-century stock exchange. At the far end of its onward pedestrian Via Dante and at the head of Parco Sempione is the 15th-century **Castello Sforzesco**, home of three museums.

Two other areas worth mentioning: the **Quadrilatero d'Oro** in the Monte Napoleone area is the place to shop for designer fashion, while trendy **Brera** is the bohemian quarter centred around Via Brera and cobbled Via Fiori Chiari.

Places to Stay Milan's closest camping ground, **Città di Milano** (☎ 02 482 00 134; w www.parcoaquatica.com; *Via Gaetano Airaghi 61; per person/tent €6/7)* is 9km west of the duomo just south of SS11 and east of the *tangenziale ovest* (western bypass). Phoning ahead is required. The HI hostel, **Ostello Piero Rotta** *(☎/fax 02 392 67 095; Via Salmoiraghi 1; B&B with card [required] €16.50)*, is in a neighbourhood called *Quartiere 'T8'* 4km northwest of the centre. In Navigli, just east of Piazzale XXIV Maggio, **La Cordata** *(Casa Scout;* ☎ 02 583 14 675; w www.lacordata.it; *Via Burigozzo 11; B&B per person €16)* is a good in-town option.

Milan's hotels are among the most expensive and heavily booked in Italy, particularly during trade fairs (nearly all the time). The area around Stazione Centrale is cheapest (and shadiest). If booking is impossible, for options try the APT or Centro Prenotazione Hotels Italia (☎ 800 01 57 72).

Around the station, **Hotel del Sole** *(☎ 02 295 12 971; Via Spontini 6; singles/doubles without bathroom €40/60)* is adequate. **Hotel Kennedy** *(☎ 02 294 00 934;* w www .kennedyhotel.it; *Viale Tunisia 6; singles/ doubles without bathroom €60/75)* is also OK. On the 3rd floor of the same building is **Hotel San Tomaso** *(☎/fax 02 295 14 747;* e hotelsantomaso@tin.it; *Via Tunisia 6; singles/doubles with bathroom €45/75)*. **Hotel Casa Mia** *(☎ 02 657 52 49; Viale Vittorio Veneto 30; singles/doubles with bathroom €80/120)* is a big step up in quality.

Elsewhere in the city, **Hotel Ullrich** *(☎ 02 864 50 156; Corso Italia 6; singles/doubles without bathroom €21/42)* is south of Piazza Duomo on the 6th floor of an old well-kept building. **Hotel Speronari** *(☎ 02 864 61 125; Via Speronari 4; singles/doubles without bathroom €45/65)*, off Via Torino near the duomo, is highly recommended. **Albergo Cantore** *(☎/fax 02 835 75 65; Corso Genova 25; singles/doubles without bathroom €45/ 75)* is a good, newly renovated choice.

Places to Eat Italians say Lombard cuisine is designed for people with no time to waste. Result? Most streets around the duomo and near the stations are riddled with **sandwich bars** and **fast-food outlets**. Italian quick-meal standbys like **Brek**, **Ciao**, **Amico** and **Autogrill** have branches in many popular areas. Self-caterers should head south to the **trattorias** and **supermarkets** in Via Torino's extensions as far as Corso Genova. The morning **market** on Piazza XXIV Maggio is a good bet too.

Wallet-friendly **restaurants** abound in two areas. In the northeast, the streets of Monte Napoleone (around Piazza Cavour) and Brera (in Via Brera and Via Fiori Chiari) are thick with eateries. In the south, the Ticinese and Navigli neighbourhoods are most promising. Corso di Porta Ticinese and the wall-to-wall pizzeria–osteria–trattoria strip along the Naviglio Grande have something for everyone.

Getting There & Away Milan is well served by public transport.

Air Malpensa international airport is a major European air hub. It's situated a few kilometres east of the Fiume Adda, along which the Navigli Milanesi bike route described on p201 runs (56km to the centre). There are express trains and buses shuttling between the airport and the city.

Bus Stations are scattered right across the city. Several major companies with national and international destinations leave from Piazza Castello in front of the Castello Sforzesco.

Train Milan is the most active rail centre in northern Italy. Services from the main Stazione Centrale go to *all* major cities in Italy (especially Turin and Genoa) and throughout Europe. FNM trains from Stazione Cadorna connect Milan with Como, Varese and Laveno. Trains from Stazione Porta Garibaldi are mostly regional trains to destinations like Varese, Como, Lecco, Sondrio/Tirano, Bergamo, Brescia, Cremona, Mantova, Piacenza, Pavia and Abbiategrasso. It's useful to compare departure times between trains from Centrale and Porta Garibaldi.

Car Milan is the primary junction of Italy's northern expressways. All roads intersect the often-jammed ring road, known as the Tangenziale. The A1 comes from the southeast via Piacenza; the A4 comes from the east via Bergamo, Brescia and Lago di Garda, and from the west via Novara, Torino and Alpine Piedmont and Aosta; the A9 comes from the north via Lugano and Como; the A8 comes from the northwest via Varese with a spur (A26) going to Domodossola; and the A7 comes from the south via Genova and Liguria.

The Alps

There is something about mountains. People just can't stay away from them. Perhaps it's because they are as complex as the human spirit: simple yet fulfilling, deceptively barren, soaring, somehow evanescent yet determinedly eternal. The dorsal alpine spine stretched across southern central Europe always draws the eye. Because they seem impassable, people have tried to conquer them; because cycling over them seems impossible…well, it's human nature to tackle the impossible.

HISTORY

Italian alpine mountain peoples, despite their distinguishing regional particularities and culture-specific customs, have a lot in common. Descended from ancient tribes, they lived for centuries coupled to a harsh environment in unfrequented regions. Singular identities developed relatively unencumbered by the squabbling and bickering of the plains denizens. However, there was contact with the outside world. Mountain valleys were valuable crossroads controlling access to the laborious passes over which pilgrims, merchants and princes had to travel. These important trade and communications choke points were first waylaid by the Romans and have been hotly contested in the centuries since. Over time the strategic locations of these mountain communities led to their development as important commercial, administrative and religious centres. In the 21st century, rekindled curiosity over cross-border identities has revived interest in high-valley culture, agricultural still, but increasingly bankrolled through controlled exploitation of outdoor adventure opportunities (particularly skiing) in the vast protected alpine parklands.

NATURAL HISTORY

The Italian Alps are the broad mountainous arc stretching north and east from Cuneo along the French and Swiss borders to the high passes north of Sondrio. Millions of years ago, they were formed by the collision and overlapping of the African and European tectonic plates. During the Pleistocene age, five great glacial waves gouged course valleys into the uplifted rock, whose features have since been somewhat softened by torrents and wind. The valley floors have also been left by the retreating ice behemoths with a thick alluvial layer of now fertile soil.

Despite differences in rock content, the superficial natural flavours remain constant. Copiously tilled low-valley land is usually thick with vegetation and creatures. Higher forests shade productive undergrowth and woodland animals. Further up, scented pine forests open onto gardens of alpine fauna and foliage, which, in turn, stretch into shrub-spotted alpine fields. Stern weather-beaten rock and the barren white tracts of everlasting ice tower over it all.

Valle d'Aosta

Duration	2 days
Distance	125.1km
Difficulty	moderate
Start	Aosta
End	Ivrea

The glacially incised Valle d'Aosta (Aosta Valley) offers a castle-spangled approach to the soul of the Alps at their highest and grandest. It has long attracted oglers and merchants seeking solace in, passage through, and control over its 13 side valleys and soaring passes. Today's governments have reaffirmed Aosta's special autonomous status, recognising rights originally bestowed in 1191. Close ties with French-speaking Europe since AD 757 often make it feel more French than Italian. In fact, the French language is equal with Italian (introduced to the valley in 1861).

PLANNING
When to Ride
Sudden Alp-prompted cold snaps and frequent rainfall aside (for weather reports in Italian call ☎ 44113), muggy summers still grip the Valle d'Aosta, especially in the lower elevations. Since this ride tackles no high passes, the best ride times are from mid-May to mid-September, with the standard caveat about August overcrowding. Prevailing daytime winds blow up the valley, but usually not fiercely enough to matter.

Maps & Books
The Touring Club Italiano's (1:200,000) *Piemonte e Valle d'Aosta* map covers everything, as does the free (1:115,000) *Valle d'Aosta* map produced by the province. The Valle d'Aosta *On the Summit of Memory* booklet is the best free guide of the upper valley. The ATL del Canavese e Valle di Lanzo produces a thorough series of *Passeggiando* booklets for appreciating outdoor activities and history in its region.

ACCESS TOWN
Aosta
Aosta, the 'Rome of the Alps', is the capital and only major city of the Valle d'Aosta, sitting at its centre on the Fiume Dora Baltea. Laid out following the Roman grid pattern, most of its historic centre (built around today's Piazza Chanoux) is closed to traffic.

Information The APT office (☎ 0165 23 66 27, W www.regione.vda.it/turismo, W www .aostavalley.com), Piazza Chanoux 8, has loads of information on the entire region. Banks are also on this large central square. A very good bike shop, Cicli Lucchini (☎ 0165 26 23 06) is 300m west of the old town walls at Corso Battaglione Aosta 49–51. Mountain bikes can be rented from Gal Sport (☎ 0165 23 61 34) at the base of the *funivia* (cable car) at Strada Paravera 6.

Things to See & Do Roman ruins are Aosta's principal attractions. Deemed the city's symbol, crucifix-strung **Arch of Augustus** is between the **Porta Pretoria/Torre dei Signori** (the main eastern gate to the Roman city) and the cobbled 1st-century BC **Roman bridge** over the Torrente Buthier. The **Roman theatre**, site of summer performances, is a skip north. All that remains of the **Roman forum**, to the west beneath Piazza Giovanni XXIII, is a colonnaded walkway known as the **Criptoportico**. The foreboding **Torre dei Balivi**, a former prison, marks one corner of the city's excellent **Roman walls**.

The **cathedral** on Piazza Giovanni XXIII has a neoclassical facade that belies the impressive Gothic interior. Original sections of the **complex of Sant'Orso** and the **Basilica di San Lorenzo** on Via Sant'Orso date from the 10th century, with excavated remains from the 5th century. Later period structures in the city include the Renaissance **Palazzo Ronca** and the **Archaeological Museum**, both on Piazza Ronca.

For **hikes** and other **outdoor activities** (rock climbing, mountain biking, hang-gliding/paragliding etc), ask at the APT office.

Places to Stay Accommodation is sometimes difficult to find. In a pinch, there are cheap and pleasant lodgings in the very near hinterland; check with the APT office.

Ville d'Aosta (☎ 0165 36 13 60; Viale Gran San Bernardo 76; per person/tent €4.80/ 8.80) is a camping ground 1km north of the town centre. **Milleluci** (☎ 0165 23 52 78; Roppoz 15; per person/tent €5.50/10.50) is about 1km to the east.

Albergo La Belle Époque (☎/fax 0165 26 22 76; Via D'Avise 18; singles/doubles without bathroom €26/46.50) has clean, basic rooms above a busy pizzeria (closed Sunday, menus from €13). **Albergo Mancuso**

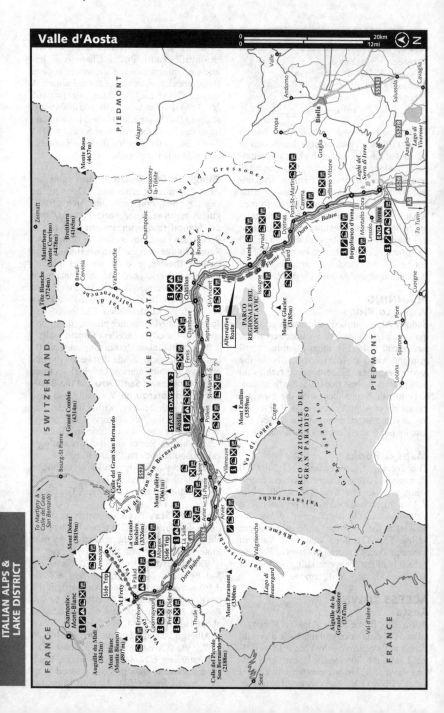

Valle d'Aosta

(☎ 0165 3 45 26; W *www.albergomancuso .com; Via Voison 32; singles/doubles €37/ 47),* just southwest of the centre, is clean, quiet and very welcoming. Also to the west, **Hotel/Ristorante Al Caminetto** *(☎ 0165 55 53 13; Via Bréan 33; singles/doubles with bathroom €26/52)* is in a leafy, calm, residential neighbourhood. Pricey **Hotel Cecchin** *(☎/fax 0165 4 52 62; Via Ponte Romano 27; singles/doubles with bathroom €60/86)* and its mid-range restaurant are perfectly situated right by the old Roman bridge.

Places to Eat The penny-conscious will find the **mercato coperto** and **supermarkets** east of the walls at Piazza Cavalieri Vittorio Veneto, and good **speciality food shops** in Via Sant'Anselmo.

For straightforward pizza, pasta and local platters at popular prices, the run of somewhat touristy **restaurants** in pedestrian Via Aubert and Via de Tillier is sure to please. Quality takeaway slices of pizza for €2 can be had from **Il Cappero** *(Via Aubert 4).* Or, for a sunshine lunch in a tranquil garden try some wine and a cheese platter (from €4.40) at **Enoteca Ad Forum** *(Via de Sales; menu from €18.50; closed Mon)* across from the cathedral.

Economical eateries away from the main strip include **Hosteria del Calvino** *(Via Croce di Città 24; full dinner from €13; closed Sun)* and **Ristorante della Torre** *(Via Torre del Lebbroso; dinner from €15.50; closed Tues).*

Getting There & Away Buses from Milan (2½ to 3½ hours, two daily), Turin (two hours, eight daily) and Courmayeur (30 minutes to one hour, five daily) arrive at the Aosta bus station (☎ 0165 26 20 27), virtually opposite the train station on Via Carrel.

The train station on Piazza Manzetti is served from most parts of Italy via Turin (two to 2½ hours, more than 10 daily). Travellers from Milan must change trains at Chivasso. Local service continues to Pré-St Didier (50 minutes), 5km short of Courmayeur.

Expressway A5 runs between Turin and the upper Valle d'Aosta. From Milan, head west on A4 and use the A4/5 connection. With the Mont Blanc tunnel reopened, Aosta can also be accessed directly from France. Another road north leads through the Great St Bernard tunnel to Switzerland.

Bicycle Of the few ways to bicycle into Aosta, two are part of the route described here. That leaves the magnificent, but brutal, road over the 2473m Colle di Grand San Bernardo from Martigny (Switzerland).

THE RIDE
Day 1: Aosta Circuit
3–5 hours, 51.1km
This ride begins in the splendid heights of the *alta valle* (upper valley). The pedal leads up 352m to a point from which nonknobby wheels will easily go no further and then back down 786m to Aosta.

The first thing today is a train ride up the hill. Since today's route is up and down the valley's only road, why not go up by locomotive? Trains to Pré-St Didier leave Aosta almost every hour and take 50 minutes. That said, there's no reason not to give the climb into the upper Aosta valley (or Valdigne) a go as an alternative route! Just follow the main road west.

From Pré-St Didier (1017m), make a beeline for even higher elevations. **Funivie Mont Blanc** *(☎ 0165 8 99 25,* W *www.mon tebianco.com)* in la Palud (1369m) is a cable car into (and even over!) the Alps beside Europe's highest peak, Mont Blanc (Monte Bianco). Cars depart every 20 minutes from 8.20am to 12.40pm and 2pm to 4.20pm (earlier and later in summer) to a number of destinations (high season return, €11.50 to €30.50). An outing to the highest point, Aiguille du Midi (3842m), and back will take around four hours. Botanists should pause at the Pavillon du Mont Fréty station for the **Alpine Garden Saussurea**.

Before heading back down the valley, ponder the side trip in **Val Ferret**, a pristine rut running along the base of the Mont Blanc monolith. It's 426m in 10.3km up to Arnouvaz where the paved road runs out. Mountain bikers with gear and gumption can continue on an epic seven-day ride around the massif (see the boxed text 'Mountain Biking' on p40-1).

Gobble down lunch in **Courmayeur** (14.4km), a town built for the love of outdoor sports and adventure; there are many good restaurants on Via Roma.

The rest of the road to Aosta is glorious: downhill, flanked by high mountains, blessed with outstanding panoramic views and peppered with quaint ancient villages.

Morgex (23.3km), capital of Valdigne, is worth a short detour for its 10th-century castle, 15th-century church, Romanesque belfry and a number of towers. Anyone planning time in Parco Nazionale del Gran Paradiso should stop at its information office (☎ 0165 9 50 55) at 39.4km. Lower down, the villages of St-Pierre (42km) and Sarre (44km) are surmounted by evocative castles: 18th-century **Castello di Sarre** was once a hunting lodge for the Italian royal family and is now a museum of the Savoy presence in the valley; fairytale 11th-century **Castello di Saint-Pierre** houses a natural history museum.

Day 2: Aosta to Ivrea
4–7½ hours, 74km
The SS26 dives 70km straight down the valley to Ivrea and the morainic hills of Canavese. It is perfect for the directionally impaired. However, for the rest, serene secondary roads creep through sedate old-world villages over the first 31.4km and toy with upslopes along the edge of the vale. The primary attractions throughout the valley are the plethora of Romanesque and Gothic castles, each within view of the next.

From Aosta, head south across the Dora Baltea River and turn east towards the magnificently restored 13th- to 14th-century **Castello de Fénis** (17km), considered the classic medieval Aosta castle, featuring rich frescoes and period graffiti.

In Chambave (24.8km), back on the north side of the river, a special microclimate favours the storage of valley-produced wines. Learn more about this at the **Cooperativa Vitivinicola 'La Crotta di Vegneron'**.

Just to the east, in Châtillon (27.5km), three castles grace the hillside. The 14th-century **Castello di Ussel** (across the river), **Castello Passerin d'Entrèves**, surrounded by gardens and visible above the centre of town, and **Castello Baron Gamba**, circumscribed by the route, are all worth a visit as is the **Roman bridge** (to the right of the Chanoux bridge just before town). Châtillon is the jumping-off point for trips (by bus and/or bike) up **Valtournenche** to Breuil-Cervinia and the back of the Matterhorn.

Clinging to the hillside at a grand curve in the valley is St-Vincent (30.4km), 'the Riviera of the Alps', famous for its **thermal spas** and **casino** (apparently Europe's largest).

Past St-Vincent, the sober 14th-century **Castello di Verrès** (42.9km) looks like an archetypal stronghold, doing sentinel duty atop its rocky perch. Across the river, the restored 15th-century **Castello d'Issogne**, built over the ruins of a Roman city, was later converted into the sumptuous Renaissance residence it now resembles. A visit here can be either a side trip or along an alternative route

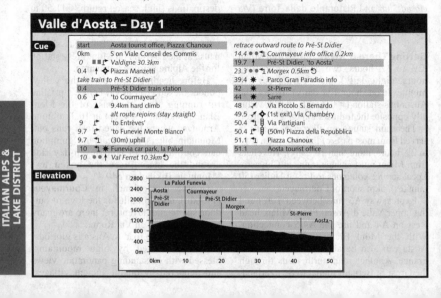

Valle d'Aosta – Day 1

Cue

start	Aosta tourist office, Piazza Chanoux		*retrace outward route to Pré-St Didier*	
0km	S on Viale Conseil des Commis		14.4 ●●↰	*Courmayeur info office 0.2km*
0	■■↱ *Valdigne 30.3km*		19.7 ↑	Pré-St Didier, 'to Aosta'
0.4	↑ ◆ Piazza Manzetti		23.3 ●●↰	*Morgex 0.5km* ↺
take train to Pré-St Didier			39.4 ✳ ·	Parco Gran Paradiso info
0.4	Pré-St Didier train station		42 ✳	St-Pierre
0.6 ↱	'to Courmayeur'		44 ✳	Sarre
▲	9.4km hard climb		48 ↙	Via Piccolo S. Bernardo
	alt route rejoins (stay straight)		49.5 ↗ ◆	(1st exit) Via Chambéry
9 ↱	'to Entrèves'		50.4 ↰ ▯	Via Partigiani
9.7 ↱	'to Funevie Monte Bianco'		50.4 ↰ ▯	(50m) Piazza della Repubblica
9.7 ↰	(30m) uphill		51.1 ↰	Piazza Chanoux
10 ↰ ✳	Funevia car park, la Palud		51.1	Aosta tourist office
10 ●●↑	*Val Ferret 10.3km* ↺			

Elevation

of rolling lanes west of the river. Return to the main route at the rocky rise of **Bard** (49.4km), once crowned by an 11th- to 13th-century fortress destroyed by Napoleon and then splendidly rebuilt in the 19th century. Try the alternative route through the bourg for a closer encounter.

There are also Roman remains along this path of the ancient route to Gaul, known to pilgrims as the Via Francigena. Donnas is the site of one of the best-preserved bits of this **Roman road** and, 3km later, the river crossing at Pont-Saint-Martin (55.1km) is just downstream of the original 1st-century BC **Roman bridge** still used until 1831.

With the passage into Piedmont, the Valle d'Aosta feel gives way to the hills and castle-capped wine villages of Canavese. Me-

dieval **Carema** (57.4km) produces one of the region's most famous elixirs. Settimo Vittone's 8th- to 11th-century **Pieve di S. Lorenzo** (62.9km) is a noteworthy example of Romanesque architecture.

Further along, past the **Castello di Montestrutto**, is Borgofranco d'Ivrea (67.4km). Little is left of its Roman origins, but the prosperity of its 13th-century *ricetto* (tax-free zone centre) survives, as does the elegant **Palazzo Marini**. Follow signs before the villages to 'Balmetti/Birreria' to examine special **natural storage cellars** of unvarying temperatures.

Montalto Dora harbours the remains of a **Roman aqueduct** and the 18th-century **Villa dei Baroni Casana**, now a Benedictine monastery. The defensive **castello** atop

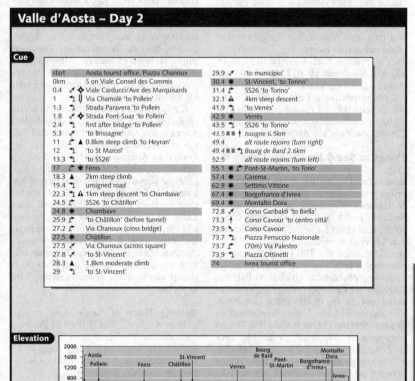

Valle d'Aosta – Day 2

Cue

start	Aosta tourist office, Piazza Chanoux	29.9	'to municipio'
0km	S on Viale Conseil des Commis	30.4	St-Vincent, 'to Torino'
0.4	Viale Carducci/Ave des Marquisards	31.4	SS26 'to Torino'
1	Via Chamolè 'to Pollein'	32.1	4km steep descent
1.3	Strada Paravera 'to Pollein	41.9	'to Verrès'
1.8	Strada Pont-Suaz 'to Pollein'	42.9	Verrès
2.4	first after bridge 'to Pollein'	43.5	SS26 'to Torino'
5.3	'to Brissagne'	43.5	Issogne 6.5km
11	0.8km steep climb 'to Heyran'	49.4	alt route rejoins (turn right)
12	'to St Marcel'	49.4	Bourg de Bard 2.6km
13.3	'to SS26'	52.5	alt route rejoins (turn left)
17	Fénis	55.1	Pont-St-Martin, 'to Torio'
18.3	2km steep climb	57.4	Carema
19.4	unsigned road	62.9	Settimo Vittone
22.3	1km steep descent 'to Chambave'	67.4	Borgofranco d'Ivrea
24.5	SS26 'to Châtillon'	69.4	Montalto Dora
24.8	Chambave	72.8	Corso Garibaldi 'to Biella'
25.9	'to Châtillon' (before tunnel)	73.3	Corso Cavour 'to centro città'
27.2	Via Chanoux (cross bridge)	73.5	Corso Cavour
27.5	Châtillon	73.7	Piazza Ferruccio Nazionale
27.5	Via Chanoux (across square)	73.7	(70m) Via Palestro
27.8	'to St-Vincent'	73.9	Piazza Ottinetti
28.3	1.8km moderate climb	74	Ivrea tourist office
29	'to St-Vincent'		

Elevation

Monte Crovero has protected the road to Ivrea, today's next and last stop, for more than 600 years.

Ivrea

Ivrea is the largest city of Piedmont's Canavese region. A few kilometres from the beginning of the Valle d'Aosta, it looks out to the wide Po River plain. Although having been established as Eporedia by the Romans, Ivrea is famous for its King Arduino, the early-11th-century first King of Italy. He and his legions built the many castles throughout the area.

Information Ivrea's main Azienda Turistica Locale (☎ 0125 61 81 31, ⓦ www .canavese-vallilanzo.it) is 1.3km east of the centre at Corso Vercelli 1. The central branch (☎ 0125 62 76 03) is on Piazza Ottinetti. Banks can be found on Via Palestro and its Corso Massimo d'Azeglio extension, and across the river in Corso Nigra. Two bike shops, Cicli Fiore (☎ 0125 64 16 95) and BiciSport (☎ 0125 4 03 48) are within sight of each other at Corso Nigra 53 and 46, respectively. Local FIAB affiliate, Amici della Bici – Legambiente (☎ 0125 4 42 02, ⓔ curzionelli@tiscalinet.it) is in the Centro Gandhi at Via Arduino 75.

Things to See & Do Peeking through the tangle of historical buildings are Ivrea's Roman foundations: the **Ponte Vecchio** (old bridge); the underwater ruins of the **Pons Maior**, once an immense river span near Via Siccardi; and a stretch of the **cardo** (main street) near Hotel La Serra. Much of the rest was covered over during the era of King Arduino, when the 10th- to 12th-century **duomo** was built over a 4th-century temple, and the **Vescovado** (Bishop's Palace), **Chiostro dei Canonici** (mostly destroyed to make way for the castle) and a vast Benedictine abbey of which only the **Campanile di Santo Stefano** (Santo Stefano Bell Tower) remains were completed. In the 14th century, the Savoys built the arresting **castello**.

You can go **canoeing** on the Dora Baltea beneath the bridges or check out the lake delights of the five **laghi della Serra di Ivrea** a few kilometres north. For an unusual week-long hiking/biking experience into Parco Nazionale del Gran Paradiso, ask at tourist information about Me Na Vòta.

Ivrea is most famous for its costumed Carnevale climax, the **Battaglia delle Arance** (Battle of the Oranges). In commemoration of a medieval rebellion, for three days in early February, nine teams of 'revolutionaries' wait in certain squares for 30 carts that are laden with helmeted 'soldiers' and then proceed to pelt them with 400,000kg of oranges.

Places to Stay & Eat About 2km northeast of town towards the eponymous lake is **Lago San Michele** (☎ 0125 61 61 95; Via Lago San Michele 13; sites per person/tent €3.10/5.30). There are two hostels in town (both temporarily closed at the time of writing): **Ostello Canoa Club** (☎ 0125 4 01 86; Via Dora Baltea 1) and **Ostello Salesiano Eporediese** (☎ 0125 62 72 68; Via San Giovanni Bosco 58).

Albergo/Ristorante Monferrato (ⓔ monferrato@iol.it; Via Gariglietti 1; singles/ doubles €40/45) is central and has a star eatery (closed Sunday). **Albergo Luca** (☎ 0125 4 87 06; Corso Garibaldi 58; singles/doubles €34/50) is on a quiet courtyard off the main loop road.

Restaurants are mostly attached to hotels, although there are several stand-alone places in Via Arduno, Via Palestro and their Corso Vercelli extension to the east. Try vaulted **La Mugnaia** (☎ 0125 4 05 30; Via Arduino 53; closed Mon), in a side vicolo (alley or alleyway) for regional fare, or **Ristorante Al Faro** (☎ 0125 64 12 29; Via Siccardi 3; closed Thur) for fairly priced pasta. **Caffe del Teatro** (☎ 0125 64 11 86; Via Palestro 29; closed Sun) is brightly lit and popular. **Ristorante Aquila Antica** (ⓦ www .aquilaantica.it; Via Gozzano 37; dinners from €23; closed Sun), in the quiet borghetto (burg) south of the river, is perhaps the city's best.

Getting There & Away Buses running to/from Aosta all stop in front of the Ivrea train station. The same train line between Turin (one hour) and Aosta (one to 1½ hours) runs through Ivrea's station, south of the centre on Via Nigra.

Bicycle On direct, busy roads, Ivrea is a flat 60km from Turin via Chivasso. Santhia, on the main train line between Turin and Milan, is 30km southeast on SS143.

Montagne Doc

Duration	3 days
Distance	244.6km
Difficulty	moderate–hard
Start	Turin
End	Pinerolo

Turin is the hub of radiating spokes of notorious high-elevation valleys. The best rides are those that slide a few lengths into the valleys and then vault the dividing ridges, giving a cyclist a little bit of everything. This three-day pedal hits three of the valleys (and the two passes dividing them!), including those elected to host the 2006 Winter Olympics: Alta Val Chisone and the Valle di Susa.

PLANNING
When to Ride
This ride goes to some high elevations, thereby escaping the heat of the plains and running the risk of hitting periodic high-elevation weather mess. The best time for pedalling is from mid-June to mid-September, although holidaying crowds in August can be a pain.

Maps
The *Piemonte e Valle d'Aosta* (1:200,000) map by Touring Club Italiano includes the area west of Turin, although part of it is in a separate box. Instead, try the free Instituto Geografico DeAgostini (1:180,000) *Province of Torino* map distributed at tourist offices. For the ride from Avigliana to Susa, ask in Turin for the *Ciclostrada Valle di Susa* map. Devoted mountain bikers should ask for the 'Montagne doc' *Due ruote tra i monti* pamphlet.

ACCESS TOWN
See Turin (p174).

THE RIDE
Day 1: Turin to Avigliana
4½–8 hours, 82.1km
Today's ride is a simple one: a gambol north into the Valli di Lazio, a scramble over the Colle di Lis and then an amble into the heart of the Valle di Susa.

Getting out of large cities is always a pain; getting out of Turin, although well supplied with bikepaths, is no different. About 10km

pass before there is real air, and almost 30km before the traffic pressing through Parco Regionale la Mandria northwest of town relaxes. Another route via Druento, San Gillio, la Cassa and Fiano in Val Ceronda is via quiet country hills on the other side of the park.

Beyond the ring of suburbs, medieval Lanzo Torinese is a short side trip from the main route (at 30.8km). Wander the *chintane* (medieval alleys) and appreciate the Gothic **Chiesa di Santa Croce**, medieval **Torre Civica** and the **Ponte del Diavolo**. Lanzo is the capital city of the Valli di Lanzo, three dead-end dales – the Viù, Ala and Grande – that slither into the mountains and are outdoor enthusiast Meccas. Today's route climbs the southernmost valley to its namesake town of Viù.

Viù is at exactly half the day's total climb. After 46.1km up 536m, now comes the hard part…and the most beautiful. A mountain lane soars the remaining 537m to the top of the **Colle di Lis** (61.8km, 1311m). The enveloping scenery is excellent recompense. So is the eye-tearing tear down!

From Almese (77km), on the edge of the Susa Valley floor, the village of Villar Dora and its storybook **castle** are 1km away. Also keep an eye out for the castle and towers of Avigliana, today's terminus.

Avigliana
The Susa Valley traces one arm of Via Francigena, a web of paths between Turin and France hiked for centuries by merchants, mercenaries and pilgrims. Avigliana, at the eastern end of the trail below Sacra di San Michele, was a focal point of valley life. Its monuments bear witness to a lasting presence.

Information Tourist information (☎ 011 932 86 50, ⓦ www.montagnedoc.it) is at Piazza del Popolo 2a. Banks are nearby on the square. The nearest bike store, Cicli Giai (☎ 011 939 93 73), Via Turin 48, is in Sant' Ambrogio.

Things to See & Do In the *centro storico* (historic centre) are a variety of medieval buildings – **Casa della Porta Ferrata**, **Casa Senore**, **Torre dell'Orologio** and **Chiesa San Giovanni**. Outside the city walls, the Gothic-Romanesque complex built around the **Chiesa San Pietro** whets the appetite for the climb to **Piazza Conte Rosso** and the

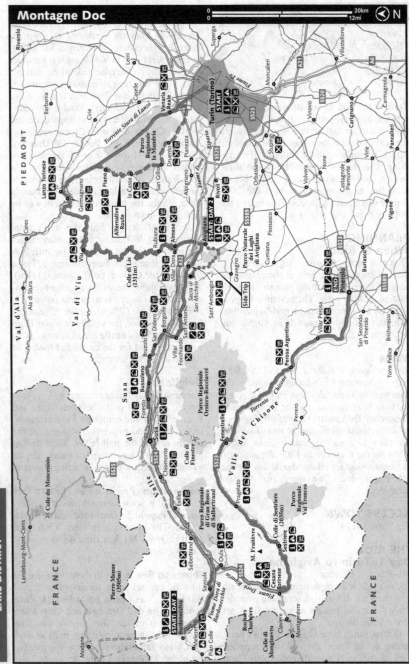

Montagne Doc

Montagne Doc – Day 1

Cue

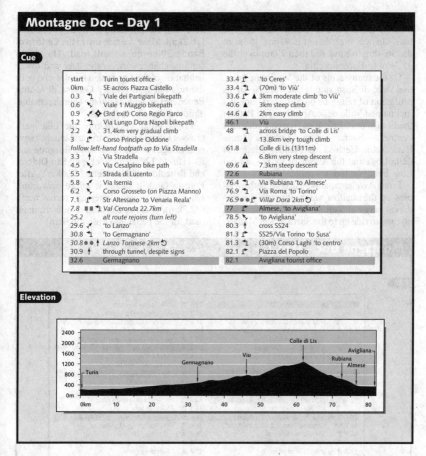

start		Turin tourist office	33.4	↱	'to Ceres'
0km		SE across Piazza Castello	33.4	↰	(70m) 'to Viù'
0.3	↰	Viale dei Partigiani bikepath	33.6	↱ ▲	3km moderate climb 'to Viù'
0.6	↘	Viale 1 Maggio bikepath	40.6	▲	3km steep climb
0.9	↗ ◆	(3rd exit) Corso Regio Parco	44.6	▲	2km easy climb
1.2	↰	Via Lungo Dora Napoli bikepath	46.1		Viù
2.2	▲	31.4km very gradual climb	48	↰	across bridge 'to Colle di Lis'
3	↱	Corso Principe Oddone		▲	13.8km very tough climb
follow left-hand footpath up to Via Stradella			61.8		Colle di Lis (1311m)
3.3	↑	Via Stradella		▲	6.8km very steep descent
4.5	↘	Via Cesalpino bike path	69.6	▲	7.3km steep descent
5.5	↰	Strada di Lucento	72.6		Rubiana
5.8	↙	Via Isernia	76.4	↰	Via Rubiana 'to Almese'
6.2	↘	Corso Grosseto (on Piazza Manno)	76.9	↰	Via Roma 'to Torino'
7.1	↱	Str Altessano 'to Venaria Reala'	76.9 ● ● ↱		Villar Dora 2km ↻
7.8	■ ■ ↰	Val Ceronda 22.7km	77	↱	Almese, 'to Avigliana'
25.2		alt route rejoins (turn left)	78.5	↘	'to Avigliana'
29.6	↗	'to Lanzo'	80.3	↑	cross SS24
30.8	↱	'to Germagnano'	81.3	↱	SS25/Via Torino 'to Susa'
30.8 ● ● ↑		Lanzo Torinese 2km ↻	81.3	↰	(30m) Corso Laghi 'to centro'
30.9	↑	through tunnel, despite signs	82.1	↱	Piazza del Popolo
32.6		Germagnano	82.1		Avigliana tourist office

Elevation

10th-century **castle** ruins at the top of Monte Pezzulano. The lakes to the south are part of **Parco Naturale dei Laghi di Avigliana**.

A 12km road climbs more than 600m to the fabulous, domineering Benedictine **Sacra di San Michele** perched at the summit of Monte Pirchiriano. The 10th-century abbey is one of the largest European religious buildings attempted during the Romanesque period. Its 13th-century **Porta dello Zodiaco** (Door of the Zodiac) is particularly striking.

Places to Stay & Eat About 500m from the lake is **Avigliana Lacs** (☎ 011 936 91 42; e campingslacs@libero.it; Via Gaveno 23; per person/site €5/6), a good camping option. **Albergo Miralago** (☎ 011 936 91 23; Via Giaveno 3; rooms without bathroom €31) also

has a restaurant with pasta and pizza from €5. **Albergo Vittoria** (☎ 011 936 73 67; Corso Torino 90; singles/doubles with bathroom €42/52) and its restaurant are north of town on the main road.

One-third of Avigliana's restaurants are on Corso Laghi. **Pizzeria del Pasché** (Corso Laghi 231) is very popular. For a view that will distract you from a top quality meal, try **Ristorante Hermitage** (Strada Sacra San Michele 12).

Day 2: Avigliana to Bardonecchia
4–7 hours, 71.7km
Today's ride is an end run of the Valle di Susa. It can be divided into two segments: the gently inclined lower-valley *ciclostrada*

from Avigliana to Susa, and the steep *alta* portion from Susa to Bardonecchia. The total change in elevation is 946m, 153m in the 36.4km to Susa and then 793m over the 35.3km to Bardonecchia.

Of the many arms of the Via Francigena, the Valle di Susa stands out because of its profusion of religious buildings; in fact, it's nicknamed Valle delle Abbazie. The Path of the Franks once linked its five core religious centres – Sacra di San Michele, Monte Benedetto, Certosa di Banda, Madonna della Losa and the Abbey of Oulx – all but Losa being on today's route.

From Avigliana, a signed bike path wobbles up the shallow valley through the medieval burgs of **Sant'Ambrogio** (if there was no time to ride up to the Sacra di San Michele

from Avigliana, there is a tough footpath from here) and **Sant'Antonio** to Villar Focchiardo (16.2km). Make the side trip to the **Certosa di Banda** 200m up a small road. This 15th-century charterhouse is the later and lower habitation of the Carthusian monks who built the original 12th-century **Certosa di Monte Benedetto**, of which only the church remains, almost 600m above Banda.

From Villar Focchiardo, the bike path crosses Fiume Dora Riparia and touches several villages on the north bank: **Borgone** and its 11th- to 12th-century chapel; **San Didero**; and **Bruzolo** and **Bussoleno** (27.5km). After Foresto (and its dramatic **gorge** backdrop), where the signed bikepath turns north (32.2km), your route instead rejoins the main road for the pedal into Susa (36.4km).

Montagne Doc – Day 2

Cue

start	Avigliana tourist office		23.6 ↰	Via Cavour bikepath
0km	NW from Piazza del Popolo		23.7 ↰	Via Umberto I bikepath
0 ↰	Via Cavalieri di Vittorio Veneto		23.8 ↱	Via della Crotte 'to Chianocco'
1.1 ↑	Largo Beato Umberto bikepath		25.6 ↰	after bridge 'to Torino'
2.1 ↰	Via Primo Levi bikepath		25.7 ↗	Via XXV Aprile/Corso Pierolo path
2.3 ↗	unsigned road (bikepath)		27.5 ✳	Bussoleno train station
2.6 ↗ ✧	(3rd exit) unsigned bikepath		27.6 ↱	Via M. d'Azeglio bikepath
4.5 ↰	Via Torino bikepath		27.7 ↰	Via Guido Olmo bikepath
4.9 ✳	Sant'Ambrogio		29.8 ✳	Foresto (gorge)
11.7 ↰	Via Rocciamelone bikepath		30.8 ↗	unsigned road
12.3 ↱	Via Maisonetta bikepath		31.8 ⚠	350m gravel path
12.5 ↰	Sant'Antonio, Via Torino bikepath		32.2 ↰	unsigned road (cross tracks)
12.7 ↰	Via Abegg bikepath		32.3 ↱	SS25 'to Susa'
16.2 ↗ ✧	Villar Focchiardo, Via di Mezzo		36.4	Susa tourist office
16.2 ●●	Certosa di Banda & M. Benedetto ↺		36.6 ↰	Via Mazzini 'to Monginevro'
16.6 ↱	Via Alighieri bikepath		36.7 ▲	4km steep climb
17 ↰	(unsigned road) bikepath		37.2 ↱	SS24 'to Monginevro'
17.2 ↑	cross SS24 to bikepath		45.7 ▲	6km steep climb
17.5 ↰	cross Doria Riparia River		47.6 ■■↰	Exilles 2.1km
17.8 ↑	cross SS25 'to centro'		49.7	alt route rejoins (turn left)
18.2 ↰	Borgone red-brick piazza		55.7 ▲	16km gradual climb
20.9 ↱	Via Abegg bikepath		71.2 ↰	Via Susa 'to Colle della Scala'
21.1 ↰	Via Roma bikepath		71.6 ↗ ✧	(3rd exit) 'to Colle della Scala'
22.6 ↱	Via Carlo Emanuele I 'to Bruzolo'		71.7	Bardonecchia tourist office
23 ↰	Via dei Mille bikepath			

Elevation

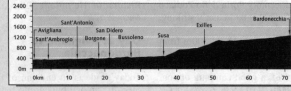

Susa started life as a Celtic town and boasts a host of charms, from its Roman **Arch of Augustus**, **amphitheatre** and **Acquedotto delle Termi Graziane**, to the 3rd-century **Porta Savoia** (Savoy Gate) and attached 11th-century **Cattedrale San Giusto**, as well as the medieval **Castello di Marchesa Adelaide**, **Borgo dei Nobili** and **Chiesa del Ponte**.

The road out of Susa immediately begins to climb. With the exception of one brief dip, it never stops. Along the way is a short alternate route to the forbidding **Exilles fort** (47.6km). It has obscure medieval origins and marked the border with Dauphiné country until the 1713 Treaty of Utrecht.

Bardonecchia, the final destination, is at the top of the valley.

Bardonecchia

Bardonecchia is the last Italian city before the tunnel to Modane (France). Spread out over a gentle slope, its oldest sections are near the top of Via Medail, the busy commercial strip.

Information The tourist office (☎ 0122 9 90 32, [w] www.comune.bardonecchia.to.it) is at Viale della Vittoria 4, just across the river from the train station. Banks line Via Medail. The only bike store for both repair and parts, Calzati (☎ 0122 9 91 44) is on Piazza Statuto 5 at the bottom of Via Medail on the far side of the tracks (use the underpass). Mountain bikes can be rented from Frejus2000 (☎ 0122 90 19 43, [w] www.frejus2000.it) at Campo Smith, the outdoor activity grounds west of town.

Things to See & Do People come here, principally in the winter, for the glory of the outdoors. During the summer, **hiking** and **mountain biking** are the top pastimes. Check with tourist information for trail maps and descriptions. The stone-built towns of **Melezet** and **Millaures** (and their frescoed chapels) are good surviving examples from the valley's past.

Places to Stay & Eat Both camping grounds are southwest of town close to Località Pian del Colle on the road to the Colle della Scala. **Pian del Colle** (☎ 0122 90 14 52; Strada Provinciale del Melezet; per site/person €3.90/3.10) is the closer of the two at 3km.

All hotels are welcomingly comfortable, have attached restaurants and offer advantageous full-board and half-board rates. **Albergo Sommellier** (☎/fax 0122 9 95 82; [e] portulano@libero.it; Piazza Statuto 3; singles/doubles without bathroom €29/42, half-board per person €44) is behind the train station at the bottom of Via Medail. **Casa Alpina** (☎ 0122 99 98 41; Via Giolitti 11; singles/doubles without bathroom €35/45, half-board per person €45) is on a quiet strip up near the old centro (centre). **Albergo Villa Myosotis** (☎ 0122 99 98 83; Via Cantore 2; singles/doubles with bathroom €30/58) is on a side street near the midpoint of Via Medail.

Purchase home-cooked meal needs from the **markets** and **stores** on Via Medail. Cheap pizza by the slice is served hot at **Pizza Medail** (Via Medail 85). In the alley behind it, **Miretti** (Via Medail 79) has the best gelato (ice cream) in town. For a bargain nonhotel dinner menu, try **La Ruota** (Via Medail 95; pastas from €5, meat dishes from €6). **L'Etable** (Via Medail 82; full meals €30; closed Tues) is the strip's gourmet stop.

Day 3: Bardonecchia to Pinerolo
5–9 hours, 90.8km

After a morning glide from Bardonecchia back down the hill to Oulx, today's route has only one climb – a 22.1km slog up 914m! – to the Colle di Sestriere. After that, it's 56.3km all downhill! Tourist authorities refer to the upper reaches of the Susa and Chisone Valleys as 'Montagne doc', an arc of quality winter resorts that in 2006 hosts the winter Olympics.

Today's fitness target is the tough uphill from **Oulx** (12.4km) via **Cesana Torinese** (23km) to the city of Sestriere at the top of the **Colle di Sestriere** (34.5km, 2035m). Sestriere is a characterless resort conceived by Mussolini and built by the Agnelli clan (of Fiat fame). The focus is on skiing and outdoor recreation, for which the surrounding mountains are ideal. Serious off-roaders will find some superb technical rides here (see the boxed text 'Mountain Biking' on p40-1).

Pinerolo, the final port of call, is 56.3km away in the plains at the bottom of the Valle del Chisone. Let gravity do its work. The villages of **Pragelato** (and its Folk Museum), **Fenestrelle** (55.7km), **Perosa Argentina**

(73km) and **Villar Perosa** (79.5km) are good pit stops along the way. The alternate route through Fenestrelle affords views of its unforgettable **fort** (commissioned in 1727 and consisting of 3km of structures connecting a series of ridgeline forts, redoubts and batteries with covered stepped corridors).

Pinerolo

A distant suburb of Turin at the foot of the mountains, Pinerolo is one of the more important cities of the upper Po.

Information The tourist information office (☎ 0121 79 55 89, W www.montagnedoc.it) is a few blocks from the train station at Viale Giolitti 7/9. There is a bank across the street, as well as others under the arches of Corso Torino and around the corner in Piazza Barbieri. Two bike shops in town are Ezio Asvisio (☎ 0121 32 21 96) at Piazza Barbieri 18 and Ciclo Sport Licheri (☎ 0121 7 39 81) at Via Monte Grappa 83.

Things to See & Do Pinerolo's greatest claims to fame are the **Museo Nazionale dell'Arma di Cavalleria** (billed as Europe's most important cavalry museum) and the **Cavallerizza Caprilli**, home of Europe's largest riding school. San Maurizio abuts the pleasant old town and its **Cattedrale San Donato**. At its heights are **Palazzo dei Principe d'Acaja** and the 11th-century **Chiesa San Maurizio**. On the way up Via Principe d'Acaja, don't miss the **Casa del Vicario** and 15th-century **Palazzo del Senato**. Clustered near the information office are a total of six other **museums**.

Places to Stay & Eat Accommodation isn't Pinerolo's strong point. There are no camping grounds or hostels in the vicinity. **La Muraglia** (*☎ 0121 7 13 61; Via Chiappero 26; singles/doubles with bathroom €18.50/ 31*) is a good-quality Chinese restaurant with basic, but acceptable, rooms overlooking a noisy inner courtyard. **Hotel Regina** (*☎ 0121 32 21 57; e hotel.regina@ noicom.net; Pizza Barbieri 22; singles/doubles €51/74*) is plush and right in the centre of town. On the outskirts, **Residence San Maurizio** (*☎ 0121 32 14 15; Via de Amicis 3; singles/doubles €35.50/47*) is pricey and quite nice.

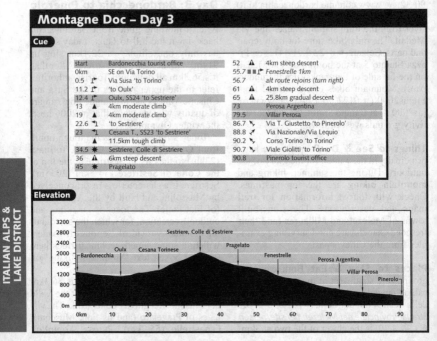

Montagne Doc – Day 3

Cue

start		Bardonecchia tourist office
0km		SE on Via Torino
0.5	↱	Via Susa 'to Torino'
11.2	↱	'to Oulx'
12.4	↱	Oulx, SS24 'to Sestriere'
13	▲	4km moderate climb
19	▲	4km moderate climb
22.6	↰	'to Sestriere'
23	↰	Cesana T., SS23 'to Sestriere'
	▲	11.5km tough climb
34.5	✳	Sestriere, Colle di Sestriere
36	▲	6km steep descent
45	✳	Pragelato
52	▲	4km steep descent
55.7	■■↱	Fenestrelle 1km
56.7		alt route rejoins (turn right)
61	▲	4km steep descent
65	▲	25.8km gradual descent
73		Perosa Argentina
79.5		Villar Perosa
86.7	↘	Via T. Giustetto 'to Pinerolo'
88.8	↙	Via Nazionale/Via Lequio
90.2	↘	Corso Torino 'to Torino'
90.7	↘	Viale Giolitti 'to Torino'
90.8		Pinerolo tourist office

Elevation

Self-caterers can find fodder in the **supermarket** *(54 Via Saluzzo)* or any of the **speciality food stores** on Via Trento. For cheap eats, two popular **pizzerias** keep Piazza Verdi hopping and the **café/restaurants** like **L'Appetito** *(Corso Torino 48)*, under the arches on Corso Torino, are worth exploring. Classic Italian fare is on offer at **Pizz'Anticha** *(Via San Pellico 7)* in the old town. **Al Cartoccio** *(Via Saluzzo 19)* serves standard Italian fare and is very popular with locals.

Getting There & Away The Pinerolo train station is the last stop on a spur line from Turin (40 minutes, 15 trains daily). A connecting bus service continues to Torre Pellice (35 minutes).

If driving, Pinerolo is best reached from Turin (35km) via SS23. Going south, head east to the A6 Torino Carmagnola exit.

Bicycle The Ciclopista Stupinigi–Vallere and Ciclostrada Pinerolo–Stupinigi cover the distance from Turin (47.8km) and the bikepaths in Basso Pinerolese and Saluzzese run to Saluzzo (57.9km), just 32km from Cuneo (see the Basso Pinerolese & Saluzzese ride in the Po River Basin on p163). Carmagnola, on the main Cuneo– Turin train line, is 37km to the east.

Alta Rezia Valleys & Passes	
Duration	4 days
Distance	276.1km
Difficulty	moderate–hard
Start	Prato allo Stelvio (Prad am Stilfserjoch)
End	Sondrio

Alta Rezia is a land of ups and downs. At its heights are the grandiose easternmost Alps in Italy, surmounted by narrow roads engineered into the mountainsides. These roads heave over passes, some of which are now part of Italy's cycling lore. The Stelvio, Gavia, Bernina, Livigno, Foscagno and Mortirolo passes are clustered in this tight zone. Between them sprawl elegant valleys, like Valfurva, the Viola, the Poschiavo, the Corteno, the Malenco and many more, all spry tributaries of the great Valtellina. This four-day ride takes you over some of these passes and into many of these valleys.

PLANNING
When to Ride
Snow can fall in the high passes in any month; weather-wise, the best time to tackle this ride is between mid-June and mid-September. Mid-August is better avoided due to the usual crowds.

Maps & Books
The Touring Club Italiano's (1:200,000) *Trentino Alto Adige* map shows this ride as far as Tirano (17km short of the end at Sondrio) and the *Lombardia* map begins in Trafoi (10.9km from the start). The free *Provincia di Sondrio* (1:115,000) map covers everything. Another good free map for the rides along the Adda River is the RegioneLombardia *Lombardia – Tourist map of rivers*.

Two comprehensive free information booklets available in English are: the *Alta Rezia Pocket Guide* (complete with a trekking/mountain-biking map) and the *Vademecum Alta Valtellina*.

What to Bring
Make sure you've got plenty of liquid and solid sustenance for the marathon high-altitude passes; there are often no services over long stretches. Also be prepared for tough weather conditions (for weather reports in Italian, call ☎ 8488 3 70 77). A bike light may be helpful in fog or snow, and for brief tunnels.

ACCESS TOWN
Prato allo Stelvio
Prato allo Stelvio derives its livelihood from its strategic location at the junction between the Val Venosta (upper Adige valley) and the Stelvio Pass road. Sitting at the gateway to the Parco Nazionale dello Stelvio, it's a small town with a distinctly Germanic flavour. Commercial life focuses on highway SS38, which doubles as the Hauptstrasse (main street). Prato's main square (Hauptplatz/Piazza Principale) is east of SS38, just uphill from the visitor centre.

Information The visitor centre (☎ 0473 61 60 34, **w** www.prad.suedtirol.com) is at

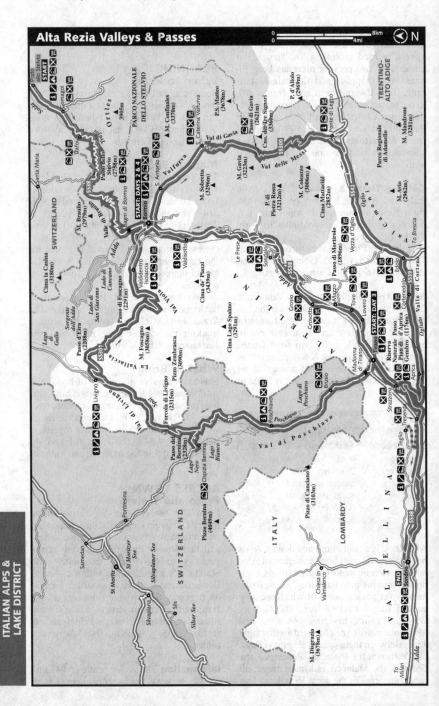

Alta Rezia Valleys & Passes

Hauptstrasse/Via Principale 29. Prato's most convenient bank is the Sparkasse/Cassa di Risparmio on Hauptplatz/Piazza Principale. Baldi Sport (☎ 0473 61 70 71), Reutweg/Via Nuova 19, rents bikes, sells a wide range of cycling gear, and repairs bikes.

Things to See & Do Prato's main tourist draw is outdoor recreation in the local mountains. **Hiking trails** abound (get a free list from the tourist office) in Parco Nazionale dello Stelvio. The **Val Venosta bike route** crosses through the heart of town on its journey from the Austrian border to Bolzano.

Places to Stay & Eat Located near the tourist office, **Camping Sägemühle** (☎ 0473 61 60 78; W www.camping.saegemuehle .suedtirol.com; Dornweg/Via delle Spine 12; per person/site €7.50/9.50) has hot showers, swimming pool and sauna.

Pension **Café Ortler** (☎ 0473 61 60 31; Hauptstrasse/Strada Principale 57; B&B per person €20) is a small, family-run place above a downtown bar/café. **Garni Wiesenheim** (☎/fax 0473 61 61 89; Hauptstrasse/Via Principale 4a; singles/doubles with breakfast €22/40) sits in a pretty field just out of town. **Gasthof Stern** (☎ 0473 61 61 23; W www.gasthof-stern.it; Silbergasse/Via Argentieri 1; singles/doubles with breakfast €33/57, half-board €44/77) is a cosy, two-star place just a stone's throw from the tourist office. **Hotel Zentral** (☎/fax 0473 61 60 08; W www.zentral.it; Hauptstrasse/Via Principale 48; B&B per person €38, half-board €52) is Prato's fanciest hotel, with sauna, solarium and fitness centre.

Groceries are available at **De Spar** supermarket in Hauptplatz/Piazza Principale. **Bäckerei/Konditorei Saurer** (Hauptstrasse/Via Principale 37) is a good bakery where you can stock up on starch. **Pizza Point** (Hauptstrasse/Via Principale 61) sells pizzas from 10am daily. Casual **Pizzeria Stern** at Gasthof Stern serves tasty pizza and pasta. The other hotels in town also have restaurants.

Getting There & Away Spondigna, a flat 3km ride north of Prato at the junction of SS38 and SS40, is the most convenient local bus stop. SAD operates bus No 401 hourly from Bolzano to Merano (40 minutes); in Merano, get connecting bus No 101 to Spondigna (1½ hours, every 30 minutes).

For a slightly higher fare, hourly trains from Bolzano to Merano (40 minutes) meet SAD's Spondigna-bound bus. The main disadvantage is paying twice for your bike (Trenitalia's bike surcharge plus SAD's fee).

For drivers, expressway A22 from Mantova and Verona goes to Bolzano, from which SS38 is a direct road to Prato.

Bicycle The Val Venosta bike route connects Prato allo Stelvio with Bolzano (87km), Merano (53km) and Nauders, in Austria (36km). At the time of research, it was poorly marked and in poor condition, though paving work was underway. For more info, check local tourist offices or the current edition of In Bicicletta Lungo L'Adige.

THE RIDE
Day 1: Prato allo Stelvio to Bormio
3–5 hours, 47.2km
This classic, challenging ride crosses Italy's highest pass (and the Alps' third highest) on the 'highest road in Europe' and is a relentless 25km climb spread out over 48 switchbacks. From the summit, the reward is a 22km plummet to Valtellina's Bormio. Today's entire ride is within the limits of Parco Nazionale dello Stelvio, Italy's biggest national park and the largest protected area in Europe.

The ascent starts out of Prato and gets steeper beyond Gomagoi (6.4km), where the Solda valley turns southeast while the route continues southwest up the Rio Trafoi. The first of the Stelvio's 48 numbered curves appears 2.2km later, signalling the beginning of the long haul ahead. Trafoi (10.9km) is the last chance for food and drink before the pass. **Hotel Bellavista** (11km; ☎ 0473 61 17 16; W www.gustav thoeni.com), run by Olympic skiing champion Gustav Thoni, is a great place to grab calories and shelter (ask about discounts for cyclists).

From Trafoi, the almost surreal succession of switchbacks heads for the pass, quickly climbing above the tree line and affording remarkable views over the surrounding mountains, glaciers and even the road itself. At **Passo dello Stelvio** (2758m, 25km), actually the largest summer ski area in the Alps, hotels and restaurants/cafés allow for a celebratory drink/snack with the throngs of other exhilarated tourists. To mark the occasion further, the tourist office (☎/fax 0342 90 30 30, w www.passo stelvio.com) issues a laser-printed colour certificate with the date, your name and address, and the time it took you to climb the pass (be honest!). There are even **memorials** to Fausto Coppi, Italy's most famous cyclist. **Carlo Donegani Museo Storico**, recounts the hows and whys of the Stelvio road (and the role it played in WWI).

What took hours to climb can take less than an hour to descend. Other than the snowscapes, extraordinary natural sights, some short, dark, wet, one-way tunnels, and tough road twists, there is nothing to stop a determined decliner from reaching record speeds. Brakes should be in working order!

Bormio

Bormio occupies a key position on a high plain met by three valleys and crisscrossed by routes over the surrounding Alps. Since the 12th century, the commercial 'Imperial German Road' and 'Ombraglio Highway' have passed through. As a result, standard feudal strife and medieval dynastic family bickering were felt even at this somewhat remote location. Still, Bormio has retained a degree of independence, formalised in 1355 by an autonomy-granting *Magna Carta della libertà bormiesi*. This ended with Bormio's pre-unification inclusion in the Kingdom of Italy.

Information Bormio's APT (☎ 0342 90 33 00, w www.bormio.it, w www.valtelli naonline.com) is at Via Roma 131b, near the southwest entrance to town. Ask here for the *Vademecum Alta Valtellina* and *Alta Rezia Pocket Guide* booklets. For information about Stelvio National Park, check with the Consorzio (☎ 0342 91 01 00, w www .stelviopark.it) at Via Roma 26. Banks are right around the corner in Via Roma.

Bobo Moto (☎/fax 0342 90 50 64), about 500m from the centre at Via Milano 56, is a good shop for repair, parts and rental. Mountain bikers will also find rental material at Baby & Sport (☎ 0342 90 16 98) on Via Morbegno (Piazzale Funivia) on the south side of the Torrento Frodolfo. For organised cycling activities, check with the Unione Sportiva Bormiese (☎ 0342 90 14 82) on Via Nesini 6.

Things to See & Do Many people come to Bormio for its nine **thermal-mineral springs**. One of them, the Cinglaccia, feeds a city **swimming pool** on the western edge of town on Via Stelvio; the rest are diverted into the private establishments (including a natural 'Sweating Grotto' and the 2nd-century remains of the Roman baths) of

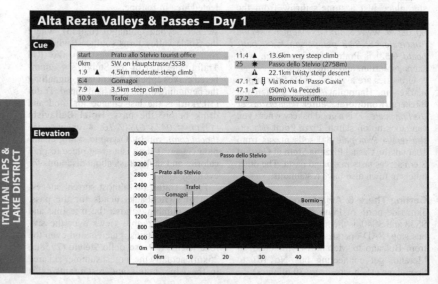

Alta Rezia Valleys & Passes – Day 1

Cue

start	Prato allo Stelvio tourist office		11.4	▲	13.6km very steep climb
0km		SW on Hauptstrasse/SS38	25	☀	Passo dello Stelvio (2758m)
1.9	▲	4.5km moderate-steep climb		▲	22.1km twisty steep descent
6.4		Gomagoi	47.1	↰ ⌷	Via Roma to 'Passo Gavia'
7.9	▲	3.5km steep climb	47.1	↱	(50m) Via Peccedi
10.9		Trafoi	47.2		Bormio tourist office

Elevation

Elevation profile chart showing the route from 0km to approximately 47km, with labelled points: Prato allo Stelvio, Gomagoi, Trafoi, Passo dello Stelvio (peak), and Bormio. Vertical axis marked from 0m to 4000m; horizontal axis marked 0km, 10, 20, 30, 40.

Bagni Vecchi above town. Otherwise, the star attractions in town are near Piazza Cavour: the 13th-century **Kuèrc**, a typical structure from which justice used to be administered, and the 16th-century **Torre delle Ore**, or Tower of Verona belfry. Elsewhere in town are two ancient churches – **Chiesa del SS. Crocefisso di San Antonio** and **Chiesa di San Vitale** – both with frescoes dating back to the 13th and 14th centuries. Fauna fans will love the **Giardino Botanico Alpino 'Rezia'** on Via Sertorelli to the north, as well as the **short hikes** possible around the city (ask at information for the *12 passeggiate nella natura* map).

Places to Stay & Eat About 5km south on the main road (SS38) is **Cima Piazzi** (☎ 0342 95 02 98; *Via Nazionale 29, Tola Valdisotto; per person/site* €6.20/10.50). Ask at tourist information about *affitta-camere* (rooms for rent).

Hotel rates change monthly (sometimes doubling) during peak seasons. Charges cited here are the highest quoted. In general, pay half-board to economise and because hotel-restaurant food quality is good. Many hotels don't even post *meublé* (room only) rates. If dining options are important, try **Sci Sport** (☎ 0342 90 43 62; e scisport@libero.it; *Via Lungo Frodolfo Credaro 3/4; singles/doubles* €50/70) situated on the river down from the information office, or, for the same rates, **Albergo Dante Meublé** (☎/fax 0342 90 13 29; e meubledante@bormio.it; *Via Trieste 2)* with sunny rooms in the centre.

Hotel Adda (☎ 0342 90 46 27; *Via Milano 70; half-board from* €28.50, *singles/doubles* €20/35), 1km west of town on the main road, is pleasant and the cheapest hotel around. **Hotel San Vitale** (☎/fax 0342 90 47 71; w www.miraparkhotels.com; *Via Roma 100; half-board from* €60) is right in the centre. **Hotel Giardino** (☎ 0342 90 31 26; *Via per Piatta; half-board per person from* €35) is on the southern outskirts of town within sight of the winter ski slopes.

Independent diners can shop in **markets** on Via Peccedi or poke around near Piazza Cavour. For pizza carbs go to **Contado** (*Via della Vittoria 6; pasta & pizzas from* €5.70; *closed Tues)*. **Notte e Di'** (*Piazza Cavour 15; closed Wed)* has very good, affordable *tavola calda* (literally 'hot table'; pre-prepared meat, pasta and vegetable selection).

Day 2: Bormio to Tirano via Gavia

5½–10 hours, 97.2km

After yesterday's heroic hike followed by a full afternoon's rest, today's labours may seem like out-and-out masochism. The climb to 2621m Passo di Gavia covers approximately the same distance, but the day's kilometre tally is 50km longer and includes a second (much easier) afternoon ascent! It's not as hellish as it sounds. The net change of elevation is 763m *down* and the surrounding natural grandeur is incomparable.

From Bormio, head straight for the Valfurva, whose lead town, **Santa Caterina Valfurva** (13.2km), is a winter ski resort and summer alpine centre for neighbouring Forni, Cedec and Zebrù Valleys. Food and drink purchased here will be the last until the top of the pass, for the right turn in town marks the start of an arduous climb. No less than 10 switchbacks force you to sweat through pine forests to the tree line, above which the Val di Gavia arena of cold, rocky, alpine desolation dominates. Never fear, there will be snow! The welcome **Rifugio Bonetta** (☎ 0364 9 18 06) at the top of **Passo di Gavia** (2621m, 26.3km) has hot and cold water, warm drinks, postcards stamped with proof of location, Giro d'Italia pictures of snow-covered cyclists at the pass, and, if necessary, lodging.

Now begins a 37.7km descent of 1922m. The steepest part – check your brakes! – covers 1363m in 18.3km down the Val delle Messi to Ponte di Legno (44.6km). The remaining 559m and 19.4km are in the verdant Val Camonica via **Vezza d'Oglio** to **Edolo** (64km).

From Edolo, the route turns back uphill the length of the Valle di Corteno to the Passo d'Aprica (1176m, 80.3km) in the same-name resort town surrounded by protected natural areas like the peat bogs of **Pian di Gembro** at Trivigno (13km north) and the **Parco Regionale Orobie Valtellinesi**.

From Aprica the route drops back to the Valtellina floor a few kilometres from Tirano. On the long hill down from Aprica, the turn to Strazzona (88.6km) can be easily missed, just 300m after the hairpin.

Tirano

At the narrowest point of the Valtellina, Tirano monitors the traffic triangle between

Alta Rezia Valleys & Passes – Day 2

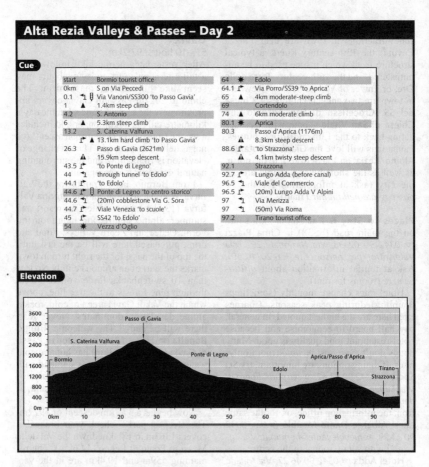

Cue

start	Bormio tourist office	
0km	S on Via Peccedi	
0.1	↰↱⊟	Via Vanoni/SS300 'to Passo Gavia'
1	▲	1.4km steep climb
4.2		S. Antonio
6	▲	5.3km steep climb
13.2		S. Caterina Valfurva
	↱▲	13.1km hard climb 'to Passo Gavia'
26.3		Passo di Gavia (2621m)
	⚠	15.9km steep descent
43.5	↱	'to Ponte di Legno'
44	↰	through tunnel 'to Edolo'
44.1	↱	'to Edolo'
44.6	↱⊟	Ponte di Legno 'to centro storico'
44.6	↰	(20m) cobblestone Via G. Sora
44.7	↱	Viale Venezia 'to scuole'
45	↱	SS42 'to Edolo'
54	✳	Vezza d'Oglio
64	✳	Edolo
64.1	↱	Via Porro/SS39 'to Aprica'
65	▲	4km moderate-steep climb
69		Cortendolo
74	▲	6km moderate climb
80.1	✳	Aprica
80.3		Passo d'Aprica (1176m)
	⚠	8.3km steep descent
88.6	↱	'to Strazzona'
	⚠	4.1km twisty steep descent
92.1		Strazzona
92.7	↱	Lungo Adda (before canal)
96.5	↰	Viale del Commercio
96.5	↱	(20m) Lungo Adda V Alpini
97	↰	Via Merizza
97	↰	(50m) Via Roma
97.2		Tirano tourist office

Elevation

Switzerland, the Alta Valtellina and Milan. Although the area has been inhabited for millennia, Tirano truly came into its own in the earliest years of the 16th century after a miraculous appearance of the Madonna. The basilica built to commemorate this was a Catholic buffer against encroaching northern Protestant reformist ideas. Now it's the most important religious building in Valtellina.

Information The tourist office (☎/fax 0342 70 60 66, ⓦ www.valtellinaonline.com) shares the train station building with the railroad on Piazzale della Stazione. Another office (☎/fax 0342 70 60 66) is hidden near the basilica at Viale Italia 183. The handiest banks are located on Viale Italia at its eastern end. For bike parts and repairs, go to Spada Biciclette (☎/fax 0342 70 50 33) at Via Benefattori 12. Bicycle rentals are possible at Ci-cli'ama' (☎ 0342 70 43 60), Via Trivigno 2.

Things to See & Do Other than the 16th-century **Santuario della Madonna di Tirano**, at the western edge of town on the hill above the Piazza Basilica is the little, frescoed, 11th-century **Chiesa di Santa Perpetua**. Back at the eastern end, **Piazza Cavour** and its **Palazzo Marinoni** are the focus of the *centro storico*. A walk east on Via XX Settembre and then northeast on Via Venosta takes in a dozen 16th- to 18th-century **palaces** and **churches**, as well as **Porta Bormina**, one of Torano's three extant 15th-century gates.

Places to Stay & Eat There is no camping anywhere near Tirano.

Al Giardino (☎ *0342 70 17 23; Via Calcagno 10; singles/doubles €18/35)* has clean rooms above a local café periodically rumbled by the infrequent trains. **Casa Mia** *(☎ 0342 70 53 00;* **W** *www.geocities.com/ eccocasamia; Via Arcari 6; B&B singles/doubles €36/62)* feels like home right in the old centre. **Albergo Gusmeroli** *(☎ 0342 70 13 38; Piazza Cavour 5; singles/doubles with bathroom €24/40)* is perfectly situated on sunny Piazza Cavour. At the western end of town, **Hotel San Michele** *(☎/fax 0342 70 13 47; Via Rascia 1; singles/doubles €18/31)* is brusquely run but is heavenly for basilica visits.

All hotels except Casa Mia have in-house restaurants serving solid Italian fare. Self-caterers will find meal makings in the **supermarket** of the shopping centre on Viale Italia. Otherwise, all of the **pizzerias** on Piazza Basilica or Via Mazzini (near the train station) are good bets for economical eats. Another pizza shop, **Chaia di Luna** *(Via Stelvio 36; closed Mon)*, just southeast of the old city, is a local favourite.

Day 3: Tirano to Bormio via Livigno

3½–6 hours, 61.3km

After two tough days of hills, isn't it time for a break? Thanks to Swiss engineering genius, it is. The day's ride *begins* at 2265m! Three passes later (none of which requires more than 400m of climbing) and a visit to the duty-free city of Livigno, Bormio is back in view. Passports are mandatory for the brief incursion into Switzerland.

From Tirano's Ferrovia Retica station, the building next door to the main station on Piazzale Stazione, the Swiss-run **trenino rosso** (℅ 0342 70 13 53; u www.rhb.ch), Europe's highest noncogwheel train, chugs up 1824m to the Ospizia Bernina station (1¼ hours, 17.20SF plus 15SF for the bicycle). The trip up the Alta Valposchiavo into the Engadin region is possible in chilly open cars with unobstructed views of the curious circular viaduct in Brusio, blue-green Lago di Poschiavo and then the Bernina mountain range glaciers. Of course, a true grimpeur will want to ride the pass. The alternative route from Tirano points 31.8km up the valley on SS38A/Swiss route 29 via Poschiavo.

Alta Rezia Valleys & Passes – Day 3

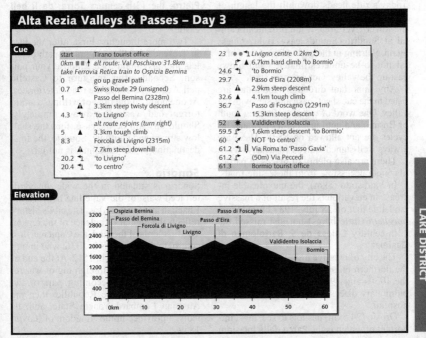

Cue		
start	Tirano tourist office	
0km ■■↑	alt route: Val Poschiavo 31.8km	
take Ferrovia Retica train to Ospizia Bernina		
0	go up gravel path	
0.7 ↱	Swiss Route 29 (unsigned)	
1	Passo del Bernina (2328m)	
▲	3.3km steep twisty descent	
4.3 ↰	'to Livigno'	
alt route rejoins (turn right)		
5 ▲	3.3km tough climb	
8.3	Forcola di Livigno (2315m)	
▲	7.7km steep downhill	
20.2 ↰	'to Livigno'	
20.4 ↰	'to centro'	

23 ●●↰	Livigno centre 0.2km ↻	
↱▲	6.7km hard climb 'to Bormio'	
24.6 ↰	'to Bormio'	
29.7	Passo d'Eira (2208m)	
▲	2.9km steep descent	
32.6 ▲	4.1km tough climb	
36.7	Passo di Foscagno (2291m)	
▲	15.3km steep descent	
52 ✳	Valdidentro Isolaccia	
59.5 ↱	1.6km steep descent 'to Bormio'	
60 ↙	NOT 'to centro'	
61.2 ↰ ▯	Via Roma to 'Passo Gavia'	
61.2 ↱	(50m) Via Peccedi	
61.3	Bormio tourist office	

Elevation

From the Ospizia Bernina station (2265m), a short climb crests at the top of the **Passo del Bernina** (2328m). The road heads down from the pass to a left turn (4.3km) back through the border and a climb to the **Forcola di Livigno** (2315m, 8.3km), from which it's 14.7km down to lunch in the centre of Livigno.

Livigno (23km) is a sunny holiday resort spread for kilometres along the single road through its valley. Most people come here for the outdoor experience, but shopping is also a draw. Livigno has been a duty-free zone since the 16th century.

Passes two and three lie above Livigno to the east. **Passo d'Eira** (2208m, 29.7km) is the lowest of the day, but the longest given the depth of the Livigno valley. The dip into **La Vallaccia** makes the 263m climb to **Passo di Foscagno** (2291m, 36.7km) a breeze.

The remaining 24.6km drops the lengths of Valdidentro to Bormio. Along the way, take in the 12th-century **Chiesa San Gallo** (in Valdidentro Isolaccia, 52km).

Day 4: Bormio to Sondrio
4–7 hours, 70.4km
Today's ride heads downhill the length of the Alta Valtellina to Tirano and then into the lower river area to the provincial capital at Sondrio. Sounds easy, right? Guess again. Starting in the early afternoon, a brutal not-to-be-underestimated wind blows east up the valley. Get an early start.

Any important directions for today are listed in the cue sheet; basically, stay with the valley. One word of warning: Starting south of Bormio and until just north of Tirano, bicycles are not allowed on SS38. There are always well-signed, quieter roads anyway.

There are also plenty of places of particular note accessible from these side roads. In Valdisotto (8km), the inexplicable increase in elevation is the result of a massive landslide that on 28 July, 1987 buried three *borghetti* (little burgs) but just missed the 13th-century **Chiesa de S. Bartolomeo di Castelaz**.

The city of massive high-rises clinging to the northern hillside is **Sondalo**, famous in the 1930s and 1940s as a curative spa for pulmonary diseases and today the region's hospital.

Grosio (24.5km) has lots to see, most important of which is the **Parco delle Incisioni Rupestri**, conserving the Bronze-Age carvings of the ancient Ráter people. Nearby are ruins of the 11th- to 14th-century **Castello Visconti Venosta** and 12th-century **Chiesa di Santo Giorgio**. The people of Grosio are some of the last in the valley to wear traditional clothes in everyday life. They used to hike the road south of Grosio to Edolo over the **Passo del Mortirolo** (1896m), one of the steepest of the Giro d'Italia.

Grosotto (27.2km) has the lovely 17th-century **Santuario B.V. delle Grazie**, and Mazzo (29.7km) the 12th-century **Torre e Contrada Pedenale**.

Tirano (38.9km) is at the dividing point between the Alta Valtellina (and an alpine climate) and the lower valley's more Mediterranean look and feel.

Further on, the side trip to Teglio, although up to 860m, is important. Teglio gave its name to the valley and, in addition to its panoramic view of the surrounding mountains, has some of its most important sites: the 16th-century **Palazzo Besta** plays host to the **'Antiquarium Tellinum' State Museum**; there are ancient frescoes in the 10th- and 11th-century **Chieso di Santo Pietro**; the 13th-century **Torre 'de li beli miri'** is all that remains of a once important castle.

Two more thoughts: First, after the turn in Tresenda (50.2km), a gravel path parallels the busy main road. Choose your poison. Second, after the turn to Castello dell'Acqua (58.1km), the road deteriorates. At one point, at the time of writing, a storm torrent had washed it away completely. Should this still be the case, ford the shallow stream and continue. Sondrio, the final destination in the Valtellina, is not far.

Sondrio
Sondrio is situated in the wide vineyard-terraced waist of the Valtellina between the Rhaetian and Orobic Alps. The city's history reflects the regular turbulence of the region. The first lords of the land, the Capitanei, lost control to the Viscontis in 1336, who in turn passed it to the Swiss in 1512. At the end of the 18th century, the foreign tug of war resulted in Sondrio becoming part of the Napoleonic Cisalpine Republic, then the Austrian Lombard–Veneto State, and, finally, a province in the Kingdom of Italy in 1859.

Information The APT (☎ 0342 51 25 00, 🅦 www.valtellinaonline.com), on Via Trieste just east of Corso XXV Aprile, is also the lead office for all of Valtellina. Detailed city historical information exists in the English *Il Filo Rosso* (The Red Thread) walking guide. Good places for banks include Piazzas Campello and Garibaldi and the connecting Corso Italia.

Try Cicli SAS (☎ 0342 21 27 03), Via Gorizia 10, for bike-related repairs and purchases. The local FIAB affiliate, with a fistful of organised cycling activities, is Amici della Bicicletta Sondrio (☎/fax 0347 922 66 82, 🅦 it.geocities.com/absondrio) at Vicolo degli Orti 3. RegioneLombardia has helped produce *Il Sentiero Valtellina*, an information folder describing local rides.

Things to See & Do The majority of Sondrio's sights are clustered around its easy-to-walk centre. East of the buzzing Piazza Garibaldi, through Corso Italia flanked by the 16th-century **Palazzo Pretorio** (now town hall), is Piazza Compello, dominated by the 18th-century **Chiesa Collegiata**, but with foundations dating back to the year 1000. This is the southern limit of the old town, whose modern shops and narrow streets distract from the elegant 15th-, 16th- and 17th-century palaces and churches, including **Palazzo Sassi de Lavizzari**, which houses the **Museum of Valtellinese History & Art**. Stretching north from Piazza Quadrivio is **Via Scarpatetti**, one of Sondrio's oldest and most beautiful streets. Stomping uphill from its outlet leads to the foot of Capitanei-built

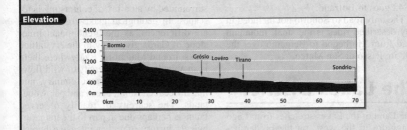

Alta Rezia Valleys & Passes – Day 4

Cue

start	Bormio tourist office		45.8 ⬏	unmarked road (after farm)
0km	S on Via Roma/SS38		47.4 ⬧	0.3km gravel path
2	⬈ 'to Valdisotto'		47.5 ⬏	unmarked road (go downhill)
7.3	⬈ before tunnel 'to Le Prese'		49 ⬏	SS39 (unsigned) through tunnel
8	⬧ 2.5km moderate climb		50.2 ⬎	unmarked road just before bridge
10.5	⬧ 2.5km steep descent		50.2 ●●↑	*Teglio 15km* ↻
21	⬧ 2.5km steep descent		52.3 ⬧	gravel begins (return to SS38)
24.5	✳ Grosio		58.1 ⬎	'to Castello dell'Acqua'
27.2	✳ Grosotto		59.1 ⬏	'to Bruga'
29.5	↑ NOT on SS38 'to Sondrio'		60.1 ⬧	jump river to 0.6km gravel
29.7	✳ ⬏ Mazzo, 'to Sondrio'		60.7 ⬊	pavement begins
31.4	↑ Tovo, 'to Lovero'		60.7 ⬏	(20m) 'to Carolo'
32.5	Lovero		62.8 ⬎	Via Streppona
33.3	↑ unmarked road		67.1 ⬎	'to Sondrio, tangenziale'
35	⬎ SS38 'to Tirano'		67.6 ⬏ 🚲	'to Sondrio via Europa'
38.9	Tirano Piazza Marinoni		69.1 ↑ 🚲	one-way wrong-way across tracks
39	⬊ Viale Italia		69.7 ⬎	Via Toti
40.2	✳ Piazza Basilica		70.3 ⬏ 🚲	Corso XXV Aprile
	⬊ Via Sondrio/SS38 'to Sondrio'		70.4 ⬏ 🚲	Via Trieste
40.7	⬊ Via Poschiavino (before bridge)		70.4	Sondrio tourist office
42.1	⬑ Lungo Adda IV Novembre			

Elevation

(Elevation profile: Bormio ~1200m descending through Grósio, Lovéro, Tirano to Sondrio over 70km)

Castello Masegra. The 15th-century **Chiesetta di San Bartolomeo** and 11th-century **Convento di S. Lorenzo** are also up here, but on the opposite bank of Torrente Mallero. On the way up to these, the 15th-century **Palazzo Carbonara** is one of the city's most architecturally appealing Renaissance buildings.

Places to Stay & Eat The only camping ground is **Dosso del Grillo** (☎ *0342 40 21 52; Località Briotti Dosso del Grillo; per person/site €5/6)*, 9km east of town and 750m above it in a suburb of Ponte Valtellina.

Sondrio offers two affordable hotels. **Il Gembro** (☎/fax *0342 21 30 81; Via Gorizia 14; singles/doubles €25/35)*, next door to the bicycle shop, has spotless rooms. Modern **Hotel Schenatti** (☎ *0342 51 24 24; ☒ www.ho telschenatti.it; Via Bernina 7b; singles/doubles €45/60)* is at the far western end of the city. For more options, check in Chiuro and Ponte Valtellina (both 9km east), and Montagna Piano (3km east).

For 'meal do-it-yourselfers', the **speciality shops** in Piazzette Rusconi and Via Beccaria are excellent. Otherwise, use the **supermarkets** in Via Parolo or Via Trieste. **Il Passatore** *(Via Trieste 41; closed Thur)* has a welcome local atmosphere and good pizzas. Ditto **Vecchio Mulino** *(Via Perego 10; closed Mon)*, hidden in a side street off Piazza Garibaldi. **Ristorante Mari e Monti** *(Via Piazza 10; dinner from €13; closed Sun)* is a sit-down treat of local specialities. **Trattoria Adua** *(Via Scarpatetti 42; closed Mon)* can't be beat for the setting.

Getting There & Away The only rail line runs from Milan (2¼ hours) to Tirano (25 minutes) via Lecco (two hours).

To Milan, the best road is the SS38 west and then SS36 down Lago di Como via Lecco. Heading east, SS39 via Aprica to SS42 goes to Bolzano.

The only road to Sondrio not included in any described rides is the small mountain road from Morbegno to Bergamo over the 1985m Passo di San Marco.

The Lakes District

The Land of the Lakes stretches from Lago Maggiore in the west, on the border between Piedmont and Lombardy, to Lago di Garda in the east on the border with Veneto and Trento. It includes the lakes of Lugano, Como, Endine, Iseo, Idro and a variety of smaller meres and tarns pooled between the pre-alpine crags at the edge of the Lombard Po plain. It's a vast land rich in art and history, and has caught the fancy of artists and poets since Roman times. Characterised by a mild climate, fresh air, varied environment and plentiful distractions, it's still a major destination for travellers seeking a small piece of paradise lost. Cycling these lakes, over the mountains dividing them and along the canals connecting them is, for some people, is an absolute dream come true.

HISTORY

Humans seem to have been drawn to the shores of Italy's northern lakes starting in Neolithic times (3rd millennium BC). Despite the vast territory, subsequent historical trends were shared: the flourishing of independent city-states; their domination by wealthy dynasties (notably those from Milan); and the fluctuating fortunes of the local economic mainstays – small industries based on local natural resources. Despite the upheavals caused by the mid-19th century campaign for independence, WWI and WWII, the Lakes have remained retreats for European nobility, and havens for transalpine travellers.

NATURAL HISTORY

The three major lakes – Lago Maggiore, Lago di Como and Lago di Garda – and their smaller satellites share their origins in the southward thrust of glaciers during the Quaternary era about three million years ago. However, they differ strikingly in the configurations of mountain ranges, ridges and valleys. Each individual lake is itself surrounded by an array of contrasting landscapes. In geological make-up, too, there are differences, as the predominant limestone of Garda gives way to the crystalline rocks around Maggiore. Everywhere there is an abundance and diversity of wild flowers, especially in limestone country, and magnificent chestnut, beech and oak woodlands. The scarcity of readily observed fauna is perhaps due in part to the long, turbulent history of rather intensive human settlement.

Navigli Milanesi

Duration	3 days
Distance	245.2km
Difficulty	easy
Start	Sesto Calende
End	Lecco

Milan wasn't built on a river. It has, however, through an astonishing web of canals, benefited from the power and utility of flowing water. Its Naviglio Grande, begun in the 12th century, was the first navigable manmade canal of the modern world. Like other area canals, it has been used for irrigation and transport (building blocks for Milan's cathedral mined near Lago Maggiore were

floated down this canal), once facilitating trade between foreign destinations and interior ports. Today, the Milanese canals' connections to nearby rivers – like the Ticino, Adda and Po – are protected nature zones.

PLANNING
When to Ride

Smouldering summers in the Po plain are tempered by the lakes and rivers in the foothills of the Alps. However, industry-rich Milan and its suburban sprawl intensify the heat, making spring and autumn ideal.

Maps & Books

Touring Club Italiano's (1:200,000) *Lombardia* map is ideal for this ride. The free Regione Lombardia *Lombardia – Tourist map of*

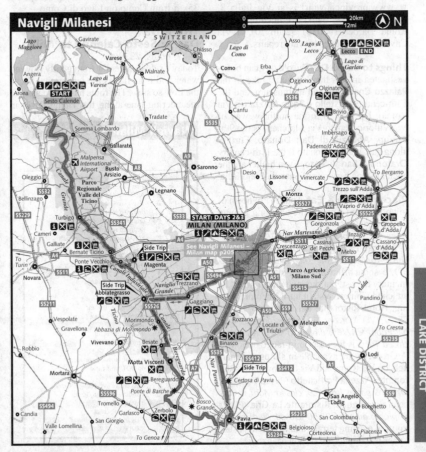

rivers is first-rate when spinning along the Ticino and Adda Rivers. For the canal traverse through Milan, find the Provincia di Milano's *Le strade azzurre in bicicletta* booklet and maps (1:10,000). The best map of Milan is the *Pianta dei Transporti Pubblici* (1:18,000) published by Azura Transporti Milanesi.

ACCESS TOWN
Sesto Calende

At the southern tip of Lago Maggiore – affluent and effluent of the Fiume Ticino – today's Sesto regroups the nine *comune* (municipalities) encircling the historic centre of the original village. Evidence traces prehistoric settlement back to the 6th century BC.

Information The IAT (☎ 0331 92 33 29, ⓦ www.provincia.va.it) is at Via Italia 3, right on the lake. Banks are lined up in Via Roma. Barberi (☎ 0331 92 46 70), at Via Cavour 21–23, does bicycle repairs.

Things to See & Do The old city can be investigated in less than an hour. Take in the **Palazzo Comunale** and its museum, and the 14th-century **Castello e Torre Mazza** (in Via Roma). Up the hill to the north by way of Via Vittorio Veneto/Via Marchetti is the 9th-century **Abbazia di Dan Donato**. Further along past Via San Donato is the 11th-century **Oratorio di San Vicenzo**. Even higher are the ancient stone carvings of **Sass de Preju Büja**.

Places to Stay & Eat About 1km north of town in Santa Anna is the camping ground **La Sfinge** (*☎/fax 0331 92 45 31; Via per Angera 1; per person/site €6.50/9*).

   Albergo La Pagoda (*☎ 0331 91 37 76; Via Umberto Maddalena*; singles/doubles €16/32), a shout from the train station, is rudimentary at best, but the lone cheap hotel. Its attached Chinese restaurant is accommodating. **Hotel/Ristorante del Parco** (*☎ 0331 92 25 77; Via Marconi 42*; singles/doubles with bathroom €47/65, dinner to €31, restaurant closed Tues) is the other mid-range option.

   Groceries are available in **shops** and **markets** on Via Roma and Via IV Novembre. **Ristorante/Pizzeria Portichetto** (*Piazza Garibaldi*; pizzas & pastas from €9; closed Mon) is very central and good. **Ristorante La Gria** (*Piazza Scipione*; dinner €23.50; closed Wed) has an inviting evening terrace and excellent pastas. Other restaurants are on Via Manzoni.

Getting There & Away Sesto is just off the Sesto C. Vergiate exit of expressway A8/26 from Milan (50km). From Turin, take A4 to A26 to A8/26.

   Sesto's train station sees locals clickety-clack through on the Milan–Domodossola line that skirts Lago Maggiore's southwest shore (one hour to Milan, one hour to Domodossola, 12 trains daily). There is also a four-times daily service between Novara (40 minutes) and Laveno (20 minutes).

Bicycle Sesto is around 50km from Milan on the very busy SS33, whereas Novara is only 35km due south on SS32 and beyond the ring of big-city industry. Laveno is an uncomplicated 30km sprint north along the lake. To the east about 20km is Varese, only 35km from Como on Lago di Como.

THE RIDE
Day 1: Sesto Calende to Milan
4–7½ hours, 73.6km

Today's ride is never far from gently flowing water and is as flat as the terrain that keeps the flow so slow. The route has four parts: the meandering lane along the Ticino River in

Navigli Milanesi – Day 1

Cue

start	Sesto Calende tourist office
0km	E on Viale Italia
0.4	Alzaia Mattea (at Piazza Guarano)
1.5	1km gravel path
2.6	unsigned main road
3.2	unsigned road (just before hill)
9.4	unsigned road (Porto della Torre)
10.7	E/1 Alleanza Assicurazioni path
10.8	0.5km cobblestones
13	Canale Industriale bikepath
17.5	cross to other side of canal
27.5	end of bike path
27.9	Via Alzaia 'to Turbigo'
28.4	Via E. Fermi
29.6	Via Milano (main road)
29.6	(10m) Via A. Boromi
29.6	(50m) along Canale Grande
29.8	Turbigo
38.1	leave E/1 bikepath
40	Bernate Ticino
44.7	Magenta
49.7	via Case Nuove (main road)
49.9	do NOT cross canal
50.9	Via per Castelletto
53.8	cross bridge over Naviglio Grande
53.9	Via Alzaia Naviglio Grande
61.7	cross canal in Gaggiano
61.7	(20m) along canal
64.7	Trezzano
73.6	Milan Piazzale XXIV Maggio

the Parco Regionale Valle del Ticino; the tranquil, car-free bikepath along the Canale Industriale; the small roads along the Canale Grande through the Parco Lombardo della Valle del Ticino; and the eastern dash along the much-storied Naviglio Grande through the Parco Agricolo Milano Sud straight into Milan's trendy Navigli area.

The first 13km pass effortlessly along the eastern bank of the **Ticino**. Starting at 10.7km, watch for the red-and-white E/1 Alleanza Assicurazioni bikepath signs guiding the route until 38.1km.

After the turn at Porto della Torre (9.4km), the 14.5km **Pista Ciclabile nel Parco del Ticino** along the Canale Industriale begins. This uninterrupted bike-only corridor doesn't get much shade, but the kilometres just whiz by. Signs pointing the path across to the east side of the canal at the Castelnovate lock complex· (17.5km) are a little confusing.

Nosate, 2.3km short of Turbigo (29.8km), is at the end of the blissfully low-horsepower *pista* and the national park. Regular roads advance the ramble. Wander inland for a pinch at Turbigo (detour through its centre for its 13th-century **Castello Visconteo**) and then ease back into the familiar canalside course. At Bernate Ticino (40km), the 15th-century **Palazzo Visconti** and a Renaissance **castle-convent** should be admired. Around 3km further, the Ponte Vecchio canal crossing (with the **bike shop** on the corner and the **park headquarters**, ☎ 02 972 10 205) is at the western edge of Magenta, site of **memorials** to an important and very bloody 1859 battle in the Italian struggle for unification. The path continues along the eastern bank of the canal, glides past sumptuous **villas**, exits the parkland and, at 53.8km, crosses the bridge over the Naviglio Grande.

The last 19.7km run the length of the Naviglio Grande through **Parco Agricolo Milano Sud**. Stop in **Gaggiano** (61.7km) at the bridge across the canal to glimpse its 15th-century **Villa Marino** and municipal palazzo. In **Trezzano** (64.7km), take in the 10th- to 12th-century **Chiesa di San Ambrogio** and 17th-century bridge. Within the Milan city limits, 13th-century **Chiesa di San Cristoforo** borders right on the canal. These few sights don't complicate directions along this arrow-straight corridor into southern urban Milan.

Milan
See p176.

Day 2: Milan Circuit via Pavia
5½–9½ hours, 94.4km
Like most terrain in the region, this route is flat, hitting the banks of three different *navigli* (canals) – the Grande, Bereguardo and Pavese – and the city of Pavia.

The morning ride is to Abbiategrasso along yesterday's Naviglio Grande, but this time from Milan and not Sesto Calende. For the already-seen averse, westbound local trains from Milan's Stazione Porta Genova, 600m west of Piazzale XXIV Maggio, make the trip in 25 minutes. Abbiategrasso has a 12th-century **Castello Visconteo** and the 15th-century **Chiesa Santa Maria Nuova**.

Navigli Milanesi – Day 2

Cue

start		Milan Piazzale XXIV Maggio
0km		W on Viale Gorizia
0.2	↘	Naviglio Grande
8.9	✳	Trezzano
11.9	↰ ✳	Gaggiano, cross canal
11.9	↱	(20m) along canal
19.7	↑	to R is bridge from Lecco route
21.1	↑	Parco Ticino bikepath
21.1	● ●↱	Abbiategrasso 3km ↻
25.2	● ●↱	Abbazia di Morimondo 3km ↻
32.4	↱	unmarked road when bikepath ends
34.1	↰	Besate, V. Fornace 'to M Visconti'
35	↰	SS526 to Motta Visconti'
38.1		Motta Visconti (go through centre)
39.3	↰	SS526 'to Bereguardo'
43	✳ ↱	Bereguardo, 'to Garlasco'
46.7	↰	'to Garlasco'
47	↰	'to Zerbolo'
63	↰	Viale Giulietti/Viale della Liberta
64	↙	Viale Battisti
64.3	↰	Via Filzi
64.4	✳	Pavia tourist office
retrace route to Piazza Dante		
64.5	↑	Viale Matteotti
64.7	↰	Via XI Febbraio
65.4	↙ ✦	(2nd exit) Viale Repubblica
65.7	↱	cross bridge over Naviglio Pavese
65.7	↰	(20m) V. Alz. Sinistra d. Naviglio
72.9	● ●↱	Certosa di Pavia 5km ↻
76.7	⚠	2km gravel path
77.8	✳	large canal lock
80.6	⚠	1.8km gravel path
80.7	✳	large canal lock
82.4	↱	rejoin main road
82.6	↙ ✦	(3rd exit) cross bridge
82.8	↱	unsigned bikepath
83.9	↑ ⚠	1.2km gravel bikepath
87.6	⚠	1km gravel bikepath
89.8	⚠	1.2km gravel bikepath
94.4		Milan Piazzale XXIV Maggio

Abbiategrasso is just west of the **Naviglio Bereguardo** along which the route then runs. This waterway is a narrow canal winding through the area's extensive agricultural meadows, much of which was once under the direction of Cistercian monks residing in the 11th-century **Abbazia di Morimondo**, just west of the canal (at 25.2km). The trail along the canal disappears and the route detours through local villages as far as Bereguardo, site of an impressive 13th-century **Castello Visconteo**.

In Bereguardo (43km), head west across to the far bank of the Ticino across a cool **ponte di barche** (boat bridge). The **Bosco Grande** (woods) after Zerbolo is a rare protected natural riparian forest.

Pavia (see the Po River Basin – Lungo Po Argine ride on p167, 64.4km) is the turnaround point and a good place for lunch.

The **Naviglio Pavese** now runs without interruption (and sometimes with gravel embankments) all the way to Milan's Piazzale XXIV Maggio. Along the way, don't dismiss the side trip (72.9km) to the **Certosa di Pavia**, a fabulous 14th- to 15th-century Carthusian monastery (church, cloister and palace) and one of the most notable Italian buildings produced during the Renaissance. Also note the impressive system of **locks** south of Binasco.

Day 3: Milan to Lecco
4–7½ hours, 77.2km

Like the previous rides, this route is very flat. It follows the same geological sequence as Day 1, only in reverse: From downtown Milan, a canal (the Naviglio Martesana) escapes the urban jungle to the shores of a river (the Adda) that cuts through a green swath of park (Parco dell'Adda Nord) to a city (Lecco) on a great lake (the Lago di Como).

The Naviglio Martesana starts just north of Milan's main train station. It's a splendid waterside terrace bounded by family parks and playgrounds, and passing through placid communities riddled with majestic 17th- and 18th-century **villas** and **farmhouses**. The bit between Cernusco and Casano d'Adda is particularly rich in architecture. Mind the direction of the canal. At three points – just after Crescenzago, just before Gorgonzola (after which the cheese is named) and before Inzago – a short detour away from the canal is required.

At Casano d'Adda (26km), the road along the canal turns north with the canal. A side trip to the centre of Casano runs by the 11th-century **Castello Borromeo** and a number of lavish **villas**. Back on the main route, a signed bikepath swings back to the west from Groppello, but your route continues north, sometimes over gravel, along the wooded bluff-base banks of the canal.

Pavement returns when a hydroelectric facility appears. The arresting, frescoed, 15th-century **Palazzo Melzi d'Eril** at Vapro d'Adda (34.8km) is atop the rock face to the left. The gravel path continues along the water.

Within sight of a pair of soaring bridges, the path crosses the canal (38km). The nearby church is Trezzo sull'Adda's 17th-century **Santuario della Maternità di Maria**. The

Navigli Milanesi – Day 3

Cue		
start	Milan Piazza Duca d'Aosta	
0km	NW on Via Galvani	
0.4	↱ Via Melchiorre Gioia bikepath	
1.3	↗ Naviglio della Martesana bikpath	
15.1	Metro Cassina de' Pecchi	
18.7	↗ follow canal bikepath	
19.3	Gorgonzola	
21	⚠ ↰ cross highway	
21	⚠ ↗ (5m) right of barrier to bikepath	
22.8	Inzago	
26	↰ follow canal bikepath	
26	●●↱ Cassano d'Adda 1km ↺	
27.7	↑ Groppello, NOT across bridge	
30.7	⚠ 3.7km gravel bikepath	
34.8	✳ ↑ Vaprio d'Adda, NOT across bridge	
35	↗ ⚠ 4km gravel bikepath	
38	⚠ cross canal (at Santuario)	
39	↘ go up ramp (to castle)	
39.5	✳ Trezzo sull'Adda	
39.5	↱ Via Visconti back to river	
39.9	⚠ 6.6km good gravel bikepath	
48.3	✳ Bertini power station	
48.8	⚠ 0.7km gravel bikepath	
51.1	✳ Paderno d'Adda bridge	
52.5	⚠ 1.2km gravel bikepath	
54.8	✳ Imbersago ferry crossing	
54.9	⚠ 3.2km gravel bikepath	
59.3	Brivio	
59.5	↑ follow river, ignore deadend signs	
61	⚠ 4km dirt single track	
66.7	↱ ⚠ unmarked road, 1.3km gravel path	
68	Olginate	
68.7	↰ Via Barozzi (last before bridge)	
68.9	↱ unsigned (main) road	
68.9	↱ cross brdge 'to Calolziocorte'	
70.1	↰ 'to Lecco'	
72.5	↰ Via della Spiaggia 'to spaggia'	
74.2	↗ unmarked nonoverpass road	
74.7	↙ Via Figini 'to Lecco'	
75.2	↰ Corso Carlo Alberto 'to Sondrio'	
76.7	↰ Via Costituzione 'to Valtellina'	
77	↱ follow curve onto Largo Isonzo	
77.2	↱ Via Saura (after Larius Rest.)	
77.2	Lecco tourist office	

Naviglio della Martesana ends here and the course along the west bank of the true Adda River begins. At the time of writing, this riverside route was blocked a short distance north. A ramp up the cliff face sufficed for a fortuitous skip into central Trezzo right by its ancient **castle**. The road just beyond the castle returns to water level and proceeds along the river.

For 6.6km, a gravel path parallels the rapid waters. A paved road briefly takes over at the **Bettini power station** (48.3km), designed by Edison and built in 1896 as the first plant for the long-distance transport of electricity. Shortly thereafter, a new canal appears, Naviglio di Paderno, and plunges into a beautiful thick wooded area of winding, sometimes-gravel paths and overgrown canal locks.

The comfortable riverside pace returns once the high 1889 bridge at Paderno wheels into view (51.1km). The barriers to the Imbersago ferry landing (54.8km) may require two people to lift the bike over. The structure and operating system of the ferry are based on drawings by Leonardo da Vinci, who spent many years studying the waters of the Adda south of Lecco.

Brivio (59.3km), the next town after a lovely wooded pedal, is the end of the effortless bikepaths. Continuing straight along the river's edge, 4km of tough **singletrack** mix with small residential-area trails to avoid the main road and then link with a fine bikepath to Olginate (68km) on its same-name lake.

Crossing the bridge here leads to the east bank of the Adda for the first time, and a fun

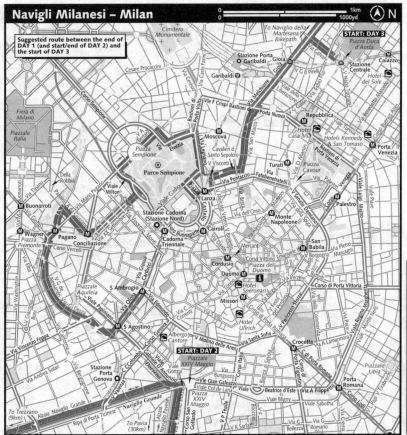

spin along Lake Garlate to Lecco, the south-ernmost city on the east leg of Lago di Como.

Lecco
See p209.

Central Lakes

Duration	5 days
Distance	329.3km
Difficulty	moderate–hard
Start	Sondrio
End	Domodossola

Lago di Como, Lago di Lugano and Lago Maggiore are the big players in the cluster of lakes laced into the mountains at the northern edge of central Lombardy. Wedged between lower ranges of the Alps, they are a surprise to all who visit and a corner many consider the most beautiful place in the world. From high valley jaunts to lakeshore shuffles and everything in between, this five-day ride traverses a territory nobody can visit only once.

PLANNING
When to Ride
The lakes region basks in a mild climate unique for the elevation. Average winter temperatures don't fall below 6°C and sum-mers rarely see days over 30°C. Thus, the best riding season is from spring to autumn, although hardy types can also enjoy winter sprints. A tangle of light afternoon breezes

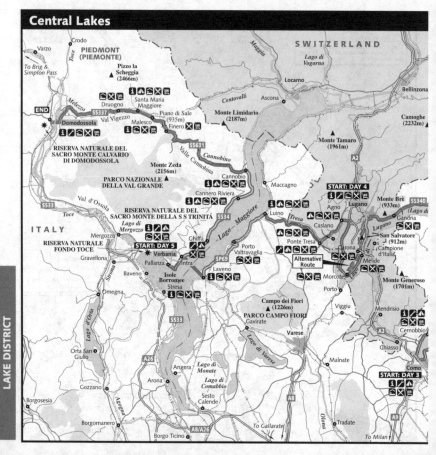

regularly kicks up on all of the lakes, blowing predominantly from the south.

Maps & Books

Touring Club Italiano's (1:200,000) map of *Lombardia* includes the full length of this ride. Kompass (1:50,000) map Nos 90 *Lago Maggiore* and 91 *Lago di Como/Lago di Lugano* also provide good coverage. The free RegioneLombardia (1:400,000) *Lombardia* map or (1:100,000) *Lago di Como* and *Lago Maggiore* maps can be used with the free *Provincia di Sondrio* (1:115,000) map too.

The Como tourist office distributes free photocopies of *Itineraries by Mountain Bike in the Province of Como* for fat-tyre fans. A consortium of Swiss *enti turistichi* (tourist organisations) joined forces to produce a folder called *Cycling Itineraries* in the Lago di Lugano region. The Comuni Ossolani Comunità Montane and Unione Ciclista Valdossola (W www.ucvaldossola.com) turn out yearly *Brevetti Ossolani* that include 11 road-cycling and seven mountain-biking itineraries in the Domodossola area.

ACCESS TOWN

See Sondrio (p198).

THE RIDE
Day 1: Sondrio to Lecco
5–9 hours, 88.3km

Although it involves no major changes in elevation, today's ride is fairly long with lots

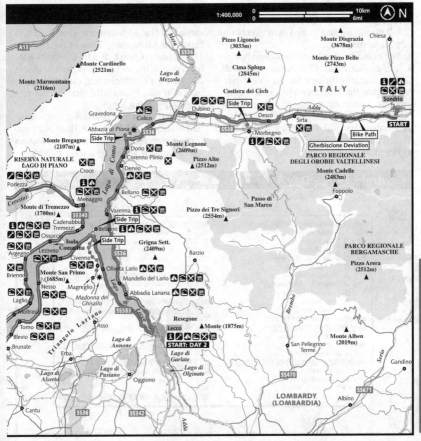

of rolling hills along the lower 44km of Valtellina to the top of Lago di Como. The next 44km follow the steep contours of the encircling mountains that plunge dramatically into the waters of Europe's deepest lake.

From Sondrio, a half-dirt, half-paved, former carriage road called the Sentiero Valtellina charts the south bank of the Adda River (with one deviation up to the main road in Gherbiscione, 11km) as far as Fusine. When it disappears into a maze of cornfields (12.4km), common sense and determination lead to small country lanes on the far side.

Shortly after Sirta (21.1km) and its **Chiesa di San Giuseppe** (with the largest dome in the region), the main road crosses the bike route. Jog over the bridge here to the north side of the Adda and then make an immediate left. A short, but steep, hill on a lovely, gravel, back road climbs to Desco (24.7km) before finally and definitively returning to pavement.

The beautiful, triple-arched, stone bridge 4.2km further is the 15th-century **Ponte di Ganda**. It marks the turn for the side trip to **Morbegno**, the last large village in Valtellina and a pleasant medieval centre. Morbegno is also the start of the Antica Via Privia that climbs the 1985m Passo di San Marco through the heart of the Alpi Orobie to Bergamo.

Back at the base of the **Costiera dei Cèch**, the last few kilometres of Valtellina unwind.

Colico (46.3km) is the first of the magical Lago di Como villages packed with history and attractions. Ruins here of the early 17th-century **Spanish fort** fit the bill. About 25km later, the side trip at Olgiasca to the 11th-century **Abbazia di Piona** takes in one of the lake's most important Romanesque structures. Crenelated **Castello Recinto** and an impressive **church** devoted to Saint Thomas of Canterbury crown the rocky spur of Corenno Plinio (55.6km). Don't speed past the fabulous **Orrido** (gorge) at Bellano formed by the Torrente Pioverna.

Varenna (66.3km) is the pearl of the Lario. Gaze up at the ruins of its medieval **Castello di Vezio** (from which the lake panorama is unrivalled) and the length of the multitiered gardens of 17th-century **Villa Cipressi** or the 1km-long botanical spread of the 13th-century former Cistercian **Villa Monastero**. Take in the 10th- to 11th-century **Chiesa di San Giovanni Battista**, one of the area's oldest. Nature lovers can visit the **ornithological museum** or the banks of the **Fiumelatte**, Italy's shortest river (only 250m long).

Further down the lakeshore, once-fortified Mandello del Lario (78.3km) is an important stop for motorcycle lovers. **Museo Moto Guzzi** is set in the former factory.

Central Lakes – Day 1

Cue

start	Sondrio tourist office		38.1	Dubino
0km	W on Via Trieste		40.9 ↰	Via delle Torre
0.2 ↱↱ 🚲	Via Bertacchi		41.9 ↰	SS36 'to Lecco'
0.3 ↙ 🚲	Via Mazzini		42.9 ↱	'to S. Agatha'
0.6 ↱↱ 🚲	Via Caimi/Via Vanoni		43.3 ↱	unsigned road after tracks
1.5 ↱	bikepath along river		44.4 ↙	merge with main road
11 ⚠	Gherbiscione deviation		46.3 ✳	Colico (train station)
12.4 ⚠	riverside bikepath ends		49.3 ↙	not into tunnel
13.7 ↱	unsigned paved road		51.8 ●●↱	Abbazia di Piona 5km ↻
14 ↰	'to Morbegno'		53.8	Dorio
14.2 ↙	unsigned road		55.6 ✳	Corenno Plinio (castle)
15.2 ↱	usigned road (stop sign)		57.1	Dervio
21.1 ✳	Sirta		61.3 ✳	Bellano
23.3 ↱	SS38 'to Sondrio'		65 ↱	'to Varenna'
23.6 ↰	unsigned road (1st after bridge)		66.3 ✳	Varenna
23.7 ⚠ ⚠	1km uphill gravel road		66.9 ↙	rejoin main road
24.7	Desco		78.3 ✳	Mandello del Lario
26.1 ↱	Via Adda		80.5	Abbadia Lariana
28.9 ↑	short steep climb		84.1 ↱ 🚲	'to lungolago'
28.9 ●●↰	Morbegno 4km ↻		88.2 ↰	Via N. Sauro
29.4 ↘	downhill (not to Mello)		88.3	Lecco tourist office

Just past Abbadia Lariana, the major vehicular road that has stuck to the upper slopes merges with the *lungolago* (lakeshore drive). It's an unpleasant 3.6km stretch, but the only road to the next and final stop at Lecco.

Lecco

Lecco has a long and interesting history. Towered over by the Grigna mountain range and Monte Resegone, but open to Lago di Como's outlet to the Adda River, Lecco is both protected and accessible. This dramatic and strategic location has attracted countless peoples – area digs have uncovered the presence of Bronze-Age folk, Romans and Byzantines, among others. It continues to draw hordes today.

Information The Lecco APT (☎ 0341 36 23 60, w www.aptlecco.com) is one block back from the lake at Via Sauro 6 and is open daily. Banks are on the square, Piazza Garibaldi, just behind it. The closest bike shop is Gilardi (☎ 0341 27 25 23), a good distance away at Via Turbada 15, inland along the Torrente Bione and off Via Tonio da Belledo.

Things to See & Do Lecco is most famous for Alessandro Manzoni, one of Italy's great writers and author of the novel *I promessi spossi* (The Betrothed*)*. Ask for information about the itinerary leading from his childhood home, **Villa Manzoni**, past many of the sites mentioned in his opus. Lecco's multisite **City Museum** includes rooms in the aforementioned Villa Manzoni devoted to the great man and also in the 15th-century **Torre del Castello** on Piazza XX Settembre; and the **Palazzo Belgioioso's** archaeological exhibits. The **Ponte Azzone Visconti** is an early 17th-century version of spans that have existed there since 300 years earlier. Hikers should ask at tourist information about one-day **treks** into the surrounding hills.

Places to Stay & Eat Campers should head 4km to the south at Chiuso's *lido* (beach) on Lake Garlate to find **Rivabella** (☎ 0341 42 11 43; Via alla Spiaggia 35, Località Chiuso; per site/person €8/5).

Lecco's cheapest lodgings are the two listed *affittacamere*: **Paroli** (☎ 0341 36 11 77; Via Balicco; rooms €17) behind the train station; and **Bartolomeo** (☎ 0341 28 24 51; Corso Martiri dell Liberazione 131; rooms €26) above the popular **Above Wildwood** bar. In Lecco's centre is **Hotel Moderno** (☎ 0341 28 65 19; Piazza Diaz 5; singles/doubles €52/68), pricey but good. **Hotel/Ristorante Bellavista** (☎ 0341 58 13 35; Via Parè 87; singles/doubles €25/40; dinner €21, restaurant closed Fri) occupies an idyllic spot 4km southwest across the lake looking at Lecco. Follow Day 2's directions to the tunnel entrance and veer right; the hotel is at the far end of the road.

Self-caterers can shop at the **supermarkets** on Viale Turati. This is also a good area for trattorias. Another restaurant row is to the east in Carlo Alberto and Via Pescatori. Downtown, **Trattoria Santa Lucia** (Via Mascari 3; closed Wed) is a local favourite for pizza and pasta, as is **Taverna ai Poggi** (Via ai Poggi 14; closed Mon). **Ristorante Dai Brambilla** (Via Cavour 36; closed Sun) is off an inner courtyard on Lecco's main shopping strip. Inexpensive, but touristy and right beside the port, is **Ristorante La Vela** (Lungolario Cadorna 20; dinner around €17; closed Wed).

Day 2: Lecco to Como

3–5 hours, 51.3km
Today's ride is like the second half of Day 1: rolling hills in an impossibly endless run of lakeside splendour. This route is on much smaller roads so traffic is vastly reduced. Whatever happens, don't skip the side trip up the hill to the Madonna del Ghisallo chapel.

From Lecco, turn north along the west side of Lago di Lecco. Claustrophobes should prepare for the two long tunnels right outside the city. To compensate, rocky beaches and lakeside turnouts rule the rest of the ride. So do groves of olive trees, a plant not usually cultivated at this elevation, but made possible by lake microclimates. The extensive olive terraces of Olivetta Lario were first planted by the Romans.

Bellagio, the 'Italian Versailles' at the tip of the *triangolo lariano* (Lario triangle), is a true gem. Built just short of Punta Spartivento, it's a holiday oasis that has attracted patrician society for centuries. Its promontory-dominating **Villa Serbelloni** (now owned by the Rockefeller Foundation),

Villa Melzi and Villa Giulia are evidence of this. Hiking and mountain-biking trails abound in the hills behind town. Ask for route information from the information office on Piazza della Chiesa across from the 12th-century Basilica di San Giacomo. Cavalcalario Club (☎ 031 96 48 14, 🖳 www .bellagio-mountains.it) runs mountain-bike day tours and rents equipment.

Patron Saint of Cyclists

In the half-light of the small Madonna del Ghisallo sanctuary (1623), you can immediately tell that it is no ordinary chapel. Cloaking the walls between votive plaques are glass-framed bike jerseys and packing the rafters is a curious collection of bicycles. On the left, amid others, is the steed *il campionnissimo* that Fausto Coppi rode to victory in the 1949 Giro d'Italia. There too is the tortured frame from Fabio Casartelli's mortal crash in 1995. On the right, the aerodynamic machine is from Francesco Moser's 1984 record-breaking one-hour ride. And how about Gino Bartali's 1948 Tour de France coup wheels? Or, yes, that's Gianni Motta's pink jersey from his 1966 Giro triumph. The other names represented are a who's who of cycling giants: Bottechia, Moser, Merckx, Hinault, LeMond, Magni, Felice. Any cycling devotee gets the shivers.

The Beata Vergine Maria del Ghisallo is the patron saint of (Italian) cyclists, a bestowment made by Pope Pious XII in 1949. Today, her sanctuary/chapel in the hamlet of Magreglio (above Bellagio) is a shrine to cycling's past and present greats. Right next door, ground was recently broken for the long-planned Museo del Ciclismo. Trinket collectors will want to purchase the tiny Madonna pendant some pros keep with them for protection when they race. The chapel grounds also have an evocative Pope-blessed Monumento al Ciclista and a panoramic lookout.

The chapel (754m) is an odd and powerful place, made more so by the 8.9km, 464m climb from the route to Bellagio. Head up the Vallassina following signs to Ghisallo, Guello and Civenna (626m, 6.7km), the last-named the only settlement with services. The ride is humbling. Perhaps that's the way it should be.

Don't miss the tough, but fantastic, side-trip climb to the Santuario Madonna del Ghisallo, which is dedicated to the patron saint of cyclists.

The ride down the eastern shore of Lago di Como to Como is one of the most dramatic on the lake, undulating with the abrupt sylvan slopes. Stop to admire Nesso's gorge (34.5km) and the medieval harbourside piazza in Torno (a walk down from the road, 45km). The 16th-century Villa Pliniana here is one of the lake's most famous, having seen Napoleon, Stendahl, Rossini and Byron as some of its guests.

Como

Como feels like a real Italian city, which is hard to find on these tourist-stuffed shores. With a compact old town retaining its original Roman layout and a good pack of attractions, it is a perfect jumping-off point for boat excursions on the lake.

Information Como tourist office (☎ 031 26 97 12, 🖳 www.lakecomo.com) is on the large lakeside square at Piazza Cavour 16. Banks are also located here. For bike problems, consult with Martinelli (☎ 03126 44 17) at Viale Lecco 95, south of the centre.

Things to See & Do From Piazza Cavour, walk along arcaded Via Plinio to Piazza del Duomo and the marble-faced 14th- to 18th-century duomo. Next to it is the polychromatic Borletto (old town hall), altered in 1415 to make way for the cathedral. Work on the nearby Basilica di San Fedele began even earlier, in the 6th century, although it has had numerous facelifts since. On Piazza Medaglie d'Oro, the Palazzo Giovio houses the Archaeology Museum and Palazzo Olginati is home to the Museum of Italian Unification. The extensive medieval walls are not far now, most striking near the Porte Torre, a 12th-century tower built as part of the defensive system that included the now-ruined 12th-century castle on the hill to the southwest. Due north of there is the huge new Museo della Seta (Silk Museum). Back by the lakeside, trails or a funicular brave the steep slopes of Brunate to a glorious lookout. If sea level feels safer, consider cruising the lake aboard the boats plying its waters and departing from the pier facing Piazza Cavour.

Central Lakes – Day 2

Cue

start		Lecco tourist office
0km		NW on Via N. Sauro
0.1	⬏1	Largo Lario Isonzo
0.3	⬐⬑	Largo Lario da Vinci
0.8	⬏	Via Italia/SS583 'to Bellagio'
3.1	⚠	1.6km tunnel
5	⚠	2.2km tunnel
14.7	✳	Oliveto Lario
17	▲	2.9km moderate climb
19.9	⚠	0.9km steep descent
20.1	⬏	'to Bellagio'
20.1	●●⬎1	Madonna del Ghisallo 17.8km ⟳
20.8	⬏1	Via Vitali 'to Bellagio'
21.5	⬏1	Via Carcano/SS583 'to Como'
21.5	●⬐⟳	Bellagio 6km ⟳
22.3	▲	1.4km moderate climb
27.9		Lezzeno
31.9	▲	4km moderate climb
34.5	✳	Nesso
38.9	▲	2.2km moderate climb
41.9	▲	0.7km steep climb
45	✳	Torno
48.2		Blevio
51.3		Como tourist office

Places to Stay Poorly situated 5km to the southwest of Como, just off the expressway, is **Campeggio International** (☎/fax 031 52 14 35; Via Cecilio, Breccia; per site/person €5/16), however, **Ostello Villa Olmo** (☎/fax 031 57 38 00; e ostellocomo@tin.it; Via Bellinzona 2; B&B per person €12.50, dinner €8; open Mar-Nov) is a superb facility bordering the lake 1km west of the centre. Next door, **Protezione della Giovane** (☎ 03157 35 40; Via Borgovico 182; B&B per person €11.50) is a hostel for women only.

In the centre of town, the budget option **Albergo Sociale** (☎ 031 26 40 42; Via Maestri Comacini 8; singles/doubles €37/47) peers out directly at the cathedral. Overlooking the nearby bus station, **In Riva al Lago** (☎/fax 031 30 23 33; w www.inrivaal lago.com; Piazza Matteotti 4; singles/doubles €29/39) is a step up to the 2nd floor and in quality. Up the street from there, **Albergo Funicolare** (☎ 031 30 42 77; Via Coloniola 8/10; singles/doubles €47/74) is somewhat dark, but good quality. Beneath the Chiesa di San Agostino bell tower, **Albergo Quarcino** (☎ 031 30 39 34; w www.hotelquar cino.it; Salita Quarcino 4; singles/doubles with bathroom €45/70) is four-star service at a two-star price.

Places to Eat Mini **markets** and **speciality food shops** are common in Como's

pedestrian grid. **Sandwich bars** and **self-service restaurants** are abundant too.

Queues can be long for the pizza and pasta at highly popular **Taverna Messicana** (Piazza Mazzini 6; closed Mon) and neighbouring **Le Colonne** (Piazza Mazzini 12; closed Tues). **Il Carrettiere** (Via Coloniola 18; closed Mon) is large and boisterous and also a local fave. Wait times are shorter at peaceful **Ristorante Piazzolo** (Viale Indipendenza 6; closed Sun) in the centre of town, and **Trattoria Sereni** (Via Borgovico 34; closed Sat) near the train station.

Day 3: Como to Lugano
3½–6 hours, 62.8km

Following another morning along Lago di Como, the route finally hits a hill – only 182m in 2.8km – and pushes into new territory: Lago di Lugano. The western half of the ride along the Lago di Ceresio arm of the lake is in Switzerland, as is the night stop in Lugano. Bring your passport.

The first 5km whiz past more of Lago di Como's most magnificent villas: neoclassical **Villa Olmo** on Como's outskirts, **Villa d'Este** and **Villa Erba** (both in Cernobbio) and many more along the narrow coastal **Via Regina** 6.8km alternative to the trafficky main road.

Argegno (19.6km) is the first town of any consequence after Cernobbio. There is a **Roman bridge** off to the left of the main bridge over the Torrento Telo and, just north of town, a quick cable car to the village of Pigra at 881m and one of the lake's best eastward-looking vistas. Around 5km up the shore, Ossuccio is famous for its Romanesque **Chiesa di Santa Maria Maddalena** and Gothic **bell tower**. A short boat trip to the east is Lago di Como's only island, **Isola Comacina**, thought of as the 'Pompei del Lario', one of Lombardy's most important archaeological sites.

Parallel with Bellagio on the 'Riviera of Azaleas' (known for its exceptionally warm climate), Tremezzo and Cadenabbia have more villas reaching for the shore through long verdant gardens. **Villa Carlotta** is the best of a very rich lot.

Finally, at Menaggio (34.1km), the route turns west and up a steep hill to the watershed between Lago di Como and its western neighbour, Lago di Lugano. Down a wide, high valley it dips past the little Lago di Piano to the town of Porlezza (46.5km). The remaining 16.3km run the length of this scenic and wild lake, cross the Swiss border and culminate in Lugano.

Lugano

Lugano is the lead city of Switzerland's canton of Ticino. It's the Italian-speaking centre of the multilingual country and a curious mix of northern and southern European qualities: easy in a Mediterranean, but also very well-ordered, Swiss kind of way.

Information The tourist office (☎ 091 913 32 32, w www.lugano-tourism.ch) is in the Palazzo Civico on Riva Albertolli. Banks can be found behind the Palazzo around Piazza della Rifomra. Two bike shops are located on Via Trevano north of the centre: Casa del Ciclo (☎ 091 972 32 34) is at No 46 and Sport Planetarium (☎ 972 22 88) at No 95.

Things to See & Do The porticoed commercial **pedestrian area** of the old town is in a close tie with the **waterfront promenade** and associated parks for most appealing area. With regard to landmark buildings, the trio of churches – 15th-century **Cattedrale San Lorenzo**, beautifully frescoed **Chiesa Santa Maria degli Angioli** and 17th-century **Chiesa San Giorgio in Casta** – tops the list. There are also a number of **art museums**.

However, it's the nonhistorical distractions in and around Lugano that really draw people in. The **casinos** of Lugano and Campione d'Italia are always busy. Also in **Campione d'Italia**, an Italian territorial enclave completely surrounded by Switzerland, is the famous 9th-century **Santuario Madonna dei Ghirli**. Hikers will find a number of signed **walks** in hills surrounding the city. The lakeside path to Gandria is highly recommended. Alternatively, funiculars motor to the panoramic caps of 912m **Monte San Salvatore** (to the south) and 933m **Mont Brè** (to the east).

Places to Stay & Eat Switzerland is an expensive country and Lugano not its cheapest city. Remember that prices here are in Swiss francs. There are neither camping grounds nor hostels in the vicinity.

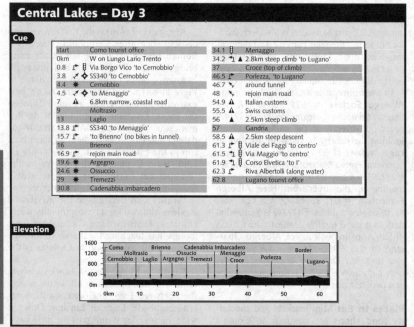

Central Lakes – Day 3

Cue

start	Como tourist office		34.1	Menaggio
0km	W on Lungo Lario Trento		34.2 ▲	2.8km steep climb 'to Lugano'
0.8	Via Borgo Vico 'to Cernobbio'		37	Croce (top of climb)
3.8	SS340 'to Cernobbio'		46.5	Porlezza, 'to Lugano'
4.4	Cernobbio		46.7	around tunnel
4.5	'to Menaggio'		48	rejoin main road
7 ▲	6.8km narrow, coastal road		54.9 ▲	Italian customs
9	Moltrasio		55.5 ▲	Swiss customs
13	Laglio		56 ▲	2.5km steep climb
13.8	SS340 'to Menaggio'		57	Gandria
15.7	'to Brienno' (no bikes in tunnel)		58.5 ▲	2.5km steep descent
16	Brienno		61.3	Viale dei Faggi 'to centro'
16.9	rejoin main road		61.5	Via Maggio 'to centro'
19.6	Argegno		61.9	Corso Elvetica 'to I'
24.6	Ossuccio		62.3	Riva Albertolli (along water)
29	Tremezzi		62.8	Lugano tourist office
30.8	Cadenabbia imbarcadero			

Elevation

Locanda Gandriese (☎ 091 971 41 81; e locanda@pacchin.ch; Sotto la Chiesa, Gandria; singles/doubles 50/100SF) is the cheapest hotel in the area. Also here is **Albergo/Ristorante Miralago** (☎ 091 43 61; singles/doubles 45/90SF), with a lovely lakeside dining terrace and good food. In Lugano, **Albergo/Ristorante del Tiglio** (☎ 091 971 24 97; Via Merlina 6; singles/doubles 40/80SF) is on a quiet side street east of the Torrente Cassarate north towards Viganello. **Villa Antica** (☎ 091 971 84 61; Via del Tiglio 5; singles/doubles 79/126SF) is also east of the Cassarate, but on a tranquil lane only two streets away from the city lido.

Some of the best sit-down food in town is served in the hotel dining rooms. Other **restaurants** can be found with the **markets** and **food shops** in the pedestrian zone, particularly around Piazza della Riforma.

Day 4: Lugano to Verbania
3½–6 hours, 58.5km

The morning is spent hugging the snaking Swiss coast of Lago di Lugano. At Ponte Tresa, the route crosses back into Italy and follows the Fiume Tresa to the lapping waters of Lago Maggiore. A gentle afternoon glide down this coast stops at a ferry to Verbania.

From Lugano, the route turns south along the shores of its homonymous lake. The main busy highway turns east at Melide, leaving behind a low-traffic shore-cuddling road. Stop in Melide (6.2km) for **Swiss Miniatur**, a 1:25 scaled-down version of Switzerland's prettiest features. Morcote (10.5km) too is worth a pause for its medieval arcaded streets and frescoed **Chiesa di Santa Maria del Sasso**. An alternative route skips Melide, hitting instead a fantastic, but difficult, high road from downtown Lugano over the hill via Carona.

The road from Morcote to Agno is a cyclist's pleasure. Unfortunately, Agno to Ponte Tresa is trafficky. Take a chocolate break at the **Shoko Land Alprose factory and museum** in Caslano (24km). In Ponte Tresa (25.9km), once across the Italian border, Lago Maggiore is a short 12.2km pedal to the west.

Luino is a bustling community best known for its shaded waterfront and extensive Wednesday street market. It also harbours the 15th-century frescoed **Chiesa**

della Madonna del Carmine. Luino sets the tone for an easy afternoon's waterview speed down to Porto Valtravaglia, over the Rocca di Caldé and on to Laveno. Weather permitting, take a trip up the **funicular** to the 1062m heights of Sasso del Ferro.

Laveno is the *imbarcadero* (embarkation point) for the cross-lake car ferry (departures every 20 minutes) to Intra, the northern of the twin cities of Verbania.

Verbania
Verbania is actually a 20th-century combination of the distinct municipalities of Pallanza and Intra, the capital of the Piedmontese province of Verbano Cusio Ossola and the largest city on Lago Maggiore. Many people bypass it for the flashier resort of Stresa, which is a good reason to stay here.

Information Verbania's main IAT (☎ 0323 50 32 49, w www.lagomaggiore.it) is in Pallanza at Corso Zanitello 8. There is a tiny (usually closed) branch office (☎ 0323 40 13 75) at the Intra ferry landing on Piazzale Flaim. Banks in Pallanza are on Piazza Garibaldi; in Intra they are around Piazza Aldo Moro and along Via Corso Mamelli. The bike shop (☎ 0323 51 95 16) in Intra is at Corso Cairoli 63. Piaggio, on Piazza Gramsci in Pallanza, will advise about bikes.

Central Lakes – Day 4

Cue

start	Lugano tourist office	
0km	SW with water on Riva Albertoli	
1.2	↘	Riva Paradiso 'to Morcote'
1.3	■■↱	alt route: Carona high road 12.2km
5.9	↱	'to Morcote'
6.2	✳	Melide
8.7		alt route rejoins (turn right)
10.5	✳	Morcote
14.5	↰	cross bridge 'to Ponte Tresa'
14.6	↰	'to Ponte Tresa'
18.7	↰	'to Ponte Tresa'
20.9	↰ ⊟	Agno, route 23 'to Ponte Tresa'
24	✳	Caslano
25.9	⚠	Ponte Tresa, Italian border
26	↱	'to Luino'
38.2	✳↰	Luino, 'to Laveno'
45.3		Porto Valtravaglia
55.3	✳	Laveno
take ferry across lake to Verbania/Intra		
55.3	↑	Intra info, cross Piazzale Flaim
55.4	✓❖	(3rd exit) Via Mameli 'to Stresa'
56.4	↰	Via V. Veneto 'to Villa Taranto'
58.5	↰	Via Zanitello
58.5		Verbania (Pallanza) tourist info

Things to See & Do Churches, *palazzi* (palaces or mansions) and villas are the noteworthy structures in both Pallanza and Intra. These can be admired best just by walking the lanes in the towns' oldest sections. In Pallanza, from **Piazza Garibaldi** climb cobblestoned **Via Ruga** past 18th-century dwellings, most notably **Palazzo Viani Dugnani**, home of the **Landscape Museum**. Of the churches, 16th-century **Chiesa San Leonardo** and **Chiesa di Madonna di Campagna**, and the 11th-century **Oratorio di San Remigio** stand out. In Intra, stroll through the ancient squares of the *centro storico* – Piazza Ranzoni, Piazza Castello and Piazza San Rocco. Little *vicoli* (alleys) snake past impressive baroque facades and little shopping lanes.

The truly must-see attraction is **Villa Taranto's botanical gardens**. The 19th-century residential mansion is perched amid 50 acres of gardens filled with 20,000 varieties and species of plants from around the world.

Verbania is also the best embarkation point for boat trips to the fairytale **Isole Borromee** (Borromean Islands) and the resort town of **Stresa**.

Places to Stay There are four **camping grounds** in Fondotoce, a few kilometres west of Pallanza. Both of the hostels are officially in Pallanza. **Villa Congreve** (☎ 0323 50 16 48; *Via alle Rose 7; B&B per person €13*) is on the promontory east of the centre. **Centro Pastorale San Francesco** (☎ 0323 51 95 68; *Via alle Fabbriche 8; B&B per person €18*) is just south of the Torrente San Bernardino bridge between Pallanza and Intra.

In Pallanza, **Albergo Novara** (☎ 0323 50 35 27; ⓦ *www.hotelnovara.com; Piazza Garibaldi 30; singles/doubles €20/38.50*) and its restaurant open onto the main square. **Albergo Riviera** (☎ 0323 50 44 45; ⓔ *pescoero@tin.it; Via Troubetzkoy 121; singles/doubles €23.50/41.50*) has charming rooms and a dining terrace overlooking the lake. **Hotel Villa Tilde Meublè** (☎ 0323 50 38 05; *Via Vittorio Veneto 63; singles/doubles €31/52*) is a notch up on the leafy bikepath between the burgs. In Intra, **Albergo Touring** (☎ 0323 40 40 40; ⓦ *digilander.libero.it/htouring; Corso Garibaldi 26; singles/doubles €38/57*) is tightly run and well placed.

Places to Eat Home cookers will find a number of **markets** off Piazza Gransci in Pallanza. In Intra, try the large **supermarket** at Piazza San Vittore. For restaurant fodder in Pallanza, stick to the well-catered pedestrian area between Piazza Garibaldi, Viale Magnolie and Via Albertazzi. One standout pizza place is **Le Magnolie** (*Viale Magnolie 12; closed Tues*). In Intra, wander along Via Mamelli, across Piazza Ranzoni and up the length of Via San Vittore. A superb and local pizza place away from the crowd is **Lago Maggiore da Gino** (*Via Roma 3a; closed Thur*). **Osteria del Castello** (*Piazza Castello 9; closed Sun*) boasts a lovely large terrace in the thick of the old town.

Day 5: Verbania to Domodossola
4½–7 hours, 68.4km
After 23.4km along the shores of Lago Maggiore, the route hits the hills. For 20.8km it climbs up the leafy Val Cannobina and then descends through the Valle Vigezzo all the way to the Ossola plain at Domodossola.

Lago Maggiore's towns are less glamorous than those of Lago di Como, but the allure is just as strong. Ghiffa (7.6km) has its curious **Museo del Cappello** (Museum of Hats) and 14th-century **Chiesa di Santa Maria Assunta** at the top of the special nature reserve around the national park **Sacro Monte della S.S. Trinità**. Cannero Riviera (16.8km) boasts two **island castles**, former refuge of the 'Mazzardini' Verbano pirates. However, the local draw is really Cannobio (23.4km) and its romantic *lungolago*.

Cannobio is at the foot of the Val Cannobina, right at the Santa Anna gorge. The **Piano di Sale** (935m, 45.2km) slouches 715m higher. All the valley villages are a short distance off the road.

On the Vigezzo side of the pass, the town of Malesco (visit the **Parish Church** and contiguous **Oratorio di San Bernardino**) heralds the arrival in Santa Maria Maggiore (51.4km), the valley's administrative centre. The **Parrocchiale dell'Assunta** here is one of Ossola's most important religious buildings, built over a 1000-year-old earlier structure of which the **campanile** remains. For the sake of oddity, who could miss the **Museo degli Spazzacamini** (Chimneysweep Museum).

After a short uphill to Druogno (54.6km), the edge of Domodossola is 11.8km and 568m down in the flats of the Ossola Valley.

Domodossola

Sadly discredited Domodossola is worth a second look. Capital of the Ossola valley and its 10 side dales, it's more than initially meets the eye, especially since the recent successful efforts to beautify the central area and renovate its 15th-century old town. Domodossola now has the renewed old feel of a hospitable transit point between the Alps and lakes.

Information Domodossola's IAT (☎/fax 0324 24 82 65, Ⓦ www.prodomodossola.it) is in the atrium of the train station on Piazza Matteotti. Banks are also on this piazza. A very good bike shop, Ciclomania (☎ 0324 24 12 03) is north of the centre at Via Giovanni XXIII 64.

Things to See & Do Finding the old medieval centre is a worthwhile challenge. The 15th- to 16th-century arcaded **Piazza del Mercato** is practically intact. Nearby **Piazza Fontana**, **Piazza Chiossia** and **Piazza della Chiesa** are also fine examples of lively public spaces surrounded by elegant **palazzi**. Just to the north of these, in Via Monte Grappa, bits of the city's original **walls** are in evidence. The 18th-century **Collegiata dei Santi Gervasio e Protasio** is the city's main house of prayer.

Places to Stay & Eat There are neither camping grounds nor hostels in the area. Run-down **Albergo Domus** *(☎ 0324 24 23 25; Vicolo Cuccioni 12; singles/doubles €18/28)* is cheap and very central. Its restaurant serves solid Italian fare at bargain prices. **Albergo/Ristorante La Pendola** *(☎ 0324 24 37 04; Ⓦ www.pendolahotel.com; Via Giovanni XXIII 93; singles/doubles €33/45)* is slightly north of town on the main road (which gets quiet at night). Next door, **Residenza Mafalda** *(☎ 0324 24 38 01; Via Giovanni XXIII 95; singles/doubles €26/41.50)* has rooms with kitchens for do-it-yourselfers. For a treat, **Albergo Eurossola** *(☎ 0324 48 13 26; Ⓦ www.eurossola.com; Piazza Matteotti 36; singles/doubles €46.50/67.50)* has a refined decor, quiet comfortable rooms and an affordable gourmet restaurant.

For sandwich fixings, a large **supermarket** hides in the northwest corner of Piazza Matteotti and **alimentari** lurk in the side streets of the old town. Cheap sit-down eats should be sought on Via Gramsci and Via Binda. **Pizzeria Due Leoni** *(Via Binda 177)* serves excellent pizza and salad on a sunny terrace. **Ristorante Terminus** *(Piazza Tibaldi*

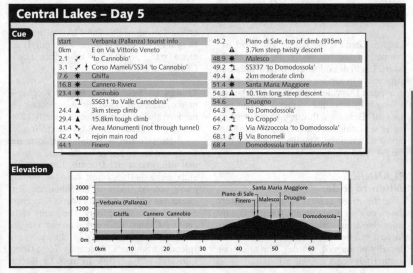

Central Lakes – Day 5

Cue

start	Verbania (Pallanza) tourist info	45.2	Piano di Sale, top of climb (935m)
0km	E on Via Vittorio Veneto		3.7km steep twisty descent
2.1	'to Cannobio'	48.9	Malesco
3.1	Corso Mameli/SS34 'to Cannobio'	49.2	SS337 'to Domodossola'
7.6	Ghiffa	49.4	2km moderate climb
16.8	Cannero Riviera	51.4	Santa Maria Maggiore
23.4	Cannobio	54.3	10.1km long steep descent
	SS631 'to Valle Cannobina'	54.6	Druogno
24.4	3km steep climb	64.3	'to Domodossola'
29.4	15.8km tough climb	64.4	'to Croppo'
41.4	Area Monumenti (not through tunnel)	67	Via Mizzoccola 'to Domodossola'
42.4	rejoin main road	68.1	Via Bonomelli
44.1	Finero	68.4	Domodossola train station/info

Elevation

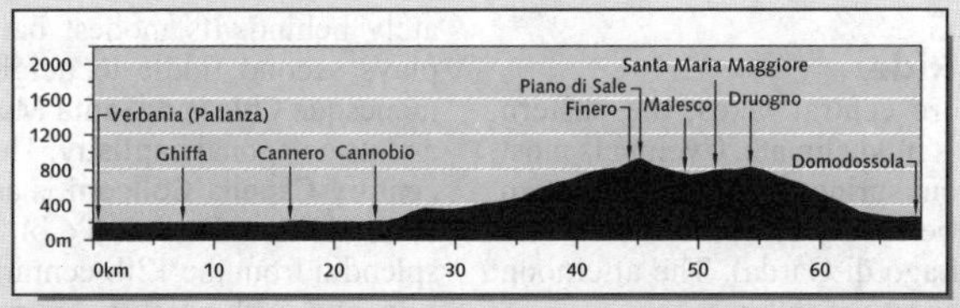

9; meals €15.50) is always busy. Savour the pasta at **Antica Trattoria da Sciolla** (Piazza Convenzione 4; pastas from €6).

Getting There & Away An important international train line from Milan (two hours) runs through Domodossola, the last Italian station before the Simplon tunnel to Brig (Switzerland) and connections elsewhere in Europe. There is also an hourly Swiss train running from Domodossola through Santa Maria Maggiore and down the Centovalli to Locarno (Switzerland).

If driving, SS30 from Domodossola flows into expressway A26, which divides south of Lago Maggiore to routes for Milan, Genoa and Turin. SS30 north of Domodossola heads over the Passo di Sempione (Simplon pass) to Brig for onward travel to Lucerne, Lausanne and Geneva.

Bicycle The 65km trip over the 1933m Simplon pass to Brig is memorable, although the road can be busy since there is no car tunnel. Lago Maggiore is only 35km away to the south via the Val d'Ossola.

Eastern Lakes	
Duration	3 days
Distance	209.3km
Difficulty	easy–moderate
Start	Bergamo
End	Mantua (Mantova)

Lago di Garda is the largest and most frequented of the Italian lot. Its tiny neighbours, Laghi di Endine and d'Iseo, although diminutive in surface area are no less grand in appeal. This ride swims through fabulous rolling hills from the former Venetian outpost of Bergamo through these eastern water sensations and down the Fiume Mincio to its terminus, Mantua, on the edge of the Po flood plain.

PLANNING
When to Ride
Like the more central lakes, the eastern basins enjoy a mild climate. Cycling is most enjoyable from spring to autumn, although August can be a very crowded month (especially on Lago di Garda). The afternoon southerly breezes are felt here too.

Maps & Books
Touring Club Italiano's (1:200,000) Lombardia map includes the full length of this ride. Alternatively, the free Department of Tourism Provincia di Brescia (1:200,000) map only misses the last few kilometres into Mantua (which are on bikepaths and not shown anyway). RegioneLombardia also distributes a 1:50,000 map of Lago d'Iseo e dintorni for a close-up of the smaller lakes, and Comunità del Garda makes a simple map of Lago di Garda.

ACCESS TOWN
Bergamo
Virtually two cities, Bergamo's enclosed hilltop città alta (upper town) is surrounded by a 16th-century circle of walls, beyond which is the città bassa (lower town), the sprawling modern counterpart to this magnificent former outpost of the Venetian empire. Although long dominated by outsiders, Bergamo has retained a strong sense of local identity.

Information The main APT (☎ 035 21 02 04, w www.apt.bergamo.it) is in the lower city at Viale Vittorio Emanuele II 20. An alternate office (☎ 035 24 22 26) in the upper city is just off Piazza Vecchia at Vicolo Aquila Nera 2. Banks are easily found in the lower city in Viale Roma and Viale Papa Giovanni.

There is a bike shop, Effendi & Merelli (☎ 035 24 79 70), on the way out of town at Via Corridoni 9a. The FIAB affiliate in Bergamo is Associazione Rilancio Bicicletta (☎ 035 36 00 53, w www.aribi.it), c/o CSI at Via Rota 22.

Things to See & Do Piazza Vecchia – medieval Bergamo's gracious commons – is hard to miss, with imposing originally 12th-century **Palazzo della Ragione** filling its southern side and, next door, the **Torre del Campanone**. The core of the burg's spiritual life, **Piazza del Duomo**, lies immediately behind. Its modest baroque **duomo** plays second fiddle to neighbouring Romanesque **Chiesa di Santa Maria Maggiore** and its octagonal **baptistry**. The gaudy 15th-century **Capella Colleoni** is an extravagant later addition. Downhill a bit the views are splendid from the 12th-century **Torre Gombito** and 14th-century fortress **La Rocca**.

They are even better from the top of **Monte San Vigilio**, last stop of the funicular from the western Porta di Sant'Alessandro. There are a number of museums in the upper city, but the eastern lower city's **Accademia Carrara**, an art centre dating to 1780, is the most important. Trekkers should take advantage of the numerous **hiking trails** by asking at the ATP for the *Carta dei sentieri della Provincia*.

Places to Stay Several kilometres north of town beyond the *stadio comunale* (municipal stadium) is **Ostello della Gioventù** (*☎/fax 035 36 17 24; Via Galileo Ferraris 1; ⓦ www.ostellodibergamo.it; B&B per person €13.50).*

The few cheapish hotels in the *città bassa* fill up quickly; it's best to call ahead. **Albergo Caironi** (*☎ 035 24 30 83; Via Torretta 6; singles/doubles €20/38),* in the eastern lower city, is very cheap and very basic, as is its restaurant. A good step up is **Albergo Novecento** (*☎ 035 25 52 10; cnr Via Statuto & Via Chiesa; singles/doubles with bathroom €24/32)* just southwest of the *città alta*. Two-star **Albergo San Giorgio** (*☎ 035 21 20 43; ⓦ www.sangiorgioalbergo.it; Via San Giorgio 10; singles/doubles €28/42)* is the nicest of the budget lot, west of the station along the tracks.

The only affordable option in the upper city is **Agnello d'Oro** (*☎ 035 24 98 83; Via Gombito 22; singles/doubles with bathroom €52/92),* southeast of Piazza Vecchia, and it has a fine restaurant.

Places to Eat There are some **markets** along Via Borgo Palazzo. In the *città bassa*, for a good, cheap bite, **Bay Bay Self-Service** *(Via Tiraboschi 73)* is hard to beat. Closer to Viale Papa Giovanni XXIII on the same street is **Nessi**, one of a chain of bakeries with popular takeaway pizza. **Gennaro e Pia** *(Via Borgo Palazzo 41)* has pizzas from €4.20. **Öl Giopì e la Margì** *(Via Borgo Palazzo 27; dinner €26)* is expensive, but the waiters wear traditional costumes.

The *città alta* is more expensive, although affordable pizza is available at the local **Nessi** *(Via Gombito 34)* and **Trattoria da Franco** *(Via Colleoni 8; pizzas from €4.20).* For a pricier meal of local specialities, try **Trattoria del Teatro** *(Piazza Mascheroni 3).*

Getting There & Away The bus station, across from the train station on Piazzale Marconi, is served by SAB with regular lines to/from the lakes and surrounding mountains. Other companies run to/from nearby big cities (Milan, Brescia, Cremona, Como and Piacenza).

Three rail lines stop in Bergamo: a direct service from Milan (50 minutes); a thrice-daily local from Cremona (1¼ hours) via Treviglio; and the busy route between Brescia (one hour) and Lecco (35 minutes).

Bicycle The *città bassa* is only 50km by busy SS525 from central Milan, although the Navigli Milanesi ride from Milan passes to within 25km at Trezzo sull'Adda via much smaller roads. Treviglio is 20km due south on SS42. Lecco, on Lago di Como, is 35km northwest by way of SS639 and SS342.

THE RIDE
Day 1: Bergamo to Iseo
4½–9 hours, 80.5km

Today's a valley and lake kind of day with two intermediate passes. From Bergamo, the route eases into the shallow lower Valle Seriana and cranks 430m up the Valle del Lujo to the Colle Gallo and then drops to the little lake gems of Laghi di Endine and d'Iseo for roars along their shores.

The Valle Seriana northwest of Bergamo is noted for its easy accessibility, one of the best for ongoing travel into the Orobian Alps. In the tight winding streets of Alzano, at the foot of the valley, are some fine medieval houses, the 16th-century **Basilica di San Martino** and Gothic **Santuario della Beata Vergine Adolorata**.

After the turn east to Casazza (15.2km), the route begins to climb more steeply. **Colle Gallo** (763m) is a gruelling 10.7km up beyond the top of an immediately visible ridge. Take a break in Abbazia for the important, intact, 12th-century, Benedictine **monastery**. Make the obligatory pilgrimage stop at the pass-top **Santuario del Colle Gallo** and its **Madonne dei ciclisti**.

The 7km plummet to the Val Cavallina and the shores of **Lago di Endine** takes only a few minutes and tears through the **spa town** of Gaverina Terme. Slip to the far side of the lake on the quieter road through Monasterolo (37.4km) for its view and

Eastern Lakes

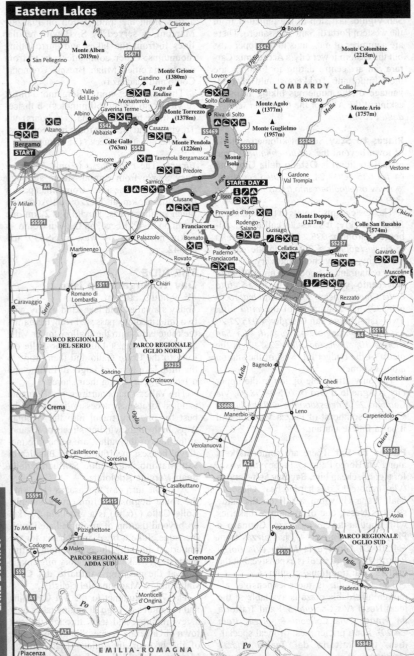

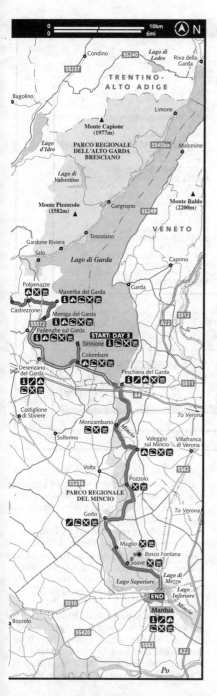

castle with 13th-century origins. Lago di Endine was Italy's first lake to forbid motorised transport on its waters. By curious contrast, **Lago d'Iseo** was the first lake in Italy to see the use of steamboats (1841).

Monolithic Monte Agolo on Lago d'Iseo is an overwhelming spectacle for anyone heading down from the top of the pass at Solto Collina (430m, 47.8km). It dominates the view until the sweet, discrete, lakeshore road bends through Tavernola Bergamasca and then to the west. Once-fortified medieval **Sarnico** (70.8km) squats at the narrow end of the lake, from which it is only 10km to the basin namesake city of Iseo. If time permits, Clusane (5km before Iseo) has an interesting 15th-century **Castello del Carmagnola**.

Iseo

After its heyday as an important command post and commercial centre at the outer reaches of the Venetian empire, Iseo slumbered for years as little more than a fishing town. Nowadays, it's a peaceful holiday resort with antique shops where fish stalls used to be.

Information The IAT (☎ 030 98 02 09, w www.lagodiseo.org) overlooks the lake at Lungolago Marconi 2. Banks can be found next door on Porto Rosa. There is a small, bike-repair storefront at Via Mirolte 90.

Things to See & Do Iseo boasts the 12th-century Romanesque **Pieve di Sant'Andrea**, the originally 11th-century **Castello degli Oldofredi**, the medieval **Palazzo dell'Arsenale** and a statue to Garibaldi, supposedly Italy's first (1883). A discerning stroller will pick out a number of other beautiful old **palazzi** in the succession of little piazzas. Otherwise, the best thing to do is get a boat to Europe's biggest lake island, **Monte Isola**, notable for its netmaking, boat yards and huts of fish drying in the sun.

Places to Stay & Eat There are 15 **camping grounds** within easy reach of downtown Iseo. The closest are just east of town, like **Punta d'Oro** (☎/fax 030 98 00 84; Via Antonioli 51/53; per person/site €4.10/8.30).

Iseo has three affordable lodges, all with wallet-friendly restaurants. Self-caterers will find a variety of **markets** in the old

ITALIAN ALPS & LAKE DISTRICT

Eastern Lakes – Day 1

Cue

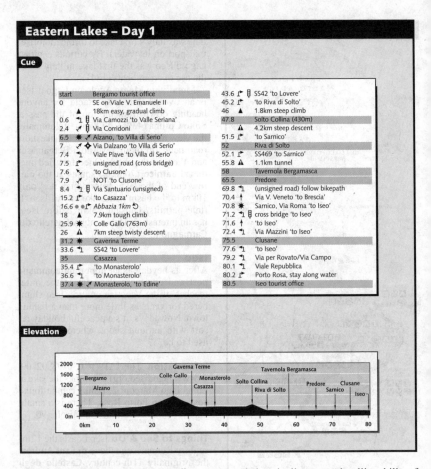

km		Direction
start		Bergamo tourist office
0		SE on Viale V. Emanuele II
	▲	18km easy, gradual climb
0.6		Via Camozzi 'to Valle Seriana'
2.4		Via Corridoni
6.5		Alzano, 'to Villa di Serio'
7		Via Dalzano 'to Villa di Serio'
7.4		Viale Piave 'to Villa di Serio'
7.5		unsigned road (cross bridge)
7.6		'to Clusone'
7.9		NOT 'to Clusone'
8.4		Via Santuario (unsigned)
15.2		'to Casazza'
16.6		Abbazia 1km
18	▲	7.9km tough climb
25.9		Colle Gallo (763m)
26	▲	7km steep twisty descent
31.2		Gaverina Terme
33.6		SS42 'to Lovere'
35		Casazza
35.4		'to Monasterolo'
36.6		'to Monasterolo'
37.4		Monasterolo, 'to Edine'
43.6		SS42 'to Lovere'
45.2		'to Riva di Solto'
46	▲	1.8km steep climb
47.8		Solto Collina (430m)
	▲	4.2km steep descent
51.5		'to Sarnico'
52		Riva di Solto
52.1		SS469 'to Sarnico'
55.8	▲	1.1km tunnel
58		Tavernola Bergamasca
65.5		Predore
69.8		(unsigned road) follow bikepath
70.4		Via V. Veneto 'to Brescia'
70.8		Sarnico, Via Roma 'to Iseo'
71.2		cross bridge 'to Iseo'
71.6		'to Iseo'
72.4		Via Mazzini 'to Iseo'
75.5		Clusane
77.6		'to Iseo'
79.2		Via per Rovato/Via Campo
80.1		Viale Repubblica
80.2		Porto Rosa, stay along water
80.5		Iseo tourist office

Elevation

town around Piazza Garibaldi. **Albergo Rosa** (☎ 030 98 00 53; Via Roma 47) and **Albergo Arianna** (☎ 030 982 20 82; Via Roma 78) both have singles/doubles from €39/47 and are a few streets back from the shore. Reflecting in the water's ripple, right next to the tourist office, is **Albergo Milano** (☎ 030 98 04 49; Lungolago Marconi 4; singles/doubles from €39/55). There are more similarly priced hotels in Clusane, 5km west of Iseo.

Day 2: Iseo to Sirmione
4–7 hours, 68.7km

Today's route goes from lake to lake. After a quick morning train through Franciacorta or a long alternative route through it to Brescia, roads climb one pass to the vine-yarded and olive-groved rolling hills of Valtenesi on the western shores of Lago di Garda. A short trip around the southern end culminates in Sirmione, a town at the tip of a narrow isthmus.

First morning responsibility: Get to Brescia the quick way. The Ferrovia Nord Milano Esercizio (w www.ferrovienord.it) station is at the end of Via XX Settembre. More than 15 trains come through daily covering the distance to Brescia in 20 minutes (€2.25).

Brescia is replete with attractions. Its historic centre is dominated by **Colle Cidneo** and its **castle** and 13th-century **Torre Mirabella**, also host to two **museums**. At the foot of the castle are the Roman ruins of **Capitolium** (a temple) and a **Roman theatre**

The city museum is housed in **Monasterio di Santa Giulia**. Heading west, on Brescia's central square, **Piazza Paolo VI**, the 11th-century Romanesque **Duomo Vecchio** is the headliner, although the Renaissance Duomo Nuovo dwarfs it. To the northwest is Piazza Loggia with its 16th-century **loggia** and **Torre dell'Orologio**. Modern, Fascist-styled **Piazza della Vittoria** is one of the best examples of the period's monumentalism.

From Brescia's Piazza della Loggia, Colle San Eusebio is 20.7km away and 425m up the Garza Valley. Beyond it are the varied terrain and quiet back roads of the world-famous Lago di Garda area of **Valtenesi**. Ruins of walls, castles and villas pepper the cultivated slopes of this region loved by Goethe, Byron, Lawrence, Ibsen, Rilke,

Gide, Pound and many others. The route takes in the villages of Polpenazze with its medieval **castle** and 16th-century **parish church**; Manerba del Garda dominated by its **Rocca** and incredible panoramic view, and host to the **Valtenesi Archaeological History Museum**; Moniga del Garda and a fabulous **castle**; and Padenghe sul Garda, with its **castle** and **palazzo**.

From Moniga, the main road is the only road around the bottom of the lake. It passes through the major hub of Desenzano del Garda before tripping north up a tapered cape to Sirmione. Desenzano has ruins of a 4th-century **Roman villa** (with excellent mosaics), a 14th- to 15th-century **castle**, and the 16th-century **Chiesa di Santa Maria Maddalena**.

Eastern Lakes – Day 2

Cue

start	Iseo tourist office		22.5		Colle San Eusabio (574m)
0km	SW through Porto Rosa			⌐ ▲	3.3km steep descent 'to Gavardo'
0.3	↰ Viale Reppublica/Via XX Settembre		31.4	↙ ✦	(1st exit) 'to Gavardo'
0.5	■■↱ alt route: Franciacort		32.3	↰	unsigned main road (cross river)
0.7	Iseo FNME train station		32.4		Gavardo
take train to Brescia			32.5	↰ ▯	Via Fossa/Viale Antonio Ferretti
0.7	Brescia train station		32.7	↰	Largo Giacobinelli 'to Muscoline'
	↘ Viale Stazione		32.8	↙ ✦	(1st exit) unsigned road
0.9	↙ ✦ (2nd exit) Corso Martiri d. Liberta		33.8	↙ ✦	3km moderate climb 'to Muscoline'
1.7	↱ Piazza della Loggia		36.1	↰	Muscoline, 'to Lago di Garda'
	alt route rejoins		38.6	↰	'to Manerba'
1.8	✳ Brescia tourist office		40.9	↰ ▲	4km steep descent 'to Manerba'
	NW across Piazza d. Loggia		42.5	↙ ✦	Via S. Antonio 'to Manerba'
1.9	↱ Via San Faustino bikepath		44.5	↘	'to Manerba' NOT Soiano
2.6	↑ ▯ Via Montesuello		46.7	● ● ↑	Manerba di Garda 3km ↻
2.8	↱ Via Apollonio 'to Lago di Garda'		46.7	↱	Via M. d. Liberta 'to Moniga'
3.2	↰ ▯ Via Galileo Galilei (unsigned)		47	↰	Via IV Novembre 'to Moniga'
3.8	↘ ▯ Via San Rocchino (against traffic)		47.8	↱ ▯	Via S. Martino 'to Moniga'
4	↙ ▲ 9.8km gradual climb 'to Ospedale'		50.3	✳	Moniga del Garda
4.3	↘ Via San Rocchino		51.3	↰ ▯	SS572 'to Desenzano'
4.4	↙ Via Schivardi bikepath		54	● ● ↱	Padenghe sul Garda 1km ↻
4.8	↘ bikepath 'to Val Trompia'		59.8	✳	Desenzano del Garda
6.7	↱ 'to Val Trompia'		65.4	↙ ✦	bikepath 'to Sirmione'
7.2	↱ 'to Nave'		65.9	↰	Via Colombare 'to Sirmione'
12.3	▲ Nave, 10.2km moderate climb		68.7		Sirmione tourist office

Elevation

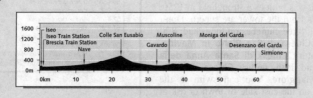

ITALIAN ALPS & LAKE DISTRICT

Alternative Route: Franciacorta

2–3½ hours, 35.6km

Franciacorta, the Tuscany of the north, is a quality wine region of rolling hills. The name Franciacorta comes from 'corti franche' (literally 'short taxes'), a hint of the area's tax-free status dating back to the Venetian Republic when privileged religious orders tilled the land. The religious centres they left behind, as well as later villas and castles, dot the landscape.

The alternate route swings through Provaglio d'Iseo (Romanesque **Monasterio di S. Pietro**, **Riserva Naturale Torbiere**), Bornato, Paderno Franciacorta (14th-century **castle**), Rodengo-Saiano (15th-century **Abbazia di San Nicola**), Gussago (10th-century **Pieve di Santa Maria**) and Cellatica on the way to Brescia.

For more local ride information (there are many signed bikepaths), contact the Brescia FIAB affiliate, Amici della Bici (☎ 030 375 60 23, W www.youthpoint.it/amicidellabici), at Via Maggi 9.

Sirmione

Catullus, the Roman poet, celebrated Sirmione in his writing and his name is still invoked in connection with the place. It's a popular bathing spot and often jammed tight with tourists. In spite of this, it retains a comparatively relaxed atmosphere.

Information Sirmione's IAT (☎ 030 91 61 14, W www.bresciaholiday.com) is at Viale Marconi 2 near the bridge to the islet at the tip of the peninsula. Banks are easy to spot along the peninsula. The closest bike shops are in Desenzano del Garda. Try Girelli (☎ 030 911 97 97) at Via Annunciata 10.

Things to See & Do The extensive ruins of the Roman villa and baths known as the **Grotte di Catullo** occupy a prime position on the northern, quieter end of Sirmione island. **Castello Scaligero**, also known as Rocca Scaligeri, was built as a stronghold in 1250; the views from the tower are superb. Don't forget the three churches on the island: 8th-century **Chiesa di San Pietro in Mavino**, 14th-century **Chiesa di Santa Anna della Rocco** and 15th-century **Chiesa di Santa Maria Maggiore**. You can swim in the **beaches** on the east side of town or ask at tourist information about water sports.

Places to Stay & Eat It's hard to believe that there are 92 hotels crammed in here. Still, always book ahead, especially at the height of summer and during long weekends. There are five camping grounds near town. **Campeggio Sirmione** (☎ 030 990 46 65; W www.camping-sirmione.com; Colombare; per tent/person €8/9), near the Colombare tourist office, is the largest.

Albergo Grifone (☎ 030 91 60 14; Via Bacchio; singles/doubles with bathroom €34/55) and **Albergo Progresso** (☎ 030 91 61 08; Corso Vittorio Emanuele 18; singles/doubles €31/47) are the cheapest Sirmione has to offer. **Albergo degli Oleandri** (☎ 030 990 57 80; W www.hoteldeglioleandri.it; Via Dante 31; singles/doubles €60/80) is near the castle in a shady, pleasant location.

Eastern Lakes - Day 3

Cue

start	Sirmione tourist office
0km	go S on Viale Marconi
2.8	↘ 'to Verona'
3.5	⬏ ⬍ SS11 'to Verona'
10	⬏ 'to Peschiera centro'
10.8	↙ 'to edificio regolatore'
10.8	↘ Peschiera del Garda 1km↻
11.1	↑ curve to right along canal
11.5	⬏ Ciclopedonale Mantova-Peschiera
20.3	Monzambano
20.7	⚠ 0.7km gravel bikepath
22.9	⚠ 1.2km gravel bikepath
24.1	⬏ unsigned road (paved bikepath)
25.2	↑ ✳ cross bridge (ignore bikepath)
25.8	⬏ uphill 'to Valeggio centro'
25.8	● ● ⬑ Valeggio borghetto 0.5km↻
26.1	⬑ 'to centro'
26.1	✳ ⬑ Valeggio, (50m) 'to Pozzolo'
32.1	⬑ Pozzolo, 'to Volta'
32.7	⬏ unsigned bikepath (before canal)
36	⬑ unsigned road (cross canal)
40	↑ unsigned main road (at 't')
42.6	⬑ SS236 'to Goito'
42.7	⬏ Strada Maglio ciclopedonale
42.7	● ● ↑ Goito 1km↻
47.3	Maglio
47.4	⬑ bikepath before Rist. al Naviglio
50.7	Soave
50.7	● ● ⬑ Bosco Fontana 5km↻
56.2	⬑ ⚠ cross wooden bridge
56.4	⚠ 0.7km gravel bikepath
57.2	⬑ through bikepath gates
57.4	end of ciclopedonale
57.8	⬑ SS62 'to Mantova'
59.1	↖ cross Via Mulini bridge
59.4	↘ Porta Mulina/Via Porto
59.6	⬏ P.za d'Arco/Via Fernelli/Via Verdi
60.1	Mantua tourist office

Albergo Villa Paradiso (☎ *030 91 61 49;* W *www.villaparadiso.3000.it; Via Arici 7; singles/doubles €34/59)* is right near the San Pietro church on the islet.

Ristorante al Pescatore *(Via Piana 20)* is one of the better, reasonably priced restaurants. Otherwise there are loads of takeaway food outlets around Piazza Carducci. This is also where the bulk of the cafés and *gelato* joints are.

Day 3: Sirmione to Mantua
4–6 hours, 60.1km

With the exception of the first 11km running along the southern fringe of Lago di Garda, today's route is entirely within Parco Regionale del Mincio, a strip of green bordering the southern edge of the river to Mantua. The road takes in a few low hills when skirting the edge of the western morainic *colline* (hills), but is essentially level.

On the road south of Sirmione, the first and last lakeside community is Peschiera del Garda (10.8km), straddling the mouth of the Fiume Mincio. Impressive ramparts dating back to the years of Venetian and Austrian domination girdle Peschiera.

In Peschiera, the route hits the beginning of the Ciclopedonale Mantova–Peschiera, a bikepath that supposedly runs the full distance between the cities. It may do just that, but its signs don't help, getting impossibly

confused with other bikepaths posted by the Associazione Turistica Colline Moreniche del Garda. Your route steers a course close to the Fiume Mincio following the *ciclopedonale* (bikepath) when fortuitously appropriate, which it is for the 13.7 riparian kilometres to Valeggio sul Mincio.

Valeggio (26.1km) is on the far side of the Mincio, across the incredible medieval **Ponte Visconteo**. The divine riverside *borghetto* visible off to the right from the bridge should be given a quick tour. Up the hill, Valeggio is topped by the **Castello Scaligeno** and a typical medieval centre. A short distance to the north, the area's crowning attraction is the 100-acre **Parco Giardino Sigurtà** installed on the grounds of the 17th-century Villa Maffei and once the headquarters of Napoleon III.

From there, a fine spin through open countryside laced with canals ends in the little town of Goito (site of medieval **tower**, 42.7km) where it rejoins the long-lost *ciclopedonale* for the final pedal into Mantua. An interesting side trip can be made from Soave (50.7km) to the protected deciduous **Bosco Fontana** complete with a 15th-century **castle**.

Mantua
See the Po River Basin – Lungo Po Argine ride on p167.

Dolomites

Unquestionably one of the most dramatic mountain ranges on earth, the Dolomites (Dolomiti) thrust their jagged spires skyward over an area of 7000 sq km in Italy's northeastern corner. While most of the rides in this chapter are extremely strenuous, excellent bikepaths along the Adige and Rienza Rivers offer flatter, scenic alternatives suitable for novices and children. This region is appealing not only for its stunning geography but also for its cultural diversity. Three languages (Italian, German and Ladin) are officially recognised in the Dolomites, and local culture is shaped by a pleasing combination of Italian, Germanic and traditional Alpine influences.

HISTORY

As glaciers receded in the Mesolithic era, hunters entered the Dolomites in pursuit of wild game. 'Living' proof of these early human migrations came to light in 1992 with the discovery of Otzi, a 5300-year-old Alpine man perfectly preserved in ice (see the boxed text 'The Ice Man Cometh', p226). A more permanent farming and herding culture had evolved by the Bronze Age, as evidenced by village sites discovered in Val di Fassa and Val Gardena.

In 15 BC, the Dolomites were conquered by the Romans and incorporated into the Alpine province of Rhaetia. The Rhaetians' traditional language mixed with Vulgar Latin, spurring the evolution of the Ladin language, which is still spoken widely in the Dolomites today. After Rome fell, the usual succession of Lombards and Holy Roman Emperors swept through the area. In 1027, political jurisdiction over the southern Adige valley and the Brenta Dolomites passed to the prince-bishops of Trent, while further north the bishops of Brixen and the counts of Tyrol grappled for control of Bolzano and the eastern Dolomites.

The 19th century brought brief periods of Napoleonic and Hapsburg rule, followed by WWI, which transformed the Dolomites into a battle zone. Austrians and Italians staked out positions in the high country and endured terrible conditions, as commemorated in numerous museums and cemeteries throughout the region. At war's end in 1918,

In Brief

Highlights
- **eight 2000m passes** (Sella, Pordoi, Gardena, Valparola, Falzarego, Tre Cime, Giau and Fedaia)
- beautiful new **bikepaths** along the Adige, Noce, Sarca, and Rienza Rivers
- the **Strada del Vino** wine route
- **Otzi**, the 5300-year-old iceman in Bolzano's archaeological museum

Terrain
Extremely steep and mountainous, except along major river valleys.

Special Events
- **Gran Fésta da d'Jstà** or Ladin Festival (August/September), Canazei
- **Val Gardena Music Festival** (July/August)
- **Val Gardena Folklore Festival** (August)

Cycling Events
- **Maratona dles Dolomites** (June), Dolomites
- **Dolomiti Superbike MTB Race** (July), Val Pusteria
- **Giro delle Dolomiti** (July/August), six days throughout Trentino-Alto Adige

Food & Drink Specialties
- *casunziei* (beet ravioli with poppy seeds), Cortina d'Ampezzo
- *sones* (apple fritters), Canazei
- *crafuncins da ula verda* (half moon-shaped spinach ravioli), Val Gardena
- *strangolapreti* (spinach gnocchi), Trentino

Italy won control of South Tyrol. Mussolini, in the Fascist spirit of nationalism, imposed new Italian names on all towns and geographical features, and divided the Dolomites into three separate political regions, attempting to dilute German and Ladin cultural influence. Almost a century later, however, the Dolomites remain proudly tricultural.

NATURAL HISTORY

The Dolomites derive their name from 18th century French geologist Déodat de

Dolomieu. While studying specimens gathered in the Adige Valley, Dolomieu discovered that, unlike normal limestone (calcium carbonate), the local rocks contained magnesium as well. This double carbonate of magnesium and limestone, which occurs elsewhere in the world as well, is today known universally as dolomite.

The Dolomites' unique landscape is the result of uneven weathering of two different kinds of rock. Millions of years ago, this part of northeastern Italy was covered by a warm sea crisscrossed with coral reefs and flanked by two large volcanoes. Over the millennia, shells from sea creatures were compacted into dolomite, while volcanic eruptions created vast areas of cooled magma. Both rock types were exposed to the elements when tectonic pressure caused dramatic uplifting of this ancient sea floor. The durable dolomite remained relatively intact, while the much softer volcanic rock eroded easily, resulting in the Dolomites' characteristic pattern of low-lying valleys and prominent spires.

The mountains' undersea origins are evident in the large number of marine fossils discovered in the area. A particularly good collection can be seen at the Regoles museum in Cortina d'Ampezzo.

CLIMATE

The Dolomites' climate is characterised by warm, wet summers and cold, drier winters. Temperatures and rainfall are highest in July and August, and lowest in January. In the mountains the best cycling weather occurs between June and September. Warmer temperatures in the Adige Valley around Bolzano and Trent permit comfortable cycling as early as April and as late as October. Average high temperatures in July and August are 30°C in Bolzano and 22°C in Val Pusteria.

INFORMATION
Maps & Books

Touring Club Italia's 1:200,000 *Trentino-Alto Adige* map provides detailed coverage of this entire region.

An excellent map of Trentino bikepaths, *Cycle Paths of Trentino*, is available free at tourist bureaus throughout the region. The map comes in English, German and Italian versions, and includes several bikepaths not covered in this book.

The spiral-bound *Raderlebnis Dolomiten* and the smaller *In Bicicletta Lungo l'Adige* cover the eastern Dolomites and the Adige Valley respectively. Published in German and Italian only, they're available at local tourist offices or direct from the publisher Schubert & Franzke (☎ +43 1 2742 78 5010, ⓦ www.map2web.cc/schubert-franzke).

Place Names

In the eastern Dolomites, place names reflect the region's trilingual heritage. In the northern valleys closest to the Austrian border (Val Gardena and Val Badia), road signs

The Ladin Language

With roots as old as Italian itself, Ladin is a Romance language spoken by roughly 40,000 people in the Dolomites. Ladin's ancestor language was once spoken throughout the Alps and evolved from the mixing of Vulgar Latin with the traditional mountain language known as Rhaetian. Rhaeto-Romanic languages other than Ladin have survived elsewhere in remote pockets of the Alps, such as southeast Switzerland's Graubunden canton, where the local variant is known as Romansh and has long been recognised as one of Switzerland's four official languages.

Geographic isolation, while ensuring the survival of Rhaeto-Romanic languages as a whole, has also resulted in the evolution of distinct dialects from valley to valley. For example, in Val Gardena, where the local dialect is called *gheirdeina*, the word for 'shoes' is *ciauzei*, while the *badiot* (Val Badia) and *fascian* (Val di Fassa) equivalents are *cialzá* and *ciuzé*.

Geographic orientation and politics have also played a role in the different dialects' development. Valleys such as Gardena and Badia, which open towards South Tyrol, have long experienced significant Germanic influence, whereas Val di Fassa and Ampezzo, which open towards Trento and the Veneto, have been more strongly affected by Italian. Ladin-speaking residents of Val Gardena and Badia, as part of the autonomous province of Bolzano, have had greater success than the others in achieving official recognition for their language, and Ladin is a now a required subject in the schools in both valleys.

can be cumbersomely complex, with Ladin, Italian and German town names all jockeying for position. South of the Alto Adige border (Val di Fassa), where German is less commonly spoken, bilingual naming conventions remain in effect, with all localities retaining a traditional Ladin name plus a modern Italian equivalent. The Ampezzo valley is the most Italianised part of the Dolomites, with signs in Italian only, although even here many people still speak Ladin at home.

In this chapter the Italian place name is always listed first, followed by the German and/or Ladin equivalent in parentheses.

GATEWAY CITIES
Bolzano
The appealing medieval city of Bolzano (Bozen) sits at the gateway to the Alps near the confluence of the Adige (Etsch), Tálvera (Talfer) and Isarco (Eisack) Rivers. The capital of Alto Adige (Südtirol), it is a thoroughly bilingual (though predominantly German-speaking) city with a relaxed feel.

Life revolves around Piazza Walther (Waltherplatz), a big square buzzing with cafés and graced with a statue of medieval lyric poet Walther von der Vogelweide.

For a city of its size, Bolzano is surprisingly cyclist-friendly, thanks to its network of bike paths following the local rivers.

Information The visitor centre (☎ 0471 30 70 00, w www.bolzano-bozen.it) is centrally located at Piazza Walther 8.

Credito Italiano (Piazza Walther 5) is one of several downtown banks that contain Bancomats.

Bolzano's best bike shop, featuring a huge selection, is Velo Sportler (☎ 0471 97 77 19) at Via Grappoli 56, one block from Waltherplatz. It is closed on Sunday.

Things to See & Do The South Tyrol Museum of Archaeology (☎ 0471 98 20 98; w www.iceman.it), Strada del Museo 43, is deservedly Bolzano's greatest tourist attraction. Most visitors make a beeline to the second floor to see Otzi (see the boxed text 'The Ice Man Cometh'), but the rest of the museum is equally fascinating, with exhibits covering everything from the Stone Age to the early medieval period. English headsets are available at the front desk.

Castel Roncolo (Schloss Runkelstein; ☎ 0471 32 98 08; w www.comune.bolzano .it/roncolo/ie), perched on a precipice above the Tálvera River, is a 13th-century castle once occupied by Tyrolean dukes and the Hapsburg Maximilian I. Fully restored and reopened to the public in 2001, its unparalleled cycle of secular medieval frescoes depicts jousting scenes, a wild boar hunt and legends from King Arthur. Don't miss the opportunity to hoist the real medieval-style 4m lance in Sala del Torneo. Access for cyclists couldn't be easier, a 2km bikepath leads north along the Tálvera to the castle's doorstep.

Churches worth visiting include the Gothic **duomo** (cathedral) and the **Chiesa dei Domenicani**, both a stone's throw from Piazza Walther, and the **Chiesa dei Francescani**, with its beautiful cloisters, just north of the centre.

The Ice Man Cometh

It's impossible to resist the magnetic draw of Otzi, the 5300-year-old man found perfectly preserved in ice west of Bolzano in 1992. People flock to the second floor of Bolzano's archaeological museum, waiting reverently in line for a chance to gaze through the tiny opening of Otzi's deep-freeze unit and make contact with their recognisably human Copper Age ancestor. As fascinating as Otzi himself are his clothing and tools, displayed on the same floor in both original and reconstructed versions. Otzi's original leggings, grass cape, soft goatskin underwear, bear fur hat, and shoes stuffed with hay are remarkable; and his goatskin coat with stripes in alternating colours is downright fashionable. Don't miss the contents of the pouch Otzi carried around his waist, on view in the adjacent room; the iceman kept glowing embers, wrapped carefully in maple leaves and enclosed in a birch container, as fire starters, plus funguses for medicinal use. Also on display is a knapsack frame made from bent hazelnut wood, and a hatchet complete with handle, blade and binding.

Otzi's status as a popular cult hero was enhanced in September 2001 when Bolzano's Nuovo Teatro Comunale launched a musical in his honour, Frozen Fritz.

Places to Stay A few kilometres north-west of the centre is **Camping Moosbauer** (☎ 0471 91 84 92; W www.moosbauer.com; Via S. Maurizio 83; basic/large sites €10/ 14.50). **Albergo Croce Bianca** (☎ 0471 97 75 52; Piazza del Grano 3; singles/doubles with breakfast €28/55) is Bolzano's most central and affordable hotel, family-run with bike storage around the back. **Albergo Gatto Nero** (☎ 0471 97 54 17; S. Maddalena 2; singles/doubles €25/40) is another family-run, very Germanic place east of the centre with a pleasant patio restaurant. **Kolpinghaus** (☎ 0471 30 84 00; W www.kolping.it/bz; Via Ospedale 3; singles/doubles with breakfast €46/70, half pension €56/90, full pension €65/108) is a third budget option west of Piazza Walther.

Hotel Feichter (☎ 0471 97 87 68; e hotel .feichter@dnet.it; Via Grappoli 15; singles/ doubles with breakfast €50/75, half pension €60/100) is an unexceptional but central two-star. **Albergo Città** (☎ 0471 97 52 21; e hotel.feichter@dnet.it; Piazza Walther 21; singles/doubles with breakfast €90/125) is an attractive four-star right on Piazza Walther.

Places to Eat The large **De Spar** (Via della Rena 5; closed Sun) supermarket is just off Piazza Walther. Bolzano's famous and bustling **fruit and vegetable market** (closed Sun) lines the streets around Piazza delle Erbe. **Caffè Città** (Piazza Walther 21; meals €4.50-7, salads €3.50-6; open daily) features good krapfen (the homemade Germanic equivalent of donuts) with coffee in the morning and gnocchetti di spinaci (spinach gnocchi) at lunch. **Ristorante Cavallino Bianco** (Via Bottai 6; meals €4-13; open Sat lunch, closed Sat evening & Sun) is a German-style beer hall with hearty Tirolese food. Try the Terlanerweinsuppe (wine soup from the town of Terlan) and Schlutzkrapfen (half moon-shaped spinach ravioli). **Pizzeria La Torcia** (Via Conciapelli 25; pizzas €4-6; closed Sun) is a popular spot for wood-fired pizza. **Nussbaumer** (Via Bottai 11; meals €5; closed Sat) has outdoor tables and a mixed German-Italian menu, including grilled vegetables.

Getting There & Away Airport Bolzano Dolomiti (☎ 0471 25 16 81), 7km south of town in San Giacomo (St Jakob), is served

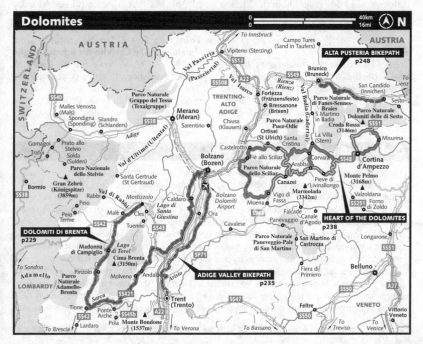

by Austrian Airlines and Lufthansa, with daily nonstops to Frankfurt (€275 return, 1½ hours,) and Rome (€225 return, 1½ hours). To reach the airport from downtown Bolzano, follow the Tálvera/Isarco bikepath south (see Adige Valley Bikepath ride), cross the Isarco River on Ponte Resia, continue straight on Via Volta, turn right on Via Buozzi, turn left on Via Einstein, and follow airport signs the rest of the way.

Servizio Autotrasporti Dolomiti, better known as SAD (☎ 800 84 60 47), Via Perathoner 4, operates an excellent network of bus routes throughout the Dolomites, allowing access to many high altitude towns not reachable by train. Bikes travel under the bus for €1 extra, regardless of trip length.

Bolzano's train station is at Piazza Stazione, one block southeast of the Piazza Walther visitor centre. The north/south service to/from Trent, Verona, Bologna, and Austria is especially good, with many daily trains. Shorter side routes to Merano and San Candido also offer frequent services. One-way fares from Bolzano include Trent €2.89 (45 minutes), Merano €3.25 (one hour), San Candido €8.83 (two hours), Bologna €12.34 (four hours), Milano €13.22 (four hours) and Venice €10.12 (four hours).

Trent

Trent (Trento) is a pleasant city on the banks of the Adige. Unaesthetic urban sprawl has greatly expanded its borders, but the historical core remains largely intact. Old palaces with painted facades fan out from central Piazza Duomo.

Already an important city in Roman times (known as Tridentum), Trent rose to prominence under a series of powerful prince-bishops who ruled it from 1027 till the time of Napoleon. Trent's biggest claim to historical fame was the Council of Trent, which convened here between 1545 and 1563, attempting to counteract the 'heresies' of the Protestant Reformation.

Information The visitor centre (☎ 0461 98 38 80, w www.apt.trento.it) is at Via Manci 2 and has excellent English-language resources, including the indispensable *Cycle Paths of Trentino* map. It's open from 9am to 7pm daily.

Convenient Bancomats include Banca Nazionale del Lavoro in the train station and Cassa Rurale di Trento, Via Belenzani 2, across from the visitor centre.

Trent's best-stocked bike shop is the chain store Sportler (☎ 0461 98 12 90), Via Mantova 12 (closed Monday morning and Sunday). Two good independent shops are Moser Cicli (☎ 0461 23 03 27), Via Calepina 37/43 (closed Monday morning and Sunday), and Andreis Cicli (☎ 0461 98 51 36), Via Prepositura 8 (closed Monday morning, Saturday afternoon and Sunday).

Things to See & Do No visitor to Trent should miss the **Castello del Buonconsiglio** (*☎ 0461 23 37 70; Via Bernardo Clesio 5*), former residence of Trent's prince-bishops. The castle, begun in the early 1200s and greatly expanded over the centuries, has a loggia with Venetian gothic arches, a porticoed courtyard with friezes of Charlemagne

---

Carbo-loading the Tricultural Way

For starch-loving cyclists, few places in the world are as fun as the Dolomites. Three cultures, all masters of the fine art of creating delectable dough, have come together here. South Tyrolean *caneder li* (dumplings) coexist peacefully on menus with the curiously named Italian spinach gnocchi *strangolapreti* (strangle-priests). Half moon-shaped spinach ravioli, called Schlutzkrapfen in Bolzano and *crafuncins da ula verda* in Val Gardena, are ubiquitously available and equally tasty, no matter where you get them. And then there are the truly exotic Dolomites pastas, like *casunziei alle rape rosse con semi di papavero* (beet ravioli with poppy seeds), a specialty of Cortina d'Ampezzo. Best of all, there seems to be a restaurant at the top of every pass serving the full range of Dolomites delicacies.

Whatever you do, save some room for dessert. Two South Tyrolean favourites are *Kaiserschmarrn* (eggy pancakes with powdered sugar and raisins) and *krapfen* (the homemade Germanic equivalent of donuts). If you're really lucky you might even encounter some *sones* or *fortaes*, sinfully delicious apple fritters and berry-covered, spiral-shaped dough thingies found at local Ladin festivals.

and the Trent bishops, and Torre Aquila's fabulous cycle of 15th century frescoes depicting daily activities for the 12 months of the year (ask for a free guided visit).

Ruins from Roman and medieval Trent can be seen at **Tridentum: Spazio Archeologico Sotterraneo del Sass** (☎ 0461 23 37 70) under Piazza Cesare Battisti.

The **Museo Diocesiano Tridentino e Basilica Paleocristiana** (☎ 0461 23 44 19; Piazza Duomo 18) has an interesting collection of religious art, including woodcarvings, tapestries, and paintings portraying the Council of Trent. Next door, adorned by a green onion dome, is Trent's eclectic **cathedral**, where most of the Council's sessions took place.

Places to Stay The closest camping ground is **Campeggio Moser** (☎ 0461 87 02 48; Via Nazionale 64, Località Nave San Felice; open May-Oct), several kilometres north of town between Lavis and San Michele all'Adige. **Ostello della Gioventù Giovane Europa** (☎ 0461 26 34 84; Via Torre Vanga 9; dorm beds €12, singles/doubles €20/40) is the best deal in town, right near the train station.

Central hotels include **Albergo al Cavallino Bianco** (☎ 0461 23 15 42; Via Cavour 29; singles/doubles without bathroom €25/36, with bathroom €34/48), dingy but cheap; **Hotel Garni Venezia** (☎/fax 0461 23 45 59; Piazza Duomo 45; singles/doubles €34/46, breakfast €5) with a great if noisy location on Trent's main square; and **Aquila d'Oro** (☎/fax 0461 98 62 82; w www.aquiladoro.it; Via Belenzani 76; singles/doubles €50/75), a more upscale establishment just around the corner.

Places to Eat There is a large supermarket, **Eurospesa** (Via Torre Vanga 7), next to the hostel and an outdoor **fruit and vegetable market** (Piazza Vittoria; closed Sun). **Gelatomania** (Via Garibaldi 9) has great ice cream in lots of flavours. **Due Giganti** (Via Simonino 14; all you can eat €5; closed Mon) is a great place to fill up on cafeteria-style pizza, pasta and salad. **Pizzeria alla Grotta** (Vicolo San Marco 6; meals €5, pizza €4-6, salad bar €2.50; closed Sun) has a cheerful atmosphere and is popular with students. **Birreria Pedavena** (Piazza Fiera 13; meals €3-4, pizza €3-5; closed Tues) is a big beer hall whose decor features mounted deer heads. **Cantinota** (☎ 0461 23 85 27; Via San Marco 22/24; meals €6-13; closed Thur) is a fancier place with a piano bar atmosphere. **Chiesa** (☎ 0461 23 87 66; Via San Marco 64; meals around €40; closed Sun) is among Trent's finer restaurants.

Getting There & Away The closest major airport is at Verona, 90km south of Trent.

The city's main FS train station is just north of the historical centre opposite the Piazza Dante park. There are direct trains to Venice, as well as to points north and south on the main Bologna–Innsbruck line. One-way fares from Trent include Venice €7.90 (three hours), Bolzano €2.89 (45 minutes), Bologna €10.12 (three hours) and Milano €11.21 (3½ hours). The private Trento–Malé train line (☎ 0461 23 83 50, w www.fertm.it), on the corner of Via Dogana and Via Romagnosi, just north of the FS station, runs daily trains northwest to points in the Val di Non and Val di Sole, including Mostizzolo, the starting point for the Dolomiti di Brenta ride.

Trent's bus station is on Via Pozzo adjacent to the FS train station. Buses run to mountain communities on both sides of the Adige Valley including Canazei, San Martino di Castrozza, Madonna di Campiglio, Molveno, and Riva di Garda. Timetables are posted at the station.

Dolomiti di Brenta

Duration	3 days
Distance	173.6km
Difficulty	moderate–hard
Start	Mostizzolo
End	Bolzano

This ride is delightful in its own right, but also makes a good warm up for the Heart of the Dolomites challenge. Taking advantage of two of Trentino's nicest bikepaths, it circumnavigates the Dolomites' westernmost peaks, cruising through the lush greenery of the Val di Sole and Val Rendena on Days 1 and 2, then following the flat and scenic Strada del Vino through vineyards on Day 3. The only challenging climb (1682m Passo Campo Carlo Magno) comes on Day 1, with a lesser climb to the beautiful mountain lake at Molveno on Day 2.

PLANNING
When to Ride
June, July and September are good months to ride this route in its entirety.

The Strada del Vino section on Day 3, due to its lower elevation, is also appealing in spring and autumn and can be combined with the Adige Valley Bikepath route to make a loop starting and finishing in Bolzano.

Maps & Books
Two useful resources for this ride are Touring Club Italia's Trentino-Alto Adige map and the free *Cycle Paths of Trentino* map, which shows all the bikepaths covered on the first two days of this Dolomiti di Brenta ride.

ACCESS TOWN
Mostizzolo
Ponte Mostizzolo is a bridge spanning the beautiful limestone canyon of the Noce River at the west end of Lago Santa Giustina, and also marks the eastern terminus of the Val di Sole bikepath. The Mostizzolo train station, just above the bridge on the northern bank of the river, offers no services of any kind. The ride begins at the station due to the easy train access and the proximity of the Val di Sole bikepath.

Getting There & Away Mostizzolo train station is best approached from Trent. Several trains daily run from Trent's Trento-Malé station to Mostizzolo (€3 one way plus €4 for bikes, 1¼ hours). Mostizzolo is

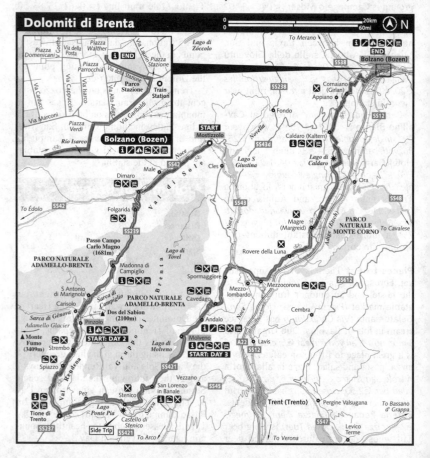

a very small station just beyond the large station at Cles. Let the *capotreno* (conductor) know where you wish to disembark.

Bicycle It's possible to cycle from Trent to Mostizzolo, although some sections of the route have heavy traffic. From Trent, take the Adige Valley bikepath 24km north to Mezzocorona, then follow the Noce River upstream towards Cles and Mostizzolo.

THE RIDE
Day 1: Mostizzolo to Pinzolo
3–5 hours, 47.5km

Today consists of three roughly equidistant segments: an initial easy stretch along a riverside bikepath, a challenging climb, and a thrilling downhill to end the day.

Leaving the train station at Mostizzolo, the route quickly descends to cross the beautiful gorge at Ponte Mostizzolo, merging with the Val di Sole bikepath after 500m. The 15km path, almost completely traffic-free, meanders languidly through forests, fields and apple orchards, following the roaring Noce River and affording beautiful views of the distant Alps to the west.

At Dimaro (15.2km) the route turns south off the bikepath and begins the climb to Passo Campo Carlo Magno, named for Charlemagne who crossed this pass in the late 700s during his campaign against the Lombards. The ascent is steep at first, then more gradual beyond Folgarida, where the Dolomiti di Brenta become visible on the eastern horizon.

From the pass, a 2.3km descent leads to the trendy but rather sterile resort town of Madonna di Campiglio. After working its way through the town centre, the route continues downhill and rejoins the main highway, offering spectacular views of huge rocky crags to the east and the Adamello glacier straight ahead. A winding descent through high meadows leads to S Antonio di Mavignola, where the bikepath resumes, plunging precipitously through a beautiful forest to the Campiglio branch of the Sarca River. The route continues downstream for 3.2km, then leaves the bikepath, navigating a maze of streets to the Pinzolo visitor centre.

Pinzolo
Pinzolo is an unpretentious town in the heart of the Val Rendena, much less glitzy

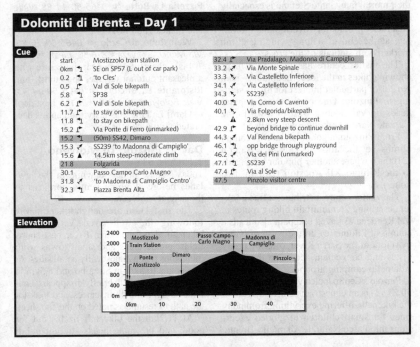

Dolomiti di Brenta – Day 1

Cue

start	Mostizzolo train station	
0km	SE on SP57 (L out of car park)	
0.2	'to Cles'	
0.5	Val di Sole bikepath	
5.8	SP38	
6.2	Val di Sole bikepath	
11.7	to stay on bikepath	
11.8	to stay on bikepath	
15.2	Via Ponte di Ferro (unmarked)	
15.2	(50m) SS42, Dimaro	
15.3	SS239 'to Madonna di Campiglio'	
15.6 ▲	14.5km steep-moderate climb	
21.8	Folgarida	
30.1	Passo Campo Carlo Magno	
31.8	'to Madonna di Campiglio Centro'	
32.3	Piazza Brenta Alta	

32.4	Via Pradalago, Madonna di Campiglio	
33.2	Via Monte Spinale	
33.3	Via Castelletto Inferiore	
34.1	Via Castelletto Inferiore	
34.3	SS239	
40.0	Via Corno di Cavento	
40.1	Via Folgorida/bikepath	
▲	2.8km very steep descent	
42.9	beyond bridge to continue downhill	
44.3	Val Rendena bikepath	
46.1	opp bridge through playground	
46.2	Via dei Pini (unmarked)	
47.1	SS239	
47.4	Via al Sole	
47.5	Pinzolo visitor centre	

Elevation

Mostizzolo Train Station — Ponte Mostizzolo — Dimaro — Passo Campo Carlo Magno — Madonna di Campiglio — Pinzolo

(elevation axis: 0m, 400, 800, 1200, 1600, 2000, 2400; distance axis: 0km, 10, 20, 30, 40)

than its uphill neighbour Madonna di Campiglio. Traditionally a rural agricultural community, Pinzolo now makes its living from tourists visiting the nearby Parco Naturale Adamello-Brenta.

Information The visitor centre (☎ 0465 50 10 07, e apt.pinzolo@trentino.to) is at Piazzale Ciclamino 32, at the south end of town.

There's a Cassa Rurale with Bancomat smack in the middle of town at the corner of Viale Marconi and Via Bolognini.

The closest bike shop is Makalù Sport (☎ 0465 80 45 12), 5km down the valley at Via Regina Elena 4 in Caderzone. The friendly owner sells, rents and repairs bicycles.

Things to See & Do Pinzolo's **San Vigilio** and Carisolo's (2km uphill) **Santo Stefano** are among several Val Rendena churches decorated with 15th- and 16th-century frescoes by the Baschenis, a family of itinerant artists from Bergamo. Both churches include striking depictions of the Danse Macabre, where shovel and scythe-wielding skeletons remind the living of their mortal fate. Santo Stefano is especially worth a visit for its impressive setting, high on a rocky promontory overlooking the valley, at the end of a long winding climb marked with stations of the cross.

The visitor centre has three free maps showing **hikes** in the local mountains – map No 2 is of particular interest for hikers starting in Pinzolo. One of the most popular heads up Val Genova west of town to the Cascate Nardis and other waterfalls.

From Pinzolo, a gondola/chairlift combo climbs to the top of Dos del Sabion (2100m), where another popular hike leads to the Rifugio XII Apostoli (2487m, two hours).

The visitor centre distributes a free booklet describing 26 **mountain biking** routes in Val Rendena. A paved bikepath also leads a couple of kilometres up the western (Genova) fork of the Sarca River, offering pretty vistas and convenient access to the Parco Adamello camping ground.

Pinzolo's **Centro Ippico Valrendena** (☎ 0465 50 23 72) is an equestrian centre adjacent to the bikepath, offering everything from pony rides for small children to guided excursions into Parco Naturale Adamello-Brenta.

Places to Stay & Eat Occupying a lovely spot between the river and the Val Genova bikepath 2km northwest of town at Carisolo, **Camping Parco Adamello** (☎/fax 0465 50 17 93; Località Magnabò; per person €6.50 plus per tent site €5) is surrounded by cornfields and old stone/wood farm buildings.

Hotel Garni Bonsai (☎/fax 0465 50 11 73; w www.hotelbonsai.it; Viale Bolognini 59; per person €36) and **Garni La Palù** (☎/fax 0465 50 36 66; e coptur@dolomitihotels .com; Via Sorano 2; per person €36) are two of Pinzolo's more affordable lodgings. **Albergo Lory** (☎/fax 0465 50 20 08; w www .albergolory.com; Via Sorano 35; per person €39) is another option, tucked off the main road with a nice vegetable garden. **Hotel Bellavista** (☎ 0465 50 11 64; Viale Dolomiti/ SS239, Giustino; per person €54) is a friendly three-star hotel just south of town.

There's a **De Spar** (cnr Via della Pace & Via Bolognini) supermarket just north of the centre. Adjacent to the camping ground in Carisolo is **Ristorante Tipico Magnabò** (☎ 0465 50 38 41), a cosy old wood and stone building with fireplace, specializing in traditional Trentino cuisine. **Ristorante Pizzeria La Botte** (☎ 0465 50 14 88; Viale Dolomiti 12; pizza €5, tiramisu €3) is lively and makes good pizza.

Weinstube al Cardo (☎ 0465 50 25 80; Via Manci 22; pizza €3-6.50, meals €4.50-10) is a cheerful place near the centre with a pleasant outdoor terrace, open until 1am. **Ristorante La Briciola** (☎ 0465 50 14 43; Viale Bolognini 27; meals €5-11), next door to Garni La Palù, has tasty food and is decorated with nice murals.

Day 2: Pinzolo to Molveno
3–5 hours, 53.6km

Today's route lingers a while in the lowlands before climbing gently northeast to the lake at Molveno.

The first 11km are delightful, primarily following the well-paved Val Rendena bikepath along the Sarca River past sports fields, picnic areas and small towns, with mountains rising majestically on all sides. At two points (6.5km in Strembo and 8.5km in Spiazzo) the bikepath briefly disappears; continue straight in both instances, and look for the path to resume as noted on the cue sheet.

At 11.2km the bikepath fizzles out for good, and the route heads straight uphill through a car park to busy SS239. A 7km downhill with fast traffic leads into Tione. (Plans are underway to extend the bikepath downstream as far as Tione, which would eliminate the need for this highway stretch. Watch for signs at 11km.)

Beyond Tione a second short (4km) bikepath heads east through cornfields to the miniature town of Pez. Here the route climbs steeply out of the valley on a wonderfully untrafficky tertiary road. Levelling out, the road snakes its way along a mountainside, crossing the steep Val d'Algone canyon, passing through a tunnel carved from solid rock and following a deep, wide limestone gorge past a waterfall into Stenico (34.2km).

Stenico offers limited services, but the short side trip to imposing **Castello di Stenico** (☎ 0465 77 10 04; admission €3; open 9am-noon & 2pm-5pm daily, closed Mon) just above town is highly recommended. Building of the present castle started in the 12th century by the prince-bishops of Trent to guard the important route between Trent and Lombardy. Among its treasures is a wonderful 13th-century

fresco of the Virgin Mary tormented by a dragon. Stenico is also noteworthy as the castle depicted in the snowball fight scene in Trent's Torre Aquila frescoes.

The final leg from Stenico to Molveno climbs and dips through beautiful pastoral country, ultimately passing through several roughly hewn limestone tunnels and levels out on the shores of Lago di Molveno.

Molveno
Molveno's setting is dramatic, with the Dolomiti di Brenta's most imposing peaks soaring dizzyingly above the lake's blue-green waters. The town itself is rather bland, but it has gained a following among British, German and Italian holidaymakers. The SS421 divides Molveno into two sections: the centre, which sprawls across a hillside above the lake; and the lower town along the lakeshore, where the camping ground, sports facilities, and some hotels and restaurants are located.

Information The visitor centre (☎ 0461 58 69 24, �SMALLW www.aptdolomitipaganella.com) is on Piazza Marconi in the heart of the centre.

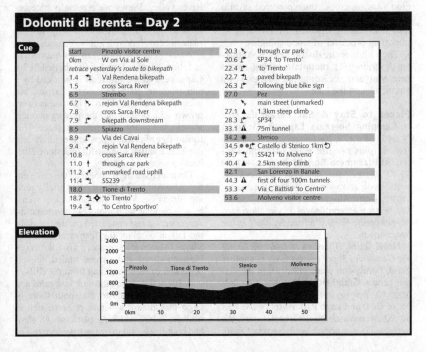

Dolomiti di Brenta – Day 2

Cue				
start	Pinzolo visitor centre	20.3 ↘	through car park
0km	W on Via al Sole	20.6 ↱	SP34 'to Trento'
retrace yesterday's route to bikepath		22.4 ↱	'to Trento'
1.4 ↰	Val Rendena bikepath	22.7 ↰	paved bikepath
1.5	cross Sarca River	26.3 ↱	following blue bike sign
6.5	Strembo	27.0	Pez
6.7 ↖	rejoin Val Rendena bikepath	↘	main street (unmarked)
7.8	cross Sarca River	27.1 ▲	1.3km steep climb
7.9 ↱	bikepath downstream	28.3 ↱	SP34
8.5	Spiazzo	33.1 ⚠	75m tunnel
8.9 ↱	Via dei Cavai	34.2 ✳	Stenico
9.4 ↗	rejoin Val Rendena bikepath	34.5 ●●↱	Castello di Stenico 1km ↺
10.8	cross Sarca River	39.7 ↰	SS421 'to Molveno'
11.0 ↑	through car park	40.4 ▲	2.5km steep climb
11.2 ↗	unmarked road uphill	42.1	San Lorenzo in Banale
11.4 ↰	SS239	44.3 ⚠	first of four 100m tunnels
18.0	Tione di Trento	53.3 ↙	Via C Battisti 'to Centro'
18.7 ↰✦	'to Trento'	53.6	Molveno visitor centre
19.4 ↰	'to Centro Sportivo'		

Elevation

Near the visitor centre, Cassa di Risparmio Trento e Rovereto (Via Cima Tosa 5) has a Bancomat, as does Cassa Rurale (Piazza delle Scuole 2b).

Andalo, 5km north along the Day 3 route, has the closest bike shop, Danilo Sport (☎ 0461 58 59 07) at Via Piz Galin 10.

Things to See & Do The lake and mountains surrounding Molveno offer endless outdoor recreation opportunities, including **rock climbing**, **windsurfing**, and **boating**. Due to the lake's icy waters, swimming is only appealing during extremely hot weather.

The Parco Naturale Adamello-Brenta, the largest protected area in all of Trentino, boasts an endless array of **hiking** trails. Chairlifts and gondolas facilitate access to the mountains. From Molveno there's summer services to Pradel (1367m, €3.50 one way) and Montanara (1505m, €4.50 one way).

An interesting excursion northwest of town follows Via Dolomiti to the Valle delle Seghe, where you can tour the water-operated 16th-century **Taialacqua Sawmill**, the last of its kind still in operation. The region's raging creeks once powered several similar mills, facilitating the cutting of large logs and helping establish Molveno as an important producer of wood shingles.

The visitor centre distributes a free booklet describing 11 **mountain biking** routes near Molveno, including one that makes a circuit around the lake.

Places to Stay & Eat Beside the lake is **Camping Spiaggia Lago di Molveno** (☎ 0461 58 69 78; Via Lungolago 25; per person €8 plus per site €12). **Albergo Lasteri/Affittacamere Bonetti** (☎/fax 0461 58 69 71; Piazza Marconi 24; per person €12) rents basic rooms across from the visitor centre. **Garni Alpenrose** (☎/fax 0461 58 61 69; e garni.alpenrose@tin.it; Via Lungolago 30; per person €28) is a friendly place in the lower town.

Hotel Garni Villanova (☎ 0461 58 63 47; Via Garibaldi 19; per person €42) is another good, family-run place uphill from the visitor centre. **Grand Hotel Molveno** (Via Bettega 18; per person half-board €76, full board €84) and **Lago Park Hotel** (☎ 0461 58 60 30; w www.dolomitiparkhotel.com; Via Bettega 12; per person with breakfast €56,

half-board €67) are among Molveno's older hotels, both commanding inspiring views of the lake and mountains from the shore opposite town.

Molveno has several centrally located grocery stores, including **De Spar** (Via Cima Tosa 10a) and **Central Market** (Via Paganella 1) across from the visitor centre. **Rosticceria Fogolar** (Piazza San Carlo 2) sells takeaway roast chicken, potatoes, veggies, pizza, strudel and panini (bread rolls). **Spaghetteria Bucaneve** (Via Garibaldi 50; meals €4-7) is a good place to fill up on pasta, just up from the visitor centre. **Birreria Pizzeria La Botte** (Via Cima Tosa 4) is a beer hall/pizzeria, which keeps its doors open until 2am. **Ristorante Pizzeria Al Caminetto** (Via Lungo Lago 8; pizza €4-6, meals €5-13) is pleasantly located near the lakeshore, with lots of outdoor seating.

Day 3: Molveno to Bolzano
4–6 hours, 72.5km
This day is longer than the first two, but less challenging, thanks to long stretches of flat and downhill riding.

After climbing gradually to Andalo, the route begins its 13km descent to the Noce River valley. Views are especially nice beyond Spormaggiore, where switchbacks drop through a landscape of long sloping plateaus covered with apple orchards.

At 19.8km, the route crosses busy SS43 to follow an abandoned road labelled SP29. Car access to the old road is blocked by a construction zone and metal barrier, but bikes pass through easily. The road is overgrown with bushes and the paving is intermittent, but guardrails remain in place. This traffic-free shortcut drops immediately into the Adige Valley's beautiful limestone cliff-backed vineyard country.

German road signs appear as the route enters Alto Adige (31.8km). After briefly joining Strada del Vino (Weinstrasse), a scenic byway popular with motorists, the route diverges onto a less congested parallel road. To the left at 37.6km, the historical centre of Magrè (Margreid) warrants a visit, with cobblestone streets and a stone-walled, flower-bedecked canal descending from the cliffs.

A 10km flat stretch through vineyards and apple orchards leads to the south shore of **Lago di Caldaro**, a nature preserve rich in birdlife. A bird-watching platform (48.4km) and boardwalk (49km) gives easy access. The

Dolomiti di Brenta – Day 3

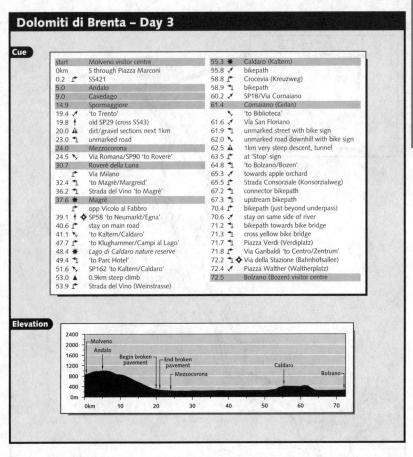

Cue

start	Molveno visitor centre	55.3 ✳	Caldaro (Kaltern)
0km	S through Piazza Marconi	55.8 ↙	bikepath
0.2 ↱	SS421	58.8 ↰	Crocevia (Kreuzweg)
5.0	Andalo	58.9 ↱	bikepath
9.0	Cavedago	60.2 ↙	SP18/Via Cornaiano
14.9	Spormaggiore	61.4	Cornaiano (Girlan)
19.4 ↗	'to Trento'	↘	'to Biblioteca'
19.8 ↑	old SP29 (cross SS43)	61.6 ↙	Via San Floriano
20.0 ⚠	dirt/gravel sections next 1km	61.9 ↱	unmarked street with bike sign
23.0 ↱	unmarked road	62.0 ↘	unmarked road downhill with bike sign
24.0	Mezzocorona	62.5 ⚠	1km very steep descent, tunnel
24.5 ↘	Via Romana/SP90 'to Roverè'	63.5 ↱	at 'Stop' sign
30.7	Roverè della Luna	64.8 ↱	'to Bolzano/Bozen'
↱	Via Milano	65.3 ↙	towards apple orchard
32.4 ↱	'to Magrè/Margreid'	65.5 ↱	Strada Consorziale (Konsorzialweg)
36.2 ↱	Strada del Vino 'to Magrè'	67.2 ↱	connector bikepath
37.6 ✳	Magrè	67.3 ↱	upstream bikepath
↱	opp Vicolo al Fabbro	70.4 ↱	bikepath (just beyond underpass)
39.1 ↑ ◆	SP58 'to Neumarkt/Egna'	70.6 ↙	stay on same side of river
40.6 ↱	stay on main road	71.2 ↱	bikepath towards bike bridge
41.1 ↘	'to Kaltern/Caldaro'	71.3 ↱	cross yellow bike bridge
47.7 ↱	'to Klughammer/Campi al Lago'	71.7 ↱	Piazza Verdi (Verdiplatz)
48.4 ✳	Lago di Caldaro nature reserve	71.8 ↱	Via Garibaldi 'to Centro/Zentrum'
49.4 ↱	'to Parc Hotel'	72.2 ↱ ◆	Via della Stazione (Bahnhofsallee)
51.6 ↘	SP162 'to Kaltern/Caldaro'	72.4 ↙	Piazza Walther (Waltherplatz)
53.0 ▲	0.9km steep climb	72.5	Bolzano (Bozen) visitor centre
53.9 ↱	Strada del Vino (Weinstrasse)		

Elevation

next several kilometres skirt the lakeshore and then climb through a sea of vineyards to the picturesque wine town of Caldaro (Kaltern) at 55.3km. Consider detouring up Caldaro's main street to visit the town square and **South Tyrolean Wine Museum** (☎ 0471 96 31 68; Goldgasse 1; open 9.30am-noon & 2pm-6pm, closed Sun afternoon & Mon). Several wine cellars also offer tastings along the main highway.

From Caldaro, a beautiful 3km bikepath follows the old railway bed towards Cornaiano (Girlan), gliding through forest with stunning views of terraced orchards dropping off to a small valley. The day's final thrill comes just beyond Girlan, where a small farm road plummets 130m from the high vineyards to the Adige Valley floor in just over 1km. From here Bolzano's fine network of bikepaths covers most of the remaining distance to the city centre.

Adige Valley Bikepath

Duration	3–6 hours
Distance	66.5km
Difficulty	easy
Start	Bolzano
End	Trent

This flat, easy ride follows a bikepath downstream from Bolzano to Trent, weaving through vineyards and fruit orchards as it ricochets between the limestone cliffs on either side of the Adige valley.

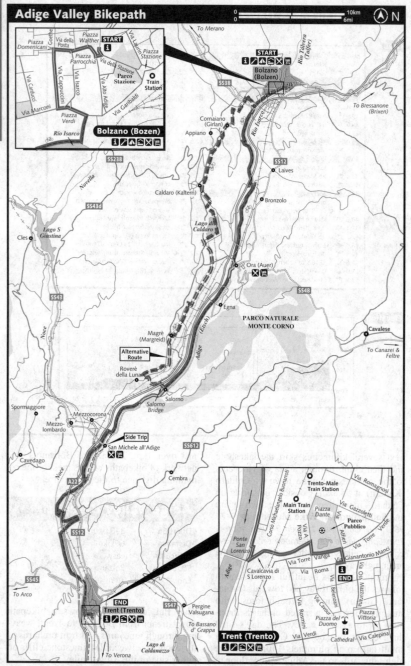

Cyclists preferring a more challenging loop back to Bolzano can follow the cue sheet for the first half of this ride, then return north via the scenic Strada del Vino route described earlier in this chapter under Day 3 (p234) of the Dolomiti di Brenta ride. To link these two routes, leave the Adige Valley bikepath at 35.1km, cross the Adige River, and follow signs towards Roverè della Luna. A right-hand turn (1.8km after leaving the bikepath) towards Magrè (Margreid) puts you on the Strada del Vino. Route directions north from this junction can be found starting at 32.4km on the Dolomiti di Brenta Day 3 cue sheet.

PLANNING
When to Ride
This ride is pleasant anytime between April and October. Fruit blossoms are at their peak in late April and early May.

Maps & Books
The northern section of this ride is covered by *Il Giardino del Sudtirolo: Bolzano e Dintorni* (€3) at tourist offices and shows additional cycling itineraries in and around Bolzano. The ride's southern half, from Salorno south, is covered by the free *Cycle Paths of Trentino* map available at Trent visitor centre.

What to Bring
Picnic benches are more common than towns along this route; avoid refuelling detours by packing your own lunch.

ACCESS TOWN
See Bolzano (p226).

THE RIDE
This ride connects Bolzano and Trent via a beautiful, flat riverside bikepath used by hordes of locals for recreation and commuting.

The route out of Bolzano passes through bustling Piazza Walther and Piazza Domenicani before joining the bikepath after 600m. After crossing a bike/pedestrian bridge over the Tálvera (Talfer), the route turns downstream towards the Isarco (Eisack) River. The path becomes scenic as it straddles the long peninsula between the Isarco and the Adige Rivers near their confluence (7km to 8km).

Crossing the Adige at 8.2km and 12.5km, the bikepath then continues downstream uninterrupted until 20km, where it crosses under a train overpass and turns onto a road.

A 3km detour off the bikepath was necessary here at the time of writing, as detailed on the cue sheet. However, construction may have since eliminated the need for this deviation.

A long straight section ensues, broken by roads crossing the valley every few kilometres. At 35.1km there's a turn-off for an alternate route to Bolzano via Strada del Vino.

Limestone cliffs loom above vineyards on the left as you enter Trentino (37.8km). At 42.3km the route again crosses the Adige, following the west bank to San Michele all' Adige (43.8km). Here a short side trip is recommended to **Museo degli Usi e Costumi della Gente Trentina** (☎ 0461 65 03 14; *Via Mach 2; admission €3; open 9am-12.30pm & 2.30pm-6pm daily, closed Mon*), one of Italy's largest ethnographic museums. Its fascinating

Adige Valley Bikepath

Cue

start		Bolzano (Bozen) visitor centre
0km		W towards Piazza Domenicani
0.2	↰	Piazza Domenicani (opp Via Goethe)
0.4	↰	Via Marconi
0.5	↱	'to Trento/Merano'
0.6	↱	bikepath towards bridge
1.0	↱	upstream bikepath
1.1	↱	downstream on riverside bikepath
1.9	↰	at T onto downstream bikepath
8.2	↱	cross Adige River
12.5	↰	cross Adige River
12.6	↱	'to Bronzolo/Branzoll'
20.0	↱	at T intersection
20.3	↰	'to Ora/Auer'
21.1		Ora (Auer)
	↱	Via S Pietro/SS12
23.0	↗	rejoin bikepath
35.1 ■ ■	↱	alt route: Strada del Vino 41.9km
42.3	↱	Via Cane (cross Adige River)
42.4	↰	bikepath
43.8		San Michele all'Adige
● ●	↰	Museo Gente Trentina 1km ↺
47.7	↰	cross Adige
47.8	↱	Località M Callianer/bikepath
53.4	↰	continue on bikepath
53.7	↱	through underpass
53.8	↱	rejoin bikepath
56.6	↱	cross wooden bike bridge
56.7	↗	unmarked westbound road
58.6	↗	stay on main bikepath
66.0	◆	Cavalcavia di S Lorenzo (no sign)
66.3	↱	Via Andrea Pozzo
66.3	↰	(10m) Via Torre Vanga
66.5	↱	Via Alfieri
	↱	(50m) Via Gianantonio Manci
		(10m) Trent (Trento) visitor centre

collection includes wonderful scale models of water-driven saws and grain mills, plus farm implements, carts and sleds, butter churns and moulds, looms, ironwork, ceramic stoves, hand-painted furniture, old wedding photos and other relics of rural mountain life.

The rest of the route zigzags across the valley, briefly making a U-turn back north at 53.4km, then swerving east to cross the Avisio River (56.6km). Increasing numbers of joggers, cyclists and picnicking families appear as you near Trent. Stay on the bikepath as you enter the city, keeping the river on your right. From Ponte San Lorenzo (66km), a 600m stretch leads to the visitor centre.

Heart of the Dolomites

Duration	6 days
Distance	317.9km
Difficulty	hard–very hard
Start/End	Fiè allo Sciliar

This circuit over the Dolomites' highest passes is one of the most breathtaking rides in Italy (both literally and figuratively). The energy expended in climbing eight 2000m passes (Gardena, Valparola, Falzarego, Tre Cime, Giau, Fedaia, Pordoi and Sella) in six days is handsomely rewarded by incomparable views and a feeling of exhilaration that will stay with you long after the trip.

The Giro d'Italia regularly crosses several of the passes, as evidenced by encouraging messages painted on the pavement. Lest you feel sorry for yourself on the long climbs, remember that Stage 13 of the 2001 Giro required cyclists to climb Passo Pordoi twice in one day, as part of a 224km route that also included Passo Fedaia!

The described route comprises one main four-day loop with side loops on Days 3 and 5. You can spread the ride out by making intermediate stops at the various *rifugi* (mountain huts) at the tops of the passes.

PLANNING
When to Ride
The ride is possible between June and September when the mountain passes are snow free. Late June, early July and early September are the best times for warm weather, without high season prices and crowds.

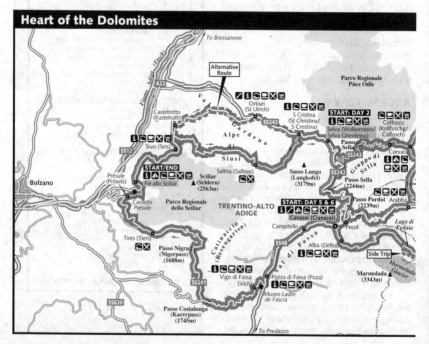

Heart of the Dolomites

What to Bring

Strong, well-adjusted brakes are imperative. Extra fluids are advisable for the many long ascents with limited services. The dirt section on Day 1 requires good tread or a willingness to walk the toughest bits.

ACCESS TOWN
Fiè allo Sciliar

Perched in verdant meadows beneath the Sciliar's giant stone hump, Fiè (Vols am Schlern) is a classic South Tyrolean mountain town. Despite its tiny size, it's a lovely place to spend a night, with a medieval main square and an onion-domed church.

Information The visitor centre (☎ 0471 72 50 47, ⟦w⟧ www.voels.it) is across from the SAD bus stop, on the corner of Via Bolzano and Via del Paese. Information is available on the Alpe di Siusi, as well as Fiè.

Banca Popolare (directly across from the visitor centre) and Cassa Rurale (Via del Paese 16) both have Bancomats.

Things to See & Do A pleasant **footpath** leads down through the town gate from the main square to the highway, affording lovely views of vegetable gardens, with steep green meadows and the Sciliar massif behind.

In summer there are **outdoor concerts** accompanied by beer and good Tyrolean food in the grounds of Castello Presule, 3km south of Fiè (see the Day 6 route).

Demonstrations of traditional grain grinding are offered on Friday at 9.30am at the historic **Moarmuller Mill** above Fiè.

Places to Stay & Eat About 3.5km up the hill along the Day 1 route is **Camping Seiser Alm** (☎ 0471 70 64 59; ⟦w⟧ www.camping seiseralm.com; tent sites €7, plus per person €5-6).

The town centre boasts three excellent hotels. **Albergo Croce Bianca** (☎/fax 0471 72 50 29; Piazza della Chiesa 2; singles/doubles with breakfast €34/68) is the most affordable. **Hotel Rose-Wenzer** (☎ 0471 72 50 16; Piazza della Chiesa 18; ⟦w⟧ www.hotel-rose-wenzer.it; singles/doubles half-board €57/95, full board €70/120) is a three-star with a sauna and a stunning terrace overlooking the Sciliar massif. **Romantik Hotel Turm** (☎ 0471 72 50 14; ⟦w⟧ www.hotelturm.it; Piazza della Chiesa 9;

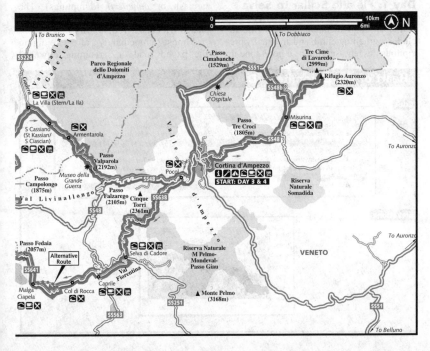

singles/doubles with breakfast €84/168, half-board €98/196, full board €115/230) is the most interesting hotel, built around a 13th-century tower, which is one of Fiè's oldest landmarks.

J Delago Markt am Platz *(Piazza della Chiesa 3)* sells groceries, cold drinks, and sandwiches. Good restaurant meals can be had in all the hotels. Albergo Croce Bianca's prices are among the lowest, while the winner for atmosphere is Hotel Rose-Wenzer, with its great panoramic terrace.

Getting There & Away There are excellent bus connections between Bolzano and Fiè. SAD (☎ 800 84 60 47) runs a bus (No 118) 20 times daily between the two towns (€1.75 one way plus €1 for bikes, 30 minutes).

Bicycle The 16.7km road from Bolzano to Fiè is steep, narrow, and heavily travelled. From downtown Bolzano, cross to the south bank of the Isarco River, follow national highway SS12 east for about 9km, then veer right following signs uphill to Fiè.

THE RIDE
Day 1: Fiè allo Sciliar to Selva
3–5 hours, 33.9km

While short in distance, today's ride includes a gruelling climb and an equally precipitous descent, serving as a good tune up for the greater challenges ahead. The main route follows a lightly travelled and partially unsealed road through the Alpe di Siusi (Seiser Alm), the largest expanse of high pastureland in the Alps. An alternate route, entirely sealed, involves less climbing and less distance, but more traffic.

The main road ascends gradually for the first 8.5km through fields at the base of Sciliar. Siusi (Seis) at 7km is the last chance for food and water before the big climb. At 8.5km the main route turns steeply uphill, while the alternate route descends straight towards Castelrotto (Kastelruth). The climb's early stages provide beautiful vistas across green fields to the onion-domed church of San Valentino. A 9km series of switchbacks offers an ever closer and more dramatic look at Sciliar, until the road finally levels off at 17.5km. At the summit is a cluster of cafés and shops.

For the next several kilometres the Alpe di Siusi's expansive meadows filled with grazing cattle and backed by the sawtooth spires of Sasso Lungo dominate the view. Smack in the middle of the Alpe lies the remote town of Saltria (Saltner), a good place to refuel on goulash or *canederli* (dumplings). The 5.9km stretch beyond Saltria is unsealed and shared with hikers (but no cars!).

Almost immediately after rejoining the paved road, a screaming downhill

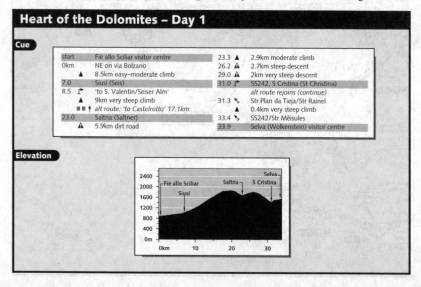

Heart of the Dolomites – Day 1

Cue

start	Fiè allo Sciliar visitor centre	23.3 ▲	2.9km moderate climb
0km	NE on via Bolzano	26.2 ⚠	2.7km steep descent
▲	8.5km easy–moderate climb	29.0 ⚠	2km very steep descent
7.0	Siusi (Seis)	31.0 ⌐	SS242, S Cristina (St Christina)
8.5 ⌐	'to S. Valentin/Seiser Alm'		*alt route rejoins (continue)*
▲	9km very steep climb	31.3 ↘	Str Plan da Tieja/Str Rainel
■ ■ ✝	*alt route: 'to Castelrotto' 17.1km*	▲	0.4km very steep climb
23.0	Saltria (Saltner)	33.4 ↘	SS242/Str Mëisules
⚠	5.9km dirt road	33.9	Selva (Wolkenstein) visitor centre

Elevation

Elevation profile showing: Fiè allo Sciliar, Siusi, Saltria, S Cristina, Selva. Vertical axis from 0m to 2400m (0m, 400, 800, 1200, 1600, 2000, 2400). Horizontal axis from 0km to 30 (0km, 10, 20, 30).

plummets to Santa Cristina (St Christina/S Crestina). Here the alternative route rejoins for the last uphill slog into Selva.

Selva

Selva (Wolkenstein/Selva Gherdeina) is the highest of Val Gardena's three main towns, scenically located at the base of two of the Dolomites' most famous rock formations, Sassolungo and the Sella massif. It's an unapologetically touristy resort offering services to skiers in winter and hikers in summer. Highway SS242, also known as Str Meisules, serves as Selva's main street, and every other building seems to be a hotel or guest house. The views from town will whet your appetite for the high country ahead.

Information Selva's visitor centre (☎ 0471 79 51 22, Ⓦ www.valgardena.com) is at Streda Meisules 213.

Cassa Rurale, just outside the visitor centre, has a Bancomat, as do several other banks along the main street.

In the town of Ortisei (St Ulrich/Urtijei), 7.5km downhill, is the valley's only full-service bike shop, Doi Rodes (☎ 0471 78 63 78), at Via Rezia 10. In Selva, Gardena Mountain Adventures (☎ 0471 79 42 47, Ⓦ www.val-gardena.com/gma), Str Ciampinoi 18, rents mountain bikes and leads adventure tours in the local mountains.

Things to See & Do There's fabulous hiking and climbing in the mountains above Selva, facilitated by cable cars climbing to Rifugio Ciampinoi (2254m) and Dantercepies (2298m). A one-way ride on each costs €5. Trails from the summits hook up with the Sella Ronda hiking circuit, which crosses the same passes you'll cover on Day 5.

A short hike from the valley floor leads to the imposing stone walls and turrets of **Castel Gardena-Fischburg**. The castle is owned by a local baron and closed to the public, but the view from the outside is still great.

Associazione Guide Alpine Val Gardena (☎/fax 0471 79 41 33, Ⓦ www.val-gardena.com/guide-alpine) offers **guided tours** throughout the summer, including glacier walks, rock climbing, paragliding, and excursions on the *vie ferrate* (iron ways) in the high country.

Ice skating at Selva's downtown Sportstadion is possible year-round.

Places to Stay & Eat Selva has no camping grounds, but intrepid souls can push over Passo Gardena to **Camping Colfosco** in Corvara (☎/fax 0471 83 65 15; Ⓔ camp .colfosco@rolmail.net; Sorega 5, Corvara; per person €5.20, site €8.80), 18.5km east along the Day 2 route.

Thanks to Val Gardena's popularity as a ski destination, Selva has no shortage of accommodation. **Garni Flurida** (☎/fax 0471 79 51 96; Ⓔ flurida@val-gardena.com; Streda Dantercepies 5; per person €35) is friendly and central, with bike storage. **Garni Villa Demetz** (☎/fax 0471 79 52 01; Streda Plan 73; per person €28) is conveniently located at Selva's eastern edge, giving you a head start on Day 2's big climb. **Garni Bon Dì** (☎/fax 0471 79 53 32; Streda Puez 41; per person €40) is a comfortable B&B. **La Majon** (☎ 0471 79 40 40; Ⓔ garni-lama jon@ val-gardena.com; Streda Larciunei 28; per person €36) has great views.

For groceries, try **Senoner Market** (Via Puez 3). **Pasticceria Perathoner** (Streda Meisules 175) has tasty baked goods. **The Goalie's Pub** (Streda Meisules 179) features Irish pub fare till 1am daily. **Pizzeria Rino** (Streda Meisules 217), with outdoor seating, serves delicious, reasonably priced food.

Restaurant Pizzeria Sal Feur (☎ 0471 79 42 76; Via Puez 6; meals €5-17, pizza €6-9) is more upscale, with Ladin specialties and a good wine list. **Medél** (Streda Meisules 22; meals €6-15) also serves tasty local dishes, often accompanied by live music.

Day 2: Selva to Cortina d'Ampezzo

4–6 hours, 55.4km
Today's route crosses three major passes en route to the grand valley of Cortina d' Ampezzo.

From Selva the climb to Passo Gardena begins almost immediately. Cyclists appear in large numbers at the junction with the Sella Ring Road (SS243) at 4.7km. Around 6.5km, the road levels out at the base of cliffs, allowing time to savour the beautiful views of green fields, hay barns and the trapezoidal profile of Sassolungo to the west. The last push up to the pass is relatively brief. Up top, restaurants with terraces offer panoramic views eastward towards Val Badia.

A steady switchbacking descent drops through Colfosco into Corvara, where the

DOLOMITES

route turns downstream, paralleling the Rio Gadera. From La Villa (Stern/La Ila) the next long climb begins gradually, then culminates in 6km of relentless uphill to Passo Valparola. At the pass spectacular views unfold to the southwest towards Marmolada, the Dolomites' biggest glacier, and southeast towards the five rugged peaks known as the Cinque Torri. During WWI Italians and Austrians faced off for three years in this desolate landscape, enduring brutal conditions, but doing little to change the border relationship between the two countries until war's end. The area's military history is commemorated in the **Museo della Grande Guerra** (37.6km). A much tackier attempt to profit from the WWII rivalry between Austrians and Italians can be seen in the gift shops at Passo Falzarego, where bottles of wine bearing the faces of Hitler and Mussolini (and inexplicably Che Guevara and Bob Marley as well!) are sold.

From Passo Valparola it's all downhill through spectacular mountain scenery to the third pass of the day (Passo Falzarego), and on into Cortina. It's worth stopping at 51.4km for the great viewpoint over Cortina's broad valley backed by sawtooth mountains.

Cortina d'Ampezzo

Cortina has grown dramatically since hosting the 1956 Winter Olympics, and the city you see today comes closer to urban sprawl than anything else in the Dolomites. Even so, the magnificence of the surrounding valley dwarfs the town centre, and Cortina remains more appealing than many other Dolomite resorts where growth has been more recent. Town life focuses on the long Corso Italia pedestrian zone near the belltower, a pleasant place for a *passeggiata* (stroll) day or night.

Information The visitor centre (☎ 0436 32 31, ⊞ www.apt-dolomiti-cortina.it) operates offices at Piazzetta San Francesco 8 and Piazza Roma 1 (cue sheets start and end at the former one.)

There are several banks with Bancomats along Corso Italia near the belltower.

Cicli Cortina (☎ 0436 86 72 15), Via Majon 148, is an excellent bike shop just north of town. Proprietor Luigi de Vila offers rentals, clothing, accessories, equipment and great advice on itineraries around Cortina. Another good local shop is Mountain Bikes Centre (☎ 0436 86 38 61), Corso Italia 294.

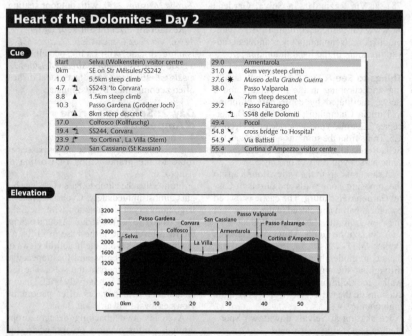

Heart of the Dolomites – Day 2

Cue

start	Selva (Wolkenstein) visitor centre		29.0	Armentarola
0km	SE on Str Mëisules/SS242		31.0 ▲	6km very steep climb
1.0 ▲	5.5km steep climb		37.6 ✳	Museo della Grande Guerra
4.7 ⬑	SS243 'to Corvara'		38.0	Passo Valparola
8.8 ▲	1.5km steep climb		▲	7km steep descent
10.3	Passo Gardena (Grödner Joch)		39.2	Passo Falzarego
▲	8km steep descent		⬑	SS48 delle Dolomiti
17.0	Colfosco (Kollfuschg)		49.4	Pocol
19.4 ⬑	SS244, Corvara		54.8 ⬊	cross bridge 'to Hospital'
23.9 ⬐	'to Cortina', La Villa (Stern)		54.9 ⬈	Via Battisti
27.0	San Cassiano (St Kassian)		55.4	Cortina d'Ampezzo visitor centre

Elevation

Passo Valparola
Passo Gardena
Corvara
San Cassiano
Passo Falzarego
Colfosco
Selva
Armentarola
La Villa
Cortina d'Ampezzo

3200
2800
2400
2000
1600
1200
800
400
0m

0km   10   20   30   40   50

Things to See & Do Ethnography, palae-ontology, and modern art museums are housed in **Ciasa de Ra Regoles** (☎ 0436 22 06; Corso Italia 69). The permanent collections are supplemented by rotating exhibits on such diverse topics as Cortina's WWI history and the Dolomites' agricultural heritage. The Museo Paleontologico, with its extensive collection of fossils from the Dolomites' coral reef days, is especially worthwhile.

Gondolas leave from two points in Cortina, permitting access to high country **hiking trails**. A free trail map is available at the visitor centre. From the southeast corner of town, gondolas (☎ 0436 25 17, €10,) climb via Mandres to Faloria (2120m); from the northwest side of town there's service (☎ 0436 50 52, €5) to Col Drusciè (1778m). The latter gondola connects to another ascending all the way to Ra Valles (2464m) and Tofana (3243m) – €5 extra per segment.

Mountain biking is great all around Cortina. The visitor centre publishes an excellent free map, *Escursioni in Mountain Bike a Cortina d'Ampezzo*, detailing 15 routes for cyclists of all abilities. Mountain Bikes Centre (☎ 0436 86 38 61), Corso Italia 294, also publishes its own booklet of mountain bike routes.

A good day ride, manageable for anyone who is in reasonable physical condition, is the 32km **Cortina–Dobbiaco bikepath**. The path is well-graded, mostly on dirt and gravel, with 300m of gradual climbing in each direction. It's possible to ride one way and take the SAD bus No 112 back to Cortina.

Places to Stay & Eat The most convenient of Cortina's four camping grounds, **International Camping Olympia** (☎/fax 0436 50 57; strada Alemagna; cyclist with tent €9, each additional person €6.50) has forested sites near the river, 4km north of town (and just slightly uphill) on the Day 3 route. **Camping Rocchetta** (☎/fax 0436 50 63; Via Campo 1; e camping@sunrise.it; up to 2 cyclists with tent €12.50, each additional person €7) is the most affordable and cyclist-friendly of three other camping grounds clustered near the river south of town, all steeply downhill from Cortina but with nice valley vistas.

The visitor centre can provide a list of rooms for rent in private homes, generally the cheapest option in high season. A few bare rooms with shared bath (€20 per person) are available above Mountain Bikes Centre (☎ 0436 86 38 61), Corso Italia 294.

Meublé Montana (☎ 0436 86 04 98; Corso Italia 94; singles/doubles €61/112) is the best central-hotel value, offering comfortable rooms, some with balcony. **Hotel Italia** (☎ 0436 56 46; e hitalia@sunrise.it; Via Marconi 2; singles/doubles €93/134) is faded but relatively affordable. **Albergo Cavallino** (☎ 0436 26 14; Corso Italia 142; singles/doubles €113/140) is well situated in the pedestrian zone but otherwise unexceptional. **Hotel Pocol** (☎ 0436 26 02; w www.pocol.it; singles/doubles half board €75/136), 6km above town at the junction between the Passo Falzarego and Passo Giau roads, is a good alternative if you're content to bypass Cortina and the Tre Cime loop on Day 3.

La Cooperativa di Cortina (Corso Italia 40) is a big department store with a great supermarket. **Osteria Pane Vino e San Daniele** (Corso Italia 137) is a trendy place for light meals and drinks. **Birreria Hacker Pschorr** (Via Stazione 7) serves affordable wurst, beer and the like in a casual setting. **Ristorante Pizzeria Cinque Torri** (Largo delle Poste 13) and **Pizzeria Il Ponte** (Via B Franchetti 8) are two recommended spots for pizza and pasta. **Croda Caffè** (Corso Italia 163) is a good place to sample the local specialty, *casunziei* (beet ravioli with poppy seeds).

Day 3: Tre Cime Loop
4–6 hours, 55.6km
This classic loop out of Cortina includes the week's steepest grade (16%) and highest summit (2320m), climbing to the base of the jagged Tre Cime di Lavaredo.

From Cortina, the initial ascent towards Passo Tre Croci traverses open fields, then enters pretty forest with a backdrop of mountain walls in every direction. After dropping into the Parco Naturale Regionale delle Dolomiti d'Ampezzo beyond the pass, the road climbs gradually to the lakeside resort of Misurina, last place to fill your water bottles before the big climb.

From Misurina, the route turns onto the Superstrada Panoramica toll road. A short

DOLOMITES

Heart of the Dolomites – Day 3

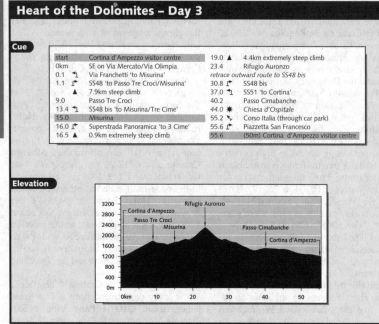

Cue

start	Cortina d'Ampezzo visitor centre	19.0 ▲	4.4km extremely steep climb
0km	SE on Via Mercato/Via Olimpia	23.4	Rifugio Auronzo
0.1 ↰	Via Franchetti 'to Misurina'		*retrace outward route to SS48 bis*
1.1 ↱	SS48 'to Passo Tre Croci/Misurina'	30.8 ↱	SS48 bis
▲	7.9km steep climb	37.0 ↰	SS51 'to Cortina'
9.0	Passo Tre Croci	40.2	Passo Cimabanche
13.4 ↰	SS48 bis 'to Misurina/Tre Cime'	44.0 ✳	Chiesa d'Ospitale
15.0	Misurina	55.2 ↘	Corso Italia (through car park)
16.0 ↱	Superstrada Panoramica 'to 3 Cime'	55.6 ↱	Piazzetta San Francesco
16.5 ▲	0.9km extremely steep climb	55.6	(50m) Cortina d'Ampezzo visitor centre

Elevation

but very steep initial climb is followed by a brief downhill leading to the tollbooth (18.3km) and a 700m flat stretch until you get to the gruelling and relentless 4.4km slog to the summit. Cars and buses must pay at the tollbooth, but bikes whiz through free of charge. Exhaust fumes from buses are an unwelcome distraction, but there are fantastic views of the stark, treeless landscape of the high Dolomites, with the tridentate Tre Cime di Lavaredo dominating the scene. The climb culminates at Rifugio Auronzo, where a bleak and lonesome café awaits. On the surrounding slopes, graffiti artists have spelled out names in big rocks.

Check your brakes before attempting the hair-raising descent to the base of the toll road! The remainder of the route, most of it downhill or flat, completes the circle back to Cortina. The final 18km through Passo Cimabanche traces an ancient trading route between Venice and Germany. At 44km is the 13th-century Chiesa d'Ospitale, built near the site of an 11th-century traders' and pilgrims' hostel and dedicated to St Nicholas, revered throughout the Alps as patron saint of wayfarers.

Day 4: Cortina d'Ampezzo to Canazei
5–7 hours, 60.4km

This is the most challenging day yet, with gut-wrenching climbs over Passi Giau and Fedaia (both over 2000m). The heart-stopping descent from Giau leaves little room for relaxation, but the views throughout are sensational.

Begin by retracing Day 2's route (with the exception of a few one-way streets in Cortina) uphill to Pocol (6.9km, last food before the summit), then turn southwest into the stupendous scenery of the quieter Passo Giau road. The climb's early stages traverse grassy glens among evergreen trees, with cowbells and a rushing river providing background music. Towards 13km the route emerges onto a vast moorland surrounded by stunning peaks, reaching the pass 4km later.

Giau is arguably the most beautiful pass in the Dolomites, and it's worth stopping to savour the view at the *rifugio*. The ensuing 9.6km descent is not for the faint of heart, with a sustained pitch of 9.2%. At Selva di Cadore (27.2km), the **Museo Civico della Val**

Fiorentina (☎ 0437 52 10 68, 0437 72 01 00) at Via IV Novembre 55 (open daily in summer from 4pm to 6.30pm) has exhibits on archaeology, history and geology, the most fascinating focusing on the Uomo di Mondeval, a 6th-century-BC man unearthed locally. Another steep descent with breathtaking southeasterly views towards Monte Pelmo leads to Caprile, a bustling tourist town.

The climb to Passo Fedaia begins in earnest at 38.3km, immediately past the side-trip turn-off for the spectacular **Serrai di Sottoguda** gorge. The ascent to Fedaia is as steep as the descent from Giau, but the road is straighter, leaving no room for doubt about the challenges ahead. A short but nerve-wracking tunnel in mid-climb doesn't help matters. From Passo Fedaia, a delightful lakeside stretch with views of Marmolada glacier leads to the junction (48.9km) where a short side trip provides access to the glacier itself.

On the exhilarating final descent into Canazei, wildflower-choked rivulets descend from high turrets on the right, competing for attention with huge rocky masses rising from the deep valley floor to the left.

Just before Canazei, the town of Alba (58.4km) offers an early chance for food and accommodation.

Canazei

Canazei (Cianacei) is a summer and winter resort surrounded by stunning mountain scenery. Here Val di Fassa runs up against the imposing barrier of the Sella group to the north, the steep face of Marmolada to the east, and the red-tinged Catinaccio (Rosengarten) to the west. Canazei's town centre is small but well-equipped with tourist services.

Information The visitor centre (☎ 0462 60 11 13, e infocanazei@fassa.com) is at Via Roma 34, providing information about Canazei and the entire Val di Fassa.

Cassa Rurale di Canazei (Via Pareda 30) and Banca Popolare del Trentino (Via Pareda 33) are banks with Bancomats along the main drag.

Detomas (☎ 0462 60 24 47), Via Pareda 29/31, is a helpful, well-stocked bike shop with excellent information about the local area.

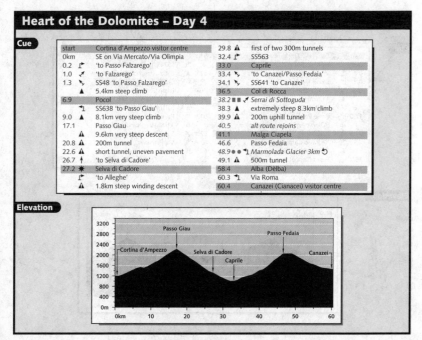

Heart of the Dolomites – Day 4

Cue					
	start	Cortina d'Ampezzo visitor centre	29.8 ⚠	first of two 300m tunnels	
	0km	SE on Via Mercato/Via Olimpia	32.4 ↰	SS563	
	0.2 ↱	'to Passo Falzarego'	33.0	Caprile	
	1.0 ↗	'to Falzarego'	33.4 ↘	'to Canazei/Passo Fedaia'	
	1.3 ↘	SS48 'to Passo Falzarego'	34.1 ↘	SS641 'to Canazei'	
	▲	5.4km steep climb	36.5	Col di Rocca	
	6.9	Pocol	38.2 ■ ■ ✓	Serrai di Sottoguda	
	↰	SS638 'to Passo Giau'	38.3 ▲	extremely steep 8.3km climb	
	9.0 ▲	8.1km very steep climb	39.9 ⚠	200m uphill tunnel	
	17.1	Passo Giau	40.5	alt route rejoins	
	⚠	9.6km very steep descent	41.1	Malga Ciapela	
	20.8 ⚠	200m tunnel	46.6	Passo Fedaia	
	22.6 ⚠	short tunnel, uneven pavement	48.9 ● ● ↰	Marmolada Glacier 3km ↺	
	26.7 ↑	'to Selva di Cadore'	49.1 ⚠	500m tunnel	
	27.2 ✳	Selva di Cadore	58.4	Alba (Dêlba)	
	↱	'to Alleghe'	60.3 ↰	Via Roma	
	⚠	1.8km steep winding descent	60.4	Canazei (Cianacei) visitor centre	

Elevation

DOLOMITES

Things to See & Do Canazei makes a great base for hiking trips into the surrounding mountains. A gondola climbs from the station at the east end of Via Pareda to Pecol (1926m), where a cable car continues up to Col dei Rossi (2383m). Alternatively, you can take the Col Rodella cable car from Campitello (2km downstream from Canazei on the riverside footpath) to 2484m Rifugio Col Rodella. Trails lead into the high country from both summits, connecting with the Sella Ronda circuit hike.

Mountain biking is also excellent in this area. The visitor centre distributes a free map, *Escursioni in Mountain Bike*, suggesting 10 itineraries in and around Val di Fassa.

Less ambitious walkers and cyclists will like the unpaved **fitness course** following the Avisio River 2km upstream and several kilometres downstream from Canazei.

The **Gran Fésta da d'Jstà** in late August/early September is an annual four-day festival celebrating Ladin culture. Attendees from all the Ladin-speaking valleys show up in traditional costume for parades, dancing, live music and traditional food served under a big tent.

Places to Stay & Eat Conveniently located near the river at the east edge of town, **Camping Marmolada** (☎ 0462 60 16 60; *Via Pareda; cyclist with tent €12, each additional person €8*) has laundry facilities and hot showers.

Garni Mia Majon (☎/fax 0462 60 12 90; *Via Pareda 48; per person €35*) is a cosy, family-run place, very central yet tucked away from traffic noise. Similarly priced are **Garni International** (☎/fax 0462 60 13 75; *Via Dolomiti 169*), **Garni Peter** (☎ 0462 60 15 79; *Via Pareda 57*) and **Albergo Alba** (☎ 0462 60 13 26; e albergo.alba@tin.it; *Via Costa 121, Alba di Canazei*). The last place, 2km east of town on the Day 4 route, is convenient for people arriving from Passo Fedaia.

Local grocery stores include **Alimentari de Bertol** (*Via Pareda 27*) and **Famiglia Cooperativa** (*Via Dolomiti 118*). **Rosticceria Le Gourmet** (*Via Dolomiti 149*) sells reasonably priced takeaway featuring roast chicken and vegetables.

Ristorante La Bolp (*Via A Costa 133, Alba; per person including drinks & complimentary grappa if you're lucky €6*) is an extremely popular and inexpensive place 2km east of town with a charmingly

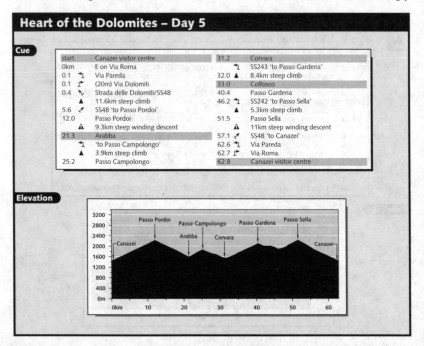

Heart of the Dolomites – Day 5

Cue

start	Canazei visitor centre		31.2		Corvara
0km	E on Via Roma			↰	SS243 'to Passo Gardena'
0.1	↰	Via Pareda	32.0	▲	8.4km steep climb
0.1	↱	(20m) Via Dolomiti	33.0		Colfosco
0.4	↘	Strada delle Dolomiti/SS48	40.4		Passo Gardena
	▲	11.6km steep climb	46.2	↰	SS242 'to Passo Sella'
5.6	↗	SS48 'to Passo Pordoi'		▲	5.3km steep climb
12.0		Passo Pordoi	51.5		Passo Sella
	⚠	9.3km steep winding descent		⚠	11km steep winding descent
21.3		Arabba	57.1	↙	SS48 'to Canazei'
	↰	'to Passo Campolongo'	62.6	↰	Via Pareda
	▲	3.9km steep climb	62.7	↱	Via Roma
25.2		Passo Campolongo	62.8		Canazei visitor centre

Elevation

eccentric owner serving local specialties. **Melester** (☎ *0462 60 20 77; Via Dolomiti 85; meals €8-18*) serves excellent regional specialties in an atmospheric old dining room.

Day 5: Sella Ronda Loop
4–6 hours, 62.8km

This is *the* classic circuit of the Dolomites, crossing four major passes as it circumnavigates the Sella massif. If you had only one day to cycle in northern Italy, this wouldn't be a bad choice.

The day's profile is fairly straightforward: steeply up and steeply down four times in a row. However, each pass has its own unique personality. The initial climb from Canazei to 2239m Passo Pordoi is the longest, but offers its own built-in encouragement in the form of words painted on the roadway for Giro d'Italia participants. The view from Passo Pordoi is one of the most dramatic in the Dolomites.

The descent from Pordoi is awe-inspiring, zigzagging through 33 numbered switchbacks into a glowingly verdant valley, occasionally checkerboarded with piles of new-mown hay. From the town of Arabba the climb to Passo Campolongo is short (3.9km) but steep. Campolongo is the lowest (1875m) and least impressive pass you'll cross all day, but the descent into Corvara, culminating in a sinuous series of steep switchbacks, provides vistas over lovely fields, forests and a stream along the right-hand side, with no ski lifts marring the view.

The next leg of the ride, from Corvara to the Passo Sella junction at 46.2km, retraces part of the Day 2 route in reverse, providing a new perspective on Passo Gardena, one of the Dolomites' prettiest passes even the second time around.

The final climb to Passo Sella is another steep one, but with stupendous views throughout. Near the 50km mark you get a great perspective on the Passo Gardena road far behind (and seemingly below). From Passo Sella, the views of Sasso Lungo and Marmolada are equally remarkable, making it hard to hop on your bike and head back down. The final 11km descent to Canazei is worth it just for the remarkable intestine-like S-curve, which looks like something straight out of Dr Seuss, at 52.7km.

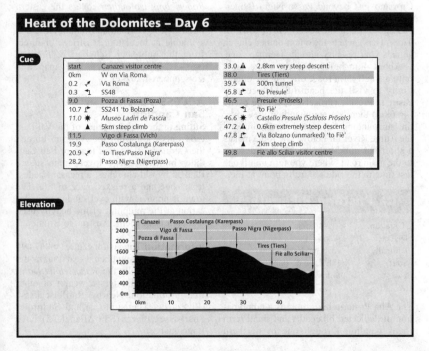

Heart of the Dolomites – Day 6

Cue

start	Canazei visitor centre	33.0 ⚠	2.8km very steep descent	
0km	W on Via Roma	38.0	Tires (Tiers)	
0.2 ↙	Via Roma	39.5 ⚠	300m tunnel	
0.3 ↰	SS48	45.8 ↱	'to Presule'	
9.0	Pozza di Fassa (Poza)	46.5	Presule (Prösels)	
10.7 ↱	SS241 'to Bolzano'	↰	'to Fiè'	
11.0 ✳	Museo Ladin de Fascia	46.6 ✳	Castello Presule (Schloss Prösels)	
▲	5km steep climb	47.2 ⚠	0.6km extremely steep descent	
11.5	Vigo di Fassa (Vich)	47.8 ↱	Via Bolzano (unmarked) 'to Fiè'	
19.9	Passo Costalunga (Karerpass)	▲	2km steep climb	
20.9 ↙	'to Tires/Passo Nigra'	49.8	Fiè allo Sciliar visitor centre	
28.2	Passo Nigra (Nigerpass)			

Elevation

Day 6: Canazei to Fiè allo Sciliar

3–5 hours, 49.8km

The return leg to Fiè allo Sciliar involves less climbing than any day on the tour, but the mountain scenery remains sensational, and visits to a museum and castle en route provide an interesting cultural dimension.

The ride out of Canazei follows the main road down the Val di Fassa, a long, gradual descent. Similar to Val Gardena, Val Badia and Cortina d'Ampezzo, Fassa is a Ladin-speaking valley with strong Ladin cultural influences. The well-organised **Museo Ladin de Fascia** (11km) showcases local culture and traditions on three floors, with interactive touch-screen videos, reconstructed traditional rooms, and displays featuring ironwork, farm implements, carnival masks and toys.

The day's toughest hill begins just beyond the museum. Compared to the previous days' ascents, however, it's mercifully short. By the time you reach Passo Costalunga (Karerpass, 19.9km) things have already levelled out, and the ride is mostly downhill from here as it skirts the bases of the Catinaccio and Sciliar massifs. The screaming descent into the lush hay barn-dotted valley of St Cipriano just beyond Passo Nigra (Nigerpass) is one of the day's highlights, as is the passage through the lovely small town of Tires (Tiers), where the onion-domed church signals your re-entry into the German zone.

About 4km before Fiè the route turns onto a small farm road, offering the opportunity to visit the beautiful 13th-century castle at Presule (Prösels). From the **castle** (46.6km) there's a commanding view over the surrounding fields and mountains and the Adige River far below. The route makes a short but mind-bogglingly steep descent to the main road, where you turn uphill one last time to the ride's starting point at Fiè.

Alta Pusteria Bikepath

Duration	2½–4 hours
Distance	40km
Difficulty	easy–moderate
Start	San Candido (Innichen)
End	Brunico (Bruneck)

The Alta Pusteria bike route is a combination of dedicated bikepaths and small farm roads winding through one of northern Italy's most scenic valleys. The region is distinctly South Tyrolean, with onion-domed churches around every corner and Germanic specialties on every menu. While more undulating than the Adige valley bikepath, this route is still manageable for cyclists of any age in reasonable physical condition. The overall trend of the ride is downhill, with a couple of steep climbs and dirt sections thrown in for good measure. The route parallels a train line and there are several bike rental locations throughout the valley, making it possible to cycle one way (or even just part of the way) and take the train back to your starting point.

PLANNING
When to Ride

This ride is enjoyable anytime from early June to mid-September, although as usual the period around the Ferragosto holiday (15 August) is best avoided due to crowds and higher prices. Many hotels close down in late September as the weather turns colder, taking a brief break before the ski season.

Maps & Books

Raderlebnis Dolomiten covers the eastern Dolomites and shows most of the route. Published in German and Italian only, it is available at local tourist offices or direct from the publisher Schubert & Franzke (☎ +43 1 2742 78 5010, w www.map2web .cc/schubert-franzke).

ACCESS TOWN
San Candido

Sitting in the upper reaches of the Val Pusteria only 7km from the Austrian border, the Germanic-flavoured town of San Candido (Innichen) has a lovely main square flanked by old churches, a pleasant pedestrian zone and a relaxed pace of life. The town is popular with cyclists due to its location at the midpoint of the heavily used bikepath from Lienz, Austria, to Brunico.

Information The visitor centre (☎ 0474 91 31 49, w www.innichen.it), at Piazza del Magistrato 1, sells the *Raderlebnis Dolomiten* guide and offers a wealth of other free information. Nearby, Raiffeisenkasse (Piazza del Magistrato 3) and Sudtiroler Sparkasse (Piazza San Michele 5) have Bancomats.

Papin Sport (☎ 0474 91 34 50), Via Freising 9, sells everything a cyclist could ever need and also rents bikes at multiple locations throughout Val Pusteria, permitting one-way rentals.

Things to See & Do San Candido has a cluster of nice churches near the centre. The lovely stone **Collegiata (Stiftskirche)** on Piazza del Magistrato, built between 1043 and 1326, is considered one of the finest examples of Romanesque architecture in the eastern Alps. There's a museum displaying religious artefacts and paintings next door. The onion-domed **Parrocchiale di San Michele (Pfarrkirche zum Heiligen Michael)** on Piazza San Michele also dates back to medieval times but was completely redone in Baroque style in the 1700s.

Dolomythos *(☎ 0474 91 32 55; Via Rainer 9)* is a museum devoted to the geological history of the Dolomites, with displays focusing on fossils, minerals, and the naturalists and explorers who have helped uncover these mountains' secrets.

There's lots of good **hiking** in nearby Parco Naturale Fanes-Sennes-Braies. The tourist office has a free brochure suggesting six hikes for people of varying fitness levels.

Places to Stay & Eat Between Dobbiaco and Villabassa, **Camping Olympia** *(☎ 0474 97 21 47; up to 2 cyclists with tent €25)* is reachable via a right turn off the San Candido–Brunico bikepath at 7.3km. **Camping Toblacher See** *(☎ 0474 97 22 94; up to 2 cyclists with tent €18)* is another option, 8km southwest of San Candido on beautiful Lagi di Dobbiaco.

Near the Drava River and city centre, **Garni Patzleiner** *(☎/fax 0474 91 32 11; Via Mantinger 3; per person €22)* has flower-filled balconies. **Garni Siebnerhof** *(☎ 0474 91 34 28; Via dei Tintori 24; per person €23)* is another central B&B.

Albergo Orso Grigio *(☎ 0474 91 31 15; W www.orsohotel.it; Via Rainer 2; singles/doubles half-board €100/176)* is an appealing historic three-star smack in the centre of town. **Weisses Rossl** *(☎ 0474 91 31 35; W www.weissesroessl.com; Via Duca Tassilo 1; per person half-board €125)* is a classy four-star place just across the street.

There's a **De Spar** *(Piazza San Michele 8)* supermarket in the heart of town. **Panificio/Backerei Wachtler** *(Benediktinergasse 1 & Via Rainer 9)* opens at 7am for delicious baked goods. **Berni's Mini-Snack** *(Piazza del Magistrato)* serves wurst and other fast food from a cart next to the visitor centre. **Miramonti Pizzeria Grillbar** *(Via Rainer 23; pizza €4-7, meals €7-14)* is open till midnight. **Restaurant Wiesthaler** *(Via Duca Tassilo 3; meals €4.50-15)* is a cosy local hangout adjacent to

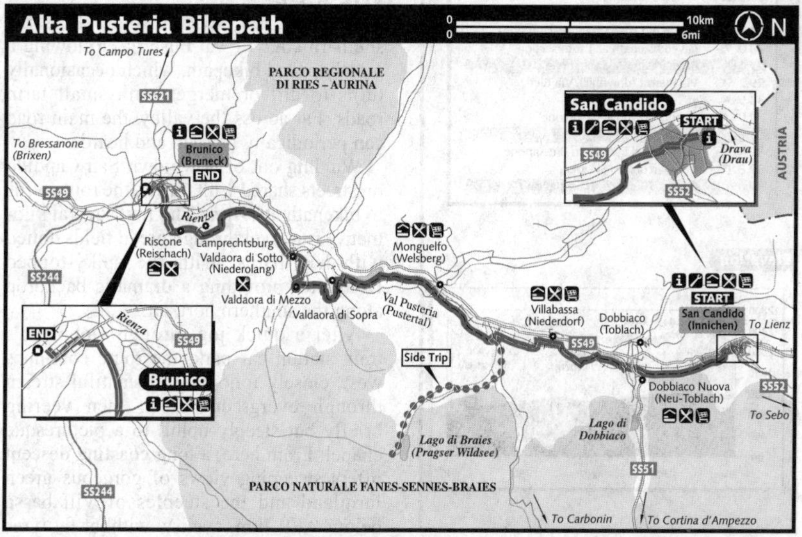

DOLOMITES

Alta Pusteria Bikepath

Cue

start	S Candido (Innichen) visitor centre
0km	W on Via dei Tintori
0.3	◿ 'to Dobbiaco/Toblach'
1.4	↘ Alta Pusteria bikepath
4.7	◿ through car park to Via Rienza
5.0	Dobbiaco Nuova (Neu-Toblach)
5.6	↰ cross stream
5.6	◿ (5m) bikepath (blue sign)
6.5	↰ under railroad bridge
6.8	◿ bikepath (blue sign)
7.3	↘ 'to Villabassa/Niederdorf'
9.7	⚠ dirt path straight ahead
9.7	↱ ⚠ (5m) steep descent under train tracks
9.8	↘ unmarked paved road
9.9	Villabassa (Niederdorf)
	↘ Via Jaeger
10.6	↰ under railroad tracks
10.6	↱ (10m) Via Platari
12.9	↱ 'to Monguelfo' (light blue sign)
	● ● ↰ Lago di Braies 14.4km ↺
13.2	↰ 'to Monguelfo' (light blue sign)
13.5	⚠ 0.9km dirt road
15.2	↰ uphill 'to Gailerhof Monguelfo'
16.8	Monguelfo (Welsberg)
	↱ 'to Brunico'
16.9	↰ following yellow-green bike sign
17.5	bikepath crosses creek
	⚠ intermittent pavement next 4.5km
18.8	↘ back onto gravel bikepath
22.4	↘ unmarked road uphill
22.8	↱ Via Salla 'to Valdaora'
23.2	↘ Via Böden 'to Brunico per i campi'
24.2	⚠ 0.3km unpaved section
24.5	↱ 'to Brunico' (downhill)
24.8	↰ into cornfield (green-yellow sign)
24.9	↱ downhill (green-yellow sign)
25.2	↰ at T intersection (no sign)
26.7	↰ 'to Brunico' (green/yellow sign)
26.8	⚠ 0.4km dirt stretch
27.2	↱ busy road downhill
27.3	↘ ⚠ 0.7km dirt road (green-yellow sign)
28.0	↰ paved bikepath at T intersection
29.1	↘ Pfarrstrasse, Valdaora di Sotto
29.2	◿ Via Rienza (downhill)/Via Ried
33.5	↘ at T intersection
34.0	◿ steeply downhill 'to Riscone'
35.7	Riscone (Reischach)
39.4	↰ Via Michael Pacher 'to Bressanone'
39.8	↱ Via Marconi 'to Stazione'
40.0	Brunico (Bruneck) train station

Elevation

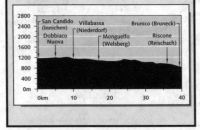

Hotel Weisses Rossl. **Uhrmacher's Wein-stube** *(Via dei Tintori 1)* is a convivial hideaway serving snacks and 300 different wines till midnight.

Getting There & Away From Bolzano, take any northbound train to Fortezza (Franzensfeste), then transfer to the slow train to San Candido. The two-hour journey costs €8.83. San Candido's station is a snarl of tracks, serving as the end of the line for both Italian trains (from Fortezza) and Austrian trains (from Lienz).

Bicycle The westbound Alta Pusteria bikepath to Brunico described here is only half the story. The same bikepath continues 45km east from San Candido to Lienz, Austria. It's a beautiful ride, well maintained and signposted, and mostly downhill. As with the ride to Brunico, it's possible to cycle one way and then return to San Candido by train.

It's also possible to connect the Alta Pusteria ride with the Heart of the Dolomites ride. Just beyond Dobbiaco Nuova (5km on the Alta Pusteria route), follow signs south towards Lago di Dobbiaco. A 32km mostly unpaved bikepath leads from here to Cortina d'Ampezzo, where you can hook up with the Heart of the Dolomites route.

THE RIDE

Throughout the day, the route skirts the southern edge of Val Pusteria, following a mostly paved bikepath, which occasionally turns to dirt or merges with small farm roads. Far across the valley, the main road can periodically be seen and heard.

Winding out of downtown San Candido on streets shared with traffic, the route turns to bikepath at 1.4km. The first several kilometres run level through green fields dotted with hay barns, with the spiky-topped Dolomites providing a dramatic backdrop along the southern horizon.

After a quick jog through Dobbiaco's train station car park, the route continues west, closely following a beautiful stream through evergreen forest, then veering briefly but steeply uphill to a picturesque chapel. From here, a long coasting descent offers sweeping views of gorgeous green farmland and the steeples of Villabassa below. At 9.7km, cyclists without fat tyres should beware of the treacherously steep, unpaved crossing under the railroad tracks.

Open fields and deep forests alternate as the route stays left of the river between Villabassa and Monguelfo. Halfway between the two towns, a side trip leads to Lago di Braies (1494m), a glittering green and turquoise lake backed by craggy grey mountains.

At 16.9km, just before central Monguelfo, yellow-green signs direct you to a section of path still under construction at the time of writing. The mostly unpaved trail descends along the rushing river to the south shore of an artificial lake, then levels out for 3km and traverses a delightfully peaceful forest. Beyond the dam, the route climbs to Valdaora di Sopra on busier roads, then re-enters farm country at 23.2km.

The next 5km require attentive navigation as the route zigzags through cornfields and open pastures, with beautiful cross-valley views to the Austrian Alps. The bumpy dirt section beginning at 27.3km

will rattle your teeth, but smooth pavement resumes at 28km. After a brief but steep downhill on a road shared with cars, the route resumes an undulating course through pastureland, with barns, woodpiles and cows jingling their bells. At 35km there's a nice view of the crenulated castle tower of Lamprechtsburg, just before the long final descent into Brunico.

Brunico

Because of the easy transportation to San Candido and Bolzano, Brunico (Bruneck) is not covered as a destination here. For information on places to stay and eat in Brunico, check with the visitor centre just east of the train station (☎ 0474 55 57 22, ⓦ www.bruneck.com) at Via Europa 26.

Getting There & Away Hourly trains run east from Brunico back to San Candido or west to Fortezza, where you can catch a southbound train to Bolzano.

Adriatic Coast

Ranging from the limestone cliffs along the Slovenian border to the dazzling Conero Riviera south of Ancona, with lagoons, beaches and vast flat wetlands in between, the Adriatic Coast offers some of Italy's easiest cycling, plus fascinating traces of the region's Byzantine, Lombard and Roman history. Also included in this chapter are rides venturing further inland, to the Euganeian Hills near Padua and across the Appenines into eastern Umbria.

CLIMATE
The Adriatic Coast has a Mediterranean climate, with hot, dry summers and moderately cold winters. Spring and autumn are the rainiest seasons, with precipitation increasing inland towards the mountains. Winter brings bone-chilling fog to the Po Delta and Venetian Lagoon, while snow falls at higher elevations.

Average highs for Venice are 28°C in July and August, 18°C in April and October and 8°C around December and January.

GATEWAY CITIES
Venice
Maligned by some as an artificial museum city ruined by tourism, Venice (Venezia) remains for others one of the world's most magical and romantic places. For cyclists, Venice is not immediately welcoming; indeed, bikes are a useless encumbrance among its bridges, canals, and narrow alleyways, and they are prohibited on the *vaporetti* (barge-like ferry boats) running along the Grand Canal between Piazzale Roma, Santa Lucia train station and Piazza San Marco. Despite these limitations, Venice is an international gateway, a convenient rail hub and an indispensable part of any northern Italian itinerary. Park your bike for a few days and enjoy!

Six *sestieri* (neighbourhoods) constitute the main nucleus of the island city. South and west of the Grand Canal are Sestieri Santa Croce, San Polo and Dorsoduro; north and east are Sestieri Cannaregio, San Marco and Castello. Street addresses commonly include the name of the appropriate *sestiere*. Santa Lucia train station is in Sestiere Cannaregio, while Sestiere San Marco to the east is Venice's tourist hub.

In Brief

- Early Christian mosaics at **Ravenna** and **Aquileia**
- Vineyards of the **Collio** and the **Colli Euganei**
- White cliffs and dazzling blue-green waters of the **Conero Riviera**
- Walled medieval towns of **Umbria** and **Le Marche**
- Island-hopping into **Venice**

Terrain
Flat along the coast except at Monte Conero (south of Ancona), Monte San Bartolo (north of Pesaro) and the Carso (east of Trieste); hilly to mountainous inland

Special Events
- **Barcolana Sailing Regatta** (October), Trieste
- **Buskers Festival** (August), Ferrara
- **Corsa dei Ceri** (May), Gubbio
- **Quintana Medieval Festival** (August), Ascoli Piceno

Cycling Events
- **Gran Fondo d'Europa** (September), Trieste-Cividale del Friuli
- **Transeuganea** (May), Euganeian Hills

Food & Drink Specialties
- *frico* (savory Friulian cheese-potato cake)
- *cappellacci di zucca* (Ferrarese pumpkin-filled pasta)
- truffles
- miniature Castelluccio lentils
- pork products of Norcia

South of the city, the island of Lido is open to traffic, and bikes are a familiar sight on its roads. Cyclists arriving from the airport or riding the Ravenna to Venice route may wish to stash their bikes here for a few days while visiting Venice. Alternatively you can lock your bike at one of the train stations.

It's impossible to do this city justice in a few paragraphs. For a comprehensive coverage, see Lonely Planet's *Venice* and *Italy*.

Information The APT visitor centre (☎ 041 529 87 11, W www.turismovenezia .it) has offices at the train station, the airport, Piazzale Roma, Piazza San Marco 71f and Gran Viale Santa Maria Elisabetta 6a in Lido.

There's a Bancomat in the train station, plus numerous banks and change offices throughout the city.

A good bike shop in Mestre (just north of Venice) is Bicimania (☎ 041 98 92 60), Via Torre Belfredo 124. Another excellent shop, Scavezzon (☎ 041 541 13 18) is 14km west of Venice on Viale Viareggio 85 in Spinea.

Things to See & Do Few public spaces in the world can match the allure of **Piazza San Marco**, opening to the Grand Canal on one side, surrounded by loggias (covered areas on the side of buildings) on three others, and enclosing Venice's two grandest architectural monuments. At the square's northeastern corner, the **Basilica di San Marco** is a Byzantine masterpiece of mosaics, domes and undulating marble pavement, showcasing the Venetians' twin gifts for artistry and plunder. Next door, the white and pink **Palazzo Ducale** was for centuries the residence of Venice's doges and seat of the republic's government.

Galleria dell'Accademia, Venice's premier art museum, houses five centuries of works by all the Venetian masters. Nearby, the **Peggy Guggenheim Collection** has a fine assemblage of modern art and a nice sculpture garden. Further down the Grand Canal, the **Basilica di Santa Maria della Salute**'s dome is one of Venice's great landmarks; the church, built to thank Virgin Mary for saving the city from plague, holds works by Titian and Tintoretto.

In San Polo, the Gothic **Chiesa dei Frari** houses masterpieces by Titian, Bellini and others. The adjoining **Scuola Grande di San Rocco** is Tintoretto's tour de force, with a remarkable cycle of more than 50 paintings.

For an incomparable view of Venice, take the elevator up the belltower of **San Giorgio Maggiore**, on an island just across from Piazza San Marco.

Easily overlooked gems include the whimsical spiral staircase at **Palazzo Contarini del Bovolo** between Rialto and Accademia bridges, and the exquisite marble-facaded church of **Santa Maria dei Miracoli** in Cannaregio.

Touristy though it may be, a **gondola ride** is an unforgettable way to see the city and reasonably inexpensive if split among several people. Whatever you do, don't forget to spend some time simply **wandering aimlessly** among the city's narrow alleyways and bridges.

Places to Stay Booking accommodation ahead is always advisable in Venice.

Ostello Venezia (☎ 041 523 82 11; e vehostel@tin.it; Fondamenta Zitelle 86; dorm beds €14) is Venice's HI hostel, on the island of Giudecca. **Foresteria Valdese** (☎ 041 528 67 97; W www.chiesavaldese.org/ venezia/foresteria; Castello 5170; dorm beds/ doubles €20/70) is a religious organisation in a delightful old mansion. **Locanda Silva**

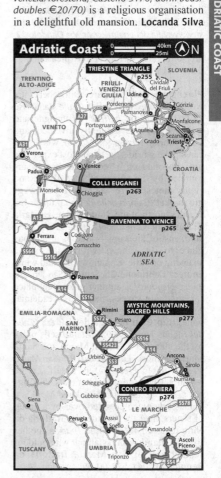

Adriatic Coast

(☎ 041 522 76 43; e albergosilva@libero.it; Fondamenta del Rimedio 4423, Castello; singles/doubles €67/104), **Hotel Riva** (☎ 041 522 70 34; Ponte dell'Angelo 5310, Castello; singles/doubles €70/100) and **Hotel Doni** (☎/fax 041 522 42 67; Fondamenta del Vin 4656, Castello; singles/doubles €50/100) are good one-star hotels near San Marco. **Casa Verardo** (☎ 041 528 61 38; w www.casaver ardo.it; Castello 4765; singles/doubles €93/197) is a classier alternative in the same neighbourhood. **Pensione Accademia Villa Maravege** (☎ 041 521 01 88; w www.pen sioneaccademia.it; Dorsoduro 1058; singles/ doubles €114/217) is a stately 17th-century villa overlooking a garden between two canals, near the Accademia. **Villa delle Palme** (☎ 041 526 13 12; w www.villa dellepalme.com; Via Dandolo 12, Lido; singles/doubles €88/130) is in a century-old house surrounded by pleasant gardens on Lido.

Places to Eat For pure atmosphere, it's worth visiting **Harry's Bar** (Calle Vallaresso 1323), where the bellini (champagne and peach juice) was reputedly invented, and **Caffè Florian** (Piazza San Marco), where you can sip the world's best and most expensive hot chocolate on a red velvet bench surrounded by the ghosts of Lord Byron and Henry James. There's a great **fruit and veggie market** (Campo della Pescaria) under the arcades, north of the Rialto bridge. **Hostaria Ai Rusteghi** (Calletta della Bissa 5529; closed Sun), east of the same bridge, is a fabulous place to rub elbows with locals while snacking on little €1 sandwiches and wine. **Enoteca Cantinone Già Schiavi** (San Trovaso 992, Dorsoduro) is another great local place for wine and snacks, near the Accademia. Try its white fragolino (a type of sweet wine). **Cip Ciap Bottega della Pizza** (Calle del Mondo Novo 5799, Castello) sells pizza by the slice between San Marco and Santa Maria Formosa. **Le Chat Qui Rit** (San Marco 1131, Angolo Frezzeria) is a self-service restaurant with good-value meals. **Ai Cugnai** (S Vio, Accademia 857; closed Mon) is a home-style place presided over by a group of sisters, near the Accademia. **Trattoria da Nino** (Castello 4668; closed Thur) is another friendly, family-run restaurant with outdoor seating east of San Marco. **Trattoria da Remigio** (☎ 041 523 00 89; Castello 3416; closed Mon evening & Tues) serves Venetian specialties like baccalà mantecata (a creamy paste made with codfish, olive oil, garlic and parsley) and sarde in saor (marinated sardines).

Getting There & Away Marco Polo Airport, 12km northeast of Venice, is served by numerous domestic and international airlines.

There are several ways of getting from the airport to the city with your bike.

Airport to Lido If you've just arrived and plan to spend a few days in Venice, the island of Lido is a convenient place to park your bike. Alilaguna (☎ 041 523 57 75, w www.alilaguna.com) provides an hourly hydrofoil service between the airport and Lido (€10, 55 minutes). Bikes are accepted as free luggage at the captain's discretion. Once in Lido, you can lock your bike and travel unencumbered into the touristic heart of Venice via a vaporetto (€3.10, 15 minutes, disembark at San Zaccaria, near Piazza San Marco).

For instructions on getting from Lido to Venice's Santa Lucia train station, see Day 4 (p272) of the Ravenna to Venice ride.

Airport to Piazzale Roma/Santa Lucia Station Another option for arriving cyclists wishing to stash their bikes is the left luggage facility at Venice's Santa Lucia train station. ATVO (☎ 041 520 55 30) runs two buses an hour from the airport to Venice's Piazzale Roma (€5.40 with bike, 20 minutes), from where you can walk your bike over the Grand Canal bridge to the train station (15 minutes).

Airport to Mestre Train Station If your plans don't include Venice, Mestre is the closest place to catch a train headed somewhere else. ATVO's Fly Bus service regularly connects Marco Polo airport with Mestre's train station (€4.20 with bike, 20 minutes).

Cyclists whose religion doesn't permit other forms of transportation can pedal the congested and uninspiring few kilometres from Marco Polo airport to Mestre. At the airport exit, turn left on SS14 (Via Triestina). After 5km, veer left (south) at the junction with Via Martiri della Libertà, then turn right towards downtown Mestre on Viale San Marco and follow signs for the station.

Treviso to Mestre & Piazzale Roma Passengers on Ryanair and some charter carriers arrive at Treviso airport. ATVO's Eurobus service (€8.60 with bike) connects Treviso's airport with Mestre train station (55 minutes) and Piazzale Roma (1¼ hours).

Train Venice has two train stations. At the island city's western edge, Venezia Santa Lucia provides arriving tourists with picture-postcard gratification, its steps descending directly to the Grand Canal. On the mainland north of the city is Venezia Mestre, which holds little interest except as a transfer point.

Several railway lines leave from Venice: east to Trieste (€8 one way, two hours); west to Padua (€2.50, 30 minutes) and Milan (€12.50, 3½ hours); northwest to Trent (€8, three hours); and southwest to Bologna (€8, two hours). Connections can be made in Bologna for Ancona (€17.50, five hours) and Pesaro (€14.50, four hours). For Ravenna (€9, 3½ hours), take a Bologna-bound train and transfer at Ferrara.

Bicycle The most atmospheric way for cyclists to approach Venice is via the lagoon islands, as described in the Ravenna to Venice ride (p265).

Friuli-Venezia Giulia

Italy's northeasternmost region, Friuli-Venezia Giulia reflects the influence of its modern Slovene and Austrian neighbours, as well as the Venetians and ancient Romans who once plied its waters. Italian, Friulian and Slovene are widely spoken. The region's cultural diversity is matched by geographic variety, ranging from spare limestone cliffs to lush vineyard-covered hills, from coastal lagoons to the rugged Carnian and Julian Alps.

HISTORY

Prehistoric settlement of the Triestine Carso is evidenced by tools, pottery and bones discovered in local caves. Excavations nearby have also revealed hundreds of Bronze Age walled settlements known as *castellieri*.

Ancient Roman influence began in 181 BC with the settlement of Aquileia, followed by the colonisation of Cividale del Friuli (Roman Forum Iulii) and Trieste (Tergeste).

All three cities were incorporated into the 10th Roman region, Venetia et Histria.

The region's low alpine passes left it vulnerable to invasion from northern and eastern tribes. Attila the Hun sacked Aquileia in AD 452, and the Lombards founded their first Italian duchy at Cividale del Friuli in AD 568.

The medieval period resulted in ongoing struggles between the patriarchate of Aquileia and the Venetian Republic. In 1420 Venice finally took Friuli, while the eastern provinces of Trieste and Gorizia (modern Venezia Giulia) fell into Austrian hands.

After a brief period of Napoleonic rule, Austria took control of the entire region in 1815. Friuli joined the Kingdom of Italy in 1866, with Venezia Giulia following in 1918.

NATURAL HISTORY

Friuli-Venezia Giulia divides roughly into three geographic zones: the Friulian lowlands, the southeastern karstic highlands (known in Italian as the Carso), and the northern Alps (not covered in this chapter).

The Friulian flatlands, drained by the great Isonzo and Tagliamento Rivers, spread south from the Alpine foothills to the sea. As elsewhere along the Adriatic, the land was historically swampy, but large sections, such as the Bonifica della Vittoria near Grado, were gradually reclaimed as farmland to feed a growing population and reduce the risk of malaria. To the west, the Marano and Grado lagoons to provide important bird habitat.

The Carso is a high limestone plateau riddled with caves, abysses and sinkholes, spreading eastward into Slovenia from Gorizia in the north and Trieste in the south. Originally called *kras* by the local Slovenes, its German name 'karst' has since been adopted by geologists to describe similar limestone formations worldwide.

Triestine Triangle

Duration	3 days
Distance	212.7km
Difficulty	easy–moderate
Start/End	Trieste

This loop showcases southern Friuli-Venezia Giulia's geographic and cultural diversity without overtaxing your legs and lungs. Highlights include the cave-riven Carso, the

ADRIATIC COAST

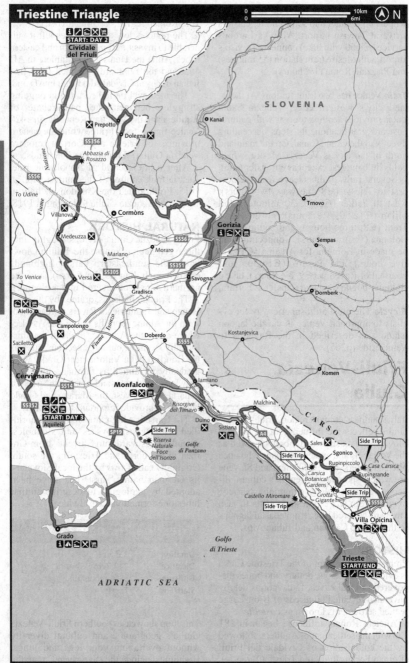

rolling Collio vineyards, the historic towns of Cividale, Aquileia and Grado, and the final scenic jaunt down the Istrian coast.

PLANNING
When to Ride
This ride is most enjoyable between April and October. August is best avoided, due to overcrowding on Grado's beaches and the closure of many Trieste hotels. In October restaurants known as *ozmizze* spontaneously pop up in the Triestine Carso, serving simple meals featuring local produce and wine.

Maps &Books
Touring Club Italia's (TCI) 1:200,000 *Veneto Friuli-Venezia Giulia* map covers this ride in its entirety.

The free brochure *20 itinerari cicloturistici in Friuli-Venezia Giulia*, available at local visitor centres, describes 20 rides throughout the region, including the Carso and Collio sections of this route.

ACCESS TOWN
Trieste
Trieste is like no other place in Italy, strongly culturally influenced by its Slavic neighbours, while architecturally retaining a faded grandeur from its former life as Austria-Hungary's principal Mediterranean port. The modern-day city is a bit gritty, and its waterfront marred by a busy main road, but there are still plenty of pleasant and intriguing places to discover. The bones of old Roman Tergeste poke out from San Giusto Hill, while the lower-lying Borgo Teresiano is filled with monumental squares and neoclassical buildings.

Information The visitor centre (☎ 040 347 83 12, w www.trietetourism.it) is on Via San Nicolo, 20.

Bancomats are available throughout the city.

Casa del Ciclo di Capponi Pierpaolo (☎ 040 63 80 09) is an excellent, helpful bike shop at Via Valdirivo 21. It leads tours in the surrounding area and is closed on Sunday and Monday.

Things to See & Do For the best panoramic and historical perspective, climb San Giusto hill, the nucleus of ancient and medieval Trieste. Don't miss the sweeping view of the city and waterfront from the ramparts of 15th-century **Castello di San Giusto** (☎ 040 30 93 62; Piazza Cattedrale 3). The adjacent **cathedral** is actually two earlier basilicas joined together, with medieval mosaics and frescoes. A few scattered reminders of Roman Tergeste survive, including ruins of a forum and theatre, and the collection of ancient stonework and pottery artfully displayed in the outdoor sculpture garden **Orto Lapidario**. Next door, the eclectic **Civico Museo di Storia ed Arte** (☎ 040 31 05 00; Via della Cattedrale 15) houses archaeological and artistic artefacts from Trieste and elsewhere.

Closer to the waterfront are two 19th-century private residences converted to museums: **Museo Revoltella** (☎ 040 30 09 38; Via Diaz 27) and **Museo Sartorio** (☎ 040 30 14 79; Largo Papa Giovanni XXIII), both displaying paintings, period furnishings and decorative art.

Fans of James Joyce and Italo Svevo can trace the authors' footsteps, following itineraries distributed free by the visitor centre.

On a promontory north of town is Maximilian of Austria's fanciful white **Miramare Castle** (☎ 040 22 41 43), now a museum surrounded by a beautiful park.

The **Val Rosandra bikepath** in the hills southeast of town runs for approximately 13km. Its hard-packed dirt course passes through a lovely narrow valley with a waterfall and Roman aqueduct.

The **Barcolana** (w www.barcolana.it) is the Mediterranean's largest competitive sailing event, taking place annually on the second Sunday in October.

Places to Stay & Eat Attractively situated high in the hills above Trieste, across from the Obelisco tram stop, is **Campeggio Obelisco** (☎ 040 21 16 55; per person/site €4/8; open year-round). Around 6km north of town on the Day 3 route is **Ostello Tergeste** (☎/fax 040 22 41 02; Viale Miramare 331; dorm beds €12; curfew 11.30pm). It's the best deal around and its dreary dorm rooms are redeemed by an airy trellised terrace offering lovely castle and ocean views. **Albergo al Viale** (☎ 040 348 08 38; Via Nordio 5; singles/doubles with bathroom €45/65) is more appealing than most budget downtown hotels. **Hotel Al Teatro** (☎/fax 040 36 62 20; Capo di Piazza Bartoli 1; singles/

doubles €40/90) has a great location on Trieste's biggest square.

There's a good **produce market** (Piazza Ponterosso; open 8am-7pm Tues-Sat), alongside the Canal Grande. **Antico Caffè San Marco** (Via Battisti 18) is a historic Viennese-style café, perfect for chess, reading, and people watching. **Buffet Rudy** (Via Valdirivo 32) is a popular beer hall serving tasty Bavarian food. **Il Pirata** (Via Boccardi 1) is a trendy late-night hangout with artsy decor, specialising in big glasses of wine and food grilled over an open fire.

Getting There & Away The train station is just north of downtown. Trieste is the easternmost stop in the Italian train system. Trains run regularly to Venice (€8, two hours), where connections can be made to other Italian destinations. There's also frequent service on the smaller line to Gorizia and Udine.

Bicycle Trieste sits at the crossroads between two international bike routes sponsored by the European Cyclists' Federation (ECF; w www.ecf.com). The Mediterranean route runs east-west from Cádiz (Spain) to Athens (Greece), while the Baltic to Adriatic route runs north-south from Gdansk (Poland) to Pula (Croatia). For more info contact ECF or its Italian affiliate Federazione Italiana Amici della Bicicletta (FIAB; w www.fiab-onlus.it).

THE RIDE
Day 1: Trieste to Cividale del Friuli
5–7 hours, 91.8km

Today descends from the stony Carso highlands to the fertile Collio vineyards. This is the tour's longest day, but still only moderately challenging.

Trieste's century-old tram line tackles the day's steepest climb (up to 26% grade!) to Villa Opicina. The 25-minute ride costs €1.40, and leaves every 20 minutes from Piazza Oberdan. Bikes travel on racks up front or in the compartment behind the driver.

From Opicina, the route undulates through stony hamlets and fields bordered by rocky walls. Side trips lead to the **Casa Carsica** (6.3km; admission free; open 11am-12.30pm & 3pm-5pm Sun), a traditional Carso farmhouse, the **Grotta Gigante** (8.9km; ☎ 040

32 73 12; admission €7; open 10am-6pm Apr-Sept, 10am-4pm Oct-Mar, closed Mon except July, Aug and holidays), listed by Guinness as the world's largest tourable cave; and the **Carsiana Botanical Gardens** (13.4km; ☎ 040 22 95 73; admission €2.50; open 10am-noon Tues-Fri, 10am-1pm & 3pm-7pm Sat-Sun, closed Mon), displaying 600 plant species native to the Carso. On autumn weekends the hills are abuzz with locals sampling jota (bean and sauerkraut soup) Terrano wine, and other regional specialties at seasonal ozmizze.

Dropping close to sea level at Sistiana, the route briefly joins the busy national highway, then turns inland again at 31.5km. The pretty cypress-lined road into the mountains passes right through one of WWII's heaviest combat zones.

Smaller roads bypass the centre of Gorizia, crossing the Fiume Isonzo at 52.5km. Aside from two short steep climbs, the remainder of the route sails blissfully along the Slovenian border, through vineyards producing Collio, Picolit, Tocai Friulano and other fine wines. The day's final highlight is the picturesque crossing of the Natisone River gorge on Cividale del Friuli's famous Ponte del Diavolo.

Cividale del Friuli
Straddling the Natisone gorge and surrounded by some of Friuli's finest vineyards, Cividale is a pleasant town with a fascinating history. Founded by Julius Caesar in 50 BC as the municipium (a self-governing town, but whose residents did not necessarily qualify for Roman citizenship) of Forum Iulii (from which the modern name Friuli derives), it became the first of 35 Lombard duchies in Italy when King Alboin invaded in AD 568, then served as seat of the Patriarchate of Aquileia from 1077 to 1238. Cividale's multilayered history is evident in its medieval and Renaissance architecture, and in the Roman and Lombard remnants preserved in its museums and monuments.

Information The visitor centre (☎ 0432 73 14 61, w www.regione.fvg.it/benvenuti/cividale/welcome.htm) is at Corso Paolino d'Aquileia 10, just a block from the Ponte del Diavolo.

A Bancomat is available at Cassa di Risparmio di Udine, Largo Boiani 33, one block west of the visitor centre.

Bicisport di Giovanni Mattana (☎ 0432 73 35 42) is an excellent, friendly bike shop on Via Udine at the northwest corner of town (closed Monday).

Things to See & Do For pretty views of the Natisone gorge and Cividale's medieval centre, start with a stroll across 15th century **Ponte del Diavolo**.

Above the Natisone upstream from the bridge, **Tempietto Longobardo** (☎ 0432 70 08 67; off Piazza San Biagio) is a small masterpiece of early medieval art. Believed to be of 8th-century origin, the temple's decoration includes statues of six female saints and a delicate arched stucco relief of grapes and vines.

Museo Archeologico Nazionale (☎ 0432 70 07 00; Piazza Duomo 1) has a superb col-

lection of Lombard goldsmithery, necropolis finds and other artefacts, plus Roman floor mosaics and carvings.

Across the square, the **duomo** (cathedral) and adjacent **Museo Cristiano del Duomo** (☎ 0432 73 11 44) hold other fine examples of Lombard sculpture and metalwork.

Ipogeo Celtico (Via Monastero Maggiore 6), an artificial cave complex presumably of Celtic origin, can be visited by arrangement with the folks at Bar All'Ipogeo (☎ 0432 70 12 11; Corso Paolino d'Aquileia).

Places to Stay & Eat The best deal in town is **Locanda al Pomo d'Oro** (☎/fax 0432 73 14 89; Piazza S. Giovanni 20; singles/doubles €40/60), a restored 11th-century inn. It's friendly, family-run, and

Triestine Triangle – Day 1

Cue

start	Trieste visitor centre		27.5 ⤴ ✦	SS14 'to Venezia', Sistiana
0km	E on Via Mazzini		32.3 ⤴	SS55 'to Gorizia'
⤴	(20m)Via San Spiridione		45.6 ⤶	'to Savogna'
0.5 ⤴	Via Galatti		47.6 ⤴	'to Savogna'
0.6	Piazza Oberdan tram stop		48.2 ⤴	SP8 'to Gorizia'
tram to Villa Opicina			53.1 ⤵	SS56 'to Udine', Gorizia
0.6	NE on SS58		53.9 ⤴	'to Gradisca/Cervignano'
1.3 ⤶	'to Monrupino'		54 ⤴	'to Piedimonte'
4.6 ⤶	'to Rupingrande'		56.4 ⤶	'to S. Floriano'
5.8	Rupingrande		57.4 ▲	1.2km steep climb
6.3 ●●⤴	Casa Carsica, 1km ⟳		59.6 ⤵	unmarked road down into vineyards
6.4 ⤵	'to Borgo Grotta Gigante'		61.0 ⤴	unmarked road
8.9 ⤴	'to Rupinpiccolo'		63.9 ⤶	'to Cormons'
●● ⤴	Grotta Gigante 2km ⟳		64.8 ⤴	'to Cormons'
11.1 ⤴	'to Carsiana', Rupinpiccolo		69.5 ⤴	'to Dolegna'
13.4 ⤴	'to Sales', Sgonico		69.6 ▲	0.9km steep climb
●● ⤶	Carsiana Gardens 1.4km ⟳		70.5 ⤵	'to Corno di Rosazzo'
14.9	Sales		73.7 ⤴	SP14 'to Dolegna del Collio'
15.7 ⤴	'to Samatorza'		79.3	Dolegna
18.4 ⤴	unmarked main road		79.7 ↑	SP21 'to Mernico'
20.3 ⤶	'to Malchina'		82.7 ⤶	'to Trattoria da Mario/Farmacia'
20.4 ⤴	'to Malchina'		83.4	Prepotto
24.1 ⤵	'to Visogliano', Malchina		84.0 ⤴	'to Cividale'
24.2 ⤴	'to Ceroglie'		91.3 ⤴	Viale Trieste 'to Centro'
27.0 ⤴	continue downhill		91.8	Cividale del Friuli visitor centre

Elevation

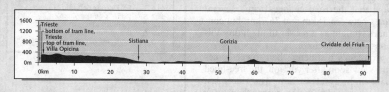

central, with an excellent restaurant. **Hotel Roma** (☎ 0432 73 18 71; Piazza Picco; singles/ doubles €55/80), the only other in-town option, is much less inspiring. **Locanda al Castello** (☎ 0432 73 32 42; ⓦ www.al castello.net; Via del Castello 20; singles/ doubles €65/90), a 19th-century castle originally built as a Jesuit monastery, sits on a hilltop overlooking vineyards north of town, with an attached restaurant and pleasant terrace.

Emporio Ortofrutticolo (3 Piazza Diacono) and **Coopca** (17 Via Ristori) are good for produce and other groceries. **Pizzeria da Carmine** (Via Cerchiari 1; pizza €4-6) is a central pizzeria. **Antica Trattoria Dominissimi** (Stretta Stellini 18; primi €5-7, secondi €5-10; closed Mon) serves fabulous frico and other local specialties in a room decorated with copper kettles and grapevine friezes. **Locanda al Pomo d'Oro** (closed Wed) also has great local cuisine. **Enoteca de Feo** (Via Ristori 29; closed Sun & Mon) is a fancy restaurant and wine bar open until midnight.

Day 2: Cividale del Friuli to Aquileia

3–4 hours, 53km

The short and easy route from Cividale to Aquileia leaves time to explore cultural attractions in both towns. The ride is entirely flat except for a short climb early in the day.

Leaving Cividale, small rural roads parallel the Fiume Natisone through farm country for 8.2km. After a brief congested stretch, the route climbs through pretty hills peppered with vineyards, cypresses, and poplars to the 11th-century **Abbazia di Rosazzo** (13.6km; open 9am-noon & 3pm-6pm daily). The well-preserved abbey commands a beautiful view of the valley below and makes a peaceful rest stop.

Descending into the vast Friulian flatlands, the route passes historical villas marked with plaques, while meandering through a series of small rural communities. Note that the road changes name several times between 18km and 26.7km, but continues straight as it passes through tiny Villanova and Medeuzza.

Aquileia's distinctive bell tower comes into view soon after you join the tree-lined main highway at 49.2km. The ride's last 1km passes old **Roman ruins**, then turns into the main square in front of the basilica.

Aquileia

At first glance you'd never guess that Aquileia once ranked among the Roman Empire's largest and richest cities, and served as its busiest Adriatic port. Aquileia was also a major ecclesiastical power, instrumental in the early diffusion of Christianity into central Europe, later ruling Friuli as a powerful patriarchate for several centuries. Nowadays the Adriatic has receded, leaving the Roman port high and dry, but the ruins, mosaics and churches left behind give fascinating glimpses of the town's illustrious past.

Information The visitor centre (☎ 0431 91 94 91) is at Piazza Capitolo 4, across from the basilica.

Triestine Triangle – Day 2

Cue		
start		Cividale del Friuli visitor centre
0km		S on Via Paolino D'Aquileia
0.3	↱	Via Manzano
1.4	↗	Via Firmano 'to Firmano'
5.3	↰	Via Strada di Ipplis
5.7	↱	Via Strada di Leproso
8.2	↰	Via Armentarezza
9.4	↱	'to Manzano'
10.2	↰	'to Rosazzo/Oleis'
10.9	↰	Via Rosazzo 'to Rosazzo'
12.8	▲	0.8km steep climb
13.6	✳	Abbazia di Rosazzo
16.6	↰	'to Corno di Rosazzo'
17.0	↱	Via Dolegnano di Sotto
18.0	↱	Via Zanon/Via IV Nov/Via Chiopris
20.2		Villanova
23.4		Medeuzza
26.7	↱	SP6 'to Versa'
29.1	↱	SS252 'to Palmanova', Versa
31.0	↱	'to Campolongo/Tapogliano'
31.3	↰	'to Campolongo'
31.6	↱	'to Campolongo'
35.0	↱	Via Puccini/SP120, Campolongo
37.7	↰	'to Ruda/Perteole', Aiello
38.0	↱	Via Petrarca
40.3	↘	'to Saciletto'
41.8	↰	SP30, Saciletto
43.0	↱	Via Garibaldi 'to Grado'
44.4	↱	'to Grado'
44.6	↰	SP54 'to Aquileia/Grado'
49.2	↘	SS352 'to Aquileia/Grado'
52.9	↰	Via Patriarca Popone
53.0	↰	through Piazza Capitolo
53.0		(50m) Aquileia visitor centre

Bancomats can be found at Cassa Rurale Artigiana and Rolo Banca, both on SS352 in the heart of town.

Motostile Nadalin (☎ 0431 9 15 72), Via Beligna 1a, can provide basic parts and repairs (or sell you a motorcycle if you get desperate!).

Things to See & Do Aquileia's **basilica** (☎ 0431 9 10 67; Piazza Capitolo), founded soon after Constantine's conversion to Christianity in the early 4th century, features a stunning floor mosaic, the largest of its kind in Western Europe. A trip up the adjacent **bell tower** offers a bird's eye view of town.

National Archaeology Museum (☎ 0431 9 10 16; Via Roma 1) has a remarkable collection of carved Roman faces, jewellery, coins and glass displayed on three floors, plus a vast courtyard strewn with broken columns, statues and floor-mosaic fragments.

Paleochristian Museum (☎ 0431 9 11 31), built on the foundations of another 4th-century church north of town (look for signs on Via Gemina), houses additional mosaics and carvings.

Between Museo Paleocristiano and the basilica, a pretty cypress-lined path follows the ancient riverbed past the ruins of Aquileia's **Roman port**. The old **forum** is nearby, alongside the main road, with additional ruins scattered throughout town.

Places to Stay & Eat Campers should head north of town, near the old Roman port, to **Camping Aquileia** (☎/fax 0431 91 95 83; ⓦ www.campingaquileia.it; Via Gemina 10; per person/site €6/9.10; open 15 May–15 Sept). Several places rent **rooms** from €15 per person; request a list at the visitor centre, or look for signs on Via Gemina and SS352. **Ostello Domus Augusta** (☎/fax 0431 9 10 24; ⓦ www.ostelloa quileia.it; Via Roma 25; per person €13) is Aquileia's newest hostel, opened in 2001. **Albergo/Ristorante Aquila Nera** (☎/fax 0431 9 10 45; Piazza Garibaldi 5; singles/doubles €27/45) is a basic but affordable one-star hotel. **Azienda Agrituristica Ca' Ospitale** (☎ 0431 91 74 23; ⓔ caospitale agritur@libero.it; Via Beligna 107; per person/site €5/6, singles/doubles €31/62) is nicely situated in the fields south of town, with a swimming pool.

De Spar (Via Giulia Augusta 17) sells groceries. **Ristorante alla Basilica** (Via della Stazione; pizza €4-6) is a friendly pizzeria near the basilica. **Ristorante ai Due Leoni** (Via Beligna 102; seafood primi €6, fish menu €13; closed Mon) is a popular place for seafood, 3km south towards Grado. **Ristorante al Pescatore** (Via Giulia Augusta 17; closed Mon) also specialises in fish, with live music on Friday and Saturday.

Day 3: Aquileia to Trieste
4–6 hours, 67.9km
Highlights of this flat final day include Grado's beaches and historic centre, plus the scenic home stretch down the Istrian coast.

From Aquileia, a beautiful canopy of sycamore trees leads to a causeway over

ADRIATIC COAST

Triestine Triangle – Day 3

Cue		
start	Aquileia visitor center	
0km	S on Via Vescovo Teodoro	
0.1	↱	Via dei Patriarchi
0.2	↖	SS352
10.4	✳	Grado
10.8	↖	Via Scaramuzza/Riva Iataper
11.3	↱	Via Galileo Galilei
11.5	↘	eastbound bikepath
12.8	↖	Viale Martiri della Liberta
13.1	↱	Viale Italia 'to Trieste'
13.3	↱	Via Saba 'to Trieste'
13.5	↱	Via Monfalcone/SP19 'to Trieste'
20.7	↱	Via Grado 'to Fossalon'
24.4	↱	Via Isonzato
27.9	↱	SP19
31.4	↱	Via del Brancolo 'to Marina Giulia'
33.9	●●☛	Riserva Foce dell'Isonzo 3km ↻
36.8	↱	'to Monfalcone'
37.5	↗	Via Boschetti
38.7	↗	Via dei Cipressi, Monfalcone
38.9	↘	Viale Cosulich
39.4	↱	SS14/Via Boito 'to Trieste'
44.5	✳	Risorgive del Timavo
46.1	↗	'to Duino'
46.7	↱	'to Trieste', Duino
48.2		Sistiana
49.7	↗	Strada Costiera Miramare/Trieste
59.3	⚠	two 300m tunnels, use footpaths
60.8	●●☛	Castello Miramare 1km ↻
67.0	↱	Piazza della Liberta
67.1	↘	Corso Cavour/Riva III Novembre
67.7	↱	Via San Nicolo
67.9		Trieste visitor centre

open water, where billboards proclaim your official entry into Grado (Mitteleuropa's Beach). Hype aside, Grado does have some nice beaches; and the beautifully preserved historic centre (on the right at 10.4km), hidden like a pearl within the ungainly oyster shell of the surrounding modern development, is filled with atmospheric cobblestone streets leading to a cluster of early Christian churches.

A bikepath from Grado's visitor centre (11.5km) squiggles out to the beach. Soon afterwards the route returns to the main Grado–Monfalcone highway, where intermittent bikepaths parallel the roadway offering broad lagoon vistas for the next 7km. A turn-off at 20.7km follows peaceful backroads through farmland reclaimed from the swamps.

After crossing the Fiume Isonzo (27.9km) on the main highway, the route detours onto another sleepy backroad for 5km, following a canal and permitting access to the **Riserva Naturale Foce dell'Isonzo**, a protected wetland bird habitat at the river's mouth (side trip on gravel road at 33.9km).

The return to 'civilisation' at Monfalcone (38.7km) is jarring, although the busy traffic along SS14 subsides somewhat when cars are lured onto the autostrada at 42.2km. At 44.5km is the mouth of the Timavo (a river immortalised in Virgil's *Aeneid*), which flows underground for 35km before emerging here.

The beautiful Strada Costiera hugs the Adriatic's edge from 49.7km all the way into Trieste, offering spectacular views of dazzling white cliffs, the sparkling sea and the dramatic Castello Miramare (side trip at 60.8km).

Po Delta & Venetian Lagoon

This section of the Adriatic Coast is overwhelmingly flat and watery, laced with canals, lakes, rivers and lagoons. Originally valued for its proximity to the sea and as a refuge easily defended from invaders, these lands gave rise to some of Italy's greatest cultural centres, including Ravenna, Padua, Ferrara and, of course, Venice.

HISTORY

Greek and Etruscan presence in the Po Delta has been documented at Spina (near present-day Comacchio) and Adria (southwest of Chiogga). Rome's many settlements in the region included the important naval port of Classis, established near modern-day Ravenna by Augustus Caesar.

In AD 402, emperor Honorius, fearing an onslaught of invaders, moved the Roman Empire's western capital to Ravenna, ushering in a new age for the city as it became successively the capital of the Ostrogoths under Theodoric (late 5th Century) and the Byzantines under Justinian (mid-6th century).

Ravenna's power slowly faded as it came under repeated siege by Lombards and Franks. Meanwhile, the nascent republic of Venice distinguished itself as the only northeastern Italian community capable of staving off the invaders. Protected on their lagoon islands, the Venetians became rulers of the Adriatic and much of the Mediterranean, increasingly declaring their independence from Byzantium and building a land empire in mainland Italy.

The entire region was incorporated into the new Kingdom of Italy in the 1860s.

NATURAL HISTORY

The Po is Italy's longest river and drains its vastest expanse of flat land, the Pianura Padana. Much of the region was historically marshy and unfit for human settlement, but over the centuries huge tracts were reclaimed for urban and agricultural development. The most substantial remaining wetlands can be found in the Po Delta near the Adriatic Coast. Here, in its eastern reaches, the Po splits into seven distinct channels (the Volano, Goro, Gnocca (Donzella), Tolle, Venezia, Maistra and Levante). In between are islands and large bodies of water known as *valli*, providing bird habitat. The Po remains heavily polluted, but with the establishment of Parco del Delta del Po, efforts are underway to protect the local environment.

Near the coast a few significant stretches of pine woods remain, as well as the Bosco della Mesola, a forest dating to Etruscan times, which shelters a herd of native deer.

West of Padua, the rugged Colli Euganei (Euganean Hills) provide a counterpoint to the region's flatness. Their cone-shaped peaks are remnants of ancient volcanoes.

Colli Euganei

Duration	5–7 hours
Distance	77.6km
Difficulty	moderate–hard
Start/End	Padua

This loop showcases the lovely vineyards, appealing small towns, and rugged topography of the Euganeian Hills west of Padua.

PLANNING
When to Ride
This ride is especially nice in spring and early autumn.

Maps
TCI's 1:200,000 *Veneto Friuli-Venezia Giulia* map shows the entire route.

ACCESS TOWN
Padua
Padua (Padova) is most famous as the site of Giotto's beautiful Scrovegni Chapel frescoes, and has also become popular among tourists as a more affordable and less crowded place to overnight while visiting Venice. Its delightful medieval centre and numerous churches and monuments deserve a visit on their own merits.

Information Padua's main visitor centre (☎ 049 875 20 77, W www.apt.padova.it) is conveniently located inside the train station.

There's a Bancomat at the station, with plenty of other banks throughout the city.

Two of Padua's best bike shops are Morbiato Cicli (☎ 049 70 64 63) at Via Pontevigodarzare 101–105, and Cicli Morello (☎ 049 871 56 50) at Via Sorio 54.

Things to See & Do Giotto's frescoes in the **Cappella degli Scrovegni** (☎ 049 820 45 50) rank among Italy's most exquisite art treasures. Painted in the first decade of the 14th century and restored in 2001, the starry ceiling and wall panels depicting the lives of Mary and Jesus shimmer with ethereal blues.

The adjacent **Museo Civico** displays Roman mosaics and statuary, plus artworks by Giotto, Bellini and others.

The 13th-century Romanesque-Gothic **Basilica di S Antonio** houses the remains of St Anthony within its frescoed walls, together with bronze reliefs and sculptures by Donatello. Pilgrims flock to seek healing here, plastering Anthony's tomb with notes and photographs, beseeching or thankful.

The 13th-century **Palazzo della Ragione**, between Piazza delle Erbe and Piazza della Frutta in the medieval centre, is famous for its large upstairs hall with vaulted wooden ceiling, an engineering feat of its time. Its treasures include a frescoed astrological calendar and a lovely wooden horse carved in 1466.

Nearby are Padua's beautiful 13th-century Romanesque **baptistery**, with frescoes influenced by Giotto, and the later **duomo**.

The **Chiesa degli Eremitani** contains the remains of beautiful mid-15th century frescoes by Mantegna, painstakingly reconstructed after the church was bombed to smithereens in WWII.

Guided tours of Padua's **university** (founded in 1221 and the second oldest in Italy) focus on the Palazzo del Bo, where you can visit Europe's oldest anatomy theatre and see the chair where Galileo once taught.

Dating back to 1545, **Orto Botanico** is Europe's oldest university botanical garden, with many rare species.

Places to Stay & Eat Padua's best low-budget option is **AIG Ostello Città di Padova** (☎ 049 875 22 19; Via A Aleardi 30; dorm beds €15), just south of downtown. **Albergo Dante** (☎ 049 876 04 08; Via San Polo 5; singles/doubles €26/36) is a simple, pleasant one-star north of the centre. **Albergo Sant' Antonio** (☎ 049 875 13 93; Via San Fermo 118; singles/doubles €55/70), a nearby two-star, has some rooms with bridge and canal views. **Hotel Leon Bianco** (☎ 049 875 08 14; W www.toscanelli.com; Piazzetta Pedrocchi 12; singles/doubles €71/96) is a nice three-star whose breakfast terrace overlooks the historic centre's rooftops.

Padua's daily **produce market** (*Piazza delle Erbe*) is one of Italy's finest. A sea of fresh fruit and vegetables fills the central area, while surrounding stalls sell everything from ice cream to horsemeat. **Caffè Pedrocchi** (*just off Via VIII Febbraio*) has been a meeting place for scholars and artists since 1831. **Pizzeria Savonarola** (*Via dei Savonarola 38; pizza from €4, pasta from €5; closed Mon*) is a good, bustling pizzeria.

Osteria dei Fabbri *(☎ 049 65 03 36; Via dei Fabbri 13; closed Sun)* is another extremely popular local hangout, worth reserving ahead. **Pizzeria dai Gemelli** *(Via Dondi dall'Orologio 11/13; pizzas from €4; meals €15; closed Wed)* and **Trattoria Mario e Mercedes** *(Via S Giovanni da Verdara 13; meals €20; closed Wed)* both serve up delicious regional specialties.

Getting There & Away The train station is just north of downtown. Padua is on the main north–south line from Venice to Bologna and also on the main east–west line from Venice to Milano. One-way fares from Padua include Bologna (€5.80, 1½ hours), Milano (€11.50, three hours), and Venice (€2.50, 30 minutes).

THE RIDE

After an easy initial cruise through the flatlands southwest of Padua, the route becomes relentlessly hilly, climbing through the forests, vineyards and lovely small towns of the Colli Euganei (Euganeian Hills). The return trip is through flat to rolling wine-growing country at the base of the hills.

It's a bit hairy navigating out of Padua, but a short bikepath paralleling Via Sorio between 4.2km and 5.2km steers clear of the nastiest traffic. Beyond the city limits, the Via dei Colli zooms through the flats for roughly 15km before climbing towards Teolo. A short side trip at 13.8km leads to **Praglia monastery**, whose attractions include lovely 15th-century cloisters and a centre for the restoration of old books.

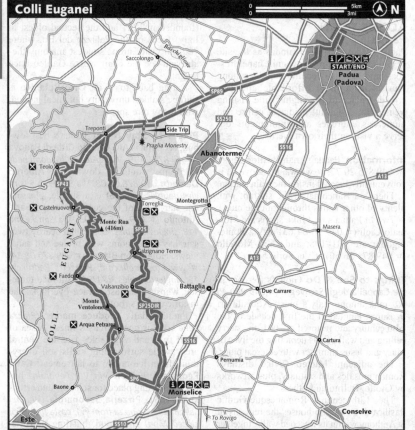

Colli Euganei

Colli Euganei

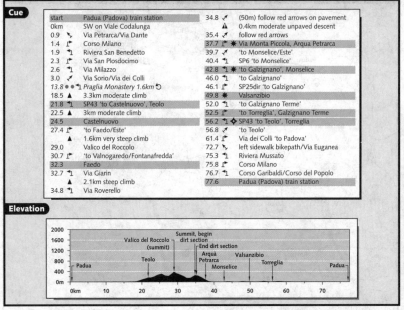

Cue

start	Padua (Padova) train station		34.8		(50m) follow red arrows on pavement
0km	SW on Viale Codalunga				0.4km moderate unpaved descent
0.9	Via Petrarca/Via Dante		35.4		follow red arrows
1.4	Corso Milano		37.7	✹	Via Monta Piccola, Arqua Petrarca
1.9	Riviera San Benedetto		39.7		'to Monselice/Este'
2.3	Via San Plosdocimo		40.4		SP6 'to Monselice'
2.6	Via Milazzo		42.8	✹	'to Galzignano', Monselice
3.0	Via Sorio/Via dei Colli		46.0		'to Galzignano'
13.8 ● ●	Praglia Monastery 1.6km ↺		46.1		SP25dir 'to Galzignano'
18.5 ▲	3.3km moderate climb		49.8	✹	Valsanzibio
21.8	SP43 'to Castelnuovo', Teolo		52.0		'to Galzignano Terme'
22.5 ▲	3km moderate climb		52.5		'to Torreglia', Galzignano Terme
24.5	Castelnuovo		56.2	◆	SP43 'to Teolo', Torreglia
27.4	'to Faedo/Este'		56.8		'to Teolo'
▲	1.6km very steep climb		61.4		Via dei Colli 'to Padova'
29.0	Valico del Roccolo		72.7		left sidewalk bikepath/Via Euganea
30.7	'to Valnogaredo/Fontanafredda'		75.3		Riviera Mussato
32.3	Faedo		75.8		Corso Milano
32.7	Via Giarin		76.7		Corso Garibaldi/Corso del Popolo
▲	2.1km steep climb		77.6		Padua (Padova) train station
34.8	Via Roverello				

Elevation

From **Teolo** (21.8km), picturesquely perched at the gateway to the hills, a densely packed series of climbs and descents leads through the heart of the Colli Euganei. Most gruelling is the 11% grade leading to Valico del Roccolo, but the views of the surrounding countryside are spectacular. The 5km stretch from Faedo to Arqua Petrarca is also appealing, snaking up through a narrow vineyard-filled valley, briefly turning to dirt at the summit, then plunging downhill and clattering onto the cobblestones of **Arqua Petrarca** (37.7km). The poet Petrarch spent his last five years in this beautifully preserved medieval town; visits to his house and tomb are possible.

Beyond Arqua the route descends to **Monselice** (42.8km), home to a splendid 11th- to 16th-century castle and several historic villas. At **Valsanzibio** (49.8km), Villa Barbarigo with its 16th-century gardens, fountains and labyrinth makes another worthwhile stop. The remainder of the route rolls along the eastern edge of the hills, continuing its course through vineyards and small towns, eventually rejoining the Teolo–Padua highway at **Treponti** (61.4km).

Ravenna to Venice

Duration	4 days
Distance	245.3km
Difficulty	easy
Start	Ravenna
End	Venice

This pancake-flat ride through the Po Delta and surrounding wetlands connects the great cities of Ravenna, Ferrara and Venice. Six ferry crossings add to the ride's appeal, culminating in an island-hopping journey across the Venetian lagoon.

PLANNING
When to Ride

Spring and autumn are the best seasons for this ride.

Maps & Books

TCI's 1:200,000 maps of *Emilia Romagna* and *Veneto Friuli-Venezia Giulia* are useful resources for most of this ride.

The Day 3 Destra Po bikepath section is covered by the free map/brochure *Destra Po*.

ADRIATIC COAST

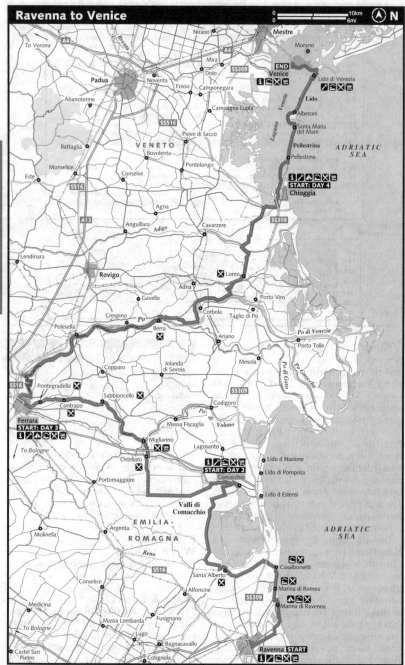

Ravenna to Venice

N

0 ———————— 10km
0 ———————— 6mi

To Verona
A4
Brenta
Nirano
Mestre
Mira
Murano
Padua
Dolo
SS309
Noventa
Fosso
Camponegara
END
Venice
Lido di Venezia
Abanoterme
Campagna Lupia
Lido
Alberoni
Piove di Sacco
Santa Maria del Mare
VENETO
Pellestrina
Battaglia
Bovolenta
Pellestrina
ADRIATIC SEA
Monselice
Conselve
Pontelongo
Este
SS516
START: DAY 4
Chioggia
Agna
A13
Anguillara
Adige
Cavarzere
SS309
Lendinara
Rovigo
Adria
Loreo
Porto Viro
Gavello
Crespino
Po
Corbola
Taglio di Po
Po di Venezia
Berra
Porto Tolle
Polesella
Ariano
Po di Goro
Porto Tolle
Copparo
Jolanda di Savoia
Mesola
SS516
Pontegradella
Sabbioncello
SS309
Po di Gnocca
Contrapo
Codigoro
Ferrara
START: DAY 3
Po di Volano
Migliarino
Massa Fiscaglia
To Bologne
Ostellato
Lagosanto
Lido di Nazione
Lido di Pomposa
START: DAY 2
Portomaggiore
Comacchio
Lido d Estensi
Valli di Comacchio
EMILIA-ROMAGNA
Molinella
Argenta
ADRIATIC SEA
Reno
Casalborsetti
SS516
Santa'Alberto
Marina di Romea
Conselice
Alfonsine
Marina di Ravenna
Medicina
SS309
To Bologne
Massa Lombarda
Fusignano
Lugo
Ravenna START
Castel San Pietro
Bagnacavallo
Cotignola

The map *Cycling in Ferrara* is also very useful for getting into and out of Ferrara. Both are available from Ferrara's visitor centre.

Tourist bureaus in this region provide a wealth of other cycling information. Of particular note is the free map/brochure *10 itinerari in bicicletta in provincia di Ferrara*, describing additional rides near Ferrara, the booklet *Cycling in Romagna*, which features rides in the Ravenna–Rimini area, and the map/brochure *The Park by Bike*, suggesting cycle itineraries in the Po Delta.

What to Bring

Carry extra water and food, as services are few and far between. Insect repellent is a must, for reasons that will become obvious as you cycle through the wetlands.

ACCESS TOWN
Ravenna

For mosaic lovers, Ravenna is nirvana. Nowhere else in Italy are so many early Christian mosaics so readily accessible; eight local churches and monuments have been designated Unesco World Heritage sites. Unlike their more austere late Byzantine successors, Ravenna's mosaics shimmer with brilliant shades of green and blue, their religious subject matter enhanced with portrayals of earthly beauty in the form of flowers, fruit, birds and animals.

Aside from mosaics, Ravenna has a pleasant and prosperous traffic-free centre where cycling is a popular way of getting around.

Information The visitor centre (☎ 0544 3 54 04, w www.turismo.ravenna.it) is at Via Salara 8.

There are many banks along Via Diaz, plus a Bancomat at the train station.

Two good local bike shops are Casa del Ciclo (☎ 0544 40 74 95), Via S Mama 148–152 (closed Thursday afternoon and Sunday), and Cicli Il Pedale (☎ 0544 40 22 74), Via F Abbandonato 293.

Things to See & Do Clumped together at Ravenna's northwest corner are two of the city's great treasures. The striking octagonal **Basilica di San Vitale** *(Via Fiandrini)* contains shimmering apse mosaics depicting Old Testament scenes, plus some fine portraits of Byzantine Emperor Justinian and Empress Theodora. Across a grassy courtyard is the starry-ceilinged **Mausoleo di Galla Placidia** *(Via Fiandrini)*, where 5th-century mosaics of a beardless Christ as Good Shepherd and San Lorenzo preparing to be roasted are complemented by decorative bird-and-fountain motifs, all illuminated by alabaster-filtered light.

The 6th-century **Basilica di Sant'Apollinare Nuovo** *(Via di Roma)*, constructed by Theodoric the Goth, has two dazzling mosaic processional scenes running the length of the church, plus smaller panels portraying the life and miracles of Christ.

Battistero Neoniano *(Piazza Duomo)* is a converted Roman bathhouse with mosaics showing Christ's baptism and the 12 apostles. Opposite, **Museo Arcivescovile** (☎ 0544 21 99 38; Piazza Arcivescovado) features additional mosaics and religious artefacts.

A single ticket, the Ravenna Visit Card (€6.50), allows access to all six of the above monuments.

It's worth travelling 5km south of town to the lovely 6th-century **Basilica di Sant' Apollinare in Classe** (☎ 0544 47 36 43; Via Romea Sud 216), whose stunning apse mosaic is one of Ravenna's finest.

Places to Stay & Eat For campers, **Camping Rivaverde** (☎ 0544 53 04 91; Viale delle Nazioni 301; per person/site €6/10) is one of several large camping grounds in Marina di Ravenna, northeast of town on the Day 1 route.

Ravenna hotels are generally bland and expensive. **Ostello Dante** (☎/fax 0544 42 11 64; Via Nicolodi 12; per person €13) is the best budget option, just off the Day 1 bikepath. **Hotel Ravenna** (☎ 0544 21 22 04; Viale P Maroncelli 12; singles/doubles €40/58) is a basic two-star near the train station. **Hotel Argentario** (☎ 0544 3 55 55; Via di Roma 45; singles/doubles €55/80) is a slightly nicer three-star near Sant'Apollinare Nuovo.

Ravenna's **Mercato Coperto** (Piazza Costa; open 7.30am-2pm daily, closed Sun) is great for fresh produce. **Standa** (cnr Via Cesarea & Via Serra) and **Coop** (across from the hostel) are large supermarkets. **L'Oste Bacco** (Via Salara 20; primi €5-7, secondi €8-12; closed Tues) has a cheerful, lively atmosphere and a varied menu. **Osteria del Santo Palato** (☎ 0544 303 51; meals €10-15; closed Mon), down a side street from San Vitale, has a creative menu and great wine list. **Araliya** (Via Pallavicini 8; meals €7-12;

closed Mon) serves tasty Indian food for people burned out on pasta.

Getting There & Away The train station is just east of the centre. Ravenna is on a secondary train line with limited direct service. Most long-distance trips require a change of train in Bologna, Ferrara, or Rimini. One-way fares from Ravenna include Bologna (€4.50, 1¼ hours), Ferrara (€4, 1¼ hours), Ancona (€7, 2¾ hours), Pesaro (€4.50, 1¾ hours) and Venice (€9, 3½ hours).

Bicycle From Ravenna, it's possible to link up with the Mystic Mountains, Sacred Hills ride at either Urbino or Pesaro. See the booklet *Cycling in Romagna* for ideas on itineraries south of Ravenna.

THE RIDE
Day 1: Ravenna to Comacchio
4–6 hours, 62.6km

Today's route makes a great S-curve through the wetlands south of Comacchio, with two ferry crossings along the way.

A quick zigzag through Ravenna's cycle-friendly streets leads to the day's first bikepath (1.4km). The route to the coast, following similar bikepaths and small roads, is often mobbed with other cyclists. A northward turn on the coastal highway passes scraggly pine forest, beaches and pizzerias en route to the Marina di Ravenna ferry landing. The port is rather grubby, but the ferry crossing is great, with little black-and-white boats bobbing in the water and hordes of bike-toting locals sharing the three-minute trip (tickets €0.50 at the dock-side machine or €0.75 on board).

From Porto Corsini, navigate north to Casalborsetti on roads interspersed with bikepaths. At 19.7km, the smell of salt and fish fills the air as the route crosses a picturesque canal bordered by fishing shacks and docks strung with cables and nets. Turning inland, another canal leads to Sant'Alberto, the last chance for food and provisions before Comacchio.

Leaving Sant'Alberto, the road narrows, crosses a dike and peters out completely at the edge of the pretty tree-lined Reno River. Here a cable-drawn ferry crosses to the opposite bank, charging cyclists €0.50.

On the north bank, a narrow dike-top road threads the needle between the broad and languid Reno and the vast Valli di Comacchio lagoon spreading away to the northern horizon. The insects can be nasty, but there's no traffic, and the wide-open vistas, with huge brick farmhouses looming like ships, are dazzling. Turning north, another long stretch follows on a narrow strip of land between canal and lagoon, with fishermen lining the banks in early morning. The home stretch into Comacchio is through flat agricultural land.

Comacchio
Surrounded by low-lying wetlands 5km inland from the Adriatic, Comacchio is better known as an eel-fishing port than a tourist destination. Optimistic local promoters have long dubbed it a miniature Venice because

Ravenna to Venice – Day 1

Cue

start		Ravenna visitor centre
0km		SW on Via Salara
0.0	↱	(50m) Via Cavour
0.1	↰	Via IV Novembre
0.2	↱	Piazza del Popolo to Via Diaz
0.6	↰	Via di Roma
0.9	↱	Via Alberoni
1.3	↰	Piazza Caduti sul Lavoro
1.4	↘	bikepath on left footpath
1.8	↱	bikepath paralleling Via Bellucci
7.8	↱	Via dell'Idrovora
9.1	↰	bikepath paralleling highway
11.0	↱	'to Marina di Ravenna'
12.1		Marina di Ravenna
14.6	↱	Via Molo Dalmazia 'to Traghetto'
14.9		ferry landing on RHS
ferry to Porto Corsini		
14.9	↱	'to Marina Romea/Casalborsetti'
15.7	↰	Via Goro
15.8	↑	bikepath (cross busy road)
16.7		Marina Romea
22.2		Casalborsetti
22.7	↱	Via Iacchini
25.4	↑	south bank of canal (cross SS309)
25.9	↰	across bridge
26.0	↱	road following north bank of canal
33.3	↙	'to Sant'Alberto/Anita'
33.5	↰	at stop sign, Sant'Alberto
35.3		ferry landing
ferry to Argenta		
40.6	↰	Via Valle Umana 'to Comacchio'
53.2	↰	Strada Fiume 'to Comacchio'
56.1	↱	Strada Canale Pega
57.7	↰	Strada Terzone 'to Comacchio'
59.8	↱	Via Spina (unmarked)
62.2	↱	'to centro'
62.2	↱	(50m) Via Alessandro Zappata
62.4	↰	Corso Mazzini
62.6		Comacchio visitor centre

of its small network of canals and unusual 17th-century bridge, but until recently there wasn't much else to see. Two new museums enhance the town's cultural appeal and visitors burned out on the tourist treadmill may even find charm in Comacchio's sleepy unselfconsciousness; while touristy enough to support a couple of good restaurants, the town's streets are still mainly peopled by local residents come sundown.

Information The visitor centre (☎ 0533 31 01 61) is in the centre of town at Piazzetta Folegatti 28.

Banca Antonveneta (Piazzetta Folegatti 23) has a Bancomat, directly across from the visitor centre.

Nordi Cicli e Moto (☎ 0533 31 15 29), Via Muratori 4, is a small bike shop offering rentals in the heart of town.

Things to See & Do The elegant **Trepponti**, Comacchio's biggest tourist draw, is an Escher-esque bridge built in 1634 to simultaneously span five canals. The bridge's five staircases meet on a central platform offering nice views.

Museo delle Valli di Comacchio (W www.vallidicomacchio.it; Località Foce 4), south of town, is an open-air museum spreading along the edges of Comacchio's lagoon. From park headquarters, where interpretive displays focus on traditional fishing life and the lagoon's natural environment, a network of pedestrian trails and bikepaths fans out along the water's edge, permitting bird-watching and visits to three *casoni*, large 17th-century structures used traditionally as bases for fishing and protection from poachers.

Museo della Nave Romana (☎ 0533 31 13 16; Via della Pescheria 2) is a fascinating new museum housing the remains of a 1st-century BC Roman ship excavated from Comacchio's mudflats. Particularly exciting is the museum's display of cargo found on board, preserved in silt for two millennia, including miniature votive temples, amphoras, fish hooks, tools, dice and more. A large mosaic photo of the excavation site shows what the ship and its cargo looked like at the time of discovery.

Across from the museum, local volunteers offer **free boat rides** on Comacchio's canals, including the obligatory passage under the Trepponti.

Places to Stay & Eat There are nine camping grounds along the beaches east of Comacchio. **Spiaggia e Mare** (☎ 0533 32 74 31; Via Strada Provincia Ferrara-Mare 4; per person/site €7/12) is the closest, in Porto Garibaldi.

Lodging options in Comacchio itself are limited. **Albergo Ristorante Tre Ponti** (☎/fax 0533 31 27 66; Via Marconi 3; singles/doubles €20/40) is the only hotel, a rather dismal one-star. **Al Ponticello** (☎ 0533 31 40 80; e resca@libero.it; Via Cavour 39; doubles €80) is a swank new B&B. **La Magnolia** (☎ 0533 31 20 21; Via Italia 61 No 13) is another B&B. The numerous beachside hotels east of town are generally dreary and overpriced but can bail you out in a pinch.

De Spar (Piazzetta Folegatti 16) supermarket is next to the visitor centre. **Panifico La Torre** (Via Filippo Carli 2) sells the eel-shaped bread called *ciambella di Comacchio*, a local specialty. **Pizza Arcobaleno** (Via Ugo Bassi 29) has pizza by the slice for under €1. **Trattoria Vasco e Giulia** (Via Muratori 21; closed Mon) is a wonderfully unpretentious place for reasonably priced local seafood. **Osteria Al Cantinon** (☎ 0533 31 42 52; Via Muratori; meals €20) has great food and front terrace views of the Trepponti.

Day 2: Comacchio to Ferrara
4–6 hours, 65km
Today starts out through flatlands rich in birdlife, then follows the Po into Ferrara.

Herons and pheasants are among the birds thronging the sleepy agricultural backroads leading to Ostellato. Continue straight at 7.8km, deviating from the main Argenta road onto an unmarked secondary road (later marked with signs 'to Porto Maggiore').

From Ostellato, tiny Strada Pioppa crosses a busy highway (29.3km) and winds through fruit orchards into Migliarino (32.4km), the day's best lunch spot. Walk your bike briefly through Migliarino's main piazza, site of a bustling outdoor market, then turn briefly against the flow of traffic, continuing straight onto Largo Zerbini towards the tiny bike/pedestrian bridge over the Po.

The remainder of the route follows the languid Po di Volano, one of the Po's biggest branches during Ferrara's medieval heyday, now reduced to a fraction of its former size. The river ducks in and out of view as you wind along dike-tops past fields, orchards and old brick farmhouses. Stay close to the Po, continuing straight onto a smaller road at 38km (the main road veers right here), then hugging the river's edge to cross under a bridge at 40.3km. An unpaved stretch starting at 44.1km makes you wonder if you've lost your way, but a sign 'to Contrapo' appears at 45.4km as pavement resumes.

The river crossing at 46.5km leads to a series of small towns along the south bank. A second crossing at 55.7km signals the beginning of the home stretch. Ferrara's excellent system of bikepaths starts in Pontegradella (60.7km), paralleling the main road from here to the town walls.

Ferrara

Traces of the past are evident everywhere in the agreeable city of Ferrara. Urban life still revolves around the Castello Estense, the moated former dwelling of the Este dukes who ruled this region between the 13th and 16th centuries. The city's medieval core and surrounding walls are largely intact, and Renaissance palaces abound.

Ferrara may well also be the cycle-friendliest city in Italy.

Information The visitor centre (☎ 0532 20 93 70, ⓦ www.provincia.fe.it/turismo) is in the heart of town, on the ground floor of the Castello Estense.

There are numerous banks with Bancomats along Corso Martiri della Libertà in the centre.

The *Cycling in Ferrara* map available from the visitor centre lists dozens of bike shops. One of the most convenient is Barlati (☎ 0532 20 68 63), at Via Adelardi 3, near the cathedral.

Things to See & Do Smack in the middle of the walled city, **Castello Estense** (☎ 0532 29 92 33; Largo Castello) has been Ferrara's most prominent landmark for more than seven centuries. Especially interesting are its dungeons, where the adulterous Marchioness Parisina and her stepson Ugo met their fate, and the Duchesses' Garden, a walled terrace affording views of the medieval city's cycle-filled streets.

Ferrara is loaded with fine palaces. The 14th-century **Casa Romei** (Via Savonarola 30) has exquisite beamed ceilings and frescoed walls. Others include **Palazzo Schifanoia** (Via

Scandiana 23) and **Palazzina di Marfisa d'Este** (Corso Giovecca 170).

North of the centre, the **Palazzo dei Diamanti** (Corso Ercole I d'Este 21) is worth a visit just to see its fanciful exterior, a nubby surface composed of more than 8000 pyramid-shaped stones. Inside are the **Pinacoteca Nazionale** and three other museums.

Ferrara's **cathedral** (Piazza Cattedrale) has a lovely tripartite facade featuring a fanciful assemblage of Romanesque and Gothic arches.

Museo Archeologico Nazionale (☎ 0532 6 62 99; Via XX Settembre 124) contains a fantastic collection of finds from the Etruscan town of Spina near present-day Comacchio. Also on display are trade goods unearthed at Spina from as far afield as Scandinavia and Africa.

The **Ferrara Buskers Festival** brings in street musicians from all over the world for a week in late August.

Places to Stay & Eat Northeast of town along the Day 3 route is **Campeggio Comunale Estense** (☎/fax 0532 75 23 96; Via Gramicia 76; per person/site €4/6). **Ostello Estense** (☎ 0532 20 42 27; ⓔ hostelferrara@hotmail.com; Corso Rossetti 24; dorm beds/family rooms per person €12.50/14; closed 10am-5pm, curfew 11.30pm) is a pleasant hostel while **Pensione Casa Artisti**

Ravenna to Venice – Day 2

Cue		
start		Comacchio visitor centre
0km		W on Via Folegatti
0.2	↰	Via Alessandro Zappata
0.5	↱	Via Spina 'to Ferrara/Ostellato'
6.5	↰	'to Anita'
20.8	↱	'to Ostellato'
28.7	↱	Via Garibaldi, Ostellato
29.0	↰	Strada Pioppa
32.4	↰	Via Gramsci, Migliarino
32.7	↱	Piazza Liberta/Largo Zerbini
32.8		(50m) cross Po di Volano
32.9	↰	Via Travaglio/Via Argine Volano
44.1	▲	1.3km unpaved stretch
46.3	↰	Piazza XXI Giugno, Sabbioncello
46.5		cross Po di Volano
46.6		(beyond bridge) 'to Ferrara'
54.4		Contrapo
55.7		cross Po di Volano
56.0	↰	Via Due Torri 'to Ferrara'
58.9	↱	cross canal
58.9	↰	(5m) Via Pontegradella 'to Ferrara'
60.7		Pontegradella
62.8	↱	Via Pomposa/Corso della Giovecca
65.0		Ferrara visitor centre

(☎ 0532 76 10 38; Via Vittoria 66; singles €18, doubles without/with bathroom €32/ 45) is the historic centre's best budget hotel. **Il Bagattino B&B** (☎ 0532 24 18 87; Corso Porta Reno 24; singles/doubles €60/80) is a nicely remodelled old palace with modern amenities, close to everything.

Supermercato Interspar and **Ipercoop Le Mura** are good places to stock up on groceries (both on Via Copparo, not far from the camping ground just outside Ferrara's north-eastern town wall). **Hostaria Savonarola** (Piazza Savonarola 14/18) is a convivial, central place for panini (bread rolls) and pasta. **Osteria Il Postiglione** (Via del Teatro 4), once a waystation for 19th-century carriage drivers, serves a devoted local clientele in an atmospheric, beamed cellar decorated with wine bottles, bricks and barrels. **Trattoria Il Cucco** (Via Voltacasotto 3; closed Wed) serves Ferrarese specialties, with a nice courtyard. **Antica Hostaria al Brindisi** (Via degli Adelardi 11) dates back to at least 1435 and features simple food and a complex wine list.

Day 3: Ferrara to Chioggia
6–8 hours, 95.8km

Today's route reaches Venice's doorstep via a combination of bikepaths, small country roads and ferryboat. Food stops are few and far between; consider bringing a picnic.

After a brief stint atop Ferrara's old town wall, the route twists through farmland north of town, following brown bike signs. The *Cycling in Ferrara* map helps with navigation.

The wonderful Destra Po bikepath begins at 8.1km, reaching the river's edge at 10.8km. Opened in September 2001, it's closed to cars except on the outskirts of towns; even here, traffic is next to nil. The path straddles a riverside dike, offering nice views of fields, vineyards, orchards and vast stands of poplars.

At 44.5km, the Berra–Villanova ferry is the last service of its kind on the Po, running daily on demand from sunrise to sunset. Service is occasionally interrupted for lunch breaks, inclement weather or maintenance; call ahead (☎ 330 24 41 43, 339 862 34 43) to avoid surprises. Cyclists pay €0.75 or €2.25 if the boat's on the far side and there are no other passengers.

For the next 20km, narrow dike-top roads offer views of the distant Dolomites to the left and the mighty Po on the right. Brief industrial and urban stretches near Loreo give way to tranquil backroads and crumbling Venetian mansions. After crossing the wide, slow-flowing Adige at 77.6km, the route follows canals through farmland to the outskirts of Chioggia.

The final few kilometres are a rude awakening, with big rigs screaming down the national highway and a gritty urban landscape unlike anything else encountered on this ride. Chioggia's calmer historic centre is a welcome relief at the end of the line.

Chioggia
During the Venetian Republic's heyday, Chioggia was Venice's proud sister city. Parallels between the two are harder to find nowadays. Modern Chioggia has more

Ravenna to Venice – Day 3

Cue

start	Ferrara visitor centre
0km	go NW on Viale Cavour
1.0 ↱	Via delle Barriere
1.0 ↰	(75m) Corso Porta Po
1.1 ↗	bikepath on top of town wall
⚠	1.2km dirt path
2.3 ⚠	steep climb down from wall
↰	bikepath along Via Azzo Novello
2.4 ↱	paved bikepath
3.4 ↰	Via Gramicia (unmarked)/bikepath
5.1 ⚠	2.6km bumpy unpaved section
5.7 ↰	bumpy dirt path
7.7 ↰	Via della Ricostruzione (unmarked)
8.1 ↱	Destra Po bikepath
43.5	Berra
44.5 ↰	down to ferry landing
ferry to Villanova	
44.6 ↰	(from dock) up to top of dike
44.8 ↱	Via Argine Po/Via Parco del Delta
53.0 ⚠	1.4km gravel-dirt road
57.6 ↗	'to Cavanella Po'
64.6 ↘	'to Cavanella Po'
64.8 ↰	away from river
65.8 ↘	to cross bridge
67.8 ↱	'to Loreo'
70.4 ↰	'to Ca' Nigra'
70.7 ↱	'to Loreo'
70.9 ↰	Via Riviera Marconi, Loreo
74.6 ↘	Via Tornova
76.1 ↰	Via Adige
77.6 ↗	'to Chioggia' (cross Adige)
77.8 ↰	'to Chioggia'
77.9 ↗	SP85 'to Chioggia'
83.4 ↱	SP4 'to Chioggia'
87.8 ↱	'to Chioggia'
87.9 ↰	'to Chioggia'
88.1 ↗	SP7 'to Chioggia'
90.9 ↰	SS309
92.1 ↗	Chioggia-Sottomarina highway exit
92.4 ↗	'to Chioggia/Stazione'
95.8	Chioggia ferry landing

vehicle traffic than canals, and is dominated by an industrial port zone with nothing to offer the tourist. Even so, if you haven't seen Venice yet, the historic centre of Chioggia gives you a watered-down but tantalising idea of what's in store. The town's northern tip retains hints of its Venetian history, with decaying waterfront *palazzi* (palaces or mansions), and sculpted lions adorning the 16th-century Porta Garibaldi arch and 12th-century Vigo Column at either end of the pedestrianised Corso del Popolo.

Information The visitor centre (☎ 041 40 10 68, ⍟ www.chioggiatourism.it) is in Sottomarina at Lungomare Adriatico 101.

Cassa di Risparmio di Venezia and Banca Antonveneto are two of the many banks along Corso del Popolo.

Ferrara, City for Cyclists

Ferrara might just be the cyclin'est city in Italy. Indeed, a 1995 study awarded it that status and surveys have shown that the Ferrarese ride their bikes as much as residents of cycle-crazed countries like Holland and Denmark, that nearly 90% of the people own bikes and that more people do their shopping by bike than by car.

In recognition of these facts, Ferrara has established itself as the first Italian member of the international Cities for Cyclists network, developing an impressive infrastructure in support of cycling. Signs at all city entrances proclaim Ferrara to be a *città per biciclette*, automobile traffic is limited or banned on many downtown streets, and there's an extensive and expanding network of well-sign-posted bikepaths, including a wonderful circuit of the city's medieval walls. The city government maintains an Office of Bicycles for Sustainable Mobility, publishes a free bike map, runs a Bicicard programme offering shopping discounts and free museum admissions to visitors willing to trade their cars for bikes, and distributes official bikes to the mayor and all city councilpeople. There are dozens of hotels and garages that provide free bikes for their clients' use, and there's even a Bicibus (☎ 0532 59 94 18) that will transport you and your bike on trips outside the city limits.

Albanese Cicli e Moto (☎ 041 40 12 55) is a bike/motorcycle shop at Corso del Popolo 970.

Things to See & Do The most pleasant tourist activity in Chioggia is simply strolling the main pedestrian thoroughfare, especially during the *passeggiata* (traditional evening stroll), when locals turn out in force. For another fascinating taste of local life, visit the early morning **fish market** along Canale San Domenico, the second canal south of Corso del Popolo (closed Sunday and Monday). The mediocre **beaches** in Sottomarina (Chioggia's window on the open Adriatic), 2km east, are the other main tourist draws.

Places to Stay & Eat One of several Sottomarina camping grounds around Chioggia is **Camping Adriatico** (☎ 041 49 29 07; ⍟ *www.campingadriatico.com; Lungomare Adriatico 82; per person/site €6.50/9.50*) with a private beach, pool, supermarket and restaurant. **Pensione Clodia** (☎ *041 40 08 13; Calle Forno Filippini 876; singles/doubles with shared bathroom €25/46*) is the cheapest place in Chioggia proper, just to the south of Corso del Popolo. **Albergo Caldin's** (☎ *041 40 35 82; ℮ becaldin@tin.it; Piazzale Peretolo 30; rooms €65*) is your basic one-star establishment overlooking the Canale Pero at the western edge of the pedestrian zone.

SISA (*Corso del Popolo*) is a large supermarket. **Punto Pizza** (*Corso del Popolo 1392*) serves tasty pizza by the slice. **Cafe Cavour** (*Corso del Popolo 1232*) is a classy vintage bar/café, popular with locals in late afternoon. **El Fontego** (*Piazzetta XX Settembre 497; closed Mon*) is a pizzeria/restaurant. **Ristorante al Buon Pesce** (*Stradale Ponte Caneva 625; closed Wed*) is one of many places serving Chioggia-style seafood.

Day 4: Chioggia to Venice
2–3 hours, 21.9km
This island-hopping odyssey across the lagoon involves as much time on boats as on your bike, but it's an unforgettably atmospheric way to reach Venice.

A single €3.50 ticket covers the first two ferry crossings, from the ACTV ferry landing in Chioggia to Pellestrina and Lido (route No 11 the whole way). Signs warn that bikes may board only at the captain's discretion, but there's usually enough space. Boats leave Chioggia roughly hourly for the 20-minute crossing to Pellestrina. There are nice views of the lagoon en route.

From the Pellestrina ferry dock, take the island's only road north, passing small residential areas and wispy vegetation on the left, with the massive 18th-century Murazzi sea wall on your right.

From Santa Maria del Mare at Pellestrina's northern tip, a larger car ferry makes the 10-minute crossing to Alberoni on Lido. Ferries that make the chug to Lido wait for passengers connecting by bus from the Chioggia– Pellestrina boat; cyclists with a litle bit of speed in their legs can usually outpace the bus, reaching the boat in plenty of time.

Hugging Lido's western shore for 8km, the route passes through the smaller communities of Alberoni and Malamocco, then circumnavigates Lido's town centre with a short run north along the island's main beach past the famous casino.

Cyclists wishing to lock their bikes in Lido de Venezia can take a *vaporetto* from the ACTV ferry dock (18.3km) into Venice (€3.10, 15 minutes). Alternatively, head north another 1.4km (briefly going against traffic) to the Tronchetto car ferry. ACTV

boat No 17 makes the 25-minute crossing every 50 minutes or so (€3.50 for passenger with bike).

From Tronchetto, signs lead the remaining 2km to Piazzale Roma, where you can catch a bus to the airport or walk your bike to the train station (15 minutes, one big bridge).

Venice
See Venice (p252).

Umbria & Le Marche

The patchwork fields, picturesque hill towns, and undulating topography of Umbria and Le Marche are classically Italian. Umbria is Italy's lone landlocked region, while neighbouring Le Marche boasts some of the Adriatic's most scenic coastline. Both have long and fascinating human histories.

HISTORY
Ancient Rome's indelible mark on this region is seen in temples, theatres, gates, bridges, roads and civic layouts, in places such as Gubbio, Assisi and Ascoli Piceno. In 220 BC Caius Flaminius opened the Via Flaminia, which passed through eastern Umbria and the northern Marche, connecting Rome to the Adriatic Coast. The Furlo Gorge tunnel stands as one of the road's enduring engineering achievements.

Umbria in particular has figured prominently in Christian religious history. Saints Benedict and Francis were born in Norcia and Assisi. The 11th-century Camaldolese Saint Romuald also walked these hills, establishing nearly 100 monasteries, including beautifully preserved Fonte Avellana.

The early Renaissance saw a flowering of courtly and artistic life in the Umbrian and Marchigian hills. The Dukes of Montefeltro in Urbino were particularly influential patrons of the arts.

Two of the regions' most famous sons are Raffaello, from Urbino, and composer Rossini, from Pesaro.

NATURAL HISTORY
Coastal Le Marche is generally flat, with notable exceptions at Monte Conero south

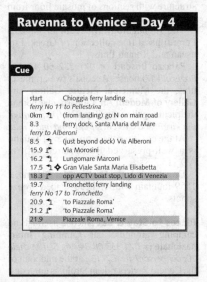

Ravenna to Venice – Day 4

Cue

start	Chioggia ferry landing
ferry No 11 to Pellestrina	
0km ↰	(from landing) go N on main road
8.3	ferry dock, Santa Maria del Mare
ferry to Alberoni	
8.5 ↰	(just beyond dock) Via Alberoni
15.9 ↱	Via Morosini
16.2 ↰	Lungomare Marconi
17.5 ↰ ◆	Gran Viale Santa Maria Elisabetta
18.3 ↱	opp ACTV boat stop, Lido di Venezia
19.7	Tronchetto ferry landing
ferry No 17 to Tronchetto	
20.9 ↰	'to Piazzale Roma'
21.2 ↱	'to Piazzale Roma'
21.9	Piazzale Roma, Venice

of Ancona and Monte San Bartolo north of Pesaro. Inland from the coast, hills rise rapidly towards the Appenine Mountains. The highest summits are in Parco Nazionale dei Monti Sibillini.

The region's underlying geology is rich in limestone. The Frasassi Caves near Fabriano rank among Italy's largest, and rivers have cut dramatic gorges, such as the Gola del Furlo, at several places in the local hills. Exposed rocky outcrops throughout the region provide fascinating opportunities for geologists. In 1978 a team from the University of California at Berkeley (USA), studying rock layers in the hills east of Gubbio, discovered unusually high concentrations of iridium, which contributed valuable evidence for their theory that a great meteorite caused the extinction of the dinosaurs.

The Piano Grande east of Norcia is one of Italy's most unusual landforms, a treeless plateau ringed by mountains, carpeted in spring with poppies, buttercups, lilies, daisies and wild tulips. The surrounding Sibillini Mountains are home to Alpine flowers such as edelweiss, and also shelter rare fauna such as the Appenine wolf and golden eagle.

Conero Riviera

Duration	3–5 hours
Distance	54.9km
Difficulty	moderate
Start/End	Ancona

This moderately hilly ride focuses on one of the Adriatic's most picturesque shorelines, the Conero Riviera south of Ancona.

PLANNING
When to Ride
This ride is possible year-round but is best in spring and autumn, and from Monday to Friday, when traffic is lighter.

Maps
TCI's 1:200,000 *Umbria e Marche* map covers the entire region in detail.

ACCESS TOWN
Ancona
Founded by Syracusan Greeks in the 4th century BC, with a harbour substantially developed by Roman Emperor Trajan in AD 115, Ancona remains the mid-Adriatic's largest port, nowadays best known among tourists for its passenger ferry service to Croatia, Greece and Turkey. The city centre, heavily bombed in WWII, is relatively uninspiring.

Information Ancona's visitor centre (☎ 071 358 99 03, ☒ www.regione.marche .it), east of town on Via Thaon de Revel 4, provides information for the city and the entire Marche region.

Banca delle Marche is at Via Marconi 217, just across from the station.

Bike Maniacs (☎ 071 218 16 00), Via Flaminia 224, is an excellent bike shop north of town along the main highway. It's closed Sunday and Monday morning.

Things to See & Do For panoramic views of the city and its waterfront, climb Monte Guasco (site of Ancona's former Greek Acropolis) to the Romanesque Cattedrale di San Ciriaco, built over the ruins of a temple to Venus and an early Christian basilica.

Other churches worth a visit include **San Domenico**, with a *Crucifixion* by Titian, **San Francesco delle Scale**, with an *Assumption* by Lorenzo Lotto, and **Santa Maria della Piazza**, a 13th-century Romanesque structure with sections of mosaic floor from its 5th-century predecessor.

The **Archaeology Museum** in Palazzo Ferretti has a fine collection of Greek, Etruscan and Roman finds.

Palazzo Bosdari (☎ 071 222 50 41; Via Pizzecolli 17) houses Ancona's two art museums, the **Municipal Picture Gallery** and **Gallery of Modern Art**. Of particular note in the picture gallery are Titian's *Apparition of the Virgin* and Crivelli's *Madonna and Child*.

At the city's northern tip, **Arco di Traiano** is a well-preserved Roman arch built in AD 115.

Downtown is the **Fontana del Calamo**, a 1559 fountain with 13 head-shaped bronze spouts.

Places to Stay & Eat Ancona itself has no camping grounds, but **Camping Internazionale** (☎ 071 933 08 84; Via San Michele 10; per person/site €7/13), at the midpoint of the Conero Riviera ride in Sirolo, is gorgeous, just below town with 230 sites overlooking the beach.

Ancona's **youth hostel** (☎/fax 071 4 22 57; Via Lamaticci 7; dorm beds €12; closed noon-4pm), the best deal in the city centre, is conveniently located 200m from the train station. **Albergo Dorico** (☎ 071 4 27 61; Via Flaminia 8; singles/doubles €31/42) is a decent one-star in the same area. **Hotel Roma e Pace** (☎ 071 20 20 07; Via Leopardi 1; singles/doubles €60/95) is a well-appointed central three-star place.

The **produce market** (Corso Mazzini 130) is your best bet for fresh fruit and vegetables. **Caffè Lombardo** (Corso Giuseppe Mazzini 59) is a fun place to watch the world go by and has with outdoor seating. **Osteria del Pozzo** (☎ 071 207 39 96; Via Bonda

2; primi €5-7, secondi €8-10; closed Sun) and **La Cantineta** (☎ 071 20 11 07; Via Gramsci 1b; primi €4-6, secondi €7-10; closed Sun) are two popular central trattorias. **Sot'Ajarchi** (☎ 071 20 2441; Via Marconi 93; primi €5-9, secondi €9-12; closed Sun) serves excellent seafood.

Getting There & Away The train station is west of downtown. Ancona sits at the junction of two major train lines, one running along the Adriatic Coast and the other heading southwest to Rome. One-way fares from Ancona include Rome (€13.50, four hours), Bologna (€10.50, 2¾ hours), Pesaro (€3, 45 minutes), Ravenna (€7, 2¾ hours), Venice (€17.50, five hours) and Milan (€19.50, 5½ hours).

ADRIATIC COAST

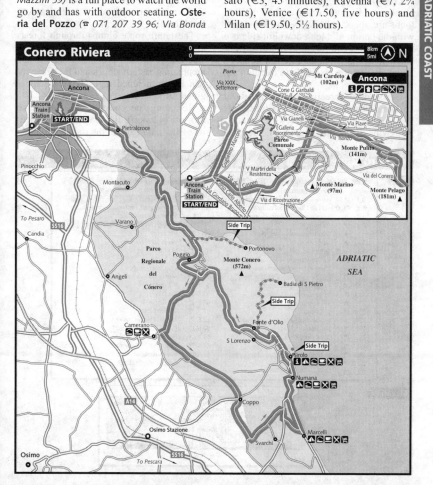

Bicycle Ancona sits near the junction of the 1000km Via Adriatica and the 500km Conero–Argentario bike routes proposed by FIAB. These routes, when completed, would connect Ancona with Venice in the north, Santa Maria di Leuca in the south, and Argentario on the Tuscan coast. Visit w www.fiab-onlus.it/bicital.htm for details.

THE RIDE

This undulating route initially parallels the Adriatic, then follows smaller backroads inland through the Rosso Conero wine country, concluding with a swing back up the beautiful Conero coast.

From Ancona's train station, the route climbs steadily out of the city. At 12.2km there are spectacular views of the coast, with the option of a long downhill side trip to the beaches and fort at Portonovo. Built by Napoleon in 1808, the fort now houses a fancy restaurant with windows overlooking the Adriatic.

Descending precipitously inland at 15.1km, the route commands a bird's-eye view of the Rosso Conero wine country. Red wine from this region has become increasingly popular in recent years, winning awards both domestically and internationally. The stretch between 17.7km and 26.1km is narrow and bumpy, but gorgeous as it threads its way through hills and vineyards.

Busier roads lead back to the Adriatic Coast. At Marcelli (29km) the route curves north to follow a flat beach popular with local families. Straight ahead, the coastline is dominated by Monte Conero's hulking profile. A steep climb leads to the medieval coastal town of Sirolo at 32km. With its stunning cliff-backed beaches (steep downhill side trip at 31.9km) and picturesque town square, Sirolo is the perfect spot to cool your heels and take a well-deserved lunch break.

The return route climbs through forests along the western edge of Monte Conero. A side trip at 34.7km provides access to the mountain's eastern slopes and the abbey of San Pietro, perched high above the blue-green Adriatic.

Rejoining the coast at the Portonovo turn-off (42.3km), the main route retraces its earlier path back to the train station.

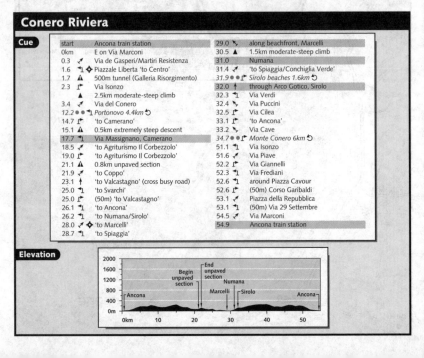

Conero Riviera

Cue		
start	Ancona train station	
0km	E on Via Marconi	
0.3	Via de Gasperi/Martiri Resistenza	
1.6	Piazzale Liberta 'to Centro'	
1.7	500m tunnel (Galleria Risorgimento)	
2.3	Via Isonzo	
	2.5km moderate-steep climb	
3.4	Via del Conero	
12.2	Portonovo 4.4km	
14.7	'to Camerano'	
15.1	0.5km extremely steep descent	
17.7	Via Massignano, Camerano	
18.5	'to Agriturismo Il Corbezzolo'	
19.0	'to Agriturismo Il Corbezzolo'	
21.1	0.8km unpaved section	
21.9	'to Coppo'	
23.1	'to Valcastagno' (cross busy road)	
25.0	'to Svarchi'	
25.0	(50m) 'to Valcastagno'	
26.1	'to Ancona'	
26.2	'to Numana/Sirolo'	
28.0	'to Marcelli'	
28.7	'to Spiaggia'	
29.0	along beachfront, Marcelli	
30.5	1.5km moderate-steep climb	
31.0	Numana	
31.4	'to Spiaggia/Conchiglia Verde'	
31.9	Sirolo beaches 1.6km	
32.0	through Arco Gotico, Sirolo	
32.3	Via Verdi	
32.4	Via Puccini	
32.5	Via Cilea	
33.1	'to Ancona'	
33.2	Via Cave	
34.7	Monte Conero 6km	
51.1	Via Isonzo	
51.6	Via Piave	
52.2	Via Giannelli	
52.3	Via Frediani	
52.6	around Piazza Cavour	
52.6	(50m) Corso Garibaldi	
53.1	Piazza della Repubblica	
53.1	(50m) Via 29 Settembre	
54.5	Via Marconi	
54.9	Ancona train station	

Elevation

Mystic Mountains, Sacred Hills

Duration	6 days
Distance	428.3km
Difficulty	moderate–hard
Start	Pesaro
End	Ascoli Piceno

This ride follows sleepy backroads through the hills and mountains of Le Marche and eastern Umbria. Highlights include the coastal scenery north of Pesaro, the beautiful hill towns of Urbino, Gubbio and Assisi, the secluded monastery of Fonte Avellana, the dramatic limestone gorge of the Furlo, the rugged grandeur of the mystery-shrouded Monti Sibillini, the stark lunar landscape of the Piano Grande, and the appealing but relatively rarely visited towns of Norcia and Ascoli Piceno.

PLANNING
When to Ride
This ride is best in May, June and September, when temperatures are warm enough to permit passage over the Sibillini Mountains but not as unbearably hot as July and August in the route's lower-lying stretches. May is festival season in Gubbio. Mid- to late June is peak wildflower season on the Piano Grande.

Maps
TCI's 1:200,000 *Umbria e Marche* map covers the entire region in detail.

What to Bring
Make sure your bike is in good shape before attempting to cross the Sibillini Mountains on Days 4 to 6. There are no bike shops between Assisi and Ascoli Piceno. Bring extra food and water, as services are limited.

ACCESS TOWN
Pesaro
Featuring a long expanse of beach and the remains of a medieval centre, Pesaro is a handy transport junction and the jumping-off point for one of the Adriatic's prettiest cycling routes, the Strada Panoramica Adriatica.

Information The visitor centre (☎ 0721 6 93 41, ⓔ iat.pesaro@regione.marche.it) is on the waterfront at Viale Trieste 164.

Banca Nazionale del Lavoro on Piazza del Popolo is one of several in the historic centre.

Biciland (☎ 0721 45 63 65), Via Carrara 7, near Via Giolitti in the Calcinari district, is a large shop selling bikes, parts, accessories and clothing.

Things to See & Do Pesaro's two best museums, **Pinacoteca** and **Museo delle Ceramiche** are housed in Palazzo Toschi Mosca (☎ 0721 38 75 41; closed Mon), near Piazza del Popolo. The Pinacoteca features Giovanni Bellini's *Coronation of the Virgin* (note the fortress of Gradara in the background; you'll be cycling past it on Day 1). The ceramics museum has a fabulous collection of majolica going back to the 14th century.

Casa Rossini (☎ 0721 38 73 57; via Rossini 34), childhood home of Pesaro's famous native son, has been a museum and national monument since 1904, housing Rossini's boyhood spinet plus portraits of the composer and prints of famous 19th-century opera performers.

Museo Oliveriano (☎ 0721 3 33 44; via Mazza 97) houses finds from an ancient Picene necropolis and other archaeological sites.

Chiesa di Sant'Agostino (Corso XI Settembre) has lovely Renaissance choir stalls with inlaid wood landscapes and other designs.

Rossini Opera Festival (☎ 0721 3 01 61; Via Rossini 37; ⓦ www.rossinioperafestial.it) is a Pesaro tradition since 1980, taking centre stage for two weeks every August.

Places to Stay & Eat Beautifully situated on a hillside overlooking the Adriatic at 11.9km on the Day 1 route is **Camping Panorama** (☎ 0721 20 81 45; ⓦ www.camp ingpanorama.it; Strada Panoramica Adriatica; per person/site €6.50/8; open May-Sept).

Pesaro has dozens of waterfront hotels. **Kappa Due** (☎ 0721 39 14 72; Strada delle Marche 15; singles/doubles €25/36) is one of the cheapest, on the south side of town. **Hotel Des Bains** (☎/fax 0721 3 49 57; Viale Trieste 221; singles/doubles €62/93) is a classier century-old three-star hotel near the tourist office. **Oasi San Nicola** (☎ 0721 5 08 49; ⓦ www.oasisannicola.it; Via San Nicola 8; singles/doubles €46/62) is a nice inland

ADRIATIC COAST

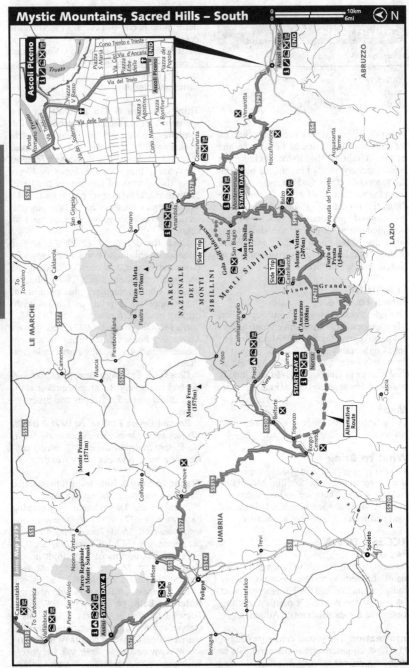

alternative, a converted 13th-century hilltop monastery surrounded by pine trees.

There's a **CRAI supermarket** at Strada Panoramica Adriatica 13 (1.9km on the Day 1 route), and a **produce market** on Via Branca behind the post office. **Black and Blue** (Viale XI Febbraio 11a) sells pizza by the slice. **C'Era Una Volta** (Via Cattaneo 26; pizzas from €3.50; closed Mon) is a popular pizzeria. **Antica Osteria La Guercia** (☎ 0721 3 34 63; Via Baviera 33; primi €4-7, secondi €6-11; closed Sun) is a great place for fish and other local specialties.

Getting There & Away The train station is southwest of the city centre. Pesaro is a main stop on the north–south Bologna–Lecce line. One-way fares from Pesaro include Bologna (€7.50, two hours), Ravenna (€4.50, 1¾ hours), Ancona (€3, 45 minutes), Venice (€14.50, four hours) and Milan (€17.50, 4½ hours).

Bicycle Pesaro is a stop on the 1000km Via Adriatica between Venice and Santa Maria di Leuca, part of a national network of bike routes proposed by FIAB.

THE RIDE
Day 1: Pesaro to Urbino
4–6 hours, 70.6km

After a brief but scenic meander along the Adriatic, today's ride turns inland through a series of attractive hill towns culminating in the Renaissance gem of Urbino.

Gently climbing from the beach at Pesaro into the coastal hills of **Parco Naturale Monte San Bartolo**, the Strada Panoramica Adriatica offers sweeping views both inland and out to sea. Pesaro's modern apartment blocks are soon replaced by farmland framed by pine and olive trees, with occasional glimpses of increasingly sheer drop-offs to the Adriatic. Traffic is relatively light, with bikes sometimes outnumbering cars.

Fiorenzuola di Focara at 15.3km is a picturesque coastal village worthy of a visit. Cobblestone streets lead up through the town gate to a grassy spot with benches overlooking the sea. It's also tempting to linger for lunch on the lovely terrace at **Ristorante La Rupe**.

At 18.1km an exhilaratingly steep and narrow descent through forest and fields leads inland toward the dramatic medieval

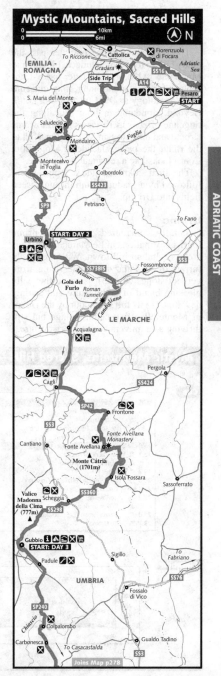

ADRIATIC COAST

hilltop fortress of **Gradara**. The heavily restored town and castle can be visited on a short side trip at 22.1km.

The undulating route continues past the pretty hilltop towns of **Saludecio** (40km) and **Mondaino** (42.4km). The latter has a 13th-century **fortress** and an interesting **museum of paleontology** (☎ 0541 98 16 74 for both). Beyond Mondaino, a long run along the ridgeline offers superb views south towards Urbino and north to San Marino. On a hill to the right, the palace facade at Montefiore Conca looks like a rectangular silhouette.

The final 20km include a long descent followed by a gradual climb through green fields into Urbino.

Urbino

Generally considered one of the prime tourist destinations in Le Marche, Urbino is a classic Italian hill town. With the lovely turrets of its Palazzo Ducale rising from verdant slopes below, it is an aesthetically pleasing blend of architecture and setting, developed to its full splendour by the Dukes of Montefeltro five centuries ago but still thriving as a university and tourist centre.

Information The visitor centre (☎ 0722 32 85 68, w www.comune.urbino.ps.it) is at Piazza Rinascimento 1, directly across from the Palazzo Ducale.

Banca Nazionale del Lavoro and Banca delle Marche both have branches on Via Vittorio Veneto, the main street running between Piazza della Repubblica and the Palazzo Ducale.

Urbino does not have a bike shop, but there's a good one (Basili Sport; ☎ 0721 79 00 77) in Cagli (34.8km on Day 2).

Things to See & Do A masterpiece of Renaissance architecture and an enduring symbol of the Montefeltro family's gracious rule, Urbino's **Palazzo Ducale** is the town's focal point. Inside is the **Galleria Nazionale delle Marche** (☎ 0722 32 90 57; Piazza Rinascimento), containing masterpieces by Piero della Francesca and numerous other artists. Especially impressive is Federico da Montefeltro's Studiolo, a small room covered in masterfully executed trompe l'oeil inlaid wood designs. Nearby, a spiral stone staircase descends to a balcony offering panoramic views over the surrounding countryside.

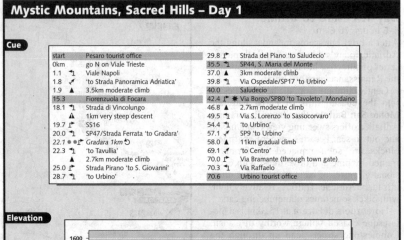

Mystic Mountains, Sacred Hills – Day 1

Cue

start	Pesaro tourist office		29.8 ↱	Strada del Piano 'to Saludecio'
0km	go N on Viale Trieste		35.5 ↰	SP44, S. Maria del Monte
1.1 ↰	Viale Napoli		37.0 ▲	3km moderate climb
1.8 ↗	'to Strada Panoramica Adriatica'		39.8 ↰	Via Ospedale/SP17 'to Urbino'
1.9 ▲	3.5km moderate climb		40.0	Saludecio
15.3	Fiorenzuola di Focara		42.4 ↱ ✱	Via Borgo/SP80 'to Tavoleto', Mondaino
18.1 ↰	Strada di Vincolungo		46.8 ▲	2.7km moderate climb
⚠	1km very steep descent		49.5 ↰	Via S. Lorenzo 'to Sassocorvaro'
19.7 ↱	SS16		54.4 ↰	'to Urbino'
20.0 ↰	SP47/Strada Ferrata 'to Gradara'		57.1 ↗	SP9 'to Urbino'
22.1 ●●↱	Gradara 1km ↻		58.0 ▲	11km gradual climb
22.3 ↰	'to Tavullia'		69.1 ↗	'to Centro'
▲	2.7km moderate climb		70.0 ↱	Via Bramante (through town gate)
25.0 ↱	Strada Pirano 'to S. Giovanni'		70.3 ↰	Via Raffaelo
28.7 ↰	'to Urbino'		70.6	Urbino tourist office

Elevation

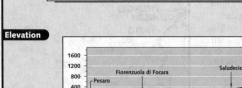

Raphael fans may enjoy visiting the house where the artist was born in 1483, **Casa Natale di Raffaello** (☎ 0722 32 01 05; Via Raffaello 57), although only one of his paintings is displayed there.

The tiny **Oratorio di San Giovanni** (Via Barocci) is well worth a visit for its lovely early 15th-century frescoes by the Salimbeni brothers.

Places to Stay & Eat Pleasantly situated 2km east of town is **Campeggio Pineta** (☎ 0722 47 10; Via San Donato, Cesane; per person/site €5/12; open Easter–15 Sept). **Pensione Fosca** (☎ 0722 25 42; Via Raffaelo 67; singles €31), Urbino's cheapest hotel, is on a top floor but allows bike parking downstairs. **Albergo San Giovanni** (☎ 0722 28 27; Via Barocci 13; singles/doubles without bathroom €20/30, with bathroom €29/45) is another affordable central option. **Hotel Raffaelo** (☎ 0722 47 84; Via S Margherita 38-40; singles/doubles €75/100) is a spiffy three-star near Raphael's house. The visitor centre has a full list of accommodation options.

Maxiconad Montefeltro (Via Rafaello 37) is a supermarket just off the main square. **Pizzeria al Taglio Il Ghiottone** (Via Mazzini 10) has cheap pizza by the slice. **Caffè Centrale** (Piazza della Reppublica) is great for people-watching, panini and pastries on the main square. **Taverna degli Artisti** (Via Bramante 52; pizzas from €3.50, primi €5; closed Tues except in summer) serves tasty pizza and pasta in a pleasant atmosphere. **Antica Hostaria La Balestra** (Via Valerio 16; pizzas €3-6, primi €5-6, secondi €6-12; closed Tues) offers a 'pizza ciclista' plus all the old standards and has a nice courtyard out front. **Vecchia Urbino** (Via dei Vasari 3-5; primi €7-11, secondi €7-18, fixed menus around €30; closed Tues) is one of Urbino's finer restaurants.

Day 2: Urbino to Gubbio
5–7 hours, 85.7km

Today's ride takes you through the rugged heart of the Appenines.

Zigzagging down to the Metauro Valley, the route offers nice parting vistas of Urbino, then joins (at 15.1km) the ancient Via Flaminia, established as a link between Rome and Rimini by Roman general Caius Flaminius in 220 BC. The most noteworthy Roman remnant is the ancient tunnel at 19.8km, bored out of solid rock by Flaminius' crew, then widened into its current form by Vespasian in AD 76.

Just beyond the tunnel (20km) is the exquisite **Gola del Furlo** gorge, where the Fiume Candigliano's jade-green waters flow beneath towering limestone cliffs shaded at the base by leafy forests. Mussolini was very fond of this area, coming here frequently to dine. A monumental profile of Il Duce was carved into Monte Pietralata west of the gorge but later damaged by partisans.

A rather gritty urban section follows, as the route emerges from the gorge into mountain-fringed flatlands paralleling the national highway. The area around **Acqualagna** (26.6km) accounts for two-thirds of Italian truffle production and hosts the National Truffle Fair in October/November.

From **Cagli** (35.7km), the route climbs through increasingly remote country along the flanks of imposing Monte Catria (1701m). A narrow, steep descent leads to 11th-century **Fonte Avellana** (53.3km), which Dante once visited and later mentioned in the 21st Canto of his Paradise. First glimpsed from above against a stunning mountain backdrop, the monastery seems lost in time. A short visit is highly recommended; the building's austere stone rooms are quite beautiful and very evocative, especially the well-preserved medieval Scriptorium.

The undulating route continues into Umbria, traversing forest and open grazing country and following another limestone chasm. From the final summit (Valico Madonna della Cima, 79.8km) a delightful winding descent reaches Gubbio via the rocky Gola del Bottaccione, famous as the site where, in the late 1970s, scientists hatched the meteorite theory responsible for the dinosaur extinction.

Gubbio

Founded by the ancient Umbrians and known to the Romans as Iguvium, the lovely stone town of Gubbio cascades down a green hillside above the fertile plain of the Saonda and Assino Rivers. The town's most prominent landmark is the amazingly tall face of the medieval Palazzo dei Consoli, rising abruptly from the square below and dwarfing all other buildings in town. With

ADRIATIC COAST

so many bumpy stone streets, Gubbio is not a comfortable place to cycle, but it's a delightful walking town and a fun place to window shop for ceramics. At sunrise or sunset, Gubbio is a dazzling study in red and gray, its stone and brick buildings exuding a warm glow.

Information The visitor centre (☎ 075 922 06 93, ℮ info@iat.gubbio.pg.it) is at Piazza Oderisi 5–6, on the corner of Corso Garibaldi and Via Cairoli near the centre of the walled city.

There's a Cassa di Risparmio di Perugia (with Bancomat) at 48a Piazza 40 Martiri.

The best local bike shop, Cicli Minelli (☎ 075 929 10 87) is 5.7km east of town in Padule on the Day 3 route.

Things to See & Do Inside the Palazzo dei Consoli is Gubbio's star attraction, **Museo Civico** (☎ 075 927 42 98; Piazza Grande). The palace's huge interior rooms and delightful panoramic loggia offer a vicarious taste of medieval noble life. Among the museum's artistic and archaeological treasures are the Eugubian Tables, seven

bronze tablets inscribed with Etruscan and Latin characters.

Palazzo Ducale (☎ 075 927 58 72; Via Federico da Montefeltro), built by Urbino's Montefeltro family, is Gubbio's finest Renaissance building.

Adjacent to the 14th-century **Bargello** on Via dei Consoli is the **Fontana dei Matti**. Tradition holds that anyone making three circles around this 'Madman's Fountain' will go insane.

Outside the walls southwest of town is Gubbio's **Roman theatre**, affording great views of the city. The nearby **Mausoleo 40 Martiri** is a moving memorial to 40 Gubbio citizens shot by the Nazis in the waning days of German occupation.

In Piazza Quaranta Martiri at the bottom of town, a statue depicts Saint Francis shaking the paw of a wolf that he legendarily convinced to stop terrorising Gubbio's medieval citizenry.

Gubbio has two wonderful festivals in May. Most colourful is the **Corsa dei Ceri** on 15 May, where teams representing Gubbio's three medieval guilds race through the streets and up the mountainside carrying

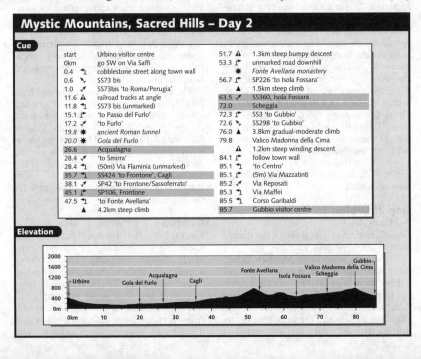

Mystic Mountains, Sacred Hills – Day 2

Cue

start	Urbino visitor centre	51.7 ⚠	1.3km steep bumpy descent
0km	go SW on Via Saffi	53.3 ↱	unmarked road downhill
0.4 ↰	cobblestone street along town wall	✳	Fonte Avellana monastery
0.6 ↘	SS73 bis	56.7 ↱	SP226 'to Isola Fossara'
1.0 ↗	SS73bis 'to Roma/Perugia'	▲	1.5km steep climb
11.6 ⚠	railroad tracks at angle	63.5 ↗	SS360, Isola Fossara
11.8 ↰	SS73 bis (unmarked)	72.0	Scheggia
15.1 ↱	'to Passo del Furlo'	72.3 ↱	SS3 'to Gubbio'
17.2 ↗	'to Furlo'	72.6 ↘	SS298 'to Gubbio'
19.8 ✳	ancient Roman tunnel	76.0 ▲	3.8km gradual-moderate climb
20.0 ✳	Gola del Furlo	79.8	Valico Madonna della Cima
26.6	Acqualagna	⚠	1.2km steep winding descent
28.4 ↗	'to Smirra'	84.1 ↱	follow town wall
28.4 ↰	(50m) Via Flaminia (unmarked)	85.1 ↰	'to Centro'
35.7 ↰	SS424 'to Frontone', Cagli	85.1 ↱	(5m) Via Mazzatinti
38.1 ↗	SP42 'to Frontone/Sassoferrato'	85.2 ↗	Via Reposati
45.1 ↱	SP106, Frontone	85.3 ↰	Via Maffei
47.5 ↰	'to Fonte Avellana'	85.5 ↰	Corso Garibaldi
▲	4.2km steep climb	85.7	Gubbio visitor centre

Elevation

massive octagonal wooden pillars surmounted by wax images of saints. The **Palio della Balestra** (last Sunday in May) is a medieval crossbow competition.

Places to Stay & Eat Pleasantly situated next to each other in the countryside 2km south of town are **Camping Città di Gubbio** (☎ 075 927 20 37; per person/site €8/9) and **Camping Villa Ortoguidone** (☎ 075 927 20 37; per person/site €8/9). **Residenza Le Logge** (☎ 075 927 75 74; Via Piccardi 7-9; singles/doubles €40/50) is an attractively remodelled old stone building with a nice courtyard. **Residence di Via Piccardi** (☎ 075 927 61 08; Via Piccardi 12; singles/doubles €25/40) has similar amenities just across the street. **Grotta dell'Angelo** (☎/fax 075 927 34 38; e grottadellangelo@jumpy.it; Via Gioia 47; singles/doubles €30/45) is on a pleasant side street at the bottom of town.

There's a **Super Conad** (1a Piazza Bosone) supermarket at the southwest corner of the walled town, plus an outdoor **fruit and vegetable market** (Piazza 40 Martiri; closed Sun). **Ristorante Pizzeria all'Antico Frantoio** (Via Cavour 18; primi €5-7.50, secondi €6-12.50; closed Mon) has a good choose-your-own contorno (side dish) bar and serves delicious pizza under an 11th-century vaulted stone ceiling. **La Lanterna** (Via Gioia 23; closed Thur) serves truffle and mushroom specialties in a medieval setting. **Locanda del Duca** (Via Piccardi 1; closed Wed) has a nice downstairs terrace beside the Camignano riverbed.

Day 3: Gubbio to Assisi
3–5 hours, 48.5km
This is the shortest day of the trip, allowing time for sightseeing or relaxing before tomorrow's long haul to Norcia.

After paralleling the main highway along the valley floor for 5.6km, the route climbs south into rolling hills, affording nice views back into the Appenines. A long descent to a small river valley is followed by an equally long climb onto a high plateau between tiny Colpalombo and Carbonesca.

From the junction at Casacastalda, the route plunges downhill on busy SS318 to Valfabbrica, then turns onto the challenging but gorgeous 12km Strada Francescana della Pace. This steep and narrow tertiary road traces part of the pilgrimage route travelled

by the young St Francis between Assisi and Gubbio. Watch carefully for the turn-off, just below Valfabbrica at a point where the main road curves right; signs are only posted for travellers coming the opposite direction.

The Strada Francescana climbs relentlessly for more than 2km at an angle that tests both patience and stamina, but the views of vineyards and open hills are magnificent, and there's virtually no traffic. A short side trip at 38.9km leads to the medieval church site of **Pieve San Nicolo**.

The basilica of St Francis comes into view just before the 40km mark. At 44.6km, in the middle of a precipitous descent, a particularly dramatic view of the church and the town unfolds, with beautiful olive groves in the foreground.

The route's final kilometres climb steeply through the medieval walls to Assisi's central piazza.

Assisi
Depending on when you visit and how long you stay, the City of St Francis may strike you more as a beautifully preserved medieval town or an oppressive tourist trap, with kitschy Franciscan souvenirs on sale in every other doorway. Either way, it's also a major site of religious pilgrimage, with people converging from all over to worship at the shrine made famous by Assisi's native son.

The massive Basilica of St Francis is the reason most people, pilgrims and tourists, visit, but the town is an appealing destination in its own right, a maze of stone streets, alleyways, gates and arches enclosed by an intact medieval wall. After the tour buses pull out, it's a nice place for an evening stroll.

Information The visitor centre (☎ 075 81 25 34, e info@iat.assisi.pg.it) is on the western side of the central Piazza del Comune.

There's a Cassa di Risparmio di Perugia with Bancomat diagonally across from the visitor centre.

For bike parts and repairs, go downhill 5km to Angelucci Cicli (☎ 075 804 25 50, w www.angeluccicicli.3000.it), Via Becchetti 31, in Santa Maria degli Angeli.

Things to See & Do The 13th-century **Basilica di San Francesco**, actually two churches stacked together, houses one of Italy's best collections of frescoes.

ADRIATIC COAST

Mystic Mountains, Sacred Hills – Day 3

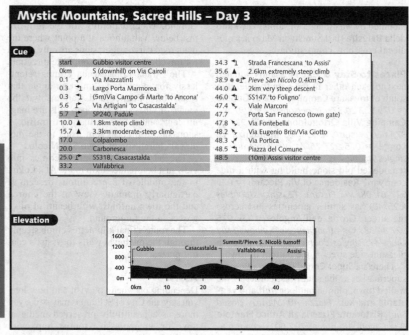

Cue

start	Gubbio visitor centre		34.3 ↰	Strada Francescana 'to Assisi'
0km	S (downhill) on Via Cairoli		35.6 ▲	2.6km extremely steep climb
0.1 ↗	Via Mazzatinti		38.9 ● ●↰	Pieve San Nicolo 0.4km ↻
0.3 ↱	Largo Porta Marmorea		44.0 ▲	2km very steep descent
0.3 ↱	(5m)Via Campo di Marte 'to Ancona'		46.0 ↰	SS147 'to Foligno'
5.6 ↱	Via Artigiani 'to Casacastalda'		47.4 ↘	Viale Marconi
5.7 ↱	SP240, Padule		47.7	Porta San Francesco (town gate)
10.0 ▲	1.8km steep climb		47.8 ↘	Via Fontebella
15.7 ▲	3.3km moderate-steep climb		48.2 ↘	Via Eugenio Brizi/Via Giotto
17.0	Colpalombo		48.3 ↗	Via Portica
20.0	Carbonesca		48.5 ↰	Piazza del Comune
25.0 ↱	SS318, Casacastalda		48.5	(10m) Assisi visitor centre
33.2	Valfabbrica			

Elevation

Summit/Pieve S. Nicolò turnoff

Gubbio — Casacastalda — Valfabbrica — Assisi

(elevation chart: 1600, 1200, 800, 400, 0m; distances 0km, 10, 20, 30, 40)

On Piazza del Comune, **Tempio di Minerva's** 1st-century facade is a striking reminder of Assisi's Roman past. Underneath the piazza, remnants of the ancient Roman forum are on view at the **Museo Archeologico e Foro Romano** (☎ 075 81 30 53; enter from Via Portica). Back above ground, **Pinacoteca Comunale** displays Umbrian Renaissance works.

Inside **Basilica di Santa Chiara** (Piazza Santa Chiara) is the talking crucifix said to have told St Francis to repair the church's moral foundations, along with the crypt of St Clare, who founded the Order of the Poor Clares, a women's counterpart to the Franciscans, in 1211.

Rocca Maggiore fortress (Via della Rocca), steeply uphill, offers great town and valley views.

In the valley below, the domed baroque monstrosity of **Santa Maria degli Angeli** is worth a visit just to see the miniature **Chapel of La Porziuncola** inside.

Less tainted by post-Franciscan influence is the bucolically situated **Convento di San Damiano**, downhill from Porta Nuova, where Saint Francis is said to have heard the crucifix speak and later to have written his *Canticle of the Creatures*.

Places to Stay & Eat In the hills east of town is **Campeggio Fontemaggio** (☎ 075 81 36 36; Via Eremo delle Carceri 8; per site/person €4/4.50) with a restaurant, hostel and hotel adjoining. **Ostello della Pace** (☎/fax 075 81 67 67; Via di Valecchie 177; dorm beds €12; closed 9.30am-3.30pm daily, curfew 11.30pm) is beautifully situated in the countryside below Assisi, with a self-service laundry. **Camere Martini** (☎ 075 81 35 36; Via S Gregorio 6; singles/doubles €20/30) is a delightful family-run place just below Piazza del Comune, with a lovely flowery courtyard and guest laundry; bookings strongly advised. **Hotel Pallotta** (☎ 075 81 23 07; ⓦ www.pallottaassisi.it; Via San Rufino; singles/doubles €30/45) is in a medieval building boasting great views from its 3rd-storey belvedere. **Hotel Ascesi** (☎/fax 075 81 24 20; Via Frate Elia 5; singles/doubles €36/52) is among the more affordable places near the basilica.

A.MI.CA. Micromarket (Via Fontebella 61) and **Alimentari da Franco** (Via S Gabriele *dell'Addolorata 3b)* are two grocery stores along the bike route. **Pizzeria Tavola Calda dal Carro** *(Vicolo di Nepis 2b; meals €5-10; closed Wed)* is a no-nonsense family-run place serving traditional Umbrian food. **Taverna dell'Arco** *(Via S Gregorio 8; primi €5-6, secondi €5-10; closed Tues)*, near Camere Martini, has a nice stone interior and excellent regional cooking. **Ristorante Metastasio** *(Via Metastasio 9; primi €7-11, secondi €8-14; closed Wed)*, near the top of town, is worth the slightly higher prices for its fantastic terrace view.

Day 4: Assisi to Norcia
6–8 hours, 99.9km

This long and challenging day crosses a remote corner of eastern Umbria. A flatter alternative route starting at 67.2km shaves off almost 15km but involves heavier traffic and several long tunnels.

After a winding descent from Assisi, an uninspiring secondary road parallels the autostrada for several kilometres. Possible diversions include a visit to historic **Spello** (13.1km), or watching for the Roman ruins poking out of weeds on the left. After a brief

stint on busy SS3, traffic decreases and the scenery improves. A steep shortcut beyond tiny Belfiore climbs to national highway SS77. This is earthquake land, as evidenced by the tunnels of scaffolding supporting damaged buildings in **Casenove** (37.5km); the epicentre of Umbria's famous 1997 earthquake was at Colfiorito, 10km northeast.

A moderate climb over a small pass leads to the beautiful Valnerina (Nera River valley). The junction at **Borgo Cerreto** (65.5km) is one of few food stops. Shortly beyond this point the road splits. The alternate route into Norcia is not advised for anyone squeamish about tunnels; the longest is more than 1km and traffic moves fast. The main route meanders up the Nera before turning back into the mountains (76.8km).

Preci (on the right at 81.2km) is an attractive hill town famous historically for its surgeons, one of whom performed cataract surgery on Queen Elizabeth of England in 1588. The valley beyond town, backed by the Sibillini mountains, is gorgeous, with a picturesque church at **Campi** (87km or so). The final push up to **Forca d'Ancarano** (1008m) yields spectacular views into Norcia's valley.

ADRIATIC COAST

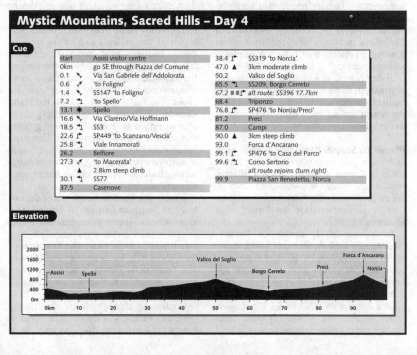

Mystic Mountains, Sacred Hills – Day 4

Cue

start	Assisi visitor centre	38.4 ↱	SS319 'to Norcia'
0km	go SE through Piazza del Comune	47.0 ▲	3km moderate climb
0.1 ↘	Via San Gabriele dell'Addolorata	50.2	Valico del Soglio
0.6 ↗	'to Foligno'	65.5 ↰	SS209, Borgo Cerreto
1.4 ↘	SS147 'to Foligno'	67.2 ∎∎↱	alt route: SS396 17.7km
7.2 ↰	'to Spello'	68.4	Triponzo
13.1 ✳	Spello	76.8 ↱	SP476 'to Norcia/Preci'
16.6 ↘	Via Clareno/Via Hoffmann	81.2	Preci
18.5 ↰	SS3	87.0	Campi
22.6 ↱	SP449 'to Scanzano/Vescia'	90.0 ▲	3km steep climb
25.8 ↰	Viale Innamorati	93.0	Forca d'Ancarano
26.2	Belfiore	99.1 ↱	SP476 'to Casa del Parco'
27.3 ↗	'to Macerata'	99.6 ↰	Corso Sertorio
▲	2.8km steep climb		alt route rejoins (turn right)
30.1 ↰	SS77	99.9	Piazza San Benedetto, Norcia
37.5	Casenove		

Elevation

Assisi | Spello | Valico del Soglio | Borgo Cerreto | Preci | Forca d'Ancarano | Norcia

2000 / 1600 / 1200 / 800 / 400 / 0m

0km / 10 / 20 / 30 / 40 / 50 / 60 / 70 / 80 / 90

Norcia

Enclosed within 13th-century walls, the remote town of Norcia sits alone in a vast valley ringed by mountains. Already a Roman city in the 3rd century BC (a fact commemorated by the 'Nursia Vetusta' inscription in one of the town gates), it gained fame in AD 480 as the birthplace of St Benedict, and in the Middle Ages as a centre for witches and necromancers.

Information The Casa del Parco visitor centre (☎/fax 0743 81 70 90), one block west of Piazza San Benedetto at Via Solferino 22, offers information about Parco Nazionale dei Monti Sibillini and Norcia itself.

There's a Bancomat at Banca Popolare di Spoleto, north of the main square at Corso Sertorio 5.

Things to See & Do At the heart of the town is the striking circular **Piazza San Benedetto**, built over the old Roman forum and ringed with solid rectilinear buildings and squared-off towers. Most interesting are the 13th-century **Basilica di San Benedetto**, a heavily remodelled shrine to Norcia's hometown saint, the **Palazzo Comunale** with its 13th-century tower, and **La Castellina**, a blocky 16th-century fortress housing a collection of religious paintings and sculptures.

Today Norcia is a popular Italian tourist destination, thanks to its many culinary specialties (pork, mushrooms, and truffles prominent among them) and its proximity to the Sibillini mountains.

Places to Stay & Eat Around 20km north of Norcia, just outside Preci on the Day 4 route is **Centro Agrituristico Il Collaccio** (☎ 0743 93 90 05; ₩ www.ilcollaccio.com; per person/site €7.25/7.25), an *agriturismo* (tourist accommodation on farms) with lovely camp sites.

In Norcia itself, **Residence Fusconi** (☎ 0743 82 83 00; Piazza Verdi 2/4/6; apartments per person €15, doubles €60) is a good deal for groups of three or more. **Albergo da Benito** (☎ 0743 81 66 70; Via Marconi x; singles/doubles €35/50) and **Hotel Grotta Azzurra** (☎ 0743 81 65 13; ₩ www .bianconi.com; Via Alfieri 12; main hotel doubles around €80, in hotel annexe around €45, slightly higher on Sat) are two good choices near the main square.

Several markets in town sell the local lentils and pork specialties, including **Fratelli Ansuini** (Via Anicia 105), whose display of hanging minipigs will provoke disgust or amusement. Restaurants tend to emphasise truffles in all courses. **Trattoria dal Francese** (Via Riguardati 16; primi €5-6, secondi €6-7; closed Fri) is simple and unpretentious, one block off the main square. **Taverna del Boscaiolo** (Via Bandiera 9; primi €5-10, secondi €7-15; closed Mon) is a trattoria with 14th-century stone and plasterwork arched ceilings. **Ristorante Granaro del Monte** (Via Alfieri 12; primi €7-14, secondi €9-20; closed Tues), attached to Hotel Grotta Azzurra, is one of Norcia's finer restaurants, offering a 'menu gastronomico' (including souvenir hand-painted ceramic plate!) for €40.

Day 5: Norcia to Montemonaco
5–6 hours, 64km

Climbing 17.4km into the mountains above Norcia, today's route crosses the otherworldly landscape of the Piano Grande, then rides a long series of ups and downs along the Sibillini's eastern slopes.

The steady climb from Norcia offers great views of the valley's patchwork quilt of fields. Traffic is light, and skies are often filled with hang-gliders. Near the summit the landscape becomes starker and more windswept, with shaggy horses roaming about. The first view down onto the **Piano Grande** (20.2km), a vast sheep-grazing plateau ringed by barren peaks, is guaranteed to leave a lasting impression. This enormous treeless bowl is ablaze with wildflowers in late spring, painted in more-subtle shades of yellow and ochre in summer and autumn.

Sitting on a knoll at the far end of the valley, the lonesome town of **Castelluccio** looks more a Tibetan monastery site than a central Italian hill town. Accessible as a side trip at 27.6km, Castelluccio is famous throughout Italy for its unique, small lentils. The **Festa della Fiorita** is held here every June in conjunction with the annual explosion of wildflowers.

Continuing through sheep country, the route climbs again to the desolate **Forca di Presta** (1540m), then drops steeply down the mountains' eastern flank, providing great close-up views of hulking **Monte Vettore** (2476m), the Sibillini's highest peak.

Another short climb and long descent leads to **Balzo**, an attractive hill community and the only chance for services before Montemonaco. The undulating profile continues, culminating in a long final ascent.

Montemonaco

Tiny Montemonaco has a picture-postcard view over the majestic eastern Sibillini. The Sibillini's countless mystical associations can best be appreciated by hiking up to legendary sites nearby, such as **Lago di Pilato**, a lake sometimes turned red by algae where Pontius Pilate reputedly met his fate, and **Grotta della Sibilla**, the subterranean domain of the prophetess from whom the mountains derive their name.

Despite its diminutive size, Montemonaco offers a range of tourist services for the visitors who flock here every summer weekend.

Information Montemonaco's Pro Loco office (☎ 0736 85 64 11, w www.montemonaco.com) at Piazza Risorgimento 2 offers general information about the town. The nearby Casa del Parco (☎/fax 0736 85 64 62, e cpchiro@tin.it) on Via Roma has information about Parco Nazionale dei Monti Sibillini.

Carisap bank is on Via Roma.

Places to Stay & Eat Basic two-star establishments along Montemonaco's main street include **Ristorante Albergo Carlini** *(☎/fax 0736 85 61 27; Via Roma 16/18; singles/doubles €40/50)* and **Albergo Sibilla** *(☎ 0736 85 61 44; Via Roma 52; singles & doubles €40)*. **Hotel Ristorante Miramonti** *(☎ 0736 85 61 18; Via Pazzaglia 25; singles & doubles €40)* is up near the top of town with a panoramic view.

Albergo Guerrin Meschino *(☎ 0736 85 63 56; w www.guerrinmeschino.com; Località Rocca; singles/doubles €26/52)* is a three-star place outside of town. A few places also rent rooms in Isola San Biagio, 4km north on the Day 6 route.

Alimentari Grilli *(Piazza Roma)* at the main junction in town sells groceries. **Il Forno Buratti** *(Piazza Roma 2)* next door is a

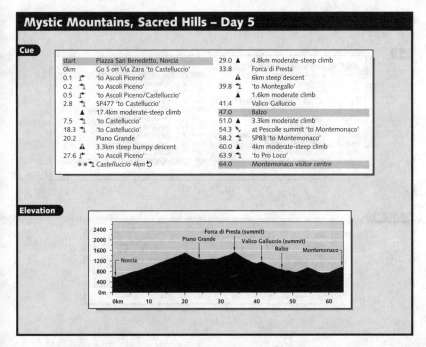

Mystic Mountains, Sacred Hills – Day 5

Cue

start		Piazza San Benedetto, Norcia
0km		Go S on Via Zara 'to Castelluccio'
0.1	↱	'to Ascoli Piceno'
0.2	↰	'to Ascoli Piceno'
0.5	↱	'to Ascoli Piceno/Castelluccio'
2.8	↰	SP477 'to Castelluccio'
	▲	17.4km moderate-steep climb
7.5	↰	'to Castelluccio'
18.3	↰	'to Castelluccio'
20.2		Piano Grande
	⚠	3.3km steep bumpy descent
27.6	↱	'to Ascoli Piceno'
	●● ↰	*Castelluccio 4km* ↺
29.0	▲	4.8km moderate-steep climb
33.8		Forca di Presta
	⚠	6km steep descent
39.8	↰	'to Montegallo'
	▲	1.6km moderate climb
41.4		Valico Galluccio
47.0		Balzo
51.0	▲	3.3km moderate climb
54.3	↘	at Pescolle summit 'to Montemonaco'
58.2	↰	SP83 'to Montemonaco'
60.0	▲	4km moderate-steep climb
63.9	↰	'to Pro Loco'
64.0		Montemonaco visitor centre

Elevation

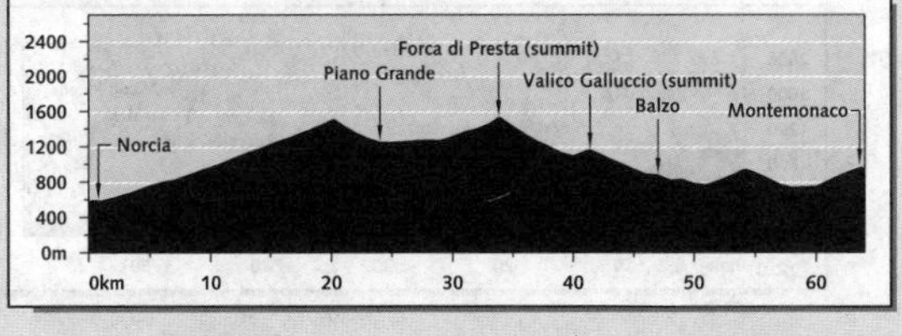

great bakery selling pizza by the slice, bread, cookies and more. There are **restaurants** at all the hotels listed in this section, specialising in the truffle dishes for which the region is famous.

Day 6: Montemonaco to Ascoli Piceno

4–5 hours, 59.6km

The final day is a breeze, with an early, long descent and only a couple of moderate climbs the rest of the way into Ascoli Piceno.

The first 12km, on a quiet road hugging the mountains' edge, are a pure delight. At 4.2km the tiny town of **Isola San Biagio** marks the beginning of a bumpy but exhilarating descent. Traffic is next to nil, and the close-up views of the Sibillini are magnificent. At 7.5km, as the paved main road hairpins right, a signposted dirt road continues straight for the side trip to **Gola dell'Infernaccio**, a narrow rocky chasm cut by the raging Fiume Tenna, accessible via a hiking trail at the end of the road.

At 12km, with lovely Montefortino perched overhead, the route veers away from the mountains and joins increasingly busy roads. The larger town of **Amandola** marks the junction with national highway SS78, which follows a sinuous course through big open fields offering lovely views back to the Sibillini. At **Comunanza** (the last major town before Ascoli), SS78 veers right, eventually crossing a small pass, then winding downhill through forest. A detour onto smaller roads at 44.8km necessitates another short climb but avoids the heavy traffic characterising other approaches to Ascoli. The grand entry into the city is via a 1st-century Roman bridge, with Ascoli's numerous medieval towers forming a picturesque backdrop.

Ascoli Piceno

While less of a tourist draw than many Italian cities its size, Ascoli Piceno is an appealing place abounding in history and fine architecture. The central Piazza del Popolo, paved in travertine, is one of Italy's prettiest squares. Ascoli's Roman origins can be seen in its straight and perpendicular street layout, the 1st-century Ponte Solesta, and the ruins of a Roman gate and amphitheatre. Ascoli is the largest city in the southern Marche, and capital of its own region.

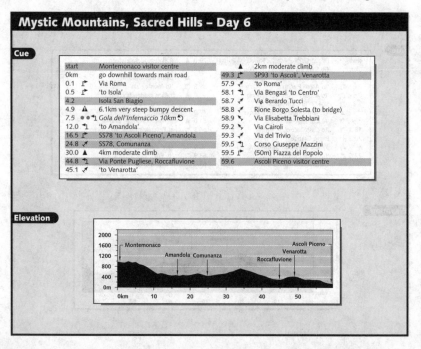

Mystic Mountains, Sacred Hills – Day 6

Cue

start	Montemonaco visitor centre		▲	2km moderate climb
0km	go downhill towards main road		49.3 ↱	SP93 'to Ascoli', Venarotta
0.1 ↱	Via Roma		57.9 ↗	'to Roma'
0.5 ↱	'to Isola'		58.1 ↰	Via Bengasi 'to Centro'
4.2	Isola San Biagio		58.7 ↗	Via Berardo Tucci
4.9 ▲	6.1km very steep bumpy descent		58.8 ↗	Rione Borgo Solesta (to bridge)
7.5 ●●↰	Gola dell'Infernaccio 10km ↻		58.9 ↘	Via Elisabetta Trebbiani
12.0 ↰	'to Amandola'		59.2 ↘	Via Cairoli
16.5 ↱	SS78 'to Ascoli Piceno', Amandola		59.3 ↗	Via del Trivio
24.8 ↗	SS78, Comunanza		59.5 ↰	Corso Giuseppe Mazzini
30.0 ▲	4km moderate climb		59.5 ↱	(50m) Piazza del Popolo
44.8 ↰	Via Ponte Pugliese, Roccafluvione		59.6	Ascoli Piceno visitor centre
45.1 ↗	'to Venarotta'			

Elevation

Castello Presule, near Fiè allo Sciliar, Trentino-Alto Adige

Traditional *casa Italiana* (Italian house), Trent, Trentino-Alto Adige

Tre Cime di Lavaredo, Trentino-Alto Adige

DAMIEN SIMONIS

Frescoes, Aquileia, Friuli Venezia Giulia

MARTIN HUGHES

ALAN BENSON

Market, Padua, The Veneto

Cathedral, Ferrara, Emilia-Romagna

JEFFREY BECOM

Priest, Assisi, Umbria

Information Ascoli's visitor centre (☎ 0736 25 30 45) is in the heart of town at Piazza del Popolo 17.

Banca Nazionale del Lavoro is centrally located on the corner of Corso Mazzini and Corso Trento e Trieste.

Cicli Falgiani (☎ 0736 34 18 66) is a good bike shop southeast of the centre at Via Amalfi 1/3.

Things to See & Do The lovely central **Piazza del Popolo**, surrounded by medieval buildings, is especially enjoyable at dusk when locals gather on its shimmering travertine pavement for the *passeggiata*.

Northwest of Piazza del Popolo are some of Ascoli's finest medieval towers, including the **Torre degli Ercolani** on Via Soderini. Spanning the Fiume Tronto just north of here is the 1st-century Roman **Ponte Solesta**. To the southwest is the **Porta Gemina**, a 1st-century Roman gate, along with the minimal remains of an old Roman theatre.

Ascoli's gaudy **cathedral** (*Piazza Arringo*) houses one of Carlo Crivelli's masterworks, the *Virgin and Saints* polyptich. Next door is the medieval **baptistery**, a beautifully simple octagonal structure built of travertine. Also on Piazza Arringo are the **Pinacoteca** and **Archaeology Museum**, the former displaying works by Crivelli, Van Dyck, and others, the latter housing a fascinating collection of treasures, including many related to the pre-Roman Picene culture.

The most atmospheric time to visit Ascoli is during the **Quintana Festival** (first Sunday in August), where trumpet-blowing, flag-throwing locals parade through the historic centre in colourful medieval garb, then proceed to the stadium for a flamboyant jousting tournament.

Places to Stay & Eat Ascoli has no camping ground. **Ostello de' Longobardi** (☎ 0736 25 90 07; Via dei Soderini 26; dorm beds €10) is the best budget alternative, housed in a medieval tower west of the main square. **Cantina dell'Arte** (☎ 0736 25 57 44; Rua della Lupa 8; singles/doubles €25/35) is the only other moderately priced place in town. **Albergo Gioli** (☎ 0736 25 55 50; Viale De Gasperi 14; singles/doubles €55/83) is a rather hideous modern four-star place.

There's an atmospheric daily **produce market** in the 16th-century cloisters just north of Piazza del Popolo. **Caffè Meletti** (Piazza del Popolo 18/22) is a classy century-old Art Nouveau café with tables set out on the travertine, great for watching the world go by at sunset. **Bella Napoli** (Piazza della Viola; pizza €4-6; closed Sun) prides itself as Ascoli's only pizzeria with two wood ovens. The **Locanda dei Longobardi** (Via Soderini 27/31; meals €5-8), near the hostel, offers discounts to hostel guests. **Cantina dell'Arte** (Rua della Lupa 5; menu including wine €8) serves hearty homemade food at bargain prices.

Getting There & Away Ascoli's train station is 1km east of the centre, connected by a short spur line to Benedetto del Tronto on the Adriatic Coast. There are three direct daily trains to Ancona (€6, two hours). Several other daily trains make the 30-minute trip to Benedetto del Tronto, allowing connections to points north and south along the coast.

Bicycle Ascoli Piceno is a stop on FIAB's 400km Via Salaria bike route between Rome and San Benedetto del Tronto. Visit **w** www.fiab-onlus.it/bicital.htm for details.

The South & Sicily

Every part of Italy's south offers a distinctly different cycling experience, each in its own way a rich and rewarding insight into a world far removed from the affluent tourist Meccas of the north. Preconceptions of the Mezzogiorno (literally 'midday' and the name for the south of Italy) are often misguided, and usually fuelled by visions of a hostile, barren landscape and uncivilised backwaters where poverty and vicious Mafiaesque corruption have created a people insular and shuttered. The reality couldn't be more different. Areas of intense natural beauty, dotted with humble villages where the people are warm and generous of spirit, contrast with sophisticated and cultivated cities steeped in history. Some parts are famous the world over, but for the most part, the rides in this chapter endeavour to uncover hidden cycling treasures, inspiring scenery viewed from lazy backroads.

CLIMATE

Sicily and the south have a mild Mediterranean climate, meaning hot, dry summers and short, mild winters with light rainfall. Spring and autumn are almost a mild extension of summer, so short is the winter. The finest weather is usually around the coast, with summer highs in the mid-30s and winter averages between 10ºC and 13ºC. The hot sirocco blows during the six hottest months of the year, bringing Saharan sand to Sicily's southern and western coasts; the Tyrrhenian coast is usually shielded from the worst effects of this by the mountainous interior.

Inland, summer days are dry and hot, with little or no respite until sundown – at altitude it can even get quite nippy. During the short winters (December to February), it can be bitterly cold, especially after dark. Substantial snowfalls are common in mountain areas above 1500m. Calabria's La Sila region, and the higher reaches of Sicily's Madonie and Nebrodi mountains are often snowbound in January. The top of Mt Etna can experience snow at almost any time of year.

GATEWAY CITIES
Bari

Bari doesn't rank high on most travellers' destination lists, but with good accommodation and transport options, plus its prox-

In Brief

Highlights
- The world-renowned **Amalfi Coast road** and its picturesque hillside towns (Campania)
- **Apulia's** verdant market gardens dotted with magical *trulli* (conical stone houses)
- The unspoilt forests and mountainous beauty of Calabria's **La Sila region**
- The awesome sight of a smoking **Mt Etna** dominating Sicily's arid centre and bustling east coast towns

Terrain
The mainland's southern half is dominated by the mountainous Apennine range. The only significant plains are the Tavoliere di Apulia and the Pianura Campana around Mt Vesuvius.

Sicily is dominated by the massive Mt Etna to the east, and the high ridges of the Peloritani, Nebrodi and Madonie mountains to the north.

Special Events
- **Festivale Musicale di Ravello** & **Wagner Festiva** (July), Ravello
- **Feast of Santa Maria della Bruna** colourful procession carrying a statue of the Madonna in a cart (2 July), Matera
- **Festival of St Nicola** celebrates the delivery of St Nicholas' bones to the Dominican friars (early May), Bari
- **Festival of Peschici's three patron saints** colourful procession through the Medieval quarter (early July), Peschici

Cycling Events
- **rofeo dell'Etna** 200km road race around Mt Etna (March), Sicily
- **rofeo Pantalica** 170km road race (March), near Syracuse, Sicily
- **iro della Provincia di Reggio Calabria** 190km road race (March), northern Calabria

Food & Drink Specialities
- Too many to mention!
- *limoncello* (a bright-yellow lemon liqueur with a hidden kick)

imity to Alberobello's *trulli* (conical-roofed stone houses) area, it's a useful gateway.

Bari is easy to negotiate. Orient yourself from Piazza Aldo Moro in the newer, 19th-century section of the city; on or around it are as many as four different train stations. From the square, it's about 1km northwards to Bari Vecchia, the old town.

Information The IAT office (☎ 080 540 11 11) is at Via Bozzi 45, and more useful than the APT headquarters (☎ 080 524 23 61) at Piazza Aldo Moro 33a (1st floor). There are plenty of banks on Corso Cavour and at the station, most with ATMs. The best place for bike spares is Simone & C Srl (☎ 080 5026829), Via della Resistenza 168, about 2km south of the centre. Tommaso De Carne, Via Gorizia 16a, is a highly respected repair specialist.

Things to See & Do Head for the tight, uneven alleyways of Bari's **old quarter**, which hides some 40 churches and more than 120 little shrines. The infamous *centro storico* (historic centre) is undergoing a gradual process of rehabilitation and restoration, with concerted efforts to chase out the bad elements that made it a definite no-go at night.

In the rejuvenated Piazza Mercantile (which also serves as a popular evening meeting place during the warmer months) is the **Sedile**, the medieval headquarters of Bari's Council of Nobles. In the square's northeast corner is the **Colonna della Giustizia** (Column of Justice), to which debtors were reportedly tied. Northwest beyond the small Chiesa di Santa Ana is the **Basilica di San Nicola** *(Piazza San Nicola)*, one of the city's main churches, the other being the **cathedral** *(Piazza Odegitria)*, a brief walk south via Strada D Carmine.

Castello Svevo, just west of the cathedral, boasts four levels of history: a Norman structure was built over the ruins of a Roman fort; Frederick II then incorporated parts of the Norman castle into his own design, including two towers that still stand; and the bastions with corner towers overhanging the moat were added in the 16th century during Spanish rule.

Places to Stay A Hostelling International (HI) youth hostel a few kilometres west of the city centre on the main coast road, **Ostello del Sole** *(☎ 080 549 11 75; Strada Adriatica 78; dorm beds/doubles €13/32, meals*

€8) is accessed from the old quarter on Via Napoli. **Hotel Adria** *(☎ 080 524 66 99; e hoadria@tin.it; Via Zuppetta 10; singles/doubles €21/37, with bathroom €37/57)* is clean and comfortable, well run and excellent value, with a good restaurant. **Albergo Romeo** *(☎ 080 523 72 53; Via Crisanzio 12; singles/doubles with bathroom €36.50/ 54.50)* is comfortable and centrally located. Upstairs is **Pensione Giulia** *(☎/fax 080 521 82 71; Via Crisanzio 12; singles/doubles with breakfast €36.50/47, with bathroom €42/ 62)*, a pleasant, family style pensione. **Grand Hotel d'Oriente** *(☎ 080 524 40 11; Corso Cavour 32; singles/doubles with breakfast €67.50/103.50)* is truly grand, with a new and an old (costlier) section.

Places to Eat Self-caterers should try the daily **produce market** *(Piazza del Ferrarese)*, the big **Supermercato DOK** *(Via De Giosa 24-28)*, one street east of Corso Cavour at the top end of town, and the **Spesa A & D** delicatessen *(Via Carulli 31-33)*.

Buy excellent savoury snacks and bread at **Magda Bar** *(Via P Petroni 32)*, just northeast of the station.

Pizzeria Enzo & Ciro *(Via Imbriani 79; meals €8)* is a no-frills eatery popular with the locals. Try the filling and delicious antipasto buffet. Also good value is the bustling and cheerful **Vini e Cucina** *(Strada Vallisa 23; meals €10)*. **Taverna Verde** *(Largo Adua 19; meals €15-18)* is stylish and justifiably popular, serving fine pasta and main dishes at very reasonable prices. For fish and seafood, try **Al Pescatore** *(Piazza Federico di Svevia 6-8; meals €25)*. The grilled squid is recommended.

Getting There & Away Bari's airport (☎ 080 583 52 04), 10km west of the city centre, services domestic flights to/from Italy' major cities. The private Ferrovia Bari–Nord train line runs right by the airport (€0.80, almost hourly). An Alitalia airport bus (for Alitalia ticket holders) leaves the main train station, calling by the airline's office at Via Calefati 37, about 80 minutes before most flight departures.

Bus services connect Bari to most major cities, with many intercity services departing from Via Capruzzi, immediately south of the main train station. ATS Viaggi office (☎ 080 556 24 46, w www.atsviaggi.com), at Via Capruzzi 224, handles bookings for most of the intercity buses. Agenzia Marino (☎ 080 521 65 54, W www.marinobus.it), Piazza Aldo Moro 15b, services Naples (€19, three hours, two daily), Parma (€38, 11 hours, one daily), Bologna (€34, 8½ hours, two daily), Modena (€34, 9½ hours, one daily), Reggio Emilia (€34, 10 hours, one daily), Milano (€34, 10½ hours, three daily) and Torino (€44, 13 hours, one daily). Marozzi (☎ 06 44 24 95 19 in Rome, ☎ 080 552 00 53 in Bari) has four buses daily to/from Rome (€25.31, 5½ to six hours), as well as services to Florence, Siena and Pisa.

From Bari's main train station (☎ 848 88 80 88), regular FS trains go to Rome (€26.20, five hours), Milan (€43.90, 8½ hours) and Foggia (with connections to/from Manfredonia). Be aware that bikes cannot be taken on Eurostar trains unless well packed and unrecognisable as a bicycle.

Catania

Catania has all the edgy chaos, traffic congestion and general decay you'd expect of Sicily's second-largest city, but if this sounds like an unsavoury prospect, fortunately someone forgot to tell the residents. With the awesome Mt Etna smoking and seething virtually on the city's doorstep, the risk of dwelling on the flanks of one of the world's most active volcanoes has left its indelible mark on the psyche of the Catanesi. A glance below the grit and grime reveals a sophisticated and vibrant metropolis with a rich and difficult history. The city was totally rebuilt in splendid baroque style after lava from the massive eruption of 1669 swallowed much of it and the subsequent earthquake of 1693 levelled what was left. No doubt such a fraught past has played a big part in the evolution of the city and its culture.

Information The APT office (☎ 095 730 62 22, W www.apt.catania.it) is at Via Cimarosa 10–12 and is open daily. There are branches at the train station (☎ 095 730 62 55) on platform No 1; at the airport (☎ 095 730 62 66); and at the port (☎ 095 730 62 09). There are several banks with ATMs on Corso Sicilia and in and around the centre. Tutto Ciclismo (☎ 095 43 49 07), Via Caronda 261–263, one street east of Via Etnea about 1km from the centre, has a large range of spares for road and mountain bikes.

Things to See & Do Stroll through the lava-hewn streets of the centre and visit its many grand buildings. The tourist office has maps with suggested walking itineraries and notes on Catania's significant sites.

Acquaterra (☎ 095 50 30 20; W www.ac quaterra.it; Via A Longo 74) is a friendly establishment run by adventure enthusiasts offering all-year **guided mountain biking** (€21-31; bike hire per day/weekend €13/21) and **guided rafting, climbing** and **river trekking.**

Nearby **Acireale** is an easy 17km ride north on the busy Lungomare (esplanade) and worth a visit. Further afield is beautiful but touristy **Taormina** and the lovely beaches on the coast around **Giardini Naxos**, which has some fine eateries. Stowing the bike under one of the regular buses on the outward leg negates the heady climb up to Taormina and leaves an easy 39km return ride.

Places to Stay An easy 5km ride north on the Lungomare, **Camping Jonio** (☎ 095 49 11 39; Via Villini a Mare 2; per person/tent €6/12) is close to a good beach. For the tight budget, **Agorà Youth Hostel** (☎ 095 723 30 10; W agorahostel.hypermart.net; Piazza Currò 6; dorm beds €16) is the best option and it's centrally located (behind Piazza del Duomo).

Lack of space can mean problems storing bikes in Catania's hotels; always ask when booking. Tucked away in a small courtyard off Via Etnea, **Hotel Rubens** (☎ 095 31 70 73; Via Etnea 196; singles/doubles €23/31, with bathroom €29/41) is central, comfortable, well priced and well run by its affable English-speaking owner. **Hotel Centrale Europa** (☎ 095 31 13 09; Via Vittorio Emanuele II 167; singles/doubles €44/62) offers excellent mid-range accommodation, with elegant singles/doubles (some overlooking Piazza del Duomo), including breakfast.

Places to Eat Fresh produce abounds in the city's two central markets, open daily except Sunday. **La Fiera** (Piazza Carlo Alberto) has bread, fresh fruit, cheese and all manner of odds and ends, while **La Pescheria** (Piazza del Duomo) is the place to buy fish.

For excellent coffee and a wide selection of mouth-watering sweet and savoury pastries, you can't go past bar **St Moritz** (Via

Etnea), 100m north of Piazza Stesicoro. **I Puritani** *(Piazza Bellini)* serves Catania's best gelati.

The oddly-named **Tex-Mex** *(Via Santa Filomena 48)* serves what could be Catania's best pizzas; its large salads also make a good meal. **Trattoria de' Fiori** *(Via Coppola 24)* isn't much in the glamour stakes, but serves as close to authentic Sicilian home cooking as you'll get without an invitation. **Trattoria La Paglia** *(Via Pardo 23)*, just behind Piazza del Duomo in the heart of La Pescheria, is one of Catania's traditional seafood restaurants.

Getting There & Away Catania's Fontanarossa airport is 7km southwest of the city centre and services domestic and European flights (the latter via Rome or Milan). It's easily accessed by bike.

Intercity buses terminate in the area around Piazza Giovanni XXIII, in front of the train station. SAIS (☎ 095 53 61 68), Via d'Amico 181, serves Palermo (€16.20, 2½ hours), Enna (€6, 1½ hours, eight daily), Napoli (€30, 8¾ hours) and Rome (€39, 10½ hours). AST (☎ 095 746 10 96), Via Luigi Sturzo 232, also services these destinations and many smaller provincial towns around Catania. Interbus-Etna Trasporti (☎ 095 53 27 16, 095 746 13 33), at the same address as SAIS, runs buses to Piazza Armerina, Taormina, Messina, Enna, Ragusa, Gela, Syracuse and Rome.

Frequent trains connect Catania with mainland cities. Supplements for bikes are €3.10 for 24 hours, but many intercity trains don't allow roll-on bikes as luggage. However, a partly dismantled and bagged bike will fit under couchette-type seats for night travel.

Train services to other towns within Sicily are often painfully slow and unreliable, while the island's bus network is vast and efficient; buses are the best option – cheaper, faster and easier.

Campania

Presided over by Naples, the only true metropolis in the Mezzogiorno, Campania is alive with myth and legend. Stories tell how sirens (sea nymphs) lured sailors to their deaths off Sorrento; how islands in the Gulf of Naples were the domain of mermaids; and how Lago d'Averno (Lake Avernus), in the Campi Flegrei, was believed, in ancient times, to be the entrance to the underworld.

In the shadow of Mt Vesuvius (Vesuvio; 1277m), southeast of Naples, lie the ruins of Pompeii and Herculaneum, Roman cities buried by the volcano, and the Greek temples of Paestum, among the best preserved in the world. Many writers have waxed lyrical about the natural beauty of the Amalfi Coast and the islands out in the Gulf of Naples, particularly Capri.

Amalfi Coast

Duration	2 days
Distance	77.3km
Difficulty	moderate
Start	Sorrento
End	Salerno

Ignore tales of foreboding about running the gauntlet on dangerously narrow roads choked with cars – the Amalfi coast would have to be one of mainland Europe's finest coastal rides. The riding is relatively easy and weekday traffic never a problem – even into early summer (when tour buses are only permitted to travel east to west). Following the route in the direction described, you'll be as close as it's safely possible to get to the edge, without sprouting wings. Coasting along a tar ribbon clinging impossibly to cliffs hundreds of metres above azure waters, and passing through idyllic Mediterranean villages, it soon becomes apparent that *la bici* (the bike) is the ultimate way to experience this amazing road.

PLANNING
When to Ride
Any time from March to mid-July. Though heat will be a factor in the warmer months, the rides are short and there are regular rest opportunities and facilities along the route. Weekends equate to major traffic congestion and potentially unpleasant riding conditions; they are to be avoided.

Maps
Touring Club Italiano's (TCI) 1:200,000 *Campania & Basilicata* map covers the route.

ACCESS TOWN
Sorrento

According to ancient Greek legend, the Sorrento area was known as the Temple of the Sirens. Sailors of antiquity were powerless to resist the beautiful song of these maidens-cum-monsters, who would lure them and their ships to doom on the reefs. In the high season this unashamed resort town is bursting with holidaymakers, predominantly from Britain and Germany, but there's still enough southern Italian charm to make a stay here enjoyable and it is handy for Capri (15 minutes away).

Information The AAST office (☎ 081 807 40 33), Via Luigi de Maio 35, is within the Circolo dei Forestieri (Foreigners' Club), an office and restaurant complex. There are several banks with ATMs in the centre, and up on Via degli Aranci. Check email at Blu Blu Internet Café (Via Fuorimura 20d), just off Piazza Tasso. Il Biciaio (☎ 081 870 57 44), Via degli Aranci 101a, has a good selection of spares for road bikes.

Things to See & Do The gleaming white and understated facade of the **cathedral** on Corso Italia gives no hint of the exuberance within. There's a particularly striking crucifixion above the main altar. Within the 18th-century **Palazzo Correale**, which has some interesting murals, is the **Museo Correale** (☎ 081 878 18 46; Via Correale), which contains a small collection of 17th- and 18th-century Neapolitan art, and a disparate assortment of Greek and Roman artefacts. Views up and down the coast from **Villa Comunale park** are breathtaking – and equally impressive from the gardens of the beautiful, if modest, cloister of **Chiesa di San Francesco**, just beside the park.

The closest beach is at **Marina Grande**, a 15-minute walk west from Piazza Tasso, which has small strips of sand. **Bagni Regina Giovanna**, a 20-minute walk or short ride west along Via Capo, is more picturesque, set among the ruins of the Roman Villa Pollio Felix. To the east is a small beach at **Marinella**.

Linee Marittime Partenopee (☎ 081 807 18 12) runs up to 10 hydrofoils daily to/from Capri, while Caremar (☎ 081 807 30 77) has one hydrofoil and three fast ferry sailings daily to/from the island. The 15-minute hydrofoil journey costs €7.75, while the ferry is €6.20.

Places to Stay There are a couple of camping grounds just west of town, an easy ride from the centre. **Camping Nube d'Argento** (☎ 081 878 13 44; w www.nubedargento.com; Via Capo 21; per person/tent €9/9.50) is only 200m from the beach and

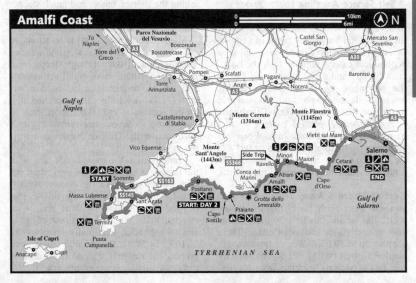

there's a pool on site. It also has bungalows (average price €62 for a twin). **Santa Fortunata Campogaio** (☎ *081 807 35 79;* W *www.santafortunata.com; Via Capo 39; per tent/person €6.50/8.50)* is set in pleasant, leafy surroundings, and has a pool and private rocky beach. Bungalows are available at €55 for a twin.

Ostello le Sirene (☎/fax *081 877 13 71; Via degli Aranci 160; dorm beds €13, singles/ doubles €39/52)* is conveniently located and all prices include breakfast. **Pensione Linda** (☎/fax *081 878 29 16; Via degli Aranci 125; singles/doubles with bathroom €42/68)* is excellent value and offers courteous, friendly service. **Hotel City** (☎/fax *081 877 22 10;* e *hotel_city.libero.it; Corso Italia 221; singles/doubles with breakfast €39/65)* is clean and friendly, but traffic noise can be a bother.

Hotel La Meridiana (☎ *081 807 35 35; Via Rota 1-3; singles/doubles €83/120)* is a good, upmarket tourist hotel. At the top end, **Grand Hotel Excelsior Vittoria** (☎ *081 807 10 44;* W *www.exvitt.it; Piazza Tasso 34; singles/ doubles €282/326)* is a venerable old hotel showcasing Sorrento's former glory.

Places to Eat There are two supermarkets within the centre: **Standa** (cnr *Corso Italia & Via Marziale)* just west of Piazza Lauro, and the **SISA** (Via *Aranci),* opposite the hostel.

Self Service Angelina Lauro (Piazza *Angelina Lauro 39-40; pasta & mains €3)* is one of several economical snack places ringing the square and has a wide range of vegetarian dishes. **Red Lion** (Via *Marziale 25)* is an economical eatery, popular with the hostel crowd; pizza and a pint of ale costs €4.70, the set menu €7.75. Enjoy reasonably priced meals under a pleasant, vine-covered terrace at **Ristorante-Pizzeria Giardinello** (Via *Accademia 7; pizza & pasta €5),* on a narrow lane west of Piazza Tasso. For a special treat, try **Ristorante Caruso** (☎ *081 878 41 76; Piazza Tasso; meals €25),* one of Sorrento's best and most expensive restaurants.

Getting There & Away To get to Sorrento you will most likely travel first to Naples, which has air and bus links to most Italian and several major European cities. There are also up to 30 trains a day from Rome to Naples. Curreri (☎ *081 801 54 20)* has a direct bus service to Sorrento from Naples'

Capodichino airport (€5.20, six per day, one hour).

SITA buses (☎ *081 552 21 76)* run from the company's main office in Via Pisanelli (near Piazza Municipio) or from Via G Ferraris (near Stazione Centrale; tickets at Bar Clizia, Corso Arnaldo Lucci 173) to Sorrento (€4.65, one per day, one hour 10 minutes).

Regular trains on the Circumvesuviana line (☎ *081 772 24 44)* make the trip to Sorrento (€1.60, every 20 to 40 minutes, one hour). There's no luggage space for roll-on bikes and permission to board with one will depend on who you ask, but it's worth a try; packed in a bike bag, there should be no problem at all.

Alilauro *aliscafi* (hydrofoils; ☎ *081 761 10 04),* Via F Caracciolo 11, make the trip from Molo Beverello in Naples to Sorrento (€6.80/4.20 per person/bike, seven per day).

Bicycle Escaping Naples by bike and making the trip to Sorrento is possible, but not recommended.

THE RIDE
Day 1: Sorrento to Positano
2–3½ hours, 34.3km

Other than the hard 3.8km climb up to Termini, this is a relatively easy day, rolling out west on quiet roads and following the coast around the Sorrento peninsula rather than taking the shorter, busier and much steeper SS145, which climbs straight over the ridge onto the peninsula's southern side.

Massa Lubrense (6.4km) is an attractive old town and worth a short stop and wander. The route then passes through sleepy olive groves and a number of small settlements with the odd restaurant or bar. Stop in **Termini** (12.1km), a little village perched high on the peninsula, and take a short stroll to the hilltop to savour the fantastic views north across the Gulf of Naples and west out to Capri.

From Termini the route heads east, with the imposing grey cliffs and rugged mountains towering above the distant Amalfi Coast. The route rejoins the SS145 just beyond Sant'Agata (18.3km) and, after swooping down in a blinding rush of twists and switchbacks, eventually leads to the SS163 (24.5km), the Amalfi Coast road proper. The run to day's end at Positano is truly exhilarating as the narrow road teeters

Positano

To say that Positano is picturesque doesn't do it justice. A veritable cascade of softly-hued, bougainvillea-laced buildings cling to a slope so steep it's hard to believe they don't tumble into the azure waters below. The town is split in two by a cliff that bears the Torre Trasita (Trasita Tower). West is the smaller, less crowded Spiaggia del Fornillo beach area and the less expensive side of town, east is Spiaggia Grande, backing up to the town centre. Travelling by bike means a long descent on one-way Viale Pasitea to the centre and a steep climb back out on one-way Via Cristoforo Colombo to rejoin the SS163, which bypasses the town in a huge hairpin high above.

Information The area below Viale Pasitea is pedestrian access only, and finding the APT tourist office (☎ 089 87 50 67), Via del Saracino 4, at the foot of the Chiesa di Santa Maria Assunta steps means locking bikes or walking them down the narrow cobbled Via dei Mulini to the seafront at Spiaggia Grande. Banco di Napoli and Banca dei Paschi di Siena on Via dei Mulini have ATMs.

Things to See & Do Positano's main cultural treasure is the **Chiesa di Santa Maria Assunta** *(Piazza Flavio Gioia)*, its ceramic dome gleaming under the sun. Inside, regular classical lines are broken by pillars and pilasters topped by gilded Ionic capitals, while winged cherubs peek from above every arch.

Diving enthusiasts should try **Centro Sub Costiera Amalfitana** (☎ 089 81 21 48), operating from Spiaggia del Fornillo.

Walking represents one of the best ways to experience the natural splendour of the area without paying for the privilege. Set aside a day for the classic **Sentiero degli Dei** (Path of the Gods; five to 5½ hours), which follows the steep, well-defined paths linking Positano and Praiano. From there you can catch a bus back along the coast road. For staggering views requiring much less effort, stroll the **Via Positanesi d'America**, the cliffside path that links the two beaches, and reward yourself with a cold drink on the terrace of Hotel Ristorante Pupetto.

Places to Stay & Eat Positano has several one-star hotels, which are usually booked well in advance for summer. Ask at the APT office about rooms in private houses, which are generally expensive.

Praiano, 5km east of Positano, has the nearest camping, **La Tranquilità** (☎ 089 87 40 84; **e** info@continental_positano.it).

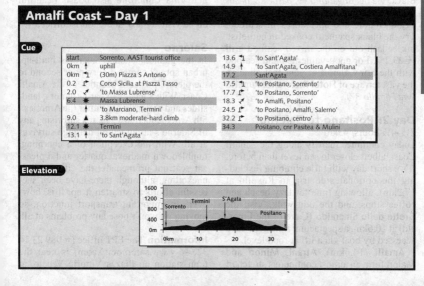

Amalfi Coast – Day 1

Cue

start	Sorrento, AAST tourist office		13.6 ↰	'to Sant'Agata'
0km ↑	uphill		14.9 ↑	'to Sant'Agata, Costiera Amalfitana'
0km ↰	(30m) Piazza S Antonio		17.2	Sant'Agata
0.2 ↱	Corso Sicilia at Piazza Tasso		17.5 ↰	'to Positano, Sorrento'
2.0 ↙	'to Massa Lubrense'		17.7 ↱	'to Positano, Sorrento'
6.4 ✳	Massa Lubrense		18.3 ↙	'to Amalfi, Positano'
↑	'to Marciano, Termini'		24.5 ↱	'to Positano, Amalfi, Salerno'
9.0 ▲	3.8km moderate-hard climb		32.2 ↱	'to Positano, centro'
12.1 ✳	Termini		34.3	Positano, cnr Pasitea & Mulini
13.1 ↑	'to Sant'Agata'			

Elevation

Ostello Brikette (☎ 089 87 58 57; W www .brikette.com; Via G Marconi 358; dorm beds €18.50, doubles €57) is clean, full of character and enjoys a staggering view of the bay. **Pensione Villa Verde** (☎/fax 089 87 55 06; Via Pasitea 338; singles/doubles €57/78) sits high above the town, not far off the SS163, and affords great views from the terrace. **Villa delle Palme** (☎/fax 089 87 51 62; Via Pasitea 252; doubles with breakfast €83, singles low season only €52) is pleasant and well-situated near the centre. The friendly English-speaking owners also run the excellent Saraceno d'Oro restaurant, just below.

Pick up all self-catering supplies at reasonable prices at **Bar Internazionale**, where Via Pasitea leaves the SS163. **La Zagara** (Via dei Mulini 10) has excellent pastries and a good selection of savoury snacks. The terrace of **Bar de Martino** (Viale Pasitea 170), with its commanding views of town and sea, makes a great place for a relaxing drink.

Most restaurants are overpriced for the food they serve. **Il Saraceno d'Oro** (Viale Pasitea 254; pizzas €5.50, meals €15-25) is a family restaurant, popular with the locals and offering good food and attentive service. **O'Capurale** (Via Regina Giovanna; pasta from €4.50) is near the main beach and serves primarily local dishes. **Chez Black** (Via del Brigantino 19; pasta €8, meals €23-35) is a popular spot overlooking Spiaggia Grande and specialises in seafood. Try the black spaghetti cooked in cuttlefish ink or lash out on the mixed seafood grill (€23.25). For good-value fish and seafood with the briny almost at your feet, dine on the vast terrace of **Hotel Ristorante Pupetto** (Via Fornillo 37).

Day 2: Positano to Salerno
2½–4½ hours, 43km
Today continues merrily along the Amalfi Coast, albeit closer to sea level than before. It's a short day with little climbing (excluding the optional side trip to Ravello at 17.2km), allowing time for lazy beach and coffee stops, and the odd walk. Visit the **Grotte dello Smeraldo** (Cave of the Emerald) at 10.6km, a spectacular limestone cave accessed by boat via a lift at road level.

Amalfi (14.6km), **Atrani**, **Minori** and **Maiori** form an almost continuous stretch of built-up, but highly picturesque, coastal resort towns. Amalfi is by far the better known, being one of Italy's most popular seaside holiday destinations. It was a major naval superpower in the 11th century, and its navigation tables, the Tavole Amalfitana, formed the world's first maritime code.

The low-key fishing village of **Cetara** (31.1km) is a nice change from the flashier coastal towns. From here to Salerno traffic increases incrementally, especially in the late afternoon. After passing through **Vietri sul Mare** (36.2km), where many workshops and showrooms display the town's renowned ceramics, the road drops down to the Salerno port area and an easy ride along the busy esplanade leads to day's end.

Side Trip: Ravello
1½ hours, 10.6km return
For those craving their daily climbing fix, the 5.3km climb through lush ravines on the side trip to **Ravello** (17.2km) will reward with spectacular views down to Amalfi, Maiori, Minori and the coast beyond. The **duomo** (cathedral) in Piazza Vescovado dates from the 11th century. It houses an impressive marble pulpit and a free museum in the crypt. Other highlights include the 13th century **Villa Rufolo**, its gardens and terrace. The villa once housed several popes and was later home to the German composer, Wagner. **Villa Cimbrone** also boasts beautiful gardens, and the city's three vineyards can all be visited – ask at the tourist office.

Salerno
In the glamour stakes, Salerno's built-up, urban sprawl comes a very poor second to the picture-postcard beauties of the Amalfi Coast. With a legacy of earth tremors, landslides and major damage after the American 5th Army landed in 1943, it's surprising any of Salerno's architectural heritage survives at all. With the exception of a charming, tumbledown medieval quarter and a pleasant seafront promenade, the city today is unexciting, although there have been successful efforts to smarten it up. It is, however, an important transport junction, so moving on won't pose any problems at all.

Information The EPT office (☎ 089 23 14 32, W www.salernocity.com) is near the train station on Piazza Vittorio Veneto, at the eastern end of town, and most intercity buses stop here. As well as information and maps, the tourist office can give you a copy of *Memo*, a fortnightly listing of what's on.

For basic (predominantly mountain-bike) spares close to the centre, try Fasano (☎/fax 089 22 64 88) at Corso Garibaldi 86–90. Ugolino Cicli (☎ 089 75 20 64), Via Annuzzi 43–47, is 3km east of town, but has a far more comprehensive stocklist. Check email and buy cheap international phone cards at Internet Point (Via Diaz 19). There are numerous banks with ATMs on Corso Vittorio Emanuele.

Things to See & Do The city's duomo in Piazza Alfano is worth a look. It was built by the Normans under Robert Guiscard in the 11th century and remodelled in the 18th century, but sustained severe damage in the 1980 earthquake. It is flanked by a Romanesque belltower and preceded by a courtyard in polychrome stone. With its 28 slender, recycled Roman columns, most plundered from Paestum, it has a decidedly Moorish air.

Museo Archeologico Provinciale (☎ 089 23 11 35), at Via San Benedetto 28, contains archaeological finds from the region, including some particularly fine classical pieces.

Places to Stay & Eat The HI Ostello Ave Gratia Plena (☎ 089 79 02 51; Via Dei Canali; B&B €10) is open year-round. **Albergo Santa Rosa** (☎/fax 089 22 53 46; e alb.srosa@fiscalinet.it; Corso Vittorio Emanuele 14, 2nd floor; singles/doubles with bathroom €23.50/34) is a friendly budget option offering good value for money. The more upmarket **Hotel Plaza** (☎/fax 089 22 44 77; e plaza@speed net.org; Piazza Ferrovia 42; singles/doubles with bathroom €52/ 78) offers comfortable rooms with telephone and TV.

Self-caterers will find **supermarkets, fruit and vegetable shops, bakeries** and **delicatessens** in and around the shopping precinct on Corso Vitorio Emanuele. There's also a daily **produce market** in Piazza Vittorio Veneto.

Vicolo della Neve (☎ 089 22 57 05; Vicolo della Neve 24; meals €15-25) is a venerable 500-year-old establishment serving excellent traditional fare. **Ristorante Cenacolo** (☎ 089 23 88 18; Via Duomo) is similarly priced and has a terrace overlooking Piazza al Duomo. **Hostaria il Brigante** (☎ 089 22 65 92; Via Fratelli Linguiti 2) is close to Ristorante Cenacolo, and more modest in price and quality.

Getting There & Away SITA (☎ 089 40 51 45) has buses for Naples (every 25 minutes, about one hour), leaving from outside Bar Cioffi (where you buy your ticket) at Corso Garibaldi 134. Buonotourist runs a weekday

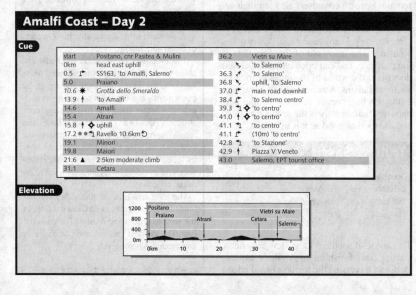

Amalfi Coast – Day 2

Cue

start	Positano, cnr Pasitea & Mulini		36.2	Vietri su Mare
0km	head east uphill			↘ 'to Salerno'
0.5	↱ SS163, 'to Amalfi, Salerno'		36.3	↗ 'to Salerno'
5.0	Praiano		36.8	↘ uphill, 'to Salerno'
10.6	✳ Grotta dello Smeraldo		37.0	↱ main road downhill
13.9	↑ 'to Amalfi'		38.4	↱ 'to Salerno centro'
14.6	Amalfi		39.3	↰ ✧ 'to centro'
15.4	Atrani		41.0	↑ ✧ 'to centro'
15.8	↑ ✧ uphill		41.1	↰ 'to centro'
17.2	●●↰ Ravello 10.6km ↺		41.1	↱ (10m) 'to centro'
19.1	Minori		42.8	↰ 'to Stazione'
19.8	Maiori		42.9	↑ Piazza V Veneto
21.6	▲ 2.5km moderate climb		43.0	Salerno, EPT tourist office
31.1	Cetara			

Elevation

1200	Positano
800	Praiano · Atrani · Cetara · Vietri su Mare · Salerno
400	
0m	
	0km · 10 · 20 · 30 · 40

express service to Rome's Fiumicino airport, departing from Piazza della Concordia (also stopping at EUR-Fermi Metropolitana in Rome). Simet (☎ 0983 52 03 15) has two buses daily to Cosenza (four hours), one daily to Rome (three hours) and Naples (one hour).

Salerno is also a major train stop between Rome, Naples and Reggio di Calabria and is served by all types of trains. It also has good train links with both inland towns and the Adriatic Coast. There's a direct train to Cosenza (€11.21 plus €3.61 per bike, 3½ hours, seven per day).

Apulia

The 'spur' and 'heel' of Italy's boot, Apulia (Puglia) is bordered by two seas, the Adriatic to the east and Ionian to the south. Its strategic position as the peninsula's maritime gateway to the east made it a major thoroughfare, and a target for colonisers and invaders.

The ancient Greeks founded Magna Graecia, a string of settlements along the Ionian coast. Brindisi marks the end of the Roman Via Appia which, completed around 190 BC, ran all the way from Rome. The Norman legacy is seen in magnificent Romanesque churches across the region. Foggia and its province were favoured by the great Swabian king, Frederick II, several of whose castles remain. Spanish colonisers also left their architectural mark, mainly in Lecce province.

Being mostly flat makes Apulia ideal cycling territory. In any case, pedal power offers a passage into many out-of-the-way parts of the province, and can open otherwise closed doors into the world of the innately friendly southern Italians. Another indirect advantage is that cycling creates an appetite, and perhaps nowhere in Italy is the produce as fresh and the food as good as it is in Apulia.

Trulli & Sassi

Duration	3 days
Distance	237.5km
Difficulty	easy–moderate
Start/End	Bari

This is one of southern Italy's few easy rides, starting and finishing in Apulia's capital, Bari, and traversing the region's broad inland

plains known as the Murge. Touch down in Basilicata to visit Matera's once infamous *sassi* (cave dwellings), then discover the magical world of the *trulli*. These quaint, conical-roofed stone houses dot the richly cultivated countryside of the Murge (between Noci and Locorotondo), a region with a justly deserved reputation as the 'garden of Italy'.

PLANNING
When to Ride
Summer heat can be oppressive in Apulia, especially out on the open plains of the Murge. Ideal riding times are March to July and September to November. If riding in the warmer months, early departures are recommended, allowing for siesta time during the hottest part of the day.

Maps
TCI's 1:200,000 *Puglia* map is fine, covering all but one or two of the minor roads

---

Trulli

Trulli are circular or cube-shaped, stone houses, conical-roofed and whitewashed, and built entirely without mortar. Their roofs are tiled with concentric rows of *chiancarelle* (evenly-shaped slate pieces) and topped with pinnacles or spheres, which are often painted with astrological or religious symbols. Their origin is obscure, with suggestions of a connection to the *nuraghe* of Sardinia, the *bories* of France and other similar structures in parts of Spain and Turkey.

The motarless construction reputedly enabled feudal lords to deny the exploited peasants who tilled their lands any civil rights, by conveniently moving them on whenever necessary. Another theory is that the dry construction enabled rapid dismantling and rebuilding of the *trulli*, thereby sidestepping decrees forbidding the construction of towns by feudal lords without express royal permission, and avoiding heavy imposts levelled on urban collectives.

The *trulli* area is in the Itria Valley and extends from Conversano and Gioia del Colle in the west to Ostuni and Martina Franca in the east. The greatest concentration of *trulli* is in and around Alberobello.

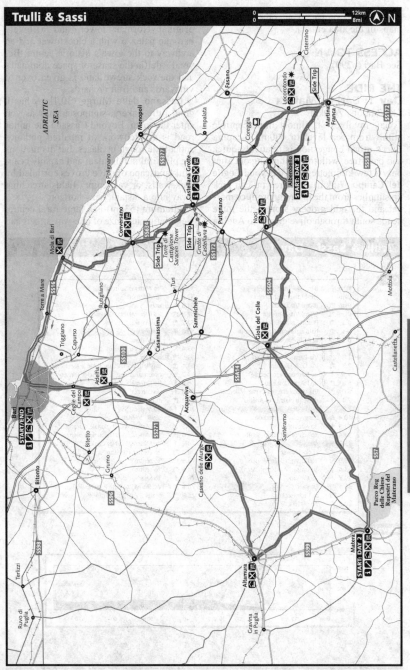

Trulli & Sassi

THE SOUTH & SICILY

(which aren't shown on any other available maps of the area either).

ACCESS TOWN
See Bari (p290).

THE RIDE
Day 1: Bari to Matera
4½–8 hours, 76.9km

Today involves an almost imperceptible climb from sea level to 400m. Escaping Bari's urban congestion is relatively quick and pain-free, with traffic thinning out after only a few kilometres. Once beyond **Ceglie del Campo** (7.5km) – where you can pick up supplies from the morning **produce market** and the odd **grocery store** – the route heads south through olive groves to **Adelfia**

(15.2km), a small rural town boasting an original Norman tower, and a lovely baroque palazzo with a clocktower and an archway to the town's historic centre. Beyond Adelfia the sense of space dominates and the rock strewn land is given over to vineyards and fruit orchards.

Cassano delle Murge (30.1km) has a good little **bakery**, signposted just as you enter the town. Beyond Cassano the minor road is a patchwork of repaired potholes and a little rough in places, but distractions are plentiful in this silent and harshly beautiful landscape of olive groves corralled by rock walls, or vast empty fields stretching away into a distant, hazy horizon.

Altamura (53km) is a large rural centre. Negotiating its maze of one-way streets can

Trulli & Sassi – Day 1

Cue

start	Bari, APT headquarters	
0km	west towards station	
0km ↰	(30m) Via Nicola	
0km ↰	(20m) Via Zuppetta	
0.3 ↰	Piazza Savoia	
0.4 ↱	hard right into Corso Cavour	
0.5 ↱	at AGIP service station	
0.7 ↰ 🍴	Viale Unità Italia	
1.8 ↱ 🍴	Via Papa Giovanni XXIII	
2.3 ↰	Via Giulio Petroni	
4.9 ↑ ◈	'to Carbonara, ospedale'	
5.8 ↱ 🍴	'to Piazza Umberto I'	
6.0 ↱	Via Vaccarella, 'to Ceglie, Valenzano'	
7.4 ↑	through piazza, 'to Adelfia'	
7.5	Ceglie del Campo	
10.4 ⚠	dangerous intersection	
13.9 ↑	'to Adelfia'	
14.4 ↰	'to centro' (at 'Stop' sign)	
15.2 ✳	Adelfia	
↱	at clocktower	
15.5 ↘	'to Cassano delle Murgie'	
23.4 ↑	'to Cassano' (at 'Stop' sign)	
29.7 ↑ ◈	'to Cassano'	
30.1	Cassano	
↰	at T intersection	
30.2 ↱	'to Matera, Santeramo'	

30.5 ↰	'to Matera, Santeramo'	
32.6 ↱	'to Altamura'	
51.8 ↑ 🍴	uphill	
52.3 ↱	'to Bari, Matera, Gravina'	
52.7 ↰	'to Matera, Gravina'	
53.0	Altamura	
↗	'to Matera'	
53.4 ↘	'to Matera, Corato'	
53.5 ↰ 🍴	no sign	
54.1 ↱	stay left of AGIP, to 'Tutte le Direzioni'	
54.2 ↘	circonvallazione, to 'Tuttel le Direzioni'	
55.0 ↑	'to Laterza'	
61.8 ↑	'to Laterza'	
64.5 ↱	at Bari provincial border sign	
70.9 ↑	'to Matera, SS99'	
72.2 ↑	SS99, 'to Matera'	
73.8 ↗	'to Matera, Via Nazionale, Taranto'	
74.0 ↱	'to Matera, Via Nazionale, Potenza'	
74.2 ↑	'to Matera, Via Nazionale'	
74.3 ↰	'to centro' (at 'Stop' sign)	
74.5 ↱	'to centro'	
74.6 ↰	'to centro'	
76.4 ↑	'to Sassi'	
76.8 ↱	Via Roma, 'to Ente Provinciale Turismo'	
76.9 ↱	Matera, APT tourist office	

Elevation

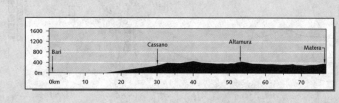

be problematic, so care should be taken to follow the cue sheet closely. The city's origins date back to Trojan times, but it's the 13th-century **Cattedrale Vergine Assunta** that is of interest. Constructed during the reign of Frederick II, it was badly damaged by an earthquake in 1316 and later suffered some unfortunate baroque renovations, when the elegant medieval main portal and rose window were moved from their original position to what had been the apse. The cathedral is in the old town's main street, Via Federico II di Svevia.

For a few short kilometres, the route traces the original Via Appia Antica (Appian Way), between 61.8km and 64.5km, but visions of Roman centurions with clanging shields and sandalled feet quickly dissipate among the roar of moderate, but fast moving traffic. The final run up to day's end at Matera is more relaxed, and reaching the centre is somewhat convoluted, but well signposted.

Matera

Matera evokes powerful images of a poor, peasant culture, which first began to hew the city's famous cave houses in medieval times or earlier. Now a Unesco World Heritage site, Matera was a troglodyte city of 20,000 until well after WWII; people and animals slept together and, despite an infant mortality rate of over 50%, a typical family cave sheltered an average of six children. Matera's famous *sassi* – buildings of tufa stone, half constructed, half bored into the rock walls of Matera's twin ravines – were home to more than 50% of the populace until the local government forcefully relocated them into new residential areas in the late 1950s.

The most striking account of how these people lived is found in Carlo Levi's *Christ Stopped at Eboli*. It took half a century and vast amounts of development money to eradicate malaria and starvation in this region. Today people are returning to live in the *sassi* – but now it's a trend rather than a necessity.

Information The APT office (☎ 0835 33 19 83, e presidiomatera@aptbasilicata.it) is at Via De Viti De Marco 9, off Via Roma. The staff are very helpful and can put you in contact with groups that provide guides to the *sassi*. Itinera (☎ 0835 26 32 59, e art tur@tin.it) and Cooperativa Amici del Turista (☎ 338 599 67 14, w www.materaturistica.it), Via Fiorentini 28–30, both organise guided tours in English. If you have time to spare and would like to explore the province of Basilicata by bike, ask about the excellent book (in Italian) on *cicloturismo* (cycling tours) in the province. Be warned that Basilicata is a very mountainous region, and the rides are quite demanding.

There are several banks with ATMs in the town centre, including the Banco di Napoli (with ATM) in Piazza Vittorio Veneto. The Internet can be accessed using a Telecom phone card in the Biblioteca Provinciale in Piazza Vittorio Veneto. Bici 2000 (☎ 0835 38 33 64), Via F P Loperfido 8–10, is well-stocked with most bike spares, and has an excellent workshop.

Things to See & Do Matera's main attraction is no doubt its *sassi*. The two *sassi* areas, **Barisano** and **Caveoso**, had no electricity, running water or sewerage system until well into the 20th century. The oldest *sassi* are at the top of the ravine. The dwellings in the lower sections of the ravine, which seem the oldest, were in fact established last century. As space ran out in the 1920s, the population started moving into hand-hewn or natural caves.

The *sassi* zones are accessible from several points around the centre. There's an entrance just off Piazza Vittorio Veneto. Alternatively, take Via delle Beccherie to Piazza del Duomo and follow the tourist itinerary signs to enter either Barisano or Caveoso. Sasso Caveoso is also accessible from Via Ridola by the stairs next to Albergo Italia.

Caveoso is the more picturesque of the two *sassi*. Highlights include **Chiesa de San Pietro Caveoso** *(Piazza San Pietro)*, plus the rock churches of **Santa Maria d'Idris** and **Santa Lucia alle Malve**, both with well-preserved Byzantine frescoes.

To see *sassi* as they were when the last inhabitants occupied them, visit **Mostra della Civiltà Contadina** *(off Via B Buozzi)* and **Casa-Grotta di Vico Solitario** *(off Via B Buozzi)*.

Back in the town centre, excavations in Piazza Vittorio Veneto have yielded some remarkable discoveries. Beneath the square lie yet more **Byzantine ruins**, including a rock church with frescoes, a castle, a large cistern and numerous houses. You can gaze down from the piazza and visit part of the complex.

Museo Nazionale Ridola (☎ 0835 31 00 58; Via Ridola 24) occupies the 17th-century convent of Santa Chiara and has a collection of primarily prehistoric and classical artefacts. Just south, on Piazzetta Pascoli, is **Centro Carlo Levi** (☎ 0835 31 42 35; Palazzo Lanfranchi), which houses paintings by Levi, including an enormous mural depicting peasant life in Matera.

Places to Stay & Eat Good accommodation for the budget traveller is available at **Albergo Roma** (☎/fax 0835 33 39 12; Via Roma 62; singles/doubles €21/36.50). Set high in Sassi Caveoso, **Sassi Hotel** (☎ 08 35 33 10 09; e hotelsassi@virgilio.it; Via San Giovanni Vecchio 89; singles/doubles with bathroom & breakfast €41.50/67.50) is unique, friendly and warmly recommended (though storage for more than two bikes could prove difficult), and has great views of Sasso Barisano. On the bottom level is a small **hostel** (dorm beds €15.50); from Piazza Vittorio Veneto, take Via S Biagio. **Albergo Italia** (☎ 0835 33 35 61; w www .albergoitalia.com; Via Ridola 5; singles/ doubles with bathroom & breakfast €75/98) is a very pleasant hotel with good rooms overlooking Sasso Caveoso and a garage for bikes.

For self-caterers, there's a daily **produce market** (off Piazza Vittorio Veneto), a **Sigma Supermarket** (Via Spine Bianche 2–6), opposite the APT office, and a good **bakery** (Via del Corso 22), southeast of Piazza Vittorio Veneto. **Caffè Tripoli** (Piazza Vittorio Veneto 17) is the ideal place in the centre for coffee and delicious pastries.

L'Osteria (Via Fiorentini 58; meals €13) in Sassi Barisano is a simple osteria (snack bar) offering 1st-class family cuisine and friendly service. Try the hearty capunti e fageoli (white beans and pasta shells simmered in a pork stock). Close by is **Oi Marí** (Via Fiorentini 66; pizza €5-8, meals €15), a popular and stylish establishment with fine food and great ambience. Back in the town centre, **Trattoria Lucana** (Via Lucana 48; meals €15-18) serves excellent meat and vegetarian dishes. Try the all-veggie antipasto then get

into your stride with the orecchiette alla materana (fresh ear-shaped pasta with a tomato, aubergine and courgette sauce).

Day 2: Matera to Alberobello
4–7 hours, 72.2km
The first half of today's ride heads back across the broad, gently rolling plains of the western Murge. Once off the main road out of Matera, the soft hues of tilled soil and wheat crops mark the long stretch to Gioia del Colle. On warmer days the silence may be broken by bizarre, squeaking crickets that do a masterful imitation of derailleur pulleys in dire need of oil!

Gioia del Colle (37.8km) is a large rural town with a **supermarket**, a **greengrocer** and several **bars** in the central piazza. Exiting town and finding Via Lamie di Fatalone (39.4km) requires careful attention to the cue sheet. This pretty little backcountry lane, bounded on both sides by rock walls, announces a major change of scenery. The sense of garden is strong, and the road, at times, seems almost engulfed in a sea of beautiful vineyards and orchards. When the first trullo appears the image becomes quite magical, a fairyland of lush gardens and little conical-roofed stone houses.

After a short interruption to negotiate the awkward southern outskirts of **Noci** (58.7km), it's back into trulli territory on another quiet backroad, and a gentle cruise to day's end at Alberobello.

Alberobello
Alberobello (translated literally as 'beautiful tree') is built on two hills: the eastern hill, made up of 'normal' buildings; and the western one, made up of several thousand fascinating stone structures with trulli conical roofs (see the boxed text 'Trulli', p300). Originally founded as a small feudal outpost some time around the mid-1400s, when heavily exploited peasants tilled the soil (and indirectly cleared the area of rocks!), the trulli area was declared a national monument in the 1930s, and a Unesco World Heritage site in 1996, even though many of these amazing stone structures now only accommodate souvenir shops, boutiques and restaurants.

Information The IAT office (☎ 080 432 51 71) is in the Casa d'Amore, just off Piazza del Popolo, the main square. Near the centre, there are banks with ATMs on Via Vittime del Fascismo, along Corso Vittorio Emanuele and in Via Trieste e Trento. Check emails at Emmegi, Via Ten, just off Piazza del Popolo behind the Palazzo Municipio. Netti (☎ 080 432 15 20), at Via Manzoni 152, may be able help with tyres and tubes.

Things to See & Do Points of interest in the town itself are naturally centred around the *trulli*. Within the more commercialised quarter of **Rione Monti**, on the south side of town, more than 1000 *trulli* cascade down the hillside. To its east, on the other side of Via Indipendenza, is **Rione Aia Piccola**, with 400 *trulli* still mostly used as family dwellings. In the modern part of town, the

16th-century **Trullo Sovrano** (☎ 080 432 54 82; *Piazza Sacramento*) has been converted into a small museum.

A few kilometres west of the town is **Chiesa di Santa Maria di Barsento**. Founded in AD 591 as an abbey, the small complex features one of Puglia's oldest churches. It is now part of a farm, but the owner is proud to show tourists around the property. Take the main Alberobello–Putignano road, turn left onto the road for Noci after 6km. Barsento is signposted 3km later on the right.

Places to Stay & Eat Accommodation ranges from camp sites to the *trulli* themselves. **Camping dei Trulli** (☎ 080 432 36 99; ⓦ *www.campingdeitrulli.it; per site/person*

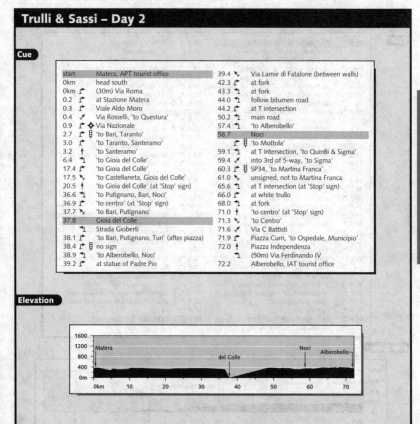

Trulli & Sassi – Day 2

Cue

start	Matera, APT tourist office	39.4 ↘	Via Lamie di Fatalone (between walls)
0km	head south	42.3 ↱	at fork
0km ↱	(30m) Via Roma	43.3 ↰	at fork
0.2 ↱	at Stazione Matera	44.0 ↰	follow bitumen road
0.3 ↱	Viale Aldo Moro	44.2 ↱	at T intersection
0.4 ⤧	Via Rosselli, 'to Questura'	50.2 ↰	main road
0.9 ↱ ◆	Via Nazionale	57.4 ↰	'to Alberobello'
2.7 ↱ 🏠	'to Bari, Taranto'	58.7	Noci
3.0 ↱	'to Taranto, Santeramo'	↱ 🏠	'to Mottola'
3.2 ↑	'to Santeramo'	59.1 ↰	at T intersection, 'to QuinBi & Sigma'
6.4 ↰	'to Gioia del Colle'	59.4 ⤧	into 3rd of 5-way, 'to Sigma'
17.4 ↱	'to Gioia del Colle'	60.3 ↱ 🏠	SP34, 'to Martina Franca'
17.5 ↘	'to Castellaneta, Gioia del Colle'	61.0 ↘	unsigned, not to Martina Franca
20.5 ↑	'to Gioia del Colle' (at 'Stop' sign)	65.6 ↰	at T intersection (at 'Stop' sign)
36.6 ↰	'to Putignano, Bari, Noci'	66.0 ↱	at white trullo
36.9 ↱	'to centro' (at 'Stop' sign)	68.0 ↰	at fork
37.7 ↘	'to Bari, Putignano'	71.0 ↑	'to centro' (at 'Stop' sign)
37.8	Gioia del Colle	71.3 ↘	'to Centro'
↰	Strada Gioberti	71.6 ↘	Via C Battisti
38.1 ↱	'to Bari, Putignano, Turi' (after piazza)	71.9 ↱	Piazza Curri, 'to Ospedale, Municipio'
38.4 ↱ 🏠	no sign	72.0 ↑	Piazza Independenza
38.9 ↰	'to Alberobello, Noci'	↰	(50m) Via Ferdinando IV
39.2 ↱	at statue of Padre Pio	72.2	Alberobello, IAT tourist office

Elevation

(Elevation profile: Matera, del Colle, Noci, Alberobello; vertical axis 0m, 400, 800, 1200, 1600; horizontal axis 0km, 10, 20, 30, 40, 50, 60, 70)

€4/5, doubles €50) is just out of town on Via Castellana Grotte. **Hotel Lanzillotta** (☎ 080 432 15 11; e hotellanzillotta@tiscalinet.it; Piazza Ferdinando IV 31; singles/doubles with bathroom & breakfast €36.50/52; dinner €13), just off the central Piazza del Popolo, represents excellent value – as does its three-course dinner of local specialities. The town's top hotel, **Hotel dei Trulli** (☎ 080 432 35 55; e htrulli@inmedia.it; Via Cadore 28; rooms €145), is a complex of self-contained trulli at the southern extremity of Rione Monti and is set in a wonderful shady garden of pine, juniper and cypress.

Pick up self-catering supplies at the **Spesa A & O supermarket** (Via Vittime del Fascismo 12), the **fruit and vegetable store** about 50m uphill or the **delicatessen** (cnr Corso Vittorio

Emanuele & Via Battisti). **Central Bar** (Corso Vittorio Emanuele 8), near the cathedral, is ideal for coffee and tasty pastries.

Hostaria del Sole (Piazza Curri 3; pizzas around €5) serves good pizzas and reasonably priced meals. **Ristorante Trullo d'Oro** (Via Felice Cavallotti 27; meals from €20) is a converted trullo, and offers great decor, loads of ambience and intimate, if overpriced, dining.

Day 3: Alberobello to Bari
5–9 hours, 88.4km

Today continues trundling along small roads backdropped by trulli and well-tended orchards and vineyards. The short side trip to **Martina Franca** (12.8km) offers the chance to admire its well-maintained

---

Trulli & Sassi – Day 3

Cue

start	Alberobello, IAT tourist office	
0km	head north on Via Ferdinando IV	
↱	'to Tutte le Direzioni' (at 'Stop' sign)	
0.4	↱ at T intersection, 'to Bari, Noci'	
1.6	↱ 'to 'Ristorante/Pizzeria di Puglia'	
10.3	↰ 'to Martina Franca, Taranto' (at 'Stop' sign)	
12.8	↰ 'to Locorotondo' (at 'Stop' sign)	
↱ ● ●Martina Franca 4km ↻		
13.0	↰ minor road before white trullo	
16.5	↑ stay left of train line	
17.2	↙ uphill	
17.5	↱ at T intersection	
17.5	✳ Locorotondo	
17.5	↰ ⑃ (40m) 'to Fasano'	
17.8	↘ 'to Ospedale Ricovero, San Marco'	
19.3	↙ 'to Contrada San Marco' (at little church)	
19.4	↰ 'to Contrada Catuscio' (white sign)	
24.2	↙ no sign	
25.1	↰ unsigned (at green gate)	
25.9	↱ at T intersection, 'to Lo Stivale'	
26.6	↑ Viale Serenissima (at 'Stop' sign)	
29.1	↰ 'to Castellana Grotte, Putignano'	
29.7	↑ 'to Putignano' (at 'Stop' sign)	
32.3	↱ rock-walled lane, trullo on right	
38.9	↰ 'to Castellana Grotte'	
39.7	Castellana Grotte	
	↑ 'to Monopoli, Polignano a Mare'	
	↱ ● ●Grotte di Castellana 6.6km ↻	
40.4	↰ 'to Brindisi, Monopoli, Polignano a Mare'	
41.2	↱ 'to Monopoli, Brindisi' (at 'Stop' sign)	
41.2	↰ (50m) 'to Polignano'	
41.4	↰ 'to Polignano'	
41.5	↱ 'to Polignano' (at 'Stop' sign)	
42.4	↰ Via Vecchia, 'to Conversano'	
43.8	↑ 'to Torre Castiglione'	
47.0	↱ 'to Conversano'	
● ●	Saracen tower 1km ↻	
48.7	↱ small road, farm sheds on right	
50.9	↱ at T intersection	
51.4	↱ at T intersection	
51.5	↰ at T intersection	
51.6	↑ ✧ 'to Conversano centro'	
52.0	Conversano	
52.3	↱ at T intersection, 'to Bari'	
52.5	↑ ✧ 'to Bari, Rutigliano'	
53.0	↑ Via Bari (white sign), AGIP on right	
53.8	✧ 2nd exit, 'to Rutigliano'	
54.0	↱ faded sign, Via Vecchia for Mola SP165	
58.0	↰ 'to Mola'	
58.5	↱ 'to Mola'	
59.2	↰ 'to Mola'	
60.5	↰ at big house	
61.2	↱ at T intersection	
61.4	↱ SP66 (at 'Stop' sign)	
65.3	Mola di Bari	
	↰ at T intersection	
65.4	↱ 'to Cozze'	
66.6	↰ onto esplanade (walk 10m of one-way)	
75.5	↙ 'to Polizia di Stato'	
78.5	↰ at restaurant (high rock wall opposite)	
79.0	↱ 'to Tangenziale, Bari'	
87.1	↰ ⑃ Via Giandomenica Petroni	
87.3	↱ Via Carulli (after traffic lights)	
88.1	↰ ⑃ Via D Cesare (after Piazza Umberto)	
88.2	↱ ⑃ around Piazza Aldo Moro past main station	
88.4	↰ no sign	
88.4	↱ (50m) Bari, APT tourist office	

Elevation

old quarter, boasting some fine examples of baroque architecture. Founded in the 10th century by refugees fleeing the Arab invasion of Taranto, Martina Franca flourished from the 14th century, when it was granted tax exemptions (*franchigie*, hence the name Franca) by Philip of Anjou.

A short pedal north of Martina is **Locorotondo** (17.5km), a completely circular town (hence the term *rotondo* meaning 'round') perched on a hill above the Valle dei Trulli. It's only a minor diversion to access the charming, rambling streets and alleys of the centre, and well worth the effort. It also offers a couple of fine restaurants serving delicious home-style food using the freshest of local produce: **U'Curdunn** *(Via Dura)* and **La Taverna del Duca** *(Via Papatodero)*.

Leaving Locorotondo, the route continues to roll along quiet roads through undulating farmland, marked by a noticeable absence of *trulli*. After the little one-bar village of Coreggia (26.6km), the route heads onto busier roads, skirting Castellana Grotte (39.7km), and beginning the long, loping descent to the Adriatic Coast at Mola di Bari (65.3km) via Conversano (52km). Don't miss the side trip (39.7km) to the incredible **Grotte di Castellana** caves. From Mola di Bari, the final 23.1km northeast is flat and moderately built up, and hugs the coast for the most part. Traffic density will vary considerably depending on the time of day and season, but it's always manageable.

Take the short side trip to **Torre di Castiglione Saracen** tower (47km; 1km return).

Side Trip: Grotte di Castellana
1 hour, 6.6km return
These spectacular limestone caves (☎ 080 499 82 11; ⓦ www.grottedicastellana.it; *Piazzale Anelli*) are Italy's longest natural subterranean network. The interlinked galleries, with their breathtaking stalactite and stalagmite formations, were first explored in the 1930s by the speleologist Franco Anelli; today's visitors can follow his route in a guided group. After trudging down 265 steps (or taking the elevator) to a huge cavern known as La Grave, you pass through a series of caves, culminating in the magnificent Grotta Bianca.

There are two tours: a 1km, 50-minute trip (€7.75) that doesn't include the Grotta Bianca; and the full 3km, two-hour trip

(€13) that does. Also worth a look is the **Museo Speleologico Franco Annelli** (€2.60).

The caves are only about 2km southwest of the main town and are well signposted. They're open 8.30am to 7pm daily, with tours on the hour. Bikes can be left at Hotel Autostello's private car park (next to the caves entrance); free if you lunch at the hotel, €2.60 if you don't.

The Gargano

Duration	2 days
Distance	169.5km
Difficulty	moderate–hard
Start/End	Manfredonia

This is an anticlockwise circuit of Apulia's surprisingly unspoilt Gargano Promontory, the 'spur' of the Italian boot. Hugging the coast one day and traversing the mountainous interior the next, the ride passes through a rich and varied landscape of limestone cliffs, ancient forests and beautiful beaches. While parts of the promontory bustle with tourists in summer, it doesn't suffer from overcrowding or overdevelopment. A midway stopover in the lovely clifftop village of Peschici offers seaside lazing and easy access to the superb beech and oak woods of the Foresta Umbra. The terrain is hilly and the two days relatively long and arduous, but opportunities abound for those wishing to linger longer.

NATURAL HISTORY
The Gargano Promontory was formed somewhere between 70 and 180 million years ago, and is predominantly composed of dolomite, limestone and sedimentary rock. Traces of human habitation date back to the Neolithic Age.

Parco Nazionale del Gargano includes the marine reserves of the Tremite archipelago and covers 120,000 hectares. The park is home to a wide variety of important plant and animal species, such as the 61 species of orchid (the highest concentration in Europe). There are 27,000 hectares of predominantly broad-leaved forest (Italy's largest), where 79 tree species such as the beech, ilex (holm oak), Turkey oak, cerris, ash and elm thrive. Coastal areas are dominated by native pines and Mediterranean maquis.

Significant and endangered native animal and bird species include the *capriolo italico* (Italy's own roe deer) that inhabits the Foresta Umbra, the *gallina prataiola* (a small native bustard) found on the dry fields of the foothills, and the *picchio dorso-bianco* (a small white-backed woodpecker). The native wild cat, several other species of woodpecker, peregrine and lanner falcons, buzzards, kestrels, owls (including the rare eagle owl) and sparrow hawks also thrive in the sanctuary of the park.

PLANNING
When to Ride
While the tourist flocks and high prices of the summer peak in August are best avoided, the beach aspect can be exploited during any of the warmer months. The promontory also offers pleasant cycling in spring and autumn, but winters are cold, wet (especially on the northern side) and windy on the coast.

Maps
TCI's 1:200,000 *Puglia* map covers the ride.

The Gargano

ACCESS TOWN
Manfredonia
Manfredonia is a port town founded by Swabian king Manfred, Frederick II's illegitimate son. Other than providing useful transport links and easy access to some great riding territory on the promontory, most will opt for a short stay. At the far end of the main drag, Corso Manfredi, is the town's majestic **castle**, started by Manfred and completed by Charles of Anjou. Within it, the **Museo Archeologico Nazionale del Gargano** displays local finds.

Information The IAT tourist office (☎ 0884 58 19 98) and the Banco di Napoli (with ATM) are in Piazza del Poplolo. Intercity buses and trains terminate in Piazza Marconi, just south of the centre. For bike spares and repairs, go to Spano (☎ 0884 53 63 06) at Via di Vittorio 105, the main road south towards Siponto.

Places to Stay & Eat There are four **camping villages** all situated within 5km south of town, but they are only open from July until around late September. **Casa per Ferie** *(☎ 0884 58 10 77; Via Scaloria 152; singles with bathroom €22)* is a convent-cum-hostel. **Hotel Sipontum** *(☎/fax 0884 54 29 16; Viale di Vittorio 229; singles/doubles with bathroom €26/42)*, located about 1.5km south of the town centre, offers basic budget accommodation.

Self-caterers will find **supermarkets**, **bakeries** and small **grocery stores** on Viale di Vittorio. **Ristorante Coppolarossa** *(Via dei Celestini 13; meals €18-26)*, just off Corso Manfredi, is a friendly, family concern. Try the seafood buffet (€6.20) as a starter, followed by fresh fish.

Getting There & Away Bus is an easy option from Bari as it doesn't involve changing trains. Unfortunately, there are only two daily SITA buses (€6.80, 1½ hours), leaving from Bari's ATS Viaggi office. Ferrovia del Gargano and SITA also operate regular services between Foggia and Manfredonia.

Hourly trains connect Manfredonia with Foggia (€1.90 per bike and person, 30 minutes, tickets from Bar Impero, opposite the station), where FS services for many major cities stop, including Bari (€6.80 plus €3.70 per bike, 1½ hours).

THE RIDE
Day 1: Manfredonia to Peschici
5–9 hours, 88km

A longish day punctuated by a number of climbs, the first (12.1km) a moderate 3km at 5% not far out of Manfredonia and necessary to avoid a ghastly 2km tunnel. After skirting Mattinata (19.1km) the road is smooth and wide, rising and falling dramatically as it negotiates the rugged coastline, offering sensational panoramas down to the sparkling waters of the Adriatic.

The south coast of the promontory is noticeably drier and the vegetation sparser than on the northern side, so noon heat should be avoided. Thankfully, shady coastal pines bring welcome relief beyond 35km. There are numerous **bars**, **restaurants**, **hotels** and **camping villages** (many of which are seasonal) dotting the route, so rest stops and accommodation options are never far away.

Vieste (61.8km) is a bright and very popular seaside resort, loaded with tourist facilities, and boasting some great beaches. The IAT tourist office (☎ 0884 70 88 06) on Piazza Kennedy is an excellent source of information on the national park and places of interest on the promontory. Worth a look in the medieval quarter are the **Chianca Amara** (Bitter Stone), where thousands were beheaded when the Turks sacked Vieste in the 16th century, and the **Museo Malacologico**, exhibiting a collection of seashells from around the world.

On the flat stretch leaving town, the road passes an endless chain of unobtrusive, low-level camping villages. At 71km there's a small **Roman ruin** on the left near the church. At 71.8km (100m along the entrance road to Camping Spiaggia Lunga), **Sinergie** (☎ 0884 70 66 35) conducts guided tours of the **Necropoli Salata**, underground tombs and burial grounds representing the earliest evidence of Christianity in the region.

There are plenty of secluded bays and little beaches to explore along the final stretch to Peschici, which includes a series of short, sharp pinches and one last hefty climb at 79.8km to test weary legs.

Peschici
Peschici is a classic medieval coastal village, perched high on a rocky outcrop

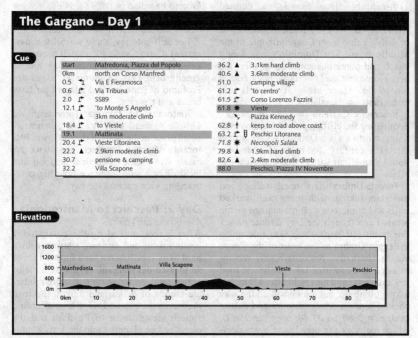

The Gargano – Day 1

Cue

start	Mafredonia, Piazza del Popolo		36.2 ▲	3.1km hard climb
0km	north on Corso Manfredi		40.6 ▲	3.6km moderate climb
0.5 ↰	Via E Fieramosca		51.0	camping village
0.6 ↱	Via Tribuna		61.2 ↱	'to centro'
2.0 ↱	SS89		61.5 ↱	Corso Lorenzo Fazzini
12.1 ↱	'to Monte S Angelo'		61.8 ✳	Vieste
▲	3km moderate climb		↘	Piazza Kennedy
18.4 ↱	'to Vieste'		62.8 ↑	keep to road above coast
19.1	Mattinata		63.2 ↱ ⛺	Peschici Litoranea
20.4 ↱	Vieste Litoranea		71.8 ✳	Necropoli Salata
22.2 ▲	2.9km moderate climb		79.8 ▲	1.9km hard climb
30.7	pensione & camping		82.6 ▲	2.4km moderate climb
32.2	Villa Scapone		88.0	Peschici, Piazza IV Novembre

Elevation

above a sweeping, sandy bay, with narrow cobbled alleyways and whitewashed houses reminiscent of villages in the Greek islands. It's not hard to see why it's becoming increasingly popular as a summer haven, but fortunately it remains relatively unspoiled.

Information There's no tourist office, but Agrifolio Tour (☎ 0884 96 27 21), on Piazza Sant'Antonio 3, is a private travel agency that can arrange hotel reservations. There are two banks with ATMs on Corso Garibaldi. Moto e Bici (☎ 0884 96 49 05), at Via Montesanto 47, stocks basic spares (tyres, tubes, chains, cassettes etc) for road and mountain bikes, and can order in if required.

Things to See & Do In warmer months, head for any of the fine **beaches**, east or west of town.

Ondazzurra (☎ 0884 96 42 34), at Corso Garibaldi 116, organises trips to the **Isole Tremite** (€23.50 return, book the day prior), a small archipelago consisting of three main islands. On **San Nicola**, take in the abbey and **Chiesa di Santa Maria**, featuring an 11th-century floor mosaic, a painted wooden Byzantine crucifix bought to the island in AD 747 and a black Madonna that probably came from Constantinople in the Middle Ages. **San Dominio's** one sandy beach and numerous small coves offer the best swimming, and a walking track circles the island. There are a few hotels and restaurants on the islands.

Peschici's **Castello** (☎ 0884 96 22 89), dominating the clifftop point 80m above the sea, is worth a visit. Dating back to around the 11th century, its restored chambers house a small art gallery and historical exhibits.

Foresta Umbra offers superb walking and mountain biking, with many well-marked trails and numerous well-maintained picnic areas. Even though the Day 2 route passes this point (30.9km), the 28km ride up to **Villaggio Umbra** in the heart of the forest, via an alternative route, is highly recommended as a day trip. Take the inland road toward Vieste and turn right after 12km. It's a long climb up, but a long roll all the way back! There's a small **museum and nature centre** (☎ 0884 56 09 44; open June-Sept), which includes a re-creation of a woodcut-

ters' and charcoal burners' camp. While there, pick up maps of walking trails and feed the roe deer in the adjacent reserve. Nearby, there's a small lake, a kiosk (open April to September) and restaurant (open July to August).

Places to Stay & Eat There are numerous camp sites along the coast east and west of town. **Camping Parco degli Ulivi** (☎ 0884 96 34 04; w www.italyis.com/parcodegli ulivi; per tent/person €6.50/9.90), downhill from the centre, offers shaded sites in a lovely, ancient olive grove.

Locanda al Castello (☎ 0884 96 40 38; Piazza Castello 29; singles/doubles with bathroom & breakfast €26/57) is a pleasant family establishment, situated above the cliffs. It's definitely the pick in the old quarter, with fine sea views. The hotel also has a decent restaurant (meals about €13) and an open-air pizzeria (evenings only).

More upmarket is **Hotel Timiana** (☎/fax 0884 96 43 21; Viale Libeta 73; full board €68), set amid mature pines, with a pool and free beach shuttle. The restaurant alone merits a visit. Another good option is **Hotel Piccolo Paradiso** (☎ 0884 96 34 66; w www .gargano.net/paradiso; full board €60), set below the old quarter near the beach.

For self-caterers, there's a **Sitis supermarket** (Corso Garibaldi), a small **supermarket-delicatessen** (Via Giamone) and a **greengrocer** (Via Montesanto). Head for **Profumo di Pane** in Via Malacera for tasty bread and pastries.

Ristorante La Taverna (Traversa di Via Castello 6; meals €20) is a cosy, character-filled place in the heart of the old town. **Ristorante Vecchia Peschici** (Via Roma 31; meals €18) serves excellent seafood and local dishes, with a terrace boasting commanding views across the bay.

Day 2: Peschici to Manfredonia
4½–8 hours, 81.5km

After a short roll along the coast, today heads inland and upward, starting with a hard 6km, levelling out for a further 1km or so to **Vico del Gargano** (17.3km), a major agricultural centre. With two more moderate climbs of 6.7km and 3.6km, the road maintains the exposed ridge line, affording superb views down to Peschici and the coast, before plunging into the leafy depths

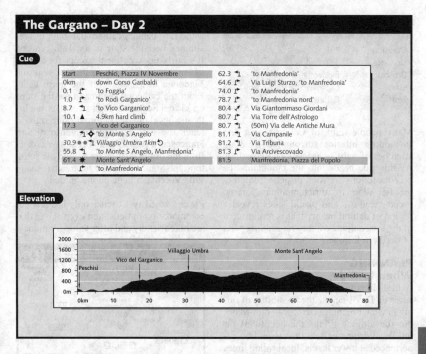

The Gargano – Day 2

Cue

start	Peschici, Piazza IV Novembre		62.3	↰	'to Manfredonia'
0km	down Corso Garibaldi		64.6	↱	Via Luigi Sturzo, 'to Manfredonia'
0.1	↱	'to Foggia'	74.0	↱	'to Manfredonia'
1.0	↱	'to Rodi Garganico'	78.7	↱	'to Manfredonia nord'
8.7	↰	'to Vico Garganico'	80.4	↗	Via Giantommaso Giordani
10.1	▲	4.9km hard climb	80.7	↰	Via Torre dell'Astrologo
17.3		Vico del Garganico	80.7	↰	(50m) Via delle Antiche Mura
	↰◆	'to Monte S Angelo'	81.1	↰	Via Campanile
30.9 ●●↰	Villaggio Umbra 1km ↺		81.2	↰	Via Tribuna
55.8	↰	'to Monte S Angelo, Manfredonia'	81.3	↱	Via Arcivescovado
61.4	✳	Monte Sant'Angelo	81.5		Manfredonia, Piazza del Popolo
	↱	'to Manfredonia'			

Elevation

The centre is just off the route. There's a useful Pro Loco (☎ 0884 56 55 20) at Via Reale Basilica 40. The Parco Nazionale del Gargano office (☎ 0884 56 89 11, ⓔ info@ parcogargano.it) is at Via Sant'Antonio Abate 121. The town's main attraction is the **Santuario di San Michele**, for centuries the last stop on a gruelling pilgrimage to the place where St Michael the Archangel is said to have appeared before the Bishop of Siponto in AD 490. Opposite the sanctuary is the **Tomba di Rotari**, not a tomb but a 12th-century baptistery. Enter through the facade of the **Chiesa di San Pietro**, its intricate rose window all that remained when the church was destroyed by a 19th-century earthquake. The town's highest point is a **Norman castle** with Swabian and Aragonese additions. Take time too to enjoy the **belvedere**, a building situated to give sweeping views of the coast.

With a scintillating switchback descent from 800m to the coast, the last leg to the ride end in Manfredonia is quick and easy.

of the Foresta Umbra. A short side trip (30.9km) to **Villaggio Umbra** leads to a **museum and nature centre**, and the leafy surrounds of the picnic areas, **kiosk** and **restaurant** nearby make an ideal rest stop.

Back on the promontory's southern side, the vegetation becomes markedly thinner and drier, slowly giving way to more open farmland as the road drops into the steep Valle Carbonara. The forbidding switchback up to **Monte Sant'Angelo** looks worse than it is, and after a steady, but exposed, 5.6km at 5% you're in the town (61.4km).

Calabria

Although it may not loom large on the average visitor's list of Italian destinations, Calabria is worth a little exploration. The province has its share of ugly holiday villages along parts of the Ionian and Tyrrhenian coasts, but its beaches are among the cleanest in Italy. Lovers of ancient history can explore the sparse reminders of the civilisation of Magna Graecia, but cyclists will love the roads heading inland, where large areas of unspoilt mountains and even the odd picturesque medieval hill top village await the more adventurous.

THE SOUTH & SICILY

La Sila

Duration	2 days
Distance	137.1km
Difficulty	moderate
Start	Fago del Soldato turn-off
End	Catanzaro

Many people think of Calabria as a dry, forbidding interior surrounded by long stretches of ugly, overdeveloped coastline. As this ride heads into the mountains the preconceptions are soon dispelled; kilometre after kilometre of rich mountain forests, green meadows and placid lakes reveal a region of natural beauty that is reminiscent of the lower alpine country resembling parts of northern Europe.

PLANNING
When to Ride
A high likelihood of snow and road closures on Day 1 negate the possibility of riding in winter months (October to mid-May), but the altitude brings the benefit of far milder midsummer heat than would be experienced at lower levels. Ideal riding times are from late May to September.

Maps
TCI's 1:200,000 *Calabria* map covers the route adequately.

ACCESS TOWN
Cosenza
Without its beautiful medieval core, Cosenza would be little more than a dismal array of cheek-by-jowl concrete high-rises. The old area, seated at the confluence of the Crati and Busento Rivers, is an unexpected pleasure, with its narrow *vicoletti* (alleys), some little more than steep stairways, winding past elegant (if much decayed) mansions.

Information The APT office (☎ 0984 274 85) is tucked away on the 1st floor of Corso Mazzini 92, but you're unlikely to find much of use there. There are several banks with ATMs on Corso Mazzini. The Casa delle Culture, at Corso Telesio 98, offers free Internet access. For bike repairs and basic spares try Barbarossa (☎ 0338 833 41 18) at Via Lungocrati 25, east of the medieval quarter on the Crati River.

Things to See & Do Up in the old town is the 12th-century **cathedral**, rebuilt in a restrained baroque style in the 18th century. It's fairly unexceptional except for a copy of an exquisite 13th-century Byzantine Madonna in a chapel off the north aisle. From the cathedral, you can take the steps up Via del Seggio through an enchanting little medieval quarter before turning right to reach the 13th-century **Convento di San Francesco d'Assisi**, which retains a chapel from the original structure behind the south transept. South of the piazza stretches shady **Villa Vecchia**, a huge public garden.

Places to Stay Cosenza only has few accommodation options, and even fewer that are bike friendly and offer value for money.

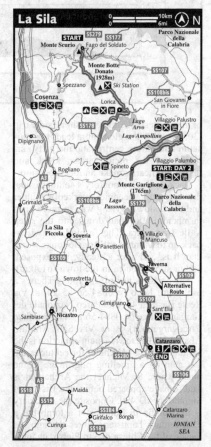

Hotel Excelsior *(☎/fax 0984 7 43 83; Piazza Matteotti 14; singles/doubles with bathroom & breakfast €34/52)*, once a grand institution, has huge, modernised rooms and is good value for money, especially for those who savour fading elegance. The pricier **Royal Hotel** *(☎ 0984 41 21 65; Via Molinella 24; singles/doubles €68/93)* is a more upmarket option offering four-star accommodation, safe bike storage and a good restaurant.

Places to Eat Self-caterers will find **supermarkets**, **delicatessens** and **greengrocers** on Via Trieste, 50m west of Corso Mazzini at the southern end of town. There's also a daily **produce market** about 500m uphill from Corso Mazzini, just west of Corso Umberto.

Grab a snack at **Rosticceria Pic Nic** *(Corso Mazzini 108)* or **Rosticceria da Giulio** *(Viale Trieste 81)*. **Ristorante da Giocondo** *(Via Piave 53; meals €13-18)* is a small, centrally located, family run restaurant. **Gran Caffè Renzelli** *(Corso Telesio 46)* is a venerable café in the old town that has been run by the same family for five generations and bakes its own deliciously gooey cakes and desserts. Sink your teeth into the *torroncino torrefacto* (a confection of sugar, spices and hazelnuts) or *varchiglia alla monocale* (chocolate and almond cake).

In the old town, there are some great places for dining, which have both character and carefully prepared cuisine. **Ristorante Calabria Bella** *(Piazza Duomo; meals €20)* is intimate and much patronised by discerning locals. **Taverna l'Arco Vecchio** *(Piazza Archi di Ciaccio 21; tourist menu €18, meals €18-23; open Mon-Sat)* is similar in style to the Calabria Bella and has attractive rooms.

Getting There & Away The city's main bus station is just northeast of Piazza Fera. Simet (☎ 0983 52 03 15) has two buses daily to Salerno (four hours).

For train travel, the national FS Stazione Nuova is about 2km northeast of the city centre. Trains connect with Villa San Giovanni, Salerno (€11.30 plus €3.70 per bike, 3½ hours, seven per day), Naples and Rome.

GETTING TO/FROM THE RIDE

In just 30 minutes – and for a mere €1.50 – one of the hourly FC buses will cover the 1100m vertical climb from Cosenza up to the ride start. The bus station is just northeast of Piazza Fera. Get the Cosenza–Camigliatello Silano bus from *binario* (platform) 1 at the main bus station and ask to be dropped off at the *bivio* (turn-off) for Fago del Soldato.

THE RIDE
Day 1: Fago del Soldato Turn-Off to Villaggio Palumbo
4½–7½ hours, 75.4km

Once on the bike, the route winds continuously upward on almost deserted (if somewhat rough) roads for another 600 vertical metres. The landscape is mostly shady beech woods and the odd meadow dotted with lazily grazing horses. The ride's high point is at the 1920m **Monte Botte Donato** ski station (18km), a good place to stop for a snack and enjoy the incredible view out across La Sila Grande to the north, and Lago Arvo and La Sila Piccola to the south.

Descending to the SS108 from the ski station, the flora changes to include oak and pine, and there are short sections of broken bitumen to look out for. Nestled on the banks of picturesque **Lago Arvo**, **Lorica** (30.6km) has all facilities and would make an excellent option for an extra day or two stopover. After skirting the north side of the lake, the remainder of the day is spent undulating through fertile farmland, and rolling easily through oak and pine forest around the smaller Lago Ampollino.

Villaggio Palumbo

Nestled on the southern shores of Lago Ampollino, Villaggio Palumbo is predominantly a winter village serving the small Palumbosila ski resort. In the off-season this position on the lake and the nearby mountains make it an excellent place to kick back and relax or head up into the myriad trails in the Cotronei forests, and further south, Monte Gariglione and the wilds of Parco Nazionale della Calabria.

Information The Palumbosila tourist office (☎ 0962 49 30 05) offers information on walks and supplies a small map of the village. All shopping facilities are in the Centro Commerciale in Piazza Ampollino, about 500m east of the information office. There are a couple of **bars**, small **supermarkets** and a **delicatessen**.

La Sila – Day 1

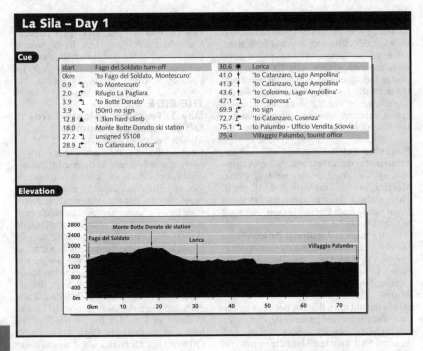

Cue

start	Fago del Soldato turn-off		30.6 ✳	Lorica	
0km	'to Fago del Soldato, Montescuro'		41.0 ↑	'to Catanzaro, Lago Ampollina'	
0.9 ⬆	'to Montescuro'		41.3 ↑	'to Catanzaro, Lago Ampollina'	
2.0 ⬈	Rifugio La Pagliara		43.6 ↑	'to Colosimo, Lago Ampollina'	
3.9 ⬆	'to Botte Donato'		47.1 ⬆	'to Caporosa'	
3.9 ↘	(50m) no sign		69.9 ⬈	no sign	
12.8 ▲	1.3km hard climb		72.7 ⬈	'to Catanzaro, Cosenza'	
18.0	Monte Botte Donato ski station		75.1 ⬆	to Palumbo - Ufficio Vendita Sciovia	
27.2 ⬆	unsigned SS108		75.4	Villaggio Palumbo, tourist office	
28.9 ⬈	'to Catanzaro, Lorica'				

Elevation

Places to Stay & Eat
The lovely grassy area along the lake shore immediately below the village is open to free camping. Outside the ski season and August, the village's central hotels offer excellent value for money. The selection includes **Hotel/Ristorante La Baita** (☎ 0962 49 30 34; *singles/doubles with breakfast €23.25/ 46.50*), **Hotel Lo Sciatore** (☎/fax 0962 49 30 98; *singles/doubles with breakfast €36.15/ 51.65*) and **Hotel Lo Scoiattolo** (☎/fax 0962 49 31 41; w www.esperia.it/loscoiattoloeng .htm; singles/doubles with breakfast €31/ 57). All have very good, reasonably-priced restaurants, specialising in *cucina tipica silana* (cuisine of La Sila) – try the (mostly vegetarian) antipasto and the porcini mushrooms (in season).

Day 2: Villaggio Palumbo to Catanzaro
3–5½ hours, 56.3km
A very easy day's ride – with only one short-ish climb after the small hamlet of **Spineto** (13.2km). Depending on the choice of route, the day culminates in an almost uninterrupted, 35km downhill roll to Catanzaro.

Leaving the main SS179 at 22.4km allows a shorter route, remaining higher for longer (so avoiding climbs), and crossing the dam wall of the picturesque **Lago Passonte** at 25.5km. The alternative route on the SS179 and SS109 through Villaggio Mancuso and Taverna is 10km longer, and arguably more scenic. It drops more rapidly and necessitates a 300m climb out of Taverna.

The terrain is mostly covered with dense, shady oak and pine until **Sant'Elia** (47.4km), when the mountain vegetation gives way to sparser, drier maquis and the more familiar sight of olive groves on harder-edged, rockier ground. There are a number of small hamlets with **bars** and the odd **restaurant** dotting the route.

The final run into Catanzaro is short and sweet, but be sure to make the right turn at 52.5km (to Catanzaro nord) to avoid a series of long, ghastly tunnels with very fast moving traffic.

Catanzaro
Catanzaro replaced Reggio di Calabria as the regional capital back in the early 1970s. Set on a rocky peak 13km inland from the

Ionian coast, it's generally overlooked by tourists – and it's not difficult to see why. Scarcely anything remains of the old city and evidence of its Byzantine origins is virtually nonexistent.

The city's seaside 'suburb' of Catanzaro Marina is 13km south and one of the Ionian coast's major resorts. Although heavily developed, it's less tacky than many others and the beaches stretching off in both directions are among the best on this coast. It also has a number of accommodation options.

Information The APT office (☎ 0961 74 39 01) is on the 2nd floor of the Galleria Mancuso building, Via Spasari 3, just north of the post office. There are several banks with ATMs along Corso Mazzinin. Tempo Libero (☎ 0961 72 59 56), Via Carlo V 15/17, can help with bike spares. Check email at La Fenice in Via Turco, northwest of Piazza Matteotti.

Places to Stay & Eat Catanzaro has few hotels and they are generally expensive.

Albergo Belvedere (☎/fax 0961 72 05 91; *Via Italia 33; singles/doubles €23.50/41.50*)

is a pleasant enough budget option. **Grand Hotel** (☎ 0961 70 12 56; *Piazza Matteotti; singles/doubles with bathroom €65/90*) is very central and has bland but comfortable rooms.

There's a big **Conad supermarket** east of Piazza Matteotti, next to the Grand Hotel. **Il Fornaio Tassone** (*Via Independenza 29a*) is a good bakery, just north of Piazza Matteotti. **Lo Spuntino** (*Via Poerio 3*), just east of Piazza Matteotti, is great for cheap takeaway pizza slices and pastries.

Ristorante La Corteccia (*Via Indipendenza 30; pizzas €2.50-6.60*) serves excellent pizzas. Across the road is **Il Mahé** (☎ 0961 74 60 34; *Via Indipendenza 55; meals €13-18*), with a good *rosticceria* (grilled-meat takeaway) downstairs, and a pizzeria and restaurant upstairs. Also on the 1st floor is a bar with nightly entertainment, including live music at weekends. **Da Salvatore** (*Salita del Rosario 28; pasta €5, meat dishes €6.50*) serves good local cuisine at reasonable prices; try the homemade gnocchi and any of the lamb dishes. **Al Vicolo 22** (*Salita Corso Mazzini 22; tourist menu €7.50*) offers á la carte dining or an excellent value tourist menu.

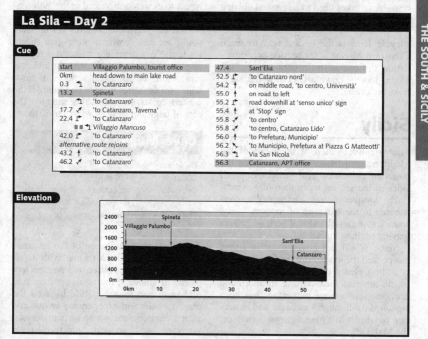

La Sila – Day 2

Cue

start	Villaggio Palumbo, tourist office	47.4	Sant'Elia	
0km	head down to main lake road	52.5 ↱	'to Catanzaro nord'	
0.3 ↰	'to Catanzaro'	54.2 ↑	on middle road, 'to centro, Università'	
13.2	Spineta	55.0 ↑	on road to left	
↰	'to Catanzaro'	55.2 ↱	road downhill at 'senso unico' sign	
17.7 ↙	'to Catanzaro, Taverna'	55.4 ↑	at 'Stop' sign	
22.4 ↱	'to Catanzaro'	55.8 ↙	'to centro'	
■ ■ ↰	*Villaggio Mancuso*	55.8 ↙	'to centro, Catanzaro Lido'	
42.0 ↱	'to Catanzaro'	56.0 ↑	'to Prefetura, Municipio'	
alternative route rejoins		56.2 ↘	'to Municipio, Prefetura at Piazza G Matteotti'	
43.2 ↑	'to Catanzaro'	56.3 ↰	Via San Nicola	
46.2 ↙	'to Catanzaro'	56.3	Catanzaro, APT office	

Elevation

Getting There & Away Regular Ferrovie della Calabria (FC; ☎ 0961 89 61 11) buses run to Catanzaro Marina (€0.52, 30 minutes), leaving from the FC train station, just north of the city centre. Foderaro (☎ 0961 72 60 06, 800-019728, w www.foderaro.it, Corso Mazzini 185) runs three buses daily to Rome (€33.10, three daily, seven hours) and one daily to Milan (€64.60, 11½ to 13 hours) via Perugia (€41.35, 9½ hours), Florence (€47, 10½ hours) and Bologna (€53.20, 10½ to 11½ hours), departing from Motel Agip.

From the Catanzaro FS station (about 2km south and downhill from the centre), trains connect with the main Tyrrhenean coast line at Lamezia Terme for services south to Sicily or north to Naples, Rome, Milan and Turin. The main Adriatic Coast line is accessed from Catanzaro Marina for connections to Bari. There are two direct trains daily to Bari (€27.70, 5¼ hours), suitable for packed bikes only, and six involving up to two changes at Paola, Taranto, Sibari, Lamezia Terme or Crotone (€19.40 plus €3.70 per bike, 5½ to 7½ hours).

FC trains leave every 30 to 45 minutes for Catanzaro Marina (€0.52). Space can be tight, so bikes need to be packed down a little.

Bicycle Bike is the easiest way to reach Catanzaro Marina – for seaside accommodation options or train connections. It's 13km, mostly downhill. Follow the signs from the centre.

Sicily

Strategically located at the heart of the Mediterranean basin, Sicily has been the target of colonisers and settlers from all sides of the sea for more than 6000 years. Each conqueror has undoubtedly contributed to the make-up of modern Sicily, some leaving a rich cultural heritage, others leaving nothing but scars.

Since WWII the government in Rome has poured trillions of lire (and now the EU is adding plenty of euros) into the island in the hope of kick-starting its moribund economy, but a huge percentage has been siphoned off through kickbacks and protection payments to a home-grown oppressor: the Mafia.

Today, Sicily's infamous cloak of insularity is being cast aside and the Sicilians have begun to open up to the outside world. Yet deep into the island's mountainous interior, away from the bustling cities and trendy beach resorts, change is not so evident, and that all-embracing shroud of mystery lives on. Hardly surprising considering that the burden of 6000 years of invasion and occupation weighs heaviest here.

NATURAL HISTORY

Sicily's precarious position over two continental plates has resulted in the island being a major centre for volcanic and seismic activity. The eastern half of the island is dominated by the imposing cone of Mt Etna, Europe's largest active volcano with more than 135 recorded eruptions.

Centuries of exploitation have taken their toll on the island's native flora and fauna. Ddeforestation that began during Roman times has seen enormous tracts of forest stripped for the large-scale cultivation of grain, particularly in the interior. Vineyards and olive trees were introduced by the Greeks and citrus groves came with the Arabs. Eucalyptus trees were introduced in the 19th century to combat malarial marshlands.

Outside the nature reserves it's unlikely you'll see any creatures other than sheep, while the coastlines are home to a regular selection of birds, mostly seagulls and cormorants. Even the great schools of tuna, which for centuries were to be found off the western coasts, are fast disappearing into the nets of large Japanese trawlers far offshore.

Lava Magic

Duration	2 days
Distance	120.8km
Difficulty	moderate
Start	Rifugio Sapienza
End	Catania

This is a circumnavigation of the immense and imposing 3350m Mt Etna. With its almost perfect conical shape and omnipresent plume of smoke, Etna is a beguiling mix of beauty and menace. Ride high on the dragon's back and experience a unique and varied environment where ancient forests, vineyards and orchards survive among unworldly, barren lava flows. The towns and villages along the way – often hewn from the lava that may have once engulfed them – offer an insight into the history of the people who have survived and thrived in the shadow of one of the world's most active volcanoes.

PLANNING
When to Ride

While it should be possible to ride almost all year, the ideal times would be March to July and September to November, avoiding the extremes of summer heat and winter cold.

Maps

TCI's 1:200,000 *Sicily* map is adequate. Another option is the free map of Mt Etna supplied by the APT office in Catania.

ACCESS TOWN

See Catania (p293).

GETTING TO/FROM THE RIDE

The 34km, 1900 vertical metre grind from Catania to Rifugio Sapienza is best tackled by the daily 8am AST (☎ 095 746 10 96) bus (€2.90, 2½ hours), departing from Catania's main bus station in Piazza Giovanni XXIII. There should be no problem fitting two or three bikes and gear under the bus. This option allows ample time to explore the barren upper slopes of Etna south, either on foot or with the (expensive) guided jeep tour (€36.15), before setting off.

Purists who opt to ride from Catania should note that roads up to Nicolosi (15km) are narrow and often heavily trafficked; head

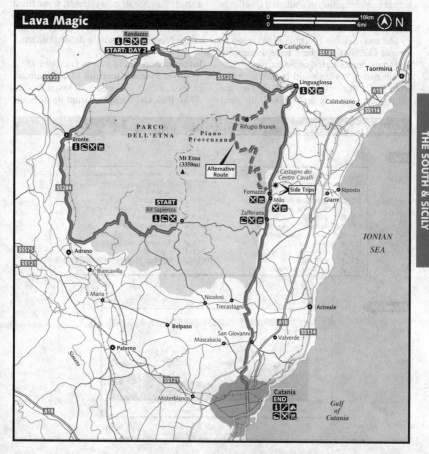

THE SOUTH & SICILY

up Via Etnea and follow signs to Nicolosi, Etna Sud and Rifugio Sapienza on the SP92 (allow at least four to five hours).

THE RIDE
Day 1: Rifugio Sapienza to Randazzo
3–5½ hours, 54.9km

In one long, uninterrupted descent, the route leaves the main Sapienza–Catania road very early (2.7km, this turn-off is easily missed) and traces minor roads down the southeast flank of Etna. Spectacular views from high lava fields are tempered by a deteriorating surface on a narrowing road with some very sharp bends. Lava soon gives way to refreshing pine and oak woods, opening out into a somewhat eerie and seemingly deserted agglomeration of shuttered dwellings and manicured orchards bound by forbidding high fences and gates.

The unavoidable 14.2km of main road to Bronte (37.9km) can be a little unpleasant due to moderate traffic and a narrow shoulder in parts – care should be taken. Apart from the 1.4km climb out of Bronte, the riding becomes easy and relaxed; the road improves and traffic thins markedly. Etna totally dominates the eastern horizon, imposing and ever present, while views left across deep valleys to the mountainous interior can be enjoyed to the full.

Randazzo
With a rich history dating back to Byzantine times, Randazzo was a strategic stopover along the only safe inland route between Messina and Palermo. Significant occupiers included the Normans and, from the 14th century, the Aragonese, under whom Randazzo reached its peak as one of Sicily's more affluent cities. Years of neglect, the plague, heavy bombardment in WWII and the unrestrained development of modern times have all taken their toll. Nevertheless, a stroll through its quiet streets, some lined with **Aragonese apartments**, is still warranted. Also worth a look are the lava walls of the Norman **Cattedrale di Santa Maria**.

Information There's a Pro Loco (☎ 095 92 38 41) at Piazza Municipio 17 and the bank in Piazza San Francesco d'Assisi has an ATM. Pick up bike spares from Ruote Sport

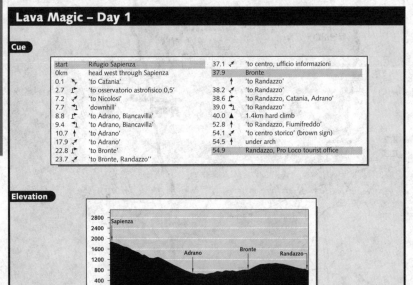

Lava Magic – Day 1

Cue

start	Rifugio Sapienza		37.1 ↗	'to centro, ufficio informazioni
0km	head west through Sapienza		37.9	Bronte
0.1 ↘	'to Catania'		↑	'to Randazzo'
2.7 ↰	'to osservatorio astrofisico 0,5'		38.2 ↗	'to Randazzo'
7.2 ↗	'to Nicolosi'		38.6 ↰	'to Randazzo, Catania, Adrano'
7.7 ↱	'downhill'		39.0 ↱	'to Randazzo'
8.8 ↰	'to Adrano, Biancavilla'		40.0 ▲	1.4km hard climb
9.4 ↱	'to Adrano, Biancavilla'		52.8 ↑	'to Randazzo, Fiumifreddo'
10.7 ↑	'to Adrano'		54.1 ↗	'to centro storico' (brown sign)
17.9 ↗	'to Adrano'		54.5 ↑	under arch
22.8 ↰	'to Bronte'		54.9	Randazzo, Pro Loco tourist office
23.7 ↗	'to Bronte, Randazzo''			

Elevation

Sapienza ... Adrano ... Bronte ... Randazzo

(elevation axis: 0m, 400, 800, 1200, 1600, 2000, 2400, 2800; distance axis: 0km, 10, 20, 30, 40, 50)

(☎ 095 7 99 21 28), Via Bonaventura 14, downhill from Piazza Loreto, or Velo e Moto (☎ 095 7 99 17 31), Via Gaetano Basile 10a, uphill from the centre (1km, Day 2).

Places to Stay & Eat Fortunately, Randazzo's only accommodation option, **Hotel Scrivano** (☎/fax 095 92 11 26; Piazza Loreto; singles/doubles €31/52) is modern and well run.

For self-caterers, there is a **greengrocer**, an **alimentari** (grocery shop) and a **panificio** (bread-only bakery) on Piazza Nino Bixio. **Ristorante-Pizzeria da Antonio** (Via Pietro Nenni 8) serves quality, reasonably priced meals, specialising in wild mushrooms and asparagus picked from the slopes of Etna.

Day 2: Randazzo to Catania
4–7 hours, 65.9km

As with Day 1, Etna towers far above, dominating the right horizon for much of the ride. After the climb out of Randazzo the route to Linguaglossa clings high above the Alcantara Valley. It's an easy cruise on a quiet road, undulating through beautifully landscaped and terraced orchards divided by lava

walls, or crossing vast lava flows, devoid of vegetation save the hardy Mt Etna broom, whose vivid yellow clusters contrast brilliantly against the stark, blackened landscape. The Peloritani mountains stretch away to the north, and on a clear day Calabria and the mainland can be seen beyond Taormina to the east.

Strong climbers, mountain bikers or those simply wishing to spend more time experiencing Etna's natural wonders may opt to turn right at the T-intersection (18.5km) and head up to Rifugio Brunek via the alternative route. If time is limited, or a 10km climb averaging 7% in gradient isn't for you, head down to **Linguaglossa**, a good spot to break before the easier climb back up onto Etna's eastern flanks. The short side trip (33.6km, signposted) to the enormous **Castagno dei Cento Cavalli** (Chestnut of the Hundred Horses) necessitates a very steep climb back out. Italy's oldest tree (estimated at more than 2000 years), the chestnut owes its name to the centuries old legend that a queen and her escort of 100 horsemen took shelter from a wild storm beneath its vast boughs. The piazza at **Milo** (38km) boasts

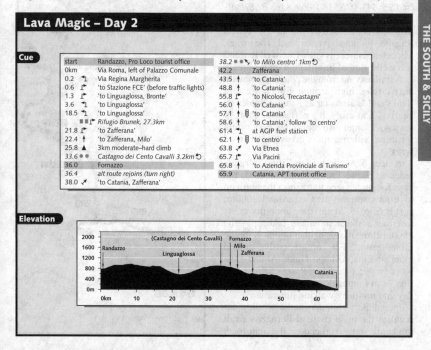

Lava Magic – Day 2

Cue

start	Randazzo, Pro Loco tourist office
0km	Via Roma, left of Palazzo Comunale
0.2 ⤴	Via Regina Margherita
0.6 ↱	'to Stazione FCE' (before traffic lights)
1.3 ↱	'to Linguaglossa, Bronte'
3.6 ⤴	'to Linguaglossa'
18.5 ⤴	'to Linguaglossa'
■■↱	Rifugio Brunek, 27.3km
21.8 ↱	'to Zafferana'
22.4 ↑	'to Zafferana, Milo'
25.8 ▲	3km moderate–hard climb
33.6 ●●	Castagno dei Cento Cavalli 3.2km ↻
36.0	Fornazzo
36.4	alt route rejoins (turn right)
38.0 ↗	'to Catania, Zafferana'
38.2 ●●↘	'to Milo centro' 1km ↻
42.2	Zafferana
43.5 ↑	'to Catania'
48.8 ↑	'to Catania'
55.8 ↱	'to Nicolosi, Trecastagni'
56.0 ↑	'to Catania'
57.1 ↑ 🅗	'to Catania'
58.6 ↑	'to Catania', follow 'to centro'
61.4 ⤴	at AGIP fuel station
62.1 ↑ 🅗	'to centro'
63.8 ↗	Via Etnea
65.7 ↱	Via Pacini
65.8 ↑	'to Azienda Provinciale di Turismo'
65.9	Catania, APT tourist office

Elevation

incredible views of the coast; pick up supplies here before rolling down to **Bosco Nicolosi** (39km), a lovely, shady oak forest
that makes an ideal picnic spot.

The long run south is mostly a gradual
descent, with villages and traffic increasing
in frequency the closer you get to Catania.
The last 10km to 15km is quite built-up and
close attention should be paid to the cue
sheet. If things get too hairy, regular buses
(with luggage vaults underneath) travel the
route into town. The stretch down Via Etnea
is the simplest way into the centre; it's
legally open only to buses, taxis and emergency vehicles, but bicycles will be toler-
ated – care should be taken.

Alternative Route: Etna North
1½–3 hours, 27.3km
This alternative high route via the steep
climb up Etna's northeastern flanks is 9.4km
longer and considerably more difficult than
the low road, but rewards for the hard work
involved are manifold. The uphill grind itself is tempered by verdant oak, chestnut
and pine forests, and at its end there is good
accommodation available. **Rifugio Brunek**
(☎ *095 643 015, 360 859 826; B&B/half-
board per person €21/31*) is a small, very
pleasant chalet set in the lovely Pineta
Ragabo, 1400m above sea level. The owner,
Michele, ensures his guests are well fed, and
is a wellspring of information on the area.

A trail leaving from the *rifugio* (mountain
hut) circles high around Etna's western
flanks and leads as far as Rifugio Sapienza,
nearly 40km away. It's perfect for short or
long walks, and also represents easy riding
for those with mountain bikes and off-road
tyres.

A steep 5km climb from Rifugio Brunek
leads to Piano Provenzana (1800m), the
base for guided jeep tours from the north up
to Etna's summit area at around 3000m;
cost is €36.15. Again, the possibility exists
to either walk or mountain bike up – the
1500m climb means neither option is for the
faint hearted! For comprehensive guided
tours of Etna, Gruppo Guide Alpine Etna
Nord (☎ *095 64 78 33*), Piazza Santa Caterina 24 in Linguaglossa, offers a number of
day and multiday walking itineraries.

Incredible panoramas and a sizzling descent to the main route at Fornazzo await
the hardy souls who choose the high road.

Centre to Sea

Duration	2 days
Distance	136.9km
Difficulty	hard
Start	Enna
End	Sant'Agata di Militello

Inland Sicily is certainly not noted as a
cycle-touring Mecca, but anyone with a
sense of adventure, a desire to experience
the true nature of rural Sicily and a thirst for
out of the way places will reap enormous
satisfaction from this strenuous, two-day
jaunt from the island's heart to its northern
shores. With Etna as a constant backdrop,
the ride passes though a rich variety of

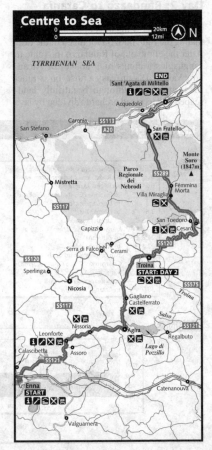

Mt Etna, on the way from Enna to Troina, Sicily

Positano, Campania

Market stall holder, Matera, Basilicata

Trulli house, near Alberobello, Apulia

Al fresco dining, old Alghero, Sardinia

Cala Gonone, Sardinia

Sunflower field, Oristano, Sardinia

Quiet back road, Gennargentu mountains, Sardinia

landscapes and some ancient and impressive mountaintop towns and villages.

PLANNING
When to Ride

Snow is common on the higher parts of the Nebrodi range and midsummer heat can be oppressive. Ideal riding is in April to July and September to October.

Maps

Use TCI's 1:200,000 *Sicily* map.

ACCESS TOWN
Enna

Enna sits almost perfectly at Sicily's scorched centre. Perched on a precipitous U-shaped ridge at around 1000m, it offers commanding views across the cultivated valleys and rugged mountains of the island's interior. It's not hard to see why it's nicknamed the *belvedere* (panorama) or *ombelico* (umbilical chord) of Sicily. With several significant archaeological treasures within easy reach, it makes an excellent base for further exploration.

Information Staff at the APT office (☎ 0935 52 82 88), Via Roma 413, are very helpful, and can give you maps and all manner of information on the city and the region. There's also an AAST office (☎ 0935 50 08 75) next to the Grande Albergo Sicilia at Piazza Colaianni 6 for information on Enna itself. There are several banks with ATMs in the Via Roma precinct and on Viale A Diaz, the main road dissecting the southern side of the U-shaped ridge. Very basic spares (tyres, tubes) are available from Trinelli bike shop at Viale A Diaz 60.

Things to See & Do A stay in Enna can be very rewarding without even venturing beyond the beautifully preserved medieval centre. Sit in Piazza Crispi and gaze out across endless valleys dotted with high hilltop towns. On an average day, Etna's smoking cone is clearly visible over 80km away, and at times of activity presents a fiery spectacle in the night sky. Enjoy fine dining or simply people-watch as the locals flood onto the traffic-free via Roma for the traditional *passeggiata* (evening stroll).

The **Villa Romana** at Casale, about 33km south of Enna, is easily the most important Roman ruin in Sicily. Made up of four connecting groups of buildings dating back to the 4th century, and said to have been maintained until around 1000, it houses a vast and breathtaking array of polychrome floor mosaics. SAIS buses travel from Enna (from the bus station at the west end of Viale A Diaz) to Piazza Armerina (€4.20 return, 45 minutes, eight per day), the closest town to Casale with transport connections. There's no public transport available to the villa itself, so a bicycle stowed under the bus can be very handy indeed. Otherwise, the 11km return trip from Piazza Armerina equates to either a long walk or a fairly expensive taxi ride. Follow the signs to *mosaici* (mosaics) or Villa Romana di Casale. Entry to the villa and mosaics costs €4.15.

Places to Stay & Eat There is only one accommodation option in Enna, and it's not cheap. Fortunately, at the **Grande Albergo Sicilia** (☎ 0935 50 08 54; Piazza Colaianni 7; singles/doubles €57/88) you do get what you pay for – a plush hotel set high in the old centre with comfortable rooms and fabulous views.

An alternative is the B&B **Da Pietro** (☎ 0935 3 36 47; Contrada Longobardi; per person €30-42), 1km along the main road up to Calascibetta, Enna's neighbour 3km away across a steep valley to the west. Da Pietro is a friendly, family-run establishment set among pleasant woods.

All self-catering supplies can be found in the Mercato S Antonio shopping precinct, one street south of Via Roma. **Ristorante Centrale** (☎ 0935 50 09 63; Piazza VI Dicembre 9; meal with wine €13-26) serves an excellent variety of regional dishes – many of them vegetarian – in an elegant, but relaxed atmosphere. Be sure to try the smorgasbord-style antipasto.

Getting There & Away SAIS (☎ 095 53 61 68) runs buses from Catania right to the centre of Enna (€6, 1¼ hours, eight daily) and from Palermo to Enna's bus station (€6.80, 1¾ hours).

Enna's train station is 5km from, and 500 vertical metres below, the town centre, making the train a less attractive option than the bus (from Catania €4.50 plus €3.10 per bike, 1¾ hours).

THE SOUTH & SICILY

THE RIDE
Day 1: Enna to Troina

3½–6½ hours, 63.1km

After the dramatic descent from Enna's lofty heights, the ride quickly establishes a rhythm of grinding and freewheeling on the rollercoaster of inland Sicily's starkly beautiful and mountainous terrain. A couple of tough climbs on the SS121 to Leonforte (23km) quickly get the legs warmed up and the blood pumping. A detour to the old centre is recommended. The highlight is the **Granfonte**, an amazing baroque fountain built in 1651 by Nicolò Braciforte, and made up of 24 separate jets playing against an ornately sculpted facade. Follow the signposts from the main cathedral.

Nissoria's (27.4km) one-way main street and most facilities can only be accessed from the far end of town (29km), where there's an excellent **bakery** that also slices cheeses and hams, ready for picnic *panini* (bread rolls). From a distance, **Agira** (35.3km) rises up in an almost perfect cone, matching in shape the incredible mass of Mt Etna that totally dominates the eastern horizon. The route bypasses the town, but all food amenities are available without entering the *centro*. After a rapid descent to the valley floor at the Salso, it's another very hard climb to **Gagliano Castelferrato** (47.9km), an amazing array of houses dwarfed by stern, craggy peaks. From here it's all hard work, as the route climbs onto the high, narrow ridge leading to day's end at Troina. A glance back to the south after cresting the final ever-steepening 2.9km lung buster (58km) affords an inspiring panorama back to the distinctive high plateau of Enna.

Troina

On a narrow perch more than 1100m high, Troina is built around a mountaintop fortress dating back to the 6th century. It was later one of the first towns taken by the Normans from the Arabs. Under Norman rule it was the 11th-century base for Count Roger I, who made major changes to the fortifications, and established the convent of San Michele and one of the island's first Christian churches here. There are also archaeological ruins dating back to the ancient Greeks in the area known as Catena, situated below Troina to the southeast.

THE SOUTH & SICILY

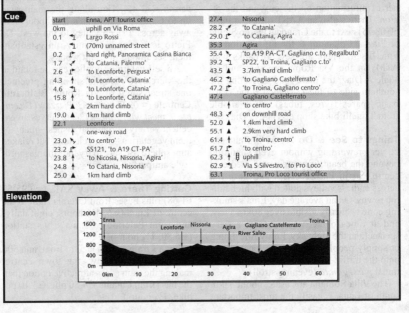

Centre to Sea – Day 1

Cue

start	Enna, APT tourist office	
0km	uphill on Via Roma	
0.1	⬐ Largo Rossi	
	⬐ (70m) unnamed street	
0.2	⬐ hard right, Panoramica Casina Bianca	
1.7	↗ 'to Catania, Palermo'	
2.6	⬐ 'to Leonforte, Pergusa'	
4.3	↑ 'to Leonforte, Catania'	
4.6	⬐ 'to Leonforte, Catania'	
15.8	↑ 'to Leonforte, Catania'	
	▲ 2km hard climb	
19.0	▲ 1km hard climb	
22.1	Leonforte	
	↑ one-way road	
23.0	↘ 'to centro'	
23.2	⬐ SS121, 'to A19 CT-PA'	
23.8	↑ 'to Nicosia, Nissoria, Agira'	
24.8	↑ 'to Catania, Nissoria'	
25.0	▲ 1km hard climb	

27.4	Nissoria	
28.2	↗ 'to Catania'	
29.0	⬐ 'to Catania, Agira'	
35.3	Agira	
35.4	↘ 'to A19 PA-CT, Gagliano c.to, Regalbuto'	
39.2	⬐ SP22, 'to Troina, Gagliano c.to'	
43.5	▲ 3.7km hard climb	
46.2	⬐ 'to Gagliano Castelferrato'	
47.2	⬑ 'to Troina, Gagliano centro'	
47.4	Gagliano Castelferrato	
	↑ 'to centro'	
48.3	↗ on downhill road	
52.0	▲ 1.4km hard climb	
55.1	▲ 2.9km very hard climb	
61.4	↑ 'to Troina, centro'	
61.7	⬑ 'to centro'	
62.3	↑ 🅿 uphill	
62.9	⬐ Via S Silvestro, 'to Pro Loco'	
63.1	Troina, Pro Loco tourist office	

Elevation

Information There's a Pro Loco (☎ 0935 65 69 81) at Via S Silverstro 71–73, but there are no regular opening hours. Banks with ATMs can be found in Piazza Martiri d'Ungheria, just off Via S Silvestro, and on Via Nazionale, the main approach road west of town.

Places to Stay & Eat There are only two accommodation options and both are outside the main town centre. About 3km west (turn left at 61.7km on Day 1 and ride 1.3km) is **Eden Hotel** *(☎ 0935 65 66 76; SS120 bivio diga Ancipa; singles/doubles with bathroom €31/47)*, a friendly, family-run establishment with excellent rooms, some with balconies and views across to Etna. It also has a very good ristorante/pizzeria downstairs where you can eat for as little as €10.50. **La Citadelle dell'Oasi** *(☎ 0935 65 39 66; Contrada San Michele; singles/ doubles with breakfast €47/73)* is a huge and somewhat bizarre multistorey complex to the east of the town, with two hotels, a restaurant and a conference centre. Definitely the lesser of Troina's two choices.

There are **bars** and a couple of good **delicatessens** on or near Via S Silvestro in the centre. There's a **Despar supermarket** and several **bars** on the main road circling south of the historic centre, and a good **bakery** and an **SMA supermarket** on Via Nazionale. **La Tavernetta** *(Via Arcirù 30; pizzas & pasta around €5)* serves good basic food.

Day 2: Troina to Sant'Agata di Militello
4–7 hours, 73.8km

After the succession of tough climbs on Day 1, today presents only one ascent, albeit a long one. Once beyond the 770m low point at the Troina River (7.5km), the route heads inexorably upwards, reaching 1530m at the top of the Nebrodi range (37.4km), near Monte Soro. Most of the climbing is on moderate gradients.

While exposure to sun and heat can be a factor during the clear days that predominate in late spring and early summer, most of the actual riding time will be spent gazing in awe across the cultivated fields and tilled soil of this starkly beautiful rural landscape to the splendour of Mt Etna. The cool, shady forests of the Nebrodi mountains beyond Cesarò bring welcome relief from the heat.

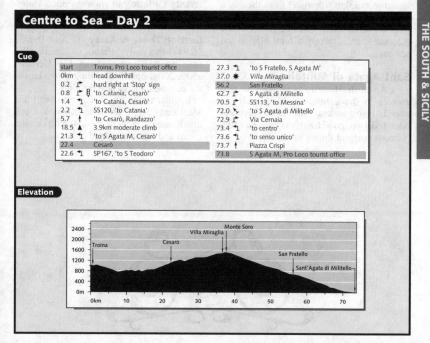

Centre to Sea – Day 2

Cue

start	Troina, Pro Loco tourist office		27.3 ↰	'to S Fratello, S Agata M'	
0km	head downhill		37.0 ✳	Villa Miraglia	
0.2 ↱	hard right at 'Stop' sign		56.2	San Fratello	
0.8 ↱ ⌷	'to Catania, Cesarò'		62.7 ↱	S Agata di Militello	
1.4 ↰	'to Catania, Cesarò'		70.5 ↱	SS113, 'to Messina'	
2.2 ↰	SS120, 'to Catania'		72.0 ↘	'to S Agata di Militello'	
5.7 ↑	'to Cesarò, Randazzo'		72.9 ↱	Via Cernaia	
18.5 ▲	3.9km moderate climb		73.4 ↰	'to centro'	
21.3 ↰	'to S Agata M, Cesarò'		73.6 ↰	'to senso unico'	
22.4	Cesarò		73.7 ↑	Piazza Crispi	
22.6 ↰	SP167, 'to S Teodoro'		73.8	S Agata M, Pro Loco tourist office	

Elevation

Elevation profile showing route from Troina to Sant'Agata di Militello, with labelled points: Troina, Cesarò, Villa Miraglia, Monte Soro, San Fratello, Sant'Agata di Militello. Vertical axis 0m–2400, horizontal axis 0km–70.

Cesarò (22.4km) is a pretty village with an almost alpine flavour, clinging high on the southern slopes of the Nebrodi mountains. An ideal place to rest, dine or collect lunch supplies, it also hosts a regional office of the Parco dei Nebrodi (☎ 095 69 60 08), situated on the main approach road at 22.3km. The office is an excellent source of maps and information on day and multiday walks in the park and also houses a small **museum** dedicated to the Nebrodi.

At 37km, buried deep in the leafy oasis of Europe's largest beech forest in the higher reaches of the Parco dei Nebrodi is **Villa Miraglia** *(☎ 095 773 21 33; half/full board €46.50/62)*, a lovely old, stone building originally built as a mountain retreat for an asthmatic count from Taormina, now serving as a small hotel. It's packed full of interesting collectables including quirky ceramics, colourfully decorated cart panels and old paintings. With good, simple food (also available as meals only), it's certainly an alluring retreat well worth considering as an overnight stop or a base for walks in and around the Nebrodi.

The day ends with an unforgettable, uninterrupted 33km freewheel from the day's high point all the way down to sea level, with the mirage-like volcanic forms of the Aeolian Islands merely a faint blur in the sea haze.

Sant'Agata di Militello

Sant'Agata di Militello is unlikely to win awards in the glamorous Mediterranean seaside resort stakes, but it does have accommodation, good transport options and a pleasant seafront dining precinct.

Information The tourist office (☎ 0941 7 22 02), Piazza Crispi, in the Castello dei Gallego (open 8.30am to 12.30pm), is a fairly basic outfit. Worth a quick browse before heading off is the **Museo Etno-Antropologico dei Nebrodi**, on Via Cosenz (also known as the Lungomare or esplanade), near the train station. There are several banks with ATMs on Via Medici, the main road through the town centre. Gomme & Service (☎ 0941 7210 61), Via Toselli 5/7, can supply very basic bike spares, tyres and tubes.

Places to Stay & Eat Offering OK, if unexceptional, accommodation are the **Roma Palace Hotel** *(☎ 0941 70 35 16; [e] hotelroma@ tiscalinet.it; Via Medici 443; singles/doubles €26/42)* and **Hotel Parimar** *(☎ 0941 70 18 88; Via Medici 1; singles/doubles €47/78)*.

For bread and tasty pastries, head to **Spiga d'Oro** bakery *(Via Medici 103)*. The huge **SMA supermarket** *(Via G Puccini)*, east of the centre and two streets north of Via Medici, has everything for self-caterers. There are several good restaurants and pizzerias along the esplanade (Via Cosenz), a short stroll from the centre. Diners at **Ristorante Carletto** can choose from a sumptuous array of Sicilian antipasto.

Getting There & Away ISEA (☎ 095 53 68 94) has a daily 5am bus to Catania (€7, four hours), leaving from Via Cernaia, about 200m uphill from the centre. This is the cheapest and easiest option.

Regular trains run to Palermo (€6) and Messina (€5.20), for connections to Catania, Rome (€36.20 or €44.50 with supplement) and other mainland cities.

Sardinia

The second-largest island in the Mediterranean, Sardinia (Sardegna) has always been considered an isolated land. Its people and culture maintain a separate identity from the mainland, which they call *il continente* (the continent), and even today many Sardinians speak an ancient Latin-based dialect and proudly maintain traditional customs and costume, especially in the remote interior.

In keeping with its tradition of isolation, Sardinia as a cycling destination offers something quite different from anywhere else in Italy, not least being its superbly maintained and lightly trafficked roads. Add to this its fabulous food, spectacular beaches and archaeological treasures, an isolated, rugged interior of intense natural beauty and people renowned for their graciousness and hospitality, and it's hard to find a reason not to head off and start pedalling – all you need is to learn to love hills!

HISTORY

While there are signs of possible human habitation that date back as far as 150,000 years, significant archaeological finds indicate that the Neolithic era saw the first widespread signs of man's presence.

Perhaps the most significant and easily identifiable of Sardinia's earlier inhabitants were the Nuraghic people, whose 7000 *nuraghi* – their conical megalithic stone fortresses – dot the island (see the boxed text 'Stone Cone Homes' on p326). These sheep-rearing people lived in separate communities led by warrior-kings and their culture flourished from around 1800 to 300 BC .

Sardinia's coast was visited by Greeks and Phoenicians, first as traders then as invaders and the island was colonised by the Romans. They, in turn, were followed by the Pisans, Genoese, Spanish, Austrians and finally, the Royal House of Savoy, the future kings of a united Italy. In 1948 Sardinia became a semi-autonomous region.

Despite the succession of invaders and colonisers, it is often said that the Sardinians (known as the Sardi) were never really conquered, they simply retreated into the hills. The Romans were prompted to call the island's central-eastern mountains the Barbagia (from the Latin word for barbarian)

SARDINIA

because of the uncompromising lifestyle of the warrior-shepherds, who never abandoned their Nuraghic customs.

NATURAL HISTORY

Sardinia and its close northern neighbour, Corsica, were originally connected to the European continent and share a similar geomorphic ancestry. The oldest of the island's rock strata, in the west coast region known as the Sulcis-Iglesiente, date back more than 500 million years. Major geological upheavals around 300 million years ago created the solid granite spine that today constitutes more than one-third of the island. Subsequent marine sedimentation helped form the lower coastal areas, but it was the massive volcanic upheaval responsible for the formation of the European Alps that forced both Sardinia and Corsica into their current mid-Mediterranean position.

Once heavily forested, centuries of fires, clearing and uncontrolled grazing have left their indelible mark on the island. In spite of this, there remain some significant tracts of oak, cork oak, chestnut and hazelnut in the higher mountain areas. On the high plateau of the Gennargentu and Sopramonte, the scent of wild herbs such as thyme, oregano, sage and rosemary perfume the air. In the sparsely vegetated coastal areas Mediterranean maquis, juniper, myrtle, rosemary, lentisk and broom dominate.

Hunters have always been active in Sardinia, but some wildlife remains, notably the *cinghiale* (wild pig), Golden and Bonelli's eagles, Peregrine falcon, pink flamingos, herons, the *mouflon* (wild mountain sheep), Sardinian deer and a colony of griffon vultures on the west coast.

CLIMATE

While extremes of temperature in summer and winter can be experienced, Sardinia's climate in general is relatively mild in comparison to other parts of Italy on a similar latitude. This is due mainly to its position within the Mediterranean whereby temperatures are often tempered by sea breezes.

There are three prevailing winds: the northwesterly Mistral (which often blows with considerable force), the sirocco from the south and the Levant from the south and southeast. Both the southerly winds can bring oppressive heat and humidity to the island.

Though the air in mountain areas is somewhat more static, altitude plays its part in keeping temperatures to tolerable levels in the warmer months. Average temperatures are 25°C in summer (a little hotter inland) and around 8°C to 10°C degrees in winter (a little colder inland, naturally decreasing with altitude). July and August are the hottest months and January is the coldest. Rain mainly falls in spring and autumn, and the mountainous interior receives the bulk of it, falling as snow on the higher peaks; the plains and coastal areas in the east and south are significantly drier.

INFORMATION

Ente Sardo Industrie Turistiche (ESIT; ☎ 800 01 31 53, ⓦ www.esit.net), Via Goffredo Mameli 97, in Cagliari covers all of Sardinia. For those planning to spend more time in Sardinia, ⓦ www.sardiniabybike.cjb.net/ is an excellent website, with suggested itineraries and information on organised cycling tours. The map on the island's official government website (ⓦ www.regione.sardegna .it/cartina.htm) has links to the major tourist offices in each region.

There are several excellent websites on Sardinia, all of which provide loads of practical information and useful links.

Ferrovie dello Stato (FdS; ☎ 147 880 88, ⓦ www.fs-on-line.com) and Trenitalia (ⓦ www.trenitalia.it) websites are one and the same, available in several languages, easy to use, and offering comprehensive information on train movements. For information on services of the two main intercity

Stone Cone Homes

Among the most dominant features of Sardinia's landscape are the 7000 or so *nuraghi* dotted around the island. Dating from 1500 to 400 BC, these truncated conical structures were made out of huge basalt blocks taken from extinct volcanoes. The towers were used for shelter and for guarding the surrounding territory. The name *nuraghe* derives from the Sardinian word 'nurra' which means 'heap' or 'mound'. Very little is known about the identity of the Nuraghic people. Judging by their buildings, they were well organised and possessed remarkable engineering skills, but appear to have left no written word.

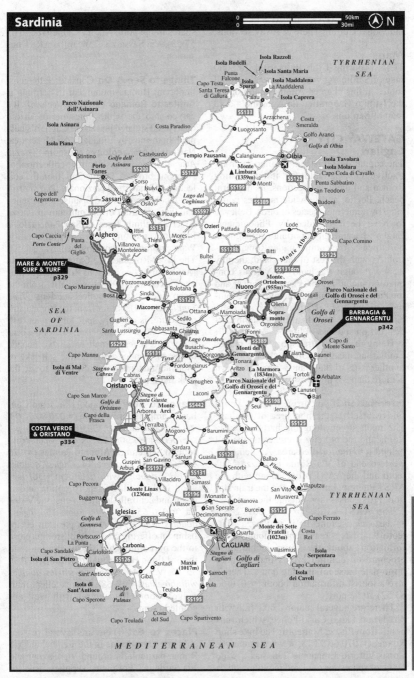

bus companies (PANI and ARST), see the individual Getting There & Away sections.

Maps

TCI's (Touring Club Italiano) 1:200,000 map of Sardinia gives good coverage of all routes in this chapter. Another good one is the Istituto Geografico de Agostino's road map of Sardinia.

GATEWAY CITY
Cagliari

The capital of the island, Cagliari is an attractive city, notable for its interesting Roman and medieval sections, its beautiful beach, Poetto, and its wide marshes populated by numerous species of birds. Believed to have been founded by Phoenicians, Cagliari became an important Carthaginian port town before coming under Roman control. As with the rest of the island, the city passed through the hands of various conquerors, including the Pisans, Spanish and the Piemontese House of Savoy, before joining unified Italy. Cagliari was savagely bombed during WWII, suffering significant destruction and loss of life.

Being a major transport hub makes Cagliari an ideal base from which to travel to other parts of the island – no major town is more than 3½ hours away by train or bus.

Information If you arrive by boat, you'll find yourself at the port area of Cagliari. The main street along the harbour is Via Roma and the old city stretches up the hill behind it to the fortified area. At the northwestern end of Via Roma is Piazza Matteotti and the AAST office, along with the ARST intercity bus station and the train station. PANI buses stop outside the port.

The AAST office (☎ 070 66 92 55, e aast.ca@tiscalinet.it) is in Piazza Matteotti 9. It has a reasonable amount of information about the town including a brochure on cultural events that includes up-to-date museum opening hours. There's also a tourist information booth (☎ 070 66 83 52) at the port.

There are several major banks (all with ATMs) on Largo Carlo Felice, which runs uphill from Piazza Matteotti. The bike shop Runner (☎ 070 66 92 18, w www.runner.it), Corso Vittorio Emanuele 296, has a wide range of spares for road and mountain bikes

and a good workshop. For repairs and basic spares in the port area, try Cimar (☎ 070 65 57 53), Via Sassari 3–7, near the ARST bus station.

Things to See & Do Considered the most important Roman monument in Sardinia is **Anfiteatro Romano** (Viale Fra Ignazio). It's carved into the white limestone of an old quarry and situated just above Cagliari's hospital. In the nearby Cittadella dei Musei area, **National Archaeology Museum** (Piazza Arsenale) has a fascinating collection of Nuraghic bronzes. On the 2nd floor, the collection at **Pinacoteca Nazionale** (Piazza Arsenale) includes local and Spanish renaissance paintings. In front of the museum in Piazza Arsenale, climb **Torre di San Pancrazio**, a Pisan tower dating from the 14th century. Wander through the nearby medieval quarter. The Pisan-Romanesque **Cattedrale di Santa Maria** houses two precious Romanesque pulpits carved in 1160 that were gifts from the Pisan rulers. The **botanical gardens** (Viale Sant'Ignazio 11), not far from the Roman amphitheatre, is a lovely spot for a quiet rest. Spend a day at Poetto beach, east of the centre, where several small bars have outside tables, or wander across to the salt lake of Molentargius, just west of Poetto, to see the pink flamingos.

Places to Stay Around 11km from Cagliari, **Camping Pini e Mare** (☎ 070 80 31 03; Via Leonardo da Vinci, Quartu Sant'Elena; per site/person €4.50/5.50) is only open from June to September. **Albergo Palmas** (☎ 070 65 16 79; Via Sardegna 14; singles/ doubles €21/31, doubles with bathroom €36) is a good budget, bike-friendly option and is clean and centrally located. **Pensione Vittoria** (☎ 070 65 79 70; Via Roma 75; singles/ doubles from €31/47) is a pleasant establishment offering clean, simple rooms close to the port although it's a bit of a climb to the 3rd floor. **Hotel Quattro Mori** (☎ 070 66 85 35; Via GM Angioi 27; singles/doubles with breakfast €47/68) is an excellent mid-range option. It's central with well appointed rooms.

Places to Eat There are several reasonably priced **trattorias** in the area behind Via Roma, particularly around Via Cavour and Via Sardegna. For picnic supplies, head for

Via Sardegna, where there are several good **alimentari**, **greengrocers** and a **forno** (bakery). **Isola del Gelato**, towards the top of Largo Felice, has sensational gelati.

Trattoria Gennargentu *(Via Sardegna 60; meals from €18)* is always packed with hungry locals looking for a fix of good Sardinian pasta and seafood. **Trattoria Ci Pensa Cannas** *(Via Sardegna 37; pasta €3.60-5.20, mains €5-16)* is very much a locals' haunt, with grilled fish and meats keeping them running back for more. **Trattoria Lillicu** *(Via Sardegna 78; antipasto €5, pasta €6)* offers excellent seafood antipasti such as deep-fried whitebait and *sardine al agrodolce* (in a sweet and sour oniony sauce); follow it with spaghetti *ai ricci* (sea urchins) or spaghetti *alla bottarga* (mullet roe). **Dulchemele Ristorante** *(Via Roma 177; meals from €21)* is a more modern alternative with a comprehensive wine list, serving superior à la carte food using traditional ingredients.

Getting There & Away Isolation isn't a problem for this island province, well-serviced with busy air and sea routes. By far the cheapest option, and a great way to arrive in Sardinia, is by sea.

Air Cagliari's Elmas airport is just off the SS130, 8km northwest of the city, and is easily reached by bike. ARST buses leave regularly from Piazza Matteotti to coincide with flights (€0.80). Alitalia has flights to all major European cities. It charges €15.50 per flight to transport bikes within Italy (get confirmation when booking whether the bike needs to be boxed). The office (☎ 070 24 00 79) is at the airport, otherwise contact the Alitalia central office on ☎ 8488 656 41. Meridiana is another airline with regular flights within Europe, also with an office (☎ 070 24 01 69) at the airport.

Sea The cheapest and easiest way to arrive with a bike is by ferry. Ferries arrive at the port just off Via Roma. Tirrenia is the main company, with connections to Civitavecchia (Rome), Palermo, Trapani, Naples and Genoa, as well as Tunisia (via Trapani). Tirrenia's Cagliari booking office (☎ 070 66 60 65) is at Stazione Marittima in the port area.

Moby Lines (☎ 02 76028132, ⓦ www.mobylines.it) runs ferries between Santa Teresa di Gallura in Sardinia and Bonifacio in Corsica (€8.50 to €12 per person and €3 per bike, plus €3 port tax, 50 minutes, 10 daily). Corsica and Sardinia Ferries (☎ 0789 4 67 80, ⓦ www.corsicaferries.com), Molo Sud, Golfo Aranci, also connect Corsica and Golfo Aranci in Sardinia.

Mare e Monte/Surf & Turf

Duration	2 days
Distance	107.9km
Difficulty	moderate
Start/End	Alghero

This two-day tour from the beautiful and upbeat port town of Alghero on La Riviera del Corallo (The Coral Riviera) to Bosa's more laid-back shores offers the very best of *il mare* (the sea) and *il monte* (the mountain): sensational and enduring panoramas across the entire northern and eastern expanses of the island on Day 1 and a return journey on arguably one of the world's better coastal cycling roads.

HISTORY
Alghero's Nuraghic heritage dates back to before 1000 BC. More recently, its strategic position in the Mediterranean made it a valuable trading port. Originally under Genovese control, it fell in 1354 to the Catalan-Aragonese who flushed out the Sardinian inhabitants and duly replaced them with Catalonians. The Catalan links are evident in the architecture, and even more so in the local language, which preserves more elements of ancient Catalan than the language spoken today in the Spanish province itself.

Bosa's post-Nuraghic history resulted in successive occupation by the Phoenicians, Romans and the Malaspina, a powerful Tuscan family who built the castle of Seravalle in 1112 to shield them from the Saracens. In the 14th century the Aragonese also left their mark, complementing the castle with extra fortifications and constructing the church of Nostra Signora di Regnos Altos.

PLANNING
When to Ride
In the warmer months (April to June and September and October), temperatures are ideal for cycling, warm enough for swimming and

SARDINIA

the summer hordes are avoided. Wind can be a factor, the Mistral sometimes howling out of the northwest for days at a time. If you ride the coast road (Day 2) on a weekday you'll feel like it's yours alone.

ACCESS TOWN
Alghero

Alghero sits on a small promontory jutting unobtrusively into the idyllic blue waters of the Mediterranean on Sardegna's northwest coast. In an area high on natural beauty, it has understandably become one of Sardinia's most popular tourist resorts. With long, sandy beaches stretching away to the north and plenty of low-key resort-style accommodation, it's thronged with sun-seeking tourists in July and August.

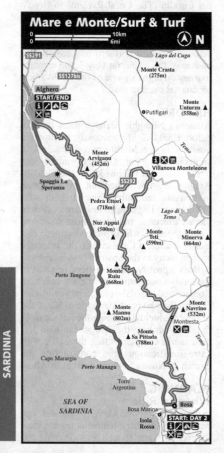

Beyond the beach umbrellas, however, is a town with an attractive historic centre reminiscent of old Spain, part of a rich cultural heritage left by the Catalan-Aragonese. A number of significant archaeological sites and areas of natural interest within easy reach make it an ideal place to explore in autumn and spring, and it'll often be warm enough to hit the beach as well.

Information The AAST office (☎ 079 97 90 54), Piazza Porta Terra 9, on the west side of the park, has material on the town's history, places of interest and available services. There are numerous banks with ATMs in town, two of which (Banca Carige and Banco Nazionale di Lavoro) are within a stone's throw of the AAST office. For bike repairs and a good range of spares for road and mountain bikes, try Velosport (☎ 079 97 71 82), Via Vittorio Veneto 90 (closed Monday morning). It also hires bikes.

Things to See & Do Start with a wander through the narrow cobbled lanes of the historic centre with three defensive towers at its perimeter. **Chiesa di San Francesco** *(Via Carlo Alberto)* is part-Gothic and part-Renaissance with a Catalan influence. In warmer months, head for the beach – the best ones are **Spiaggia di San Giovanni** and **Spiaggia di Maria Pia**, a few kilometres north of town.

At around 55km return on the SS127, **Le Grotte di Nettuno** *(Neptune's Caves; ☎ 079 94 65 40)* at Capo Caccia make an interesting day ride. To access these vast limestone caverns with their massive stalagmites and stalactites you'll need to negotiate – down and up – the 654 steps from the car park to the caves' entrance at sea level. If the thought of the steps doesn't appeal, regular Navisarda boats (☎ 079 95 06 03) make the trip to the caves, departing from Alghero's marina downhill from the tourist office.

About 10km from Alghero on the Capo Caccia road are the impressive **Nuraghe di Palmavera** *(Cooperativa SILT; ☎ 079 95 32 00)*. The two towers and adjoining fortified village of around 50 houses dating back to around 1000 BC.

Places to Stay There's no shortage of accommodation options. Outside August you shouldn't have too much trouble finding a room, but booking ahead is advised.

SARDINIA

Camping Calik *(☎/fax 079 93 01 11; SS127, Fertilia; per bicycle/person/tent €1/4.20/9.50; open June-Sept)*, about 6km north of Alghero, has pleasant, shady sites. **Camping La Mariposa** *(☎ 079 95 04 80;* W *www.lamariposa.it; Via Lido 22; per tent/person €5/10.50; open Apr-Nov)* is only 1km from Alghero, but has limited shady sites. Both camping grounds have a shop and Calik has a restaurant-pizzeria.

Ostello dei Giuliani *(☎ 079 93 03 53; Via Zara 1, Fertilia; B&B with 1 hot shower €10, meals €7.75)* requires you to produce a hostel card and has only 25 beds, so book early.

Pensione Normandie *(☎/fax 079 97 53 02; Via Enrico Mattei 6; singles/doubles €23.50/44)* is a friendly, budget option. It's a little out of the centre and rooms are shabby but large.

Hotel San Francesco *(☎/fax 079 98 03 30;* e *hotsfran@tin.it; Via Ambrogio Machin 2; singles/doubles with bathroom €39/62)* is a popular hotel located in the heart of the *centro storico* (historic centre). **Hotel El Balear** *(☎ 079 97 52 29; Lungomare Dante 32; singles/ doubles €41/70)*, on the esplanade, is more your upmarket holiday digs, but with easy access to the *centro storico*, quiet, comfortable rooms and a pleasant terrace with a sea aspect.

Places to Eat For self-caterers, there's a **produce market** *(cnr Via Sassari & Via Cagliari; open 8am-1pm Mon-Sat)* one block from the tourist office. There are numerous **supermarkets**, closest are: **Mura** *(Via La Marmora 28)*, on the far side of the park from the tourist office, and **SISA** *(Via Sassari 55)*.

Caffè Costantino *(Piazza Civica)* is the best spot to sit and take in the atmosphere while enjoying a beer or cappuccino. **Al Vecchio Mulino** *(Via Don De Roma 3; pizzas €3.70-6.80, pasta €5.20-8.30, mains €7.30-13)* is an attractive trattoria with an atmospheric vaulted ceiling. *Gamberoni alla griglia* (grilled prawns) and *cozze alla marinara* (clams with white wine, garlic and onion) are house specialities. **Posada del Mar** *(Vicolo Adami 29; pasta €6.80-10.50, mains from €10.50)* offers excellent (but pricey) fish dishes served in an outdoor dining area. **Mabroux** *(☎ 079 97 00 00; Via Santa Barbara; 4-course set menu €21)*, located in a tiny *vicolo* (alley) between the cathedral and the sea wall, is one of

Alghero's best finds – a true mamma's kitchen where the menu is limited but you get the best fish-based dinner in town. Be sure to book.

Getting There & Away Alghero is easily reached from all parts of the island.

Air The airport, about 12km north of town and inland from Fertilia, has domestic flights to major cities throughout Italy. It's easily reached by bike, and regular buses (€1.90, 30 minutes) leave from the corner of Via Vittorio Emanuele and Via Cagliari to coincide with flights.

Bus Your best transport option is the bus. Intercity buses terminate on Via Catalogna, on the north (downhill) side of the public park. Between 5.35am and 7pm, FdS (Ferrovia della Sardegna) and ARST buses make the trip to Sassari approximately every hour (€2.60, one hour). Timetables are posted outside the tourist office and also in the ticket office (☎ 079 95 01 79) beside the bus stop area.

From Sassari, PANI runs six buses per day to Cagliari (€13, 3½ hours), four of which pass through Oristano (end of the Costa Verde ride, €7.20, two hours) and connect with Nuoro (end of the Gennargentu ride, €7.50, 2½ hours, change at Macomer). They leave Sassari from the PANI office (☎ 079 23 69 83) at Via Bellieni 25.

ARST also runs a special service to Olbia to coincide with night ferry departures to Genova and Civitavecchia. ARST and PANI both have services to Porto Torres (for ferry connections to Corsica).

Train The FdS station is on Via Don Minzoni, 1km north of town, where local trains leave almost hourly for Sassari (€1.80 plus €2.60 per bike, one hour). From Sassari FdS trains connect with Olbia (€7.30 plus €2.60 per bike, six daily, two hours) and the main north–south line (change at Chilivani) for Cagliari (€15 plus €2.60 per bike, five daily, 3½ to four hours).

Bicycle The 35km ride to Sassari (for all main transport connections) is a feasible alternative. Leaving from the tourist office, follow Via Vittorio Emanuele directly onto the SS127.

SARDINIA

THE RIDE
Day 1: Alghero to Bosa
3½–6 hours, 62.2km

This is your classic up-and-over day. Much of the work is expended early in gaining the high ridge (around 600m) that is maintained for most of the ride until the drop to the Fiume Temo at Bosa. The roads are excellent and the traffic is so light as to go almost unnoticed.

The theme for the day is 'panorama' – the vistas that dominate virtually from the outset are a just reward for a little sweat expended on the climbs. It's not all hard work, though, with the road at times undulating through beautiful open country dotted with cork oak and criss-crossed by low stone walls.

Perched like a natural balcony on the upper slopes of the Colle di Santa Maria is **Villanova Monteleone** (23km), a lovely village commanding stunning views over Anglona to the north and Gallura to the east. The centre of town is just off the main route (go straight at 24.1km instead of turning right as the cue sheet indicates and follow the 'centro' signs), where you'll find a daily **produce market** (open mornings Monday to Saturday, follow signs to 'mercato'), **supermarket** and a couple of **bars** within easy reach. The ristorante-pizzeria **Cocobamba** is a few kilometres out on the Bosa road.

Once a major cork-producing centre, today the region is renowned for its fine hand-woven rugs and excellent *pecorino* (sheep's cheese), the latter available from a sales outlet on Piazza G Casula.

In a distinctive brown-and-white stone building below the main piazza is **Calarinas** (☎ 079 96 04 00; e *calarinas@tiscalinet.it*), a small cooperative involved primarily with promoting the town and region and preserving the strong cultural traditions of its people. The staff is incredibly friendly and can offer information on the town's history and places of interest, arrange guided tours, even find a cheap bed for the night for those who wish to explore further. It also oversees the small **artefact museum** in the same building, where you can see, among other treasures of centuries past, the ingenious ways cork could be put to use.

On the high road beyond Villanova Monteleone, some great coastal views are on offer as the road bobs and weaves through shady woods and across a lacework of pretty, rock-walled meadows. The final 5km climb is far outweighed by the sizzling 10km descent into Bosa.

Bosa
Bosa is becoming more popular as a tourist destination, but it is yet to show signs of becoming touristy. Sitting in a deep valley at

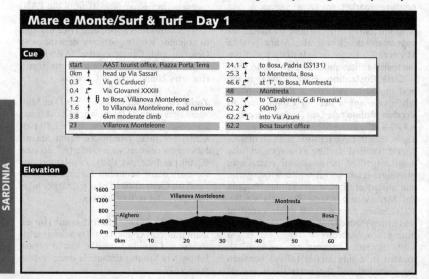

Mare e Monte/Surf & Turf – Day 1

Cue

start	AAST tourist office, Piazza Porta Terra		24.1 ↱	to Bosa, Padria (SS131)
0km ↑	head up Via Sassari		25.3 ↑	to Montresta, Bosa
0.3 ↱	Via G Carducci		46.6 ↱	at 'T', to Bosa, Montresta
0.4 ↱	Via Glovanni XXXIII		48	Montresta
1.2 ↑ 🅑	to Bosa, Villanova Monteleone		62 ↗	to 'Carabinieri, G di Finanzia'
1.6 ↑	to Villanova Monteleone, road narrows		62.2 ↱	(40m)
3.8 ▲	6km moderate climb		62.2 ↰	into Via Azuni
23	Villanova Monteleone		62.2	Bosa tourist office

Elevation

Elevation profile (m) showing the route from Alghero (0km) over Villanova Monteleone (around 23km, ~600m), past Montresta (around 48km), descending to Bosa (around 62km). Vertical axis marked 0m, 400, 800, 1200, 1600; horizontal axis marked 0km, 10, 20, 30, 40, 50, 60.

SARDINIA

the mouth of the Fiume Temo, its easy pace, fine historic centre and proximity to clean beaches make it a very pleasant little seaside haunt.

Information The Pro Loco M Melis tourist office (☎ 0785 37 61 07), Via Azuni 5, is open daily and can provide a town map and useful local information. Within the main town centre, Banco di Sardegna (Piazza IV Novembre) and Credito Italiano (Corso Vittorio Emanuele) have ATMs. The IP service station (☎ 0785 37 31 78) next to Hotel Mannu in Viale Alghero can provide very limited budget bike spares such as cables, tyres and tubes. Access the Internet at ristorante-pizzeria Al Gambero Rosso (☎ 0785 37 41 50), Via Nazionale 12.

Things to See & Do A wander through the pedestrian-only medieval quarter, known locally as Sa Costa, and a visit to the imposing **Castello di Seravalle** is the ideal way to get a feel for the town's history. Built on the slopes below the castle, the historic centre is a fascinating labyrinth of narrow, cobbled alleys, stairways and close-knit dwellings. Also of interest is the **Romanesque church** of San Pietro Extramuros, 2km east of the old bridge on the south bank of the Temo.

In warmer months, head for the **beach**, either nearby at Bosa Marina or along the north coast (Day 2 ride). Access to the northern beaches is only possible between Sa Badrucche and Torre Argentina. **Scuba-diving** aficionados are sure to enjoy an undersea adventure in the crystal clear waters. Contact Diving Malesh (☎ 0330 92 92 58). The whole northern coastal region also offers great **walking** in any season.

Places to Stay & Eat There are several hotels in Bosa Marina, a somewhat ordinary, modern resort town at the mouth of the Temo about 2.5km south of the centre, but Bosa has the best options. All prices rise considerably in late July and August.

Ostello della Gioventù (☎ 0785 37 50 09; *Via Sardegna 1, Bosa Marina; dorm beds €9.30, half-board €19.50*) and **Hotel Perry Clan** (☎ 0785 37 30 74; *Via Alghero 3, Bosa; singles/doubles with bathroom €18/36*) are budget places close to the centre, with functional rooms and a decent restaurant.

Hotel Sa Pischedda (☎ 0785 37 30 65; [e] *asapischedda@tiscalinet.it; Via Roma 2, Bosa; singles/doubles with bathroom €31/47*), across the river from the centre, has an older-style ambience and clean, spacious rooms, some with balconies. **Hotel Mannu** (☎ 0785 37 53 06; *Viale Alghero 28, Bosa; singles/doubles with bathroom & breakfast €31/52*) offers clean, modern rooms and a good restaurant specialising in seafood.

Stock up on supplies at the large **supermarket** (*Viale Alghero*), opposite the Hotel Mannu. **Arcobaleno**, back towards the centre, has the best gelati. The ristorante-pizzeria at **Hotel Sa Pischedda** has pizzas from €4.50 or very comprehensive meals from €18.50. It's an unexpected surprise offering superior dining and an extensive list of excellent local wines. **Ristorante Borgo Sant'Ignazio** (*Via Sant'Ignazio 33; pasta €5.20-7.30, full meals from €15.50; closed Mon*), tucked away in the medieval quarter, is a respected eatery serving excellent, well-priced dishes. Try the *culinzones e calameda*, home-made ravioli stuffed with ricotta and mushrooms and served in a rich meat sauce.

Day 2: Bosa to Alghero
2½–4½ hours, 45.7km
On a wide and almost empty road with a flawless surface, weaving and bobbing its way along a truly spectacular stretch of rugged, deserted coastline, this ride is a true gem. There's only one significant climb of 6.2km to 350m, but the work involved is more than offset by the commanding views gained in the process. The brilliant white cliffs of **Capo Caccia** (16km) can often be seen on the northern horizon through the Mediterranean haze. A head wind from the northwest is the only thing that could realistically spoil the fun.

In spring, the scent of wildflowers fills the air and often the only signs of life are the jangle of goats' bells from the rugged, high slopes soaring steeply to the right, or a bird of prey winging on thermals high overhead. The area is one of the last habitats of the griffon vulture and it's quite an experience if you are lucky enough to spot one of these huge birds, with wingspans reaching up to 2m.

Other than the path to the beach (5.4km), just south of Torre Argentina, there's no

SARDINIA

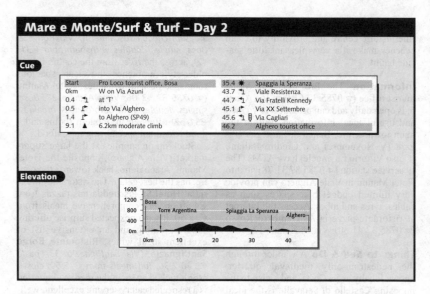

Mare e Monte/Surf & Turf – Day 2

Cue

Start		Pro Loco tourist office, Bosa	35.4	✳	Spaggia la Speranza
0km		W on Via Azuni	43.7	⬑	Viale Resistenza
0.4	⬑	at 'T'	44.7	⬑	Via Fratelli Kennedy
0.5	⬐	into Via Alghero	45.1	⬐	Via XX Settembre
1.4	⬐	to Alghero (SP49)	45.6	⬑ ⛛	Via Cagliari
9.1	▲	6.2km moderate climb	46.2		Alghero tourist office

Elevation

chance to swim until **Spiaggia La Speranza** (35.4km); the long sandy beach lapped by crystal clear aquamarine waters looks inviting indeed, especially if the weather is hot. A **bar** and the very good **Ristorante La Speranza** (specialising in seafood) make it an ideal place to break the ride before the final 10.8km run into Alghero.

Costa Verde & Oristano

Duration	3 days
Distance	147.4km
Difficulty	moderate
Start	Iglesias
End	Oristano

This three-day ride is 'one with the lot'. For the beachcomber: lazy little Mediterranean villages and secluded bays, long, unspoilt sandy beaches and stretches of rugged coastline, all caressed by an emerald sea. For the culture vulture: beautiful medieval towns rich in architectural treasures. For the adventurer: mining ghost towns reminiscent of the wild west, open spaces and high, rocky peaks in some of the more isolated and sparsely populated parts of the island. You get all of this on smooth, empty roads where a tourist coach can be a very rare sight indeed.

HISTORY

The rugged and remote mountain region north of Iglesias (known as the Iglesiente) was originally home to the Nuraghic people. It was later colonised by the Phoenicians, but passed successively to the Carthaginians, Romans and Pisans, who all exploited its rich lead, zinc and silver resources. Mining activity began to decline during the centuries of Aragonese control until a boom in the 19th century saw it become Italy's most important mining region. Falls in productivity and demand after WWII led to inevitable mine closures and the eventual death of the industry.

While the area around Oristano lacked the mineral resources of the Iglesiente, it reflects a similar history of Phoenician, Carthaginian and Roman occupation. The Phoenicians established the port town of Tharros, whose later inhabitants moved inland and laid the foundations of Oristano.

NATURAL HISTORY

The Iglesiente is an area of major geological significance and provides an incredible keyhole into the past. In the rock strata of the coastal cliffs and the mountains inland, there is clear evidence of the upheavals that created the major massifs of Western Europe more than 500 million years ago. Prized fossil remains from the area, such as the

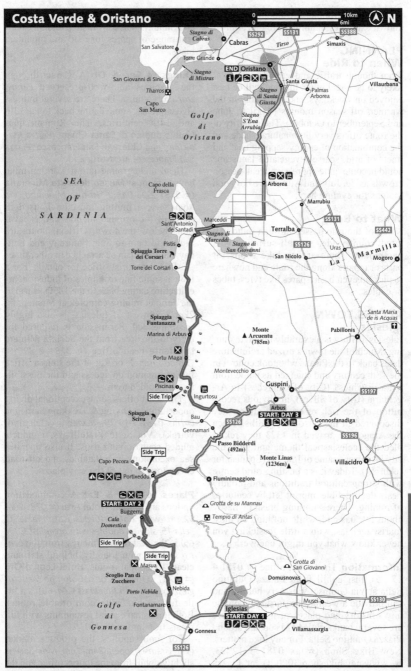

Pre-Cambrian trilobite, are among the oldest known examples of animal life on earth.

PLANNING
When to Ride

Even though traffic and crowds are never likely to be a real issue, the ride will be best enjoyed on weekdays, and preferably in the warmer, off-season months (April to June and September to October). The majority of the route offers very little natural shade and the combination of energy-sapping heat and tracts of arid, sparsely vegetated landscape could become quite oppressive. Peak-season crowds aside, July and August are not good months for cycling here.

What to Bring

Much of the ride passes through quite isolated countryside, so self-sufficiency is paramount. There are no bike shops for parts or repairs along the route and nowhere to pick up even basic spares like tyres, tubes or cables.

ACCESS TOWN
Iglesias

Iglesias' history is inexorably linked to mining. Much of the town's prized architecture dates back to the Pisans who took control in the 13th century and changed its name from Villa di Chiesa (City of Churches) to Argentaria (City of Silver), in obvious recognition of the rich reserves of silver they discovered in the surrounding hills. When the Aragonese arrived in 1323 they rekindled the ecclesiastical theme and gave the city its current name of Iglesias (Spanish for 'church'). Today it is a bustling rural centre with strong cultural traditions and proudly bears the indelible imprint left by centuries of mining. There's nothing brash or flashy about Iglesias and, while not high on most tourist agendas, with a little fossicking you never know what you might uncover!

Information The tourist office (☎ 0781 4 17 95), just uphill from Piazza Quintino Sella at Via Gramsci 9, is very helpful and can provide a wealth of information on the city's history and places of interest. There are several banks with ATMs on and around Piazza Quintino Sella. For any bike matters, New Bike Shop (☎/fax 0781 3 12 23, ⓦ www.newbikeshop.3000.it), at Piazza

Cavalleria 2–3 (closed Saturday afternoon and Sunday), has a workshop and an excellent range of spares for road and mountain bikes.

Things to See & Do A wander through the gracious and well-preserved *centro storico* is a must. There are several impressive churches, some dating back to the 13th and 14th centuries. The Romanesque-Gothic **duomo di Santa Chiara** *(Piazza Municipio)* and **Chiesa di San Francesco** *(Piazza San Francesco)* are worth a look.

Head underground into a working mine environment at **Museo dell'Arte Mineraria** *(☎ 0781 2 23 04; c/- Istituto Minerario, Via Roma 47)*, a mining museum housed in some of the original tunnels and excavations below the town. Official hours are limited to 6pm to 8pm Saturday and Sunday, but visits can be arranged at other times – ask at the tourist office for details. For a look at some fine examples of industrial architecture dating back to the 1850s, a trip to the defunct **mining complex** at Monteponi, 2km southwest of Iglesias, is also highly recommended. Permission is required for entry to the area from the **Società Miniere Iglesiente** head office *(☎ 0781 2 39 19; Campo Pisano)*, or ask at the tourist office for information on access and the possibility of a guided tour.

The coast offers some exceptional **diving** opportunities. Diving & Trekking Sardegna *(☎/fax 0781 3 19 29, ⓦ web.tiscalinet.it/divetrek)*, Via Sette Fratelli 38, conducts guided scuba-diving trips. It also operates **sea excursions** in inflatables and **off-road excursions** to out of the way places.

Places to Stay & Eat Accommodation options are limited. **Hotel Artu** *(☎ 0781 2 24 92; ⓦ www.hotelartuiglesias.it; Piazza Q Sella 15; singles/doubles with breakfast €39/ 65)* is the best option, metres from the *centro storico*, with friendly, helpful staff and clean, functional rooms. **Hotel Leon d'Oro** *(☎ 0781 335 55; Corso Colombo 72; singles/doubles with breakfast €44/68)* is a little further out, with comfortable rooms. Both hotels have good restaurants with full meals from around €18.

For food supplies, the **produce market** *(Via Gramsci; open 8am-1pm Mon-Sat)* is slightly uphill from the tourist office and the

SISA supermarket *(Via dei Cappuccini)* is in a small street just opposite the train station. There are numerous **pastry shops**, **take-aways** and **grocery shops** in the shopping area around Via Martini and Via Azuni in the *centro storico*. **Bar Capocabana** *(Via Gramsci 4)* is a friendly place for a drink and a snack.

Il **Medievale** *(Via Musio 21; meals from €21)*, off Corso Matteotti in the *centro storico*, is an elegant restaurant and one of Iglesias' best. **Italia 2** *(Via Valverde 54; pizzas from €4.20, full meals from €18; closed Tues afternoon)*, 400m downhill from Piazza Q Sella, serves simple pizzas or tasty regional dishes.

Getting There & Away Ferrovie Meridionali Sarde (FMS; ☎ 0781 3 28 00, 🅆 www.ferroviemeridionalisarde.it), Via Crocefisso 92, buses leave from the main bus terminal in Cagliari (€3.50, one hour, around 10 per day) and arrive at Via Oristano, one block south of the tourist office.

Hourly trains also leave from Cagliari (€3.70 plus €2.60 per bike, 50 minutes).

Iglesias is a relatively easy 55km ride from Cagliari. Head north past the airport and turn left just before Assemini onto the secondary road running parallel to and south of the busy and fast SS130.

THE RIDE
Day 1: Iglesias to Buggerru
2–3½ hours, 34.2km

Day 1 is quite short, leaving plenty of time to enjoy some magnificent stretches of unsullied coastline and marvel at the ruins from mining endeavours of centuries past.

Once off the Iglesias–Sant'Antioco road (8km), any concerns about traffic quickly dissipate as the route heads north on a lovely quiet road, lolling and bobbing its way past pristine white beaches and imposing cliffs. Stop for a swim at **Fontanamare** (11km), which has a **pizzeria-ristorante** on the beachfront. Just beyond **Nebida** (14.5km), the aptly named Pan di Zucchero (Sugar Loaf), an enormous 132m-high mass of pure white limestone, looms above the sea.

Set in a bay below towering grey cliffs, **Masua** (17.7km) is just off the main route. The side trip to its small **beach** offers great views out to Pan di Zucchero and across the bay to the ancient **Porto Flavia**, a mining facility carved directly into the cliff face. It involves a 2km descent from 130m, but any urge for a quick dip may be tempered by fears of the monster waiting back on the main route, a 2.6km lung-busting climb over the pass from Masua – the sign says it all: 'average gradient 13%'!

Cala Domestica (27.3km) is a stunning, secluded bay lapped by emerald waters, and makes a very easy and worthwhile side trip. A short tunnel to the right of the beach accesses another pristine cove. Other than a dusty car park, it has no facilities and the beach is only accessible on foot – without a bike. A little lateral thinking is required to find a secure place to lock up.

Buggerru
Set within the natural walls of a steep valley, Buggerru (buh-jeh-ruh) is a quiet Mediterranean delight. This little seaside town's origins date back to around 1860 when it was established to serve a thriving zinc- and lead-mining industry. Production reached its peak in the early 20th century when the population swelled to more than 12,000. A gradual decline in mining activity from around 1940 onwards saw many

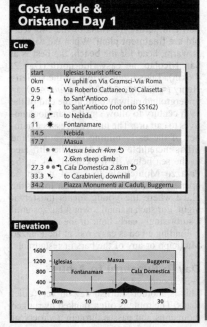

Costa Verde & Oristano – Day 1

Cue

start	Iglesias tourist office
0km	W uphill on Via Gramsci-Via Roma
0.5 ↰	Via Roberto Cattaneo, to Calasetta
2.9 ↑	to Sant'Antioco
4 ↑	to Sant'Antioco (not onto SS162)
8 ↰	to Nebida
11 ✳	Fontanamare
14.5	Nebida
17.7	Masua
••	Masua beach 4km ↷
▲	2.6km steep climb
27.3 ••↰	Cala Domestica 2.8km ↷
33.3 ↘	to Carabinieri, downhill
34.2	Piazza Monumenti ai Caduti, Buggerru

Elevation

move away and today the town harbours only around 1300 permanent inhabitants.

While the main preoccupation these days is trying to attract the valuable tourist dollar, there's little evidence of crass development. The atmosphere is relaxed, and the people are warm, friendly and welcoming.

Information All shops and services, including a bank with an ATM, are on Via Roma, the main drag running straight down the hill from the coast road to the port. There's very little in the way of tourist infrastructure – the Pro Loco (☎ 0781 5 45 22), Via Roma 17, only opens in high summer, but the Palazzo Municipio (town hall; ☎ 0781 5 40 23), Via Roma 53, is open 7.30am to 2pm Monday to Saturday. The staff is happy to offer information on places of interest or to help find a bed in a private home. Any of the bars or supermarkets in town can also help in finding a cheap bed. Expect to pay around €20 per night. There are plenty of places to free-camp on the road south of town.

Things to See & Do There are plenty of **off-road trails** in the rugged inland hills to explore by mountain bike or on foot, but perhaps the best way to enjoy Buggerru is to kick back and relax. Stroll down to the port and peruse the ruins of the 140-year-old **ore treatment plant**. When the weather is warm, head for the **beach**; the best is at **San Nicolao**, an easy ride north (Day 2, 4.6km). Take a guided tour of the **Galleria Henry** (☎ 339 484 66 40; open July-Aug), an underground railway built at the end of the 19th century to allow small steam locomotives to cart ore. The tunnel accesses a number of the early mining excavations and offers incredible views down the cliff face to the sea below. If it's closed, ask at the Palazzo Municipale to see if it can be opened. For nightlife, **La Baia da Tore** is the place where the young locals muster at night. For such a small town, it buzzes until a surprisingly early hour of the morning.

Finding a bed is easy. Ask at the Palazzo Municipo or any of the bars or restaurants.

Day 2: Buggerru to Arbus
2–3½ hours, 33.2km
This is another shortish day on very quiet roads. The route is often flanked by rugged mountains and passes through a variety of terrain from open sandy beaches to high rolling plains dotted with tracts of cork oak. Other than the hard 7.2km climb to the 492m **Passo Bidderdi** there isn't a great deal of hard work involved. The only services available on route are at the small village of **Portixeddu** (6.9km; also written 'Portisceddu'), nestled in a small bay 500m off the main road. There are a couple of beachfront **bar-restaurants** and a **hotel** and **camping ground** nearby. The 9km side trip from Portixeddu to the windswept promontory at **Capo Pecora** involves a hard climb in both directions to 115m, an easier task if heavy bags are left at one of the obliging restaurants. It's worth the effort for the views alone and, weather permitting, offers good snorkelling possibilities.

An early departure from Buggerru should also leave plenty of time to reach the day's end at Arbus. Unload, and ride out to **Montevecchio** (see Things to See & Do under Arbus on the following page).

Arbus
The small town of Arbus has always relied on agriculture and grazing, but the mining

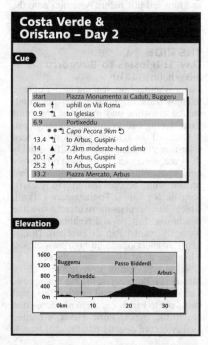

Costa Verde & Oristano – Day 2

Cue

start	Piazza Monumento ai Caduti, Buggeru
0km ↑	uphill on Via Roma
0.9 ↰	to Iglesias
6.9	Portixeddu
●●↰	Capo Pecora 9km ↻
13.4 ↰	to Arbus, Guspini
14 ▲	7.2km moderate-hard climb
20.1 ↗	to Arbus, Guspini
25.2 ↑	to Arbus, Guspini
33.2	Piazza Mercato, Arbus

Elevation

boom of the 19th century signalled a new era of prosperity. Production peaked after WWII until a gradual decline in profitability led to total mine closures in the 1970s. Today, Arbus strives to attract tourists, overseeing and promoting not only the areas of natural beauty like the Costa Verde and the wilderness areas of Monte Arcuentu, but also the heritage left by 150 years of mining – what the Sardinians call *arceologia industriale* (industrial archaeology).

Information The main road through town is Via Repubblica and most services can be found scattered along it. The small Pro Loco (☎ 070 9 75 62 81) is at No 132, uphill from the church of San Sebastiano. If the tourist office is closed the president of the Pro Loco can usually be found in his bar at No 62. Banco di Napoli, downhill at No 53, has an ATM.

Things to See & Do Down from central Piazza Mercato, the **Museo del Coltello Sardo** (☎ 070 975 92 20; ⓦ *www.coltelleriarbu resa.com; Via Roma 15*) is a celebration of Sardinia's long tradition of producing fine knives. Established by master knife craftsman Paolo Pusceddu, it houses a collection of superbly crafted knives of every conceivable shape and size, and the tools and equipment that have been used to hand manufacture them over the centuries. The museum also boasts the largest knife in the world, 3.35m in length and weighing in at a hefty 80kg!

The abandoned 150-year-old **Montevecchio mining complex** (☎ 070 97 25 37; ⓦ *www.europroject.it/montevecchio*) is an easy and rewarding 14km return trip. Head up Via Repubblica to the pass and take the small signposted road to the left. Detailed maps with historical information (in Italian and English) on the entire mining area from Montevecchio to Piscinas are available from the Pro Loco or from Hotel Meridiana.

Places to Stay & Eat The only accommodation in town is **Hotel Meridiana** (☎ 070 975 82 83; Via Repubblica 172; B&B €36.50, half-board €46.50), but fortunately it is a very good one. It has large, well-appointed rooms, many with balconies and great views. This is a friendly, modern, family-run establishment with a good ristorante-pizzeria.

Pick up supplies from the **ISA supermarket** (Via Repubblica 163-165) and satisfy sweet cravings at **Paradiso del Dolce** (Via Repubblica 77), the pasticceria opposite the church.

Ristorante Sa Lolla (Via Libertà 225) is one of Arbus' best eating options, with good pasta and pizzas, and full meals for €25.

Day 3: Arbus to Oristano
5–8 hours, 79.7km
Day 3 offers a little off-road adventure, more superb deserted coastline viewed from equally deserted roads and the opportunity to ride what may be the longest stretches of uninterrupted flat road in Sardinia.

SARDINIA

After retracing the last 8km of Day 2, the route passes through (and literally under in the case of the old mine management building!) the eerie mining ghost town of **Ingurtosu** (12.1km). This signals the start of the loose gravel section that descends to Piscinas and the Costa Verde, maintaining the south bank of the rather toxic looking Rio Naracauli. A slow and steady pace here will ensure a safe passage. As the road nears the dunes area there are also a few short, soft sand sections, where walking the bike through may be the most upright option.

The 3.4km return side trip to **Piscinas** (19.3km) arrives at a wide beach and vast protected area of dunes, in places reaching almost 200m in height. Other than the restaurant at **Le Dune**, a hotel in a reconstructed mining building, there are no facilities whatsoever in the area.

Crossing the **Rio Piscinas** (19.3km) should present no dramas – it has a firm base, but check the depth if it's running fast and walk the bike through if necessary. Once you're back on the bitumen the road flows for more than 30km through the remote maquis-covered wilderness of the **Costa Verde**, punctuated only by the odd coastal hamlet or summer holiday village, some of which have **bars** or **ristoranti** open all year. There are any number places to stop and **swim**.

The left turn (onto the very narrow road that accesses the even narrower causeway to the tiny fishing village of **Marceddi** is not signposted and is easily missed. It comes immediately after the small bay close to the left verge. The long, straights of the pancake-flat road grid on the **Arborea flatlands**, a swamp reclamation project initiated by Mussolini in the 1930s, are almost hypnotic after days of up-and-down on *strade nervose* (nervous roads). The final section into Oristano from Santa Giusta can be busy, but is easily navigated.

Oristano

Proud capital of the province of the same name, Oristano is believed to have been founded sometime in the 11th century by the people of Tharros, who abandoned their ancient coastal town and headed inland in search of more secure lodgings. It grew to prominence in the 14th century, particularly under the *giudicessa* (queen-judge) Eleonora d'Arborea, who opposed the Spanish occupation of the island and drew up a body of laws known as the Carta de Logu, a progressive legal code which was eventually enforced throughout the island.

Today, Oristano is the commercial hub of a thriving agricultural industry and an important trading port. Its historic centre, rich in architectural monuments, is a fine showcase

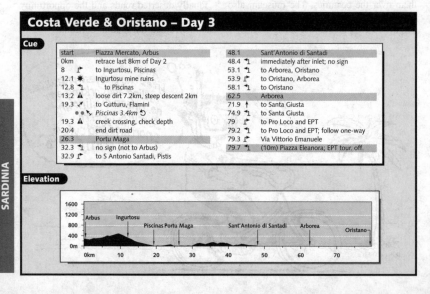

Costa Verde & Oristano – Day 3

Cue

start	Piazza Mercato, Arbus		48.1	Sant'Antonio di Santadi
0km	retrace last 8km of Day 2		48.4 ↰	immediately after inlet; no sign
8 ↱	to Ingurtosu, Piscinas		53.1 ↰	to Arborea, Oristano
12.1 ✳	Ingurtosu mine ruins		53.9 ↱	to Oristano, Arborea
12.8 ↰	to Piscinas		58.1 ↰	to Oristano
13.2 ⚠	loose dirt 7.2km, steep descent 2km		62.5	Arborea
19.3 ↙	to Gutturu, Flamini		71.9 ↑	to Santa Giusta
● ● ↖	*Piscinas 3.4km* ↺		74.9 ↰	to Santa Giusta
19.3 ⚠	creek crossing, check depth		79 ↱	to Pro Loco and EPT
20.4	end dirt road		79.2 ↰	to Pro Loco and EPT; follow one-way
26.3	Portu Maga		79.3 ↱	Via Vittorio Emanuele
32.3 ↰	no sign (not to Arbus)		79.7 ↰	(10m) Piazza Eleanora; EPT tour. off.
32.9 ↱	to S Antonio Santadi, Pistis			

Elevation

of its medieval heritage. The vast wetland areas of the surrounding bays and inlets are an important stopover to abundant species of migratory birds, the most significant being the *fenicotteri* (flamingos), which in summer can number up to 8000.

Information The EPT office (☎ 0783 3 68 31), Piazza Eleonora d'Arborea 19, has loads of information on the town and the province and will advise on accommodation. There's a Pro Loco office (☎ 0783 7 06 21) around the corner at Via Vittorio Emanuele 8. There are several banks with ATMs on and around Piazza Roma. Ciclo Sport (☎ 0783 7 27 14), Via Busachi 2, in the area east of Via Cagliari, is an excellent place for any spares or repairs.

Things to See & Do A look through the attractive *centro storico* is obligatory. Of significance are the 13th-century **Torre di Mariano II** (Piazza Roma), the 19th-century **statue** (Piazza Eleonora d'Arborea) of Oristano's *giudicessa* heroine, the neoclassical **Chiesa di San Francesco** (Via Sant'Antonio) and the **duomo** (Piazza del Duomo), built in the 13th century but completely remodelled in the 18th century. Also of interest is the 14th-century **Convento & Chiesa di Santa Chiara**, between Via Parpaglia and Via Garibaldi. **Museo Antiquarium Arborense** (Via Parpaglia) on Piazza Corrias contains interesting finds from the ancient Phoenician port of Tharros.

Sinis Peninsula about 15km east of Oristano makes an excellent day trip by bike. Between the sleepy villages of **Putzu Idu** and **Su Pallosu** at the northern end of the peninsula, are marshes which are home to vast numbers of pink flamingos and various other species of water birds. At the southernmost end of the peninsula is the village of **San Giovanni di Sinis**, with its 6th-century **Byzantine church**. Immediately south are the impressive Phoenician and Roman ruins of **Tharros**. The peninsula's best beach is at **Is Arutas**.

Places to Stay & Eat Oristano lacks good budget hotel options and the nearest camping grounds are at Marina di Torre Grande, about 7km west. Prices for camp sites jump in high season.

    Camping Torregrande (☎/fax 0783 2 22 28; Località Marina di Torre Grande; per person/tent €4.20/6.70; open June-Sept) and **Spinnaker** (☎ 0783 2 20 74; Località Marina di Torre Grande; per person/tent €5.20/2.10; open Apr-Oct) are the town's two camping options.

    Piccolo Hotel (☎ 0783 7 15 00; Via Martignano 19; singles/doubles with bathroom €41.50/51.70) is Oristano's cheapest deal, a pensione-style place with clean rooms and a central position. **Hotel ISA** (☎ 0783 36 01 01; Piazza Mariano 50; singles/doubles with breakfast €50/83) has excellent rooms and a prime location. **Hotel Mistral** (☎ 0783 21 03 99; Via XX Settembre; singles/doubles with breakfast €54.50/83) is Oristano's four-star hotel. It's a bike-friendly, upmarket option.

    Agriturismo (farm stays) is another excellent accommodation option, with half-board in a double room costing around €31 per person. Contact the **Consorzio Agriturismo di Sardinia** (☎ 0783 7 39 54; e cas.agr iturismo@tiscalinet.it; Piazza Duomo 17).

    For food supplies, the **Vinci supermarket** and covered **produce market** are at Via Mazzini 54, between Piazza Roma and Piazza Mariano. The bakery/pasticceria **Nino Vacca** (Piazza Mannu) has sublime pastries. **Al Piatto Pronto** (Via Mazzini 21; meals & snacks from €4.20), just off Piazza Roma, is good for snacks and picnic dishes. **Trattoria del Teatro** (Via Parpaglia 11; seafood antipasto €6.20, pasta from €7.75; closed Sun) has a good selection of local wine and a cosy, comfortable setting. **Il Faro** (Via Bellini 25; full meals from €36.50; closed Sun) is one of Oristano's best (and most expensive) restaurants. Excellent food and service and an impressive local wine selection make this a top place for a special treat.

    Socialise over a Guinness at **Dubb Linn**, an Irish-style pub hidden away in the backstreets of the centro in Vico Antonio Garau.

Getting There & Away Buses are cheaper and more convenient than trains, but less frequent. Four PANI buses leave daily for Cagliari (€6, 1½ hours) and Sassari (for connections to the start of Mare e Monte ride, €7.20, two hours). They depart from Bar Blu (Via Lombardia 30), off Via Tirso about 500m west of Piazza Roma.

    All trains on the main north–south line stop in Oristano. The station is in Piazza Ungheria, about 1km east of Piazza Mariano along Via Vittorio Veneto. There are trains about every two hours to both Cagliari (€4.50 plus €2.60 per bike, one hour) and Sassari (for connections to the start of Mare e Monte ride, €7.60 plus €2.60 per bike, 2½ to three hours), and almost hourly to Abbassanta/Ghilarza (start of the Gennargentu ride, €2.20 plus €2.60 per bike, 30 to 40 minutes).

Barbagia & Gennargentu

Duration	4 days
Distance	293.4
Difficulty	hard
Start	Ghilarza
End	Nuoro

This arduous four-day jaunt through Sardinia's central–east region takes in the island's high country, circling the mountains of the Gennargentu, dominated by Monte La Marmora (at 1834m, the island's highest peak), and tracing the SS125 through the awesome massifs and gorges of the Parco Nazionale del Golfo. Stopovers in the lazy coastal Meccas of Arbatax and Cala Gonone are the ideal places to recuperate after the hard climbs of Days 2 and 3. The roads are uncluttered and boast an almost blemish-free surface; they cling to rugged mountainsides, swoop down long, steep valleys, meander through dense green forests, hug the banks of deep lakes and visit picturesque villages. This is some of Sardinia's most remote territory – some call it the 'real' Sardinia for the lack of major tourist development and the open and friendly nature of the people.

PLANNING
When to Ride
With some mountain sections at altitudes over 1000m, snow and ice can be a factor. April to June and September and October are ideal; warm enough to allow beach days and comfortable passage over the mountains.

ACCESS TOWN
Ghilarza
Ghilarza is a small town of around 4500 people that sits just west of Sardinia's mountainous heart. It is the larger of three towns (the others being Abbassanta and Norbello) that have grown to the point where they virtually merge; these 'triple-towns' are perched on the western rim of a broad volcanic high-plain that provided the basalt for the construction of many of their striking stone buildings.

Information Ghilarza's primary importance in this ride is its proximity to the main rail line at Abbassanta, making it an effective gateway to the fabulous cycling territory of the Gennargentu to the east. With little tourist infrastructure it has a Pro Loco (☎/fax 0785 52396; w www.sardiniacnos .it/ghilarza/), Piazza A. Gramsei 3, but only one fairly average hotel. Most riders will be keen saddle up and head into the hills.

The main thoroughfare, Corso Umberto, has a couple of banks (with ATMs) and supermarkets within easy reach. Ciclomania (☎ 0785 52768), Via Nessi 22, is a surprisingly good bike shop with spares and repair facilities for road and mountain bikes.

Things to See & Do Visit **Casa Gramsci** (☎ 0785 5 41 64; Corso Umberto 37), a museum established in the home of Antonio Gramsci, one of the founders of Italy's communist party; he was imprisoned by Mussolini's fascist regime until his death in 1937.

Places to Stay & Eat Your only hotel choice is **Su Cantaru** (☎ 0785 5 45 23; Via

Aah! Snake!

Grinding hard up a steep backroad high in Sardinia's Gennargentu, a snake suddenly slithered unavoidably into my path. As both wheels bump-bumped right over it, I did as any self-preserving Australian would do, feet snapping from the pedals like lightning and heading skyward, accompanied by a loud and involuntary scream. The cause of this unbridled terror was a green reptile about 1m in length whose wriggle quickly turned to blur as it hurtled to the sanctuary of roadside bushes, its shock seemingly even greater than my own. Relating the tale to an elderly Sardinian woman that evening induced roars of laughter – the *biscia*, it seems, is one of Sardinia's totally harmless reptilian inhabitants. Wish I could say the same about some of its Antipodean cousins!

Quentin Frayne

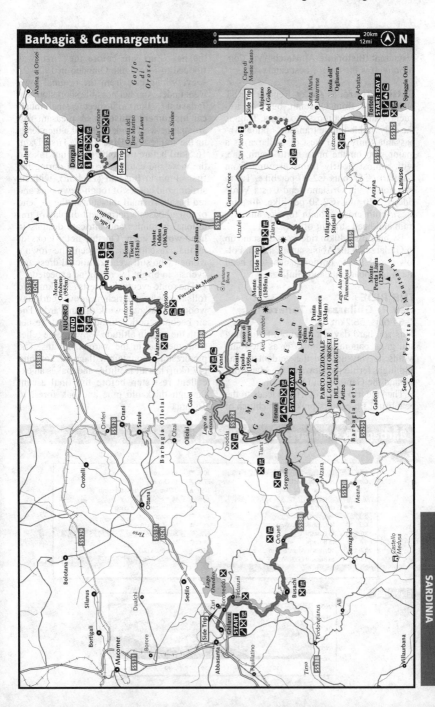

Monsignor Zucca 2; singles/doubles €33.57/ 54.23). It has average digs with an average restaurant. **Ristorante Al Marchi** *(Via Concezione 4)* is the town's best eatery.

Getting There & Away Regular ARST buses arrive from Oristano, but stop frequently and take almost two hours. Train is the only viable public transport option. Abbassanta (only 2km west of Ghilarza) is a major stop on the main north–south line, with almost hourly trains arriving from Cagliari (€67 plus €2.60 per bike, 1½ to two hours) via Oristano (end Costa Verde ride, €2.20 plus €2.50 per bike, 40 minutes), both close enough to take an early train and head straight off on Day 1.

By bike it's a 40km ride from Oristano up to Ghilarza on the Abbassanta Plateau. Follow the SS388 to Fordongianus, then head north to Abbassanta and Ghilarza.

THE RIDE
Day 1: Ghilarza to Tonara
3–6 hours, 56.2km
This is a hard day with plenty of climbing and great panoramas on offer as the route winds its way up into the verdant forests and high, fertile meadows of the Mandrolisai and the Gennargentu mountains.

The side trip to **Zuri** (4.1km) leads to the beautiful 13th-century pink basalt **church of San Pietro**. The work of Lombard, Anselmo da Como, it was relocated brick-by-brick to the new Zuri site before the Tirso was flooded to form Lake Omodeo in 1922–23 – everything else from the original town went under. Another possible short stop is at **Tadasuni** (5.3km) to inspect its small **musical instrument museum**. A pleasant roll around the west bank of the lake then leads to the impressive **Diga Tirso** (Tirso Dam, 16.5km) before the route heads up. Take in the view and catch your breath during the first climb in **Busachi** (20.4km), with its striking old houses of rough-hewn pink and red basalt. A small museum at the top end of town houses a permanent display of traditional costumes and intricate designs in hand-woven linen. On this note, looks of mutual fascination between the town's women who still wear traditional dress and cyclists in bright Lycra can be expected.

The route eventually crests (32.2km) and rolls through some rich meadows, cork-oak woods and a latticework of vineyards. The air becomes noticeably cooler and fresher with the gain in altitude – a welcome relief from the heat in the warmer months. The picturesque mountain village of **Sorgono** (47.6km) has all facilities and makes an excellent rest stop before the final ascent through thick old pine and oak forest to Tonara.

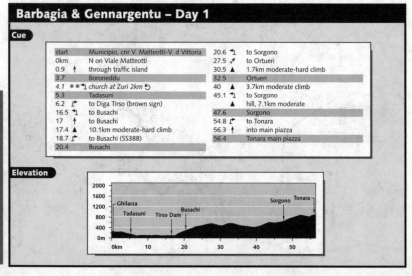

Barbagia & Gennargentu – Day 1

Cue

start	Municipio, cnr V. Matteotti-V. d Vittoria	20.6		to Sorgono
0km	N on Viale Matteotti	27.5		to Ortueri
0.9	through traffic island	30.5 ▲		1.7km moderate-hard climb
3.7	Boroneddu	32.5		Ortueri
4.1 ● ● church at Zuri 2km ↻		40 ▲		3.7km moderate climb
5.3	Tadasuni	45.1		to Sorgono
6.2	to Diga Tirso (brown sign)	▲		hill, 7.1km moderate
16.5	to Busachi	47.6		Sorgono
17	to Busachi	54.8		to Tonara
17.4 ▲	10.1km moderate-hard climb	56.3		into main piazza
18.7	to Busachi (SS388)	56.4		Tonara main piazza
20.4	Busachi			

Elevation

Tonara

At around 950m, Tonara is one of Sardinia's highest towns and is often under snow during the island's colder winters. Perched like a sentinel on the southern slopes of Monte Muggianeddu (1467m), this picturesque town serves as a commercial centre for the surrounding region and proudly maintains its centuries-old traditions, most notably the hand manufacture of Sardinia's jangling *campanacci* (herd-animal bells) and the prized *torrone* di Tonara, recognised as Italy's best.

The town itself is divided into the four distinct *rioni* (quarters/precincts) – Arasulè, Su Pranu, Toneri and Teliseri – with several hundred vertical metres separating the highest from the lowest. The hillsides above the town are covered with thick forests of native chestnut, hazelnut, walnut, cherry, holly and numerous species of oak, and in spring and autumn the fabulous and flavoursome *porcini* mushrooms – some of which can grow to 1kg – are gathered there.

Information There is no tourist office in Tonara, but the amicable president of the Pro Loco association, Mr Gabriele Casula (☎ 0784 6 36 47), can be contacted for information on services, places of interest and things to do and see in and around the town. The Comune (☎ 0784 6 38 23), Viale della Regione 8, is also a good point of reference. There is a bank with ATM on Via Sant'Antonio in the town centre. Sulis Gomma (Via Monsignor Tore 18), on the main road into town, may be able to supply a tyre or a tube.

Things to See & Do The hills above the town offer exceptional **walking** and **mountain biking** possibilities; for general information contact the **Caserma di Vigilanza Ambientale** (☎ 0784 6 36 16; *Via Dante*); for cycling-specific information ask at the Comune for Pierluigi La Croce, an avid cyclist with a vast knowledge of the area.

Don't leave Tonara without popping into one of the **torrone factories** to pick up some of the scrumptious nougat that has made this town famous; it's also the ultimate pick-me-up when cycling legs seem spent. There are two main commercial producers: **Fabbrica Pili** *(Via Vitttorio Emanuele 68)* and **Pruneddu Torronificio** *(Via Ing Porru 5)*. Tonara takes its *torrone* heritage very seriously – the town's annual feast day, held in late March–early April, even bears its name – **La Sagra del Torrone**.

There are a number of **campanacci workshops** where hand-manufacture of the distinctive animal bells can be viewed; ask any local for directions.

Places to Stay & Eat For such a small centre, accommodation options are excellent and offer great value. **Ostello della Gioventù Il Castagneto** (☎ *0784 61 00 05;* e *ilcastagneto@tiscalinet.it; Via Muggianeddu 2; camping per person €5.20, 6-8–bed rooms per person €10.50, pizzas €2.60-6.20, pasta from €5.20)*, 1km up a rather steep hill from centre, offers a lovely panoramic aspect with terrace and evening ristorante-pizzeria.

Locanda del Muggianeddu (☎/fax *0784 6 34 20; Via Monsignor Tore; singles/doubles with bathroom €18/34)* is a pleasant pensione-style establishment with four rooms. It has an award-winning restaurant downstairs serving excellent local cuisine. Full meals range from €10.50 to around €21.

Hotel Belvedere 1 (☎ *0784 637 56; Via Belvedere 24; singles/doubles €26/47)* has great views and clean rooms. It's a friendly family-run hotel, serving excellent local cuisine in a downstairs restaurant.

Hotel Belvedere 2 (☎ *0784 61 00 54;* e *hotelbelvedere@tiscali.it; Via Monsignor Tore 39; singles/doubles/triples €36.50/52/67.50, half/full board €41.50/52)* is the high quality sister to Belvedere 1, offering large, very comfortable rooms with balconies and all facilities, and a restaurant serving fine local dishes.

Self-caterers will find everything they need in and around the small centre.

Day 2: Tonara to Tortoli/Arbatax
6–10 hours, 103.6km

This is a long day on quiet roads covering myriad terrains, from shady forests and clear mountain lakes to high, rugged, treeless plains and vast coastal bowls. The kilometres spent climbing are more than offset by some long descents, especially the unforgettable drop at day's end.

Dropping out of Tonara, the route hugs the west side of the River Tino valley as it meanders and descends through oak and chestnut woods to **Lago di Gusana** (25km), passing through the small hamlets of **Tiana**

SARDINIA

(10.5km) and **Ovodda** (14.7km) along the way; both have small **supermarkets** and a couple of **bars**. The pleasant public **rest areas** around the lake make an excellent place for a short break before the climbing begins. At 1000m **Fonni** (31.8km) is Sardinia's other high town. Stop for a sit-down lunch or pick up picnic supplies. There are several **bars**, **supermarkets**, **alimentari**, **ristoranti** and **pasticcerie** scattered along the main street. It's also the last water for some time, an essential commodity in hot conditions during the exposed climb up to the 1246m pass of **Arcu Correboi** (47.6km) and beyond. Traffic of any sort is rare on this old high-road (the new road hugs the valley floor and passes through a tunnel many hundreds of metres below). It isn't maintained and is quite rough in places; cows and goats roam freely so care should be taken on the long, fast descent.

After meeting the new road in the Calaresu river valley floor, the route heads up onto the southern rim of the vast, open high-plains of the northern Gennargentu. At the eastern edge below Monte Genziana (1505m) are the impressive nuraghic ruins of **Bau 'E Tanca** (70.4km), an easy 500m side trip – look for an unsigned gravel track on the left. The switchback descent into **Talana** (75.8km) hails the beginning of a scintillating 20km freefall – the road literally

drops off the edge of the Gennargentu as Sardinia's east coast explodes into view. The scene will take your breath away and the drop is surely the closest thing to riding the face of a 1000m wave! Be sure to keep one eye on the road – the allure of the spectacular panorama is strong indeed.

Tortoli/Arbatax

Set about 4km inland of Capo Bellavista, Tortoli is a bustling business town that becomes a bit of a summer haven for the tourists lured by the nearby beaches and a lively holiday scene. About 4km east is Capo Bellavista, with Arbatax (the major central east–coast port for ferries from Civitavecchia and Cagliari) to its immediate north and Tortoli's other resort 'suburb', Porto Frailis, to the south.

Information The Pro Loco tourist office (☎/fax 0782 62 28 24, **w** www.prolocotortoliarbatax.it) is at Via Mazzini 7. It has excellent maps and loads of information in English on the town and area. It also has an office (☎ 0782 66 76 90) on the Arbatax esplanade, Via Lungomare. There are several banks with ATMs in and around the main centre of Tortoli. The large Porra hardware (Via Baccasara), in the industrial zone about 1km east of town, has only very basic budget bike spares.

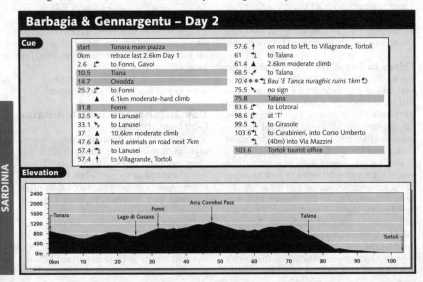

Barbagia & Gennargentu – Day 2

Cue

start	Tonara main piazza		57.6 ↑	on road to left, to Villagrande, Tortoli
0km	retrace last 2.6km Day 1		61 ↰	to Talana
2.6 ↱	to Fonni, Gavoi		61.4 ▲	2.6km moderate climb
10.5	Tiana		68.5 ↙	to Talana
14.7	Ovodda		70.4 ●●↰	Bau 'E Tanca nuraghic ruins 1km ↻
25.7 ↰	to Fonni		75.5 ↘	no sign
▲	6.1km moderate-hard climb		75.8	Talana
31.8	Fonni		83.6 ↱	to Lotzorai
32.5 ↘	to Lanusei		98.6 ↱	at 'T'
33.1 ↘	to Lanusei		99.5 ↰	to Girasole
37 ▲	10.6km moderate climb		103.6 ↰	to Carabinieri, into Corso Umberto
47.6 ⚠	herd animals on road next 7km		↰	(40m) into Via Mazzini
57.4 ↰	to Lanusei		103.6	Tortoli tourist office
57.4 ↑	to Villagrande, Tortoli			

Elevation

Things to See & Do Tortolì lacks major attractions, but the lovely stretch of sandy coastline to the east is within easy cycling distance. Stroll around the **port** at Arbatax, with its spectacular backdrop of red granite cliffs, or take a dip on its long white **beach**. There are also excellent beaches at **Porto Frailis**, **San Gemiliano** and further south at **Orri**. The tourist office has information on **boat trips** and **guided diving**.

Places to Stay & Eat Other than camping, there are no good budget options and all prices rise in mid summer. **Camping Telis** (☎ 0782 66 71 40; Località Porto Frailis; per person/site €6.20/6.20), set in a protected bay, enjoys a very pleasant beach location. **Locanda da Angelo** (☎/fax 0782 62 35 33; Via Piemonte 15; singles/doubles €34/55) offers average digs in a convenient, central location, with a moderately priced pizzeria-trattoria downstairs. **Hotel la Perla** (☎ 0782 66 78 00; Viale Europa, Arbatax; singles/doubles with breakfast €44/68) is a pleasant, low-key establishment in a quiet location close to good beaches and it has modern, clean rooms. **Hotel Victoria** (☎ 0782 62 34 57; W www.hotel-victoria.it; Via Monsignor Virgilio 72; singles/doubles with breakfast €60/85) is a very comfortable upmarket hotel in central location with an excellent restaurant.

For self-caterers, try the big **Standa** supermarket (cnr Via Marmilia & Via Piemonte), two streets south of Via Monsignor Virgilio. There's a large **bakery** a few doors down from Hotel Victoria in Via Monsignor Virgilio. Sample pastry delights at **Pasticceria del Corso** (Corso Umberto 56), 50m from the Pro Loco.

Try **Locanda da Angelo** (pizzas from €4.30) for budget meals. Tortolì's best dining is at **Hotel Victoria** (meals from €21) where seafood is a speciality. There are a number of reasonably priced eateries serving average fare in Arbatax, all within easy reach of the port area.

Day 3: Tortolì to Dorgali

3½–6½ hours, 65.7km

This is an 'up-and-over' day spent entirely on the SS125 (also known as the Orientale Sarda). This section is renowned as one of Sardinia's most panoramic roads and it's not hard to see why – it's a wild, rugged landscape and there isn't a single kilometre that fails to impress with stunning, uninterrupted panoramas unfolding from the moment the road begins to head upwards at Lotzorai (5.2km). While the long ascent to more than 1000m from sea level is hard work, once beyond Baunei at 400m (15.4km) the gradient and the effort ease noticeably. From Baunei, consider a very worthwhile stopover or side trip to explore the **Golgo region** (see the boxed text 'Guided Excursions' below).

Guided Excursions

From Baunei into the Golgo

Cooperativa Goloritzé (☎ 0782 61 05 99, E goloritze@tiscalinet.it) is a well-organised excursion company, run by young locals, offering guided treks in the magical Golgo area – on foot, horseback or by donkey. Its base is on the high plain, about 8km from Baunei via a very steep road to the north of the town centre (15.4km, Day 3), indicated by a sign to the church of San Pietro. The coop is located in a group of low buildings (visible from the road), accessed via a road to the left about 300m before you reach the church. It can also organise pick-ups from Baunei.

From Sa Domu E s'Orcu & Urzulei

For inexpensive and efficient guided tours and walking in the Urzulei area call **Società Gorropu** (☎ 0782 64 92 82, E francesco murru@virgilio.it), a group of young expert guides based at Sa Domu E s'Orcu (38.1km, Day 3). They can help you make the exciting descent into the Gola di Gorropu or explore the area's fascinating underground caves and rivers. This company also organises treks in other parts of the Barbagia and can offer help with renting rooms in private homes in Urzulei – an excellent way to get a feel for the real Sardinia. Expect to pay around €15.50 to €21 per night.

From Dorgali

Coop Ghivine (☎/fax 0784 9 67 21, W www.ghivine.com), Via Montebello 5, is a highly professional outfit that organises guided walks or horse trekking in the Supramonte and treks to the Gola di Gorropu or the Codula di Luna.

SARDINIA

Just left of the road at 24km there's a shady pine forest with picnic and barbecue facilities – a path leads to a **small pinnacle** offering unbeatable 360 degree views – an ideal place for a break. Fill up bidons at the signposted *sorgente* (spring; 27km).

The only semblance of flat road encountered is a 4km traverse of the northern rim of the vast Gennargentu high plains (31km), an open, rolling meadow bordered by rugged peaks where horses, cows, sheep, goats and enormous wild pigs graze lazily under the watchful eye of their herders. **Sa Domu e S'Orcu**, a bar/ristorante at **Passo Genna Croce** (38.1km), offers a welcome respite from the day's toil. For those wishing to explore this fascinating region in depth, it's also the base for Società Gorropu (see the boxed text 'Guided Excursions').

From the day's high point of 1017m at **Passo Genna Silana** (43km), it's a superb downhill roll all the way to Dorgali. The road clings high to the steep east walls of the spectacular **Gola di Gorropu** (Gorropu gorge).

Dorgali & Cala Gonone

Whether visitors choose to stay in Dorgali or Cala Gonone will probably be determined by the desire for sea or mountains. Dorgali is dominated totally by the Supramonte to its south, the vast 500 sq km high plain (around 1000m above sea level) and the awesome Gola di Gorropu gorge that cuts deeply into it. Opportunities for excursions on foot abound – guided walks, from day trips to week-long excursions come highly recommended (see the boxed text 'Guided Excursions' on p347).

The coastline that extends south from Cala Gonone, the sleepy fishing village turned coastal resort town immediately east of Dorgali, is truly exceptional, even by Sardinian standards. Much of this vast, unspoilt stretch of coast is accessible only on foot or by boat. It's a seemingly endless line of limestone cliffs and crags dotted with caves of every dimension, interrupted only by pristine beaches nestled in secluded bays. It's a 6km ride into or out of Cala Gonone or there's always the option of catching the bus with your bike.

Information Dorgali's main street, Via Lamarmora, is one way and the town can only be entered from the lower, western end. The helpful staff at the Pro Loco (☎/fax 0784 9 62 43), Via Lamarmora 108, can provide maps and information on accommodation and the vast array of natural and archaeological wonders in the area, including particulars on guided excursions. There's also a tourist office (☎ 0784 9 36 96) at Cala Gonone open from April to October.

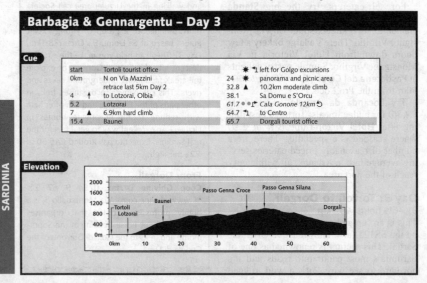

Barbagia & Gennargentu – Day 3

Cue

start	Tortoli tourist office		✳ ⌐	left for Golgo excursions	
0km	N on Via Mazzini		24	✳	panorama and picnic area
	retrace last 5km Day 2		32.8	▲	10.2km moderate climb
4	↑ to Lotzorai, Olbia		38.1		Sa Domu e S'Orcu
5.2	Lotzorai		61.7 ● ● ⌐		Cala Gonone 12km ↻
7	▲ 6.9km hard climb		64.7 ⌐		to Centro
15.4	Baunei		65.7		Dorgali tourist office

Elevation

Tortoli, Lotzorai, Baunei, Passo Genna Croce, Passo Genna Silana, Dorgali

Banco di Sardegna and Banca Commerciale Italiana, both with ATMs, are on Via Lamarmora. For limited bike spares, try Ditta Pier Paolo Melis (☎ 0784 9 62 30), Via Lamarmora 74. Six daily ARST buses run between Dorgali and Cala Gonone. The bus stop in Dorgali is on Via Lamarmora, in front of the post office.

Things to See & Do In Dorgali, visit the small **archaeological museum** (☎ 0784 961 13; Via Lamarmora) with finds from digs in the Nuraghic and other sites in the area.

By far the most rewarding way to experience this fascinating region is on a **guided excursion**. See the boxed text 'Guided Excursions' on p347 for details.

From Cala Gonone's small port, you can catch a boat to the spectacular entrance of **Grotta del Bue Marino** (Cave of the Monk Seal), one of the last habitats of the rare monk seal, which has not been sighted for some years. A guide will take you on a 1km walk to see vast caves with stalagmites, stalactites and lakes. There are also boats to the beautiful **Cala Luna**, a stunning, isolated cove accessible only on foot or by boat. For information on all boat trips contact Nuovo Consorzio Trasporti Marittimi (☎ 0784 9 33 05), Via Vespucci, Cala Gonone.

There is a **walking track** along the coast linking Cala Gonone and **Cala Luna**. The track starts at Cala Fuili, which is about 3.5km west of Cala Ganone. It's then about 4km between the two coves on rocky terrain, but with breathtaking coastal views; the walk takes about 1½ hours one way. You can organise with the boat operators at Cala Ganone to be dropped off at Cala Luna and walk back to Cala Gonone or to be picked up at Cala Luna at a specified time.

Places to Stay & Eat Accommodation and dining choices in Dorgali are a bit slim.

Hotel S'Adde (☎ 0784 9 44 12; ᴡ www .hotelsadde.it; Via Concordia 38; singles/doubles/triples €46/76/82) is a good, centrally located hotel with clean rooms and a decent pizzeria/ristorante downstairs. It can also organise walking and 4WD excursions in the Sopramonte, with traditional lunches.

For self-caterers, there's a huge **SISA supermarket** at the bottom end of Via Lamarmora and several smaller stores located close to the centre. **Ristorante Colibri**

(Via Floris 7; full meals from €18) offers excellent regional dishes. Follow the signs from Via Lamarmora.

Cala Gonone offers far greater choice. Note that free-camping is strictly forbidden in the area.

Camping Cala Gonone (☎ 0784 931 65; ᴡ www.campingcalagonone.it; Via Collodi 1; per person €16, 4-bed bungalows €113; open June-Oct) is one of Sardinia's best camping grounds, with excellent facilities including a nice pool.

Piccolo Hotel (☎ 0784 9 32 32; Via Cristoforo Colombo; singles/doubles with bathroom €31/51) is near the port and has very pleasant rooms. **Hotel La Plaia** (☎/fax 0784 931 06; Via Collodi; singles/doubles €34/50) offers all mod cons and very comfortable rooms. **Pop Hotel** (☎ 0784 931 85; Via Marco Polo; singles/doubles €47/78), conveniently located at the port, has good accommodation and an attractive, inexpensive **restaurant**.

There are a couple of small **supermarkets** in the centre of town. **El Bocadillo** (Via Colombo 8; panini around €2), one street back from the port, is a hip bar/café that does excellent coffee and great panini. **Due Chiacchiere** (Via Acquadolce 13; pizzas from €5.20, full meals from €15.50) is a ristorante-pizzeria overlooking the sea near the port. **Ristorante Il Pescatore** (Via Marco Polo; full meals from €21), just near the port, specialises in fish and seafood.

Day 4: Dorgali to Nuoro
4–7 hours, 67.7km

The final day follows a fairly circuitous route to Nuoro and continues the trend for experiencing the rugged, natural beauty of the region, highlighted by the spectacular backdrop of the Sopramonte. While the small towns of Oliena, Orgosolo and Mamoiada lack major tourist facilities or sights, cycling through them offers the unique possibility to see how locals live in Sardinia's interior. Often regarded as quite guarded and insular, locals are far more likely to warm to travellers arriving under pedal-power.

The route drops quickly out of Dorgali, crossing the narrow Lago Cedrino before dropping to the valley floor at the Oliena river with the enormous pale-grey mass of Monte Sos Nidos (1349m) looming large beyond. Traffic between Dorgali and Oliena (21km) is light but fast-moving and the road lacks a good shoulder – from Oliena onward, roads are close to empty. The turnoff for Orgosolo on the far side of Oliena (22km) is easily missed.

After the meandering 8.2km climb out of Oliena through shady woods, the sudden sight of the Sopramonte's jagged escarpment 700m above as the road crests the pass at Cantoniere Iannas (30.2km) is simply breathtaking. The rocky, maquis-speckled terrain of the next valley is like another world, seemingly deserted but for Orgosolo, perched like a lonely eagle's nest high above and reached after a stiff climb from the Fiume Cedrino (36.6km).

Orgosolo (40.9km) became famous for its tradition of *banditismo* (banditry), immortalised by the 1963 Italian film *The Bandits of Orgosolo*, but not a locals' favourite subject. Also of interest are the **murals** decorating the facades of many of Orgosolo's buildings. Dating back to 1973, they originally reflected fairly extreme political views on international issues such as the Vietnam war, South African apartheid and the Palestinian question – these days the murals deal mainly with domestic social issues.

The road to Mamoiada remains high, traversing the oak woods and hayfields of the fertile Pratobello plateau, then sweeping through a lush valley of vineyards, crops and orchards – a welcome relief in warmer months from the persistent glare of the sun. Once beyond the sleepy mountain hamlet of **Mamoiada** (50.5km) and onto the superb, swooping 'old' road down to Nuoro (*quella vecchia tortuosa* – 'that twisty old one', as the locals call it with disdain), sighting a car would be rare indeed.

Nuoro

There isn't a lot to see and do in Nuoro, but it is a major transport hub and offers good possibilities for a speedy exit, if desired. The old centre of town is around Piazza delle Grazie, Corso Garibaldi and Via Italia, near the tourist office.

Information The EPT office (☎ 0784 3 00 83) is at Piazza Italia 8. There are also several banks with ATMs around Piazza Italia. For bike spares (mostly mountain bike), try Soddu Tonino (☎ 0784 20 07 50), Via della Resistenza, about 2km east of the centre.

Things to See While in town, you might as well take a look at the neoclassical **cattedrale di Santa Maria delle Neve** (*Piazza Santa Maria della Neve*) and the **monument and square** dedicated to the local poet Sebastiano Satta. **Museo della Vita e delle**

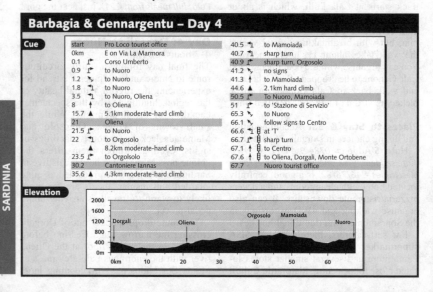

Barbagia & Gennargentu – Day 4

Cue					
start	Pro Loco tourist office		40.5 ↰	to Mamoiada	
0km	E on Via La Marmora		40.7 ↰	sharp turn	
0.1 ↱	Corso Umberto		40.9 ↱	sharp turn, Orgosolo	
0.9 ↱	to Nuoro		41.2 ↘	no signs	
1.2 ↘	to Nuoro		41.3 ↑	to Mamoiada	
1.8 ↰	to Nuoro		44.6 ▲	2.1km hard climb	
3.5 ↰	to Nuoro, Oliena		50.5 ↱	To Nuoro, Mamoiada	
8 ↑	to Oliena		51 ↱	to 'Stazione di Servizio'	
15.7 ▲	5.1km moderate-hard climb		65.3 ↘	to Nuoro	
21	Oliena		66.1 ↘	follow signs to Centro	
21.5 ↱	to Nuoro		66.6 ↰ ☐	at 'T'	
22 ↰	to Orgosolo		66.7 ↱ ☐	sharp turn	
▲	8.2km moderate-hard climb		67.1 ↑ ☐	to Centro	
23.5 ↱	to Orgolsolo		67.6 ↑ ☐	to Oliena, Dorgali, Monte Ortobene	
30.2	Cantoniere Iannas		67.7	Nuoro tourist office	
35.6 ▲	4.3km moderate-hard climb				

Elevation

Tradizioni Popolari Sardi (*Museum of the Life & Traditions of the Sardinian People;* ☎ *0784 24 29 00; Via Antonio Mereu 56*), south of the cathedral (up the hill behind it), is well worth a visit. It houses a magnificent collection of traditional costumes (many of which are still used during local festivals), jewellery, masks, textiles and musical instruments.

Places to Stay & Eat There are no real budget accommodation options in Nuoro. From the outside, **Hotel Grillo** (☎ *0784 386 78; Via Monsignor Melas 14; singles/doubles with bathroom €47.50/63*) is pretty ugly, but inside its rooms are pleasant. The **Hotel Paradiso** (☎ *0784 3 35 85; Via Aosta; singles/doubles with bathroom & breakfast €49/70*) is a better option than it seems, even if it's a little out of the centre. It has good, clean, quiet rooms.

Pick up food supplies at the **Emanuela market** (*Via Isonzo*), off Via Trieste just near Piazza Italia. There's also a great **grocery shop** (*Corso Garibaldi 168*), with a good **cheese shop** next door.

Caffè Venezia (*Via B Sassari 1; fruit juice €1.30, panini from €1.60*), diagonally opposite the tourist office on the corner of Piazza Italia, is good for a snack or light meal. **Pizzeria-Trattoria Il Rifugio** (*Vico del Pozzo 4; pizzas from €4.65*) is in a narrow street parallel to Via La Marmora in the old centre near Le Grazie. The pizzas are tasty and filling.

Getting There & Away Bus is the easiest transport option. Four PANI (☎ 0784 3 68 56) buses travel daily to Cagliari via Oristano (€11.70, 3½ hours) and to Sassari (connections to Mare e Monte ride, €7.50, 2½ hours) via Macomer (on the main north–south rail line). They leave from Via Brigata Sassari 15, about 100m south of Piazza Italia.

ARST (☎ 0784 29 41 73) has one direct bus daily to Cagliari (€12.40, 2½ hours), leaving from Viale Sardegna, about 1km southeast of the centre.

The train station is about a 20-minute walk from Piazza delle Grazie along Via La Marmora. Five Trenitalia trains connect with Macomer on the main north–south line (€6.90, 2¼ hours).

Travel Facts

TOURIST OFFICES
Local Tourist Offices

The offices most likely to have opening hours for passing tourists are either provincial or local. Their names and acronyms may differ, but the services are the same. Contact details for relevant offices are provided throughout this book.

A provincial office is called either an Ente Provinciale per il Turismo (EPT) or, more commonly, an Azienda di Promozione Turistica (APT). More often than not it has information about the province and town in which it's located. It is the office most likely to carry cycling trail maps for a large area, and details about outdoor activities and organisations.

Local offices come in two flavours: Informazioni e Assistenza ai Turisti (IAT) and Aziende Autonome di Soggiorno e Turismo (AAST). In very small communities, you may come across a Pro Loco office. In all cases, information will be restricted to local area accommodations, transport, cycling routes and services. Some sell maps and guidebooks, especially where cycling is popular. In larger towns you may find an after-hours accommodation contact kiosk displaying a range of establishments. A free telephone with which to check availability is sometimes part of the set-up.

Small information offices can sometimes be found in train stations (particularly the large ones). Towns with no information centre at all provide question-answering services (and often printed information) through the *municipio*.

Tourist Offices Abroad

The Ente Nazionale Italiano per il Turismo (ENIT), or Italian State Tourist Board, has an extensive website at ⓦ www.enit.it (and, in English, ⓦ www.italiantourism.com) and offices in several countries, including:

Australia (☎ 02-9262 1666, fax 9262 1677, ⓔ enitour@ihug.com.au) Level 26, 44 Market St, Sydney, NSW 2000
Canada (☎ 416-925 4882, fax 415-925 4799, ⓔ enit.canada@on.aibn.com) 175 Bloor St East, Suite 907 South Tower, Toronto, Ontario M4W3R8

France (☎ 01 42 66 66 68, fax 01 47 42 19 74, ⓔ enit.parigi@wanadoo.fr) 23 rue de la Paix, 75002 Paris
Germany *Berlin:* (☎ 030-247 83 97, fax 247 83 99, ⓔ enit.berlin@t-online.de) Karl Liebknecht Strasse 34, 10178
Frankfurt am Main: (☎ 069-25 91 26, fax 23 28 94, ⓔ enit.ffm@t-online.de) Kaisterstrasse 65, 60329
Japan (☎ 03-3478 2051, fax 3479 9356, ⓦ www.tabifan.com/italia) 2-7-14 Minamiaoyama, Minato-ku, Tokyo 107-0062
Netherlands (☎ 020-616 8244, fax 618 8515, ⓔ enitams@wirehub.nl) Stadhouderskade 2, 1054 ES Amsterdam
UK (☎ 020-7408 1254, fax 7399 3567, ⓔ enitlond@globalnet.co.uk) 1 Princess St, W1R 2AY London
USA *New York:* (☎ 212-245 4822, fax 586 9249, ⓔ enitny@italiantourism.com) 630 Fifth Ave, Suite 1565, New York, NY 10111
Chicago: (☎ 312-644 0996, fax 644 3019, ⓔ enitch@italiantourism.com) 500 North Michigan Ave, Suite 2240, Chicago, IL 60611
Los Angeles: (☎ 310-820 1989, fax 820 6357, ⓔ enitla@earthlink.net) 12400 Wilshire Blvd, Suite 550, Los Angeles, CA 90025

VISAS & DOCUMENTS
Passports & Visas

Citizens of European Union (EU) member states can travel to Italy with their national identity cards (if issued) alone. All others (European and non-European) must have a valid passport.

Visas for travel in countries (like Italy) that have signed the Schengen Convention are not required of legal residents of other Schengen countries, or of Ireland, the UK and a few European states. Nationals of several other countries, including Australia, Canada, Japan, New Zealand and the USA, do not need visas for tourist visits of up to 90 days. Everyone else must acquire a Schengen visa valid for travel in all signatory countries.

Among those who do need visas are South Africans. Visa fees depend on exchange rates, but a transit visa should cost about US$10, a 30-day visa around US$26, and a multiple-entry visa of up to three months about US$32. Visas must be obtained (only twice in any 12-month period) in the country of residence and from the embassy of the first Schengen country to be visited.

Several of the northern mountain rides described in this book dip briefly into France or Switzerland. Officially, there should be no border-crossing formalities at the French frontier. However, the non-EU, non-Schengen Swiss may have different visa requirements and are scrupulous about rules and regulations – even at the tops of mountain passes. Check that there won't be problems getting in or out, even for a quick transit pedal or one-night stay.

Non-EU travellers are required to have proof of onward travel. Passports also must be valid for six months, or more for some countries, from the date of arrival in Europe. Schengen visas *cannot* be extended (except in an emergency) once in Europe.

Travel Insurance

A travel insurance policy to cover theft, loss and medical problems is a good idea.

Some policies offer lower and higher medical-expense options; the higher ones are chiefly for countries such as the USA, which have extremely high medical costs. A wide variety of policies is available, so check the small print. Some policies specifically exclude 'dangerous activities', which can include scuba diving, motorcycling and even trekking, so check carefully what it says about cycling and any other planned activities while on the road. Check that the policy at least covers ambulances or an emergency flight home.

Many people prefer policies that pay doctors or hospitals directly rather than you having to pay on the spot and claim later. Later claims require lots of documentation; keep every scrap of related paper – bills, medical certificates, police reports. Some policies may ask that contact be made (reverse charge) with a home-country centre where an immediate assessment of the problem is made prior to treatment.

Other Documents

Should car rental be necessary, a driving licence is compulsory. Many non-EU licences are valid in Italy, but bringing an International Driving Permit as well avoids many potential problems.

A Hostelling International (HI) card is required for overnights in any establishment run by the Associazione Italiana Alberghi per la Giovent. Cards are issued in your home country with membership in the national Youth Hostel Association (YHA), but they are also available at hostels. In the latter case, on each of the first six nights spent in a hostel, a €2.50 stamp charge is added to the hostel fee, after which you become a full international member. With membership come various discounts.

The International Student Identity Card (ISIC) for full-time students, and the International Teacher Identity Card (ITIC) for full-time teachers and professors also entitle bearers to a range of discounts. The Euro<26 card (CartaGiovani) offers similar advantages to anyone under 26, whereas seniors over 60 or 65 need only present proof of age. The Centro Turistico Studentesco e Giovanile (CTS) youth and student travel organisation with branches throughout Italy can issue ISIC, ITIC and Euro<26 cards, but you have to join first, which costs around €25.

EMBASSIES
Italian Embassies

Italian embassies abroad include:

Australia (☎ 02-6273 3333, e embassy@ambitalia .org.au) 12 Grey St, Deakin, Canberra 2600

Canada (☎ 613-232 2401, w www.italyincanada .com) 275 Slater St, 21st floor, Ottawa, Ontario KIP 5H9

France (☎ 01 49 54 03 00, e ambasciata@ ambi-italie.fr) 51 rue de Varenne, 75007 Paris

Germany (☎ 030-254 400, w www.ambasciata -italia.de) Hiroshimastrasse 1-7, 10785 Berlin

Ireland (☎ 01-660 1744, e italianembassy@eir com.net) 63–65 Northumberland Rd, Dublin 4

Japan (☎ 03-3453 5291, w www.sunsite .sut.ac.jp/embitaly) Mita 2-chome 5/4, Minato-ku, Tokyo 108-8302

Netherlands (☎ 070-302 1030, w www.italy.nl) Alexanderstraat 12, 2514 JL Den Hague

New Zealand (☎ 04-473 5339, w www.italy -embassy.org.nz) 34 Grant Rd, Thorndon, Wellington

South Africa (☎ 021-43 55 41) 796 George Ave, Arcadia/Pretoria

UK (☎ 020-7312 2200, w www.embitaly .org.uk) 14 Three Kings Yard, London W1Y 2EH

USA (☎ 202-612 4400, w www.italyemb.org) 3000 Whitehaven St NW, Washington, DC 20008

Embassies in Italy

Some embassies in Rome are:

Australia (☎ 06 85 27 21, e consular-rome@ dfat.gov.au) 250 Corso Trieste

Canada (☎ 06 44 59 81, w www.canada.it) Via Zara 30, 00198

France (☎ 06 68 60 11, w www.france-italia.it) Piazza Farnese 67

Germany (☎ 06 49 21 31, w www.ambger mania.it) Via San Martino della Battaglia 4

Ireland (☎ 06 697 91 21) Piazza di Campitelli 3

Japan (☎ 06 48 79 91, w www.ambasciatajp.it) Via Quintino Sella 60

Netherlands (☎ 06 322 11 41, w www.olanda.it) Via Michele Mercati 8

New Zealand (☎ 06 440 29 28, e nzemb.rom@ agora.stm.it) Via Zara 28

South Africa (☎ 06 841 97 94) Via Tanaro 14–16

UK (☎ 06 422 00 001, w www.britain.it) Via XX Settembre 80A

USA (☎ 06 467 41, w www.usembassy.it) Via Veneto 119/A

CUSTOMS

Goods that are purchased in and moved between EU countries incur no additional taxes, provided duty has been paid somewhere within the EU and the goods are for personal use.

Travellers coming to Italy from outside the EU can import, duty free, 200 cigarettes, 100 small cigars, 50 cigars or 250g of tobacco; 1L of strong liquor or 2L of spirits, plus 2L of wine; 50ml of perfume; 500g of coffee and other goods up to a total value of €175. Anything over this limit must be declared on arrival and the appropriate duty paid; carry all receipts.

No duty need be paid for a bicycle.

MONEY
Currency

On 1 January, 2002, the euro (€) became legal tender, a common currency shared with 14 other European Union countries (Austria, Belgium, Denmark, Finland, France, Germany, Greece, Ireland, Luxembourg, the Netherlands, Portugal, Spain, Sweden and the UK). One euro comprises 100 cents. Euro banknotes come in seven denominations: €5, €10, €20, €50, €100, €200 and €500. Coins come in eight denominations: 1c, 2c, 5c, 10c, 20c, 50c, €1 and €2.

Exchange Rates

The Universal Currency Converter posts daily exchange rates at w www.xe.net/ucc. As this book went to print, currency conversions were calculated as follows:

country	unit		€
Australia	A$1	=	0.56
Canada	C$1	=	0.64
Japan	¥100	=	0.77
New Zealand	NZ$1	=	0.51
South Africa	R10	=	1.21
UK	UK£1	=	1.45
USA	US$1	=	0.92

Exchanging Money

Cash on hand is always crucial, especially in remote areas. Fortunately, one rarely has to look far for an exchange facility. Banks and/or other *cambio* services have offices at airports, train stations in most cities, information points and busy tourist centres. A *cambio* is faster and easier to deal with than banks, has longer hours, and sometimes offers better rates. Banks, post offices and bureaus de change may give a better rate for travellers cheques than for cash, but banks' commissions on cheques are higher. Post offices charge a flat rate for all transactions.

Cash & Travellers Cheques There is little advantage in bringing large quantities of foreign cash to Italy. Commissions are often lower for cash than for travellers cheques, but the risk of loss or theft far outweighs any petty gains. In fact, cheques are sometimes more easily cashed due to counterfeiting concerns (particularly for US$50 and US$100 bills). Get most of the cheques in largish denominations to save on per-cheque charges. Large, reputable, international brands (such as Visa, American Express and Thomas Cook) are familiar in Italy.

Credit/Debit Cards & ATMs Credit, debit and bank cards are more and more routinely accepted in stores, hotels and restaurants, further reducing reliance on cash. For getting cash with plastic, the easiest option is an Automatic Teller Machine (ATM) – called a 'Bancomat' – found in just about every population centre in the country. ATMs provide bankcard users with direct access to home cash reserves at advantageous exchange rates. Cash advances may also be had using

Visa or MasterCard, although local and credit card company fees can sometimes be brutal (check your company's policy). ATMs blink merrily on the outside walls of most banks, at major train stations and even in many very large stores. Italian ATMs commonly reject foreign cards for no apparent reason. Just try a few more machines at major banks (where your card's logo, like Cirrus or Maestro, is displayed) until it works. The local system is usually at fault, not the card. Italian ATMs dispense only €10, €20 and €50 bills.

Security

Petty theft is a problem throughout Italy. Keep only a limited amount of money as cash. While on the road, it is best to carry all cash, money substitutes (cheques, plastic), important documents and valuables in one safe dry place that you can easily remove from the bicycle when you leave it by itself.

Costs

Long-haul transport costs aside, life can be lived comfortably on €50 to €75 per day. Individual travel styles will dictate a budget, but typical daily costs per person for two penny-wise travellers sharing food and accommodation could be:

item	cost (€)
camping ground	6.50–10
hostel/B&B	10–15
albergo/hotel	10–25
continental breakfast	2.50
picnic lunch	5
pizzeria dinner	8–15
small beer/inexpensive wine	2–5
coffee/gelato	2

Tipping & Bargaining

While there is no expectation that tips will be offered on top of the service charge usually included in restaurant bills, Italians commonly round up or leave a small amount (unless service was bad). In the absence of a service charge, consider leaving 10% extra, although this isn't required. In bars, Italians often leave small change as a tip. Most Italians do not tip taxi drivers.

Bargaining in shops is generally unacceptable, although attempts to finagle small discounts on very large purchases are routine. Some hotel rates are based on length of stay; ask at check-in about special prices.

Receipts

Government has continued to crack down on unregistered commercial transactions. Greymarket dealings whereby normal purchases made in recognised stores do not make it into the shop's accounts (and escape the notice of tax collectors) have fed Italy's 'parallel economy' for decades. Unfortunately, recent laws to tighten controls on tax payment place the onus on the buyer to ask for and keep receipts for *all* goods and services. Although it rarely happens, an officer of the Guardia di Finanza (Fiscal Police), uniformed or under cover, has the right to ask for proof-of-purchase receipts immediately after you leave a shop or restaurant. Hefty penalties can be imposed on both the consumer and the shopkeeper if a *scontrino* (chit) is not forthcoming.

Taxes & Refunds

Another good reason for amassing receipts is the possibility of refunds when leaving the country. Non-EU big-spenders can file for reimbursement of about 60% of the 20% value-added tax (IVA) added to just about everything in Italy. The total worth of all acquisition must be greater than €150 purchased in one day and in one shop of a store affiliated with the system. Look for 'Tax-free for tourists', 'Cash Back' or 'Global Refund' signs and/or ask the shopkeeper. Fill out the form at the point of purchase and have it stamped and checked by Italian customs when leaving the country.

POST & COMMUNICATIONS
Post

Italy's postal service is notoriously slow, unreliable and expensive.

Post offices and authorised tobacconists (look for the official *tabacchi* sign: a big 'T' on white or black) sell *francobolli* (stamps). Tobacconists will not weigh anything, so for precise amounts and overseas mailings, go to the *posta*. An airmail letter can take up to two weeks to reach the UK or the USA and up to three weeks to Australia. Postcards take much longer. Within Italy, local letters take from three to seven days.

Letters (up to 20g) sent *posta ordinaria* (extra slowly) and postcards cost €0.41 to all European and Mediterranean countries and €0.52 to all other destinations. *Posta prioritaria* (airmail) costs €0.62 and €0.77 respectively (up to 20g). Aerograms (available only at post offices) cost €0.41 plus the appropriate *priorita* surcharge. *Raccomandata* (registered mail) or *assicurata* (insured mail) may be quicker than normal mail. A standard *raccomandata* envelope to European/Mediterranean countries costs an additional €2.17 and for *assicurata* the surcharge varies with both destination and the value for which the mailing is insured. Very important documents weighing less than 3kg will be reliably delivered the next working day for €7.23 via *Postacelere*.

To receive mail while on the road, try *fermo posta* (poste restante).

Telephone

Italy's country code is ☎ 39. Area codes of up to four digits are an integral part of the Italian phone number, including the initial 0. Mobile phone numbers also begin with a four-digit prefix, such as ☎ 0330, ☎ 0335 or ☎ 0347. The 0 at the start of some mobile prefixes no longer needs to be dialled.

When calling Italy from abroad, the 0 in the area code (eg, ☎ 010 11 22 33) must be retained after the country code (eg, ☎ 39 010 11 22 33), except when calling mobile phones.

For calls from Italy to outside the country, dial ☎ 00 followed by the relevant country and city codes, and then the telephone number. International direct dial (IDD) calls to almost anywhere in the world can be placed from public telephones. Country codes are usually posted in phone booths.

Numeri verdi (freephone or toll-free numbers) begin with the code ☎ 800. The

Useful Numbers

The following are all free calls from public phones. The emergency numbers are also free from mobile phones.

directory inquiries	☎ 12
international directory inquiries	☎ 176
reverse-charge (collect) calls to European countries	☎ 15
reverse-charge calls for anywhere else	☎ 170
carabinieri	☎ 112
police/emergency	☎ 113
fire	☎ 115
ambulance	☎ 118

prefix ☎ 147 indicates that a national number is charged at a local rate.

Telecom Italia, Italy's leading telecommunications company, operates most of the orange payphones found throughout the country. Fewer and fewer take coins – most only use phonecards – and a new generation accepts major credit cards, allows for the sending of faxes and even has a separate jack for data connections. The minimum charge for a call from a public phone is €0.10.

Phonecards *Carte/schede telefoniche* are available at post offices, *tabaccherie*, newspaper stands and from vending machines in Telecom offices in four main values: €1, €2.50, €5 and €7.50. They can be used for both local and long-distance/international calls. Remember to unclip the perforated triangle or the card won't work.

Telecom Italia also now issues the Welcome card (€5 and €10) with special rates to all international destinations. Lonely Planet's ekno Communication Card, aimed at travellers, gives competitive international rates (avoid using it for local calls), messaging services and free email. Visit ⓦ www.ekno.lonelyplanet.com to join or to access the service, including toll-free access numbers in Italy.

Email & Internet Access

There are Internet cafés in all major cities and most larger towns. Many public libraries, even in smaller towns, also have Internet access. Telecom Italia operates an Internet Corner in some of its major offices. For a fairly comprehensive list of Internet cafés throughout Italy see ⓦ www.net cafeguide.com. Rates vary greatly with the speed of connection and quality of service, but count on €2.50 to €7.50 per hour.

TIME

Italy operates on the 24-hour clock, although the 12-hour system is also seen. The country is one hour ahead of GMT/UTC; France and Germany are on the same time as Italy; the UK is one hour behind. When it's noon in Rome, it's 3am in San Francisco, 6am in New York and Toronto, 11am in London, 9pm in Sydney and 11pm in Auckland. Daylight-saving time starts on the last Sunday in March, when clocks go forward one hour. Clocks go back an hour on the last Sunday in October.

ELECTRICITY

The electric current is 220V, 50Hz. Power sockets/plugs have two or three round pins, some fatter than others. Electrical and hardware stores sell adapter plugs. Travellers from North America will need a voltage converter if appliances do not automatically convert 220V to 110V.

WEIGHTS & MEASURES

Italy uses the metric system: see the standard conversion table on the inside back cover of this book. Note that, like other continental Europeans, Italians indicate decimals with commas; points indicate thousands.

BUSINESS HOURS

The following is a guide only:

Banks Open 8.30am to 1.30pm and 3.30pm to 4.30pm Monday to Friday. Change facilities in larger cities and major tourist towns will be open on weekends; also try the tourist office.

Bars/Cafés Open 7.30am to 8pm (sometimes later)

Bike Shops Open 9am to 1pm and 3pm to 7.30pm (or 4pm to 8pm) Monday to Saturday

Grocery Shops (alimentari) Open 9am to 1pm and 3.30pm to 7.30pm (or 5pm to 9pm in summer) Monday to Saturday. They may close on Saturday afternoon and Monday or Thursday afternoon.

Museums & Attractions Open 9.30am to 7pm daily (sometimes as late as 10pm in summer). Many close on Monday.

Pharmacies Open 9am to 12.30pm and 3.30pm to 7.30pm; closed Sunday & usually Saturday afternoon. When closed, they must display the nearest open pharmacies.

Post Offices Open 8.30am to 5pm or 6pm Monday to Friday and 8.30am to noon Saturday. Small offices usually close in the afternoon.

Restaurants Open noon to 3pm and 7.30pm to 11pm (later in summer and in the south)

Supermarkets Many open 9am (or earlier) to 7.30pm Monday to Saturday and 9am to 1pm Sunday. Some open for a day/half day on Monday or Thursday.

Tourist Offices In summer, open 8.30am to 12.30/1pm and 3pm to 7pm Monday to Saturday, and often Sunday. Closed Saturday afternoon and Sunday outside summer.

Restaurants and bars are required to close for one day each week, which varies between establishments.

PUBLIC HOLIDAYS

Many businesses and shops close for at least part of August, when most Italians take their annual holiday, particularly during the week around Ferragosto (Feast of the Assumption) on 15 August. National public holidays include:

New Year's Day 1 January
Epiphany 6 January
Easter March/April
Liberation Day 25 April
Labour Day 1 May
Feast of the Assumption (Ferragosto) 15 August
All Saints' Day 1 November
Feast of the Immaculate Conception 8 December
Christmas Day 25 December
Feast of Santo Stefano 26 December

Getting There & Away

AIR
Airports

Italy's main international gateway is Rome's Leonardo da Vinci (Fiumicino) airport, but regular international flights also serve Rome's Ciampino, Venice's Marco Polo, and Milan's Malpensa and Linate airports. Plenty of flights from other European cities are available direct to most regional capitals.

Buying Tickets

If you are flying with your bicycle, simply buying the cheapest ticket may not be the best option. Check each airline's bicycle policy: how much will they charge for your bike, and how do they require you to pack it? Also consider how many connections you will have to make en route (the fewer the better).

The plane ticket will probably be the single most expensive item in your budget. Start searching early: some of the cheapest tickets must be bought months in advance, and some popular flights sell out quickly.

Return (round-trip) tickets are usually cheaper than two one-way tickets, and sometimes even cost less than a single one-way fare. The cheapest tickets often come with restrictions: minimum and/or maximum stays, advance reservation requirements, nonrefundable conditions and so on.

If Italy is only one stop on your grand world tour, you may want to consider a

Packing for Air Travel

We've all heard the horror stories about smashed/lost luggage when flying, but a more real threat to cycle tourists is arriving in a country for a two-week tour and finding their bike with broken wheels or in little bits spread out around the baggage carousel. Fixing a damaged bike could take days, and the delay and frustration could ruin your holiday.

How do you avoid this? Err on the side of caution and box your bike. Trust airline baggage handlers if you want (we're told some people actually do) and give your bike to them 'as is' – turn the handlebars 90°, remove the pedals, cover the chain with a rag or bag (to protect other people's baggage) and deflate your tyres (partially, not all the way) – but is it worth the risk? If you want to take that sort of risk do it on your homeward flight, when you can get your favourite bike shop to fix any damage.

Some airlines sell bike boxes at the airport, but most bike shops give them away. Fitting your bike into a box requires a few simple steps and only takes about 15 minutes:

1 Loosen the stem bolt and turn the handlebars 90°; loosen the clamp bolt(s) and twist the handlebars as pictured.

2 Remove the pedals (use a 15mm spanner, turning each the opposite way to how you pedal), wheels and seat post and saddle (don't forget to mark its height before removing it).

3 Undo the rear derailleur bolt and tape it to the inside of the chainstay. There's no need to undo the derailleur cable. You can remove the chain (it will make reassembly easier) but it isn't necessary.

4 Cut up some spare cardboard and tape it beneath the chainwheel to prevent the teeth from penetrating the floor of the box and being damaged.

5 Remove the quick-release skewers from the wheels and wrap a rag (or two) around the cluster so it won't get damaged or damage anything else.

If you run your tyres at very high pressure (above 100psi), you should partially deflate them – on most bikes this won't be necessary.

6 Place the frame in the box, so it rests on the chainwheel and forks – you might want to place another couple of layers of cardboard underneath the forks.

Most boxes will be too short to allow the front pannier racks to remain on the bike; if so, remove them. The rear rack should fit while still on the bike, but may require the seat stay bolts to be undone and pushed forward.

Packing for Air Travel

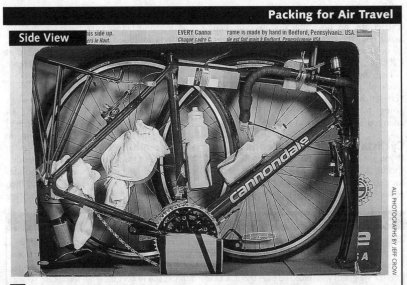

Side View his side up. ers le Haut. EVERY Cannoi rame is made by hand in Bedford, Pennsylvania, USA. Chaque cadre C ile est fait main à Bedford, Pennsylvannie USA

ALL PHOTOGRAPHS BY JEFF CROW

7 Place the wheels beside the frame, on the side opposite the chainwheel. Keep the wheels and frame separate by inserting a piece of cardboard between them and tying the wheels to the frame (to stop them moving around and scratching the frame).

8 Slot the saddle and seat post, your helmet, tools and any other bits and pieces (eg, tent, sleeping bag) into the vacant areas. Wrap the skewers, chain and other loose bike bits in newspaper and place them in the box. Add cardboard or newspaper packing to any areas where metal is resting on metal.

9 Seal the box with tape and write your name, address and flight details on several sides.

Now all you need to do is strap your panniers together and either take them with you as carry-on luggage or check them in.

Top View

Bike Bags

If you're planning on travelling between regions via train, plane or bus then consider taking a bike bag. The simplest form of zippered bike bag has no padding built into it, is made of Cordura or nylon, and can be rolled up and put on your rear pannier rack and unfurled when you need to travel again.

Some of the smaller ones require you to remove both wheels, the front pannier racks, pedals and seat post to fit inside the bag. However, these make for (relatively) easy and inconspicuous train, plane or bus transfers so the extra effort is worthwhile.

round-the-world (RTW) ticket. There may be restrictions on how many stops you can make, and the tickets are usually valid for 90 days to one year. Prices begin at around UK£800, A$2500 or US$1300.

Use the fares quoted in this book as a guide only. They are based on the rates advertised by travel agencies at the time of going to print and are likely to have changed by the time you read this.

Cyclists with Special Needs

If you are travelling with a child or have other special needs – vegetarian or kosher meals, for example – let the airline know as soon as possible so that it can make arrangements.

Departure Tax

The departure tax for passengers leaving Italy by air is included in airline ticket prices. However, there is a port tax, payable at check-in when you leave the country by ferry.

The USA & Canada

Council Travel (☎ 800-226-8624, ⓦ www .counciltravel.com) and STA Travel (☎ 800-781-4040, 800-777-0112, ⓦ www.statravel .com) are quality agencies specialising in student and budget travel, with offices in major cities throughout the USA. Other discount travel agencies, known as consolidators, buy in bulk from the airlines and then pass on some of the savings to you. They are

---

Cycle-Friendly Airlines

Not too many airlines will carry a bike free of charge these days – at least according to their official policy. Most airlines regard the bike as part of your checked luggage. Most carriers working to routes to Europe, Asia and the Pacific usually allow 20kg (44 lbs) of checked luggage (excluding carry-on), so the weight of your bike and bags shouldn't exceed this. If you're over the limit, technically you're liable for excess-baggage charges.

Carriers flying routes to Europe from or through North America use a different system. Passengers are generally allowed two pieces of luggage, each of which must not exceed 32kg (70 lbs). Excess baggage fees are charged for additional pieces, rather than for excess weight. On some airlines a bike may be counted as one of your two pieces; others charge a set fee for carrying a bike, which may then be carried in addition to your two other pieces. Check whether these fees are paid for the whole journey, each way or per leg.

Some airlines require you to box your bike, while others accept soft covers, or just ask that you turn the handlebars, remove the pedals and cover the chain. Check this policy before getting to the airport; only a few airlines sell sturdy boxes at the check-in counter.

When we looked into the policies of different carriers, we found that not only does the story sometimes change depending on who you talk to – and how familiar they are with the company's policy – but the official line is not necessarily adhered to at the check-in counter. If a company representative or agent reassures you that your bike travels for free, ask them to annotate your passenger file to that effect. If your flight is not too crowded, the check-in staff are often lenient with the excess charges, particularly with items such as bikes.

The times when you are most likely to incur excess baggage charges are on full flights and, of course, if you inconvenience the check-in staff. If you suspect you may be over the limit, increase your chances of avoiding charges by checking in early and being well organised, friendly and polite – a smile and a 'Thankyou' can go a long way!

◀ LUGGAGE

◀ LUGGAGE

DON HATCHER

another good source of budget fares. Look for their ads in the Sunday travel sections of the *New York Times*, *LA Times*, *Chicago Tribune* and *San Francisco Chronicle*.

Alitalia flies several nonstop routes from the USA to Italy; Rome-bound flights leave from New York and Atlanta, while Milan flights leave from New York, Chicago, Boston, and Miami. Delta Airlines has nonstops from New York to Venice, Rome, and Milan, and United Airlines flies nonstop from Washington, DC to Milan. (Nonstops from the west coast had been discontinued at the time of writing as a result of the September 11, 2001 terrorist attacks.) Low season return tickets from New York to Rome or Milan can be found for as little as US$450, or around US$700 in high season. Return fares from the western USA are generally US$100 to US$200 more expensive.

From Toronto, Alitalia and Air Canada both have nonstop flights to Rome and Milan. Travel CUTS (☎ 866-246-9762, 800-667-2887, Ⓦ www.travelcuts.com), specialising in discount fares for students, has offices in all major Canadian cities. Other good resources are the budget travel agents' ads in the Toronto *Globe & Mail*, *Toronto Star*, *Montreal Gazette* and *Vancouver Province*.

The UK & Ireland
London is one of the best centres in the world for discounted air tickets, including RTW tickets.

An excellent source of UK-based travel information is the free publication *TNT* (Ⓦ www.tntmagazine.com). Also check out the travel page ads of the Sunday newspapers,

---

Warning

⚠ The information in this chapter is particularly vulnerable to change: prices for international travel are volatile, routes are introduced and cancelled, schedules change, special deals come and go, and rules and visa requirements are amended.

You should check directly with the airline or a travel agent to make sure you understand the conditions of your ticket. The details given in this chapter should be regarded as pointers and are not a substitute for your own careful, up-to-date research.

Time Out (Ⓦ www.timeout.com) and *Exchange & Mart* (Ⓦ www.exchangeandmart .co.uk). All are available from most London news stands or outside some train stations.

In the UK, two reliable travel agencies are STA Travel (☎ 08701-600 599, Ⓦ www .statravel.co.uk) and Trailfinders (☎ 020-7628 7628, Ⓦ www.trailfinders.co.uk), each with numerous branches nationwide. In Ireland a good resource is USIT (☎ 01-602 1600, Ⓦ www.usitnow.ie).

Advance purchase return fares from London to Rome on major airlines start at around UK£125. Even better fares can sometimes be found with budget carriers such as Ryanair (Ⓦ www.ryanair.ie), which flies from London to 12 destinations in Italy.

A great web resource listing cheap flights from the UK and Ireland is Ⓦ www.cheap flights.com.

Australia & New Zealand
Good airfares can be found through agencies like Flight Centre (☎ 133 133, Ⓦ www .flightcentre.com.au) and STA Travel (☎ 300 733 035 in Australia, Ⓦ www.statravel .com.au • ☎ 0508 782 872 in New Zealand, Ⓦ www.statravel.co.nz). The travel sections of the *Sydney Morning Herald*, the *New Zealand Herald* and the *Age* in Melbourne are also good resources.

Return fares to Italy on major airlines start around A$1800 low season and A$2050 high season. Some of the best deals are routed through Asia. Fares from Perth are generally a bit cheaper. Because Australia and New Zealand are so far from Europe, a RTW ticket can sometimes be more attractive than a simple return flight. Cyclists considering RTW tickets from Australia or New Zealand should note that eastbound RTW routes through North America sometimes have more generous weight allowances than westbound routes through Asia.

Continental Europe
Rome and Milan are well served by air connections from cities throughout Europe. At the time of writing, typical return prices to Rome were as follows: Frankfurt €265, Madrid €280, Berlin €285, Paris €285 and Amsterdam €310. The train is more attractive than the plane for certain itineraries, such as Paris–Milan and Munich–Bologna, thanks to fast international services.

Ryanair flies from Frankfurt to Milan, Pisa, and Pescara, and from Brussels to Rome, Pisa and Venice, offering great deals on all flights.

STA Travel (w www.statravel.com), Nouvelles Frontières (w www.nouvelles frontieres.fr), and Kilroy Travels (w www .kilroytravels.com), all with multiple offices on the continent, are among the many reputable travel agencies offering discounted air travel.

South Africa

STA Travel has numerous locations throughout South Africa, including Cape Town (☎ 021-418 6570) and Witwatersrand University (☎ 011-717 9341). Its services are aimed primarily at students, with discounted youth fares to Rome and Milan costing around R4625 from Johannesburg, R6105 from Cape Town and R5880 from Durban at the time of writing.

BUS

Eurolines, Europe's leading long-distance bus operator, won't take bikes. Luckily for cyclists, there's a great alternative bus service called European Bike Express (☎ 01642-251 440, fax 232 209, w www .bike-express.co.uk). EBE operates four distinct routes, picking up passengers at 15 points in England, from Middlesbrough to Dover, then crossing by ferry to the continent and branching out into France, Spain, Switzerland, and Italy. Cyclists ride in a comfortable coach, with bikes travelling behind in a covered trailer (handlebars must be turned before loading). EBE's weekly Adriatic service from the UK to Cavallino, Italy (just east of Venice) departs every Saturday from early May to late September, plus every other Wednesday from May to August, stopping in Como and Verona prior to reaching its terminus at Cavallino. There are services from the UK to the Italian destinations of Como (UK£169, 19 hours), Verona (UK£179, 22 hours) and Cavallino (UK£179, 24 hours). Return trips to the UK are on Sundays and alternate Thursdays. You can choose your own return date, and even opt to return to the UK on one of EBE's other bike buses from France or northern Spain. Once you have chosen a particular itinerary, penalties apply for any changes you make.

TRAIN

Train travel from the UK and France goes much more smoothly if you travel with a bike bag, or *housse*, required by the British, French, and Italian railways for travel on their fastest international services.

The UK

The most direct train route from the UK to Italy is via Paris. The speedy Eurostar train (☎ 0990-186 186, 0870-5186 186, w www .eurostar.com) operates through the Channel Tunnel between London's Waterloo station and Paris' Gare du Nord. The journey takes about three hours, with frequent daily services. Passport and customs checks are usually done before boarding. In order to fit in the luggage racks, your bike bag must measure no more than 120cm by 80cm by 50cm, requiring you to remove wheels, pedals, racks, and fenders, and turn your seat 90°. If your bike won't fit into a bag of this size (some large bikes won't), an alternative is to use Eurostar's affiliated parcel service Esprit (☎ 0870-5850 850), which charges UK£25 to carry your bike from London to Paris in a luggage car; there's no guarantee that you and your bike will travel on the same train.

Continental Europe

The quickest route from France to Italy is aboard one of the two daily TGV trains connecting Paris' Gare de Lyon with Milan's central train station. Travel time is just under seven hours, and the one-way fare is €94 (2nd class). An equally fast option is the TGV Meditérranée from Paris to Ventimiglia on Italy's west Ligurian Coast (€76, just under seven hours). Almost all TGV's bikes must be stored in a bag of the allowed dimensions (120cm by 90cm). You also need to reserve a seat for yourself to travel on any TGV.

If you don't want to dismantle your bike, there are a few other options. In summer (June to September) a specially equipped TGV Meditérranée with storage space for up to four unboxed bikes runs daily between Paris and Ventimiglia; you'll need to reserve a bike space and pay €10 over and above the regular TGV fare. There are also a few other international trains permitting transport of unboxed bikes as luggage. These are marked with bike icons on French train timetables and travel mostly at night or in the wee hours of the morning. One such overnight service is train No 261 from Paris to Munich, allowing connections in Munich to the Italy-bound Brenner Express or Eurocity Val Gardena. Another overnight service equipped with a bike car is train No 469 from Paris to Chur, Switzerland, via Basel and Zurich; transfers are possible in Basel to the bike-friendly Intercity Riviera dei Fiori, continuing nonstop to Milan (5½ hours) and Genova (7½ hours), or in Zurich to the Intercity Cinque Terre train, which continues nonstop to La Spezia (eight hours). Note that bikes travel for free on almost all French trains, but you will have to pay a bike supplement and/or make a special reservation for the Swiss or German part of the above itineraries.

It's possible to carry your bike unboxed from Germany to Italy on certain trains, including the Brenner Express connecting Munich with Bolzano, Bologna and Milano, and the Eurocity Val Gardena from Munich to Bolzano. International trains which carry bikes are noted on German timetables and mostly travel at night. There's typically a special car with bike racks for at least 16 bikes. It's essential to pay a bike supplement and reserve a numbered space for your bike (this can be done up to three months in advance). It's also possible, though not obligatory, to reserve a seat for yourself in the car adjacent to the bike compartment for an additional fee.

Austria and Switzerland are cyclist-friendly countries where most regional trains, and some Italy-bound Intercity and night trains, carry bikes, usually in a luggage car or designated bike compartment. As always, it's important to check locally to make sure the train you're boarding accepts bikes, and to pay the appropriate reservation fee and bike supplement.

Austrian, Swiss, German and French trains returning north from Italy generally have the same bike services as they did travelling southbound.

SEA

Thanks to its central geographic location, Italy is a hub for ferry services all over the Mediterranean. Routes connect Italy with Greece, Croatia, Montenegro, Albania, Turkey, Spain, France, Tunisia, and Malta. A good website listing all the principal companies is w www.traghetti.com. The main points of embarkation are Trieste, Venice,

Ancona, Bari and Brindisi on the Adriatic coast; Genoa, La Spezia, Livorno, Piombino, Naples and Salerno on the Tyrrhenian coast; Palermo and Trapani in Sicily; and Cagliari and Porto Torres in Sardinia. Prices vary according to the time of year and are most expensive during summer. Bicycles incur a small fee on some ferries and travel free on others. There is also a port tax, payable at check-in when you leave the country.

Some of the leading companies and their routes are:

Greece, Albania, Croatia & Montenegro

Adriatica (☎ 041 78 18 61, fax 041 78 18 18, w www.adriatica.it) From Bari to Durres; Ancona to Split (Croatia); and Ancona to Bar (Montenegro)

Agoudimos Lines (w www.agoudimos-lines .com) From Bari to Durres, Albania and from Brindisi to Igoumenitsa

Anek Lines (w www.anek.gr) From Trieste and Ancona to Patras and Igoumenitsa

Hellenic Mediterranean Lines (w www.ferries .gr/hml) From Brindisi to Patras, Igoumenitsa, Corfu, Cefalonia, Paxi and Zante (Greece)

Jadrolinija (w www.jadrolinija.hr) From Bari to Dubrovnik (Croatia); and from Ancona to Split and Zadar (Croatia)

Minoan Lines (w www.minoan.it) From Venice and Ancona to Igoumenitsa and Patras

Strintzis Blue Star Ferries (w www.bluestar ferries.com) From Ancona, Venice and Brindisi to Patras, Igoumenitsa and Corfu

Superfast Ferries (w www.superfast.com) From Ancona and Bari to Patras and Igoumenitsa

Ventouris Ferries (w www.ventouris.gr) From Bari to Corfu, Igoumenitsa and Durres (Albania)

Turkey

Turkish Marmara Lines (w www.marmaralines .com) From Venice and Brindisi to Cesme (Turkey)

Spain & Malta

Grandi Navi Veloci (w www.forti.it/grandinavi) From Genoa to Barcelona (Spain)

Grimaldi Ferries (w www.grimaldi-ferries.com) From Salerno and Palermo to Valencia (Spain); and from Salerno to Malta

France (including Corsica) & Tunisia

Happy Lines (w www.forti.it/happylines) From La Spezia to Bastia (Corsica)

Linee Lauro (w www.forti.it/LineeLauro) From Naples, Trapani and La Spezia to Tunis (Tunisia); and from Naples to Corsica

Moby Lines (W www.forti.it/moby) From Genoa (Livorno) and Piombino to Bastia (Corsica)

SNCM (W www.sncm.fr) From Porto Torres (Sardinia) to Toulon and Marseille (France); from Genoa and Livorno to Porto Vecchio and Bastia (Corsica); and from Genoa to Tunis (Tunisia)

Tirrenia (W www.tirrenia.com) From Trapani and Cagliari to Tunis (Tunisia)

South America, Africa, Israel & Northern Europe

A more adventurous alternative is to travel on one of the cargo boats operated by Grimaldi Freighter Cruises (W www.grimaldi-freighter cruises.com). Grimaldi offers cabin space on its long-haul services from Italy to Brazil, Argentina, and West Africa, plus services to Mediterranean and European destinations including Egypt, Israel, Portugal, Ireland, the UK, Sweden, Denmark, and Belgium.

Getting Around

Public transport is well organised and is relatively inexpensive. In this guide, there has been an effort to ensure that bus or train services are accessible to the beginning and end of the rides. However, before setting out, check timetables and plan accordingly.

AIR
Domestic Air Services

Unless you're travelling from one end of the boot to the other in one fell swoop – from Milano to Reggio Calabria, for example – it generally makes better sense to use the efficient and considerably cheaper train, bus and ferry services, especially when you consider the additional hassle of getting to/from airports and packing your bike for air travel.

The main domestic carriers are Alitalia (☎ 06 656 41, 848 86 56 41, W www.ali talia.it), Meridiana (☎ 199 11 13 33, W www .meridiana.it) and Air One (☎ 06 48 88 00, 848 84 88 80, W www.air-one.it), all offering roughly comparable fares. Alitalia flies to most Italian cities; Meridiana, based in Sardinia, flies to 10 cities on the mainland, plus Catania and Palermo in Sicily, and Alghero, Cagliari and Olbia in Sardinia. Air One, in partnership with Lufthansa, emphasises southern coastal cities in its route network.

These airlines offer a range of discounts for young people, seniors, families and weekend travel, as well as occasional promotional fares. It should be noted that airline fares fluctuate, and that special deals sometimes only apply when tickets are bought in Italy, or for return fares only. The following gives an idea of return fares at the time of writing.

Rome–Venice	€128
Rome–Catania	€129
Rome–Milan	€145
Milano–Naples	€162
Milano–Palermo	€166
Rome–Cagliari	€174

Prices shown include departure tax and are for advance-purchase economy return fares. By comparison, return train fares for these same routes are roughly two-thirds the price.

Domestic flights can be booked directly with the airline or through a travel agency. One good travel agency with 170 offices throughout Italy is Centro Turistico Studentesco e Giovanile (CTS; ☎ 06 462 04 31; W www.cts.it) with its headquarters based in Rome at Via Genova 16.

Carrying Your Bicycle

Rules for flying with a bike in Italy seem to vary depending on airline and which agent you talk to. Always check the airline's bike policy when making a reservation, and ask for your file to state any specific information you're given about price or appropriate packaging. As a general rule, it's safer to box your bike for airline travel (both for the bike's sake and to avoid hassles at check-in); however, Italian airlines have been known to allow bikes to travel unpackaged. Regarding cost, if your bike doesn't exceed the airline's weight and dimension requirements, it should qualify as one of your allowed pieces of checked luggage; otherwise you'll get a per-kilogram excess baggage charge.

TRAIN

Travelling by train in Italy is often the most convenient and affordable option. Trenitalia (W www.trenitalia.com), also known as Ferrovie dello Stato, is the partially privatised state train system which serves most destinations. There are also numerous private train services throughout the country.

Your experience with trains may vary depending on which part of the country you're travelling in. Facilities for bikes tend to be more dependable, more heavily used, and better supported by train personnel the further north you go.

There are several types of trains, only some of which accept bicycles. In order of speed and amenities, from slowest and simplest to fastest and fanciest, they are the *diretto* (D), *regionale* (R), *interregionale* (IR), Intercity (IC), Eurocity (EC) and Eurostar (ES). The faster trains require you to pay a supplement and are less cycle-friendly.

Carrying Your Bicycle

Thanks to the ongoing efforts of organisations like Federazione Italiana Amici della Bicicletta (FIAB; **w** www.fiab-onlus.it), amenities for cyclists have greatly improved over the past decade. Currently the biggest problem is the difficulty of transporting bikes on the faster trains.

Bicycle icons displayed on timetables and train station departure boards indicate which trains are bike-friendly. As a rule of thumb, almost all *diretto*, *regionale* and *interregionale* trains will carry bikes, and most have a special bike car at the front or back end of the train marked with a bike symbol. The bike compartment is typically a big open space equipped with hooks along one side, allowing several bikes to be hung parallel to one another. When the bike compartment is not full, it's also possible to simply lean your fully loaded bike along one wall of the compartment and secure it with a bungee. The bike car is usually staffed, but there's no guarantee that he or she will help with bike loading/unloading; you should always come prepared to hoist the bike yourself. Doors on bike cars are wide enough to allow a fully loaded touring bike to pass through.

Unfortunately nobody ever seems to know in advance which end of the train the bike car will be on; the best strategy is to arrive early, watch carefully as your train pulls into the station, and head for the appropriate end of the train as quickly as possible. On trains with tight connections, if you guess the wrong end of the train, you may find yourself running the length of the platform to reach the bike car before the train pulls out again! It's also worth noting that lift services in Italian train stations are often nonexistent or out of service, requiring you to lug your bike up and down staircases to reach the desired platform.

To carry your bike on any Trenitalia train, you must purchase a *supplemento bici* (bike supplement) ticket which costs €3.50 (slightly higher on some long distance trains) and is valid for 24 hours regardless of the distance travelled or number of trains used. If you're staying in Italy a long time and travelling frequently by train, it may be more economical to purchase an annual bike supplement, good for 12 months from the date of issue and available for €42 at major train stations (list available from FIAB). Private train lines also usually accept bikes, charging separate supplements.

Fast trains labelled IC and EC officially only accept bicycles stored in a bag, with wheels removed. Super-fast Eurostar trains will generally not take bikes at all, meaning that they must be sent as registered luggage or packed creatively to avoid notice. Shipping your bike as baggage can take a few days and will probably mean that your bike won't be on the same train that you travel on.

The situation with trains and bikes is continuously evolving; check with Trenitalia or FIAB for updated information.

Classes & Costs

There are 1st and 2nd classes on all Italian trains, with a 1st-class ticket costing a bit less than double the price of 2nd class.

To travel on the Intercity, Eurocity and Eurostar trains, you are required to pay a *supplemento*, an additional charge determined by the distance you are travelling. Supplements increase with the speed of the train, and Eurostar service requires a seat booking fee as well. For instance, a 2nd-class ticket on the super-fast Eurostar Pendolino train between Rome and Florence (1½ hours) costs €30 one way (including applicable supplements and booking fees), while the Intercity (2½ hours) costs only €22, and the *diretto* (3½ hours) costs a mere €15. Always check whether the train you are about to catch requires a supplement, and pay it before you get on; otherwise you'll pay extra on the train.

On overnight trips within Italy it can be worth paying extra for a *cuccetta* (sleeping berth; €11.50 extra in a six-berth compartment, €16 in a four-berth compartment). A typical *cuccetta* compartment should have just enough room under the seats to fit a tightly packaged bike.

Additional examples of point-to-point train fares can be found in the Getting There & Away section at the beginning of each ride.

Reservations

Reservations are generally not required (or even possible) on slower trains with special bike compartments. On the faster EC and IC trains, it's recommended that you book tickets ahead, particularly if you're travelling on weekends or during holiday periods; otherwise you could find yourself standing in the corridor for the entire journey. On the Eurostar trains, it is obligatory to make a booking, since they don't carry standing room passengers. You can get timetable information and make train bookings at most travel agencies, or simply buy your ticket on arrival at the station. There are special booking offices for the Eurostar services at the relevant train stations.

If you are doing a reasonable amount of travelling, it may be worth buying a train timetable. There are several available at newspaper stands in or near train stations for around €3, including the official Trenitalia timetable.

Discounted Tickets

It is not worth buying a Eurail pass or Inter-Rail pass if you are going to travel only in Italy, since train fares are reasonably cheap. Trenitalia offers its own discount passes for travel within the country. These include the Carta Verde for people aged 12 to 26 years, and the Carta Argento for people 60 years and older. Each costs €26, is valid for one year and entitles the bearer to a 20% discount on all train travel, although you'll need to do a bit of travelling to get your money's worth.

Another money-saving option for frequent train travellers is the *biglietto chilometrico* (kilometric ticket). Costing €117 (2nd class) or €181 (1st class), it is valid for two months, can be shared by up to five people, and allows you to cover 3000km, or take a maximum of 20 trips, whichever comes first; this is roughly a 15-20% discount per trip. You must still pay the normal bicycle supplement plus any additional charges for fast trains.

Children aged between four and 12 years are automatically entitled to a 50% discount, and under four years they travel for free.

Validating Your Ticket

Before boarding any Trenitalia train, you must validate your tickets (personal ticket and bike supplement) by inserting them into one of the ubiquitous yellow machines found in train station lobbies and along platforms. The machine will stamp your ticket with the time and date, ensuring that you don't use the same ticket twice. Passengers who fail to validate tickets are subject to reprimand (at best) or a fine. Foreigners who are honestly unfamiliar with the system may be treated a bit more leniently.

Before validating your ticket, make sure you're ready to travel; most tickets are valid for two months from the date of issue, but expire within six hours after validation.

Left-Luggage

There are left-luggage facilities at most train stations. They are often open 24 hours, seven days a week (or in some cases closed in the wee hours of the morning). The price per piece of luggage ranges from €2.50 per day upwards.

BUS

Numerous companies provide bus transit within Italy. Services vary from slower regional routes linking small villages to faster ones making major intercity connections. By combining bus and train travel, it's possible to reach most locations in the country. Buses can be a cheaper and faster way to get around if your destination does not cover a major train line.

Luggage space permitting, most Italian bus companies will allow unboxed bikes to travel underneath the bus free of charge or for a nominal fee. You're most likely to run into difficulties in peak summer season, when suitcase-toting tourists vie for limited luggage space, or in certain rural locations where minibuses are the vehicle of choice.

The giant Lazzi transportation group operates buses under a variety of names, including Lazzi, with services from Florence to other points in Tuscany; Alpinbus, providing a direct service from Tuscany to the Dolomites; Freccia dell'Appennino, with services from Siena and other Tuscan cities to Umbria, Le Marche and Abruzzo; and Sena, providing services from Siena and other points in Tuscany to Rome, Milan, Emilia Romagna, Campania, Calabria and Sicily. Other companies providing long-haul services include Marozzi, with services to Bari, Brindisi, Sorrento, the Amalfi Coast and Pompeii; SAIS and Segesta, both specialising in Rome to Sicily services; and SITA, offering services to a variety of destinations.

A helpful website for researching Italian bus routes is W www.italybus.it. You can enter a departure and destination city and see which companies offer a service between the two. For useful information on major intercity bus companies, try W www .trioviaggi.com.

It is often possible to get bus timetables for the provinces and for intercity services from local tourist offices. In larger cities most of the main intercity bus companies have ticket offices or operate through agencies, and buses leave from either an *autostazione* (bus station) or from a particular piazza or street. In some smaller towns and villages tickets are sold in bars – just ask for *biglietti per il pullman* – or on the bus. Note that buses generally leave on time.

It is usually unnecessary to make reservations on buses, although it is advisable in the high season for overnight or long-haul trips.

CAR

Car travel in Italy presents numerous disadvantages, including high petrol, toll and parking costs, the difficulty of navigating through urban centres, and the high incidence of theft in places like Naples and Sicily. At the time of writing petrol cost more than €1.10 per litre. Still, cars can offer flexibility and independence if you're trying to reach a part of the country not well served by public transit.

For rules of the road, especially as they apply to cyclists, see Safety on the Ride in the Health & Safety chapter on p57.

Rental

It is usually far cheaper to arrange car rental before leaving your own country, for instance through some sort of fly/drive deal. Most major international firms, including Hertz and Avis, will arrange this, allowing you to simply pick up the vehicle at a chosen point when you arrive in Italy. If you must rent on the spot, shop around for the best price. Car rental agencies tend to be clustered together in airports and near train stations, making your job easier, and if you let people know you're actively comparison shopping, you'll often find a friendly manager willing to do a bit of wheeling and dealing.

You will need to be aged 21 years or more (23 years or more for some companies) to rent a car in Italy, and you will find the deal far easier to organise if you have a credit card. Most firms will accept your standard licence, sometimes with an Italian translation (which can usually be provided by the agencies themselves) or International Driving Permit.

Major car rental agencies in Italy include Maggiore (☎ 848 86 70 67, 06 229 15 30), Avis (☎ 199 10 01 33), Hertz (☎ 199 11 22 11, 02 694 30 007) and Europcar (☎ 800 01 44 10, 02 703 99 700).

BOAT

Navi (large ferries) serve the islands of Sicily and Sardinia, and *traghetti* (smaller ferries) and *aliscafi* (hydrofoils) serve the Aeolian Islands, as well as other islands such as Elba, the Tremiti, Ischia and Capri. The main embarkation points for Sardinia are Genova, Livorno, Civitavecchia and Napoli; for Sicily the main points are Napoli and Villa San Giovanni in Calabria. The main points of arrival in Sicily are Palermo and Messina; in Sardinia they are Cagliari, Arbatax, Olbia and Porto Torres.

Tirrenia Navigazione (W www.tirrenia .com) is the major company serving the Mediterranean and it has offices throughout Italy. Trenitalia also operates ferries to Sicily and Sardinia. Travellers can choose between cabin accommodation (men and women are usually segregated in 2nd class, although families will be kept together) or a *poltrona*, an airline-type armchair. Deck class is available only in summer and only on some ferries, so ask when making your booking.

Most ferries will carry bicycles. Cyclists are usually allowed to ride onto the ferry's car deck, leaving their bikes locked and/or bungeed to a railing during passage and paying a fee for the bike over and above the cost of a normal passenger ticket.

Certain boats will not take bikes, including hydrofoils in the northern Lake District and *vaporetti* (barge-like ferries) on Grand Canal in Venice. Further details about local boat services are provided in the relevant sections.

LOCAL TRANSPORT

Thanks to pressure from FIAB, Milan's subway now allows bike transport on weekends, holidays and evenings after 8pm, while Rome's allows them on Sundays only. See individual chapters for additional information on local transport services.

Language

ITALIAN

Italian is a Romance language related to French, Spanish, Portuguese and Romanian, all of which are directly descended from Latin.

Although it's commonly accepted that modern standard Italian developed from the Tuscan dialect, history shows that Tuscany's (and in particular, Florence's) status as the political, cultural and financial power base of the nation ensured that the region's dialect would inevitably be installed as the national tongue.

Before the creation of an official national language, the people of Italy's various geographic regions spoke only local dialects, the majority of which are still in common use today. Some of these dialects are in fact so different from modern standard Italian that they could class as languages in their own right. Don't be surprised if you fail to understand a word of some conversations – it's entirely possible that what you're hearing is a regional dialect.

Today's standard Italian is something of a composite. What you hear on the radio and TV, in educated discourse and indeed in the everyday language of many people is the result of centuries of cross-fertilisation between the dialects, a process of change that was greatly accelerated in the postwar decades by the modern media.

Visitors need to be aware that many Italians still expect to be addressed in the third person formal (*lei* instead of *tu*). Also, it's not considered polite to use the greeting *ciao* when addressing strangers unless they use it first; it's better to say *buongiorno* (or *buona sera*, as the case may be) and *arrivederci* (or the more polite form, *arrivederla*).

We've used the polite address for most of the phrases in this guide. Use of the informal address is indicated by 'inf' in brackets. Italian also has both masculine and feminine forms (often ending in 'o' and 'a' respectively). Where both forms are given in this guide, they are separated by a slash, the masculine form first.

For a more comprehensive guide to the language, get a copy of Lonely Planet's *Italian phrasebook*.

Pronunciation

Vowels

a	as in 'art', eg, *caro* (dear); sometimes short, eg, *amico/a* (m/f) (friend)
e	as in 'tell', eg, *mettere* (to put)
i	as in 'inn', eg, *inizio* (start)
o	as in 'dot', eg, *donna* (woman); as in 'port', eg, *dormire* (to sleep)
u	as the 'oo' in 'book', eg, *puro* (pure)

Consonants

c	as 'k' before a, o and u; as the 'ch' in 'choose' before e and i
ch	a hard 'k' sound
g	as in 'get' before a, o and u; as the 'j' in 'job' before e and i
gh	a hard 'g' sound, as in 'get'
gli	as the 'lli' in 'million'
gn	as the 'ny' in 'canyon'
h	always silent
r	a rolled 'rr' sound
sc	as the 'sh' in 'shed' before e and i; as 'sk' before h, a, o and u
sch	a hard 'sk' sound
z	as the 'ts' in 'lights', except at the beginning of a word, when it's as the 'ds' in 'beds'

Note that when **ci**, **gi** and **sci** are followed by **a**, **o** or **u**, the 'i' is not pronounced unless the accent falls on the 'i'. Thus the name 'Giovanni' is pronounced 'joh-**vahn**-nee'.

A double consonant is pronounced as a longer, often more forceful sound than a single consonant.

Word Stress

Stress often falls on the second-last syllable, as in *spa-**ghet**-ti*. When a word has an accent, the stress is on that syllable, as in *cit-tà* (city).

Greetings & Civilities

Hello.	*Buongiorno.*
	Ciao. (inf)
Goodbye.	*Arrivederci.*
	Ciao. (inf)
Yes.	*Sì.*
No.	*No.*
Please.	*Per favore/ Per piacere.*
Thank you.	*Grazie.*

That's fine/ You're welcome.	*Prego.*
Excuse me.	*Mi scusi.*
	Scusam. (inf)
Sorry (forgive me).	*Mi scusi/Mi perdoni.*
What's your name?	*Come si chiama?*
	Come ti chiami? (inf)
My name is ...	*Mi chiamo ...*
I'm pleased to meet you.	*Piacere!*
Where are you from?	*Di dov'è?*
	Di dove sei? (inf)
I'm from ...	*Sono di ...*
Do you like ...?	*Ti piace ...?* (inf)
I (don't) like ...	*(Non) Mi piace ...*

Language Difficulties

I (don't) understand.	*(Non) Capisco.*
Please write it down.	*Può scriverlo, per favore?*
Can you show me (on the map)?	*Può mostrarmelo (sulla carta/pianta)?*
Do you speak English?	*Parla inglese?*
	Parli inglese? (inf)
Does anyone here speak English?	*C'è qualcuno che parla inglese?*
How do you say ... in Italian?	*Come si dice ... in italiano?*
What does ... mean?	*Che vuole dire ...?*

Paperwork

name	*nome*
nationality	*nazionalità*
date of birth	*data di nascita*
place of birth	*luogo di nascita*
sex (gender)	*sesso*
passport	*passaporto*
visa	*visto*

Getting Around – General

What time does ... leave/arrive?	*A che ora parte/ arriva ...?*
the (city) bus	*l'autobus*
the (intercity) bus	*il pullman/corriere*
the ferry	*il traghetto*
the hydrofoil	*l'aliscafo*
the plane	*l'aereo*
the ship	*la nave*
the train	*il treno*

I'd like a ... ticket:	*Vorrei un biglietto ...*
one-way	*di solo andata*
return	*di andata e ritorno*
1st-class	*di prima classe*
2nd-class	*di seconda classe*

I want to go to ...	*Voglio andare a ...*
How long does the trip take?	*Quanto dura il viaggio?*
Do I need to ...?	*Bisogna ...?*
change buses	*cambiare autobus*
change trains	*cambiare treni*
change platform	*cambiare binario*
The train has been cancelled/ delayed.	*Il treno è soppresso/ in ritardo.*

the first/last	*il primo/l'ultimo*
platform number	*binario numero*
station	*stazione*
ticket office	*biglietteria*
timetable	*orario*

I'd like to hire ...	*Vorrei noleggiare ...*
a car	*una macchina*
a motorcycle	*una moto(cicletta)*

Getting Around – With a Bike

Does the (bus/ hydrofoil/train) carry bikes?	*(L'autobus/l'aliscafo/ il treno) trasporta le bici?*
The bike must be in a bag.	*La bici dev'essere in una sacca.*
When is the next train allowing non-bagged bikes?	*Quando è il prossimo treno che permette bici non smontate?*
Where on the train does the bike go?	*Dove nel treno dovrei mettere la bici?*
Where is the luggage car?	*Dov'è il bagagliaio?*
I'd like to send my bike to ...	*Voglio spedire la mia bici a ...*
Will it be on the same train as me?	*Si porterà nello stesso treno con me?*
When will it arrive?	*Quando arriverà?*
Where do I collect it from?	*Da dove la riprendo?*

Around Town

I'm looking for ...	*Cerco ...*
an ATM	*un bancomat*
a bank	*un banco*
a bike-touring club	*un club di cicloturismo*
the church	*la chiesa*
the city centre	*il centro (città)*
my hotel	*mio albergo*
the market	*il mercato*
the museum	*il museo*

the post office	*la posta*
a public toilet	*un gabinetto/*
	bagno pubblico
the telephone	*il centro telefonico*
centre	
the tourist office	*l'ufficio di turismo/*
	d'informazione

I want to change ...	*Voglio cambiare ...*
money	*denaro*
travellers cheques	*degli assegni per*
	viaggiatori

beach	*la spiaggia*
bridge	*il ponte*
castle	*il castello*
cathedral	*il duomo/la cattedrale*
island	*l'isola*
(main) square	*la piazza (principale)*
market	*il mercato*
old city	*il centro storico*
palace	*il palazzo*
ruins	*le rovine*
tower	*la torre*

Accommodation

I'm looking for ...	*Cerco ...*
a guesthouse	*una pensione*
a hotel	*un albergo*
a youth hostel	*un ostello per la*
	gioventù
a room in a	*una camera in una*
private house	*casa privata*

Where is a good	*Dov'è un albergo a*
budget hotel?	*buon prezzo?*
What is the address?	*Cos'è l'indirizzo?*
Please write down	*Può scrivere l'indirizzo,*
the address.	*per favore?*
Do you have any	*Ha camere libere/C'è*
rooms available?	*una camera libera?*
Are bikes a prob-	*È un problema portare*
lem at the hotel?	*le bici all'albergo?*
Do you have a safe	*Avete un posto sicuro*
place to store	*lasciare bici?*
bikes?	

I'd like ...	*Vorrei ...*
a bed	*un letto*
a single room	*una camera singola*
a double room	*una camera*
	matrimoniale
a room with	*una camera doppia*
two beds	
a room with a	*una camera con*
bathroom	*bagno*

Signs

Ingresso/Entrata	Entrance
Uscita	Exit
Informazione	Information
Aperto	Open
Chiuso	Closed
Proibito/Vietato	Prohibited
Polizia/Carabinieri	Police
Questura	Police Station
Camere Libere	Rooms Available
Completo	Full/No Vacancies
Gabinetti/Bagni	Toilets
Uomini	Men
Donne	Women

| to share a dorm | *un letto in* |
| | *dormitorio* |

How much is it ...?	*Quanto costa ...?*
per night	*per la notte*
per person	*per ciascuno?*

May I see it?	*Posso vederla?*
Where is the	*Dov'è il bagno?*
bathroom?	
I'm/We're leaving	*Parto/Partiamo oggi/*
today/tomorrow.	*domani.*

Shopping

a bike shop	*un negozio di bici*
a bookshop	*una biblioteca*
a chemist/	*una farmacia*
pharmacy	
a laundry/	*una lavanderia*
laundrette	
the market	*il mercato (civico)*
a newsagency	*una giornaleria*
a supermarket	*un supermercato*

I'd like to buy ...	*Vorrei comprare ...*
How much is it?	*Quanto costa?*
I (don't) like it.	*(Non) Mi piace.*
May I look at it?	*Posso dare*
	un'occhiata?
I'm just looking.	*Sto solo guardando.*
It's cheap.	*Non è caro/a.*
It's too expensive.	*È troppo caro/a.*
I'll take it.	*Lo/La prendo.*

| Do you accept | *Accettate carte di* |
| credit cards? | *credito?* |

| more/less | *più/meno* |
| smaller/bigger | *più piccolo/più grande* |

At the Bike Shop

Where can I find a bike repair shop?	*Dove posso trovare un riparatore di bici?*

I'd like to buy ...	*Vorrei comprare ...*
arm warmers	*manicotti*
an elastic (ocky) strap	*un elastico per attaccare i bagagli*
glasses	*occhiali*
gloves	*guanti*
a helmet	*un casco*
knicks	*pantaloncini*
a jersey	*una maglia*
leg warmers	*gambali*
tights	*calzamaglia*
a tube	*una camera a aria*

I'd like to hire ...	*Vorrei noleggiare ...*
a (road) bike	*una bici (di strada)*
a mountain bike	*una 'mountain bike'*
a child's seat	*un sediolino per bambini*
a ... trailer	*un carrello ...*
child's	*porta bambini*
luggage	*porta bagagli bambini*

Could you ...?	*Potresti ...?*
adjust the gears	*regolare il cambio*
adjust the saddle	*regolare la sella*
inflate the tyres	*gonfiare le gomme*
true the wheel	*centrare il cerchione*
tighten the ...	*serrare il/la ...*

I have a flat tyre.	*Ho una foratura*
I have a broken spoke.	*È rotto un raggio.*

front	*anteriore*
rear	*posteriore*

Time & Dates

What time is it?	*Che ora è?*
	Che ore sono?
It's (8 o'clock).	*Sono (le otto).*
in the morning	*di mattina*
in the afternoon	*di pomeriggio*
in the evening	*di sera*
When?	*Quando?*
today	*oggi*
tomorrow	*domani*
yesterday	*ieri*

Monday	*lunedì*
Tuesday	*martedì*
Wednesday	*mercoledì*
Thursday	*giovedì*
Friday	*venerdì*
Saturday	*sabato*
Sunday	*domenica*

January	*gennaio*
February	*febbraio*
March	*marzo*
April	*aprile*
May	*maggio*
June	*giugno*
July	*luglio*
August	*agosto*
September	*settembre*
October	*ottobre*
November	*novembre*
December	*dicembre*

Numbers

0	*zero*
1	*uno*
2	*due*
3	*tre*
4	*quattro*
5	*cinque*
6	*sei*
7	*sette*
8	*otto*
9	*nove*
10	*dieci*
11	*undici*
12	*dodici*
13	*tredici*
14	*quattordici*
15	*quindici*
16	*sedici*
17	*diciassette*
18	*diciotto*
19	*diciannove*
20	*venti*
21	*ventuno*
22	*ventidue*
30	*trenta*
31	*trentuna*
40	*quaranta*
50	*cinquanta*
60	*sessanta*
70	*settanta*
80	*ottanta*
90	*novanta*
100	*cento*
1000	*mille*
2000	*due mila*

Emergencies

Help!	Aiuto!
There's been an accident	C'è stato un incidente!
I'm lost.	Mi sono perso/a.
Go away!	Lasciami in pace! Vai via! (inf)
Call ... !	Chiami ... !
a doctor	un medico
the police	la polizia

Health & Toiletries

I'm ill.	Mi sento male.
It hurts here.	Mi fa male qui.
I'm ...	Sono ...
asthmatic	asmatico/a
diabetic	diabetico/a
epileptic	epilettico/a
I'm allergic ...	Sono allergico/a ...
to antibiotics	agli antibiotici
to penicillin	alla penicillina
to nuts/peanuts	alle noci/noccioline
antiseptic	antisettico
condoms	preservativi
contraceptive	anticoncezionale
diarrhoea	diarrea
headache	mal di testa
medicine	medicina
sunblock cream	crema/latte solare (per protezione)
tampons	tamponi

ON YOUR BIKE

Where have you ridden from?	Da dove hai pedalato? (inf)
Where are you riding to (today)?	Dove pedali oggi? (inf)
I'm going from ... to ...	Vado da ... a ...
Would you like to ride together?	Vuoi pedalare insieme? (inf)

Directions & Road Conditions

Where is ...?	Dov'è ...?
How do I get to ...?	Quale strada devo prendere per ...?
Is it near?	È vicino?
Is it far?	È lontano?
How many kilometres to ...?	Quanti kilometri per ...?
Is it hilly?	È collinoso?
Is it steep?	È ripida?
There are lots of hills.	Ci sono tante salite.
The road climbs.	La strada sale.
The road drops.	La strada scende.
Is there a lot of traffic?	È molto trafficato?
Is there a bikepath near here?	C'è una piste ciclabile qui vicino?
Is there a shortcut?	C'è una scorciatoia?
Can you show me on the map?	Potrebbe mostrarmi sulla carta?
Is this road OK for bikes?	Va bene per bici, questa strada?
Go straight ahead.	Si va sempre diritto. Vai sempre diritto (inf).
Turn left.	Gira a sinistra.
Turn right.	Gira a destra.
at the traffic lights	al semaforo
at the next corner	al prossimo angolo
at the next x-road	al prossimo incrocio
via ...	per mezzo di .../ attraverso ...
behind	dietro
in front of	davanti
opposite	di fronte a
to cycle/ride	andare in bici/pedalare
to stop off at ...	fare una tappa a ...
north/south	nord/sud
east/west	est/ovest
bitumen road	strada asfaltata
gravel/unpaved road	una strada bianca/ sterrata
shoulder (of road)	spalla
in good condition	in buona condizione
potholes	buche
headwind	vento contro
tailwind	vento a favore

Glossary of the Bicycle

The masculine/feminine Italian article, equivalent to 'a' (un/una) or 'the' (il/la) in English) is included to identify a noun's gender. See the numbered picture on p373 for more parts.

Allen key/wrench	una chiave (a brugola/ esagonale)
Allen-head bolt	un bullone (a brugola) esagonale
alloy	lega (di metalli)
aluminum	alluminio
anodized	anodizzato

axle (of wheel)	*il perno (asse)*	crankset	*la guarnitura*
bar ends	*corna ('horns')*	derailleur (general)	*il deragliatore*
a battery/	*una batteria/*	disc brake	*un freno a disco*
some batteries	*delle batterie*	down tube	*il tubo diagonale (del*
bearing/s (ball)	*il cuscinetto/*		*telaio)*
	i cuscinetti (a sfere)	dynamo	*una dinamo*
bike carrier (for	*una porta bici*	flat/a flat	*sgonfiato/una foratura*
car)		frame	*il telaio*
bolt	*un bullone*	freewheel	*la ruota libera*
brake pad	*un pattino del freno*	glue (for patch)	*il mastice*
cable housing	*la guaina (di cavo)*	grease	*il grasso (lubrificante)*
caliper (of disc)	*una pinza*	grip	*una manopola*
carbon fibre	*carbonio*	handlebar tape	*nastro manubrio*
cassette	*il pacco pignoni a*	lever (brake,	*una leva*
	cassetta	change etc)	
chain breaker	*uno smagliacatena*	link (of chain)	*una maglia (della*
cleat	*una placchetta/*		*catena)*
	piastrina	light bulb	*una lampadina*
clipless pedals	*pedali a sgancio*	lube/lubricant	*il lubrificante*
	rapido	mountain bike	*una mountain bike (as*
cog/sprocket	*un pignone*		*in English)*
computer	*un computerino*	mudguard	*un parafango*

1	*mozzo* (hub)	**9**	*pedivella* (crank arm)	**19**	*manubrio* (handlebars)
2	*denti* (cogs)	**10**	*pedale* (pedal)	**20**	*cavo* (cable)
3	*pacco pignoni a cassetta*	**11**	*valvola* (valve)		*di freno* (brake)
	(cassette)	**12**	*cerchione* (rim)		*del cambio* (gear)
4	*cambio* (rear derailleur)	**13**	*copertone* (tyre)	**21**	*borraccia* (water bottle)
5	*catena* (chain)		*camera a aria* (tube)	**22**	*sella* (saddle)
6	*deragliatore delle corone*	**14**	*raggio* (spoke)	**23**	*cannotto reggisella*
	(front derailleur)	**15**	*borsa* (pannier)		(seatpost)
7	*movimento centrale*	**16**	*portapacchi* (carry rack)	**24**	*freno/i* (brake/s)
	(bottom bracket)	**17**	*forcella* (fork)		
8	*corona* (chainring)	**18**	*serie sterzo* (headset)		

Road Signs

Attenzione!	Danger!
Strada Accidentata	Rough Road
Strada Scivolosa	Slippery Surface
Passo/Valico Chiuso	(Road Over) Pass Closed
Strada Sterrata	Gravel Road
(...) Obligatorio	(...) Compulsory
Dare Precedenza a Destra	Give Way to Right
Strada Chiusa	Road Closed
Senso Unico	One Way
Divieto di Sosta	No Parking
Tutte le Direzioni	All Directions
Lavori in Corso	Roadworks
Strade Ghiacciate	Icy Roads

patch (for tube)	*una pezza/toppa*
pin (for chain)	*un perno*
pressure (eg, tyre)	*la pressione*
pump/small pump	*una pompa/pompetta*
puncture	*una foratura*
quick-release (for wheel)	*uno sgancio rapido (di ruota)*
rim tape	*nastro di protezione del cerchio*
(a) screw	*una vite*
(a) seal	*una guarnizione*
seat bag	*una borsetta*
shifters	*i comandi del cambio*
shifting system	*il cambio*
shock absorber	*un'ammortizzatore*
shoes	*scarpe*
slick/semi-slick (tyre)	*un (pneumatico) liscio/ semi-slick*
skewer	*un bloccaggio*
spanner/wrench	*una chiave (fissa)*
spoke nipple/s	*un nipplo/dei nippoli*
spoke spanner/ wrench	*un tiraraggi*
sprocket	*un pignone*
steel	*acciaio*
steering/head stem	*l'attacco/la pipa*
suspension fork	*una forcella ammortizzata*
tooth/teeth (of sprocket)	*un dente/i denti*
tread	*la battistrada*
to true (a wheel)	*centrare*
bidon/bottle cage	*un porta-borraccia*
weight	*peso*
weld/to weld	*una saldatura/saldare*
wheel	*una ruota*

FOOD
Basics

breakfast	*(prima) colazione*
lunch	*pranzo*
dinner	*cena*
restaurant	*ristorante*
grocery shop	*alimentari*
I'd like the set menu.	*Vorrei il menù turistico.*
Is service included in the bill?	*È compreso il servizio?*
I'm a vegetarian	*Sono vegetariano/a.*

Useful Words

affumicato	smoked
al dente	firm (as all good pasta should be!)
alla brace	cooked over hot coals
alla griglia	grilled
arrosto	roasted
ben cotto	well done (cooked)
bollito	boiled
brodo	broth
cameriere/a	waiter/waitress
coltello	knife
conto	bill/cheque
cotto	cooked
crudo	raw
cucchiaino	teaspoon
cucchiaio	spoon
forchetta	fork
fritto	fried
menù	menu
minestrone	vegetable soup
piatto	plate

Staples & Condiments

aceto	vinegar
burro	butter
formaggio	cheese
limone	lemon
marmellata	jam
miele	honey
olio	oil
olive	olives
pane	bread
panna	cream
pepe	pepper
peperoncino	chilli
polenta	cooked cornmeal
riso	rice
risotto	rice cooked with wine and stock
sale	salt

uovo/uova	egg/eggs
zucchero	sugar

Meat & Fish

acciughe	anchovies
agnello	lamb
aragosta	lobster
bistecca	steak
calamari	squid
coniglio	rabbit
cotoletta	thin cut of meat
cozze	mussels
fegato	liver
gamberi	prawns
manzo	beef
ostriche	oysters
pesce spada	swordfish
pollo	chicken
polpo	octopus
salsiccia	sausage
sarde	sardines
seppia	cuttlefish
sogliola	sole
tonno	tuna
vitello	veal
vongole	clams

Vegetables

asparagi	asparagus
carciofi	artichokes
carote	carrots
cipolla	onion
fagiolini	string beans
melanzane	eggplants/aubergines
patate	potatoes
peperoni	capsicum/peppers
piselli	peas
spinaci	spinach

Fruit

arance	oranges
banane	bananas
ciliegie	cherries
fragole	strawberries
mele	apples
pere	pears
pesche	peaches
uva	grapes

Pasta Sauces

all'arrabbiata – tomato and chilli
alla carbonara – egg, bacon and pepper
alla matriciana – tomato and bacon
napoletana – tomato and basil
al nero – made from cuttlefish ink

con panna – cream, prosciutto and sometimes peas
pesto – basil, garlic and oil; often with pine nuts
al ragù – meat sauce (bolognese)
alle vongole – clams, garlic and oil; sometimes with tomato

Pizzas

All pizzas listed have a tomato (and sometimes mozzarella) base.

capricciosa – olives, prosciutto, mushrooms and artichokes
frutti di mare – seafood
funghi – mushrooms
margherita – oregano
napoletana – anchovies
pugliese – tomato, mozzarella and onions
quattro formaggi – with four types of cheese
quattro stagioni – like a capricciosa, but sometimes with egg
verdura – mixed vegetables

DRINKS

almond milk	orzata
bitter cola	chinotto
lemonade	limonata
orangeade	aranciata
orange juice (bottled)	succo d'arancia
orange juice (fresh)	spremuta d'arancia
soft drink	bibita
(cup of) tea	(un) tè
(cup of) coffee	(un) caffè
with/without ...	con/senza ...
milk	latte
sugar	zucchero
... water	acqua ...
boiled	bollita
mineral	minerale
sparkling	frizzante
still	naturale
non-drinkable	non potabile
wine	vino
red	rosso
rose	rosato
sparkling	spumante
white	bianco
a bottle of ...	una bottiglia di ...
a glass of ...	un bicchiere di ...

Glossary

AAST – Azienda Autonoma di Soggiorno e Turismo; local tourist office

abbazia – abbey

ACI – Automobile Club Italiano; Italian Automobile Association

aereo – aeroplane

affittacamere – rooms for rent

agora – (Latin) marketplace, meeting place

agriturismo – tourist accommodation on farms

AIG – Associazione Italiana Alberghi per la Gioventù; Italian Youth Hostel Association

albergo – hotel (up to five stars)

alimentari – grocery shop, delicatessen

aliscafo – hydrofoil

Alleanza Nazionale – National Alliance; neo-Fascist political party

alloggio – lodging (cheaper than a *pensione* and not part of the classification system)

alto – high

ambasciata – embassy

ambulanza – ambulance

anfiteatro – amphitheatre

antipasto – starter, appetiser

appartamento – apartment, flat

APT – Azienda di Promozione Turistica; regional tourist office

assicurato/a – insured

AST – Azienda Soggiorno e Turismo; local tourist office

autostazione – bus station or terminal

autostop – hitchhiking

autostrada – motorway, freeway

bagno – bathroom; toilet

bambino – child

bancomat – ATM

belvedere – panoramic viewpoint

benzina – petrol

benzina senza piombo – unleaded petrol

bicicletta – bicycle

biglietto – ticket

biglietto chilometrico – kilometric card (train pass)

binario – (train) platform

borghetto – burg

calcio – football (soccer)

cambio – money exchange

camera – room

campanile – belltower

campeggio – camp site

campo – field

cantine – wine cellars

cappella – chapel

carabinieri – police with military and civil duties

Carnevale – carnival period between Epiphany and Lent

carta – menu

carta d'identità – ID card

carta telefonica – phonecard; see also *scheda telefonica*

cartoleria – stationery shop

casa – house

case abusive – (literally, abusive houses) illegal construction usually associated with the Mafia

castello – castle, citadel

cattedrale – cathedral

cava – quarry (as in the pumice quarries at Campobianco)

cena – evening meal

centro – centre

centro storico – historic centre

chiave – key

chiesa – church

ciclopedonale – bikepath

cin cin – cheers (a drinking toast)

CIT – Compagnia Italiana di Turismo; Italian national travel agency

città – town, city

codice fiscale – tax number

colazione – breakfast

colline – hills

comune – equivalent to a municipality or county; town or city council; historically, a *commune* (self-governing town or city)

consolato – consulate

contorno – side dish

contrada – district

convalida – ticket stamping machine

coperto – cover charge in restaurants

corso – main street, avenue

cortile – courtyard

Cosa Nostra – alternative name for the Mafia

CTS – Centro Turistico Studentesco e Giovanile; Centre for Student and Youth Tourists

cuccetta – couchette

Democrazia Cristiana (DC) – Christian Democrats; centre-right political party

deposito bagagli – left luggage

digestivo – after-dinner liqueur
diretto – direct; slow train
distributore di benzina – petrol pump
dolce – sweet, dessert
duomo – cathedral

elenco – list
elenco degli alberghi – list of hotels
ENIT – Ente Nazionale Italiano per il Turismo; Italian Tourist Board
enoteca – wine bar
enti turistichi – tourist organisations
espresso – express mail; express train; short black coffee

faraglione – rock stack
farmacia (di turno) – pharmacy (open late)
fermo posta – poste restante
Ferragosto – Feast of the Assumption, 15 August
ferrovia – rail system
festa – festival
fiume – river
focaccia – flat bread
fontana – fountain
forno – bakery
fortezza – fortress
Forza Italia – Go Italy; centre-right political party
francobollo – postage stamp
FS – Ferrovie dello Stato; State Railway
funivia – cable car

gabinetto – toilet, WC
gasauto or **GPL** – liquid petroleum gas (LPG)
gasolio – diesel
gelateria – ice-cream parlour
gelato – ice cream
gola – gorge
golfo – gulf
granita – drink of crushed ice flavoured with lemon, strawberry, coffee and so on
grappa – grape liqueur
grotta – cave
guardia di finanza – fiscal police
guardia medica – emergency doctor service

IC – Intercity; fast train
imbarcadero – embarkation point
interregionale – long-distance train that stops frequently
isola – island

IVA – Inposta di Valore Aggiunto; valued-added tax of around 19%

lago – lake
largo – (small) square
lavanderia – laundrette
lavasecco – dry-cleaning
lido – beach
locale – slow local train
locanda – inn, small hotel
lungolago – lakeshore drive
lungomare – esplanade, seafront road, promenade

mare – sea
menù del giorno – menu of the day
mercato – market
merceria – haberdashery shop
mescita di vini – wine outlet
mezza pensione – half-board
Mezzogiorno – literally, midday; name for the south of Italy
monte – mountain
motorino – moped
mototraghetto veloce/tradizionale – car ferry
meublé – room only
municipio – town hall, municipal offices
museo – museum

Natale – Christmas
nave – large ferry, ship
navigli – canals
necropoli – (ancient) cemetery, burial site
Novecento – 20th century
numero verde – toll-free phone number

oggetti smarriti – lost property
Ognissanti – All Saints' Day, 1 November
ospedale – hospital
ostello per la gioventù – youth hostel
osteria – snack bar, cheap restaurant

Pagine Gialle – Yellow Pages; telephone directory
palazzo – palace or mansion; large building of any type, including an apartment block
panetteria – bakery
panino – bread roll with filling
paninoteca – sandwich bar
Pasqua – Easter
passeggiata – traditional evening stroll
pasta – cake; pasta; pastry or dough
pasticceria – shop selling cakes, pastries and biscuits

Partito Comunista Italiano (PCI) – Italian Communist Party; political party
Partito Democratico di Sinistra (PDS) – Democratic Party of the Left; political party
pedaggio – toll
pensione – small hotel, often with board
pensione completa – full board
permesso di lavoro – work permit
permesso di soggiorno – residence permit
pianta della città – city map
piazza – square
piazzale – (large) open square
pinacoteca – art gallery
pinoli – pine nuts
polizia – police
poltrona – airline-type chair on a ferry
ponte – bridge
porta – gate, door
portico – covered walkway, usually attached to the outside of buildings
porto – port
posta – post office
posta aerea – airmail
pranzo – lunch
primo – first; starter (meal)
Pro Loco – local tourist office
pronto soccorso – first aid; casualty ward
pullman – (English) long-distance bus

Quattrocento – 15th century
questura – police station

rapido – fast train
regionale – slow local train
ricetto – tax-free zone centre
rifugio – mountain hut
riserva naturale – nature reserve
rocca – fortress; rock
ronda – roundabout
rosso – red
ruderi – ruins

sagra – festival (generally dedicated to one food item or theme)
sala – room
salumeria – delicatessen
santuario – sanctuary
scalinata – staircase, steps
scheda telefonica – phonecard; see also *carta telefonica*
servizio – service charge in restaurants
sindaco – mayor
sopra – over, above

sotto – under
spiaggia (libera) – (public) beach
stazione – station
stadio comunale – municipal stadium
stazione di servizio – petrol or service station
stazione marittima – ferry terminal
strada – street, road
strada provinciale – main road; sometimes just a country lane
strada statale – main road; often multi-lane and toll free
superstrada – motorway; highway with divided lanes
supplemento – supplement, payable on a fast train

tabaccheria – tobacconist's shop
tavola calda – literally, 'hot table'; pre-prepared meat, pasta and vegetable selection, often self-service
TCI – Touring Club Italiano; automobile association with retail outlets; produce the most common road maps of Italy
teatro – theatre
tempio – temple
terme – thermal baths
tonno – tuna
torre – tower
torrente – stream
torrone – nougat (the best comes from Sardinia and uses pure honey instead of sugar)
traghetto – ferry, boat
tramezzino – sandwich
trattoria – cheap restaurant
Trenitalia – Italian national railway (see also *FS*)
treno – train

ufficio postale – post office
uffizi – offices

vacanza – holiday, vacation
via – street, road
via aerea – by airmail
viale – avenue
vicolo – alley, alleyway
vigili del fuoco – fire brigade
vigili urbani – traffic police; local police
villa – town house or country house; also the park surrounding the house
vino alla mandorla – almond wine

zona rimozione – vehicle removal zone.

Index

Text

For a listing of rides, see the Table of Rides (pp4-5).

Boxed Text

ABOUT LONELY PLANET GUIDEBOOKS

Lonely Planet published its first book in 1973 in response to the numerous 'How did you do it?' questions Maureen and Tony Wheeler were asked after driving, busing, hitching, sailing and railing their way from England to Australia.

Written at a kitchen table and hand collated, trimmed and stapled, *Across Asia on the Cheap* became an instant local bestseller, inspiring thoughts of another book.

Eighteen months in South-East Asia resulted in their second guide, *South-East Asia on a shoestring*, which they put together in a backstreet Chinese hotel in Singapore in 1975. The 'yellow bible', as it quickly became known to backpackers around the world, soon became the guide to the region. It has sold well over half a million copies and is now in its 10th edition.

Today an international company with offices in Melbourne (Australia), Oakland (USA), London (UK) and Paris (France), Lonely Planet has an ever-growing list of books and other products, including: travel guides, walking guides, city maps, travel atlases, phrasebooks, diving guides, wildlife guides, healthy travel guides, restaurant guides, world food guides, first time travel guides, condensed guides, travel literature, pictorial books and, of course, cycling guides. Many of these are also published in French and various other languages.

In addition to the books, there are also videos and Lonely Planet's award winning Web site.

Some things haven't changed. The main aim is still to help make it possible for adventurous travelers to get out there – to explore and better understand the world.

At Lonely Planet we believe travellers can make a positive contribution to the countries they visit – if they respect their host communities and spend their money wisely. Since 1986 a percentage of the income from each book has been donated to aid projects and human rights campaigns.

> Lonely Planet gathers information for everyone who's curious about the planet – and especially for those who explore it first-hand. Through guidebooks, phrasebooks, activity guides, maps, literature, newsletters, image library, TV series and Web site we act as an information exchange for a worldwide community of travellers.

LONELY PLANET OFFICES

Australia
Locked Bag 1, Footscray, Victoria 3011
☎ 03 8379 8000 fax 03 8379 8111
e talk2us@lonelyplanet.com.au

UK
72 – 82 Rosebery Ave, London EC1R 4RW
☎ 020 7841 9000 fax 020 7841 9001
e go@lonelyplanet.co.uk

USA
150 Linden St, Oakland, CA 94607
☎ 510 893 8555 TOLL FREE: 800 275 8555
fax 510 893 8572
e info@lonelyplanet.com

France
1 rue du Dahomey, 75011 Paris
☎ 01 55 25 33 00 fax 01 55 25 33 01
e bip@lonelyplanet.fr
w www.lonelyplanet.fr

World Wide Web: www.lonelyplanet.com *or* AOL keyword: lp
Lonely Planet Images: www.lonelyplanetimages.com